Pretty Good for a Girl

MUSIC IN AMERICAN LIFE

A list of books in the series appears at the end of this book.

PRETTY

GOOD *for a Girl*

Women in Bluegrass

MURPHY HICKS HENRY

University of Illinois Press
Urbana, Chicago, and Springfield

LIBRARY OF CONGRESS CATALOGING-IN-PUBLICATION DATA
Henry, Murphy.
Pretty good for a girl : women in bluegrass / Murphy Hicks Henry.
p.   cm. — (Music in American life)
Includes bibliographical references and index.
ISBN 978-0-252-03286-8 (hardcover : alk. paper) —
ISBN 978-0-252-07917-7 (pbk. : alk. paper)
1. Women bluegrass musicians—United States—Biography.
2. Bluegrass musicians—United States—Biography. I. Title.
ML394.H457   2013
781.642092'52—dc23   2012036560
[B]

*To my favorite
bluegrass musicians:
my husband, Red; my
daughter, Casey; and
my son, Chris.
With special thanks
to Casey for
her unwavering
enthusiasm and help
with this project.*

CONTENTS

Acknowledgments ix

Introduction 1

IN THE BEGINNING: THE 1940S 9

Sally Ann Forrester 13

Wilma Lee Cooper 20

Rose Maddox 28

Ola Belle Campbell Reed 35

THE SECOND DECADE: THE 1950S 41

Bessie Lee Mauldin 46

Vallie Cain 54

Grace French 59

The Lewis Family: Miggie, Polly, Janis 63

The Stonemans: Patsy, Donna, Roni 69

Margie Sullivan 84

THE NUMBERS ARE GROWING: THE 1960S 93

Jeanie West 96

Betty Amos with Judy and Jean 100

Gloria Belle 104

Hazel and Alice 113

Dottie Eyler 135

Vivian Williams 138

Bettie Buckland 143

Rubye Davis 146

Ginger Boatwright 150

The Whites: Pat, Sharon, Cheryl, Rosie 157

Wendy Thatcher 161

Martha Adcock 168

The McLain Family: Alice, Ruth, Nancy Ann 175

THE FLOODGATES OPEN: THE 1970S 181

Beck Gentry 186

Suzanne Thomas 192

Delia Bell 202

Buffalo Gals 207

Betty Fisher 216

Katie Laur 221

Dede Wyland 229

Lynn Morris 233

The Women in California 241

Laurie Lewis 250

Kathy Kallick 260

Claire Lynch 269

Lee Ann Lenker Baber 275

LEADERS OF THE BAND: THE 1980S 281

Missy Raines 284

Alison Brown 293

All-Female Bands 304

Alison Krauss 316

TOO MANY TO COUNT: THE 1990S AND BEYOND 331

Kristin Scott Benson 337

Rhonda Vincent 346

The Dixie Chicks 361

Cherryholmes 374

Conclusion: Not Just Pretty Good for a Girl! 381

Sources 385

Bibliography 403

Author Interviews and Emails 425

Index 431

ACKNOWLEDGMENTS

During the ten years that I have been working on this book I have had an amazing amount of help from the bluegrass community. My first and biggest thanks go to the women who shared their life stories with me. In the midst of hectic schedules they carved out time for interviews, answered a long list of questions, endured endless follow-up emails, and trusted me with their revelations. Their belief that I would take them seriously, listen without judgment, sympathize with their choices, refrain from prying into personal issues, and respect their confidences meant the world to me. Thank you for this trust. I was ever aware of it as I was writing, and I have tried hard to present your stories with the admiration I feel for your accomplishments. Any errors of fact or interpretation are mine alone.

My research almost always began in the pages of *Bluegrass Unlimited,* and I am greatly indebted to everyone who keeps this venerable publication rolling off the presses. Pete Kuykendall has been at the helm (or very close to it) since its inception in July 1966, and he and the entire staff were only a phone call away. (It did help that I've been writing the magazine's "General Store" column since 1987.) Thanks to Linda Shaw, Kim Yates, Katie Blankenship, Pat Jeffries, Sally Pontarelli, Lisa Kay Howard, and Sharon McGraw for always taking my calls with good cheer, even when they were up against their own deadlines.

I was consistently aided and abetted in my quest for corroborative detail by a number of other talented bluegrass writers. Three of these became my "go-to guys," whose vast knowledge of all things bluegrass was ever at my disposal. For an entire decade Walt Saunders, Dick Spottswood, and Frank Godbey answered questions both deep and trivial at the drop of a hat—or rather the click of a mouse. Special thanks to Walt for insisting that I include Delia Bell and then lending me all of her albums, and to Dick for sending a complete list of Alex and Ola Belle's 45 rpm recordings.

Other exceptionally knowledgeable folks who were quick to reply to whatever information crisis I was facing at the moment include Tom Adler, Fred Bartenstein, Nancy Cardwell, David Dees, Jon Hartley Fox, Ken Irwin, Dan Hayes, Cherrill Heaton, Tom Henderson, Randy Pitts, Gary Reid, Neil Rosenberg, and Jon Weisberger. Their replies were often lengthy and thoughtful.

A host of musicians who worked closely with the women profiled here graciously filled in some elusive biographical tidbits. Many thanks to James Brooks, Andrew Buckland, Pat Cloud, Wayne Clyburn, Dudley Connell, Ed Dye, Tony Ellis, Bill Emerson, Pat Enright, Kristin Ericsson, Bill Evans, Bob Forrester, Joe Forrester, Bob French, Troy Gilchrist, Tom Gray, Jim Greer, Marvin Gruenbaum, Dave Harvey, John Hedgecoth, Bill Keith, Keith Little, Barbara MacDonald Magone, David McLaughlin, Ann Milovsoroff, Bruce Nemerov, Andy Owens, Todd Rakestraw, Wayne Rice, Mike Seeger, Elmo Shropshire, Rick Shubb, Tim Stafford, Peter Thompson, Tony Trischka, Butch Waller, Peter Wernick, Marshall Wilborn, and Mark Wingate.

The Bluegrass and IBMA Listservs kept me connected to the worldwide bluegrass community. Any time I posted a question ("Does anyone know who played banjo with Ola Belle before Ted Lundy?" "Does anyone have the Good Ol' Persons' first album?"), someone would shoot back an answer, offer to copy the album ("Don't tell Laurie Lewis!"), or provide a telephone number. My heartfelt thanks to all of you. As Charlie Monroe used to say, "I'd like to buy you all a drink . . . and I would if I thought one would go around!" Some of the fine folks who came through with recordings or information include Tom Armstrong, Cary Banks, Nick Barr, Cindy Brooks Baucom, Geoff Berne, Andrea Broadstreet, James Bryan, Meredith Bub, Mike Bub, DeeDee Bunnell, Joe Bussard, Lauren Calista, Jean-Mark Delon, Debbie Durant, Leo Eilts, Stewart Evans, Tom Ewing, Mark Freeman, Lena Taylor Isner, Rienk Janssen, Fred Jasper, Mike Kelley, Paul Kenny, Jerry Keys, Bill Knowlton, Kitsy Kuykendall, Kevin Lynch, Art Menius, Rod Moag, Harry Moore, Terry Moorehead, Julia Mottesheard, Alan Munde, Brad Paul, Jeremy Raven, Archie Warnock, Andy Wilkinson, Joe Wilson, and Ellen Wright. Pam Bock transcribed interviews early on. My apologies if I failed to mention any of you who extended a helping hand. The blame rests squarely on my faulty memory and less-than-stellar record keeping.

Other fellow travelers who went to great lengths to help out include Elena Sky, who Xeroxed Ola Belle Reed's entire unpublished autobiography; Richard D. Smith, who shared copies of his own original research into Bessie Lee

Mauldin's life; and Eddie Stubbs, who duplicated cassettes of his live, on-air interview with Wilma Lee Cooper. Writers who generously provided entire unedited transcripts of interviews they conducted themselves include Ira Gitlin, Derek Halsey, Casey Henry, Henry Koretzky, and Carolyn Wright. Ira also interviewed Dede Wyland specifically for this book. And near the end of my journey, dozens of wonderful photographers, along with the women themselves, dug through old photos and then generously granted permission to use those I selected. I am greatly in your debt.

I was also blessed to have not one but two editors during this long labor. Judy McCulloh offered the initial idea for the book and was unwavering in her support. Her suggestions were always insightful and kind. Laurie Matheson, who took over when Judy retired, has been patient with my numerous questions and my hit-and-miss work ethic. Her enthusiasm over early portions of the book boosted my confidence and fired me up to write more while her hand-holding eased my angst. This is a better book thanks to my copyeditor, Jill R. Hughes.

My thanks would not be complete without mentioning those who have been with me for the long haul. My sisters, Claire, Argen, Nancy, and Laurie, were my first singing partners. We learned to sing from our mama, who eased us into slumber with songs like "Chattanooga Choo Choo," and "Way Down Yonder in the Paw Paw Patch." Daddy didn't sing so much but supported our early bluegrass endeavors by listening and saying, "Stop tuning and play!"

My final thanks goes to my own family, to whom I have dedicated this book. To Red for keeping the Murphy Method going so that I could write, for proofreading, and for going above and beyond the call to scan and tweak more than a hundred photos; to Casey for carving her own feminist bluegrass path, banjo in hand; to Chris for his stellar songwriting, which always makes me smile and sometimes moves me to tears. And to my first grandson, Dalton Whitfield Henry, whose favorite song of the moment is "Larry Perkins Had a Dog and Banjo Was His Name."

A few years ago I decided life is too short not to dance. By chance, fate, or kismet, I found square dancing. A great big THANK YOU to my square-dancing friends and angels for keeping me sane during the final push to finish this book, making me laugh out loud, and telling me I look good in a short skirt with a huge petticoat! And, as always, to Karen and Bonnie.

INTRODUCTION

This book has had a long gestation period. In fact you might say I've been prepar-
ing to write it all my life, since I am both a woman and a banjo player. That combination has always been fraught with some amount of tension, which occasionally
found voice in my *Banjo NewsLetter* column. The second article I wrote, in 1983,
was titled "For Girls Only" and contained the sage advice, "And finally, ignore
all Slack-Jawed Bimbos who have the audacity to try to strike up a conversation
with the comment, 'You're pretty good for a girl.'" When you hear that often
enough, it makes an impact. You understand the intent is to offer praise, but at
the same time the compliment comes with the hidden dagger "for a girl." When
I was growing up in the fifties, that line was the ultimate put-down. "You throw
like a girl." "You run like a girl." "You pick like a girl." "*You are a girl.*" I fought
back the only way I knew how: by becoming a tomboy.

Still, this book might not have sprouted wings at all if I hadn't been at the International Bluegrass Music Association Awards (IBMA) show in September 1993.
My banjo-picking daughter, Casey, fifteen, and I sat in the audience and watched
as a band of young male musicians, the Bluegrass Youth All-Stars, was referred
to by one of the hosts as the "future of bluegrass music." I was livid. When told
that the show's organizers had tried but couldn't find a young woman to be part
of the group, I decided to start a database of women in bluegrass so that no one
could ever use that excuse again. The database grew into a quarterly newsletter,
Women in Bluegrass, which was published for ten years, from 1994 to 2003.

During this time period, fired up by the IBMA incident and inspired by the
writings of feminist Carolyn Heilbrun, who authored the seminal *Writing a
Woman's Life,* I began working on my master's degree at George Mason University in the summer of 1995. In 1999 I was awarded the Master of Arts degree
in interdisciplinary studies with an emphasis in women's studies. I wrote my
thesis on Sally Ann Forrester, the first woman in bluegrass. Her story became
the opening chapter in this book.

But as I learned in my feminist studies, my own history informs every aspect of my research, my writing, and my thought processes. I once described my first twenty years of growing up in Georgia as "barren of bluegrass but not of music." My musical roots are planted deep in the *Broadman Hymnal* and the Baptist Church, in sing-alongs at myriad Girl Scout and 4-H camps, and in the piano lessons that were requisite for well-rounded little girls in the June Cleaver era. I have had a stringed instrument in my hands ever since I got a ukulele for Christmas in the fourth grade. Guitar came next, allowing me to follow in the footsteps of my idol, Gamble Rogers, and become a folksinger in college. Finally in 1972, at the advanced age of twenty, following a suggestion from Gamble, I went to my first bluegrass festival in Lavonia, Georgia, where, as so many other women have testified, I got "bitten by the bug." I also met my husband-to-be, mandolin player Red Henry. Shortly thereafter I got myself a good-sounding banjo and joined Betty Fisher and the Dixie Bluegrass Band—as bass player. I had entered the world of bluegrass and there was no turning back.

To me this new world seemed to be populated by "men, men, and more men" as Hazel Dickens once noted. The bands I shared the stage with, the bands I worshipped, were all made up of men: Bill Monroe and the Blue Grass Boys, Lester Flatt and the Nashville Grass, Ralph Stanley and the Clinch Mountain Boys, the Osborne Brothers, and Jim and Jesse and the Virginia Boys. Even the hottest regional bands were all male: the Shenandoah Cut-ups, the Bluegrass Tarheels, the Sunshine Bluegrass Boys, Marty Raybon and the American Bluegrass Express.

Culturally conditioned to dismiss women and their accomplishments as unworthy, I failed to even see, much less give credit to, the many women I worked shows with: Margie Sullivan; Miggie, Polly, and Janis Lewis; Frances Mundy Mooney; Gwen Biddix Flinchum; Connie Freeman Morris; Louisa Branscomb; Martha Adcock; Barbara and Gwen White; Pam and Connie Hobbs; Alice and Ruth McLain; Sharon and Cheryl White; Marlene Hinson; Betty Fisher; and even my own sisters, Claire, Argen, Nancy, and Laurie Hicks, who were budding musicians. I always had some excuse to dismiss the women I saw: she's "just" a guitar player and singer, she's "just" a bass player, she's a wimpy banjo player. Many of the women who were interviewed for this book felt the same way and often said, "I was the only woman I knew playing bluegrass." Although later on they would casually say, "Of course there was Wilma Lee." Or Gloria Belle. Or Ola Belle. Or Donna Stoneman. Or the Lewis Family sisters.

But I was not the only one who was blind to the presence and accomplishments of women in bluegrass. The idea that bluegrass was "man's music" was shared by others more experienced and knowledgeable than I was. In the first scholarly work about the music, "An Introduction to Bluegrass," folklorist Mayne Smith wrote, "Bluegrass bands are made up of from four to seven *male musicians* who play non-electrified stringed instruments and who also sing as many as four parts [emphasis mine]." Smith's article was originally published in the *Journal of American Folklore* (1965) but was reprinted in *Bluegrass Unlimited* (1966), thus not only propagating that myth in academic circles but also injecting it into the bluegrass community.

The glaring fact that Bessie Lee Mauldin had been playing bass—and recording—with Bill Monroe, the Father of Bluegrass, from 1952 to 1964 is somehow blithely ignored. She was undoubtedly dismissed because she was a girl—Monroe's girlfriend. Still, Mayne Smith's own band, the Redwood Canyon Ramblers, from California, used bass player Betty Aycrigg on some of their earliest gigs. Then there were all the other women who were playing bluegrass before 1965: Sally Ann Forrester; Wilma Lee Cooper; Rose Maddox; Ola Belle Campbell Reed; Vallie Cain; Patsy, Donna, and Roni Stoneman; Peggy Brain; Miggie, Polly, and Janis Lewis; Margie Sullivan. And these are just the better-known female musicians. The list goes on. *What about these women?* By his own admission Smith arrived at his definition by "following the ideas of the musicians themselves" to arrive at the "defining traits of bluegrass." One wonders if any of those musicians were women.

Earlier Ralph Rinzler had written a biographical sketch of Roni Stoneman in which he opined, "Just as it is rare for women to play 'bluegrass' style music it is even more rare for them to play this banjo style." He expressed these thoughts in the liner notes to the LP *American Banjo: Three-Finger and Scruggs Style* (Folkways, 1957). As late as 1985 preeminent bluegrass historian Neil Rosenberg, author of *Bluegrass: A History,* does not challenge Mayne Smith's definition, but instead makes the tiniest alteration, saying, "The band members are *almost always men*; in fact, in its formative years bluegrass was *virtually a male music* [my emphasis]." Eight years later, *Finding Her Voice: The Saga of Women in Country Music* (1993), that wonderful work by Mary Bufwack and Robert Oermann, would echo Rosenberg's words, bearing the myth onward: "Bluegrass music remained an *almost completely male domain* [my emphasis] during its first twenty-five years." Twenty years later this definition was still being quoted in other scholarly works, such as William Lynwood Montell's *Grassroots Music in the Upper Cumberland* (University of Tennessee Press, 2006). And Mark Humphrey, writing in the liner notes to a 1992 Bill Monroe boxed set, would actually use the phrase "man's music" and speak in sneering tones of the mandolin as a "woman's instrument": "[Bill Monroe] would create a *ferocious and hell-bent man's music* [my emphasis] on an instrument disparaged as a kid's or a woman's."

Fittingly, it was Alice Gerrard, herself a pioneer woman in bluegrass, who would challenge Neil Rosenberg's thinking. Neil wrote the liner notes to Hazel Dickens and Alice Gerrard's second Folkways album, *Won't You Come and Sing for Me*, which was recorded in 1965 but not released until 1973. The eight-year delay required Neil to revisit his original liner notes. In the rewritten notes Neil talks candidly about what happened. In his 1965 notes he had quoted Mayne Smith as saying, "'Bluegrass bands are made up of from four to seven male musicians.'" Neil then went on to suggest two reasons for this. He wrote, "Few women seem to possess the technical skill necessary to play bluegrass instruments properly and few women can sustain the 'punch' or 'drive' so essential for the successful presentation of bluegrass vocals." On reading this, Alice wrote back to articulately explain that "one reason most women in bluegrass or even country music have tended not to possess the above-mentioned skills is not for lack of inherent ability, but more because they have not been encouraged to develop these skills and qualities; or have felt or been made to feel that the skills were not in keeping with their oft-defined roles as women." To Neil's everlasting credit, he printed Alice's remarks as part of the new liner notes and graciously admitted that her writing "points out the flaws in my reasoning quite concisely."

I myself had absorbed what I had read so unconsciously and so well that in the liner notes to my own album *M & M Blues* (Arrandem, 1992) I wrote, "Twenty years ago there were not many women in this [bluegrass] world, let alone women who played banjo Scruggs-style." What I failed to recognize back then was that I didn't want to acknowledge the other women out there, because if I had, then how could I have been that "rare woman who has known this instrument [the banjo] understandingly enough to become a virtuoso," which is what Nat Winston declared in his foreword to the instructional book *Earl Scruggs and the 5-String Banjo* (1968). I wanted to be that Rare Woman. I told myself that I was. As this book will show, however, I was not. Roni Stoneman, Gloria Belle Flickinger, Sally Wingate, Lynn Morris, Janet Davis, Betty Amos, Bettie Buckland, Susie Monick, Connie Freeman Morris, Mary Cox, Connie Hobbs, Louisa Branscomb, and undoubtedly many others were also developing a fine understanding of the banjo. And if there are so many of us, then we are not Rare Women at all. We're just banjo players.

Thank goodness for Charles Wolfe, that fallen giant among country music historians, who wrote in the *Old-Time Herald*, "One of the sillier myths being bandied about these days . . . involves the role of women in the history of country music. It is said . . . that before the advent of Kitty Wells in the late 1940s, women had little to do with country music's development . . . This is, of course, nonsense and an account of the significant women artists who contributed to the development of the music would take up the rest of this issue."

It is worth noting that the "first full description" of bluegrass, written in 1959, does not mention gender. In fact Mike Seeger opens the door to all comers by saying, as he closes out the liner notes to *Mountain Music Bluegrass Style* (Folkways, 1959), "*Young people* [my emphasis] will continue to play and sing and make up songs for fun, and some will hope for the day that they might go professional." Perhaps Mike was influenced by the time he had spent playing in a band with Hazel Dickens, or by seeing Ola Belle Campbell Reed on stage at Sunset Park and New River Ranch, or by watching Roni Stoneman and Gloria Belle compete in banjo contests. Perhaps the fact that he grew up with a mother, three sisters, and a housekeeper (Elizabeth Cotton) who played a variety of instruments helped him see music as a non-gendered activity. And Wayne Daniel at least gives women a place at the table when he says, "If bluegrass and country music have been dominated by males, the domination has not been complete." Dominated, yes. Defined by, no.

As the cultural blinders began to fall from my own eyes, I could finally see that women—many women—have always had a presence in bluegrass music. So if this book has had a guiding force, a mission, an underlying objective, it is to lay that tired myth of bluegrass being "man's music" to rest. Bluegrass was and is no more "man's music" than country music was "man's music," than jazz was "man's music," than this globe is a "man's world."

The question then becomes, How do we find these women? When reporters, historians, and even photographers have been culturally trained to disregard women and their achievements, then women don't make it into print—the magazines, the history books, the photograph collections, the advertising, and the fronts of T-shirts—or the International Bluegrass Music Association Hall of Fame.

Sherrie Tucker, who writes about "all-girl" jazz bands of the 1940s, says that jazz scholars are "critically reevaluating some of the timeworn patterns of how mainstream jazz histories have been written." She points out that "the jazz historical record is too reliant on the very small portion of music which gets made into jazz records." And as the introduction to her book *Swing Shift* loudly proclaims, "It Don't Mean a Thing If It Ain't in the History Books." Again, as Tucker points out, "The dominant swing texts are not 'gender neutral' . . . they are histories of musical men." *Pretty Good for a Girl* sets out to add some balance to the bluegrass texts by presenting the histories of musical women.

Musical women, too, are easiest to find if they have made recordings, and these are the woman I primarily spotlight in this book. Finding the other women who played bluegrass, the local women who played for only a short time, is a task that still lies ahead. As James Nelson wrote about hillbilly music, "To avoid neglecting the significant roles played by these countless lesser knowns, it is imperative that researchers turn their efforts toward the activities with which most country [and bluegrass] music performers were involved, live radio shows and personal appearances. Then and only then will the whole story be told."

This book leaves out many women of bluegrass, and for that I am in the depths of despair. If you do not find your name written here, I am truly sorry. Because this book focuses entirely on women as musicians, it omits those who are primarily singer-songwriters (Emma Smith) as well as songwriting women from other genres (Gillian Welch); women like Louise Scruggs who were business managers and booking agents; women who produce festivals such as Grey Fox (Mary Tyler Doub) and Wintergrass (Earla Harding and Trish O'Neill); women who are bluegrass deejays (Katy Daley and Cindy Baucom); women at the helm of various bluegrass publications from local newsletters like *Bluegrass Breakdown* (Suzanne Denison) to the full-fledged magazines like *Bluegrass Now* (edited by Deb Bledsoe for much of its eighteen-year life) and the long line of women who have served as managing editors for *Bluegrass Unlimited:* Diane Sims, Sally Gray, Marion Kuykendall, Sharon McGraw, and the latest, Linda Shaw. Nancy Cardwell, before her 2012 appointment as executive director of the IBMA, did most of the writing and organizing for the association newsletter, *International Bluegrass*, and for twenty years (1974–2004) Dobro player Beverly King published her own magazine under the various names *Dobro Nut, Resophonic Echoes,* and finally *Country Heritage*. Keeping this project manageable also meant that I dared not delve into the contributions of women outside the United States, even though fiddler Colleen Trenwith of New Zealand's Hamilton County Bluegrass Band was one of the earliest female musicians to grace the cover of *Bluegrass Unlimited* (September 1969).

It is my great pleasure in this book to bring to light the stories of some of the pioneer women in bluegrass. When I started this project, even I had no idea that I would uncover so many women playing bluegrass, especially so early in the history of bluegrass. Finding them has brought me immense satisfaction and great joy. And if there are this many women who are clearly visible—who recorded and who were written about—imagine how many more are lurking in the shadows, unknown and unseen.

IN THE BEGINNING: *The 1940s*

Bluegrass music has many "starting" dates, depending on whom you talk to. However, a significant number of historians cite 1945 as the year it all began, because that was the year Earl Scruggs and his fancy five-string banjo joined the Blue Grass Boys, bringing him together with Bill Monroe and Lester Flatt, the classic "big three" of bluegrass. What most people don't realize or find significant is that this first pairing of Lester, Bill, and Earl included a woman, Sally Ann Forrester, on accordion.

Bluegrass music also has myriad definitions, and heated, all-night discussions can be launched with the simple question, "What is bluegrass?" For the sake of simplicity and to provide this book with some much-needed boundaries, I have defined a bluegrass band as one that features the five-string banjo played in the three-finger Scruggs style. I readily admit this is an extremely limiting definition, which is perhaps why I chose it.

Because this book uses 1945 as a starting point and Scruggs-style banjo as a defining element, the many women who played in string bands or hillbilly bands are not included. Some of the best known of these include Sara and Maybelle Carter, Molly O'Day, Lulu Belle Wiseman, Lily May Ledford and the Coon Creek Girls, Cousin Emmy, Samantha Bumgarner, Moonshine Kate, and a host of others. Many of these women are included in Bufwack and Oermann's *Finding Her Voice: The Saga of Women in Country Music.*

In addition, my self-chosen and admittedly narrow definition of bluegrass prevents the inclusion of those wonderful modern-day groups that don't feature Scruggs-style banjo but are in other ways closely related to bluegrass, such as Robin and Linda Williams and the now-defunct Nickel Creek. These groups often appear at bluegrass venues and are written about in the bluegrass press, but from my vantage point they fit more comfortably into the overarching genre of music now known as Americana. Nor will you find new old-time groups such as the Be Good Tanyas, Uncle Earl, Misty River, or primarily old-time artists such as Cathy Fink and Marcy Marxer.

And one further note on terminology: In the interest of avoiding the tedious repetition of the phrase "bluegrass music," I use the word "bluegrass" to mean "bluegrass music." And when I say "banjo," I mean five-string banjo played in the three-finger Scruggs style.

With these defining elements in place, we can now turn our attention to the women we are aware of who were playing bluegrass during its first half decade. Because it was such a new kind of music at the time, we do not find many women playing bluegrass professionally in the 1940s. Bands were still in the process of transitioning from early country music to bluegrass by adding a banjo, and most female musicians were still playing in these early hillbilly bands. Sally Ann Forrester, Wilma Lee Cooper, Rose Maddox, and Ola Belle Campbell Reed all started out in hillbilly music.

Born in the 1920s or earlier and coming from various parts of the country, these four women were surprisingly well educated. All made it through several years of high school, and Wilma Lee earned a one-year-college business diploma. And with the exception of Rose Maddox, whose family worked as sharecroppers, these women were raised in families of schoolteachers, store owners, barbers, and coal miners. These parents found a place for a piano or an organ in their homes and made sure that their daughters took lessons. Playing music was an integral part of family life and the girls were always included. In addition to playing guitar, each woman played at least one other instrument. Rose Maddox played bass, Ola Belle and Wilma Lee played old-time banjo, and Sally Ann played accordion and fiddle. All left behind numerous recordings, beginning with the eight numbers Sally Ann cut with Bill Monroe in 1945 and continuing all the way through Rose Maddox's final Grammy-nominated bluegrass CD, *$35 and a Dream* (Arhoolie), in 1994.

Not surprisingly, all four women married, and three were in longtime, seemingly compatible relationships. Rose, on the other hand, seemed to be unlucky in love and divorced twice. All had children, but just barely. Sally Ann, Wilma Lee, and Rose had only one child, while Ola Belle had two. Did they purposely limit their families? We don't know. But larger families and numerous pregnancies would certainly have made a musical career more difficult.

In addition to these professional players, this decade also found other younger women taking an interest in this new, bluegrass music. In addition to thirteen-year-old Betty Amos, from Virginia, who began learning banjo from her brother Ed in 1947, over in North Carolina eight-year-old Betty Harper (b. 1930) was learning guitar from her brother Bud so that she could play and sing in their family band. Eventually, though, there were "too many guitars, so I just sang." She began "going out" with the band when she was around fourteen, and by 1947 she was fronting her own band, Betty Harper and the Black Mountain Boys, which included two of her brothers and a cousin. The group released two titles (78s) for Blue Ridge Records in 1952, "I'm Lonely Tonight" and "Don't That Moon Look Lonesome," on which Betty sang but did not play an instrument. In 2010, at age eighty, Betty was still musically active with the group Farmington Bluegrass.

Then there are the virtually unknown women like Ginny Payne Glaze (1909–1978), of Virginia, who, according to her daughter, "learned to play the banjo three-finger style from Myrtie Payne (possibly a relative) when she was very young [and] always played and sang old-time hillbilly music." Although her earliest banjo playing predates Scruggs-style bluegrass, Ginny performed at clubs in the Washington, D.C., area, with a guitar player until the late 1950s and, on at least one occasion, sat in with the Stoneman Family and Jimmy Dean's Wildcats. Was she bluegrass? Without recordings it's hard to say, but photos of her five-string banjo show some well-worn grooves in the fingerboard.

With these three musicians as examples, imagine the numbers of other young women all across the country who were playing bluegrass but never had the opportunity to record. Or who were learning to play bluegrass, or even heading in the direction of playing bluegrass, but who got derailed by marriage, family, children, and a culture that did not encourage women to follow their own muses or dance to a different drummer. The fact that Sally Ann, Wilma Lee, Rose, and Ola Belle did so is a testament not only to their love for the music and their own inner drive to play but also to that sometimes seemingly capricious force we often term fate.

Come prepared to stay. Bring fiddle.

—Telegram from Howdy Forrester
to Sally Ann Forrester, 1940

SALLY
ANN
FORRESTER

Sally Ann Forrester (b. 1922) occupies a special place in the annals of bluegrass history. Because she played with Bill Monroe and the Blue Grass Boys from 1943 to 1946, she is, by definition, the first woman in bluegrass, the original bluegrass girl. She and her accordion were in the band where bluegrass originated before the term "bluegrass" had even been coined. She played—and sang—on Monroe's 1945 Columbia recordings, which included "Footprints in the Snow," "Kentucky Waltz," "True Life Blues," and "Rocky Road Blues," bluegrass standards all.

Sally Ann was part of Monroe's band when he was still experimenting with his music, trying to find a combination that would be commercially successful while satisfying his own not-quite-formulated musical vision. But the fact that she played the accordion, a nonstandard bluegrass instrument, coupled with the fact that she was a woman, has made it hard for the bluegrass music community—pundits, historians, and fans—to accept Sally Ann as a "real" musician.

Complicating matters further is the presence of her husband, Howdy, whose two stints on fiddle with the Blue Grass Boys were separated by his service in World War II. For years Sally Ann was known merely as Howdy's wife, a woman who was "holding Howdy's place" in the band until he got out of the navy, a woman who was hired as a "favor" to Howdy while he was overseas. Some people undoubtedly assumed (wrongly) that she was Monroe's girlfriend. For all these reasons her tenure with Monroe has been ignored, blown off, or smirked about. But Sally Ann had her own rich musical life long before she met Howdy Forrester or Bill Monroe.

Born Wilene Russell in Raton, New Mexico, Sally Ann was raised by her maternal grandparents, George and Sudie Robbins, in Avant, Oklahoma. George, owner of a pool hall and barber shop, was a fiddler who played locally for dances. By the sixth grade Sally Ann was playing piano, violin, and her favorite, the guitar. She adored Bob Wills and the Texas Playboys and loved going with her grandfather to their dances at Cain's Academy in nearby Tulsa.

In 1937 Sudie sent her granddaughter to the high school academy at Southwest Baptist College in Bolivar, Missouri, where Sally Ann helped pay her way by working in the kitchen. Here her friends began calling her "Bill" or "Billie." In addition to regular high school courses, she took glee club, orchestra, piano, and voice. In her autograph book the phrase "I like to hear you sing" appears so often that it sounds like a broken record. Her piano playing was pronounced "marvelous." One friend wrote, "I'll always remember you as the Hillbilly singer of Southwest." Sally Ann and a female friend are pictured with their guitars in the 1939 yearbook. She also played in a violin quartet that toured the surrounding area.

There are indications that Sally Ann may have been performing on radio before she entered Southwest Baptist, and she almost surely did so in the summer of 1938. An intriguing autograph from April 1938 reads, "Please don't forget to let me know when you go back on radio." Two other friends say they hope to hear her on the radio "this summer." In May 1939, after Sally Ann's second year at the academy, she returned to Oklahoma with every intention of coming back in the fall to complete her high school education. But fate had other plans.

By June 1939 Sally Ann had landed a spot playing guitar and singing on the newly formed barn dance program the *Saddle Mountain Roundup* on KVOO in Tulsa. Billed as the Little Orphan Girl, she was dressed, somewhat ironically, in a cowgirl outfit. Herald Goodman, who had recently relocated to Tulsa from Nashville's Grand Ole Opry, was the driving force behind the *Roundup,* which featured his group, the Tennessee Valley Boys. The band included seventeen-year-old Howdy Forrester on fiddle and his brother Joe, twenty, on bass along with Arthur Smith and Robert "Georgia Slim" Rutland on fiddles. As historian Charles Wolfe points out in his book *The Devil's Box,* these were "three of the most famous fiddlers in southeastern music. What this band must have sounded like, God only knows."

Howdy and Joe had been raised on the sounds of old-time fiddling in Hickman County, Tennessee, where their father, grandfather, and uncle all played. The brothers had both dropped out of high school to join Herald Goodman and the Tennessee Valley Boys in 1938 and had gone west with the band.

The *Saddle Mountain Roundup* began on April 1, 1939, and ran for eleven weeks in the Tulsa Convention Hall, playing to thousands, before taking to the road. The musicians couldn't travel far, though, because they had to be back for their early morning appearances on KVOO. The Little Orphan Girl had her own spot as a featured artist, backed by the Tennessee Valley Boys. When Arthur Smith left the group, the Little Orphan Girl was also featured as one of the Three Fiddlers, with Howdy and Slim. Soon she and Howdy were dating on the sly.

The *Saddle Mountain Roundup* lasted one short year. By March 1940 Goodman had let the Tennessee Valley Boys go. Howdy and Joe and two other musicians headed to Wichita Falls, Texas, to try to find work. Sally Ann stayed behind with the understanding that Howdy would send for her when they landed a job. He hated to leave her. In a letter he said, "Boy, that ride from Oklahoma City down here was the lonesomiest [*sic*] thing I ever did in my life . . . I would rather be in Tulsa right now than any other place I know of and would I like to see you—but don't tell anyone I'm homesick." Sally Ann apparently still had work at the radio station. In another letter Howdy says, "You're in 'seventh heaven' up at that radio station and don't deny it. It gets in your blood, don't it?"

The Tennessee Valley Boys finally found steady work at KWFT in Wichita Falls. In May Howdy sent a telegram to Sally Ann saying, "Come prepared to stay. Bring fiddle. Howard Forrester KWFT." "And she did," said their son, Bob, "for forty-seven years." On June 29, 1940, Sally Ann and Howdy were married.

Sally Ann then joined the Tennessee Valley Boys at KWFT, performing again as the Little Orphan Girl. She, Howdy, and Joe often sang trios, with Sally Ann taking the lead and the brothers harmonizing beneath her. The Forresters worked together at several different radio stations in Texas and Illinois until Joe received his draft notice in May 1941. Sally Ann and Howdy continued to play in Texas, but when Pearl Harbor was bombed they headed back to Nashville, where Howdy signed up with the navy. It would be over a year, however, before he was called into service.

In Nashville, Sally Ann and Howdy hooked up with Grand Old Opry stars and blackface comedians Jamup and Honey. Honey Wilds had taken out the first major Grand Ole Opry tent show in the spring of 1941, using Roy Acuff as headliner. In spite of the naysayers the venture proved lucrative, and when Roy Acuff started his own tent show the next year, Honey hired Bill Monroe as his star.

A Grand Old Opry tent show was a traveling assemblage of country music acts that toured from early spring until late fall. David Wilds, son of Honey, says, "My dad just crossed a carnival with the Grand Ole Opry and hit the road." Like a circus, it was totally self-contained with tent crew, cooking facilities, its own generator, and a tent that could seat two thousand or more people.

In the spring of 1942, when Sally Ann and Howdy were traveling with Jamup and Honey, the group heard Dixie Belle and Goober Buchanan singing on the car radio. Sally Ann began harmonizing with Dixie Belle and said, "We could make a good duet." Honey, who was looking for a female act for that year's tent show, stopped by the radio station and hired the husband-and-wife duo on the spot. The two women joined forces as the Kentucky Sweethearts with Sally Ann on guitar and Dixie Belle on bass. They were backed by the Blue Grass Boys with Art Wooten on fiddle. Howdy served as fiddler for singer Tommy Thompson, and Goober did a comedy act. However, when Art Wooten was called into service that summer, Howdy stepped into his shoes as the fiddler for the Blue Grass Boys. Goober had also been tapped by Uncle Sam, and he and Dixie left in early June. Sally Ann and Howdy remained with the tent show until the end of the season, and Howdy stayed with Monroe until he went into the navy in the spring of 1943. It is unclear whether Sally Ann played with the group over the winter. She is not included in the band's publicity photo.

The outrageous financial success of Honey Wilds inspired Bill Monroe to take out his own tent show in the spring of 1943. Although Howdy was now in the navy, Sally Ann was still in Nashville, living with Howdy's mother, Emmie. Monroe knew that Sally Ann was a seasoned performer who could pull her own weight with the show. And having a woman on the show was considered an asset. Roy Acuff went out of his way to find a woman, banjoist Rachel Veach, to play in his band. He believed that "men in the audience like to see a girl on stage." Paradoxically, he also said, "Don't ever headline a show with a woman . . . people just don't go for women." In addition to performing, Sally Ann also took up the tickets and looked after the often considerable sums of money.

Since there is no indication that Sally Ann was playing accordion at this time, it is most likely that she continued to play guitar and sing as she had done in the past. In her earliest publicity picture with the band, she does not have an instrument but is positioned in front of the microphone as if she were a featured singer. Only in a later band photo do we see her with the accordion.

Although Sally Ann was originally hired only for the tent show season, in a September 1943 letter Howdy says, "I hope you can keep on with Bill and the boys throughout the winter as it will keep you busy and your mind free from worry. Nobody could worry around that outfit." A June letter from a friend in Kansas City indicates that Sally Ann was putting out feelers for a job at a radio station there, probably looking ahead to when her work with the tent show ended.

The question of when and why Sally Ann began playing the accordion with the Blue Grass Boys remains the most puzzling piece of her career, especially since there is nothing to indicate that she had played accordion previously. Of course, as a piano player and versatile musician, playing the accordion probably came easily to her. The most likely scenario is that when Roy Acuff added accordion to his group in September 1943, Monroe—or Sally Ann—realized the commercial appeal of the instrument and followed suit. Joe Forrester thought it was Sally Ann herself who suggested to Monroe that she play the accordion. Perhaps she was looking for a way to stay with the band after tent show season, and the accordion provided the perfect opportunity.

Then, too, by August old-time banjo player String Bean (David Akeman) had left the band (he would return), and as Howdy wrote after hearing the group on the Opry, "Bill's program was fair enough, but String Beans leaving really left an empty spot in it." Perhaps the accordion helped fill that "empty spot." By October, Sally Ann was a full-fledged member of the band—she was singing on the Opry with the Blue Grass Boys. Some of the solos she sang were "Put Me in Your Pocket," "Goodnight Soldier," "Bury Me Beneath the Willow," and "I'm Just Here to Get My Baby Out of Jail."

In February 1945 Sally Ann went with Bill and the band to Chicago to record eight songs for Columbia Records. In addition to the four mentioned earlier, the numbers included "Nobody Loves Me," "Come Back to Me in My Dreams," "Goodbye Old Pal," and "Blue Grass Special." On "Kentucky Waltz" and "Rocky Road Blues" the accordion plays prominent and colorful backup, while on "Blue Grass Special" Sally Ann takes a swinging instrumental solo, documenting for all time her impressive improvisational capabilities.

Unfortunately, the two vocal trios on which Sally Ann sings tenor to Monroe's lead, "Come Back to Me in My Dreams" and "Nobody Loves Me," were not released until 1980 and 1984, respectively. (An alternate take of "Nobody Loves Me" was released in 1992.) These were the first vocal trios that Monroe had ever recorded—and they featured a woman singing tenor! If these trios had been become part of the bluegrass canon early on, it might have been more difficult to muster an argument that bluegrass was "man's music."

In November 1945 Howdy was discharged from the navy, and by December he had returned to his job with the Blue Grass Boys, a group that now included Lester Flatt on guitar and Earl Scruggs on banjo. Howdy also brought brother Joe along to play bass and do comedy. Having Lester, Earl, and Bill in the same band raises the question, Was *this* the first bluegrass band? That is to say, was it the first band to feature Monroe-style mandolin rhythm paired with Scruggs-style banjo? Did the first bluegrass band include a woman? Live recordings from the Opry lend some credence to this observation. Unfortunately, on these recordings Earl's banjo is the primary instrument you can hear. As there are no studio recordings of this group, and since Monroe's next configuration—with Lester, Earl, Chubby Wise, and Cedric Rainwater—has already been crowned the "original bluegrass band," the argument is intriguing but moot.

The Forresters remained with Monroe until the last of March 1946, working one week into tent show season. Thus ended Sally Ann Forrester's trailblazing connection with bluegrass. A different era in her life was opening. She was twenty-three and newly pregnant.

The three Forresters headed back to Tulsa, where they worked with Art Davis and the Rhythm Riders before moving on to Dallas, where their old buddy Robert "Georgia Slim" Rutland was reorganizing his Texas Roundup. Sally Ann was not a part of this group. Possibly her advancing pregnancy was a factor. In January 1947 Sally Ann and Howdy's only child, Bob, was born.

That same year the Texas Roundup added three new members—Sally Ann on accordion, Ludie Harris on bass, and Felipe Sanchez on drums—and began playing at a nightclub called Bob's Barn. With Sally Ann's grandmother Sudie now living with the Forresters and looking after Bob, Sally Ann was free to play music.

In November 1947 Sally Ann filmed some movie shorts with Rambling Tommy Scott, of medicine show fame, and his Hollywood Hillbilly Jamboree. Tommy's show featured a folksy kind of hillbilly music and included songs such as "Buffalo Gals," and "She'll Be Coming Round the Mountain." Tommy does all the lead singing but is joined by the entire band, including his wife, Frankie; daughter, Sandra; and guitarist Jenny Vance on the choruses.

Now in video format these clips testify to what a confident, gifted, talented, and beautiful performer Sally Ann was. As viewers can see, not only is she quite the show person, but she also carried the rest of the group with her accordion playing. She plays the majority of the introductions, most of the solos, and her backup holds the performances together. Looking like a 1940s-era movie star, she comes alive on camera and performs with smiling grace and ease. The Forresters worked in Dallas until 1949 when they, along with Sudie and Joe, moved back to Nashville. In 1951 Howdy began his thirty-six-year-tenure as Roy Acuff's fiddler. Sally Ann got out of show business entirely and went to work for the Social Security Administration, where she stayed for thirty years, retiring as a mid-level manager. She and her accordion came out of retirement a couple of times to join Roy Acuff's band on tour, but for the most part she was content to play at home gatherings with Howdy and Joe and friends. She later developed Alzheimer's disease and died on November 17, 1999, in a nursing home with her son, Bob, by her side. Howdy had died in August 1987.

The story of Sally Ann's life demonstrates how the first woman in bluegrass carved out space for herself. She began as a single girl playing in a non-family situation, played in several bands with her husband before the war, played in an all-male band with whom she had no personal connections during the war, played again with her husband in several bands after the war, took some musical jobs that did not include her husband, and finally quit the music business entirely—all in the space of ten years. Except for the year of her pregnancy, her musical career was not radically different from that of many men. As Robert Coltman points out, it is "rather typical for a country artist to quit performing after five or six years, to settle down, raise a family, and go to working steadily at something near home."

Did Sally Ann's presence in the Blue Grass Boys have an influence on any other women in bluegrass? That's a hard question to answer. In recent years the all-female group Tennessee HeartStrings has revived "Nobody Loves Me," one of the trios Sally Ann sang with Monroe. Another all-female group, Misty River, performs with an accordion. But for many years Sally Ann's playing and her accomplishments were generally disregarded. After all, it was only an accordion. And she was only a woman. But the fact is, she was there at the beginning, showing us that women have always been a part of bluegrass. Others would follow.

WILMA
LEE
COOPER

Often when first-generation women in bluegrass are asked if they recall seeing any other female players, their answer is no. However, many quickly add, "Of course, there was Wilma Lee." Indeed there was. In the world of hillbilly music, before country and bluegrass became separate genres, Wilma Lee Cooper was out there pounding the road and making records with her husband, Stoney, as Wilma Lee and Stoney Cooper and the Clinch Mountain Clan. Their music started out "hillbilly" in 1947 with the strong sound of the resonator guitar (Dobro), included a not-always-prominent banjo in the early 1950s, and became more "modern country" in the early 1960s with the addition of heavy drums, electric guitar, and piano. Then, as country music changed and their popularity and radio airplay waned, the Coopers found a new home in the world of bluegrass, a world that would continue to sustain Wilma Lee's career long after Stoney's death in 1977. But through all these changes, Wilma Lee's gutsy, belt-'em-out voice remained the foundation of the music.

Wilma Lee and Stoney themselves did not consider their music bluegrass. To them it was simply "pure, old country." Wilma Lee called her music "the old mountain style of singing." A reviewer in *Bluegrass Unlimited* captured the essence of the conundrum: "While Wilma Lee and Stoney never played bluegrass exactly, their music paralleled it to a certain degree, especially in spirit and basic instrumentation, and they have had considerable influence on many who do play bluegrass." Much of Wilma Lee and Stoney's early music could be called bluegrass without banjo. The Coopers had a foot in both worlds. And both worlds honored them. Wilma Lee and Stoney became members of the Grand Ole Opry in 1957, and in 1994 Wilma Lee received the IBMA Distinguished Achievement Award. In 2007 Bear Family Records issued a four-CD boxed set of their music titled *Wilma Lee and Stoney Cooper: Big Midnight Special*.

Wilma Leigh Leary (1921–2011), the oldest of three sisters, was raised near Elkins, West Virginia, by a schoolteacher mother, a coal-mining father, and a woman called Aunt Liney who lived with the family and looked after the girls. Both parents sang in church, where Wilma Lee's mother played the pump organ, and the Leary Family performed gospel music at picnics, funerals, and camp meetings, generally for free. As the girls got older they added secular songs to the repertoire. As a youngster Wilma Lee (who changed the spelling of her name sometime after high school) took piano lessons, and when she was around ten, her parents got her a mail-order guitar. From then on she and a fiddle-playing uncle provided accompaniment for the Leary Family. Having skipped several grades in grammar school, Wilma Lee graduated from Elkins High School in 1937 when she was sixteen. Her senior yearbook pronounces her "Wistful . . . Ladylike . . . Lovable." Wilma Lee entered nearby Davis and Elkins College that fall, earning a business diploma in 1938.

The Leary Family might have remained strictly a local group, but in 1938 they won a statewide band contest and were selected to appear at the National Folk Festival, which had moved to Washington, D.C., that year. When they attended again in 1939 as honorary guests, the Leary Family made some recordings for the Library of Congress.

On their way back from their first appearance at the folk festival they stopped by WSVA in Harrisonburg, Virginia, where they were offered a full-time job on the radio. Jake Leary was not interested in that but agreed to play on Saturdays. Soon, though, Wilma Lee says, "They talked my dad into coming down regular every day, and that's how we started in radio, there." The Leary Family had become full-time musicians. Their uncle, however, had to go back to teaching school, leaving them short a fiddle player. They found a replacement in Dale Troy "Stoney" Cooper, who joined the group probably in the fall of 1938. Stoney (b. 1918), from nearby Harmon, West Virginia, had gone to work as a fiddler in a local band when he graduated from high school. Blending his fiddle with her guitar and his voice with hers, Stoney began a partnership with Wilma Lee that would end only with his death.

Thrown together every day by work, travel, and music, it was almost inevitable that Wilma Lee and Stoney would pair up romantically. She, the dark-haired oldest sister, was extremely good looking, outgoing, personable, a small girl with a big voice. Stoney, tall, slim, friendly, talkative, and debonair with a thin mustache, looked a bit like Clark Gable. They married in June 1941 and in the fall moved with the Leary Family to WWVA in Wheeling, West Virginia. When their only child, Carolee, was born in March 1942, the newlyweds decided to give up the music business. Wilma Lee stayed home with their daughter, and Stoney drove a soda pop truck. Six months of living a conventional lifestyle convinced the Coopers that this was not for them. They resumed their musical career and never looked back. Instead of rejoining the Leary Family, they decided to strike out on their own, hoping to find work at a radio station that would pay enough so that they "wouldn't have to make personal appearances to make ends meet." This would, of course, allow them to spend more time at home with Carolee.

In the fall of 1942 they found that job at KMMJ in Grand Island, Nebraska. Here they drew a regular salary working as a duet on various shows throughout the day and going home at night. They found a woman to keep Carolee during the day. To Wilma Lee, "It was like a regular job." Between programs Wilma Lee did typing for the station to make extra money; Stoney shot pool. But the next summer the Coopers got a better offer and moved on, first to a radio station in Indianapolis, then to Chicago, and finally back to Fairmont, West Virginia, in 1944. Stoney recalled that it was there that Wilma Lee told him, "I think we could take our own band out and do just as well." Stoney, not as confident, said, "It kinda scared me." Nevertheless, that's exactly what they did, calling themselves Stoney Cooper and His Blues Chasers, the name taken from a line in a song they sang. The group included an electric steel guitar, a bass, and a guitarist who yodeled.

During their next move, to Blytheville, Arkansas, at the end of 1945, they picked up Bill Carver, a Bill Monroe–style mandolin player who also doubled on steel guitar and Dobro. Wilma Lee had begun singing some Roy Acuff numbers like "Wreck on the Highway," with Stoney backing her up on the Dobro. Robert Cogswell says, "The popularity of the Acuff material and style was so strong that it influenced the basic direction of [their] sound—it utilized Wilma Lee's strength as a 'heavy' vocal solo and allowed Stoney to play instrumental backup and sing harmony." Wilma Lee's voice, backed by the Dobro, would become the defining element in their music.

A jump to WWNC in Asheville, North Carolina, in March 1947 was short-lived, but here they made their first recordings: eight sides for Jim Stanton's new Rich-R-Tone Records. In July they were hired back by WWVA, now a powerful fifty thousand watts. That December in Wheeling they cut eight more sides for Rich-R-Tone. Wilma Lee said that these recordings were her favorites. "Our heart and soul were in those records. I just felt that's the best work we ever did." Those songs included "The Little Rosewood Casket," "Wicked Path of Sin," "This World Can't Stand Long," "Tramp on the Street," and "Matthew Twenty-Four." These hard-core, no-frills recordings are, as Grand Ole Opry announcer Eddie Stubbs says, the "real deal."

As indicated by the labels on these early 78 rpm recordings, the band name was still in flux. Today the name Wilma Lee and Stoney Cooper and Their Clinch Mountain Clan seems non-gendered and equitable. But most of these first Rich-R-Tone releases list the group as Stoney Cooper and His Clinch Mountain Boys or simply as Stoney Cooper and Wilma Lee. It was only at the insistence of Carter Stanley, who headed up the Clinch Mountain Boys, that the name was changed to Clinch Mountain Clan. Stoney's name undoubtedly came first because, according to Robert Cogswell, he was the "front man and decision-maker." Since Stoney did most of the emceeing, it was easy for fans, especially radio fans, to assume that Wilma Lee "was a bit passive and let Stoney run things." But Bill Carver, a longtime side musician, said that Wilma Lee was actually never very far from the decision-making process.

The Coopers would remain in Wheeling for almost ten years. Many musical changes marked their stay here. Wilma Lee taught herself to play clawhammer banjo, which she called "flog style," by listening to performer Cousin Emmy. She recorded one number with the instrument, "I Ain't Gonna Work Tomorrow" (1950), which she learned from Ola Belle Reed, but she did not play banjo on a record again until 1963. In 1951 the Coopers hired Buck Graves, a pioneering Dobro player best known for his work with Lester Flatt and Earl Scruggs. Then in the late forties or early fifties they added a bluegrass-style banjo player to the group, although this instrument did not make an appearance on their records until November 1955 when Johnny Clark stepped up to the plate.

In Wheeling the Coopers were able to settle down for the first time. Although they pulled a house trailer up there, they eventually bought their own home. They also bought a record shop, which Wilma Lee ran from 1948 to 1956. "I made sure there wasn't an entertainer who could come through Wheeling but what he could find his record in our store." They not only stocked country music; they also stocked "Sepia music"—black gospel. Wilma Lee points out that her black customers did not come in on Saturdays because of the large numbers of country music fans, mostly white, who were in town then. She says there was one black lady, however, who bought every record she and Roy Acuff made. Wilma Lee also did a big mail order business, sending out a catalog with new listings every month.

In April 1948 Wilma Lee and Stoney signed with Columbia Records, where their big sellers were "Walking My Lord up Calvary's Hill," "West Virginia Polka," "Legend of the Dogwood Tree," and "Thirty Pieces of Silver." Many of their Columbia recordings were the "story songs" that Wilma Lee liked so well. She said, "When I sing a song, I see it happening in front of my eyes." These numbers would remain popular for Wilma Lee throughout her long career. They also recorded "Stoney, Are You Mad at Your Gal," a re-gendering of Cousin Emmy's "Ruby, Are You Mad at Your Man."

In May 1955 Wilma Lee and Stoney made the switch to Hickory Records, where they would stay until 1964. They released only three LPs, however, because Hickory's Wesley Rose didn't think the new format, which featured blue-grass banjo, would sell. Carolee, now fourteen, made her recording debut with the group in 1956, adding vocal harmony on several sessions. She would play rhythm guitar and sing with the band for a number of years and eventually go on to form the Carolee Singers, a prominent backup group that still performs on the Grand Ole Opry.

If chart action is considered to be the pinnacle of commercial achievement, as it is by some, then Wilma Lee and Stoney's most successful years were on Hickory from 1956 to 1961. Seven singles would make *Billboard*'s country music chart, with "Come Walk with Me," "Big Midnight Special," "There's a Big Wheel," and "Wreck on the Highway" landing in the top ten. But by the sixties country music had begun to change and newer sounds were in vogue. Wilma Lee and Stoney, now in their early forties, were starting to seem dated.

Propelled by their chart success, Wilma Lee and Stoney achieved country music's highest honor when they were inducted into the Grand Ole Opry on January 12, 1957. They sold their house and record store and moved to Nashville. For six years things were looking good for the Coopers, but in 1963 Stoney suffered a heart attack and never quite regained his health. In the years that followed, Wilma Lee often found herself working without him. Her attitude was pure mountain pragmatism: "I'm sure I don't do it like Stoney would . . . but he's not here, so I've got to do the best I can."

In 1965 the Coopers signed with Decca Records, where they stayed for four years. But the death of Harry Silverstein, who looked for songs that would fit Wilma Lee's "mountain style of singing yet be accepted by the Nashville sound," ended their tenure there.

During the sixties Wilma Lee had became increasingly frustrated with record producers who "didn't understand our kind of music" and wanted her to record songs she would never sing on stage. She preferred to choose her own songs, because "when you have to do songs you don't care for, it's hard to sing them and do them justice." Perhaps she was more satisfied with the two albums that came after Decca: *A Tribute to Roy Acuff* (Skylite, 1972) and the gospel *Walking My Lord up Calvary's Hill* (Power Pak/Gusto, 1973). Gospel music had always been a big part of the Coopers' repertoire, and Wilma Lee once said, "As far back as I can recall, I always wanted to be a preacher."

By the early seventies Wilma Lee and Stoney's old-fashioned country music could no longer find a home on a major label. Fortunately they were welcomed with open arms by the bluegrass community. The first bluegrass festivals were starting to spring up, and it was here, as *Bluegrass Unlimited* noted, that the Coopers began "winning over a whole new audience to their unique mountain style."

Wilma Lee and Stoney sealed their departure from commercial country music by recording a self-titled album for the new bluegrass label Rounder in 1976. And though the *Bluegrass Unlimited* reviewer called Wilma Lee "the most powerful, exciting, and enduring of all the female singers of traditional country music," he deemed the album a "musical disappointment" due to the loud electric bass, the drums, and the "insipid Nashville humming of the Carolee Singers." But Wilma Lee had other things on her mind. Stoney was becoming increasingly ill, and on March 22, 1977, he died.

Wilma Lee was fifty-six years old. She had been partnered with Stoney in music and in life for almost forty years. "It was hard because Stoney and I were together constantly. We were never apart like most families are, where the husband goes to work and leaves the wife. When we worked, we worked together, we traveled together, and when we were home, we were together." And now he was gone.

Wilma Lee could have quit playing entirely or at least gotten off the road, but she didn't. Two years after Stoney's death she released her first solo album, *Daisy a Day* (Leather, 1979). She was happy again to be choosing her own material, and some of her choices are poignant. The title number tells of a man who puts a "daisy a day" on his wife's grave. Wilma Lee pours out her heart in song, perhaps putting some of her grief into her music. The *Bluegrass Unlimited* reviewer, a longtime devotee of Wilma Lee's singing, declared the disc "a joy to review" and said the high point was "the intense, gutsy singing of one of the most remarkable women country music has ever produced."

In 1981 Rounder released a second album, titled simply *Wilma Lee Cooper,* which included six songs she had recorded with Stoney during their 1976 sessions. *Bluegrass Unlimited* called this one a "rare delicacy." That same year Wilma Lee recorded a second album for Leather using top-notch young bluegrass musicians, including Dobro player Gene Wooten, whom she would take on the road with her. The album, *White Rose*, eventually came out on the Rebel label in 1984. There was nothing ambiguous about her music now—it was bluegrass all the way. Of course, many of the songs were ones she and Stoney had done down through the years, but if there's one thing bluegrass audiences love it's an old song. After Stoney's death, instead of hunting new material, she "tended to stay with the authentic music . . . those good old songs."

Wilma Lee stayed on the road for years, often using her sister Gerry in the band to sing and do comedy as she had done long ago with the Leary Family. Then on February 24, 2001, Wilma Lee suffered a stroke while performing at the Opry. As the liner notes to her boxed set tell it, "Her mountain heritage and perseverance intact, she struggled to finish the song. Still in her trademark crinoline skirt and high spiked heels at eighty years old, she left the stage to a standing ovation." She was never able to return to performing and lived for years in a nursing home. She died on September 13, 2011.

Over the years, Wilma Lee Cooper has been called many things. *Bluegrass Unlimited* called her "the first lady of traditional country music," and historian and writer Robert Oermann called her "our matriarch, our musical conscience, our living legend." But in 2001, when WSM announcer Eddie Stubbs asked Wilma Lee in a live on-air interview how she would like to be remembered, she replied, "I wouldn't change my life. I would live it the same way. It's been a good life. I just want to be remembered as being a fair, moral, upstanding person. When they speak of me they think I'm a good person. And I try to live like that. And they might say, 'She's a right good country singer.'"

Indeed they might.

Rose Maddox was the consummate professional
entertainer, giving herself to the
audience above all things.

—Jody Stecher, liner notes
to *Heart of a Singer*

ROSE
MADDOX

Rose Maddox, the powerful lead singer for America's "most colorful hillbilly band," the Maddox Brothers and Rose, was playing rockabilly music before the term was even invented. As her biographer, Jonny Whiteside, notes, "She exploded the previously inconsequential role of the 'girl singer' in country music, established herself as one of country music's first national female stars, and set the tone for every woman who followed her." After parting ways with her brothers, Rose went on to have a successful solo career, putting a number of songs in *Billboard*'s top ten country singles. Then toward the end of her life she found a warm welcome from bluegrass fans. But her initial claim to fame in bluegrass circles was the one album, *Rose Maddox Sings Bluegrass* (Capitol, 1962), on which Bill Monroe played mandolin. Long thought to be the first bluegrass LP by a woman, it was actually released two years after the lesser-known *Roamin' the Blue Ridge with Jeanie West* (Prestige, 1960). The third bluegrass album by a woman, *Dian and the Greenbriar Boys* (Electra, 1963), by Dian James, would show the influence of Rose Maddox herself.

The life of Rose Maddox (1925–1998) is so melodramatic that if someone had written it as fiction, readers would scoff and say, "That could never happen!" It's a little like John Steinbeck's *Grapes of Wrath* with a musical twist. Born to the dirt-poor sharecropping Maddox family in Boaz, Alabama, Rose was the sixth of seven children, including five brothers. Her grandfather was a fiddler; her father, Charlie, played banjo; her mother, Lula, played banjo and mandolin; and her uncle Foncy was a traveling multi-instrumentalist who also taught music. Music was in the family's blood.

Lula was a strong-willed, determined woman, and in 1933 she, Charlie, and five children ages five to seventeen headed west, hitchhiking, walking, hopping freights, and living in hobo jungles. Arriving in Northern California, they began "following the crops" and picking fruit. They bought a radio and started listening to groups like the Carter Family, Patsy Montana, and the Sons of the Pioneers. Her brother Cal heard an ad for a "mail-order course in guitar playing," which included a guitar, and he signed up. Cal and brother Cliff, who already owned a guitar, started singing together for fun, and where there was singing there was Rose.

It was eighteen-year-old Fred, a nonmusician at the time, who came up with the idea to form a band after hearing that the hillbilly group he'd seen at a rodeo had been paid a cool one hundred dollars. Fred, raconteur nonpareil, talked the owner of a furniture store into sponsoring the band on radio. The agreement came with one caveat: they had to have a "girl singer." Eleven-year-old Rose fit the bill perfectly, even though her only previous performing experience had been in school talent shows. Nevertheless, in 1937 Rose, Cliff, Cal, and Fred, thumping on his brand-new bass, hit the airwaves on KTRB in Modesto. They played for free in exchange for being allowed to announce their personal appearances. They began following the rodeos on weekends, playing in rough bars at night for tips. As Jonny Whiteside so eloquently put it, "And the focal point was Rose Maddox, all of twelve years old, singing at the top of her lungs for this mob of rowdies." Thus the Maddox Brothers and Rose was born, a group who earned the title America's Most Colorful Hillbilly Band not only for their no-holds-barred approach to the music but also for their glamorous, colorful Western outfits.

At some point Rose learned to play bass, inspired by seeing Juanita Starks playing bass with her father's group, Arkie and His Hillbillies. This stood Rose in good stead when World War II came along and Fred and Cal were called into service. She and brothers Cliff and Don were able to keep playing for a while with her on bass. Later during the war she also sang and played bass with a western swing band in Fresno.

When Rose was sixteen she married a serviceman, primarily at the insistence of her mother. The marriage was a disaster from the start and the couple eventually divorced, but it did produce Rose's only child, Donnie, in 1943. What to do with her child was the problem every working mother faces. Rose says, "I was on the road all the time, and he couldn't get to school without me, and I couldn't find reliable babysitters to do all this stuff, so I enrolled him in military school when he was in first grade." But having to do that "just about tore me up." However, she told him, "It's the only way I got of makin' a livin',' and I've got to be gone to do it." In the summers he went to camp.

The Maddox Brothers and Rose remained together until 1956, when Rose split off to start a solo career. In the early sixties she had three top ten country hits, with her peak year of popularity being 1963. For a short time she was a member of the Grand Ole Opry. But bluegrass was not her métier until she was presented with the opportunity to record an album with Bill Monroe. According to Rose, it was Monroe himself who suggested that she record a bluegrass album. When she told him that she couldn't sing bluegrass, he replied, "If any woman can sing bluegrass, you can." And while Rose and Bill may have had this conversation, Carlton Haney, who was booking both Monroe and the pioneering bluegrass act Don Reno, Red Smiley, and the Tennessee Cut-Ups, says the idea was his. As Carlton pointed out, if Monroe had arranged it, why didn't he use his band to back Rose up?

According to Carlton, who was operating the Old Dominion Barn Dance in Richmond, Virginia, at the time, he asked Rose to stop by and play the show sometime. When she was in the area visiting her son, she obliged. At her rehearsal with the house band, Rose started off with a lively number she had recently recorded, "Down, Down, Down," but had barely gotten into it before she turned to the musicians and said, "Hold it! Y'all gotta get with me. I'm gonna start again." And she did. Another misfire. She stopped the band again. "Drummer," she said, "you see my right leg? You get with it. Don't pay any attention to my left leg." And as the drummer began hitting the off beat between the words—"I'm going down [*whop*], down [*whop*], down [*whop*]"— Carlton said, "You know what I heard? I heard Bill Monroe's mandolin beat." He told Rose, "You have got the timing."

Shortly after that, Rose and Buck Owens had two hit singles, "Loose Talk" and "Mental Cruelty," which were released in April 1961. Carlton booked them on a show together in Indiana that also featured Don Reno and Red Smiley's band. When Buck's bus broke down and he missed the gig, Carlton asked Rose if Don and Red could back her. "You betcha," said Rose. "If Red Smiley'll put that guitar to me, I'll be fine." The combination brought the house down and once again Carlton heard the beat. This time he asked Rose, "If I can get Bill Monroe to play and Reno and Smiley to back you up, will you record a bluegrass album?" Yes, she would. Don and Red would provide banjo and guitar and sing harmony.

With the go-ahead from Capitol Records, Carlton called Bill Monroe and asked him to play. Bill's first question was, "Is she gonna do some of my numbers?" When Carlton responded that she would probably do a quite a few of them, Bill agreed to play. Rose would record seven of Bill's compositions, including "Uncle Pen," "Molly and Tenbrooks," and "The Old Crossroads." Although he was uncredited at the time on the album, many bluegrass fans were well aware that Monroe was doing some of the mandolin playing.

Bill's absence on the second day of recording is a mystery. He told Carlton he had to be out of town. Carlton says Bill refused to play because Rose wanted to use a pedal steel guitar on the session. Rose says, "They all throwed a fit when Wayne Gailey showed up with me to play steel on it; 'You do not use steel on bluegrass!'" She replied with a classic: "Watch me." It is true that the second day's sessions use the steel extensively, while on the first day only "Footprints in the Snow" has a short pedal steel solo (which could possibly have been overdubbed later). So perhaps Monroe really did object to the steel.

The whole issue of Monroe's leaving the session would be of supreme unimportance here except for the fact that he was replaced by Donna Stoneman. Carlton says when Bill told him he wouldn't be there the second day, he (Carlton) told the producer he knew a "little girl mandolin player" who "keeps time almost as good as Monroe's beat." Donna, twenty-eight, had just moved to town and was glad to get the work. This is perhaps the first instance of a female bluegrass musician being hired specifically as a side musician for a recording session. Unfortunately, Donna's work did not open doors for other women in bluegrass.

Donna says she was originally hired just to chop rhythm on the mandolin, but while they were in the studio working up the songs, some of the men couldn't get the instrumental solos the way Rose wanted them. When Donna played something on the mandolin and asked, "Is this what you want?" Rose said, "Let her do it." Donna takes leads on four songs, including the kickoff to "The Old Crossroads" (which she patterned after Monroe's kickoff to "Precious Memories"). Donna was a hard-core bluegrass player who had studied Monroe's work extensively, and her substitution for him is so seamless that one has to listen closely to realize that a change in players has taken place.

In keeping with her forceful personality and star status, Rose pitched bluegrass standards like "Roll in My Sweet Baby's Arms" and "Blue Moon of Kentucky" in keys where she could sing them, including C-sharp, B-flat, E, and F. She even moved Monroe's "Footprints in the Snow" from the sacred key of E to the higher key of G. Rose also changed the gender in "Footprints in the Snow," singing, "*He* traced *my* little footprints in the snow." And in the last verse, it's the man who ends up in heaven with the angel band.

Unlike most women playing and recording bluegrass during this era, including Jeanie West, Rose did not play an instrument on this bluegrass album—or any other album. Although she could play guitar and bass, when she recorded with the Maddox Brothers and as a solo artist, she performed as a vocalist only. She thus unintentionally serves as a model for female singers in bluegrass today who choose to not play an instrument.

Throughout the sixties and seventies Rose kept a brutal schedule performing country music, but as Jonny Whiteside wrote, "she never regained a high national profile." The business was changing and making way for younger talent, and Rose was old by commercial country music's demanding standards, especially for a woman. As her star status waned, she found refuge on the folk and bluegrass festival circuit as a single, picking up a band when she got there. Here she was treated as a "revered pioneer" rather than an "aging star." The Good Ol' Persons were one of the bluegrass groups who occasionally backed Rose at festivals on the West Coast in the late 1970s and early 1980s. Bandleader Kathy Kallick says, "She was always dishing out tips on performance and professionalism. She was very tolerant."

Perhaps in conjunction with Rose's emerging status as a musical pioneer, California's Arhoolie Records began reissuing some long-out-of-print Maddox Brothers recordings in 1976. Although these were not bluegrass by any stretch of the imagination, *Bluegrass Unlimited* apparently thought *Maddox Brothers and Rose, 1946–1951, Vol. 1 and 2* had enough connection with the music to mention them in the magazine. The reviewer called Rose "one of the truly all-time great female vocalists in country music" and waxed eloquent about these "marvelous reissues."

Rose ventured close to bluegrass territory again with *Reckless Love & Bold Adventure* (Takoma, 1977). *Bluegrass Unlimited* opined, "It's not bluegrass as such, but the fiddle, steel, banjo, and piano bring a similar drive and lilt to the proceedings." Her backup band included bluegrass greats Byron Berline on fiddle and John Hickman on banjo. Again Rose made gender shifts on a well-known bluegrass number, boldly changing "Shelly's Winter Love," recorded by the Osborne Brothers, to "Willie's Winter Love."

Arhoolie would eventually release four bluegrass CDs by Rose, including one compilation. The Vern Williams Band had been backing Rose frequently on personal appearances, and *This Is Rose Maddox* (1981) and the all-gospel *A Beautiful Bouquet* (1983) would surround Rose with the talents of this great traditional group. Rose had recorded most of these numbers during her rockabilly days, and the fact that the songs easily make the transition to bluegrass shows how closely related the two genres were. The fifty-something singer, still in strong voice, sounds as if she is enjoying herself with her exclamations such as "Swing 'em low!" and "One more time! Whoo! Lord, yes!" The compilation of the two projects was aptly titled *Rose of the West Coast Country* (1990).

Keith Little, the banjo player with the Vern Williams Band, recalls his days of working with Rose with much pleasure and affection. Keith was impressed by Rose's insistence on "making the audience an equal partner in the creative process . . . She paid as much attention to the flow of energy coming from offstage as she did the energy being created onstage." Keith describes Rose as a "blue-collar artist who was amazing in her capacity to perform under duress." He says that once, in Reno, "after getting a dose of food poisoning, Rose subsequently spent the twenty-five minutes between her six shows either in the bathroom or on the dressing room floor. When the curtain went up, no one was the wiser."

Rose's final album, *$35 and a Dream* (1994), would be nominated for a Grammy (1996) in the Best Bluegrass Album category. Many of the selections were newer compositions, such as "Sin City" and "Old Train," and numbers by Buck Owens and Merle Haggard. Rose's voice is finally starting to lose a bit of its power, which was no surprise. She was almost seventy and had survived the death of her son, Donnie, and two heart attacks. Her 1989 heart attack had put her into a coma for three months. Still she rallied to perform again, singing first from a wheelchair. In 1995 the Grand Lady of the West Coast was honored with the IBMA's Distinguished Achievement Award.

Rose kept working almost up to the end. She made it to the big screen, playing Woody Harrelson's mother in the Western *The Hi-Lo Country* (1998). Possibly her last public appearance was at the Sugar Shack in Hollywood, California, on July 22, 1997. As reported on one Internet website, "Looking tiny and frail, she had to be helped up onto the foot-high stage. Wearing what looked like a warm-up suit, she didn't look the image of a country music pioneer. But any doubts about that were erased the moment she started singing." Rose died nine months later, on April 15, 1998, of kidney failure in a nursing facility in her longtime home of Ashland, Oregon.

Although Rose's biographer Jonny Whiteside says that Rose "set the tone for every woman who followed her," he was talking primarily of women in country music. Was this true for women in bluegrass? Both Laurie Lewis and Kathy Kallick, pioneers themselves in the California bluegrass scene, believe Rose had a large impact on the West Coast. Kathy says:

> Rose was still quite iconic when I first came on the scene here [1973]. I first saw her at a folk festival in Santa Rosa, put on by Kate Wolf. Rose was a headliner. Butch Waller and I stood in line to get her autograph and he was quite reverential. He played that album for me, and I was puzzled at her not playing an instrument but still being thought of as a bluegrasser. I had the early indoctrination that everybody in a bluegrass band played an instrument. Anyway, I feel lucky to have met her and to have played music with her, and to have been made fun of by her and to have been part of her era. She was undaunted by living in a man's world, and sexism didn't slow her down as far as I could see. Yeah, I think she did a lot of paving the way.

I've endured, I've endured . . .

—Ola Belle Reed composition

OLA BELLE
CAMPBELL
REED

"I'm a hillbilly and I sing hillbilly music," declared Ola Belle Campbell Reed, singer, songwriter, guitarist, clawhammer banjo player, and National Heritage Award winner. And this remained the gospel truth even after Alex and Ola Belle and the New River Boys and Girls took on a bluegrass-style banjo player in the mid-fifties.

She could have just as easily pronounced herself a folk artist, for in her un-published autobiography she says, "All my life I knew the folk field existed and that someday . . . I'd be part of it." In fact, the music she is best known for today is found on the four folk albums she recorded in the 1970s. These LPs feature her at her old-timey best, playing clawhammer banjo and singing her original songs. But even as a folksinger Ola Belle refused to be stereotyped. As she says,

"I didn't exaggerate my hillbilly ways by putting on a gingham dress. The things I wear fit me good."

Ola Belle's songs also cross musical boundaries. Her best-known, "High on a Mountain Top," landed on the *Billboard* chart courtesy of country star Marty Stuart, was recorded by bluegrass great Del McCoury, and found its way into the repertoire of the alt-country band Blood Oranges. Old-timer performers Cathy Fink and Marcy Marxer have waxed "I've Endured" and "Hopelessly in Love," and Cathy's album *The Leading Role* (Rounder, 1985) includes "Only the Leading Role Will Do" and "Where the Wild, Wild Flowers Grow." The Demolition String Band devoted an entire album, *Where the Wild, Wild Flowers Grow* (Okra-Tone Records, 2004), to her songs. There is an Ola Belle Reed Homecoming Festival in her home state of North Carolina and a jamgrass group from New York named Olabelle in her honor. Who is this woman who has inspired so much admiration and whose spirit still endures?

Ola Wave Campbell (1915–2002) was born in Lansing, North Carolina, in that musically fertile area where the western part of the state meets southern Virginia. She was the fourth of thirteen children; her brother Alex, who would become her musical partner, was six years younger. Both her father and grandfather played fiddle. Grandfather Campbell, a Primitive Baptist preacher, had gotten kicked out of his church for winning a fiddle contest—and for being unrepentant about it. He continued to preach and to fiddle, starting a Sunday meeting at the Campbell home. People would come to hear him preach and stay to hear him fiddle. Thus did he balance heaven and earth and serve as a powerful example for his granddaughter.

Her father, Arthur, a schoolteacher turned general-store owner, had played in a band with his brother Dockery, sister Ellen, and their friend Rebecca Jones on old-time banjo. The New River Boys and Girls (named for the nearby New River) performed locally at homes and socials, as well as for medicine shows and sales. Thus from the beginning Ola Belle was part of a community where it was possible for women to play music—even the five-string banjo—outside their own homes. Uncle Doc taught her to play old-time banjo, and Aunt Ellen taught her to play guitar and organ. Ola Belle paid it forward by teaching Alex to play guitar when he was ten.

The Depression hit Arthur Campbell hard, and in 1934 the family headed north, joining an exodus of Southerners looking for work. They eventually wound up in the area around Rising Sun, Maryland. Ola Belle, who had had to leave high school just a few months before she graduated, found work as a housekeeper, and she and Alex began to play music at community gatherings and local auctions.

In 1936 Ola Belle met Arthur "Shorty" Woods, who was looking for a lead singer for his band, the North Carolina Ridge Runners. She would stay with this group for twelve years, playing guitar and clawhammer banjo. During this time she added the "Belle" to her name, perhaps drawing on the example of other established "hillbilly" singers such as Lulu Belle, from the WLS Barn Dance, and Maybelle Carter.

The Ridge Runners were a hillbilly band who dressed in Western outfits complete with hats. Over the years the group had a number of girl singers who would harmonize with Ola Belle. The group cut two 78 rpm records (Security, 1947), and at least one of them was credited to "Ola Belle and the North Carolina Ridge Runners." In 1942 the Ridge Runners became the house band at Sunset Park, a country music park that had opened in 1940 in West Grove, Pennsylvania.

Ola Belle's life took some new turns in 1945 when Alex returned from the war to join the Ridge Runners and she started dating Ralph "Bud" Reed, also back from service. Bud, a Maryland native, was from a musical family who had moved to Rising Sun in 1928. He played a fine harmonica and guitar and had been performing regularly at dances in the area since the late 1930s. The two would marry in 1949 when Ola Belle was thirty-four.

By the time 1948 rolled around, Alex and Ola Belle had formed their own band, the New River Boys and Girls, with Sonny Miller on fiddle and Ola Belle occasionally playing clawhammer banjo. (Though often shortened in print, the name was clearly intended to carry on the spirit of their father's mixed-gender group.) At some point they added Dobro and bass, and at one time they had a Merle Travis–style electric guitar player. Around 1951 they cut one 78 rpm record for the Chesapeake label.

Then in 1950 Ola Belle and Alex signed a five-year lease to do the booking and be the house band at Rainbow Park in nearby Lancaster, Pennsylvania. When that didn't work out and Sunset Park couldn't use them as the house band, they decided to build their own country music park. New River Ranch in Rising Sun, Maryland, opened in the spring of 1951 with Lester Flatt and Earl Scruggs. It ran for seven years until a blizzard destroyed the stage in the spring of 1958. Ola Belle and Alex, thinking practically, moved to Sunset Park, where they became the house band and "Uncle" Alex served as the genial emcee. During this time period, Ola Belle's two sons were born, Ralph Jr. in 1950 and David in 1953.

Times were changing, as always, and young musicians were starting to pick the banjo "Scruggs style." The popularity of this new and exciting music was probably what led Ola Belle to feature twenty-two-year-old James "Jim" Brooks, a transplanted banjo player from Lansing, North Carolina, on the show as a guest. He joined full-time around 1954, but little about the music altered. Sometimes Ola Belle and Jim played clawhammer and bluegrass banjo together; sometimes fiddler Sonny Miller would play twin bluegrass banjo with Jim. When Jim's brother Harold came back from service in 1955, he joined the band as a guitarist, enabling the group to play some of the up-tempo bluegrass numbers that Harold and Jim liked to sing. Their instrumental capabilities also allowed Sonny Miller to play fiddle tunes such as "Katy Hill" at blistering bluegrass tempos. According to Jim, when they started playing fast, Ola Belle and Alex would "back off" and let them shine. The music Ola Belle and Alex played was "not as fast." Jim and Harold stayed with the band until around 1959 when they went back to North Carolina. This apparently left the band without a banjo player until Ted Lundy joined the group around 1961. Jim remembers their schedule like this: Fridays they played firemen's carnivals, Saturdays they played radio and TV shows, Sundays they played at Sunset Park or New River Ranch. Sunday nights they would "work out their shows" at Alex's house.

Ola Belle and Alex recorded a number of singles and EPs on their own New River label. These thirty-two songs, recorded around 1961 or 1962 after Ted Lundy joined the band, give us a chance to hear the early sound of the group. Most of these numbers were packaged on two Starday LPs: *Sixteen Radio Favorites* (1963) and *Travel On* (1965). Many of these selections reflect the early "not-quite-bluegrass" sound of the band, which features fiddle and the old-fashioned Dobro work of Deacon Brumfield. Some, however, such as "[Gotta] Travel On" and "When I Lay My Burdens Down," feature the strong, crisp banjo playing of the young Ted Lundy.

If these sides are an indication of what the band did in a live show, Ola Belle certainly did not have a "leading role," something she sang about in a song she wrote. She played no clawhammer banjo and sang little lead. She mostly sang tenor to Alex or even Ted Lundy, and in the mix her voice does not stand out. In addition, according to Jim Brooks, Alex did the emceeing for the show, although Ola Belle did some "talking and cutting up." Perhaps this is one reason she made a conscious choice to redefine her music and find acceptance as a folk artist. In the world of bluegrass and country music, there was no place for Ola Belle to tell stories or expound on her philosophy of life as she did so eloquently on her album *My Epitaph*.

In 1965 two students from the University of Pennsylvania, Henry Glassie and Gei Zanzinger, began documenting Ola Belle's music on film and tape. Their interest in her music and her as a person ushered Ola Belle into the world of folk music. Here her old-time banjo playing, her singing, and her original songs—her very "authenticity"—were treasured. Folk music brought wider audiences, more extensive traveling, and a broader appeal. With help from Henry, Ola Belle began to find steady work in the folklore field, playing in college classrooms and for historical societies and museums. A whole new world was opening up for her music. Still, every Sunday found her and Alex playing with the New River Boys and Girls at Sunset Park.

In 1969, now fifty-four, Ola Belle began performing regularly with Bud and their son David, playing colleges and folk festivals across the country, where she and her music were warmly received. In the seventies she recorded four albums, two for Rounder, *Ola Belle Reed* (1972) and *Ola Belle Reed and Family* (1976), and two for Folkways, *My Epitaph: A Documentary in Song and Lyric* (1976) and *All in One Evening* (1977).

No story of Ola Belle's life would be complete without mentioning the generosity she and Bud showed in opening their home to people in need. From the time they were married, they always had someone else living with them. Folks stayed for weeks, months, and even years. Sometimes they were white, sometimes they were black. All in all, Ola Belle says, "I have helped raise twenty-one little ones and maybe more if you count those who stayed for just a couple of years."

In 1978 Ola Belle was awarded an honorary doctorate degree from the University of Maryland, and in 1986 she received the National Heritage Award. The IBMA recognized her many contributions to bluegrass music with its Distinguished Achievement Award in 1988. She was the second woman to receive this award. Unfortunately, Ola Belle was not able to personally accept her IBMA award. In 1987 she had had an aneurysm and a stroke. She would remain bedridden and unable to speak for fifteen years, living with her sister Darthula in Rising Sun. Bud visited her every day.

Ola Belle died on August 17, 2002, leaving behind a rich legacy not only in performance and song but also in the memories of the folks who knew her as a deeply caring person who always went the extra mile, had a big heart, and believed religion means that those who have should look after those that don't have.

THE SECOND DECADE: *The 1950s*

As bluegrass enters its second decade, the list of visible women has grown longer. Some musicians such as Bessie Lee Mauldin and the Stoneman sisters played out their careers on the national stage. Grace French, however, stayed primarily in the New England area, as did Vallie Cain in the Washington, D.C., metropolis. The Sullivan Family and the Lewis Family started out as regional groups but over the years found that their audiences stretched far beyond the boundaries of the South.

As did their predecessors, many of these women had some experience playing hillbilly music before they ventured into bluegrass, although the Lewis sisters and Bessie Lee (as far as we know) began their professional careers in full-fledged bluegrass bands. For the most part, these women still came from the blue-collar families of mill workers, carpenters, sharecroppers, and machinists. Educationally, a number graduated from high school, while others like Margie Sullivan and Donna Stoneman had to drop out early on to help their families. Husband-and-wife teams and family bands were still the rule, with only Patsy Stoneman breaking out of the pattern to lead her own all-male band in the sixties.

But most significantly, while the majority of these women continued to play supporting roles on guitar or bass, a few brave souls were venturing into tes-tosterone territory and beginning to step up to the plate instrumentally. Roni and Donna Stoneman were studying Earl Scruggs and Bill Monroe just like the men and becoming proficient on banjo and mandolin. Their sister-in-law (for a time), Peggy Peterson Brain, was also showcasing her finely honed skills on the Dobro. These three would become the first women to record bluegrass music on their respective instruments.

But these relatively well known artists were by no means the only women playing bluegrass in the fifties. Others performing at the local level have left behind their own musical footprints. In 1951 Lou Osborne (Williams), sister to the Osborne Brothers, Bobby and Sonny, recorded four songs that she wrote, including "New Freedom Bell." Featuring Sonny, Bob, and Jimmy Martin, the numbers were released on the Kitty label as Lou Osborne and the Osborne Family and Lou and Sonny Osborne and the Stoney Mountain Boys. Lou sang but did not play an instrument. Bill and Mary Reid and the Melody Mountaineers, from Virginia, had a decade-long career in country music and were beginning to dabble in bluegrass when their marriage broke up in 1958. Two of the eight songs the group recorded for Columbia in 1955 featured banjo, and Mary sang high baritone on both of these. Although Mary played bass on their stage shows, only a male musician would do in the studio.

Other women followed the time-honored tradition of both singing and play-ing. One of the best known was guitarist Lillimae Whitaker (b. 1940), from Ohio, who was described by *Bluegrass Unlimited* as a "gospel performer from the singin'-shoutin' school whose voice is rough-hewn and forceful." Lillimae first played with her dad and sister Wilma Jean as the Haney Family, performing at churches and camp meetings. When Wilma Jean married and gave up traveling, Lillimae and her father added mandolin player Charlie Whitaker and kept going. Then in 1956, as Lillimae tells it, "I run off and married him. And that's how I kept a mandolin player all these years!" Her father retired shortly thereafter and Noah Hollon joined on banjo. Known throughout the early sixties as the

Southern Gospel Singers, the group changed its name to Lillimae and the Dixie Gospel-Aires around 1966 after the success of *The Old Crossroad*, an LP they made with gospel singer J. D. Jarvis. Additional albums quickly followed: *Lo, I Am with You* (Arco, 1967), *Jesus Has Called Me* (Rural Rhythm, 1968), and *Working on a Road* (Down Home, 1972). Although in her later years, Lillimae would occasionally "retire" from the road, the group continued to play and record well into the twenty-first century.

Bonnie Lou and Buster is also a familiar name to those who are well versed in the history of early country music. The wife-and-husband team had been playing hillbilly music together since their marriage in 1945, with Buster Moore on mandolin and Bonnie Lou (birth name Margaret Bell, b. 1927) on guitar. Although the Moores performed together with their own group in various Tennessee and North Carolina locales, in 1958 and 1959 they worked with Carl Story, known as the Father of Bluegrass Gospel, and recorded a number of songs on Starday Records. Bonnie played guitar or bass and did some singing. In the seventies they began hosting a nightly bluegrass and country show in Pigeon Forge, Tennessee.

Well known in the Bluefield, West Virginia, area were Rex and Eleanor Parker (b. 1922), another mandolin and guitar duo, who had been together since they married in 1941. They crossed the line into bluegrass when Rex began adding banjo to their shows in the mid-fifties. Their daughters, Conizene and Rexana, had joined the group by the late 1950s. The Parker Family released several recordings in the early 1960s, and Eleanor and Rex continued to play on into the 1990s.

Then there are those women who were usually known only to family and friends, but whose names somehow made it into print. LaVaughn Lambert (Tomlin) could represent every woman who has played in a bluegrass band for a while and then dropped out only to later remain uncounted, unremembered, and unrecognized. She joined her brother L. W. Lambert in his band, the Carolina Neighbors, in 1952, playing guitar to begin with and then switching to bass. She left the group around 1955. Decades later she was pictured in an article about her brother in *Bluegrass Unlimited*. Wilma Martin (b. 1925) is also pictured in the magazine, playing bass with Bill Monroe's brother Charlie in 1953. She and her husband, Slim, on banjo, worked with Charlie off and on for years, but Wilma did not record with him. When Charlie resurrected his career in the 1970s, Wilma and Slim signed on again.

Way up north in New Hampshire, Dottie Lou Martin was learning to play the bass fiddle so that she could join her husband's band, Tiny Martin and the

Countrysiders, in 1957. She also sang lead and tenor. The band appeared regularly on radio and TV, and in 1959 they began a three-year stretch playing at the Hillbilly Ranch in Old Orchard Beach, Maine. They were still going strong in 1970, with Dottie Lou now on autoharp. Farther south, in 1954 Juanita Saylor and her husband, Lucky, who had been performing as a duo, took over the leadership of the Maryland-area Blue Ridge Mountain Boys around 1954. The group continued on with weekly radio shows in Rockville and Wheaton. Juanita played bass and sang.

Down in Georgia, Iona "Onie" Baxter (b. 1934) had "started into a bluegrass-type music in the early 1950s when a fiddle and banjo player asked me to play with them. I really liked the sound so I kept it up." She married J. N. Baxter in 1954, taught him to play guitar, and they began to jam with a couple of friends on banjo and fiddle. They were starting to get calls to play out when J. N. was drafted. When he got out of service in 1959, they resumed their jams with their old banjo player and added a mandolin and bass player to the group. By 1963 they had become the Bluegrass Five, and they carried that name and their music right into the twenty-first century. Onie and J. N. were inducted into the Atlanta Country Music Hall of Honor in 1998.

Guitarist Jackie Dickson had been playing country and gospel music when she married her banjo-playing husband, Larry, in Louisiana in 1957 and joined him in his brother's band. Later she and Larry moved to Little Rock, Arkansas, with mandolin player Clyde Baum. As Jackie told *Bluegrass Unlimited* in 1984, "At first it was just us and the Wootens playing bluegrass in Arkansas. As Larry taught others, bluegrass began to spread in the state. But there still weren't any women in bluegrass at that time. Even when we went to the first festival held at Hugo, Oklahoma [in 1969], I was still the only woman in bluegrass."

Jackie's comments provide a perfect example of how easy it is for female musicians to be unaware of other women who are playing, as that first festival in Hugo featured a band, the Down Homers, that included at least two women, Pat White (wife of Buck White) and Peggy Johnson, and probably also included Pat and Buck's daughters, Sharon and Cheryl. Also performing were Delia Bell and her singing partner, Bill Grant, whose family was putting on the festival.

Grassroots Music in the Upper Cumberland, a study of local music in the Upper Cumberland area of Kentucky and Tennessee, reveals several women playing at the community level. Nell Walker, from Nabob, Kentucky, started out as a young girl playing mandolin and guitar for her father's band in 1946. In the late fifties she organized her own group, the Little Nell Walker Band, which played both bluegrass and country music. The group broke up in the mid-sixties when her father died. The Lantana Ramblers, "the first bluegrass band from Cumberland County," officially formed in 1953 and included Willie Gene Warner on bass, her sister Creola Warner on guitar, and their brother Greer on mandolin. A reorganized version of the group played on into the nineties. Clyde and Marie Denny, who began singing together when they married in 1958, went on to have a long career in bluegrass and recorded a number of albums with their group the Kentuckians.

And of course this is only part of the story. We don't know the rest. Careful research at the local level will surely reveal even more female musicians and help paint a clearer picture of the number of women in bluegrass in its early days. As the saying about banjos goes (slightly reworded), they're out there, girls.

On the right-hand side with the bass fiddle,
from North Carolina, is Bessie Lee,
the Carolina Songbird.

—Bill Monroe
stage introduction

BESSIE
LEE
MAULDIN

Bessie Lee Mauldin (1920–1983), the bass player for Bill Monroe and the Blue Grass Boys from 1952 until 1964, was also Bill's girlfriend—or, as he called her in song, his "sweetheart." Richard D. Smith, Monroe's biographer, calls Bessie Lee "the great love" of Monroe's life. The fact that Bill was still married to his wife, Carolyn, for much of Bessie Lee's tenure made things tricky but ultimately workable. Many people who saw Bessie Lee and Bill together assumed they were married, and Bessie Lee has said that Monroe often introduced her as his wife. Ralph Rinzler's pivotal 1963 *Sing Out!* article, which positioned Bill Monroe as the Father of Bluegrass Music, refers to her as Bessie Lee *Monroe*.

Bessie Lee played bass on a whopping 35 of Monroe's recording sessions, a total of 111 cuts, which is more than any other player except fiddler Kenny Baker. She played on Monroe's first six albums, including *Knee Deep in Bluegrass* (1958),

I Saw the Light (1958), and *Bluegrass Instrumentals* (1965). She is the prototype of women in bluegrass everywhere who have been tapped by men—husbands, fathers, sons, brothers, and boyfriends—to play bass in bluegrass bands and who have risen gloriously, if unheralded, to the challenge.

That Grand Ole Opry star Bill Monroe would depend on his girlfriend to play bass for twelve formative years is remarkable. That bluegrass writers in general have not remarked on Bessie Lee's presence is unfortunate but understandable. The title of a Bill Monroe song perhaps says it best: "How Will I Explain about You?" In a bluegrass community that seemed to hold what we now call "traditional family values" and appeared to be deeply religious, how could anyone explain about Bessie Lee? Since there was no way to explain her, the community ignored her. Except when they were snickering about her.

Richard D. Smith changed all that in 2000 with his Monroe biography, *Can't You Hear Me Callin.'* In fact, he "aroused considerable consternation" among some outspoken Monroe fans who thought parts of Bill's life, such as the rumor that he and Bessie Lee had had a child together, were better left alone. What little we know of Bessie Lee's personal life comes from Smith's work.

Bessie Lee was raised in Norwood, North Carolina, a town near Charlotte, where Bill Monroe and his brother Charlie were on the radio in early 1936. It is unclear when Bessie Lee met Bill, but it was probably around this time, when she would have been sixteen. Bill's relationships with women were never simple, and in October of this same year he had married Carolyn Brown, who had given birth to their daughter, Melissa, the month before. Bill had met Carolyn in Iowa in 1934 when he and Charlie were on the radio out there. But the brothers had moved to Columbia, South Carolina, in 1935. Had Carolyn come with Bill? Did she come later? Had Bill gone back to Iowa to visit? Was Bill already married when he and Bessie Lee met? In a suit filed against Monroe in 1975, Bessie Lee claimed that Bill had initially told her that he wasn't married. The questions are myriad, the answers unknown.

After the Monroe Brothers broke up in 1938, Bill was in and out of the Carolinas until October 1939, when he and the Blue Grass Boys made their first appearance on the Grand Ole Opry. No one knows where Bessie Lee was in all of this, but the relationship obviously survived, because by September 1941 she had moved to Nashville and was traveling on the road with the band as Monroe's girlfriend. Carolyn stayed at home with the now two children and kept the books for the band. According to Smith, Carolyn was well aware of what was going on.

The situation gets even more complicated. As Smith goes to some pains to document, Bessie Lee most likely had a child by Bill Monroe, probably in the early 1940s, who was given up for adoption. In the mid-forties she had an on-again, off-again marriage to Nelson Gann, but by 1949 she had returned to Bill, who had left Carolyn. She and Gann divorced for good in November 1951, but Bill and Carolyn would not officially divorce until 1960.

By 1952, perhaps as early as mid-1951, Bessie Lee had become something more than Monroe's girlfriend. She had become the bass player for the Blue Grass Boys. As Alice Gerrard, herself an early woman in bluegrass, noted, "The word going around was that she was just in the band because she was Bill Monroe's girlfriend." And on one level this is true. Nothing that we know about Bessie Lee's life indicates that she was a musician before she met Monroe, and after her stint with the band, as far as we know, she never played again. But the bottom line is that she would not have been in the band—for twelve years—if she hadn't been able to play the music the way Monroe wanted. Bass players may be underrated, unrecognized, and unrewarded, but they are the rhythmic foundation of a bluegrass band. Those who can't cut it don't last long.

If Bessie Lee had been a man, no one would question why she was in the band. But because she was a woman and Monroe's girlfriend, we must answer the inevitable question: why did Bessie Lee begin playing bass with the band in the first place? The most likely answer is that she was there. In the early 1950s, with rock-and-roll sweeping the country, Monroe was finding it hard to keep a band together, because he, like many other country musicians, did not have steady work. He often had to rely on pickup musicians. With unrehearsed players, however, a solid rhythm section is essential. With Bill himself on mandolin and a dependable bass player who knew the material, he could hire pickup musicians and get the job done. And who was always on the road with Bill? Bessie Lee. Carlton Haney, Bill's one-time manager, says, "Bill told her she oughta learn to play the bass so he wouldn't have to hire another man. In three or four months she was just as good as anybody was on straight bluegrass." Carlton adds, "She was the only one I heard that could keep time like Bill Monroe." And with apologies to bass players everywhere, at an elementary but stage-worthy level, bluegrass bass is not difficult to learn—if you have a sense of rhythm, which Bessie Lee had in spades.

Bessie Lee began her recording career with Bill Monroe on September 16, 1955, recording three tunes, the vocal "Used to Be," in the key of C; the fast and furious instrumental "Tall Timber," in G; and the mellow "Brown County Breakdown," in E. These varied keys point to the fact that Bessie Lee was competent in all the keys, as anyone who played with Monroe would have to be. A study of the numbers she recorded reveals she played in the keys of A, B-flat, B, C, possibly C-sharp, D, E, F, G, and possibly G-sharp. She played in 4/4 time, 3/4 time, 6/8 time, at blistering speeds, medium speeds, and at slow speeds. She did not take any bass breaks on records or in any live shows that have surfaced.

During the next nine years Bessie Lee participated in all of Monroe's sessions except one (December 3, 1960), when she asked Tony Ellis to play bass because her fingers were blistered, presumably from the two sessions a few days earlier. Yet it must be noted that, as far as anyone can remember, she never played bass on the Opry. As Tony Ellis points out, there was always a staff bass player there, usually the great Junior Husky, hauling the big bass fiddle around was a lot of trouble, and "she didn't care to go in there." Did propriety enter into it? One can only speculate.

How good was Bessie Lee? The recordings show that she played more than the basic "root-five" pattern and quite often added inventive bass runs. It is enlightening to hear what some of her bandmates had to say. Banjo player Tony Ellis talked about her use of "passing notes" and praised the fact that all her notes were played at the same level. Tony said she had excellent instincts and timing and compared her playing to that of Jack Cooke, longtime bass player with Ralph Stanley. Banjo innovator Bill Keith said he liked her playing and described it as "better than adequate" although "never adventurous." And Del McCoury praised her bass playing as "highly underrated."

Tom Gray, bass player with the Original Country Gentlemen and the Seldom Scene, who is in the IBMA Hall of Fame, first saw Bessie Lee play in 1957. He says, "Let it not be thought that Bessie was just there because of her friendship with Bill . . . She played a driving bass line, not just keeping time, although her timing was always right in the pocket." Tom also points out that "Bill must have recognized talent in Bessie, for none of the . . . other women with whom he had an affair were ever asked to be part of the band." Tom has named his own bass Bessie in her honor.

In spite of the album credits, rumors circulated as late as the 1980s that Bessie Lee had not played bass on these sessions at all. According to these tales, either the bass parts were all replaced after she recorded them, or her studio microphone was turned off and there was another bass player somewhere in the studio doing the actual recording. It has also been suggested that Monroe listed Bessie Lee as a musician on the sessions just to get the recording fee. These rumors indicate the lengths some people went to in order to discredit Bessie Lee's accomplishments.

Bessie Lee not only played bass, but she also sang at live performances, although never on any of Monroe's commercial recordings. In a 1955 radio interview Bill Monroe said, "Bessie Lee sings in the quartet, in the Shenandoah Valley Trio, and also does solos." In live recordings that have surfaced, her high-pitched voice has a fair amount of vibrato (unusual in bluegrass), but even so it blends in nicely. On one live radio show, probably from 1952, she sings the huge Kitty Wells hit "It Wasn't God Who Made Honky Tonk Angels." (One has to wonder what Bessie Lee was thinking when she sang the line "Too many time married men think they're still single / That has caused many a good girl to go wrong.") Later in the show she takes the tenor on the quartet "Walking in Jerusalem," a part that Monroe himself sang on his 1952 recording. Her voice is smooth and controlled, and she's more of a crooner than a belter. On other shows from the 1950s, Bessie Lee sings high harmony on the quartets "Wait a Little Longer Please, Jesus" and "Hills of Glory." By the early 1960s Bessie Lee no longer seems to be singing when she takes the stage. Bill's daughter, Melissa, was starting to appear as a guest, and one can imagine that two featured female singers might have been too many.

Tony Ellis has said Bessie Lee didn't like to sing. He describes her voice as "operatic" and "educated sounding" and says that often the "rednecks in the audience would make fun of her." In spite of that, he says, Monroe would frequently make her sing, solely "to upset her." At a gig in Chicago, Bill was "egging the audience on, saying, 'Don't you wanna hear Bessie Lee, the Carolina Songbird?'" Finally Bessie Lee got so mad she walked off the stage.

Apparently Monroe's teasing Bessie Lee was not uncommon, as this tidbit from a live show in south Georgia in 1963 seems to indicate. At one point in the show Bill says, "Now we would like to try to do a hymn on the program here, a quartet. And Bessie Lee wants us to do a number entitled 'Somebody Touched Me.' What did you say, Bessie Lee?" Her reply is too muffled to hear, but one gets the sense that Bill is making a private joke at Bessie Lee's expense.

In addition to singing and playing bass, Bessie Lee helped out in other ways on stage. At a live show at the Newport Folk Festival on July 1963, during the first set, when Bill is introducing the band, you can hear Bessie Lee in the background telling Bill the name of the fiddle player he'd forgotten (Billy Baker). After the introductions, perhaps reading an expression on Bill's face, she says, "'Muleskinner,'" the name of the next song he was going to do. After Bill sings that, he asks in a low voice, "What's next?" Bessie Lee says, "'Uncle Pen.'" The next day you can hear Bessie Lee say, "Bill, stand back from the microphone," as someone has apparently asked him to do. Bill then asks, "What shall we do next?" and Bessie Lee says, "'Rawhide,'" which the band performs. Later in the show Bill's mischievous comment, "Really, I play the best time of any man in the United States," draws much appreciative laughter and applause. Bill then adds, "Bessie Lee says I brag too much." When someone in the audience asks if Bill ever sings any unaccompanied ballads, it is Bessie Lee who immediately says, "'Pretty Little Miss.'" Bill then sings the song. This interaction indicates that Bessie Lee was looking out for Bill and that their relationship, at least for the moment, was a comfortable one.

Pictures show Bessie Lee as a curvaceous, well-proportioned woman with bleached-blonde hair. On stage she wore a dress and high heels. Hazel Dickens and Alice Gerrard, musicians themselves, saw Bessie Lee play a number of times. When asked about her, both immediately got a strong mental picture. Hazel said, "I get this image of a great big blonde Amazon of a woman. She was always fixed up—her nails, her makeup, her bleached-blonde hair. She was classy and tasteful, but always on the edge." Alice said, "I have a very powerful picture of her in my head. I didn't really notice anything about her bass playing. I was more intrigued by the way she looked and the fact that she was a woman doing this. She was a very vivid-looking person. Her bearing was very dignified. She seemed big, she stood straight, she didn't smile on stage, she was very contained."

Richard Smith has made a conscious effort to acknowledge other aspects of Bessie Lee's influence. He positions her as Monroe's "muse," the woman whose often tempestuous relationship with the bandleader "inspired his greatest and most passionate love songs." These songs included "Can't You Hear Me Callin'," "Letter from My Darlin'," "I Believed in You, Darling," "In Despair," "On and On," and "Little Georgia Rose."

Smith also gives Bessie Lee credit for encouraging Monroe to allow Ralph Rinzler to conduct "the first in-depth interview that Bill Monroe had ever granted" and credits her with convincing Bill that Rinzler should become his booking agent. Bessie Lee knew that Ralph could book Bill into places, such as colleges and folk festivals, that he had never played before. And Ralph did, introducing Bill—and Bessie Lee—to a whole new audience of Northern college students. And, Smith says, she also acted as the band's "de facto road manager," sitting up front with the map and doing the navigating for the driver. Banjo player Bill Keith says that "getting a call from Bessie was like getting a call from Bill."

Bill Keith also tells a fascinating story about a time, early in his tenure as a Blue Grass Boy, when Bill Monroe didn't show up to go on tour. Fiddler Kenny Baker, finding out that Monroe was not going, also bailed. That left Bessie Lee, who picked up Bill Keith and guitarist Del McCoury in her car at their Nashville hotel. For the four-day tour in Alabama and Louisiana that they were doing with the Sullivan Family, Bessie Lee, Del, and Bill Keith performed as the Blue Grass Boys. When they left Friday night to drive back to Nashville, they were stunned to hear Bill Monroe on the Opry with a pickup band.

Bessie Lee did her last session with the band on April 9, 1964, recording four songs. On Monroe's next recording session a year later, his son, James, would be playing bass. Sometime during that year, Monroe told her that she would no longer be traveling with the band. She would be staying home on their farm, a farm that Bessie Lee would later say she had put her "life savings" into. Bill had a new girlfriend. Bessie Lee had been replaced. She was now wearing the shoes Carolyn Monroe had worn for so many years. But it wasn't until 1970 that Bill actually moved away from the farm, "completely abandon[ing]" Bessie Lee.

In 1975 Bessie Lee filed for "divorce" from Bill, claiming that she was, in fact, his common-law wife. She received a settlement of seventy-five thousand dollars and left the farm in 1976. For a time she worked for Johnny and June Cash as a receptionist. By the fall of 1982, in poor health with diabetes and heart problems, she moved back to Norwood to be cared for by her sisters. She died of heart trouble in 1983 and was buried in the Norwood cemetery. Bill Monroe did not attend the funeral.

Was Bessie Lee an inspiration or role model for other women? Historian Neil Rosenberg postulated that she had served as a role model for his then-wife, Ann Milovsoroff, who started playing bass in 1964 only after having seen Bessie Lee on stage with Bill Monroe. (Ann played autoharp before.) Ann herself doesn't quite see it that way. She says that back then "bluegrass was a guy's gig with the wives or significant others hanging around being the outskirts (good term). I can't say I saw Bessie Lee and said, 'Oh, wow, I want to do that.' I think I started playing more to have something to do to avoid boredom while all the get-togethers and rehearsals were going on, which may have had something to do with why she was playing. Can you imagine being on the road with nothing to do?" Ann also says, "I liked her [and] thought she had a tough row to hoe—Bill could be very crusty and moody—but she genuinely cared for him. She was dignified in what may have been a lifted-eyebrow situation."

Fiddle player Vivian Williams mentions a more indirect influence. In the mid-sixties Vivian played fiddle in the Tall Timber Boys from Washington State, the only woman in the group. She said, "It seemed okay to us at first to use the word 'Boys' in the band name, because Bill Monroe's Bluegrass Boys sometimes had a woman playing bass."

It is hard to calculate the influence Bessie Lee might have had on women who saw her perform with the Blue Grass Boys. In this overwhelmingly male musical genre, here was a striking-looking woman playing bass and singing in a top-level professional bluegrass band, a band that played on the Grand Ole Opry, and a band that traveled all over the country. Women everywhere could see that there was a space for them—singing and playing—in a bluegrass band. To be sure, it was a supportive role, a role women have always been assigned and were used to filling, a role that placed them in the back of the band. Still and yet it was a space. Bessie Lee was on the road with the band, on stage with the band, in the recording studio with the band. And if she shared Monroe's bed, so what? Maybe that was one of the perks of the job.

We're not in it for the money.

—Vallie Cain

VALLIE
CAIN

When banjo player Johnnie Whisnant left the house to play his first gig with Vallie and Benny Cain in October 1962, he told his wife, "I may be back in a few minutes 'cause I just happened to think, they's a woman playin' that guitar and it'll probably be some helluva mess." But when Johnnie arrived, he found out "there wasn't nothin' wrong" with Vallie's guitar playing. It was so good, in fact, that he played with Benny and Vallie for the next ten years; so good that Johnnie would ask Vallie to play rhythm guitar on a single he cut in 1964; so good that Vallie backed him in some of the numerous banjo contests he would win. Vallie played the old-fashioned way, with a thumb pick, and she was solid.

Benny and Vallie Cain, a husband-and-wife team, were stalwarts on the Washington, D.C., bluegrass scene from 1950 until Vallie's death in 1993. Their group, the Country Clan, was one of the first bluegrass bands in the D.C. area.

During the 1950s and 1960s they played locally five to six nights a week in addition to broadcasting regularly on several radio stations. With their steady work, they attracted some of the best musicians in the region, players who would later make their own marks on bluegrass: Tom Gray, Pete Kuykendall, Bill Emerson, Tom Morgan, Donnie Bryant, Johnnie Whisnant, Don Stover, John Hall, Scotty Stoneman, Roni Stoneman. When *Bluegrass Unlimited* spotlighted them in 1972, they became only the fourth band with a female member to make the magazine's cover.

Vallie Redinia Marion Kave (1927–1993), the seventh of eight children, was born in Maryland but moved to Berkeley Springs, West Virginia, in 1934. Many members of her family played music informally, and Vallie started playing guitar when she was about twelve, picking out her first song, "You Are My Sunshine," note by note. She said, "That guitar meant more to me than anything in the world." She graduated from Berkeley Springs High School in 1945 and was working for a clothing manufacturer in town when she met Benny Cain in 1947 at a musical gathering his aunt had put together.

James Bennett Cain (1921–1998) was born in New Haven, Connecticut, and moved with his family to Berkeley Springs when he was three. He, too, started playing guitar when he was twelve, and by his teens he was playing for local square dances. After graduating from high school in 1939 and attending college for a time, he served in the navy from 1942 through early 1946 and then went to work for the Bureau of Alcohol, Tobacco, and Firearms.

Vallie and Benny's first meeting turned into regular weekend picking parties whenever Benny was home. In 1949 these sessions materialized into a formal band called Benny Cain and His Country Cousins, with Benny and Vallie on guitars, Vallie's sister Virginia on bass, their brother Ford on guitar, and Kenny McBride on electric lead guitar. Pictures of the Kave sisters show them dressed to the nines in full country regalia, including skirts and vests, Western shirts, and neckerchiefs, with white cowgirl boots and white hats. The group played the modern country music of that era—Ernest Tubb, Hank Snow, Hank Williams—and soon got a job on WINC radio in nearby Winchester, Virginia. Much of the vocal work was done by Vallie and Virginia. Home recordings spotlight some of their duets, which included "When He Reached Down His Hand for Me," "Just a Closer Walk with Thee," "I Believe I'm Entitled to You," and "Snow Deer." Vallie sang the high part, Virginia the low.

At this time Vallie didn't know much about bluegrass, but Benny was learning. "Footprints in the Snow" was already in his repertoire. Soon he took up the mandolin, the group added a fiddler, and Benny and Vallie began experimenting with bluegrass harmony. Slowly but surely, the band began gravitating toward a bluegrass sound. Benny and Vallie's vocals kept the pattern established by the Kave sisters: Benny singing in a low range, almost always doing the leads, and Vallie singing high, catching the tenor.

Vallie said it was her idea to start singing in the higher, bluegrass keys. "We were singing very low . . . We thought if we're going to add a banjo to this thing—you know, the banjo's loud—you're not going to be able to stand up there and sing this low stuff and get it through unless you've got a powerful mike and they didn't have them back then. So I said, 'Benny, we're going to have to start tempoing this music up.' I said, 'Benny, you're going to have to sing the high lead and pitch it up in C or B.' And he did."

In August 1950 Vallie and Benny married and moved to Washington, D.C., to be closer to Benny's job. The Country Cousins broke up, but shortly thereafter the Cains formed an all-bluegrass group, the Country Clan, hiring a banjo player for the first time and continuing their show on WINC. Vallie was now the lone female member. The genderless name was perhaps inspired by Wilma Lee and Stoney Cooper's Clinch Mountain Clan.

The band name might have been genderless, but Benny still did all the emcee work and seemed to run the show (with Vallie occasionally interjecting caustic remarks if she thought Benny wasn't playing well enough). According to their friend and champion Walt Saunders, who wrote a detailed article about the couple for *Bluegrass Unlimited* in 1972, "Vallie did not seem to mind being second banana. She seemed comfortable in her role as tenor singer and rhythm guitarist. She complained all the time about everything, but did not seem to resent Benny's role. She just liked to complain. But she knew her job and was totally professional as far as their performances were concerned."

Like many bluegrass musicians, Vallie and Benny never tried to make a living solely from the music, and with Benny's government job, they didn't have to. Vallie also worked at a convenience store for fifteen years. Having day jobs made it easy for Vallie to say, "We're not in it for the money." They didn't have to be. On the other hand, Benny and Vallie never let their day jobs stand in the way of playing music. Somehow they found a way to do it all. For roughly fifteen years they played music anywhere from three to seven nights a week at restaurants, taverns, fire departments, roller rinks, and dances. Many of their jobs were short-lived—a couple of months, a few days—but sometimes they stayed as long as a year in one place, such as the B and J Restaurant (1955–1956) or Jimbo's (1964–1967). These venues usually paid from thirty to sixty dollars a night for the entire band, with tips no doubt raising the total. In 1962 they played at least 141 dates, in 1963 at least 125. One reason Benny and Vallie were able to hire such excellent side musicians is that they had so much work.

In March 1951 their only child, Andre Paul, was born. What Vallie did for child care the first four years of Andre's life while she was out playing music is a mystery. But when Andre was four, Erma Kidwell came to live with them and to look after the boy. She stayed for thirty-nine years. Andre would join the band on electric bass in 1968 and remain for over fifteen years.

Bennie and Vallie's first recording, "Angry Brown Eyes" and "Roving Gambler," a 78 rpm single (Adelphi, 1956), was among the earliest in bluegrass to feature a woman. Vallie's solid guitar playing, complete with runs, can be heard throughout. The trio on both songs is very tight, with Benny singing lead on the verses and Vallie and Pete Kuykendall (banjo) adding tenor and baritone to the choruses. While both songs are solid bluegrass, Benny's mild voice doesn't have the power and drive to propel either song into the hard-driving, high lonesome category.

Six years later they recorded a 45 rpm single for the new Rebel label featuring "New River Train" and the instrumental "Rag Time Annie." Two more singles followed in 1963. That same year they recorded nine more songs, which appeared, along with four of their singles, in a four-album package called *Bluegrass Spectacular, 70 Songs* (Rebel, 1963). The set featured other artists from the Washington-Baltimore area such as Buzz Busby, Earl Taylor, Frank Wakefield, Red Allen, and the Country Gentlemen. Vallie was the only woman on the project. The Cains' song selection was indicative of the musical path they would follow throughout their careers: old and obscure songs done professionally and competently but without that added level of excitement that the younger bands in the District area would supply.

Benny and Vallie recorded two albums for Rebel: *Benny and Vallie Cain and the Country Clan* (1968), with Andre Paul on electric bass, and *More of Benny and Vallie Cain* (1974). The *Bluegrass Unlimited* review of the second disc chastised them for waxing overdone songs like "Lorena" and "Mary Dear" but gave them high marks for singing all the verses to "My Little Girl," an "ancient chestnut," which was "the sort of thing the Cains do best." Unfortunately, this was their last recording.

Although the fifties and sixties were the heyday for Benny and Vallie, they continued to play throughout the 1970s, even making an overseas tour in 1982. But locally they seemed to have "dropped out of sight," according to Washington's bluegrass newspaper, *Blueprint*. Editor Mike Pittard tracked them down at their

Falls Church, Virginia, home in 1983 for an interview. Unfortunately the article perpetuates a number of tired gender stereotypes. The piece begins by saying, "One thing about Vallie, she makes good chili. Good, down-home, no frills chili." The same article describes her as a "wonderful, jolly lady," and later, in talking about her tenor singing, refers to her as having a "little girl voice." So we see Vallie portrayed as a jolly cook who sings like a little girl. Benny, on the other hand, is described as a "regular G-man . . . he carries a badge and it all sounds rather dangerous, having to do with raids and busts and things." Still, the writer shows a deep reverence for the Cains' music and closes with a description of their impromptu performance: "They sang like they have sung for as long as anybody can remember, half turned to face each other, each voice anticipating the other, supporting the other. Like the song and the chili, they seemed very much the right combination."

By the late 1980s the Cains had stopped booking shows entirely, primarily for health reasons. Vallie died in 1993 of complications from diabetes, Andre Paul died in 1997, and Benny followed them home in 1998 after a series of strokes.

Although Bennie and Vallie were one of the first bluegrass bands in the Washington, D.C., area and played there regularly for thirty years, their accomplishments have been overshadowed by other early District artists such as Buzz Busby, the Country Gentlemen, and the Stonemans. Perhaps this is partly because neither Benny nor Vallie had an impressive solo voice, although they did have a solid duet. Or perhaps it is because they were never on the cutting edge musically. They favored the old songs, the obscure songs, and their singing style was reminiscent of the mellower hillbilly brother duets like the Blue Sky Boys, rather than the fiery Monroe Brothers. Although bluegrass as a musical genre was new, Vallie and Benny performed in an almost pre-bluegrass style—with banjo.

Possibly their greatest contribution to bluegrass was providing steady work and a training ground for so many younger musicians. And Vallie's very presence in the D.C. bluegrass scene for so many years proves yet again that bluegrass was not completely a male domain. Walt Saunders says, "Vallie was the first female singer that I ever saw playing bluegrass." Undoubtedly that was true for many other bluegrass players and fans in the area. Yet few women mention her as an influence. Unlike Wilma Lee, Ola Belle, and Rose Maddox, Vallie never stepped out to take the "leading role." She was neither songwriter, commanding performer, nor darling of the folk movement. She was simply Vallie Cain, pioneer bluegrass musician, a woman who, in company with her husband, carved out a little piece of bluegrass history for herself. Perhaps that was enough.

Life was a happy rollercoaster.

—Grace French

GRACE
FRENCH

In 2002 *Bluegrass Unlimited* magazine featured an article titled "Bob and Grace French: Pioneers of Bluegrass Music in New England." The piece was a retrospective of their long career. But in spite of the article's title and the accompanying photographs, all of which feature Grace, the piece focuses primarily on Bob and often refers to "his band" and "his home." It includes no quotes from Grace. According to Grace, when Bob saw the final draft of the story, he called the author and said "he was tired of hearing only about himself. I was the other half, not only of him, but of the shows we played. I was an integral part of what he was in the music. I played rhythm guitar, did solo singing, most of the harmony, all the yodeling, and the train whistle. I was also the clothing manager." Like many women in all walks of life, Grace's contributions had been rendered invisible.

Born and raised near Boston, Grace Haley French (b. 1930) has always been a hillbilly at heart. As a young girl she loved to sing old country songs. Active in music from the time she could walk, she began entertaining at the age of twelve in a variety of ways: ballet, tap dancing, acrobatics, rope tricks, and, of course, singing. She was named "Most Talented" by her senior high school class. When she met Bob, also from the Boston area, on a blind date when they were both sixteen, she was already singing with a country band. This seemed perfectly normal to Bob, whose sister also sang with a country group and had made him learn to sing all her songs so that she could practice her harmony. Grace and Bob continued to date for four years, graduating from high school in 1948 and tying the knot in 1950. Before their marriage, Grace worked office jobs, went to college for a year, and worked as a professional model.

Soon after they were married, Grace and Bob bought guitars and learned to play. By 1952 they were working with the Rainbow Valley Boys, a country band. During the next three years, Bob took over leadership of the band, which added "and Sweetheart" to its name to acknowledge the presence of Grace. By 1954 the couple had three children, with a fourth arriving in 1961. Having kids kept Grace off the stage for only a little while. "After they were weaned," she says, "I went back to playing music." The couple would stay in the music business from then on (with minor breaks), although Bob, and often Grace, continued to work day jobs.

In 1953 the Frenches heard their first live bluegrass band, fiddler Toby Stroud and the Blue Mountain Boys, in which Toby's wife, Blue-Eyed Janie, played guitar and sang. Bob decided he needed to learn to play the banjo. Years later when Grace was asked why she started playing bluegrass, she would say, "I had to. We were playing country and my husband was playing banjo." In the developing bluegrass arena, Grace "seemed to be very much alone at that time. There just weren't any women playing bluegrass in our area. It was a man's world."

Grace and Bob worked with the Rainbow Valley group until 1955, when they took a hiatus from performing to spend more time with their three young children. Grace says, "Bob kept his day job and spent the rest of the time practicing the banjo." During this time Grace waitressed at night while Bob stayed home with the kids.

After two years off, Grace and Bob were back in the saddle again. They played on local television (Manchester, New Hampshire) every Wednesday night with Clyde Joy and the Country Folk and worked with this mostly country band throughout New England. Around 1959 Bob and his banjo joined Fred Pike,

Randy Hawkins, and the Country Nighthawks. When Grace weaned her last child, she, too, joined the band.

How did Grace handle the babysitting issue during these early years of playing? The couple often had live-in babysitters who received room and board in exchange for sitting with the kids on nights they were performing. The children's godmother, Lil Wamboldt, was a "tremendous help." When the Frenches played fairs and festivals, they took the kids and Lil usually came along. Grace says, "I never had any dire problems when the kids were little, but in their teens, Mom needed to be home for them."

In 1962 the Frenches reorganized the Rainbow Valley Boys and Sweetheart. They began playing every Tuesday night at Boston's famous Hillbilly Ranch so that the Lilly Brothers, the bar's regular bluegrass band, could have some time off. Bob did the emceeing for the group, and much of the lead singing, while Grace provided harmony and the occasional solo. She also yodeled and had the ability to make her voice sound like an old-fashioned train whistle, which always delighted and mystified audiences. Grace says, "Bob and I loved bluegrass, but to get the audience to really listen and feel the warmth of the music we had to play old country tunes and intermingle them with the bluegrass." Slowly but surely their fans began requesting bluegrass songs and asking where they could get bluegrass records. Grace and Bob had become ambassadors for bluegrass in New England.

Four years later the band released its first album on its own R-V-B label, *Green Green Grass of Home* (1966), on which Grace sang and played guitar. The recording, a mixture of country and bluegrass standards, also shows a strong influence from the West Coast group the Dillards, with the inclusion of "There Is a Time," and "Feudin' Banjos" (the latter tune recorded before it gained popularity in the movie *Deliverance* as "Dueling Banjos"). Grace provided harmony on most numbers and sang two solos: "Jambalaya" and "Shackles and Chains." Her voice shows the influence of her favorite singers Kitty Wells, Jean Shepherd, Patsy Cline, and Wilma Lee Cooper. The *Bluegrass Unlimited* review noted that the material was "performed in a competent bluegrass style" and that the singing was "professional." The album was reissued in 1973 with several additional cuts on which Beverly Raymond played bass. Rainbow Valley Boys and Sweetheart released a second album, *Authentic Bluegrass*, in 1967.

Around 1968 Grace decided she wanted to spend more time at home with her growing teenagers. During this time Bob played with several groups, including Joe Val and the New England Bluegrass Boys. When asked how she felt about staying home while Bob was out playing, Grace replied, "Bob was always very attentive to me, so it really didn't bother me too much that he was playing and I was home. Yes, I missed him, but I could go with him and sit in the audience whenever I wanted to. The band would always get me up to sing or do the train whistle." When the Frenches moved to Maine in 1970, Bob continued to play with Joe Val.

In 1974 Grace and Bob again reorganized their band, with Margaret Gerteis on bass, and changed the name to the Rainbow Valley Folks. The group remained active until 1990, when they disbanded due to Bob's health. In April 2002 Grace and Bob were recognized by the IBMA for their contributions to the development of bluegrass during its formative years, 1940–1954. Their names are inscribed on a large plaque at the International Bluegrass Music Museum in Owensboro, Kentucky, along with those of more than two hundred other First Generation pioneers. There are only sixteen women on the list, and Grace French is one of them.

I don't think there were many
women in bluegrass playing
when we got started.

—Janis Lewis

THE LEWIS FAMILY
Miggie, Polly, Janis

One might say that the Lewis Family, from Lincolnton, Georgia, had its genesis late one night in 1925 when twenty-year-old Roy Lewis (not yet known as Pop) and fifteen-year-old Pauline Holloway (not yet known as Mom) eloped, using the clichéd ladder-up-to-the-second-story-window ploy. All of the children from this union except Mosely, who died at age four, would go on to play in the family gospel group: Miggie (b. 1926), Wallace, Esley, Talmadge, Polly (b. 1937), Janis (b. 1939), and Little Roy. Mom and Pop stayed married for seventy-seven years until Mom's death in 2003 at ninety-two. Pop died a year later at ninety-eight.

Although the youngest child, Little Roy, became the "star" of the show with his world-class banjo playing and his comedy, the heart of the singing was the trio of sisters: Miggie, Polly, and Janis. From the beginning the women made a striking impression on stage, looking resplendent in high-heel pumps and fashionable matching dresses (hand-stitched by their mother until the mid-seventies), their hair fixed in the latest style. Early on the sisters began keeping a list of the outfits they wore at each show so that when they returned they could be sure to wear something different. Their wardrobe—and coiffures—always kept pace with the times, so today a review of their album jackets is an education in Southern fashion. Although Miggie never played an instrument, Polly and Janis did time on the bass, and if a piano was available Polly would tickle the ivories, since she and Janis had taken several years of piano lessons from Pop's sister.

Oldest brother, Wallace, was the first sibling to play an instrument, learning his first chords from Mom, who played guitar in a Mother Maybelle Carter style. Polly says, "We had to beg her to play for us. She never played on stage." Then, as Pop said, "The rest joined in." First it was the boys, as the Lewis Brothers, but in 1951 the group, including Miggie, who sang, did its first performance as the Lewis Family for a Woodmen of the World supper. Polly joined a short time later, and fourteen-year-old Janis joined in 1953. In the band's early days Polly and Janis were still in high school, and after graduating they, like many in the family, went to work in a nearby mill.

The group found its first jobs at church suppers and singing conventions, homecomings, schools, and supermarkets. In the early fifties the Happy Good-man Family recommended them to Southern gospel promoter Wally Fowler, who began using them on his thousand-seat auditorium shows. Their first long-distance booking was in Alabama. "We thought Birmingham was at the end of the world," said Pop. Although they were a gospel group, the Lewis Family let their music do the talking for them—they didn't evangelize or preach from the stage.

In 1954 the group began doing their own television show at WJBF in Augusta, Georgia, a show that would run for thirty-eight years without missing a telecast. For ten years they broadcast live every Sunday from noon until 1:00 P.M. As Polly said, "We had to plan our marriages, honeymoons, and pregnancies around the show day." Around 1963 the show, now being videotaped, moved into syndication and was shown on nearly twenty-five stations from Arkansas to Indiana to the Carolinas. Elvis Presley, who saw it in Memphis, said it was his favorite show. Freed from the confines of live TV, the family was now able to travel longer distances. By 1964 everyone but Wallace had quit their jobs at the mill. He hung on until 1967. The band had bought a bus in 1960, and the family members were now able to devote their considerable energies to music full-time. Mom almost always traveled with the group. She managed the record table while the family was performing, and at home she handled the financial records, paid the bills, and answered the fan mail.

The group's long recording career began in 1954 when they released two 78 rpm singles on Sullivan Records. Their next four songs were done for the Hollywood label, and in 1957 they signed with Starday and released their first album, *Singing Time Down South*. They would go on to record fifteen albums for Starday.

The first of their many *Bluegrass Unlimited* reviews appeared in May 1967 for the Starday LP *Shall We Gather at the River*. The reviewer, familiar with their earlier work, was irked here by their "artificially cheerful" performances and called them a "honky-tonk Chuck Wagon Gang." A few months later in a review of *Time Is Moving On* a different writer called them one of the best of the "country gospel singing groups." He also recognized what would become one of the strengths of the group, "material written by relatively current gospel song writers" such as Randall Hylton. They would also record gospel-flavored songs from the pens of Billy Joe Shaver, Tom T. Hall, and Johnny Cash. Their third *Bluegrass Unlimited* review, however, revealed the prejudice that many female singers in bluegrass ran up against: "The girl's [sic] singing tends to take the music away from bluegrass." To some, if it didn't sound like Bill Monroe or Flatt and Scruggs, it wasn't bluegrass. By 1975 a reviewer in the magazine opined, "There is not really much need to write a review of the new Lewis Family album. Take a look at the reviews of the last three or four LP's these folks have released . . . and you'll have a fairly accurate idea of what to expect . . . highly professional, well engineered, and tastefully performed."

The Lewis Family would continue to release albums at the rate of about one (sometimes two) a year up through the 1990s, when they slowed down a bit. After a fifteen-album run with Starday they moved on to Canaan Records for twenty-five albums, then Riversong/Benson, and in 1995 Thoroughbred/Daywind. By the early seventies they had begun to use Nashville studio musicians such as Buddy Spicher on fiddle, Pig Robbins on piano, and Buddy Harmon on drums to enhance their sound. But the singing was always their own.

Ever alert for opportunities to promote the band, in 1966 they began sending in their schedule of personal appearances to the brand-new publication *Bluegrass Unlimited,* a practice they continued for years. The Lewis Family was one of the earliest and most consistent groups to take advantage of this free advertising. Already they were traveling throughout the Deep South, but they were also going out west to Arkansas, Texas, and Oklahoma as well as all the way up to North Dakota.

These dates in the West paved the way for their first appearance at a bluegrass festival. In August 1970 they performed at the Grant's Oklahoma Bluegrass Festival in Hugo, where they were extremely well received. They continued to play there for more than twenty-five years. That festival was followed by a September appearance at Carlton Haney's Camp Springs, North Carolina, show. Bluegrass festivals were a logical extension of the work they had already been doing at fairs and country music parks. And they had always worked venues like schoolhouses with big-name bluegrass acts such as the Stanley Brothers and Mac Wiseman. For the next four decades the Lewis Family's big bus would become a familiar sight at festivals from Maine to California.

Pop Lewis credits the show Shindig in the Barn, which began in the fall of 1968 in Lancaster, Pennsylvania, for giving their career a big boost. The Lewis Family first played there in May 1969 and continued to appear two or three times a year for almost thirty years. Shindig in the Barn gave the Lewis Family exposure above the Mason-Dixon Line, which undoubtedly led to bookings at some of the larger Northern festivals. Playing this close to *Bluegrass Unlimited* headquarters in northern Virginia probably helped land them on the cover of the magazine in June 1970. They were only the third group featuring women to appear in this vaunted space.

Anchored by the maniacal comedy of Little Roy, the Lewis Family's show was unlike any other. Polly often performed the straight role for Little Roy's many routines and served as the butt of his jokes, but no one on stage was exempt, including Miggie, whom Little Roy consistently referred to as the "old maid." Miggie took his teasing with good grace as did everyone. *Bluegrass Unlimited* said, "They probably give more show for the money than any other group on the circuit, be they Gospel or straight bluegrass."

At bluegrass festivals the modus operandi of the group was professionally consistent. When they hit the stage, resplendent in their colorful outfits, they would immediately launch into a fast-paced song from their newest album, which Little Roy propelled with his driving banjo. Polly did much of the emceeing, introducing the songs and pleading with Little Roy to stop cutting up and get on with the show. She also advertised their records and future dates and always invited the audience to visit their record table, where Mom was sitting with a gargantuan display of merchandise. In addition to all that, Polly did the lion's share of the singing, participating in most of the trios and performing many solos.

To many people the Lewis Family radiated a sincerity and down-home friendliness that never seemed false or crossed the line into cloying sweetness. Others seemed unable to get past their deep south Georgia accents, as if this, coupled with their gospel music, automatically turned them into the dreaded Bible thumpers.

When asked about their influences, Polly mentions Martha Carson, Mahalia Jackson, and Sister Rosetta Thorpe as being "ladies I admired when I was growing up." Janis says, "I don't think there were many women in bluegrass playing when we got started. I can't think of any." But, she says, "There were a few women who played. I guess some of my influences were Wilma Lee Cooper, Anna Carter (now Mrs. Jimmie Davis, who was with the Chuck Wagon Gang), and it was a real treat to hear Melissa Monroe (Bill's daughter) sing occasionally on the Grand Ole Opry."

Although the sisters do not mention her, Gloria Belle was one of the women who shared the stage with the Lewis Family in the early seventies. Gloria Belle says she became friends with the Lewis sisters because "there weren't any girls around in the business to talk to except them." Festival ad after festival ad from the early seventies includes boy band after boy band, and then, often on Sunday, the Lewis Family.

The Lewis Family endured through the years as a family band with only occasional changes. In 1972 Talmadge left the group, and in 1974 the third generation came aboard with the addition of Wallace's son Travis on bass. Janis said, "Pop, Polly, and I alternated the bass playing, but when we heard Travis we realized we were not playing as well as we thought we were. The three of us haven't played since." Lewis Phillips, Janis's son, joined full-time a few years later. Wallace retired in 1995 due to illness and died in May 2007. When Mom began to have health problems in the mid-nineties, Miggie stayed at home with her. Still in 1995 the band traveled more than one hundred thousand miles, playing two hundred dates, including fifty or so bluegrass festivals.

Over time the Lewis Family has accumulated numerous awards, including the Distinguished Achievement Award from the International Bluegrass Music Association in 2002. In 1992 they were inducted into the Georgia Music Hall of Fame. In 2006 they received bluegrass music's highest acclaim when they were inducted into the IBMA Hall of Fame.

The long career of the original Lewis Family band came to an end in 2009. Little Roy and his banjo joined forces with multi-instrumentalist Lizzie Long in the group Little Roy and Lizzie, while Janis, Lewis Phillips, and Travis Lewis put together a group they call the Lewis Family Tradition. So in one way or another the music of the Lewis Family lives on into the twenty-first century in bands that continue to feature women.

I felt kinda bad sometimes that the Stonemans
were not kinda pampered a wee bit
by the bluegrassers.

—Roni Stoneman

THE
STONEMANS
Patsy, Donna, Roni

The Stonemans—Patsy (b. 1925), Donna (b. 1934), and Roni (b. 1938)—occupy an important place in the history of women in bluegrass. Roni, whom many people know from the television show *Hee Haw*, was the first woman to play Scruggs-style banjo on an LP, in 1957. That same year Donna became the first woman to play bluegrass mandolin, on a single she cut with her brother Scott's band, the Bluegrass Champs, which also included their brother Jimmy. Peggy Brain, married to Jimmy at the time, also appeared on that recording, making her the first woman to record bluegrass Dobro. And Patsy, who played guitar and autoharp, was one of the first women to lead her own bluegrass band, beginning around 1962. That's a lot of firsts.

Born into a family with deep musical roots in southwest Virginia, all three Stoneman women began playing publicly at young ages. For major parts of their lives they were in and out of various family musical aggregations whose flexible lineups usually included genius fiddler Scott along with stalwart brothers Jimmy and Van, and "Pop," the patriarch. Their mother, Hattie, herself an old-time fiddler who had taught Scott to play, joined them only occasionally.

The Stonemans' accomplishments were myriad. After becoming one of the best-known bluegrass bands in the Washington, D.C., area during the late fifties, they broke onto the national scene in the mid-sixties, appearing on television shows hosted by luminaries such as Steve Allen, Danny Thomas, and the Smothers Brothers. Their constant touring took them coast to coast, where they played prestigious night spots, including the Ash Grove in Los Angeles and the Bitter End in New York City. Relocating to Nashville during this time, they recorded six albums for MGM Records and three for RCA, headed up their own syndicated television show, and were named Vocal Group of the Year by the Country Music Association in 1967.

Still, for all their accomplishments, the Stonemans have remained somewhat outside the loving embrace of the bluegrass community, although the IBMA did honor them with a Distinguished Achievement Award in 2002. Of the three instrumentalists in the group, only Scott is recognized as a brilliant musician. Even those conversant with the overall history of the music are remarkably silent about the accomplishments of Donna and Roni, who carried the instrumental load in the family for years when Scott was not with the band. This lack of appreciation for two gifted performers is puzzling. One has to suspect that the miniskirts and white go-go boots of Donna and Roni were a serious distraction from what their fingers were doing. A look at their lives will tell us more.

Ernest "Pop" Stoneman, a carpenter by trade, was one of the stars of the early country music industry. Primarily a vocalist and guitarist, he recorded more than two hundred numbers for various labels between 1925 and 1929. Sometimes he recorded alone; sometimes he was joined by his wife, Hattie Frost, on fiddle or banjo or other area musicians. When Pattie Inez, the fourth of fifteen children (who lived long enough to be named), was born near Galax, Virginia, in May 1925, her father had just made his first recordings for Okeh Records in New York.

Thanks to his recording career, Ernest became quite prosperous. By 1927 he had built a home with electricity for Hattie and their then six children. They had a car and hired help in the house. But by 1932 changes in the recording industry coupled with the Depression had put the Stonemans on the road to ruin. Records were not selling well, and Ernest was having trouble finding work as either carpenter or musician. House, land, and furniture were all repossessed. Now with nine living children (Nita, age five, had died), the Stonemans made a hasty exit to Alexandria, Virginia, outfoxing the sheriff who had come to take their car. Still, things didn't seem to be much better in northern Virginia, where carpentry work was also scarce. Ernest and Eddie, the oldest child, played music whenever they could for a dollar or two a performance, but times were hard and the Stonemans lived in direst poverty.

In the midst of all of this, Donna made her appearance in February 1934, child number eleven and the first to be born in a hospital. Roni (short for Veronica), number fourteen, arrived in May four years later. Patsy's memories of these years often center on being hungry and being called a "dumb hill billie" at school. When she was about eleven, Patsy started working some music jobs with her father and Eddie, playing guitar or banjo. In 1941 the family moved into a partially finished home that Ernest was building for them in Carmody Hills, Maryland, a "suburban slum area" three miles outside of Washington, D.C. The one big room had no electricity, no water, and a roof partially covered with a tarp, but it was theirs. The family would live here for more than twenty years.

The first momentous musical event in this Stoneman era occurred in 1947 when Pop, along with Hattie and the youngest children, won a talent show at Washington, D.C.'s Constitution Hall. Their prize was a twenty-six-week gig on a local country music television show called *Gay Time*, after promoter Connie B. Gay. This was the first step on the long, slow road back to musical prominence.

Around this time Patsy faded from the musical picture, not to reappear until 1963. Already separated from the abusive husband of a disastrous first marriage, in 1947 she moved to California, where she married again. She later spent several years farming with her new husband in Mississippi, seeing her family only occasionally. Her thinking was, "If the family gets in real bad shape, they'll know where to come to eat." (Several siblings would take her up on this.) Things were working out pretty well until Patsy developed cancer and had to have both breasts removed. She also lost the use of her hands for a while. As she tells it, "Then my husband said, 'Nobody's hanging around me that don't produce.' So he divorced me." He received custody of the three girls they had adopted.

Even before her first marriage Patsy had already moved away from home, leaving Donna, eight, as the oldest girl. And in the Stonemans' world, as biographer Ivan Tribe notes, girls "existed for the purpose of helping their mothers in the home, especially with housework and the younger children." Thus Donna, whose formal education would end in the seventh grade, spent the next eight years as a "household servant while her mother tended her flower garden and looked after the yard." But there was always the music. According to Donna, the children who played instruments—usually made by Pop—were the ones who received attention, so she chose the mandolin, debuting on stage at seven or eight. Her ability to dance while playing earned her the nickname "little dancing Donna."

Roni, the next to youngest, also began playing music at a young age. She claims it was Scott who sparked her interest in playing. "Just being around him made you want to play an instrument." Scott taught both Donna and Roni to play, admonishing them, "Don't play like a girl!" Although today that phrase sounds condescending, Scott was insisting that they become the best players they could be. He knew they could be as good as any of his musician friends who came to the house—Charlie Waller, Bill Emerson, Buzz Busby—and he refused to settle for anything less. He showed them how to slow down records to study the playing of Earl Scruggs and Bill Monroe. In all things musical, from stage presence to set lists, Scott was their teacher. Donna, in particular, showed a knack for Scott's wild, unfettered approach to improvising.

In addition to learning from Bill Monroe and Scott, Donna also purloined a few tricks from the mandolin playing of Buzz Busby, who had moved to the D.C. area in 1951 at age seventeen and had become friends with Scott. According to Buzz, Scott and Donna would come to his house on Sundays. "Donna was wanting to learn the mandolin at this time, so I taught her quite a bit, got her started, and she took it from there." Of course, by this time Donna, who was a year older than Buzz, had been playing the mandolin for years. Donna herself claims that although she did learn some things from Buzz, when she began catching on too quickly he refused to show her anything more.

In 1950 sixteen-year-old Donna married Bob Bean, who was a year older, and continued to play music with her family. In 1953, when Bob joined the army, Donna moved with him to Washington State, where she joined a country band for a short time. By 1955 she and Bob were back in Carmody Hills.

With Donna gone and the older children wanting to play the newer country music, Pop put together Pop Stoneman and His Little Pebbles with Roni; youngest son, Van; and two other teenagers. They found work on weekends, primarily in bars.

Around 1955, with Donna back in town, Scott organized a band he called the Bluegrass Champs expressly in order to play at a bar called the Famous in Washington, D.C. The group also included Jimmy on bass, Jimmy Case on guitar, and the talented Porter Church on banjo. The group played six nights a week and became quite popular locally. Located next to the Trailways bus station in downtown D.C., the Famous was what Roni called a "skull orchard," a rowdy place that hosted a rough, drunken crowd, many of them from the military. Fights and knifings were common occurrences.

At the urging of club owner Sam Bomstein, the Champs auditioned for the CBS television show *Arthur Godfrey's Talent Scouts* and were accepted on the condition that Donna sing. Singing was not Donna's forte, but for this occasion she and Scott worked up a version of "Salty Dog Blues" with her stepping in on the chorus to tenor Scott's lead. A tape of the program shows Donna taking a mandolin break in an already-distinctive style that features a fast and furious tremolo. Positioned between power players Scott and Porter, Donna easily holds her own, performing with an infectious grin. Attired in fringed Western outfits, the group won the 1956 contest and was featured on the daily show for two weeks.

During their second week Peggy Brain, who played Dobro and was dating Jimmy, came in to replace Porter, whom Scott had fired to make room for a woman to sing with Donna. Peggy had played steel guitar in a band in Pennsylvania and after high school had moved to the D.C. area, where the Stonemans persuaded her to switch to the Dobro. On stage she stood next to Scott, who, she said, "filled me full of praise." The Bluegrass Champs now included two women playing lead instruments, which was extremely unusual for the time. Peggy would quit the group in late 1957, and she and Jimmy would later divorce.

Peggy did stay long enough to play Dobro on a single the Champs cut in the winter of 1957. Here she and Donna made history by becoming the first women to record bluegrass mandolin and Dobro. Their playing is strong on both songs: "Heartaches Keep on Coming," which Scott sings, and "Haunted House," an instrumental with a minor flavor, which Peggy kicks off. By 1958 the Champs were doing a weekly show on a Washington television station and playing frequently on the *Don Owens' Jamboree* on that same station.

Meanwhile Roni, who had quit school at sixteen, continued to play with Pop and the Pebbles. In April 1956, a week shy of eighteen, she married Gene Cox, a novice banjo player who was perhaps as attractive for his Gibson banjo as he was for his smile. During their courtship Roni, the seasoned professional, taught him the three-finger banjo roll and "Foggy Mountain Breakdown." After they married, however, Roni felt obligated to let Gene assume the role of family banjo player, because "he was more important. He was the man." And she didn't want to hurt his feelings. So he took Roni's place playing banjo with Pop, and Roni began playing bass.

Shortly after their marriage, Roni, who was pregnant with the first of their four children, became the first woman to play Scruggs-style banjo on a recording. *American Banjo: Three-Finger and Scruggs Style* (Folkways, 1957) featured Roni and fourteen men, including Gene, playing instrumentals in the modern three-finger style. It was produced by Mike Seeger, who recorded Roni and Gene in their home. Gene backed Roni on guitar for "Lonesome Road Blues" as she backed him for his tune "Wildwood Flower." Mike's focus for the recording was Roni; Gene was included simply because it would have been impolitic not to do so. Sensitive to marital harmony, Mike recorded "Wildwood Flower" first. As Gene struggled to get his tune down, Mike kept thinking, "Boy, I hope we can get this done before Roni has to go or do something else." When Gene finished, Roni took the same banjo and, according to Mike, "ripped off the piece in one take and went back to whatever she was doing." Today the educated listener might find Roni's playing somewhat unpolished, but closer listening reveals a confident musician with a solid sense of rhythm who is learning to command her instrument. The cut also highlights the countless hours Roni had spent studying the playing of Earl Scruggs.

Roni's banjo playing showed considerable improvement on her next recording, a 1958 session that included Donna, Scott, Jimmy, and brother Billy. The five numbers were eventually released as *Country Favorites* (Wyncote, 1964) with five cuts by Jimmy Dean. The instrumental "Bluegrass Breakdown," in particular, is the best early example of Donna and Roni's expert handling of classic bluegrass material. Here they attack Bill Monroe's rapid-fire number with vigor, purposefully speeding it up at the end in true Stoneman fashion. Not only have they studied the original 1949 recording, but they also have taken the concepts and made them their own. (Interestingly, there is no fiddle break.) Donna's playing puts her right up there alongside the best mandolin players of the era. And Roni's banjo work on the vocal "Daddy Stay Home" is some of the finest straight-ahead playing she would ever do. (Scruggs fanatics will recognize Earl's classic kickoff to "Little Girl in Tennessee.")

Roni had been happy early in her marriage, but after the birth of their first child, in 1957, Gene quit his factory job. By now the Little Pebbles had disbanded and Pop and Van had joined the Bluegrass Champs. With no money coming in, life turned into a living hell as Roni, who would deliver four children in five years, struggled to support her babies. Simply finding a place to live was a challenge. Gene would come and go, dropping in occasionally to babysit and get Roni pregnant again. For years Roni took in washing—using a scrub board—to make ends meet.

Shortly after her third child was born, in 1960, Roni found work as a bass player, playing for tips, working six shows a night, six nights a week. Pregnant at the time, she miscarried at four months. After losing her job playing bass, Roni played banjo for a time with Benny and Vallie Cain and then landed a steady job as banjo player for a country band that was playing at the Famous.

Meanwhile the Bluegrass Champs would occasionally ask Roni to fill in, and when Porter Church quit, Roni became the regular banjo player. With Van on guitar and Pop on autoharp, the group was now all-Stonemans all the time. Roni loved playing in a group with Donna, even though she was well aware that the audience considered her sister the pretty one. Since most of their jobs were in honky-tonks, Donna added an electric pickup to her mandolin, which allowed her to dance all over the stage and still be heard. Not only did this move alienate bluegrass purists, but the pickup also made the recorded sound of her mandolin less than optimal, tinny and thin rather than resonant and woody.

In 1962 the family, yearning for the big time, made a short-lived foray into Nashville. They appeared on the Grand Ole Opry and recorded a couple of singles that went nowhere, but they couldn't find enough work, so they returned to Maryland. While in Nashville, however, Donna made another piece of bluegrass history when she filled in for Bill Monroe during the recording of the album *Rose Maddox Sings Bluegrass*. Donna plays on four songs, all done in nonstandard keys (E, F, and B-flat) to accommodate Rose's higher female voice. To Donna, whose family routinely played in keys such as E and F, "Playing in an off-key wasn't too much of a bother." Having studied Monroe's playing extensively, Donna made an excellent substitute, and the listener must be a considerable expert to decipher who is playing mandolin on each cut.

The Stonemans' presence in Nashville had not gone totally unnoticed. Don Pierce at Starday Records asked them to come back that summer to record an album. They would record a second Starday album the next fall. The recordings, now available on CD as *The Stoneman Family: 28 Big Ones* (King, 2000) give us a better look at Donna's unique mandolin style and Roni's more restrained but still serviceable banjo playing. (Being eight months pregnant with her fourth child during the first recording undoubtedly had an effect on Roni's playing. Also, as she herself noted, "When you got a bunch of babies you can't sit and woodshed.")

Unfortunately these albums don't capture the excitement and energy of a Stoneman stage show. Seventy-year-old Pop, who does a hefty amount of the lead singing, was rooted in the old-time country ballad tradition, not the brash new bluegrass sound. Donna's aggressive mandolin playing shines in spots, and she does some amazingly inventive improvising, but Roni's banjo is often in the background. The only truly exciting cuts are Scott's two fiddle showpieces, "Talking Fiddle Blues" (also known as "Lee Highway Blues") and "Orange Blossom Special," on which Donna and Roni provide only rhythmic support. Donna's own magnificently raucous rendition of "Orange Blossom Special" would emerge later when Scott's appearances with the group became erratic due to his drinking.

Donna's playing had not gone totally unnoticed by the bluegrass community. Her original instrumental "Girl from Galax," from the first Starday album, became the focal point of a *Bluegrass Unlimited* review in 1967. By then the Stonemans were riding high and cuts from the two Starday albums had been repackaged into one LP. After ignoring Donna's and Roni's contributions, but praising Scott and mentioning Pop, the reviewer turns critical. "Donna said in a recent fan-club magazine piece that she thinks her mandolin playing has gone beyond Bill Monroe; 'Galax' is a mandolin piece which should show who has gone beyond whom." Donna, who has always had the utmost respect for Bill Monroe, felt as if her remarks had been misquoted or taken out of context. Focusing on something Donna supposedly said, rather than on her playing, gives an indication of how casually her abilities were dismissed. Perhaps, too, she was serving as a lightning rod for the reviewer's own ambiguity toward what he called their "pop-oriented" music.

By 1963 the Stoneman Family was beginning to break into the college scene as a folk music act. A glowing review of their appearance at the University of Illinois sheds some light on an aspect of their performance that may have made hard-core bluegrass fans uncomfortable. The male writer says that their show "has a certain quality not usually attributed to folk music concerts—sex." By "sex," of course, he meant female sex—Donna and Roni. He went on to say, "Both are dressed in tight skirts that seem barely capable of confining their obvious charms." To be sure, he also mentioned that Roni picked a "mean banjo." He concluded by saying, "The result was straight country music, with the real brand of wild country humor and liberal use of sex."

In 1961 Patsy Stoneman returned to the D.C. area, the survivor of a double mastectomy and two disastrous marriages. She got a job as a waitress at the Famous. Choosing not to join the family band, because she didn't think she was good enough, she instead bought herself a small guitar and began to play solo at bars around Washington for seven dollars a night plus tips. She called it her "gypsy act." When her arm started hurting, she said, "I'd stop playing and

I'd talk to the audience." Eventually she organized her own band, the Patsy Stoneman Show, whose rotating membership included some of the area's best musicians—Buzz Busby, Red Allen, Porter Church, Bill Emerson, Ed Ferris, and sometimes Scott.

Bill Emerson, who played with Patsy off and on for about a year, says:

Wayne Yates and Ferrell and Earl Brown and I had a band at the time and she up and hired our whole group to perform with her. We were working with her when her husband Don Dixon was killed [1964]. We were pallbearers at his funeral. Patsy was a total professional package and not the least bit shy. She was the group's emcee, lead singer, and rhythm guitar player. She sang country and bluegrass songs that were popular at the time. We sang harmony with her. I never had a better boss and nobody laughed at us [for working for a woman]. They better not have. We all loved Patsy and still do.

Patsy did not like to call herself the boss—"because they knew what they could do better than I did"—but preferred to think that the musicians were working together because they needed each other. "They helped me out an awful lot," she says. "But then I helped them—I found their jobs." When asked specifically if the name of the group was the Patsy Stoneman Show, Patsy quickly replied, "Well, of course it was. 'Cause I didn't know who was going to show up. I knew I was."

Being labeled a folk act worked for the Stonemans, and during the next two years, 1964–1966, they spent much time on the West Coast appearing at such venues as the UCLA Folk Festival, the Monterey Folk Festival, the Steve Allen television show, the Danny Thomas television special, the Ash Grove, and the Hollywood Troubadour. Their new album, *Big Ball in Monterey* (World Pacific, 1964), obviously aimed at the folk market, included a cut of "Dominique," popularized by the movie *The Singing Nun* (Scott played banjo on this). The disc, which purported to be "live," was actually done in a studio with canned applause. Hard-core bluegrass numbers like "I Wonder How the Old Folks Are at Home" and "Lost Ball in the High Weeds" finally give Roni an opportunity to strut her stuff. Her picking wasn't fancy, but it was solid. She herself once said that she would put her right hand up against any man, but her left hand didn't get developed because of raising her four babies. Purists might flinch at the funky twelve-string guitar lead on "Groundhog," but with the brothers doing most of the lead singing, *Big Ball in Monterey* is a strong bluegrass showing from the Stonemans.

In 1965 the family began a long-term engagement at the Black Poodle, a Nashville nightclub. The Stonemans were in the right place at the right time, and their energetic, freewheeling stage show—supported by their solid, tight musicianship—touched a nerve in Music City. Soon they were playing to standing-room-only crowds. They began recording for MGM Records, eventually turning out six LPs and a number of singles from 1966 through 1969. The Stonemans were hot. Family members, including Pop and Mom, Donna and Bob, and Roni, who was still married to Gene, moved to the Nashville area.

Listening to these MGM albums today is not easy. There is little bluegrass (*Bluegrass Unlimited* did not review these discs), and many of the numbers are folk-pop hits such as "Bottle of Wine" and "Winchester Cathedral" and current country fare like "There Goes My Everything." Much of the singing (including, unfortunately, the bluegrass standard "Muleskinner Blues") is done choral style with everyone pitching in, and there is frequent "oohing." There was less and less banjo and mandolin, and with Scott now gone from the group there was no fiddle. Yet for the persistent listener there are grains of wheat among the chaff. Bluegrass standards like "Cripple Creek," "Shady Grove," "Slewfoot," and even the instrumental "The World Is Waiting for the Sunrise" allow Donna and Roni to ring like silver and shine like gold. Perhaps Roni says it best: "Don't pay any attention to our records—because they were really not us. The big guys at RCA [and MGM] would tell us what to record. They took us away from our hillbilly roots and made us do more pop-like songs." The albums sold well, however, and some singles even made the *Billboard* charts.

What none of the Stonemans records include is Roni's comedy, which was an important aspect of their stage shows. Numbers such as "Dirty Old Egg-Suckin' Dog," "My Dirty, Lowdown, Rotten, Cotton Pickin' Little Darlin'," and "All the Guys Who Turn Me On Turn Me Down" give a hint of the role assigned to Roni, who always played up the "dumb hill billie" aspect of her life. In later years one of her favorite stage bits was the true story of falling into the outhouse.

Since the Stonemans were a hot property, television was the next logical step. Their half-hour nationally syndicated series, *The Stonemans,* debuted in April 1966. New shows were filmed through 1969, although reruns were broadcast for a few years after that. Thirteen of these cuts have been assembled on a CD, *The Stonemans: Live!* (Old Homestead, 2000), which also includes selections from a concert in 1981. The outstanding number here is Bill Monroe's instrumental "Rawhide," a tour de force that Donna and Roni successfully tackle at a blistering pace.

The Stonemans' popularity also led to their inclusion in two 1967 low-budget movies, *Hell on Wheels* and the *Road to Nashville*, both of which feature a number of country music acts. The band now included Donna, Roni, Van, Jimmy, Jerry Monday (on harmonica or Dobro), and Pop in a limited role. The Stonemans had forsaken Western wear in favor of an early "folksinger" look for the men—cardigan sweaters and ties—and modern country attire for the women—matching dresses, short colored boots, and bouffant hair.

These four performances allow us to see how easy it was for Donna to steal the show not only with her dancing and her exuberant stage personality but also with her fiery mandolin playing. Her earlier recordings were just a warm-up for the flights of fancy her mind took when ripping through a standard like "Cripple Creek" or her own boogie-woogie piece "Donna Mite." Few people back then, except possibly Frank Wakefield and Bill Monroe in his wilder moments, were playing mandolin in this far-out and furious, almost manic style.

Roni's part in the films was much more subdued, since her comedy was not featured. She takes a banjo lead only on "Cripple Creek," turning in a solid performance at a breakneck tempo. But so does Donna, and she gets to dance around and "make show," as Roni would say. Here Roni's "making show" was limited to standing rigid before the microphone and not cracking a smile. Roni once said that it didn't matter who got the applause in the family "as long as it was got," but for this immensely gifted woman to be shunted to the side while Donna basked in the spotlight had to hurt. On the other hand, maybe Roni was simply glad to be working.

In October 1967 all the roads the Stonemans had been traveling converged at the top when they were named Country Music Association Vocal Group of the Year in the inaugural presentation of these awards. (The only other bluegrass act to receive this honor has been the Osborne Brothers in 1971.) Although this was a major coup for the Stonemans, nothing seemed to change. On the advice of their management they passed up an opportunity to become members of the Grand Ole Opry, a decision they would later come to regret.

Less than a year later, on June 14, 1968, the family sustained a major blow when Ernest Stoneman died at the age of seventy-five. Pop, whose role in the band had shrunk to one song per album, was still the emotional linchpin of the group. While he was in the hospital, he asked Patsy to take his place in the band, saying, "You seem to be the young'un with the strongest backbone . . . Will you keep the kids together as long as you can?" Patsy took his request as her life's mission. From the start she insisted on keeping Pop's old songs in the show, even though the others were resistant to the idea. "I said either that, or I ain't here." Their RCA albums, which include Patsy playing autoharp and singing the old chestnuts "Wildwood Flower" and "Somebody's Waiting for Me," indicate that she had indeed won that battle. Eventually Patsy moved to Nashville, where she and her fourth husband, John Murphy, the jewel of her life, lived happily until his death in 2004. They were married for thirty-nine years.

With Pop gone, things rocked along for a few years as the Stonemans continued to record and to work the road. The three RCA albums they released in 1970 featured little bluegrass and many trendy rock songs, such as "Bad Moon Rising" and "Who'll Stop the Rain." Still the rapid-fire version of the tricky instrumental "Banjo Signal" shows that Donna and Roni could still put the pedal to the metal. Although *Bluegrass Unlimited* did not review the RCA material, in December 1971 readers voted Donna one of their favorite mandolin players. She was the only woman honored in the entire poll. Scott was named as a favorite fiddler.

In 1971, however, the family unit began to slowly unravel. Roni was the first to go. Divorced from Gene Cox, she had been living in North Carolina since 1968 with a physically abusive spouse. In spite of how it might appear, she was not making a lot of money with the Stonemans, and George, her second husband, thought she could do better on her own. Roni, ever eager to please the men in her life, acquiesced. She would try to make it as a single. Her slot was filled first by Jerry Monday on banjo, and then, when Jerry quit at the end of 1971, by singer Cathy Manzer on electric organ, making the group banjo-less for most of a year.

Patsy was the next to go. Upset with the musical direction the group was taking, she quit in August 1972. Meanwhile, Donna had discovered that her twenty-year marriage to Bob Bean was on the rocks. She separated from Bob, who continued to manage the band, and moved in with Cathy. Distraught and even suicidal at times, she remained with the group until November 1972, when she and Cathy both quit. After she and Bob divorced, Donna found a new direction for her life by dedicating herself to Christ, doing solo work as a gospel singer, and eventually becoming an ordained minister. When Donna left, Patsy filled in to help out and then decided to stay. While away she felt as if she had reneged on her promise to Pop to keep the group together. Scott also rejoined the group briefly, but in March 1973 this exasperating but lovable brother and mentor died of alcohol-related causes. He was only forty years old.

With Patsy back at the helm, supported by the ever faithful Van and Jimmy, the Stonemans carried on, using various side musicians. As Ivan Tribe points out, although the remaining family members were competent musicians, it was

Donna, Roni, and Scott who had the "stage charisma that made crowds go wild." The Stonemans continued to work, but things were never quite the same.

Roni's work as a single didn't pan out, but in 1973 she hit pay dirt when, thanks to her comedy, she was tapped to play Ida Lee Nagger, the "Ironing Board Lady," on *Hee Haw.* Although not hired for her banjo playing, she eventually became part of the Banjo Band with Roy Clark, Grandpa Jones, and Bobby Thompson. Since *Hee Haw* taped only twice a year—June to July and October to November—Roni was free to make personal appearances the rest of the time. As the character Ida Lee became more popular, these outside engagements became more frequent and quite lucrative.

Roni stayed with *Hee Haw* until 1991, when she and other regulars were fired as the show revamped itself out of existence and into reruns. She had been with the show for eighteen years. The importance of *Hee Haw* in Roni's life and career cannot be overestimated. First of all it enabled her to make a good living, even while in a disastrous marriage. Second, her popularity and name recognition propelled her solo act into a career that is still successful today. As Roni says, "Thank God I got the part, because it kept me out of nightclubs and I was able to support my children and educate 'em. 'Cause to me that was a sign of success. Educating your children. Getting 'em out of the poverty you were raised in." This she has done.

Grateful or not, Roni couldn't help thinking "it would have been nice to be able to sit down and pick the serious stuff instead of doing all that comedy." She also was well aware of the *Hee Haw* Honeys. "Being around all those beautiful girls could be depressing. I was playing ugly characters, that was my job, and I understood that, but still sometimes it was stressing on my soul."

Still and yet, when she first lost her *Hee Haw* job, unbelievable as it sounds, Roni had trouble finding work. It was a classic catch-22. Music jobs were hard to find because of potential legal problems arising from the use of the *Hee Haw* characters, and no one would hire Roni for menial labor, such as motel maid, because she was a star from *Hee Haw.* Finally she returned to the one job that had never let her down: playing in honky-tonks. Sometimes she was backed by a country band; sometimes it was just her and a boom box.

After husband number two, Roni would go through three more marriages, all terrible. In 2007 she talked freely about these and other aspects of her life in her autobiography, *Pressing On.*

Meanwhile Patsy, Jimmy, Van, and various side musicians continued to record, albeit less frequently than in their heyday. Two of their three CMH albums,

Cuttin' the Grass (1976) and *On the Road* (1977), featured their usual mixture of popular songs and old favorites, and Patsy continued to honor Pop's memory with her autoharp playing. But the best project the Stonemans did for CMH was *The First Family of Country Music* (1982), a double disc that features almost all of the Stoneman siblings, along with some of their children. Among the standout numbers are the instrumentals "Under the Double Eagle" and "Cripple Creek," both of which showcase Donna's still rapid-fire, idiosyncratic mandolin playing. Her amazing version of "Orange Blossom Special" reveals the tremendous influence that Scott's fiddling had on her own approach to this foot-stomping crowd-pleaser.

Although Donna kept a low profile once she left the Stonemans, she did surface long enough to play mandolin on Tom T. Hall's bluegrass album, *Magnificent Music Machine* (1976). She was the only woman featured. After the completion of the Stonemans' CMH album in 1981 Donna returned to the group, but they were not playing enough for anyone to make a living solely from the music. As is often the case in bluegrass, bills got paid because spouses—and sometimes the musicians themselves—were working day jobs.

In the ensuing years Patsy, continuing her quest to preserve her family's musical legacy, has released a number of cassettes and CDs on her own Stonehouse label, featuring old and new music by the Stonemans, including two cassettes of Roni's music. Old Homestead and Rutabaga Records also issued Stoneman albums in the late eighties. And Donna released a cassette of gospel numbers. It was Patsy's persistence that finally resulted in the well-documented biography *The Stonemans: An Appalachian Family and the Music That Shaped Their Lives* (1993) by Ivan Tribe. Today Patsy, Roni, and Donna are the last surviving children of Ernest and Hattie Stoneman. They continue to play together occasionally. In 2009 the sisters recorded a new CD of old tunes for Patuxent Music called *The Stonemans: Patsy, Donna & Roni*. The *Bluegrass Unlimited* reviewer commented that the women were "returning to the sounds they grew up on in the thirties and forties. I think Pop and Hattie Stoneman would be proud."

As we have seen, much of the Stonemans' music does not fit neatly into the bluegrass matrix. Though they had the authenticity of deep southwest Virginia musical roots, they were first and foremost entertainers. Ivan Tribe wrote, "The Stonemans . . . concerned themselves more with the basics of daily sustenance and survival than whether the purity of their musical virtue had been compromised." As late as 1978 a *Bluegrass Unlimited* reviewer would say, "For a variety of reasons, perhaps quality control, the Stonemans have yet to make a serious mark among bluegrass listeners, and that is curious because virtually no other bluegrass band produces a more vital and varied live show."

Yet there are women in bluegrass who claim Donna Stoneman as an influence. When the teenage Rhonda Vincent saw Donna performing, she says, "I knew I wanted to play just like her. I was reinvigorated. She was so aggressive. It was like watching a madwoman up there on stage." Mandolin player Beck Gentry caught Donna's performance at a county fair in the mid-seventies. She was the first woman Beck had seen playing the mandolin. Beck says, "It's kind of a cool night, so she's got these white gloves on with the tips cut out of the fingers so she can play. It doesn't seem to impede her playing at all. I was just knocked out. She was wearing a mini-skirt and white go-go boots! I mean she was rock solid. How could you not like her playing?"

Perhaps, as Tribe postulated, the Stonemans were simply too country for bluegrass and too bluegrass for country. Perhaps bluegrass fans, unable to wade through the profusion of pop-rock and country material on their MGM and RCA albums, have been simply unaware of how good Donna and Roni really are. The fact that the Stonemans were not fielding their strongest lineup when bluegrass festivals—and the bible of bluegrass, *Bluegrass Unlimited*—were beginning to take off in the mid-sixties can't have helped. Furthermore, until Tribe's book in 1993, the Stonemans never had anyone in academia to speak for them as Ralph Rinzler spoke for Bill Monroe and as Louise Scruggs spoke for her husband, Earl. But one cannot rule out gender as a factor. Perhaps the Stonemans were not taken seriously because two of their lead instrumentalists were women. Donna's dancing (and her electric mandolin) and Roni's comedy were also barriers to being considered top-notch players.

One has to suspect that if Donna and Roni had been Don and Ron, bluegrass pundits would have been singing their praises alongside mandolinists Frank Wakefield, Buzz Busby, and Pee Wee Lambert and early banjo players such as Lamar Grier, Rudy Lyle, and Porter Church. Fortunately, thanks to the Internet, the music of the Stonemans is still accessible, just waiting for someone to listen to it, to appreciate it. It's not too late to reclaim the playing of Donna and Roni Stoneman and to elevate them into the ranks of the exalted company they should be keeping.

I can't apologize for something
the Lord called me to do.

—Margie Sullivan

MARGIE
SULLIVAN

Women in bluegrass often wear many hats—wife, mother, booking agent, chief cook and bottle washer, wardrobe consultant, emcee, bus driver, merchandise manager—but Pentecostal preacher is not usually one of them. Unless you are Margie Sullivan (b. 1933), who took her guitar and went on the road with a female evangelist when she was only thirteen. She's been on the road preaching, praying, and singing ever since.

Born in the northeast corner of Louisiana, near Winnsboro, Margie Brewster was the sixth of twelve children in a sharecropping family. "My dad played guitar, three-finger style. I learned to sing before I could pick, and I begged my dad to go and play for me at church, and he was real timid and didn't want to be before people, but I'd beg in such a way that he couldn't refuse. He bought me my first guitar in August before he died, when I was thirteen."

With seven children still at home and no one to do the farming when her husband died, Margie's mother had no choice but to go on welfare. Margie, then in the ninth grade, dropped out of school because there was no money for clothes or school supplies. She was desperate to help her mother, but what could a young teenage girl do? Margie, who had been saved at a brush arbor meeting when she was nine, also "felt an urge to do work for the Lord." An opportunity presented itself to do both when she saw an advertisement in an Apostolic newspaper. Hazel Chain, who was starting her ministry as a traveling evangelist, was looking for a woman to travel with her and help with the music. With her mother's permission, Margie answered the ad, and soon Ms. Chain was visiting in their home. When she left, Margie went with her. Margie would stay on the road with Ms. Chain for three years, completing her high school education by taking correspondence courses.

Traveling by bus, the two women found accommodations in the homes of preachers and church members. Early on they wound up in a southern Alabama home for a service. Here Margie met fifteen-year-old Enoch Sullivan (b. 1931) from St. Stephens, Alabama, who was playing music with his father, Arthur, and brother Aubrey. Thanks to a late-life conversion experience, Arthur had became a Pentecostal minister. From then on he and his family played only religious music. Margie and Enoch were shy but smitten, and after a courtship that was mostly by mail, they married on December 16, 1949. Two weeks later the Sullivans played their first radio broadcast, in Picayune, Mississippi, as the guests of another minister. Brother Arthur, as he was known, played mandolin and did the emceeing, Aubrey and Margie were on guitars, and Enoch played fiddle. As of yet there was no banjo. Enoch's brother Emmett (b. 1936), would add that sound in the early fifties and stay with the band until his death in 1993.

A few months after that first broadcast the Sullivan Family landed their own Sunday morning show in Jackson, Alabama, on a station close to home. By then the band had grown to include Arthur's brother J. B. on guitar; sister Susie and friend Hob Williams on vocals; along with bass player Hilton Taylor, whose business sponsored part of the program. Originally contracted for thirteen weeks, the Sullivans stayed for seven years.

By early 1951 the group had expanded its radio ministry to Thomasville, Alabama, where they were sponsored by a furniture store. Brother Arthur preached and Margie and Enoch provided the foundation for the music, using whomever they could drum up to help them. They stayed there for five years, broadcasting live five days a week from 5:45 till 6:00 A.M. Radio shows not only provided them an opportunity to preach the gospel but also allowed them to advertise their personal appearances at churches, family reunions, and revivals.

The Sullivan Family always played for what they called a "free will offering." Only once did Enoch convince his father to let them charge an admission for a show at a high school auditorium. They packed the place, but Brother Arthur couldn't preach, because people had paid to get in. This was the last time they tried that while Brother Arthur was alive.

In February 1951 Margie, expecting her first child, went back to Louisiana to be near her mother. But after a few weeks she returned to Alabama and the radio shows. Usually there was someone to take care of the baby at the station, but when there wasn't, Margie put him on a little pillow in her guitar case. "That was my babysitter for the radio broadcast." By 1961 she and Enoch had five children. Margie continued to play up until the last stages of pregnancy. Asked how she managed to play her guitar during these latter days, she said, "I took the strap off of it and rested it on the Bible stand." If anyone had a problem with her playing while in the family way, she said, "They never mentioned it to me."

As the band became more popular, they would often remain on the road for two or three weeks at a time. Enoch's mother, Florence, who still had young ones herself, frequently took care of Margie and Enoch's children, too. Margie says, "A lot of the reason the Sullivan Family was able to go on was that she was dedicated to seeing us play our music. That was her contribution." But they also had a lot of babysitters. Some lived with them, some just came and went.

When the Sullivan Family made their first 78 rpm recording in 1954 for Revival Records, Margie was not present. She was in the hospital having her second baby. Emmett played banjo on one side and Dobro on the other.

In November 1957 Arthur Sullivan died after preaching a sermon, leaving the Sullivan Family bereft. Not only had they lost a father, but they had also lost their patriarch, preacher, and emcee. In the midst of their grief they also had the radio show to think about and a recording session coming up. They didn't know whether to continue on with the music or not. Encouraged by friends, ministers, and their own prayers, they decided that the Lord had called Brother Arthur home—his work was finished. Theirs, however, was still ahead. They would carry on.

Enoch assumed the role of emcee and turned out to be a natural. Until his death in 2011 the genial stage patter rolled with ease off his silver tongue, which in his later years matched his bountiful head of hair and jaunty mustache. A cross between Billy Graham and a carnival barker, Enoch had the audience in the palm of his hand from the time the band stepped on stage, be it festival, church, or theme park. Margie was by no means the silent, dutiful wife. She advertised upcoming dates, pushed the merchandise, and if she felt the Spirit move her, she testified.

The Sullivans rescheduled their recording session for January 1958 and cut two songs for Sandy Records: a solo by Margie, "I Can See God's Changing Hand," and "Happy on My Way," written by Enoch. The core trio of Margie, Enoch, and Emmett was fleshed out by mandolin and bass. This disc marks the real beginning of the Sullivan Family's recording career, since it was the first session to include Margie.

By now the band was doing well enough for Enoch to quit his day job at the chemical company in Mobile, Alabama. Before this he occasionally had had to miss some of their personal appearances, although he was always on hand for important gigs and the radio shows. Around 1959 the Sullivan Family made their first appearance on television, guesting on *The Friendly Variety Show,* in Mobile, where they soon became regulars.

On July 2, 1960, their lives were turned topsy-turvy when Enoch was diagnosed with a virulent form of cancer and given just a short time to live. He underwent several surgeries and fifty cobalt treatments, and, against all odds, became a survivor. Not only did Margie have to deal with Enoch's illness, but she also was pregnant, and with Enoch unable to work or play music, the family was without a source of income. But friends and family chipped in to help with expenses and the young couple pulled through. In April 1961, in the midst of all this trauma, Margie gave birth to their last child, daughter Lesa. But as soon as she could, she took a job at Vanity Fair Mills and the band continued with their gospel singing on weekends.

In 1960, with Enoch still very weak, the group recorded four songs for an extended play album on Walter Bailes's Loyal Records. They would stay with the label for fourteen years. Jerry Sullivan shared bass-playing duties with Patsy Jones.

As soon as Enoch got well enough, they hit the road again. By now they were broadcasting on a fifty-thousand-watt station in Magee, Mississippi. Soon they were traveling throughout the South: Louisiana, Florida, Texas, Arkansas, Georgia, Kentucky, and Tennessee.

In 1962 Enoch convinced Bill Monroe to do a series of "string band gospel concerts" with the Sullivan Family. Although Monroe wanted to split the take down the middle, Enoch insisted that they structure it sixty-forty, with Monroe getting the larger portion. According to Margie, Enoch said, "Bill, you're away from home and you've got other expenses that we don't have. We're at home and we're just not gonna do it that way." Margie did the booking, and the tour was so successful that Bill did one again in 1963 and again in 1964. These were the lean years for Bill Monroe, and the Sullivan Family, who had developed an audience through their hard work and long exposure over the years, was drawing good crowds. Not only did they want to help Bill out, but they also wanted to get personally acquainted with the man they revered so highly.

Around 1964 the Sullivan Family met J. G. Whitfield, the legendary Southern gospel concert promoter and disc jockey. He invited them to be on his television show in Pensacola, Florida, and began booking them on some shows on the Southern gospel circuit, one of the earliest bluegrass bands to be included. Some of his all-night gospel sings were so big they had to be held in football stadiums.

Just because they were Pentecostal didn't mean Margie and Enoch weren't political. In addition to holding strong religious beliefs, Margie also holds strong political beliefs. In the sixties the Sullivans were on the political trail playing music for Governor George Wallace and then later for his wife Lureen's gubernatorial campaign in 1965. In 1966 the Sullivan Family moved to Hattiesburg, Mississippi, for eighteen months to support Jimmy Swan in his campaign for governor. Swan, a disc jockey and hillbilly singer who owned a radio station in Hattiesburg, was running on much the same platform as George Wallace. His campaign bought the Sullivans a mobile home and put it right behind the station, from which they broadcast daily. Secretaries at the station looked after Margie and Enoch's children while the couple hit the campaign trail with Swan, playing at churches and courthouses. They campaigned again for Swan in 1971. In spite of their best efforts, however, he lost both elections.

In March 1967 the album *Presenting the Sullivan Family in Blue Grass Gospel* (Loyal, ca. 1966) was reviewed in the new magazine *Bluegrass Unlimited*. Unfortunately the packaging—a printed paper bag—was so off-putting that the reviewer spent half of the six-line review railing about that. He commended the Sullivans for a "creditable job" and concluded by saying, "The recorded sound is good." Later reviews in the magazine would consistently single out Margie's voice as the strong point of the group: "The most exciting part of this album is the lead singing of Margie Sullivan who recalls the era of Molly O'Day," and "she belts out these numbers as few women can."

Like many regional bands of the era, the Sullivan Family recorded often; they depended on selling albums to help out financially. They have released more than thirty recordings to date. A "free will offering" might sound good, but selling merchandise helped keep gas in the tank and food on the table.

In 1970 a young Marty Stuart heard the Sullivan Family play a show with Bill Monroe in Jackson, Alabama. Two years later he spent the summer traveling with the Sullivans, playing mandolin and fiddle. He was joined by two older teenagers: Carl Jackson, who had already spent a number of years playing banjo with bluegrass stalwarts Jim and Jesse and the Virginia Boys, and Ronnie Dickerson on bass.

By the early seventies the Sullivan Family had made a firm entrance into the world of bluegrass festivals, playing events across the Deep South along with Ralph Stanley's Virginia festival and Bill Monroe's show in Bean Blossom, Indiana. They also had their own television show in Jackson, Mississippi, which they taped once a month. A number of these programs, some of which include the young Marty Stuart, survive in video format.

In 1972 Margie and Enoch partnered again with the Father of Bluegrass to launch the Bill Monroe Dixie Bluegrass Festival in Chatom, Alabama. The event was so successful that they added a spring show three years later. The festival eventually moved to the Sullivan's old homeplace near St. Stephens, Alabama, where it continued on into the twenty-first century.

In 1976 the Sullivans made their first appearance on the Grand Ole Opry and journeyed all the way to Nova Scotia for their first performances out of the country. Then in March 1977 they were in a terrible automobile accident in Mississippi, in which they slammed into a car that had fallen off a trailer. As a result of their injuries—Margie's left leg was broken in four places, and Enoch had five broken ribs—they had to stop playing for a year. Margie, who finally returned to the stage in a cast using a walker, says that going back on the road was the best therapy she could have had.

The Sullivans came back stronger than ever in 1978 with a band that included their daughter Lesa, seventeen, on bass. She would stay with them until 1983. The group soon included two other teenagers: Joe Cook on mandolin and his sister Vicki on lead guitar and occasionally banjo. With three women in the band, the group often featured a ladies trio.

In October 1980 this version of the band graced the cover of *Bluegrass Unlimited,* and in November they made their first trip overseas, going to Holland. Everything for the trip fell right into place except the seventy-five hundred dollars they needed for plane tickets. As always, Margie prayed about it, and it seemed to her that the Lord was telling her to mortgage the house. She and

Enoch had had to go the mortgage route before for various reasons, and they had made a pact to never do it again. Margie was reluctant to mention this idea to her husband, but catching him in a mellow mood one day, she suggested it. He said, "Well, if it means that much to you to go, then go ahead." So Margie went to the bank and secured the financing for the trip. While they were there, they recorded the album *Live in Holland*. They would make two more visits to Holland, in 1981 and again in 1983. In 1983 Lesa retired from playing bass and was replaced by Joy DeVille, from Louisiana, who stayed with them for twenty-eight years.

In 1989 they were dealt the hardest blow of their lives when their oldest son, Wayne, died. Troupers that they were, they left his funeral and went right back out on the road. The year 1993 brought both sorrow and joy to the couple: in April, Emmett Sullivan passed away, and in September the Sullivan Family was inducted into Bill Monroe's Hall of Honor in Bean Blossom, Indiana.

To mark their fiftieth anniversary in bluegrass gospel, Enoch and Margie told their life story to Robert Gentry, who, with the help of editor Patricia Martinez, turned these memories into the book *The Sullivan Family: Fifty Years in Bluegrass Gospel Music* (Sweet Dreams Publishing, 1999). The year 2005 saw the Sullivan Family receive the IBMA Distinguished Achievement Award as well as the Alabama Folk Heritage Award. Through all these many years, Margie and Enoch kept hitting the road hard with their music, often still playing at small churches for a donation.

In 2005 *Banjo NewsLetter* profiled a Sullivan Family show at a one of these small churches in Romney, West Virginia. The article noted, "When Enoch asked Margie to say a few words, she stepped up to the plate and delivered like an old-time preacher woman. She would have been powerful in the pulpit." The writer concluded by saying, "All I want from music is for it to make me feel something. Margie Sullivan does that every time she reaches down into the depths of her Louisiana soul and pulls out a song. With her low, almost husky voice (imagine Lauren Bacall with a Southern accent) and her no-holds-barred delivery, she packs an emotional wallop."

In April 2009 Margie suffered a heart attack and underwent a five-way by-pass. By August, however, she was back to traveling and playing full-time. In November the Sullivans celebrated sixty years in the gospel music business with a show at the Texas Troubadour Theater in Nashville. Pictures of the seventy-six-year-old Margie show her looking positively radiant as she and Enoch cut their anniversary cake.

The long partnership of Margie and Enoch came to its earthly end on February 23, 2011, when Enoch passed away. Margie, however, continues to perform, primarily locally, with her son-in-law Richard Tew on guitar and Darrell Lloyd on banjo. In a recent conversation when I expressed admiration for her courage, she said, "Well, darlin,' what else would I do?" Further talk centered on publication of this book, with her asking for ten copies to sell at her shows as soon as it comes off the press. "Just send me the bill," she says. "You know I'll pay it. You have to be willing to put some money in your work. And I'm more willing to put money into my *own* work—because I believe in me and what I do."

Sally Ann Forrester, guitar, and Dixie Belle Buchanan, bass, the Kentucky Sweethearts, ca. 1942. (Courtesy of Bob Forrester)

Wilma Lee and Stoney Cooper, mid-1970s. (Photo by Phil Straw, courtesy of *Bluegrass Unlimited*)

Rose Maddox performing at Watermelon Park in Berryville, Virginia, 1995. (Photo by Penny Clapp, personal collection of author)

Ola Belle Campbell (Reed) with the North Carolina Ridge Runners, 1947.
Back row, L-R: Alex Campbell, Lester "Slick" Miller, Earl Wallace,
Arthur "Shorty" Woods, Johnnie Miller. (Courtesy of Walt Saunders)

Bessie Lee Mauldin with the Blue Grass Boys, ca. 1959. L-R: Bobby Hicks, Bessie Lee,
Bill Monroe, unidentified banjo player, Jack Cooke. (Courtesy of *Bluegrass Unlimited*)

Sisters Virginia Kave, bass, and Vallie Kave (Cain), guitar, ca. 1949. (Personal collection of author)

Grace and Bob French. (Personal collection of author)

The Lewis Family Sisters, L-R: Miggie, Polly, Janis, at the 1975 Kerrville, Texas, Bluegrass Festival. (Photo by Rick Gardner)

The Bluegrass Champs, ca. 1956. L-R: front, Donna Stoneman, Peggy Brain; back, Jimmy Case, Scotty Stoneman, Jimmy Stoneman. (Personal collection of author)

Roni Stoneman at the Maryland Banjo Academy,
1997. (Personal collection of author)

Margie Sullivan with Emmett Sullivan on banjo and Enoch Sullivan
on fiddle, ca. mid-1980s. (Courtesy of *Bluegrass Unlimited*)

Jeanie and Harry West, ca. 1970s. (Courtesy of *Bluegrass Unlimited*)

First bluegrass album by a woman, *Roamin' the Blue Ridge with Jeanie West,* 1960. (Photo by Red Henry)

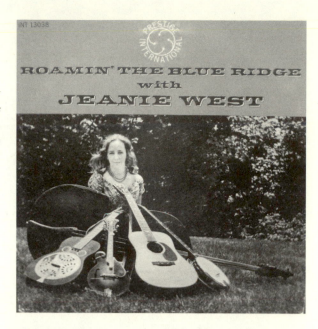

Betty Amos with Judy and Jean. L-R: Judy Lee, guitar; Betty Amos, banjo; Gloria Belle, mandolin; Jean Amos, bass guitar, ca. 1966. (Personal collection of author)

Hazel Dickens, guitar, and Alice Gerrard, banjo, 1964.
(Photo by Jeremy Foster, courtesy of Alice Gerrard)

Hazel Dickens pretending
to mow the grass at Murphy
Henry's house before they
headed to the 1996 IBMA
World of Bluegrass. (Per-
sonal collection of author)

Dottie Eyler, mid-1980s.
(Courtesy of Bonnie Eyler)

Vivian Williams with Bill Monroe and His Bluegrass Boys in Seattle, Washington, 1967. L-R: Bill Monroe, Vivian Williams, Paul Wiley, Doug Green, Phil Williams. (Photo by Irwin Nash, courtesy of Vivian Williams)

Bettie Buckland playing banjo at her Massachusetts home in 1962 while Sonny Osborne looks on. (Photo by Bob French, courtesy of Bob French and the Buckland Family)

Ginger Boatwright, Clarksville, Tennessee, 1980.
(Courtesy of Ginger Boatwright)

The Season Travelers at Nashville's Bluegrass Inn, ca. 1976. L-R: Hubert Davis, Shelby Jean Davis, Rubye Davis. (Photo by Dan Loftin)

Buck White and the Down Homers, late 1960s. L-R: Byron Berline, Buck White, Pat White, Sharon White, Cheryl White. (Courtesy of *Bluegrass Unlimited*)

The IInd Generation at the Indian Ranch Bluegrass Festival, Webster, Massachusetts, 1972. L-R: Jimmy Gaudreau, Wendy Thatcher, Eddie Adcock, Randy Stockwell. (Photo by Fred Robbins)

Martha Adcock, Kerrville, Texas, Bluegrass Festival, 1975. (Photo by Rick Gardner)

THE NUMBERS ARE GROWING: *The 1960s*

By the 1960s growing numbers of women, often from solid middle-class backgrounds, were finding their way into the bluegrass fold. For the first time college-educated women like Vivian Williams, Alice Gerrard, and Ginger Boatwright were turning their musical talents from pop, folk, and classical to bluegrass. Although most women were still being nudged toward bluegrass by husbands, fathers, or boyfriends, others such as Martha Adcock, Wendy Thatcher, Gloria Belle, and Bettie Buckland were driven solely by their own inner fires. On hearing her first Carter Family album, Martha Adcock said, "It was like manna from heaven."

Although women had been appearing regularly on recordings since the forties and fifties, both as side musicians and featured singers, the sixties would deliver the first bluegrass album to be marketed solely under a woman's name, *Roamin' the Blue Ridge* (1960) by Jeanie West. It would be followed shortly by three others: *Rose Maddox Sings Bluegrass* (1962), *Dian & the Greenbriar Boys* (1963), and *Gloria Belle Sings and Plays Bluegrass in the Country* (1967), the first album to showcase a woman singing and playing several lead instruments. In addition, *Who's That Knocking* (1965), the debut project from Hazel Dickens and Alice Gerrard, was the first album to showcase two women singing bluegrass together. The strong feminist songwriting of these two women, however, would not surface until the seventies.

For the most part, women continued to perform in bands with husbands, fathers, brothers, or boyfriends, but Betty Amos and Bettie Buckland were leading their own groups. And while the majority of women were still playing rhythm guitar or bass, more were taking up flashier instruments like the fiddle (Vivian Williams), banjo (Bettie Buckland), and mandolin (Alice McLain). Gloria Belle, marching to her own drummer, played whatever the gig called for, be it mandolin, banjo, bass, or even snare drum.

Houston native Janet Davis began teaching herself banjo around 1964 when she was at the University of Texas in Austin. Trained in classical piano but always "fascinated with the stringed instruments," she had first heard the banjo via the Kingston Trio. After college she and her husband, Jim (mandolin and guitar), formed the group Crosstown in San Antonio in 1977, with Sue Coats on bass and Sue's husband, Bill, on guitar. About 1980 the group morphed into the Blue Ridge Connection, which included Janet, Jim, all three of their sons, and Mary Ann Cornelius on bass. Janet became well known for her long-running *Banjo NewsLetter* column, which originated in 1976, as well as for her instructional books like *Splitting the Licks*. Today she runs Janet Davis Music Company in Bella Vista, Arkansas. She says, "My mission has always been to have the world fall in love with as well as respect the banjo as a true and valid musical instrument, especially professional musicians. Of course, the first challenge was being accepted by banjo players as a female banjo player. Fortunately, it is all fun, too."

Beverly King (b. 1949) became enamored of the Dobro in 1961 and finally acquired one in 1967, but did not begin to make real progress on the instrument until she saw an actual Dobro player, Oswald Kirby, in 1969. A fast learner, she recorded her first LP, *A Dobro Dozen*, in 1971. More would follow, including *Instrumental Tribute to Brother Oswald* in 1977 and two albums with Oswald in the eighties. Bev's music was never exactly bluegrass, but rather the old-time country music of Roy Acuff and Wilma Lee Cooper. Still, between 1970 and 1975, while living in Pennsylvania, she would join Alex and Ola Belle on stage at Sunset Park whenever she could, and in 1979 and 1981 she won first place in the Dobro contest at the Hugo, Oklahoma, bluegrass festival. From 1974 until 2004 she published a magazine devoted to the Dobro, the final name of which was *Country Heritage*. Along the way she also wrote several instructional books for Dobro, and in 1998 she opened her own Country Heritage Music store in Clarksville, Arkansas.

Other early female Dobro players included Bonnie Greer, who started playing with her sister Valeda (guitar) and brother Jim (banjo) in the late 1950s, first as the Greer Sisters and Little Brother Jimmy, which later became Ohio's Mac-O-Chee Valley Folks, and Carolyn Smith, who was playing with Clyde and Marie Denny and the Kentuckians by the late sixties. As *Bluegrass Unlimited* said, "The Dobro would seem a formidable instrument for a girl, but Miss Smith handles it quite well. More power to her; that big ugly thing could stand having a little glamour attached."

The time-honored family band was by no means a thing of the past. One of the groups that would take the bluegrass world by storm in the mid-seventies was the gospel-singing Marshall Family, with sisters Judy and Donna, who started playing professionally in Ohio in 1967, having moved there from West Virginia. Singer-songwriter Judy played guitar while Donna contributed lead and harmony vocals. When the group made an unadvertised appearance at Ralph Stanley's Virginia festival in May 1974, they landed not only a recording contract with Rebel Records but also the patronage of Ralph Stanley himself. The Marshalls already had two Gloryland albums under their belts, *The Valley* (1969) and *Beautiful* (1973), but the three LPs they recorded for Rebel secured a spot for them in the history of bluegrass gospel music. *Bluegrass Unlimited* waxed effusive over their second, *Requests* (1976), saying, "If you don't like the Marshalls' music you've got stone ears and a lead heart." The group was featured on the cover of *Bluegrass Unlimited* in June 1977, but unfortunately, except for two "Best of" LPs, they would record no more albums.

In short, while women were still occupying plenty of traditional roles, more were beginning to move into what was stereotypically considered male territory: bandleader, instrumentalist, album headliner. They were beginning to bridge the gap between what they were capable of doing and what the culture—including their own internalized cultural voices—would support. They stood on the shoulders of the women who came before, and would provide an even stronger foundation for the ones who would follow. As Bob Dylan intoned, the times were, indeed, a-changin'.

JEANIE
WEST

Jeanie West. The first woman to have solo billing on the cover of a bluegrass album. The title of the LP even bears her name: *Roamin' the Blue Ridge with Jeanie West* (Prestige, 1960). Yet that recording is so little known that for years the 1962 disc *Rose Maddox Sings Bluegrass* was considered to be the first bluegrass album recorded by a woman. And while Rose did not play an instrument on her project, Jeanie carried the rhythm guitar playing throughout her entire album. How could Jeanie West have gone unheralded for so long? There are several probable reasons: Prestige was an independent jazz label; Jeanie was not an established country music star; living in New York City, the Wests were far away from the bluegrass heartland; and Bill Monroe did not play on her recording.

Jeanie West (b. 1933, with the birth name West), from Asheville, North Carolina, had been playing music with her husband, Harry West, who was from southwest Virginia, since 1951. In that banner year she had graduated from high school, met her future spouse at Asheville's Mountain Folk Dance and Music Festival, married him, and moved to New York City. There they became part of the newly developing bluegrass scene that had sprung up in Greenwich Village's Washington Square. As far as Jeanie remembers, she was the only woman there who was playing bluegrass. The Wests also had a foot in the folk music scene, as indicated by an early album called *Shivaree!* (Esoteric, 1955), on which they appeared with Jean Ritchie, Tom Paley, and Oscar Brand. Other early recordings include *Banjo Songs of the Southern Mountains* (Riverside, 1956) and *Southern Mountain Folksongs and Ballads* (Riverside, ca. 1957), on which they appear with a number of other old-time musicians; the duet album *Favorite Gospel Songs* (Folkways, 1957); and *Smoky Mountain Ballads* (Esoteric, 1958), with Dobro player Artie Rose on several cuts.

As many of the numbers on these albums reveal, the Wests' core sound, which they never changed, was basically pre-bluegrass, vocal duets with Jeanie on guitar and Harry on mandolin. Occasionally Harry would play primitive Scruggs-style or clawhammer banjo or Dobro. Their music was patterned after the brother duets they loved so well: Bill and Charlie Monroe, the Blue Sky Boys, Wade and J. E. Mainer. Many of these songs eventually became part of the standard bluegrass repertoire, including "Wild Bill Jones," "Nine Pound Hammer," "Banks of the Ohio," "Bury Me beneath the Willow," and "Knoxville Girl." In general, Harry sang lead and Jeanie sang high harmony, although there were times when Jeanie sang lead and Harry sang a low harmony. Occasionally Jeanie would sing a solo.

Roamin' the Blue Ridge, however, featured a full-fledged, honest-to-goodness bluegrass band. This album and *Harry and Jeanie West: Country Music in the Bluegrass Style* (Prestige, 1960) were recorded one weekend in Washington, D.C., and included the same backup musicians: banjo colossus Bill Emerson, Artie Rose on Dobro, and Tom Morgan on bass. The cover of *Roamin' the Blue Ridge* pictures Jeanie alone, kneeling behind an array of bluegrass instruments propped up against a bass fiddle. Releasing the album under Jeanie's name with a big photo of her on the front was clearly a marketing ploy. Jeanie remembers it as being Harry's idea, and she thought it was a good one. Joan Baez's first solo album, *Joan Baez* (Vanguard), was also released in 1960. Clearly, female folksingers were hot.

The liner notes, by prominent folklorist D. K. Wilgus, mention that *Roamin' the Blue Ridge* is the first album by the Wests to feature the "new sound" of "bluegrass."

(He himself put both words in quotes.) Of the fourteen songs, eight are solos by Jeanie. The rest feature her singing the verses and Harry joining her with a lower harmony on the choruses. Among the songs included on this first female bluegrass album are "Greenback Dollar," "The Girl in the Blue Velvet Band," "Poor Ellen Smith," "Single Girl, Married Girl," "You're a Flower Blooming in the Wildwood," "Little Margaret," and "The Girl I Left in Sunny Tennessee." The sources for these are many, including the brother duets previously mentioned, but there is a healthy dose of female influence as well: Molly O'Day, the Carter Family, the Coon Creek Girls, and the hillbilly singer Georgia Dell. Jeanie herself cites Molly O'Day, Sara and Maybelle Carter, and Samantha Bumgarner as female influences. The songs tend to be on the folk and ballad side of the bluegrass repertoire, with none of the high-powered Bill Monroe originals that Rose Maddox would include on her bluegrass album.

The second Prestige album from the Wests, *Country Music in the Bluegrass Style,* features a picture of the full band on the cover. Of the fourteen songs, thirteen are duets, with Harry singing the lead and Jeanie singing the higher harmony. The song selection leans slightly more to the "hard-core" bluegrass sound and includes Bill Monroe's "Blue Moon of Kentucky," sung as a duet all the way through. However, D. K. Wilgus, who also wrote these liner notes, points out that "this album is not strictly a bluegrass performance. To the duet harmonies of the Wests . . . have been added the additional components of the bluegrass band . . . But instead of a restyling of the Wests' performance into the syncopation of bluegrass, the result is that the young bluegrass musicians are blending their style with the 'old-timey' Wests'." This is the same thing that happened when Wilma Lee and Stoney Cooper added a banjo to their band—their sound didn't magically change to "bluegrass"; it was the same sound they'd always had, only now with a banjo.

As historian Neil Rosenberg notes, these Prestige albums were "products of the New York–centered folk scene." The Wests had moved to the Big Apple because Harry already had a job there. Jeanie soon found work with AT&T as a long-distance telephone operator. Her Southern accent did not go unnoticed by her potential employer, but Jeanie won the job when she pointed out that she spoke both cleanly and clearly. Like many professional bluegrass musicians, the Wests performed their music as a sideline. Jeanie admits that having four children, beginning in 1955, made it "kinda rough." Luckily Harry's mother, who was in New York, could help out, and often the couple took their kids along to gigs. Jeanie said that during the weekend musical gatherings in Washington Square, their children often played in the sprinkler. When asked if she remembered seeing any other women playing bluegrass in those early years, Jeanie replied, "I was it." But she also says, "It didn't really bother me."

Jeanie and Harry made other recordings down through the years, including *Songs of the Southland* (Folkways, 1963) with Artie Rose. In the liner notes Harry writes, "Our music is much the same now as it was some years ago . . . Strange to say, we used the same instruments as in 'Blue Grass' before the latter became popular . . . and while we enjoy all the current 'Blue Grass' groups we do not mimic."

Fifteen songs that they recorded bluegrass style in 1964 never made it to an album until 1982, when they were released as *Roots of Bluegrass* on West Germany's Folk Variety label. Although the recording includes banjo, the sound is still more akin to string-band music, in which all the instruments play the melody at the same time and there is no mandolin chop. Jeanie does the lead singing on only three songs, one of these being the solo "I Know What It Means to Be Lonesome."

Another group of recordings from 1969 was also lost but resurfaced as *I Need the Prayers of Those I Love: Old Time Sacred Picking & Singing* (Old Homestead, 1988). This LP featured the bass playing of the Wests' son Everett, who died before the album came out. The couple also recorded *In a Little Village Churchyard*, a new set of old songs with just mandolin and guitar, in 1981 for the same label.

In 1980 the Wests moved back to North Carolina. For years their ad for "Fine Bluegrass Instruments" could be found in the classified section of *Bluegrass Unlimited*. Today Jeanie and Harry live in Statesville, where they run a music store, Harry and Jeanie West Fine Musical Instruments. They continue to play music but mostly for their own enjoyment. When asked if they liked to jam with other musicians, Jeanie wrote, "Seldom do. Most folks can't play our music as they learn from the new recordings. We mostly do the older repertory and haven't updated." Their two Prestige albums were released in 2000 on the Fantasy label as a combined CD titled *Jeanie West: Country Bluegrass Featuring Harry West.*

They have to pour water on me
twice a day to calm me down.

—Betty Amos

BETTY AMOS
WITH JUDY
AND JEAN

One of the earliest women to take up the Scruggs-style banjo was Betty Amos (b. 1934), who grew up near Roanoke, Virginia. Although photographed holding a five-string for a promotional shot when she was with the Carlisles in 1953, she maintains that she didn't play banjo professionally until she teamed up with Judy and Jean in 1960. Her first recordings with the instrument were made in 1964. Her introduction to three-finger picking began at age thirteen when her brother Ed "showed me the roll." (Ed would go on to play banjo with the Bailey Brothers and Mac Wiseman.) Not wanting to copy anyone, even Earl Scruggs, Betty would take her banjo "deep into the woods" to practice. In her family band with her father and brothers, the Buck Mountain Ramblers, however, she played guitar.

In 1952 Betty went on the road with country music artist Bill Carlisle as the female lead singer and guitar player, replacing Martha Carson. For the sake of propriety, because she was eighteen and single, her father and Bill decided that she would be known as the bandleader's niece, Betty Carlisle. While she was with Bill, she appeared on several of his *Billboard* hits, including "No Help Wanted" and "Is Zat You Myrtle." When she left to go solo around 1954, she reclaimed the birth name she had loathed giving up. Working as a country singer, she recorded a number of singles, including "Hello to the Blues" and "Jole John" and played places such as the Louisiana Hayride, where she shared the stage with Elvis Presley.

Meanwhile, up in St. Marys, Pennsylvania, fourteen-year-old Alice Schreiber (b. 1934), who would later change her name to the more country-sounding Judy Lee, was learning to play guitar and bass and joining her father's band, Barney Schreiber and the Hayshakers. Her younger sister, Betty Schreiber, soon joined on bass, and the sisters sang duets and often traded instruments.

When Judy Lee was sixteen, she and sister Betty went out on their own, playing with a group of friends that included brothers Buddy and Bobby Spicher and Donna Darlene and calling themselves the Golden West Girls. Eventually Judy Lee's "dream came true" and she was able to leave St. Marys to play country music. In 1957 she wound up in West Virginia and met Betty Amos at the WWVA Wheeling Jamboree.

In 1960 Betty Amos, her sister Jean, and Judy teamed up as a country band with Judy on electric lead guitar, Betty on electric rhythm guitar, and Jean on bass. Betty did all the solo singing, and their three-part harmony featured her lead. For bluegrass numbers Judy would switch to rhythm on her Martin guitar and Betty would play banjo. The group played often at USO shows and military bases and occasionally they traveled overseas. In January 1961 they survived a plane crash while heading to a USO show near Labrador. Undaunted by their brush with death, they borrowed instruments from the men at the base and gave the troops a rousing performance. Judy said, "I think that was the best audience we ever had."

In 1963 Betty Amos with Judy and Jean (as they were usually billed) signed with Starday Records and moved to Nashville. Although most of their recordings were "hard-core country," as Jean calls them, two from around 1964, "Eighteen Wheels A-Rolling" (co-written by all three women) and "Franklin County Moonshine" (written by Betty), are decidedly bluegrass, with Betty's prominent banjo powering both songs. She kicks off both numbers and takes all the instrumental solos in a style that is clean, clear, and forceful. She also plays the banjo while singing the lead vocals, an impressive feat. With Jean and Judy providing harmony, the women have a strong, tight trio. Betty would go on to write many more country songs, including "Second Fiddle to an Old Guitar," which Jean Shepherd would take to number five on the *Billboard* chart in 1964.

Many people who have heard these recordings may have assumed that the banjo playing was being done by a studio musician as did this male record collector:

> "Franklin County Moonshine" and "Eighteen Wheels A-Rollin'" both go at lickety-split tempos and feature Scruggs-style banjo as the lead instrument, instead of steel guitar. I know Betty played banjo live, but I have always assumed it's a session player and not Betty herself playing the banjo on those sides. It's really hotshot pro chops stuff, and if she could burn like that I can't believe she wouldn't have featured it on more of her records. That's just a total guess though, I could be completely wrong about that. It could be her, who knows?

Unfortunately, these two numbers and Betty's fine banjo playing are practically unknown to the bluegrass community. Almost certainly part of the reason is that the trio was primarily a country music act whose other recordings were solidly in that musical vein. Also, that redoubtable magazine *Bluegrass Unlimited* did not begin publishing until 1966, thus there is no review of these records in this respected repository of bluegrass history.

These are some of the earliest songs to be written by the women in bluegrass who sang them. Even if the stories are not personally drawn from the lives of the writers, both songs are told from a woman's point of view and reflect her experience. "Eighteen Wheels A-Rolling" relates the somewhat conventional story of a waitress at a truck stop waiting for her truck-driving man to come rolling in. However, it is the waitress herself who spins the tale, singing, "I'm waiting for that Big Mac, number two-oh-three." On the other hand "Franklin County Moonshine" has a sassier narrator, a spouse who is not happy with her moonshining husband and the marital arrangement he came up with: "You said I'd watch the cook stove and you would watch the still." It ends with the singer saying, "Something's gotta change" and "I'm gonna put my foot down."

Betty, Judy, and Jean were a working band who spent much time on the road. One of the strengths of their show was that they could switch instruments, so in a typical program they might do a set of country music, a set of bluegrass, and even a set of light rock-and-roll. As Betty says, there was something for everybody.

Betty, Judy, and Jean stayed together until 1977. Other women who played with them during these years included Shirley Wood, Bobby Sills, Connie Barnett, Gilda Jordan, Lois Johnson, Gloria Belle, and Sudie Callaway, about whom Betty and Judy's song "If Mommy Didn't Sing" was written. The three friends reunited in 2003 for the Louisiana Hayride Reunion Show in Shreveport.

Today all three women live near one another in Hendersonville, Tennessee. Judy is a pioneer in the growth of women's senior softball and in 2007 became the national women's director of the Softball Players Association. As Judy said, "I am still playing with the Tennessee Senior Stars 65-Plus team; we have been the world champions for the past five years. I have battled numerous health problems, including open-heart surgery, a hysterectomy, back surgery, a knee cartilage transplant, several strokes and more. I've even survived a plane crash. But I ain't out yet. I am the phoenix of softball. I rise from the ashes. I'm still in the game."

In talking to Betty today, it's easy to tell that she is extremely proud of the fact that she did all of the maintenance work on her banjo herself. She was playing in the era of skin banjo heads (not plastic), which required much upkeep. Betty liked to keep her banjo head as tight as she could get it without breaking it. She says this gave her a loud sound that often drew comments from other players.

Betty, who lives just a few doors down from Judy, takes a great interest in natural medicine and says, "I am satisfied with my body and my health." She has so much energy, she says, "They have to pour water on me twice a day to calm me down." Which just goes to prove that you can take the girl from the show, but you can't take the show from the girl!

I just wanted to play music.

—Gloria Belle

GLORIA BELLE

Gloria Belle is best known to bluegrass lovers for the years she spent playing bass, guitar, and mandolin with the legendary Jimmy Martin and His Sunny
Mountain Boys. She went to work with Jimmy full-time in March 1969 and
played off and on with him until 1978. She sang on a number of his albums, and
her high baritone on his classic recording "Milwaukee, Here I Come" is instantly
recognizable. But Gloria Belle was an established professional musician years
before she became a Sunny Mountain Boy.

Gloria Belle's musical journey has been markedly different from that of her
peers. Most early women followed a musical path that included marriage, children, and participation in a band that included a family member, be it husband,
partner, father, or sibling. Gloria Belle, however, chose music over marriage,
consciously not marrying until she was fifty. Her thinking was this: "I don't want

to stop playing music when I get married, and it won't work for me to go out on the road and play music and him sit home. Because he'll be imagining things even if there is nothing bad happening." So Gloria Belle did it her way.

Gloria Bernadette Flickinger (b. 1939) was raised in Hanover, Pennsylvania, an only child. At age three she began singing on a church radio program in Frederick, Maryland, with her parents. Her mom played piano and guitar; her dad, harmonica. By her teens she could play guitar and piano (taught by her mother) along with mandolin and banjo. (The great Don Reno showed her the three-finger banjo roll.) This makes Gloria Belle one of the earliest female banjo players right alongside Roni Stoneman and Betty Amos.

Gloria idolized the "girl singers" of the day: Wilma Lee Cooper, Rose Maddox, and "the late, great, one and only Molly O'Day." However, it was hearing the Bailey Brothers on the Wheeling Jamboree that made her decide to play music for a living. "They were my idols. They were the first ones I really idolized besides the girl singers." Gloria admits that their girl singer, Miss Evelyn (Evelyn Bryan), was "probably another influence on me."

Gloria attended only one year of high school, dropping out at fifteen, "because all I wanted to do was play music." It would be six years before she landed her first professional job. "I didn't know the right people. I didn't have the connections," she says. In the meantime she took a job in a potato chip factory in Hanover, telling her mother all the while, "This is not what I want to do. I wanna play music!" Her parents supported her goal, buying her a Gibson mandolin for her sixteenth birthday.

Gloria spent those years learning to play her instruments, making guest appearances on shows, and entering contests. Mike Seeger, reporting on the 1959 banjo contest at Pennsylvania's Sunset Park, lists twenty-two players, including "Gloria Flickinger," who played "Dixie Breakdown," a difficult banjo tune. Mike notes that she is "the only girl in the contest this year and better known for her Molly O'Day–style singing and mandolin playing." (She didn't win or place.) Finally, around 1958 she began working with Gary Epley and the Cheerful Valley Gang, a local band who played on the radio in Hanover.

Gloria and her mother, playing mandolin and guitar, eventually secured a guest spot on Cas Walker's live radio show in Knoxville, Tennessee, in 1959, where Gloria sang "Do Lord." Although she did not land a job then and went back to the potato chip factory feeling "a little discouraged," the audition eventually paid off. Six months later Gloria joined the cast, becoming duet partners with none other than Danny Bailey, who had split with his brother Charlie. Since

Cas Walker could not pronounce "Flickinger" easily, he christened his newest musician "Gloria Belle." At twenty-one she was finally getting to play music for a living. She would stay with the Cas Walker show for five years.

Duetting now with Danny Bailey, Gloria played mandolin and sang tenor. She was also featured playing banjo on solo numbers like "Banjo Picking Girl," "Slewfoot," and "Little Birdie." For variety, she sometimes played twin mandolin numbers, such as "Soldier's Joy" and "Old Joe Clark," with mandolin whiz Red Rector.

In 1963 Gloria Belle, playing lead mandolin and doing the solo singing, cut two singles for the Redwing label with the help of Bill Monroe's banjo player Bill Keith and fiddler Tater Tate. These were the first bluegrass mandolin solos to be recorded by a woman other than Donna Stoneman. Four years later, the year-old magazine *Bluegrass Unlimited* reviewed one of these singles in conjunction with that of another "girl singer," Trigger Star. After dismissing Trigger's voice as "mediocre," the reviewer says, "Gloria Belle sings only a little better, with a voice that's not really suitable for bluegrass." He does not mention her mandolin playing, but spends most of the review praising Tater Tate and Bill Keith, declaring the single "well worth having" only because of them.

In the summer of 1965 Gloria and a number of her cohorts were laid off by Cas Walker. She immediately found a seasonal job as the "banjo picking girl" at Ghost Town in Maggie Valley, North Carolina. Banjo player Raymond Fairchild was also with the show and backed Gloria Belle on guitar. She did seven shows a day, six days a week, and had to sing "Banjo Picking Girl" in every show. She says, "I was singing that song forty-two times a week. Can you imagine? I felt like a robot." In the fall she worked for a short time with the McCormick Brothers, who ran an old-time square dance near Gallatin, Tennessee, and also did a few road shows. Gloria was featured as the "girl vocalist" and also played a little Mother Maybelle–style lead guitar.

In the spring of 1966 Gloria joined Betty Amos and Her All-Girl Band, who were working out of Roanoke, Virginia. This group played primarily country music but included a smattering of bluegrass in all of their shows. Gloria Belle, playing electric bass, replaced Lois Johnson, who had been the "girl singer" with Jimmy Martin in the early sixties. When they played bluegrass, Gloria switched to mandolin, since Betty Amos played banjo.

Playing in an all-girl band was a new experience for Gloria Belle, and it was the first time she had experienced jealousy from other members in a band. As

Gloria tells it, "Girls have a tendency to feel competitive with each other, where boys don't feel that way [toward women]. They're not competing with a woman. The woman just adds to the show, she's totally different, so they do their thing and she does her thing. The majority of men don't feel threatened by a woman because they figure a woman can't play my instrument or can't play it as well as I do anyway. And in a lot of cases it is true."

By 1967 Gloria Belle had left Betty Amos and was back in Hanover working on her first album with the help of Paul Gerry, whom she was dating. Paul later went on to found Revonah Records. (Revonah is Hanover spelled backward.) *Gloria Belle Sings and Plays Bluegrass in the Country* (Rebel, 1967) showcases Gloria Belle's singing and her picking. She plays banjo on three songs, lead guitar on one, and takes mandolin leads on five others. The twelve vocals include two Molly O'Day songs and one from Rose Maddox. Four numbers are solos, and the rest include harmony singing from Paul Gerry, who also played guitar. Part of the album was recorded with Red Smiley's fine band: Billy Edwards on banjo, Tater Tate on fiddle, and John Palmer on bass. This recording, the first album from Rebel Records to feature a woman, is not well known, but it is a milestone for women in bluegrass. Only the fourth solo bluegrass album by a woman, it is the first of these to feature a woman playing a lead instrument.

May 1967 found Gloria at Sunset Park again, filling in as bass player of the day for Ralph Stanley. Alice Gerrard and Hazel Dickens, performers themselves at this time, would often see Gloria when she made guest appearances at the country music parks. Alice recognized that Gloria "was a good banjo player," but she and Hazel were a bit put off by Gloria's willingness to ask bands if she could get up and play a number with them. They were not used to such assertive behavior from a woman. Alice says, "I think we were a little jealous. Maybe there was a piece of us that wished we were up there. We weren't learning to play banjo like that; we were just kinda sliding by on whatever we were doing."

That summer Gloria was asked to become the leader of an all-male band from Frederick, Maryland, the Bluegrass Travelers, whose leader had been killed in an automobile accident. She had never thought of herself as a bandleader but took the job anyway, changing the name to Gloria Belle and the Green Mountain Travelers. Today it is not unusual to see a woman leading a bluegrass band, but back in 1967 female bandleaders were rare. Gloria Belle played banjo and mandolin and sang lead and harmony. Unfortunately the group broke up after a short time.

What we are seeing here is a picture of the quintessential bluegrass side musician, only this had never been done before by a woman in bluegrass. Versatile on many instruments, Gloria Belle went where the work was.

Enter Jimmy Martin, Decca recording artist and bluegrass music star. Jimmy had used "girl singers" before: Lois Johnson and Penny Jay (Helen Morgan). Lois had joined in 1961 (along with her husband on snare drum) and had recorded eleven songs with Jimmy in 1962. Penny Jay, who was on board by 1963, recorded two songs with Jimmy, including his hit "Widow Maker," which she co-wrote. On stage Penny played bass and Lois played guitar, but in the studio the women were vocalists only, singing high baritone.

Jimmy had first seen Gloria Belle on the Cas Walker show. She had even talked to him about using her in the band, but he wasn't interested. Eventually, though, he asked her to play some dates that specifically called for a "girl singer." Gloria Belle had gotten a break. Jimmy Martin was the big time.

For the rest of 1968 Gloria worked part-time with Jimmy, as the "girl singer," playing mandolin or guitar. Although Gloria Belle had been playing mandolin professionally for years, Jimmy allowed her to play lead on just two songs, the kickoffs to "Lord I'm Coming Home" and "Train 45." As Gloria said, "Jimmy Martin didn't want a girl playing mandolin." Then in March 1969 Jimmy told Gloria that if she would move to Nashville, he would give her a full-time job in the band—as the snare drum player. Gloria Belle accepted. She was off to Nashville to become a real, live Sunny Mountain Boy.

She had not been with the band long when in May 1969 they went into the studio to cut a spine-tingling version of "Milwaukee." Like her female predecessors, Gloria Belle never played an instrument when recording with Jimmy. He would always bring in studio musicians. As she said, "He wanted me to concentrate on the singing." Needless to say, the men in the band were somehow able to concentrate on their singing while they played.

Gloria stayed on snare drum for about a year and then moved to acoustic bass. In the spring of 1970 she recorded ten more songs with the band, including "I've Got My Future on Ice" and "Singing All Day and Dinner on the Ground." Her vocal contributions did not go unnoticed. The *Bluegrass Unlimited* review of Jimmy's *Singing All Day and Dinner on the Ground* called her high baritone vocal "unsurpassingly lovely." The reviewer went on to say, "The use of a girl's voice in a vocal ensemble gives a feeling of old time family revival meetings . . . An indispensable album."

Although Gloria Belle was working full-time for Jimmy, for eight years she drove cars for an auto auction on Wednesdays and worked in a short-order restaurant. This money paid her living expenses so that her earnings with Jimmy could go into savings. In 1974 she was able to buy a house near Nashville. Never free with compliments, Jimmy liked to brag that Gloria Belle was "the only Sunny Mountain Boy that owns her own home."

Playing for Jimmy Martin was no picnic for any of the band members. He could be abrasive both on and off stage. His treatment of Gloria Belle was captured in a *Bluegrass Unlimited* article in November 1969. The writer says that while she was singing her solo number, "Jimmy cavorted from one end of the stage to the other, making ungodly faces at her, sticking out his tongue, and inviting the audience to boo her performance." After noting her "ample physical attributes" the writer then criticized her singing, saying she "actually has a rather raucous voice which does not lend itself to bluegrass."

How did Gloria Belle feel about Jimmy's treatment of her? She said, "Jimmy is a very critical person. He works with this theory: I have to keep 'em on their toes all the time." He was afraid to praise his band members for fear they would "let down." Gloria says, "I wouldn't argue with him. The more I could ignore it, the better it was."

Is it any wonder that she decided to take a break from Jimmy Martin? The spring of 1972 found her playing electric bass with the all-female Nashville Kitty Kats, a country dance band working out of Richmond, Virginia. She wouldn't commit to the group until they promised she could play some bluegrass, so every show included fifteen minutes of Gloria Belle playing the banjo and singing standards like "Rocky Top."

In the summer of 1973 Gloria Belle worked with Charlie Monroe, Bill's older brother, then seventy. She sang tenor and played banjo, mandolin, and guitar and helped his wife, Martha, with the driving. They worked primarily as a duo, except at festivals where Jimmy Martin was booked, when his band backed them up. Then in 1975, as she says, cackling with laughter, "I went back to Jimmy Martin again." As before, she played bass, eventually moving to electric bass at Jimmy's insistence so that she would be louder. The band made a ten-day tour of Japan that year.

While still a member of the Sunny Mountain Boys, Gloria Belle began work on her second album, *A Good Hearted Woman,* in 1976. Jimmy and the band played on part of the album, and when they bailed, Tom Gray, Mike Auldridge, and

Randy Graham stepped in to help her finish it. Originally slated to be released by Rebel, the album eventually came out on Gloria Belle's own label, Southern Belle, in 1978. In a huge departure from her other recordings, Gloria Belle did not play a single lead instrument. And she took up the rhythm guitar only after Jimmy Martin pulled out. Perhaps—unfortunately—she was following the Jimmy Martin model and concentrating on her singing. The *Bluegrass Unlimited* reviewer called this a "satisfying effort" by a "true bluegrass veteran."

In January 1978 Gloria Belle did her last recording with Jimmy Martin, singing high baritone on numbers such as "White Dove," "Uncle Pen," and a remake of "Widow Maker." These were eventually released on several Gusto albums. In June she left the band for good.

Being a side musician with Jimmy Martin had been a high-profile job. If she had been a man, Gloria Belle almost certainly could have moved right into another top-tier band as many of Jimmy's side musicians did. But those opportunities were not open to women then, and few are open to women now. Nevertheless, Gloria Belle would continue to find work as a bluegrass musician.

The next two years, she says, found her in "limbo," taking various music jobs until she could "settle in on something." After being on the road constantly, Gloria was ready to stay in one place for a while. In 1980 she contacted Cas Walker in Knoxville, who again teamed her up with Danny Bailey. The show was now being taped twice a week, freeing Gloria to take other jobs in the Tennessee area. She worked as a fill-in banjo player with the Bonnie Lou and Buster show at Pigeon Forge, she subbed on electric bass for a band in Gatlinburg, and she played guitar and sang in a local band that worked conventions in the area. She played the 1982 World's Fair with the Bailey Brothers and also was paired with a woman guitarist, Joy King, as a duo during the fair's Women's Week. "That wasn't my idea, but I had to go along with it." She calls 1982 "one of the busiest years of my life."

In April 1983 the Cas Walker show went off the air and Gloria Belle headed to South Florida for the winter. Never content to be without a band, she helped put together a local all-girl group called Foxfire, in which she played mandolin. They played a few dates in Florida in 1984. Gloria liked Florida so much that she bought a second home there in 1985 and from then on spent every winter in the Sunshine State.

For her third album, *The Love of the Mountains* (Webco, 1986), Gloria Belle had the backing of one of the hottest bands on the circuit, the Johnson Mountain Boys. Again she did not play an instrument, except on one cut, the instrumental

"Maple Sugar," where she ripped through her mandolin break in a solid, old-fashioned style. The testosterone-charged Johnson Mountain Boys were used to a rapid-fire pace, and Gloria Belle says, "They did a lot of things faster than I anticipated. I don't know how in the world I ever played 'Maple Sugar' that fast." The *Bluegrass Unlimited* reviewer opined that "Gloria Belle still manages plenty of spirited bluegrass that makes for worthwhile listening."

Finally in 1989 Gloria took the plunge and married guitarist and luthier Mike Long, with whom she had picked informally since the mid-seventies. Mike was not a professional musician, but he was "in the league" with them. While Gloria Belle had always led a "very normal dating life," she had been cautious about getting seriously involved, especially with someone who didn't play music. On the other hand, many of the musicians she dated "weren't marriage material." So it was hard for her to find the right combination, someone who could "play music with me and go with me on the road" and who was also a "stable, secure, thinking person." Gloria Belle could see that Mike was "gonna be serious about playing music. And he wouldn't stop me from playing." They formed a band in 1990, Gloria Belle and Tennessee Sunshine, with Gloria on mandolin and Mike on guitar. They have released five recordings, including *A Tribute to Molly O'Day* (1996). *Bluegrass Unlimited* called their gospel CD *He Leadeth Me* (2000) one of Gloria Belle's "most impressive" recording efforts.

In 2000 Gloria Belle and sixteen other women participated on the Rebel project *Follow Me Back to the Fold: A Tribute to Women in Bluegrass,* headlined and coordinated by Mark Newton. Mark said that "starting with Gloria Belle" there had been a lot of women who had had an impact on his music, and he wanted to acknowledge this female influence. The CD was named Recorded Event of the Year by the IBMA in 2001. At the IBMA Awards show in October of that year, Gloria Belle participated in the grand finale with the rest of the album cast. When she stepped up to the mike to belt out her verse of the title song, the audience broke into spontaneous applause for her energetic performance.

Today Gloria Belle is not some old-timer who is content to stay at home curled up in front of the television. She is present every year at the IBMA World of Bluegrass and is always eager to take part in anything musical. She participated in the World's Largest All-Female Jam (1995); a storytelling session at the International Bluegrass Music Museum (1996); a Women in Bluegrass performance at Fan Fest, where she played killer mandolin on the rapid-fire instrumental "Dixie Breakdown" (1997); and a Women in Bluegrass workshop (1999) where she and Hazel Dickens stole the show by singing a hair-raising version of "Banjo

Picking Girl." In 1999, in recognition of her long career in bluegrass and her many accomplishments, Gloria Belle was given a Distinguished Achievement Award by the IBMA, only the ninth woman to receive the award.

The paths for women in bluegrass have widened and diversified since Gloria Belle dropped out of high school to play music in 1954. But even today we don't see many female side musicians. Two women, however, come immediately to mind: bass player extraordinaire Missy Raines (who has now formed her own band) and banjo player Kristin Scott Benson. (The fact that both of these women have supportive husbands who don't mind their being on the road is a positive development!) Both play bluegrass full-time, both play in bands without husbands or family, and both have moved from band to band as circumstances demanded—just as Gloria Belle did. They may not realize it, but Gloria Belle carved out this path and took the first steps along it forty years ago when she left home to play on the Cas Walker show.

This brings to mind Robert Frost's poem "The Road Not Taken." Frost writes about two roads that diverge in the woods and the choice he makes to take the one less traveled. When Gloria Belle came to these same woods, the two paths had signs over them. The wider path said: "CONVENTIONAL LIFESTYLE. GET A JOB, GET MARRIED." The much narrower path said: "PLAY BLUEGRASS MUSIC." Gloria liked that one. But there was some fine print. It said: "WOMEN WHO ENTER MUST PLAY IN A BAND WITH FAMILY OR HUSBAND." Gloria Belle didn't like that choice, so she just hauled off and headed down through the woods where there was no path. And then years later, when Missy and Kristin made their visits to these same woods, they saw this rough path. It was almost invisible, because not many people had taken it, but it was there. And they didn't know who made it, but they liked the sign, which said: "GROUNDBREAKING WOMEN IN BLUEGRASS ENTER HERE." They didn't know at the time that they *were* groundbreaking women, but they didn't like the restrictions on the other signs, so they headed down this new path. They were all excited about their future, so they didn't stop to read the fine print on this sign. In very tiny letters it said: "PATH CARVED BY GLORIA BELLE."

> if they had any more drive it'd take you
> a week to get home again to turn the
> record over. if they had more punch
> the first cut would give you a black
> eye. dis is black-belt bluegrass.
>
> —jon da peripatetic poet, 1973

HAZEL
AND ALICE

Hazel Dickens. Alice Gerrard. Hazel and Alice. Alice and Hazel. The legendary duo whose four groundbreaking albums proclaimed the revolutionary idea that two women could sing bluegrass with the same passion and intensity as men. The two composers who proved that women could write powerful bluegrass numbers based on their own personal experiences. The pioneering duet whose first Rounder album inspired the country music careers of Naomi and Wynonna Judd. Hazel and Alice. Like Simon and Garfunkel, their names are forever bound.

Of course their partnership inevitably unraveled. Thankfully, each woman, strong enough to bend, went on to have a stellar career in her own right. Hazel, known for her powerful mountain singing, won the National Heritage Award in 2001, received an honorary doctorate in 1998, and starred in the documentary film of her life, *It's Hard to Tell the Singer from the Song* (2002). Her songs have been recorded by bluegrass artists such as Lynn Morris, Laurie Lewis, the Johnson Mountain Boys, Hot Rize, and the Dry Branch Fire Squad. Acts as diverse as Dolly Parton and the New Riders of the Purple Sage have covered her compositions. Alice, in addition to raising four children, founded the *Old-Time Herald* magazine in 1987 and served as editor for fifteen years. She received an apprenticeship to study old-time fiddling with the great Tommy Jarrell and helped produce a documentary film of his life, *Sprout Wings and Fly* (1982). She herself is featured in the documentary *Homemade American Music* (1980). Both women have been honored by the IBMA with Distinguished Achievement Awards. When Hazel accepted hers, she walked up to the podium and boldly declared, "I was wondering if any women's names were ever going to be mentioned."

Although the two women were drawn together by their love of traditional music, their early lives—Hazel in West Virginia and Alice on the West Coast—could not have been more disparate. What twisted paths led to this unconventional pairing?

Hazel Dickens

It's a long way from the coal-mining country of southern West Virginia to the cover of the *Washington Post Magazine*. And nobody knows that better than Hazel Dickens. As she once said, "I guess my biggest accomplishment is the miracle that I am here."

Born near Bluefield in 1925, Hazel was the eighth of eleven children. Her father, H. N. Dickens, who drove a truck for a mining company, had given up playing the banjo at dances to become a preacher in a Primitive Baptist church. He was also a powerful singer who "lined out" hymns for his congregation. This unaccompanied church singing had a profound influence on Hazel's own music. But equally important were the secular offerings of the Grand Ole Opry, hillbilly records, and country radio. Hazel not only absorbed the sounds of Bill Monroe, Molly O'Day, the Carter Family, and the Stanley Brothers, but she also loved the "modern" honky-tonk sounds of Ernest Tubb and Kitty Wells.

In Hazel's mountain culture, as she doesn't hesitate to point out, a woman "stayed home and had the babies and kept the house and did the cooking and generally kept her mouth shut if she knew what was good for her." Her mother, Sarah, never went anywhere without H. N., unless it was to the next-door neighbor's house. The one exception was the time she carried a very sick three-month-old Hazel clear across the mountain—all by herself—to a doctor. As Hazel says, "My mother is not the kind of person that would give up on one of her children . . . She pulled me through." Hazel survived but says, "I was not in good shape for a long time. I was late starting school. I was so thin."

Although her six brothers all played a variety of stringed instruments, Hazel took only minimal interest in the guitar until she moved to Baltimore. Singing was her passion. Early on she began copying down the words to songs. "I had a terrific recall. When I would hear something on the radio I would write down what I remembered." The next time she heard the song, she would write down the rest—or fill in what she thought should go there. She laughingly calls this the "folk process."

Like her older siblings Hazel dropped out of school, going through only seventh grade, because she "didn't have clothes to wear." She stayed at home, helping her mother, who was not well. When she turned sixteen she went to Radford, Virginia, to live with a relative, taking a job at the mill the next year when she was old enough to get a work permit. Then, in 1950 she followed her older sister Velvie and some of her brothers to Baltimore. Eventually her parents and most of her siblings would join them. Hazel moved in with Velvie and her husband and their two boys, sleeping on their couch.

Baltimore slammed Hazel with a big dose of culture shock. Apartments boasted signs that read, "NO DOGS OR HILLBILLIES." Hazel says, "I was so scared of everybody." The city, while exciting, was noisy and filled with unfamiliar faces. "I was very unsocialized and I didn't know how to talk to people . . . When you're that shy, you don't relate, you don't communicate very well, and you try to find people that you can be close to that are like you." What happened to Hazel happened to many displaced people. "We ended up in these hillbilly ghettos. As a result you never got away from your own kind . . . Even in the factories, you were around the same kind; not many city people worked those jobs." Hazel felt "terribly inferior." People made fun of her. "I couldn't understand which way I was supposed to be or what I was supposed to be."

At least in Baltimore there was work. After several factory jobs and a stint at waitressing, Hazel landed a "good job" at Continental Can, a unionized work-place. She says, "That was the first time I'd ever encountered working people speaking up for themselves and having other people like the union looking out for you." That was also the first time she got a paid vacation. Hazel would work here for three or four years until she got fired for taking off so much time to play music. "That shows what a passion I had for playing." With some of her first money, Hazel had bought an inexpensive used guitar.

So for four years Hazel lived a life that was not too different from that of many other mountain folks who had moved north. During the week she worked in a factory. On weekends she would go to a bar to hear country music or to someone's house to make homegrown music. She was insulated and isolated among her own people. As far as Hazel could see, she was looking at the rest of her life.

In 1954, however, things began to change. Hazel met Mike Seeger, the catalyst who would open the doors into a different world. Mike (b. 1933), the son of ethnomusicologists Charles and Ruth Seeger, had been raised on Library of Congress field recordings and already played a number of instruments. He also had a keen interest in "hillbilly" music. A conscientious objector during the Korean War, he had moved to Baltimore in 1954 to fulfill his service requirement by working in a tuberculosis hospital. As fate would have it, Hazel's brother Robert was a patient there, and soon he and Mike were playing music to pass the time. As Hazel says, Mike, "being the historian he was, was curious about the rest of the family." He was invited to meet them at the apartment of Hazel's parents. Hazel couldn't understand why Mike, an educated man from a middle-class family, was interested. "I think we were the first live hillbilly family that he met."

As Hazel tells it, when Mike came over, he and her brother Arnold immediately hit it off and started playing. Hazel, however, says, "I was stand-offish at first. I was not gonna buy a pig in a poke." In addition to being shy, Hazel was also "suspicious as to what he wanted of us." She watched from the other side of the room, where she had the radio on. Then she says, "I thought I'd really test him. I turned the radio up and said, 'This is the way it should really sound.'" But Mike was not intimidated. "He stood his ground. He passed the test." And Hazel joined in the playing.

Mike's interest in hillbilly music "validated" that music for Hazel, giving her a "whole new perspective on what I could become." In addition, Mike introduced her to people from another culture, paving the way for a radical personal transformation in Hazel's own life.

Hazel, Mike, and her brothers Arnold and Robert started picking together at parties in the homes of friends. Soon mandolin player Bob Shanklin (whom Hazel would date for a while) and banjoist Dickie Rittler joined the jams. It was Bob, Dickie, Hazel, Mike, and Arnold who first ventured out of the living room and into a club. It wasn't long before they invited Bobby Baker, who had led a band in Kentucky, to join them. He became the leader of the group, re-naming it the Pike County Boys. Did being a Pike County "boy" bother Hazel? "I just wanted to play. I didn't care who with or what. I just wanted to do it. And I persevered through all of that stuff, being unrehearsed, getting up there without hardly even knowing the chords to the songs. I was just sticking my nose out there. I knew that I knew all of the songs." In addition to singing tenor, Hazel served as the "girl singer," who could sing the current jukebox offerings of female country singers such as Wanda Jackson, Rose Maddox, and Kitty Wells, as well as the hits of George Jones, Lefty Frizzell, and Hank Williams. As she said, "I knew every bluegrass song coming and going and most country songs."

Today it is almost impossible to understand what a monumental leap this was for Hazel, moving out of the supportive behind-the-scenes mountain woman's role and into the public arena with a group of men. She was violating the moun-tain taboo of "keeping her mouth shut if she knew what was good for her." And in public. Having her brothers in the band helped to make this possible.

Hazel eventually moved out of her sister's house and into her own small apartment, where she lived until she moved in with social worker Alyse Taub-man. Alyse, whose home was a center for music parties as well as intellectual discussion groups, was another pivotal person in Hazel's life. Hazel says, "When I went to live in the same house as Alyse, I think that was probably the turning point. I was really wrestling with myself then. I really admired Alyse . . . she got me to see another way of putting something, another way of thinking about it—it wasn't done overnight."

By now Hazel had bought a used bass. "I would have done just about anything to keep playing music. And that was one way that I could be involved, to play bass with them." Now she could freelance. In addition to her work with the Pike County Boys, she worked some locally with Jack Cooke and with Danny Curtis, and she even went to New Jersey for a weekend to play bass in a country band. Later she would fill in on bass with the Greenbriar Boys during their 1962 tour with Joan Baez.

A sample of Hazel's work with the Pike County Boys can be heard today on the CD reissue of *American Banjo: Three-Finger and Scruggs Style* (Folkways, 1957), where she sings tenor and plays bass on "Cindy." A later cut that is reminiscent of her early sound is the duet with Mike Seeger, "You'll Find Her Name Written There," on his *Second Annual Farewell Reunion* (Mercury, 1973).

A year or so after Hazel met Mike, a young woman from California started showing up at some of the Baltimore music parties. Although it would take a few years for the seeds of these meetings to bear fruit, the eventual partnership of Hazel and Alice Gerrard would make bluegrass history. So now we turn to the life of Alice.

Alice Gerrard

In some ways Alice Gerrard seems to live in the shadow of Hazel Dickens. Not in the old-time community, of course, where she is well known as a musician, singer, songwriter, and founder of the *Old-Time Herald*. But the bluegrass community is somewhat ambivalent about its relationship to old-time music. Even the IBMA, which presented Hazel with a Distinguished Achievement Award in 1993, took another eight years to honor Alice in the same way. One could argue that after their breakup, Hazel continued to play bluegrass while Alice turned her energies to old-time music, but it's a fine distinction.

Questioned about this, Alice reluctantly admits that sometimes it seems like it's "Hazel, Hazel, Hazel." However, she immediately adds, "I feel like it's great that Hazel's gotten the recognition that she's gotten. The only time it bothers me is when I feel like people ignore my contribution to the two of us. Because it was a very equal contribution, it wasn't just Hazel. It was our vision and it was just as much my contribution to material and arranging as it was hers."

Except for her love of music, Alice (b. 1934) was the opposite of Hazel in almost every way. Born in Seattle, Washington, to middle-class parents who played classical music in their spare time, Alice and her younger brother lived there until their dad died in 1942. The family then moved to Guadalajara, Mexico (a good climate for her mother's rheumatoid arthritis), where Alice learned to speak fluent Spanish. A year later they moved in with Alice's aunt and her four children in a rural area south of Oakland, California.

Tomboy Alice was crazy about horses and loved living on the farm. Once a week her mother took both children out of their multicultural school and into the city for dance lessons, foreign movies, and tours of art galleries. Following in her mother's footsteps, Alice took piano lessons, but she never felt at home reading music. Later she learned to play piano by ear so that she could provide accompaniment for fiddle tunes. When Alice reached high school age, her mother married a professor and the family moved into Oakland.

Although Alice says that folk music was all around while she was growing up, she was into the pop music of the day, although "not Frank Sinatra." She liked the "slightly more weird stuff" such as "Come On-a My House," "The Cry of the Wild Goose," "Nature Boy" by Nat King Cole, and hits by the Weavers. She also loved ragtime and honky-tonk piano. She was listening to music, but not in a serious way.

In 1953 Alice entered Antioch College, a small liberal arts school near Dayton, Ohio, chosen by her mother. It was, as historian Neil Rosenberg writes, "a center of student interest in folk music." Here Alice started dating Jeremy Foster, grandson of the brilliant physicist Albert Michelson and a friend of Mike Seeger's. Jeremy, who was already into old-time music, gave Alice a copy of Harry Smith's *Anthology of American Folk Music* (Folkways, 1952), a six-LP set of traditional songs that included both black and white artists such as the Carter Family, Uncle Dave Macon, Dock Boggs, and Mississippi John Hurt. Alice says, "That was a very pivotal thing in so many people's lives. That anthology just opened doors for people. I loved the sounds, like Clarence Ashley playing 'Coo Coo Bird.' I've always been attracted to the hard edge, the darker side." In the college library she found a 78 rpm recording of Virginia ballad singer Texas Gladden singing "One Morning in May" unaccompanied. "I wore that 78 out," she says. Surrounded by these old-time sounds, Alice started teaching herself guitar and three-finger banjo.

Alice was also influenced by other women. She thought Wilma Lee Cooper and Mollie O'Day were "fabulous singers." She listened to the Coon Creek Girls with Lily May Ledford, and later would watch Ola Belle Campbell Reed and Gloria Belle at the country music parks back east. There was also Katy Hill, the "great fast clawhammer banjo player" who recorded with Charlie Monroe. "These were powerful women. And they were out there and I was listening to them. At the same time I was listening to Bill Monroe and the Stanley Brothers."

The year 1955 found Jeremy and Alice in Washington, D.C., where they had taken co-op jobs as part of their course work at Antioch. Jeremy, who already knew Hazel through Mike, told Alice, "There's this little girl with this great big voice and you've gotta meet her." Living close to Baltimore made it easy to drive over and hear Hazel play in the clubs, and naturally they attended many of the same picking parties. Alice says, "It was a weird mix of people all mingling together, and the common denominator was the music. We couldn't have been further apart from some of them culturally and in other things. Education, outlook. But somehow it all sort of worked in this weird way."

Strange as it may seem, according to both Hazel and Alice, they did not sing together at this time. For one thing, Alice was more interested in the instrumental side of the music than the singing. Plus she was not playing or singing much at the parties at all. When asked if this was gender related, she says:

I think what was working there, more than a gender thing, was a cultural thing. I was getting to know people, and I'll take things in for a long time and see where the lay of the land is, and see what's appropriate and what's not.

If we'd go over to some musician's house, and they were married, the women always ganged together in the kitchen, and I felt as though I needed to be with them. There was definitely a sense that if you didn't adhere to this particular rule, you would be *frowned on,* and they would talk about you or they'd think you were trying to steal their husbands. It's also true that their husbands were cheating on them all the time. So they had good reason to speculate about this and be nervous about it. But of course that wasn't what was on *my* mind. And I remember having this real conflict. I wanted to be out there listening to the music; I didn't want to be in here talking about whatever. But I had to be here—it was my *role* as the accompanying woman.

I don't remember feeling angry about it; I just remember being frustrated by it. And if there was any way to move the conversation into the other room so at least I could be near the music, I would do it. But it didn't always happen. I've tried and tried to think about when did I finally break out of this listening role and started actively participating, and I don't remember.

Later when Mike [Seeger] and I would go traveling around the South, visiting this musician and that musician, his role was taping stuff and my role was always talking to the wife, or the daughter, or the mother, and it's not that I didn't find that interesting a lot of times, but it is a secondary role. I didn't think about it like that at the time, but I always did feel a certain frustration at not being able to be part of the musical side of the thing as opposed to the wind under his wings. [She laughs.] I hate that song.

Hazel, on the other hand, who was already singing professionally, was not inclined to sing with just anyone. Her memory is that she and Alice first sang together at a picking party a few months after Alice and Jeremy had gotten married in 1956. Everyone had gone home except the "diehards."

So we were kinda all jamming together a little bit, which was unusual for me to sing with some of those people, because I was used to singing with people that were really a little bit more established as far as knowing the music. Like for instance Mike and I, because Mike was in the band. And I remember being a little shy about singing with her, because I didn't know if she would know our songs. She was very shy. And we sang something and it sounded good. And everybody says that sounds good, you should try some more.

However, in 1957, before anything could develop seriously, Alice and Jeremy both dropped out of school. Jeremy, who was drafted, did two years in service before he and Alice returned to Antioch, where he finished up his degree in 1961. Alice did not go back to school but assumed the role of housewife, looking after one daughter while another was on the way. When asked how she felt about this, Alice replied, only slightly facetiously, "He had to get his degree. He had to get a job and support us, of course."

Back at school Alice and Jeremy became deeply involved in the traditional music scene. In February 1960 they brought in the Osborne Brothers for the first college bluegrass concert ever. Alice and Jeremy's band, the Green County Stump Jumpers, was the opening act, with Alice, the only woman in the group, playing guitar. In May of that same year they booked the Stanley Brothers.

In 1962 Jeremy took a job in Washington, D.C., and they moved back east, where their two sons were born. Here the young couple began to host picking parties in their home. These parties were different from the Baltimore parties in that they attracted primarily middle-class urban musicians: banjo player Lamar Grier, who worked for IBM; Pete Kuykendall, founder and editor of *Bluegrass Unlimited* magazine; Jack Tottle, who would start the bluegrass program at East Tennessee State University; Dick Spottswood, another *Bluegrass Unlimited* founder; and Greenbriar Boy Ralph Rinzler, who later worked for the Smithsonian Institution. Alice says, "They were the [parties] at which Hazel and I were playing and singing a lot. She'd be playing bass, I'd play guitar."

Hazel and Alice Unite

Comfortable singing together now, in 1962 Hazel and Alice made their first public appearance at the Galax, Virginia, Fiddlers Convention, where Hazel also entered the folk song contest, singing the unaccompanied ballad "Little Bessie." Although Hazel considers this their first job, to Alice "playing at Galax was not a big deal. We were just at the fiddler's convention. It was not like a concert."

It was at one of these picking parties, around 1962 or 1963, that budding recording entrepreneurs Peter Siegel and David Grisman first heard Hazel and

Alice singing. They asked the women if they'd ever thought about making an album. They had not. But spurred on by Peter and David's interest, the two women made a demo (with full bluegrass backing) in Pete Kuykendall's home studio. Moe Asch of Folkways was interested. Hazel and Alice started practicing and paring down a list of songs.

Of this first recording Alice says, "Hazel and I didn't push ourselves in any way. Nothing would ever get done if somebody didn't push us to do it. But we had these people who were very encouraging, who were pushing us, and helping make arrangements." Jeremy was one of these. According to Alice, Jeremy's interest in playing music was secondary. "His role was being the person around which stuff centered and happened. He was charismatic, he brought people together. He very social and could relate to people at many levels." And he was very much involved in the planning of this album.

But in September 1964, before they could begin recording, Jeremy was killed in an automobile accident, leaving Alice with four children under the age of eight. Fortunately there was insurance money, which a trusted friend helped Alice invest. Since she knew how to live frugally, and was comfortable doing so, she did not have to take an outside job in order to make ends meet. She also had the music, a strong support network from the musicians, and the friendship of Hazel. Incredibly, they were able to go ahead with the recording in early 1965.

This first album, *Who's That Knocking?* (Verve/Folkways, 1965), features Hazel and Alice on bass and guitar, backed by fiddling Chubby Wise, banjoist Lamar Grier, and David Grisman on mandolin. Although Hazel and Alice were not the first women in bluegrass to sing together on a record (Roni and Donna Stoneman had recorded several duets, and Betty Amos with Jean and Judy had sung trios), Hazel likes to point out that this was the first time two women had selected their own songs and done them the way they wanted to. Alice sees it in a slightly different light: "I don't recall we had to stand up to a bunch of guys. It wasn't like there was this big battle going on to retain our integrity. But it's true that we made the decisions about what was going to be on the album. I think we welcomed suggestions from our peers. But we were also playing with side musicians who were respectful, who liked us, who were not a bunch of assholes that you had to do battle with all the time. And I think that made a big difference."

Five of the fifteen numbers came from the original Carter Family. The point has been made that Hazel and Alice patterned their singing after that of men, but Sara Carter, with her low lead voice (like Alice's), and Maybelle Carter, with her close tenor, were also a strong influence. As Alice says, "They were *huge* in the musical lives of people like myself. And they were very influential on Hazel and me as a duo [although as Hazel points out, Maybelle did not sing the "high bluegrass tenor" at which Hazel herself excelled]." Still, as much as they admired all the women singers, they were "trying for more of a Stanley Brothers, Bill Monroe duet sound." The two original numbers "Cowboy Jim" and "Gabriel's Call," with their traditional-style lyrics, give no hint of the powerful personal compositions that were yet to come.

Who's That Knocking? garnered some favorable remarks from the press, mainstream and otherwise, and several reviewers commented on the gender of the singers. The small mention in *Time* magazine (1965) referred to the "youngsters" as "almost the only successful girl duo in the [bluegrass-country] field." A review in *Broadside* magazine noted that many of the young urban performers of traditional country music were men and said, "Now two young urban females have come to the forefront to show that you don't have to be a guy to interpret well and tastefully." The *Village Voice* chose to focus on the "encouraging example of city folk meeting country." The album obviously had staying power, as it was reissued on LP in 1978 and on CD in 1996, coupled with their second album. Of the reissue *Bluegrass Unlimited* had this to say in 1979: "These performances . . . proved for many that bluegrass was not necessarily for men only." Fiddler and songwriter Laurie Lewis, who heard a bootlegged copy of the album around 1974, says, "That set of songs was the only recording of real straight-ahead Monroe- and Stanley-inspired bluegrass sung by women that I had ever heard, and I was an instant fan."

The year of the album's release was also a big one for Hazel in a more personal way—she married Joe Cohen, whom she had been dating for three years. As Hazel tells it, "The first thing my father said when I got married was 'Well, I don't guess you'll play anymore now.' That was a very hard thing for me to cope with—to still continue with the music and be what I thought was a good wife." The union lasted a brief three years, and the painful breakup would provide Hazel with the raw material for some of her finest personal songs, including "My Better Years" and "Scars from an Old Love."

On the heels of this first LP, Hazel and Alice went to New York City in 1965 to record again with engineer Peter Siegel. The lineup was basically the same with the exception of Billy Baker on fiddle. *Won't You Come and Sing for Me*, which has much in common with their first Folkways album, already shows growth in several ways. Hazel wrote the title song, which was drawn from her own experience in the Primitive Baptist Church, while Alice shows off her clawhammer banjo playing on "Train on the Island," which Hazel sings. And their friend Bill Monroe had given them "The One I Love Is Gone," a powerful modal number he had written but never recorded. Unfortunately, for some unknown reason, this second Folkways album was not released until 1973.

Even with an album to their credit, Hazel and Alice did not tour much. By now Hazel was married, and as she says, "All my married life, I wasn't even that involved with my music." For Alice, "It was hard for me with the kids. It was always a huge problem about who was going to babysit. I found that to be extremely difficult in my life. I didn't have family around. That was something I was always having to think about." In July 1966, however, they played the Newport Folk Festival, where they were backed by Tex Logan, David Grisman, and Smiley Hobbs. Big-name bluegrass acts had graced the stage at Newport for years, along with numerous women performers, but as the liner notes to the *Newport Folk Festival* CD (2001) note, the appearance of Hazel and Alice "gave bluegrass a feminine face." The duo also made regular appearances at Bill Monroe's Bean Blossom Bluegrass Festival from 1969 to 1971.

In July 1966 *Bluegrass Unlimited* magazine began publication. Many of its founders were regulars at the Washington-area picking parties that Alice and Hazel attended. Alice became a member of the staff the next year (staying through October 1970) and began to contribute the occasional article, something few women did in those early years (although, interestingly enough, several of the early managing editors were women).

One of Alice's articles (April 1969) spotlighted the Southern Folk Festival, a politically active, twice-a-year tour of colleges and small communities in the South. Its goal was to present Southern music, by both black and white artists, as a positive reflection of Southern culture. Organized by Anne Romaine, the traveling concert often included Dock Boggs, Elizabeth Cotton, Ola Belle Campbell Reed, the Reverend Pearly Brown, and the Balfa Brothers. Alice and Hazel joined the tour in the spring of 1968 and participated in it until their breakup in 1976. The event would have a profound effect on the lives and music of both women. Many of the small towns they visited were in the heart of coal-mining country. Alice says, "If there was a political event going on, like a strike or people having a benefit, we'd go there and we'd do a little concert."

Since the tour did not have a lot of money, Alice and Hazel played as a duo, relying solely on themselves for instrumental support. Hazel played guitar; Alice played clawhammer banjo, lead guitar (in the style of Maybelle Carter), and autoharp. Accustomed to playing with a band, they now worked up songs that sounded good with just the two of them. They were beginning to develop the powerful yet sparse sound they would showcase on their first Rounder album in 1973. "And that's the record that people really remember," says Alice.

Anne Romaine was incredibly supportive of what Hazel and Alice were doing. Alice says: "It was a very consciousness-raising time. Certainly it was for me. And Hazel, for her it was like going home in a way. But it resonated in such a way that it encouraged us—and Anne encouraged us too—to write songs. And so that's really when Hazel started writing a lot of songs I think. And certainly it was true for me. It just brought stuff to the front that wasn't to the front before. I feel like it was a *very* pivotal time in both of our musical lives." And what did Alice do with her kids while on tour? "Ahhhhhhhh," she says, very softly. "It was a huge problem. And I was just so happy to have somebody that very often I'd get people who weren't the greatest people to get. Everybody survived, not unscarred, but everybody survived."

With their next Folkways album still languishing in the can, Hazel and Alice's second appearance on record would be with the Strange Creek Singers, a loose old-time aggregation they'd been playing with since the late 1950s. The group usually included Mike Seeger and Tracy Schwarz, both members of the New Lost City Ramblers, and Lamar Grier. In 1969 the Strange Creek Singers recorded a self-titled album (Arhoolie, 1972) on which the various vocal configurations allow the women's and men's voices to blend and shine equally. There was only one Hazel-and-Alice duet, "No Never No," on which their intertwined voices are closer than ever. Still, when Hazel steps up to take the lead on "Will the Circle Be Unbroken" and her own powerfully chilling "Black Lung," the intensity of her performance, perhaps by comparison, is shocking. With "Black Lung," recorded live at a concert in 1970, Hazel had arrived at a potent combination: her own hard-hitting song paired with her equally hard-hitting delivery. Written in 1969, after her brother Thurman's painful death from the disease, the a cappella rendition was a raw outpouring of grief and anger. As Hazel says, "It wasn't my first song but it might have been my first attempt at a strong social statement song."

Other political protest songs followed. Many of these focused on current mining events. "The Mannington Mine Disaster," "The Yablonski Murder (Cold Blooded Murder)," and "Clay County Miner." These, along with "Black Lung," all appeared on *Come All You Coal Miners* (Rounder, 1973), an album that sprang from a workshop on coal-mining songs held in 1972 at the Highlander Center in New Market, Tennessee. Neither Alice nor the Strange Creek Singers participated in these recordings, which were done with a different group of musicians, including Ralph Rinzler. Not only was Hazel writing protest songs, but she was also showing up at rallies and performing. Even listeners who enjoy Hazel and Alice's music and Hazel's solo work may be largely unacquainted with Hazel's larger body of political songs, and Hazel herself thinks this aspect of her career has been overlooked.

Meanwhile the personal lives of the two women were undergoing significant changes. In the winter of 1969, Hazel, now separated from her husband, moved to Washington, D.C., where she lived with Alice before getting her own place. She took a job in retail sales at Old Mexico, a prestigious women's clothing store in Georgetown. In 1970 Alice married Mike Seeger, and she and her four children moved with him to southern Pennsylvania. In the summers they often had Mike's three kids living with them as well. For a time Alice took Mike's last name, but later she reverted to Gerrard.

On the musical front, the folks at the young Rounder Records, which had released its first album in 1970, had heard Hazel doing some of her "work songs and coal mining songs," at the Smithsonian Folklife Festival (whose director was Ralph Rinzler) and had approached her about doing an album for them, but Hazel was "leery." As she says, "I didn't have a lot of self confidence, because I'd never done anything on my own." Finally Hazel told them that if she did do an album with them, she would want to include Alice. And as Hazel reports, "After they heard what we were doing, of course they were all for it."

The two albums Hazel and Alice did for Rounder, *Hazel and Alice* (1973) and *Hazel Dickens and Alice Gerrard* (1976), are now classics. Although the heart of the music—their duet—remains the same as on their Folkways albums, the brash, rollicking bluegrass sound is gone. In its place is a leaner, meaner, starker, more intense sound that often features just the two of them. Following in the footsteps of the Strange Creek Singers, there are even some a cappella numbers. When there is additional accompaniment it is most likely to be Tracy Schwarz and Mike Seeger, who brought an old-time feel to the music (although on the second album their sound was expanding to include piano, drums, and pedal steel). But by far the most exciting aspect of these albums is the original material. The three original songs from each woman on each disc are some of the earliest bluegrass songs to be written by women from a woman's point of view. And unlike the lighter, rollicking fare from Betty Amos, these numbers carry powerful political messages. The Folkways albums had proved that women could sing traditional bluegrass like men. And perhaps that had to come first, especially in an era when there seemed to be few women doing so. But the Rounder albums proved that bluegrass songs could reflect the modern personal experiences of women.

As their titles boldly proclaim, many of these songs are squarely in the feminist camp: "Don't Put Her Down, You Helped Put Her There," "Working Girl Blues," and "Ramblin' Woman" from Hazel, and "Custom Made Woman Blues" from Alice. On the other hand, "Beaufort County Jail," which, according to Alice, almost didn't make it onto the album due to its overt racial content, carries its message in its lyrics ("Black woman in a white man's jail"), as does Alice's "Mary Johnson," which turns the classic country barroom song on its ear by telling the story from the woman's point of view: "I been working hard and I just stopped in before I head on home / And if you're thinking something different, friend, you sure are thinking wrong."

The selections on these Rounder albums reflect the tremendous influence participating in the Southern Folk Tour had had on the two women, both in their choice of material (many of these numbers had been worked up especially for the tour) and in their songwriting. Not only was it political, but it was also personal and it was feminist. But as many feminists have learned, the personal *is* political.

To quote historian Charles Wolfe, the CD *Hazel and Alice* would "go where no Rounder record had gone before." And one of the groups it appealed to was women. As Hazel put it, "The longer it stayed out there, the more legs it acquired. It kinda became the bible for women that were just coming into the music or women that were going through changes in their lives and wanted to listen to women sing. They wanted to hear someone like themselves singing."

Naomi Judd, who had not yet embarked on a singing career, picked up the album in a discount bin in 1975. She and her daughter Wynonna were just starting to play guitars for fun. In her autobiography Naomi writes, "What a concept, I thought, a record with two women singing together." As she and Wynonna listened to it, she says, "we became absolutely transfixed." They learned every song on the album.

Hazel and Alice could tell something was afoot from the response of the crowds at their concerts. Alice says the first time she sang "Custom Made Woman Blues" in public at a workshop, "people stood up and cheered and I had to do it again, right there on the spot. It began to sort of sink in that there was something going on here." They found their shows, which Hazel insists were still infrequent, packed with people—mostly women—who did not usually come out to hear bluegrass or old-time music.

On the strength of "Don't Put Her Down, You Helped Put Her There," they were asked to appear on *Woman Alive!* (1975), a series of PBS television specials that focused on the feminist movement. Backed by Mike Seeger and Tracy Schwarz, they sang the song that got them there, Hazel's compassionate defense of the "pathetic" women she would see in the Baltimore bars: "There's more to her than powder and paint, than the men she picks up at the bar." She takes the men to task, saying, "You abuse her, accuse her, turn around and use her, then forsake her any time it suits you." Few things made Hazel as mad as the way she saw and experienced women being treated not only in her mountain culture but in Baltimore as well. She poured her anger into this song.

Sometime after the release of their first Rounder album, Hazel began dating Ken Irwin, one of the founders of the label. They would remain together, off and on, for seventeen years. As Hazel readily admits, "I'd have been dead in the water long ago if it hadn't been for him." Together they went to auditions, listened to demos, worked on Rounder reissues, and sought out new bands. It was Hazel who brought the Johnson Mountain Boys to Ken's attention. She was there when Ken heard the first four-song cassette from a very young Alison Krauss. While other people made much of Alison's fiddling, Hazel recognized her potential as a singer. Ken often played the role of producer, sometimes uncredited, on Hazel's albums. Together they would produce Hazel's second and third solo albums for Rounder.

Unfortunately, Hazel and Alice's second album for Rounder would be their last. By the time the LP came out in 1976, the duo had split up. It was an awkward, emotional affair with feelings of betrayal on both sides and little in the way of real communication. Even today the subject remains sensitive. As Alice readily admits, "It was my idea, I wanted to end it." Now, however, she acknowledges that "it wasn't a great career move." It still pains Hazel to think that some people thought the split was initiated by her. "We were on the verge of doing something. We could have become very big." She goes on to say fatalistically, "It always happens. It happened with Simon and Garfunkel and it happened with the Johnson Mountain Boys."

Not surprisingly the folks at Rounder were "extremely upset" over the demise of an act in which they had just invested thousands of dollars. With no one to tour in support of the new album, there was no point in promoting it. And that's a shame, because, as Hazel says, "I think it's a damn good record. The material is just fantastic. Some of the material on there is some of my favorite." Luckily the album survives in CD form.

Although the two women refused to speak ill of each other in public, the breakup destroyed their friendship for years. As time went by, however, the whole thing got "shoved under the rug," according to Alice, and they resumed their camaraderie. But it was on a different level and they didn't play together. It would take *Pioneering Women of Bluegrass*, the 1996 reissue of their Folkways albums on CD, to get the two friends back on stage together.

Although Hazel was devastated by the breakup, she landed on her feet. As Alice said, "She's a survivor." And it was Hazel's solo work that provided an opening. Barbara Koppel, who was producing the Academy Award–winning documentary *Harlan County, USA* (1976), was already using songs from *Come All You Coal Miners* in the film, including Hazel's "Mannington Mine Disaster" (sung by someone else), "Black Lung," and "The Yablonski Murder." Now she asked Hazel to write the closing number. Hazel, who had never written on commission before, rose to the task, coming up with the jaunty, defiant "They'll Never Keep Us Down." Political grassroots organizations began showing the film and invited Hazel to perform songs from the movie. In 1978 and 1979 she did a number of benefits for the striking coal miners in Stearns, Kentucky.

Harlan County would bear fruit in big ways. Producer John Sayles, who viewed the documentary as part of the prep work for his own coal-mining movie, asked Hazel to sing in his film *Matewan* (1987). Hazel appeared on screen several times, and her powerful rendition of "Gathering Storm" (which she did not write) at a funeral for one of the miners is one of the highlights of the production. She also sings the traditional "Beautiful Hills of Galilee" as the credits roll. Her hard mountain voice provides the perfect ending to a gut-wrenching film.

Hazel went on to appear in or contribute songs to other movies, including the documentary *Coal Mining Women* (Appalshop, 1982), for which she wrote the title song; *Songcatcher* (2000), in which she appears as a singer at the barn dance; *Journey of August King* (1995), which features "Fly Away Pretty Little Bird" at the end; and *With Babies and Banners* (1979), for which she rewrote Joe Hill's "Rebel Girl." More of Hazel's political songs were included in the album *They'll Never Keep Us Down: Women's Coal Mining Songs* (Rounder, 1983). Eventually Rounder compiled the two coal mining albums into one CD, *Coal Mining Women* (1997).

Hazel also got back into the saddle with her own projects, recording three solo albums for Rounder: *Hardhitting Songs for Hard Hit People* (1980), *By the*

Sweat of My Brow (1983), and *It's Hard to Tell the Singer from the Song* (1987). A fourth album, *A Few Old Memories* (1987), would comprise the best songs from these three recordings. Among the rich offering of original songs, eighteen in all, are several jaw-dropping standouts such as "You'll Get No More of Me," "A Few Old Memories," "Scraps from Your Table," and "It's Hard to Tell the Singer from the Song." Lynn Morris's recording of the now-classic "Mama's Hand" would win IBMA Song of the Year in 1996. A few numbers were undisguised protest songs such as a rerecording of "They'll Never Keep Us Down" and "Will Jesus Wash the Bloodstains from Your Hands."

Aside from the a cappella "Beautiful Hills of Galilee," almost all of the numbers are performed with various full-bluegrass band configurations. Through the years Hazel would stockpile an assemblage of top-notch players such as David McLaughlin, Marshall Wilborn, Richard Underwood, Barry Mitterhoff, Tom Adams, and Tim Stafford, whom she could call on as needed while never having to maintain a full-time band. She also used a number of different harmony singers, one of the most successful pairings being with Dudley Connell, of the Johnson Mountain Boys and Seldom Scene, who came the closest to matching Hazel in intensity. Dudley had become familiar with Hazel's music from the *Hazel and Alice* album. He says, "I was stunned not only by the power of her singing, but also by this indescribable vulnerable and honest quality of her voice. Hazel has played an enormous role in my musical career and I continue to be influenced by her singing and songwriting."

After her three solo projects, Hazel would not record again for eleven years. When she finally went back into the studio, it was to record *Heart of a Singer* (Rounder, 1998) with friends Ginny Hawker and Carol Elizabeth "CE" Jones. The album includes two of Hazel's originals, "Old River" and "I Can't Find Your Love Anymore." Ginny, who had several albums under her belt with singer Kay Justice, was now married to and playing music with Hazel's old pal Tracy Schwarz. Carol Elizabeth and her then-husband, James Leva, recorded for Rounder as Jones and Leva. One of her main musical influences had been the records of Hazel and Alice. "She learned every one of their songs," say Jody Stecher's liner notes. If any women could rise to the challenge of recording with Hazel, who was already practically an icon, Ginny and Carol Elizabeth could, as they proved by sharing the lead singing and providing harmony for each other.

But recording was never a picnic for Hazel. After *Heart of a Singer,* she says, "I came out of the studio this last time and I walked into the other room and said, 'I just figured out why I don't like recording. It's too damn hard.' I just didn't realize it. It's very taxing on your nerves. It taxes your brain. You know it's going to go down there forever and you think, 'Oh, god, I can never live up to this. Even if you get it really, really good you know you're probably not going to emulate that again on stage."

Meanwhile, time had been busy healing old wounds. With the reissue of Hazel and Alice's Folkways albums as *Pioneering Women of Bluegrass* (Smithsonian Folkways, 1996), enough water had gone under the bridge for the two women to once again share a stage. They did so on many occasions during the next few years. One of their first reappearances was at the Smithsonian's presentation of "Hazel Dickens: A Life's Work" at the second annual Ralph Rinzler Memorial Concert in Washington, D.C. The stage was full of performing women (hand-picked by Hazel), including Alice, Ginny Hawker, Kate Brislin, Kay Justice, Lynn Morris, Suzanne Thomas, Mary Jo Leet, Elaine Purkey, and Laurie Lewis, who said, "Getting the tap on the shoulder from Hazel was deeply gratifying."

Then in the fall Hazel and Alice played the IBMA Fan Fest in Owensboro, Kentucky, where they received a warm welcome from the crowd. In May 1997 they did a monthlong tour of the West Coast, which they kicked off by appearing on *Prairie Home Companion*, where Alice dedicated "You Gave Me a Song" to her grandchildren. And Alice was on hand in May 1998 to watch Hazel receive an honorary doctor of humanities degree from West Virginia's Shepherd College. Hazel closed her acceptance speech with these words: "I especially would like to thank Mike Seeger and Alice Gerrard for their encouragement and support in the music world and in my life."

In 2007 Hazel was honored by her home state as one of the inaugural inductees into the West Virginia Music Hall of Fame. She was presented with her award by none other than Alison Krauss, who has long been an admirer. As Alison says in the documentary of Hazel's life, "She has it on ten. She's all the way up to ten."

Although Hazel continued to play occasionally through 2010—and was a headliner for years at the Hardly Strictly Bluegrass Festival in San Francisco— her health was becoming increasingly frail. Unbeknownst to the world at large, she was actually ten years older than reference books indicated. She died at the age of eighty-five on April 22, 2011. As Alice said, "Yes, [she was] a complicated and talented woman; sometimes aggravating (as I was to her, I'm sure) and always wonderful—a *huge* part of my life and a dear friend." And as her friend Ron Thomason said, "She never held back, even at the end. Her voice above all others had the power to flay, and when combined with her words, did just that

. . . She expressed herself in aphorisms you could live by. The one I chose was, 'Just playing bluegrass is political.'"

The further adventures of Alice, also a survivor, returned her to her deepest love: old-time music, which from the outside appears to be a bit friendlier to females who are often seen playing fiddle and banjo. But according to Alice, "It traditionally is a male thing, too. There's a lot of testosterone."

Fortunately Alice found a number of women to play with, including multi-instrumentalists Irene Herrmann and Jeanie McLerie, who joined her in forming the Harmony Sisters in the late seventies. The group's two albums for the Flying Fish label, *Harmony Pie* (1980) and *Second Helping* (1982), included several Alice originals. The LPs were eventually combined into one CD, *The Harmony Sisters: The Early Years* (1999). Later Alice would join Gail Gillespie and Sharon Sandomirsky in the Herald Angels. The group, whose name gave a nod and a wink to the magazine Alice founded, released one cassette, *You've Been a Friend to Me (1994)*, and a CD, *Alice, Gail, & Sharon: The Road to Agate Hill: Music from Southwest Virginia and Beyond* (2007).

After ten years of marriage, Alice and Mike separated around 1980. But before parting they released an album, *Alice Gerrard and Mike Seeger* (Greenhays, 1980) and participated in the documentary *Homemade American Music* (1980), which features them playing together and with old-time greats Lily May Ledford, Roscoe Holcomb, and Libba Cotton. Alice then followed her heart to Galax, Virginia, an area known for its profusion of old-time musicians, many of whom were still active in 1981. Surrounded by these "classic practitioners," Alice immersed herself in the music and its culture. Her friendship with her fiddle mentor, Tommy Jarrell, resulted in the documentary of his life mentioned earlier and in his receiving a National Heritage Award in 1982. In addition she helped produce *The Old-Time Way* (1986), an album featuring Luther Davis and siblings Roscoe and Leone Parish, which came with a fifty-four-page booklet. She also played a big part in seeing that banjo player Bertie Mae Dickens received the North Carolina Folk Heritage Award in 1992 at the age of eighty-nine.

Alice was extremely conscious of the role of women role in this Southern mountain culture:

> When I lived in Galax I went around and talked to lots and lots of older musicians, and without reservation, there was always an aunt or a [female] cousin or a mother who played the banjo or the fiddle. Always. But they never played out. They just played around the home. The men all went out and played for dances, but dances

were really rough places. People got cut and killed and shot. Women did not play out but they did play, only not in huge numbers like the men. So there they all are, these shadow figures.

She was also aware of her own position as a woman and an outsider. "It was fine for me to come down there and play and spend a lot of time with Tommy Jarrell trying to learn how to play some of his tunes on the fiddle, and he was very supportive, but in general, his daughter didn't learn how to play. So there's some sort of cultural thing where it's just not cool for women to [play]. I mean this [the fiddle] is the Devil's instrument."

In 1987, concerned about the health and direction of old-time music and remembering how *Bluegrass Unlimited* had pulled that community together, Alice thought "maybe something like that would work for old-time music." She was willing to try. With some monetary input from friends, she started the *Old-Time Herald*, a quarterly publication that would be her primary focus for the next fifteen years. After two years she moved the magazine to Durham, North Carolina, where she continued to serve as editor in chief until 2003, when she turned the reins over to her friend Gail Gillespie. Alice had not wanted the magazine to interfere with her music, but of course it had. Now she said, "I felt I needed to pay more attention to my own music." She continued to maintain ties with the *Herald* as a board member and consultant.

With a publication to turn out every quarter, it took Alice a number of years to release a solo album. *Pieces of My Heart* (Copper Creek, 1994) featured six of her lovely, introspective original songs, including the stunningly sad "Agate Hill," a song she wrote after her mother died. As Alice says in the song notes, "We never were able to get past all our garbage to any real communication . . . I wish we had gotten to know one another better." Writing in the liner notes, well-known author Lee Smith opines that when she was listening to "Agate Hill," she "cried so hard I drove off the road." Smith would title her 2007 novel *Road to Agate Hill*. Alice's second solo album, *Calling Me Home: Songs of Love and Life* (Copper Creek, 2004), would come ten years later.

Today Alice stays busy with her current band, the trio Tom, Brad, and Alice (fiddler Brad Leftwich and banjoist Tom Stauber). The group, which officially came into existence in 1994, has released four CDs for Copper Creek: *Been There Still* (1998), *Hollyding* (2000), *We'll Die in the Pig Pen Fighting* (2001), and *Carve That Possum* (2006). She reunites occasionally with the Harmony Sisters and does solo gigs with various backup bands. Summers usually find her teaching at numerous music camps across the country. She also enjoys spending time with her nine grandchildren.

Alice and Hazel have a stunning list of musical accomplishments both together and apart. Their musical influence is undoubtedly greater now than ever as upcoming—and uppity—women discover their recordings. Their lives represent the journey every woman takes, each in her own fashion. Perhaps the *Old-Time Herald* said it best: "If Hazel and Alice were pioneering anything, it was themselves."

I seemed to be alone.

—Dottie Eyler

DOTTIE EYLER

In February 1968 Dottie Cullison Eyler (b. 1931) became the first woman to be pictured in a band in the not yet two-year-old *Bluegrass Unlimited*. The fact that the group, the Carroll County Ramblers, and the magazine were both based in Maryland, was undoubtedly a factor. The dark-haired young woman, holding her guitar in the center of the photo, is surrounded by four men including her mandolin-playing husband, Leroy. The couple, each from the Baltimore area, had been playing hillbilly music together since forming the Covered Wagon Gang in 1954, but by 1961 they had decided to devote their musical energies to bluegrass. They began recording in 1963 (with Dottie on guitar and Leroy on bass), released their first album in 1972, and eventually welcomed their two children into the group. Daughter Bonnie (b. 1953) took over on bass in 1971, and son Dale (b. 1964) became their fiddler in 1978. Dottie not only wrote songs for all of their albums, but she also contributed original artwork for one of the covers. Although Leroy died in 1995, the Carroll Country Ramblers continued to perform and Bonnie and Dale are still keeping the band active today.

Ten-year-old Dottie learned to play guitar from a "neighbor lady" and she loved it. But, she says, "[My family] tried to talk me into playing piano, saying that *girls* don't play guitars, they play pianos. *Boys* play guitars." One boy who didn't play guitar until Dottie taught him was Leroy Eyler. The two met as teenagers and married in 1951. "He must have fell in love with the guitar," says Dottie. When they formed their first band, Leroy was still watching Dottie's hands to figure out the chord changes. The Covered Wagon Gang, which lasted about two years, worked as many as three or four nights a week, often in "beer places." Dottie brought Bonnie to many of the jobs they played. "When she would get tired she'd just curl up and fall asleep in my guitar case." At one point the Eylers thought about going full-time but decided they preferred the security of Leroy's day job.

Somewhere along the line Dottie heard her first bluegrass, and "as soon as I heard it, I loved it." Leroy learned to play mandolin, and in 1961, with the addition of a banjo and fiddle, the Carroll County Ramblers were born. Like many early women in bluegrass, Dottie doesn't recall seeing other females playing this kind of music when she started. She says, "I seemed to be alone." Later she would get to know Vallie Cain, Delia Belle, and Wilma Lee Cooper.

In 1963 the Carroll County Ramblers recorded an EP with six songs on it. By 1968 they had a radio show and a fan club. Over the years they recorded a total of three 45s, six LPs on a variety of local labels, and three cassettes. And in 1986 they fulfilled one of Dottie's dreams by starting their own bluegrass festival in Kingsdale, Pennsylvania, near their Maryland home.

Beginning in 1973, five of their seven LPs were reviewed by *Bluegrass Unlimited,* all garnering favorable comments. Their music was described as "well-done, down home bluegrass," and as having "a solid country sound that needs no improvement, only more exposure." The banjo playing of the mighty Chris Warner contributed greatly to this solidity. That same review rightly pegged them as "one of those versatile regional bands that . . . are largely (and undeservedly) unknown nationally." But national recognition was not to be, as day jobs curtailed extensive touring. In their last review the Eylers were acknowledged as "thirty-year veterans of the bluegrass scene" who were still primarily a local group. What they did have was staying power. The reviewer, struck by their "simple honest approach" to the music, struggled to find the proper words to praise this "good" but not "superlative" album. He recognized that *The Best of All Things* (1994) was their "strongest recorded outing to date," yet he also recognized that it lacked "world class excitement."

When Leroy died in 1995, the band slowed down but did not stop playing. It did, however, take the family several years to feel comfortable working with another mandolin player. In 2005, when I interviewed Dottie for this book, the seventy-four-year old musician gushed enthusiastically about the bluegrass music she was still performing: "I just love it, I just love it, I just love it! I'm gonna pick until I die!" Alas, although her spirit was willing by 2007 her health had begun to fail. However, in October 2011 when the Carroll County Ramblers celebrated fifty years in the business with a show that included many former band members, Bonnie made sure that Dottie, then eighty years old, was there. Afterward Bonnie asked her mother how she liked the music. Her reply? "It was the best music I ever heard!"

I have never heard a lady fiddler that could beat
Vivian and a lot of men fiddlers can't beat her.

—Bill Monroe

VIVIAN
WILLIAMS

Fiddler Vivian Tomlinson Williams (b. 1938), from Seattle, has a well-deserved reputation as one of the top fiddlers in the Northwest. She has competed at the National Oldtime Fiddlers' Contest in Weiser, Idaho, for over
thirty years, where she was named the National Ladies Champion for the
years 1966 to 1968. She has also placed in the top ten in the general division.
Bandleader Del McCoury is well aware of her prowess on fiddle. When the
Del McCoury Band toured near Seattle in the 1990s, Del made sure that his
fiddler Jason Carter—then three-time IBMA Fiddle Player of the Year—spent
some time with Vivian so that she could show him the finer points of fiddling
along with some old-time tunes. Her tune "Chicken under the Washtub" was
a regular feature on Del's stage show for a time, and Jason recorded it on his
1997 fiddle album, *On the Move*.

Vivian has been partnered with her husband, Phil, an attorney, in a number of bluegrass bands around Seattle since 1962. Although Seattle may seem off the beaten path for bluegrass, the area has always had a strong contingent of transplanted Southerners, many from North Carolina, who came to Washington state to work in the timber industry. Vivian says, "We learned our traditional music from the Tar Heel community in Darrington, Washington."

Raised in Tacoma, Vivian took up piano at six and violin at nine, continuing with both through college. Self-described as a "social misfit" in school, she compensated by being a "brain." She entered Reed College in Portland in 1955 and got into folk music when her future husband dragged her to a Pete Seeger concert. In fact Vivian observes that she and Phil, who played baroque chamber music in college, were well on their way to becoming "cultural snobs" when the folk music revival rescued them. The two married in 1959 and were soon settling into the Seattle folk music scene and then moving on to bluegrass. Or as Vivian said, "My husband Phil started learning banjo and I had to do something in self-defense!" She switched to the fiddle. At first she didn't like bluegrass fiddling, finding it too "harsh." But she soon learned to love those "nasty slides" and "discordant fifths." Old-time fiddling helped ease her into bluegrass. In the meantime, while working on her PhD in anthropology, she "lost interest in the whole academic thing" and dropped out to focus on music.

Vivian and Phil's first group, the Turkey Pluckers, formed in 1962 with two other men, played both bluegrass and old-time music. The name was chosen to make fun of the folk singers (whom they had outgrown) and whom they privately referred to as "turkeys." The four played at coffeehouses and on local television shows. They also jammed and performed with some of the Tar Heel bands in Darrington "which were chronically in need of a bass or a fiddle player."

These transplanted Tar Heels were old-fashioned, traditional country people, and jam sessions were usually held in someone's home. The men would be in the living room playing, and the women would be in the kitchen "cooking and talking about children." Vivian says, "And guess where I was? Not in the kitchen!" She readily admits that she "kind of enjoyed being the only woman playing in the living room."

Vivian postulates that she was accepted as a musician because she was a "freak" in several ways: "I was a city girl who played the fiddle and liked their music, and I had long hair and wore no makeup (which some thought was a sign of being religious), and besides I was with my husband, so I was probably not a threat to their husbands." Also, as she points out, fiddlers were in short supply. There was also her considerable talent, enhanced by her classical training, which often earned her the highest accolade of the era: "She fiddles as good as a man!"

Vivian speaks articulately about the cultural clash that can occur between college-educated middle-class musicians and working-class players with less formal education. She says, "Meeting loggers and mill workers who spoke with heavy mountain accents and had radically different political and religious views from our own suddenly broadened our cultural horizons." She adds that some of the initial appeal, in addition to the music, was undoubtedly the "typical intellectuals' romantic ideas of the 'authentic folk.'" But working with musicians who did not share their basic values was "sometimes difficult." At times she felt it took "extra effort" to play with musicians who were the "real thing" and that she and Phil often had to "make a lot of accommodations" to work with them. One can only wonder what accommodations the Tar Heels felt they were making for Vivian and Phil!

The Turkey Pluckers released three 45 rpm recordings of fiddle tunes for Crossroads Records around 1963. Both Vivian and Phil had worked for the Seattle label, Phil as a recording engineer and Vivian as a producer. The single with "Lee Highway Ramble" and "Back Up and Push," listed solely under Vivian's name, was reviewed in *Bluegrass Unlimited* in 1967. The first line reveals much about how women in bluegrass were viewed at the time: "Lady fiddlers, especially in bluegrass, have never been in great supply, and Miss [*sic*] Williams performs acceptably."

The Turkey Pluckers lasted until 1964, when Vivian and Phil formed a strictly bluegrass band, called the Tall Timber Boys, with three other men. "All the bluegrass bands we knew of were called the Something Something Boys, and we were very consciously conforming to that bluegrass band image." By the late sixties "we started to sense the weirdness of our group name with a woman as a featured member (not 'just' a bass player), so we changed the name to the Tall Timber Gang."

Sometime in the mid-sixties Vivian played in a just-for-fun trio, the White Pine Girls, with Barbara Hug on banjo and a folksinger named Carol Crist on guitar. Barbara used to tell Vivian that she got a lot of flack about being a female bluegrass banjoist.

In 1967 Vivian and Phil launched Voyager Recordings with the LP *Fiddle Jam Sessions,* which received an enthusiastic review in *Bluegrass Unlimited.* Vivian wrote the liner notes and played lead on a twin version of "Devil's Dream," which was called "top-caliber" by the reviewer. Since then the label has issued more than fifty albums, most of which Vivian co-produced. She is also the publisher of the *Brand New Old-Time Fiddle Tunes* books.

That year Vivian also had the honor of being Bill Monroe's fiddle player for two shows. Bill's bus had broken down on the way to Seattle, and he flew out with his guitar player Doug Green (later Ranger Doug of Riders in the Sky), planning to find musicians in the area to fill in as his band. In addition to Vivian, Phil, on bass, and banjo player Paul Wiley were also tapped to play the two concerts in Seattle. Vivian says, "Of course I was petrified at the prospect of playing with Monroe, so Paul, a professional-caliber musician who played some fiddle as well as banjo and mandolin, showed me the fiddle breaks to some of the standards." Bill expected even a pickup band to know his material, and thanks to Paul, who was originally from Kentucky, Vivian did. The Father of Bluegrass was more than pleased with her performance. It was after Vivian played the challenging fiddle tune "Grey Eagle" at their second show that Monroe praised her by saying "a lot of men fiddlers can't beat her."

Vivian didn't like being beaten in anything. Even in high school it was important for her to be the best, even if "best" meant playing first chair in the school orchestra, which was definitely uncool. Entering fiddle contests in the 1960s allowed her to give her competitiveness free rein and even win prizes for it. She says winning wasn't hard, because there "weren't many competent women fiddlers around the scene then." But now, she says, "the competition has gotten much stronger so that I haven't won anything for years—so I don't give a damn anymore about winning or losing." She also finds the current generation of women fiddlers "extremely competitive" and the competition much tougher. (Danita Hartz, from Meridian, Idaho, became the first woman to win the Grand National Championship at Weiser in 1998. She also won in 2000 and 2001.) Vivian won the senior division in 1999, but says, "I haven't been able to get past third since then!"

By the 1970s the Tall Timber Gang had reformed as Tall Timber. Around this time Vivian became fiddle teacher and musical mentor to the young, vivacious Barbara Lamb, who would go on to become a founding member of the all-female Ranch Romance and who now works as a studio musician in Nashville. As Vivian tells it, "Barbara was about twelve years old, playing fiddle in a Scandinavian dance music band, when she heard me play 'Orange Blossom Special' with Tall Timber. She decided that that was what she wanted to do, and so I took her on as a student. She learned awfully fast, and I finally had to fire her because she learned everything I could show her!" Vivian adds, "But while she was my student she never beat me in a fiddle contest; that only came later."

When Barbara was sixteen, she and Vivian released an all-instrumental twin fiddle album called *Twin Sisters* (Voyager, 1975), with Vivian playing harmony to Barbara's lead. This was among the first bluegrass twin fiddle albums ever released. At the time, as far as Vivian knows, there were only two other twin fiddle LPs, both by men (*High Country* by Kenny Baker and Joe Green, and one side of an album by Bill Mitchell and Red Taylor). The *Bluegrass Unlimited* review said the fiddling on *Twin Sisters* was "smooth, clean, and together." The reviewer also noted, "Except as singers, women have been featured too rarely in country music. A nice album like this one goes a little ways toward filling the gap."

In 1979 Vivian released her first solo album, *Fiddler,* backed by Tall Timber. The *Bluegrass Unlimited* reviewer, recognizing her classical training, called her style "very polished and exact" and suggested that those who were into "clean, well-executed fiddle playing" should enjoy the album.

For a while Tall Timber became a two-woman group in 1981 with the addition of Sue Thompson on guitar. Then in 1985 Vivian and Phil joined forces with another couple, Harley and Shera Bray, first in a band called Friends of Sally Johnson and then simply as Williams and Bray, which continues to this day, "a band as exciting as its name." They frequently use Nancy Katz on bass.

Shera Bray (b. 1943), from Chicago, was already playing folk guitar when she got interested in bluegrass about 1961. During her first week at the University of Illinois, she had a "life-altering experience" when she heard the Bray Brothers singing "Harbor of Love" on the student union jukebox. She immediately got a banjo, only to be told, "Ladies don't play the five-string!" She had graduated from college and was working when she met the banjo player on that very record, Harley Bray himself. They started hanging out musically and became "fret buddies." But she says, "Because Harley was so good on the banjo, I felt stupid asking him to show me stuff (I liked him and didn't want to embarrass myself), so I just played the guitar. We sang duets, too." She and Harley married in 1967, and eventually his job with the phone company took them to Washington State, where they hooked up with Vivian and Phil.

To date Vivian has appeared on many albums, including a number of Weiser Oldtime Fiddlers' Contest records from the 1960s and 1970s, along with *Phil and Vivian Williams Live!* (2000) and *Bluegrass Hoedown* by Williams and Bray (2003). In the last few years she and Phil have been exploring the historical side of fiddle music with projects such as *Pioneer Dance Tunes of the Far West* (2006) and *Fiddling Down the Oregon Trail* (2007). Today she stays busy with Voyager Records and, as ever, playing the fiddle.

She was better than me!

—Bob French on why he quit
teaching Bettie the banjo

BETTIE
BUCKLAND

Except for family and friends, few people today know much about Bettie Buckland (1933–1968) from Rome, New York. Yet along with Roni Stoneman, Betty Amos, and Gloria Belle, Bettie Buckland was one of the earliest women to take up the banjo professionally, as she did in 1962. She was also one of the first women to lead her own band, the Moonlighters. After getting the group off the ground, however, she found herself having to make the excruciating choice between band and family, and she chose family. Perhaps after her four children were grown, Bettie might have chosen to revive her musical career, but she was killed in an automobile accident in 1968 at the young age of thirty-five. Her story comes to us courtesy of her son Andrew.

Like many girls of her era, Bettie took piano lessons. In her teens she was a social musician, playing guitar and singing folk songs at parties with her friends.

Her two years at Vassar found her performing with a female group called the G-Stringers. She married in 1954 and continued playing guitar and singing at parties. She moved with her husband and growing family to the Boston area in 1959, and then in 1961 to West Acton, the Massachusetts home of bluegrass pioneers Grace and Bob French.

In late 1961, after her fourth child was born in April, Bettie went to the French home, which was the local gathering place for bluegrass musicians. She had heard that Bob played banjo and she wanted lessons. Why banjo? No one knows. Bettie introduced herself, stayed for two or three hours, and went home knowing several banjo rolls. According to Bob, she was a quick study who learned everything he showed her and was soon figuring out things on her own. She took regular if informal lessons for the next two years, and finally Bob found he couldn't teach her anymore. As he said, "She was better than me."

Even as a student she was good enough to sit in with Grace and Bob and their band on Tuesday nights at Boston's Hillbilly Ranch. Also by early 1962 she had been getting together regularly at her house with Charlie Patterson, who provided guitar rhythm for her banjo practice. Her son Andy said they were practicing three or four nights a week, staying up until two or three A.M. Soon they developed a repertoire of songs, both instrumental and vocal, with Bettie singing tenor harmony. A teenage Peter Rowan, who was just discovering bluegrass, sometimes jammed with them.

One night when Bettie was playing with Grace and Bob, mandolin player Louis Arsenault also sat in. Shortly thereafter Bettie asked Louis to join her in a band she was forming. Coincidentally, Bob French asked Louis the same question shortly after Bettie. But Louis had committed to Bettie. The student had stolen a player from under the teacher's nose!

By late 1962 Bettie had a band: Louis on mandolin, Charlie on guitar, Dave Nickson on bass, and herself on banjo. Although it was simply called the Moonlighters (perhaps influenced by the folk group the Limelighters), everyone knew that it was Bettie Buckland and the Moonlighters. She did the booking, handled the business, and organized rehearsals. In 1963 they were busy with gigs in the Boston area, playing venues like Club 47 on Harvard Square and college mixers. They also opened the Boston Folk Festival in 1963. Charlie remembers that the band wore black suits and white shirts while Bettie wore a red dress. She "looked like a million dollars," Charlie told her son. Andy said she had a magnetic personality and lit up any room she entered.

The Buckland house also became a center for bluegrass. One night Bob French brought banjo great Sonny Osborne by, and they stayed up into the wee hours, passing the banjo around and playing. Sonny showed Bettie a number of banjo licks, making them progressively harder. Bettie learned them all. Sonny later told Andy that after she learned the last one, an amazingly complex lick, "That's when I knew she had a mind." Andy interprets this left-handed compliment to mean his mother had passed some sort of test. One wonders if a man would have been tested in this particular way. Bettie was no doubt under an incredible amount of pressure to prove herself as a female banjo player.

Pressing onward, the Moonlighters recorded a demo tape in October 1963. The music they laid down offers a glimpse of Bettie's skill level. For someone who had been playing banjo for a mere two years, she is amazing. She has a solid right hand, a good Scruggs approach, and a liking for unusual tunes such as "Stoney Creek" and "Turkey Knob." She was also tackling hard tunes like "Flint Hill Special" and "Under the Double Eagle." Three numbers—"Doug's Tune," "Old Home Place," and "Old Man at the Mill"—are from the Dillards' hot-off-the-press *Back Porch Bluegrass* (1963). Her playing is by no means letter-perfect, but it shows drive and promise. In addition to playing, she sings tenor on the choruses of the vocals.

The Moonlighters were full of potential, but unfortunately by the end of the year the band had broken up. In spite of Bettie's seemingly limitless energy and her organizational abilities, the conflict between band and family had reached a critical point. Her husband, while supportive, was opening his own business, which required Bettie's help. When push came to shove, Bettie chose family. Louis and Charlie moved on to Grace and Bob French's band, and Peter Rowan eventually joined Bill Monroe and the Blue Grass Boys.

Bettie went back to being a social musician. She started playing guitar with Ed Robbins, a jazz guitarist, and in 1966 she played in a jazz band with another guitarist and a female vocalist. In 1968 her life ended tragically in the car accident.

Bettie's story is offered not only to showcase her place in bluegrass history but also in honor of other women in bluegrass whose contributions have not yet been uncovered.

I do have a name. And I was
part of that band, too.

—Rubye Davis

RUBYE
DAVIS

When Rubye Davis (1937–2002) was interviewed for the *Women in Bluegrass* newsletter in April 2002, she was undergoing chemotherapy for the lung cancer that would take her life four months later. She could barely talk. Yet she did talk. Perhaps with Death hovering nigh, she felt emboldened to tell her story. Surely she would not have spoken so freely if Hubert, her husband and musical partner, had not died a decade earlier. "We was in business a long time . . . But just about everywhere we went we'd see people who'd say, 'I know you.' And it was always, 'You're Hubert Davis's wife.' And I got to one day when I said, 'I'm Rubye. I'm Rubye Davis.' . . . I know I was never the star, Hubert was, and I never will be. But I do have a name. And I was part of that band, too."

Rubye was *the* lead singer and guitar player for Hubert Davis and the Season Travelers, a full-time, no-day-jobs, traditional bluegrass band that formed in the mid-sixties. From 1973 until 1993 the group played four nights a week in Nashville, Tennessee. Rubye, a tall, thin woman who often had big hair, has been called "the soul of the Season Travelers." At a time when the most visible women who played bluegrass were primarily singing harmony or being featured on the occasional solo number, Rubye was belting out bluegrass standards like "Head over Heels" and "Why Did You Wander." Standing alongside Rubye on stage were Hubert, banjo player and genial emcee, and starting in 1968 their daughter, Shelby Jean (b. 1956), on bass. With Rubye singing lead, Shelby Jean singing tenor, and Hubert (or sometimes Gene Bush) singing baritone, the group maintained a traditional bluegrass sound. The fact that Hubert almost always played the banjo in G position, even in the keys of C or D, contributed to this. In 1977 a *Bluegrass Unlimited* reviewer called Rubye and Shelby Jean "the best women singers of straight bluegrass. They aren't folky, high lonesome, or old-time; instead they have a solid country-bluegrass style which is completely infectious."

Over the years the Season Travelers boasted some of the finest young players in the business, including Mike Compton, Gene Bush, James Bryan, and fiddler Ingrid Herman Fowler (later Reece), whose presence was a rare instance of a woman (with no family connections) filling the role of side musician.

Hubert, from Shelby, North Carolina, had been playing banjo pretty much all his life and had recorded four songs with Bill Monroe in 1954. Rubye, who was raised near Albany, Georgia, married him in 1955, and their only child, Shelby Jean, arrived a year later. Rubye knew Hubert was going to make his living playing music, but as she put it, "I never dreamed of music being my career."

Like many other women whose husbands play, Rubye became a member of the band by default—the guitar player quit. So in 1965 Rubye took over on guitar and started doing the lead singing. Thirteen-year-old Shelby joined the band three years later. The Season Travelers performed traditional material, but since Rubye was the lead singer, the band had to play in higher keys to accommodate her higher voice. Rubye said their fiddler Richard Hoffman "used to get mad because he said, 'All you women want to do is sing in B-flat.' And it's hard for a fiddle player to play in B-flat. So he'd want us to change our songs to fit his fiddlin' . . . We couldn't do that and we wouldn't do that."

In 1972, at the urging of Bill Monroe, the Davises moved from Brookhaven, Mississippi, to Nashville. Rubye held a day job for a short time until the band landed steady work, first at the Bluegrass Inn, near Vanderbilt University (from 1973 to 1978), and then at Wind in the Willows (from 1978 to 1982). In 1983 they bought the Bluegrass Inn. When they played out of town, Buck White and the Down Home Folks, with sisters Cheryl and Sharon White, often filled in for them.

But even before the Davises bought the club, Rubye had been managing it.

> I had a lot of responsibility on me . . . Because even though Hubert was the leader of the band, I had to take care of the club and take care of everything that was going on down there, and it was hard. Buddy, I stood on that stage and I didn't want to see no customer having to get up and go to no bar and wait on themselves . . . And I had plenty of waitresses that could clean up and everything, but I ended up always having to help 'em when I got through. So when you get through playing, your job is not over.

The Travelers recorded five albums between 1971 and 1980, two for Stoneway and three on their own RHD label. The *Bluegrass Unlimited* review of their first, *Down Home Bluegrass,* is inadvertently hilarious. "There is a respectable blend of the male and female parts which always lends an added demention [*sic*] to a bluegrass band." One supposes the writer meant "dimension," but clearly the inner workings of his mind were conflicted. Since their albums were designed to be sold at gigs, many of the songs are warhorses, such as "Rocky Top" and "Fox on the Run," that would entice college students to reach for their wallets.

In 1990 Hubert and Rubye relocated the Bluegrass Inn to downtown Nashville because they were losing their lease. Unfortunately the move proved to be unsuccessful primarily because Hubert got sick and was almost never able to play again. (He died in 1992.) Rubye kept the band together by hiring other banjo players, and Shelby Jean took over the emceeing, but it wasn't the same. If Hubert wasn't on stage, the crowd simply wasn't interested. "People would come to the door, and if they didn't see him on stage, they wouldn't even come in." As Rubye told *Bluegrass Unlimited* matter-of-factly, "He was the showman and he's the one people came to see." But to the *Women in Bluegrass* newsletter she was more candid:

> It kindly hurts in a way, you know, but it was like I was nobody . . . After Hubert [died]—and it's bad to say it, because God knows I'm proud that people loved him and cared that much for him—but I was part of that [band], too. But I never felt recognized. He didn't make me feel that way, but a lot of people did . . . [A]s hard as I was standing on that stage trying, but they'd walk up there and turn around and walk off . . . And yeah, it hurt. It hurt bad.

Rubye closed the Bluegrass Inn in 1993, later saying, "It was too much for me." Yet the article that ran in *Bluegrass Unlimited* marking the closing of Nashville's "original and oldest" bluegrass room is titled "Hubert Davis and the Bluegrass Inn," even though the name of the inn, clearly visible in the accompanying photo, is "Davis's Bluegrass Inn." It's no wonder that Rubye would say, "It's like I was nobody."

Quitting bluegrass was hard. "[I was] upset for a long time," Rubye says. "And still, I try not to think about it." She didn't go out to listen to bluegrass, either. "It brings back so many memories, I can't stand it." When asked if she thought it was harder because she was a woman, Rubye replied,

> No, I didn't. I'll tell you what, before I started playing . . . I always felt like people looked down on me. And when I first started just a little bit of playing . . . I always felt like I was not good enough or there was people above me . . . And it took me a long time to get out of that, that I felt people were looking down, because we *were* musicians.
>
> Being a woman playing, naw, that never bothered me . . . But we played a lot of churches with the Sullivan Family back in those days, and of course there was Margie on stage. I guess I just didn't pay any attention to being a woman playing music.

When it was suggested that her circumstances were special, since she worked in a band with her husband, Rubye admitted, "I probably could not have worked with anybody or for anybody else. See, I started out with Hubert and after he passed away I tried to carry on the best way I could, but as far as working with anybody, no. There's no way I could."

Banjo player Dan Loftin, who first saw the Season Travelers playing at the Bluegrass Inn, says, "I went to hear Hubert play the five but got blindsided by this tall, dark-complected woman singing bluegrass standards with soul like I've never heard . . . I always thought of Rubye as the soul of the Season Travelers . . . That's the way I remember her: singing her heart out to a crowd of fans that knew she was singing just to them."

Quit music? I'd rather rip my heart out
still beating. As long as there's breath
in this body, I intend to sing.

—Ginger Boatwright

GINGER BOATWRIGHT

Alabama's Ginger Hammond Boatwright (b. 1944) has been making a lasting impression on women in bluegrass for years. The redoubtable Claire Lynch, also from Alabama, says, "Ginger was the first gal I saw on stage in a bluegrass band who sparkled so bright that I couldn't turn away. She had charisma, humor, savvy, timing, and a pretty voice. She and her cohort Dave Sebolt showed us comedic timing, stage dignity, and interesting songs done in a bluegrass setting. She was beautiful to me and whether I knew it at the time or not she was my mentor."

Ginger grew up with a mom and dad who sang country music on the radio in the forties as the duo Kate and Bill. Her dad started a bluegrass band in the mid-fifties. Originally from Palmetto, the family later moved to Birmingham. As Ginger says, "There's nothing I ever wanted to do besides sing in my whole life." She was always plunking around on the guitar, and at twelve she started taking piano lessons.

Married briefly as a teenager and with a daughter, Danae (b. 1963), to support, Ginger found a job as a bookkeeper in a finance company. Entering the University of Alabama at Birmingham in 1966, she studied accounting. That same year she met guitarist and singer Grant Boatwright. The two teamed up as Grant and Ginger, which became Grant, Dale, and Ginger in 1967 with the addition of her cousin Dale Whitcomb on banjo. The group played around Alabama and Georgia and were regulars on the *Sunday Show* on Birmingham television for two years. Ginger says, "I was working days in a finance company, I was going to school nights, and on weekends I was playing. Every weekend."

While Ginger could and did play guitar at times, she most often sang and played tambourine and jaw harp. Even this had an influence on Claire Lynch, who says, "That was a little different than the 'norm,' but it didn't matter to me. Just as many beginning guitar flat-pickers learn Tony Rice licks, I picked up a tambourine and learned to bang on it while I sang. It was only later that I took up guitar in a band setting."

Shortly after Ginger and Grant married in 1969, she was diagnosed with a rare form of cervical cancer and forced to drop out of college just a few hours short of graduating. She had a hysterectomy but was still given only three weeks to live. She thought, "Well, if I've only got three weeks left to live, what do I do with my time? Do I lie in bed and feel sorry for myself, or do I go out singing? I decided that I wanted to sing, and I've been singing ever since."

As Ginger tells it, "I got out of the hospital, drove to the *Sunday Show*, did a song sitting down to hide the fact that I couldn't stand up, and then we piled into Dale's old Chevy and went to Chicago." Here a club owner pushed for a name change, and when Ginger, in a moment of pique, suggested the "Red, White, and Bluegrass Old-Time Banjo Pickers and Hoss Hair Pullers without Portfolio," the group found themselves billed instead as Red, White, and Blue(grass). The name stuck and became the fodder for Ginger's quirky and sometimes self-deprecating emcee work. As she told *Bluegrass Unlimited*, "I used to say the band's name stood for redneck, white trash, and old blue 'cause I was the dog in the group."

Still, with a young daughter, Ginger was not exactly footloose and fancy free. When Danae was not in school, she toured with the group. When school was in session, she stayed with Grant's parents, often flying to gigs on weekends or during breaks if the band was close by. Ginger would write and record the cleverly worded "She Has Wings (and She Knows How to Fly)" for Danae. When Ginger and Grant moved to Nashville in 1974, a family in nearby Madison took care of her when they were on the road.

In 1970 the band, with Dave Sebolt on electric bass, landed a steady job at Muhlenbrink's Saloon in Underground Atlanta, where they held forth for eighteen months until they decided to go back on the road with Norman Blake in the group. At Muhlenbrink's they came to the attention of Michael Thevis, who owned the GRC label in Atlanta. According to Ginger, Michael said, "I don't know anything about your music but I have enough money to get you played." And he did. "July, You're a Woman," sung by Grant on their first album, *Very Popular* (GRC, 1973), reached number seventy-one on the *Billboard* country music chart and stayed for nine weeks. Ginger did much of the lead singing on the disc and contributed several original songs, including the fast, banjo-propelled lead-off number, "High Ground."

In its first review of the group, *Bluegrass Unlimited* wrongly speculated that the name Red, White and Blue(grass) was a "deliberate appeal for middle American listeners." But the magazine was correct in thinking that their music was "designed for mass appeal." Anticipating airplay and pushing the boundaries of bluegrass, the band experimented with using the Atlanta Symphony string section on many of the songs. In addition the vocals were fattened up and layered, a sound achieved, as Ginger notes, by the "stacked tracks." The reviewer also took note of Ginger's voice, saying she "sings with persuasive force, somewhat in the manner of a cross between Janis Joplin and Karen Carpenter (if such a thing be possible)."

By their second album, *Pickin' Up* (GRC, 1974), which included the talents of fiddlers Byron Berline and Vassar Clements, Ginger was doing most of the lead singing. She pitches Bill Monroe's "It's Mighty Dark to Travel" in the "girl's key" of D, where Byron and Vassar take a twin fiddle break. This time the *Bluegrass Unlimited* reviewer commented, "[T]he acceptance of their album will depend largely on how one feels about the role of the female voice in bluegrass."

The eye-catching album jacket, conceived by Ginger, was laid out like an old-fashioned newspaper, complete with advertisements. Ginger wrote all the "copy," which is an everlasting testament to her twisted sense of humor. In her commentary about one of the songs, she writes, "If Byron and Vassar don't quit pickin' it, it won't ever get well!" Unfortunately, as Ginger points out, the credit for the jacket went to somebody at the label. "It kinda burned my buns.

They did flip me some money but they gave him the credit. But I wanted the credit. It seemed like nobody wanted to give me credit because I was a girl. And that was the only thing I really ever ran into. I didn't really run into much prejudice because I was unique on the circuit. Because there weren't many of us [women]."

One of Ginger's contributions to the band that wasn't found on the albums was her engaging ability to front the show. She has been called "one of the most entertaining band emcees to ever step foot on a bluegrass stage." She began talking to audiences early on partly because she didn't have an instrument to tune. Her natural gift of gab and Southern predilection for storytelling, combined with her wacky sense of humor, created a dynamic stage personality. *Women in Bluegrass* noted that "she would have made a great Baptist preacher." Her recitation of the Mason Williams poem "Them Toad Suckers" was as unexpected as it was hilarious.

In addition to signing the band, Michael Thevis had also signed Ginger as a solo artist for GRC. She released several singles but didn't complete a solo album, because, as she says, "It was causing real conflict within the group and within my marriage."

In 1974 Ginger and Grant moved to Nashville, where Grant went into partnership with Randy Wood and Tut Taylor in the Old Time Picking Parlor. However, Ginger notes that the arrangement was only "on paper." She says, "They wouldn't do business with a woman. But I'm the one who put up the money." And "when cash was needed, I had to come up with the funds, and Grant would put it into the business." Not only was Red, White, and Blue(grass) doing well, but Ginger was still working as an accountant. After a year or so, Randy Wood bought everyone out and ran the business until 1978. Two years later Ginger bought the Picking Parlor back, but as she says, "My heart wasn't in it." It was "fun for about a year," but then she let someone else take over the lease and eventually the club folded.

During this time, their third album, *Red, White, and Blue(grass) and Company* (Mercury, 1977), was released. Although it included two bluegrass standards, its opening number, a banjo-inflected cover of the Beatles' "Eleanor Rigby," indicated the direction the music was heading. Ginger contributed four of her own songs and took the lead on the Stephen Stills number "Love the One You're With."

By 1979 Red, White, and Blue(grass) had run its course, and Ginger and Grant had divorced. Ginger immediately put together the Bushwhackers, an all-female group with Ingrid Herman Reece on fiddle, Susie Monick on banjo, and April Barrows then Kathy Chiavola on bass. The quartet got their start playing as the house band at the Old Time Picking Parlor, and when Ginger gave that up, they went on the road. As Ginger said, "We may not have been the best musical band in the world, but nobody had a more splendid time together making music than we did." The group, together for two years, recorded one project, produced by Vassar Clements, which remained unissued until 1994, when with some additional work from the "salvage crew" it was released as *Sentimental Journey*. The disc included clarinet work from Ingrid's father, big band leader Woody Herman, and featured six of Ginger's original songs.

When the Bushwhackers disbanded, Ginger contemplated quitting the music business. After all, as she said, "I'd been on the road seventeen years." But the great banjo player Doug Dillard was putting together a group and asked her to join, and how could she turn down Douglas, whose playing she admired so much? She would play guitar, sing lead, and front the Doug Dillard Band for almost twenty-two years, until 2003. She appears on two of the band's Flying Fish albums, *What's That?* (1986) and *Heartbreak Hotel* (1988). Joining the group for several years on electric bass (although not on these LPs) was former Bushwhacker Kathy Chiavola. The group, more traditional than Red, White, and Blue(grass), recorded several of Ginger's songs. Not surprisingly, Ginger and Doug became romantically involved. As Ginger dryly puts it, "When you're in close proximity, things happen."

During this time, Ginger recorded her first solo CD, *Fertile Ground* (Flying Fish, 1991). *Bluegrass Unlimited* described it as falling somewhere in the "stylistic middle ground between bluegrass-influenced folk and acoustic country music." Ginger wrote or co-wrote seven of the songs. Two more solo CDs featuring more originals would follow, *Sipsey* (GFA, 1999) and *Inside the Gate* (GFA, 2001).

Never one to sit around with time on her hands, in 1991 Ginger got her BS degree from Trevecca Nazarene University in Nashville. She then started work on a nursing degree at Tennessee State University in Nashville but had to drop out in 1993 due to health problems. Fourteen years later she would receive her registered nursing degree from the University of Alaska in Anchorage.

In 1994 Ginger married Buck Kuhn, whom she had met in 1993 while playing a gig in Alaska. On their honeymoon Buck discovered a lump in Ginger's breast that her physician had thought was a cyst. Buck insisted on consulting another doctor, who found the lump to be malignant. The mastectomy and reconstructive surgery that followed were difficult, but Ginger pulled through and was later able to laugh about her tribulations. She described to *Bluegrass Now* how the surgeons had taken tissue from her stomach to reconstruct her breast. She said, "Now when I get hungry, my hooter rumbles!"

But Ginger and Buck's troubles were not over. In 1998 Buck, who owns a blasting company, was severely injured when a half a pound of dynamite detonated in his left hand. Although he survived, he lost his hand and much of his hearing. Ginger had long been playing an extremely valuable D-45 Martin guitar. As she tells it, after Buck "got blown up" he was

> worried about what a toll the accident was taking on his business. So after a *lot* of soul searching, I called George Gruhn and told him I wanted to sell the guitar, but in the next tax quarter (always the good accountant). George called me the next day and said he had a buyer. I didn't want to know who was getting it, because I was just sick about selling it. I cried for four days and threw up six or seven times. I guess I finally found someone I loved more than myself! Last year a friend took my husband and me to the movies to see Neil Young's *Heart of Gold*, and towards the end, Neil starts playing a D-45. I blurted out in the theater, "That's my guitar!" After all, I played it for twenty-seven years, and I know every ding and patch on it! I'm glad Neil got it, because he'll love it the same way I did.

Buying and selling instruments has always been a hobby of Ginger's, and at one point she and Grant owned sixty-nine vintage instruments. Her passion nowadays, however, is "getting good instruments into the hands of beginning musicians." She sells to these young people at cost, often calling on her network of dealer friends to help her out. She knows that "young people are the future of everything and there are some out there who are just waiting to be megamusicians." One of the youngsters she has befriended is Megan McCormick, who played lead guitar with Missy Raines and the New Hip for a time. She calls Megan "one of my babies." It is Ginger's firm belief that Megan will be the first woman to win the IBMA's award for Guitar Player of the Year.

Ginger Boatwright could arguably be considered the first "modern" woman in bluegrass, and not only because Red, White, and Blue(grass) was one of the earliest "hippie" bands who played a "newgrass" type of music. Although she was raised on traditional country and bluegrass sounds, her first professional experience was in a folk duo, her first stage instrument was the tambourine, and her performing attire was a long, sixties-style prairie skirt. Then there was her humor. From her recitation of Mason Williams's poems on stage; to her design of the cover for the band's second LP ("Sale of this album prohibited by copyright"); to the risqué name of her all-female group, the Bushwhackers, Ginger's idea of funny was definitely grounded in the wild and crazy 1960s.

But perhaps her most important modern contribution was something she was simply born with: the way she sang. Her vocals were not in the shouting style of Wilma Lee Cooper or Gloria Belle, nor did they have the hard edge of Hazel Dickens or Rubye Davis. She was one of the first women in this musical genre to bring a softer, smoother, more lyrical quality to the singing, paving the way for other women with similar vocal gifts. Nancy Blake, Kathy Chiavola, Elizabeth Burkett, Teri Chism, and Debbie Peck all claim her as an influence.

Today Ginger and Buck divide their time between Alaska and Alabama. Her latest group is her own Sipsey River Band, and she has another solo project in the works that will feature more of her original songs. As Ginger says in her inimitable way, "I'm so old now, I figure I better write *a lot*! I'm too old for a label and too young to be an icon. Maybe that should be the title!"

We know that your heart should
really be your only guide.

—Sharon White Skaggs

THE
WHITES
Pat, Sharon, Cheryl, Rosie

Stars of the Grand Ole Opry, backup singers for Emmylou Harris, top ten
Billboard artists, and featured performers in the movie *O Brother, Where Art Thou?*
Sharon and Cheryl White were part of the new wave of young women who
were beginning to grace bluegrass stages everywhere. Yet they performed, and
continue to perform, in the most traditional of formats—the family band—with
their father, Buck, and early on their mother, Pat.

Texas-born sisters Sharon (b. 1953) and Cheryl White (b. 1955) grew up
around Wichita Falls with their father holding down two jobs: plumber by day,
piano and mandolin player by night. Tiring of the dance hall environment, Buck
and Pat moved the family to Fort Smith, Arkansas, in 1962, where they soon put
together the Down Homers with friends Arnold and Peggy Johnson on fiddle
and bass and Ralph Thomas on banjo. (Their children even formed a group

called the Down Home Kids.) They started a weekly Saturday night show at a community center in nearby Witcherville, taped radio shows from their house, and eventually had a television show for a couple of years.

Early on Sharon and Cheryl began singing with their parents on stage. Sharon took up the bass when she was twelve, moving to guitar when Cheryl took over on bass. The sisters played their first road show at a Walker, Louisiana, festival in 1967. Buck said, "They took to it like ducks to water, and it's been that way ever since. The bigger the crowd, the better they like it!" They spent the next four years playing festivals in the summer and taking weekend music jobs in the winter. But Buck was still working as a plumber, and they considered themselves part-time professionals. That all changed in the fall of 1971 when they moved to Nashville.

In Music City, as Sharon says, "things got going right away," although Buck had to hang on to his day job for a while. They soon released their first album, *Buck White and the Down Home Folks* (County, 1972), which included Pat as a vocalist along with Kenny Baker on fiddle and Jack Hicks on banjo, both of whom were playing with Bill Monroe. With songs from the country repertoire like "Making Believe," "Dixieland for Me," and "Each Season Changes You," it is no wonder that the *Bluegrass Unlimited* reviewer noted that the band played "country-style bluegrass." They were, as Sharon would comment in 2001, never "a real hard-core bluegrass band." And though their first four albums would include banjo, by 1979 they had replaced the banjo with the resonator guitar of Jerry Douglas.

It would be five years before the group released its second record, *In Person at Randy Wood's Old-Time Picking Parlor* (County, 1977), which featured country tunes like "Good Morning Country Rain" and "Tumbling Tumbleweeds" mixed in amongst the bluegrass. In the interim, father and daughters were featured on two of Doug Green's albums, *In God's Eyes* (1972) and *Liza Jane and Sally Anne* (1973). Cheryl's bass playing here was some of the earliest instrumental studio work for a woman not playing with her primary band. (Sharon sang but did not play guitar.)

Doug was so impressed with the band that he wrote a cover article about Buck White and the Down Homers for the May 1973 issue of *Bluegrass Unlimited*. They were only the sixth band with women members to be pictured on the front of the magazine in seven years. Doug takes special note of the group's female aspect and says the band has been "involved in a crusade" to "make their audience realize that Pat, Sharon, and Cheryl are as good musicians as any." He finds bluegrass audiences at times "reluctant, at best, to accept women in a bluegrass band," but he thinks the Down Homers are helping people to realize that "women can be as capable as men as musicians and singers." He also asserts, incorrectly, that there have never been three women in a bluegrass band before. He was apparently unaware of or had forgotten about the Lewis Family, the Stoneman Family, Betty Amos with Judy and Jean, and the Buffalo Gals. Shortly after the article came out, Pat retired from the music business to tend to her younger daughters, Rosie and Melissa.

By the time their third album, *That Down Home Feeling* (Ridge Runner, 1977), came out, Sharon had married banjo player Jack Hicks, who also appeared on this recording. With the switch to the Sugar Hill label for *Poor Folk's Pleasure* (1978), the group was starting to veer into what *Bluegrass Unlimited* called "contemporary country with a bluegrass flavor." The album included Buck on piano and Jack on banjo along with drums and electric guitar. The Whites were beginning to spread their musical wings.

Things began happening in a big way for the band in 1979. Not only did they tour Japan with Jerry Douglas (resulting in *Buck and Family Live* in 1982), but they also appeared on Emmylou Harris's album *Blue Kentucky Girl* and served as her opening act. They would guest on a number of Emmylou projects, including her acoustic *Roses in the Snow* (1980). As a result of this national publicity, they signed with Capitol Records in 1981 and began a string of country music recordings for various major labels that would put fifteen songs on the *Billboard* charts between 1981 and 1989. Even though the Whites, as they were now called, were still doing "basically the same music," as Sharon said, their backup was decidedly country and these albums were not reviewed by *Bluegrass Unlimited*.

Big changes took place during these years. By 1982 Sharon and Cheryl had both married (Sharon, for the second time, to Ricky Skaggs) and had had children. Sister Rosie, who had stepped into the band on percussion during Cheryl's maternity leave, would stay for eight years. But career-wise the group's most important achievement was joining the cast of the Grand Ole Opry in 1984. They can often be seen on that hallowed stage today.

Still the Whites continued to be somewhat of a musical paradox, and in spite of not reviewing their country albums, *Bluegrass Unlimited* featured them on its cover again in 1986. By then the shoes of Jerry Douglas, who had amicably left the group that January to concentrate on his studio work, had been filled by a pedal steel player.

In December 2000 *Bluegrass Unlimited* readmitted the Whites to its review section with glowing praise for their new acoustic project, *A Lifetime in the*

Making (2000), on Ricky Skaggs's Ceili Music label. Of course the reviewer had to ask the question, "Is this bluegrass?" He then answered his own question by saying, "There's no banjo . . . and there's no high-velocity, high-lonesome edge. But in this case, who cares? It's gorgeous acoustic music." In the eighteen years since the Whites had been reviewed in the magazine, bluegrass music had actually become more accepting of banjo-less bands with female singing. And the Whites themselves had helped pave the way.

The Coen Brothers gave bluegrass and acoustic music a huge shot in the arm in 2000 with the release of their movie *O Brother, Where Art Thou?* and the accompanying sound track. The Whites were among those featured and even had a small role in the movie as a family band who sang "Keep on the Sunny Side." Artists featured on the sound track, including the Whites, toured together as part of the successful Down from the Mountain Tour (2002) and again with the Great High Mountain Tour (2004).

On June 16, 2002, Pat White, sixty-eight, died unexpectedly. Buck, Sharon, and Cheryl were able to rush home from their touring to be with her before she passed on.

In the middle of the *O Brother* hoopla, Sharon and Cheryl sang on Mark Newton's noteworthy, albeit smaller, project *Follow Me Back to the Fold* (Rebel, 2000). As Mark said in the liner notes, "When I realized this project was actually going to become a reality, there was one name at the top of my list: the Whites." The sisters sang "If It Ain't Love (Let's Leave It Alone)," a song the Whites had taken to the number twelve spot on the *Billboard* chart in 1985.

The latest project from the Whites, *Salt of the Earth* (Skaggs Family, 2007), teams Sharon, Cheryl, and Buck with Ricky Skaggs for an album of acoustic traditional and contemporary gospel music. The Whites had done one previous gospel album, *Doing It by the Book* (1988). The recording, which also includes Sharon and Ricky's daughter Molly playing autoharp, won the Grammy for Best Southern, Country, or Bluegrass Gospel Album. Could you call it bluegrass? Probably not. But as Sharon told *Bluegrass Unlimited* way back in 1986, "We have never let other people tell us that we have to do a certain type of song or do it a certain way or dress a certain way. We have to be true to ourselves because if we don't we won't be happy and won't be believable."

But the ultimate goddess of
bluegrass was Wendy Thatcher.

—Bluegrass writer
Caroline Wright

WENDY
THATCHER

Wendy Thatcher was not supposed to be the guitar player and lead singer in the nascent newgrass band IInd Generation. Tony Rice was slated for that honor. She was going to be the booking agent. It was only when Tony took a job with someone else and Eddie Adcock and Jimmy Gaudreau couldn't find another man to fill his shoes that Wendy was allowed to step in. As she says, "I was not a professional. And I was a girl. How were *they* gonna be accepted?"

Born in Washington, D.C., and raised in nearby Arlington, Virginia, Jan Erin "Wendy" Thatcher (b. 1948) started piano lessons in first grade and began playing guitar around age thirteen, singing folk songs for her younger brother and sister. However, her passion for music didn't really kick in until she learned to fingerpick tunes like "Deep River Blues" and "Freight Train" on the guitar when she was fifteen. But she wouldn't play around anybody outside her home. "I was terribly shy. Introverted. Insecure. I was the kid in junior high school that nobody would remember because I didn't make any noise." She and her friend Beth rehearsed for hours to perfect songs to play on the open stage at the Cellar Door in Georgetown, only to have Wendy chicken out every time. Although she was comfortable hanging out backstage with the performers, "I could not get on that stage. I was petrified."

Teaching guitar was something she could do, however, and she soon landed a job as guitar instructor at Arlington Music, where she herself had taken lessons. Here, mandolin player John Duffy, who had quit the Country Gentlemen in 1969, was doing repair work; his wife, Nancy, was behind the counter; and the great Bill Emerson was teaching banjo. Blues legend Mississippi John Hurt would often drop by, as would Elizabeth Cotton, composer of "Freight Train." In spite of her immersion in this musical world, Wendy says, "I'm still not listening to music in my spare time. I never did. The only thing I ever heard was AM music on the radio in my little room, the horrible teen stuff, like 'Teen Angel.' And I had to endure what my mother played on her phonograph, Jerry Vale and Frank Sinatra. I didn't buy records, I didn't listen to records, or to music. Friends of mine would sometimes play Joan Baez or something, and so I'd hear it. But I didn't pursue it." But she liked the ambiance of the scene. "I got to hang around all these heavies, but I didn't know they were heavies. They were just the people who were at work with me. I was so ignorant. I had *no* background in music. I couldn't stand bluegrass or country. So I never listened to it and knew nothing about it."

It was through John Duffy that she met Eddie Adcock, who had played with John in the Country Gentlemen. Wendy was not taken with Eddie at first. "I had no idea he could really play. I was polite, but the last person I would have ever gone anyplace with was Eddie Adcock." But singing had become fun, and she and Eddie, who was ten years older, started hanging out. "We'd do some duets and we sounded pretty good; we had a good blend, and we were all full of ourselves, you know. But still I'd never performed and I didn't *want* to perform." Nevertheless, by 1968 she and Eddie were playing together in public, sometimes during the breaks at Country Gentlemen performances. "The stage fright was never there with him. And I didn't remember that it had ever been there. It wasn't an issue."

By March 1969, though Eddie was still with the Country Gentlemen, he and Wendy had formed a trio with bass player Ed Ferris to play Wednesday through

Sunday at Hall's Seafood Restaurant in Washington, D.C. Hall's was a "ritzy yacht club piano bar. The other act was a lady in an evening gown who played the piano."

In early 1970 Eddie left the Country Gentlemen, and he and Wendy took off for California, renaming themselves Clinton Codack and Wendy Special and playing together in a country band called the Codack Special. With Wendy singing lead and Eddie providing harmony, they played country standards and bluegrass in bars in Sacramento, and then at military bases all over Northern California. They were "wildly successful" at this and could have played seven nights a week at officers clubs and NCO clubs. Wendy says, "It was like slave work, playing rhythm [guitar]. I'd never had to keep up with any bluegrass. Boy, oh, boy, that was some kind of apprenticeship. My arm would hurt *so* bad after every song, but I'd just keep going and going." When asked if this was an equal partnership, Wendy just laughs. She then says, "Even though I did my share of the work, it was because of him that I could even do the work." Wendy and Eddie recorded one 45 rpm single for an MGM subsidiary. Clinton Codack and Wendy Special are also credited as co-writers of "Another Lonesome Morning," which has been recorded by a number of artists, including Emmylou Harris and the Seldom Scene.

California soon paled for Eddie, and in 1971 he and Wendy came back east, where, at a festival, Eddie

> hooked up with Jimmy Gaudreau and they hatched this super-duper plot for this super-duper bluegrass band. *Of course* I wasn't gonna be in it. I couldn't play blue-grass. I didn't know anything about bluegrass. And I was a girl. Come on. Give me a break. I was going to be their booking agent. So I got a little office in Silver Spring, Maryland. And I arted up the brochures for this band. I did the drawing and the hype and the mailings and the telephone calls. All this before the band was actually even firmed up, because they still didn't have a guitar player. I filled in. They needed somebody to work up the songs, so I played guitar and sang the way the real guitar player would when he stepped in. They allowed me the honor of being the clone rhythm while they worked up the songs. So the band's all booked for six or eight weeks and there's no guitar player. And by now I'm getting kind of possessive because I liked singing with them. I just liked the sound.

Eddie and Jimmy, who had played with Eddie for a brief time in the Coun-try Gentlemen, had envisioned Tony Rice as their guitar player and finally ap-proached him at a festival. Wendy, who didn't know Tony or his playing, was thinking, "Boy, he better be good, because we sound really good." But they were too late. Tony had just taken a job with J. D. Crowe and the Kentucky Mountain Boys. Undaunted, Eddie and Jimmy still wanted a man for the role and tried to enlist A. L. Wood. No dice. When their first gig at WWVA's Wheeling Jamboree rolled around, they still hadn't found their man. As Wendy says, "They had to go on with me." She continues, "Maybe Eddie didn't mind but he never told me. But he didn't want anybody to think he couldn't play with a *real* guitar player. He didn't want to be *weak* or anything." Wendy also felt that Jimmy was not comfortable with her on guitar. She felt "invisible" around him.

That first night, Wendy says, both Eddie and Jimmy were nervous about having to use her. When asked if all her playing in Codack Special counted for nothing, she said:

> That was different. That was scratching a living. Nobody cared if there was a girl in the band there. Ed and I were a couple, so that didn't matter. But Ed's reputation was on the line now. This is back in his world. I had no background. Who was I? I was a cipher. I didn't even like bluegrass. I knew nothing about it except the songs we did. And I wouldn't listen to it if you paid me. There wasn't anybody cool playing bluegrass yet that I knew about. Bluegrass grew on me. And the last things I fell in love with were the best things like Ralph Stanley and Bill Monroe.

Eddie's take on this is not substantially different, although he does say that Tony Rice worked up all the material and then left. A *Bluegrass Unlimited* cover story on IInd Generation sans Wendy reports:

> With two days before their first show they were desperate. *The only one left was Wendy Thatcher* [my italics], who had been Eddie's partner during his folk and folk-rock days in California. [Eddie says,] "With two days left I called Wendy over and said, 'You are the IInd Generation's guitar picker.' We hadn't worked up anything much, and she really had not appeared in front of an audience to speak of other than the coffee house we played at in California. She did a hell of a job."

And it was a hell of a way to get the job.

Wendy found the Jamboree house at WWVA to be "just the weirdest place in the world. It was dark in there and people sat on benches, and they looked liked Appalachia personified, not that I knew what that was. They were so alien to me. I knew that I had to smile and be pretty and innocent. And believe you me, it wasn't that hard." The reception, however, was "unbelievable." Wendy had a ball. "I was so focused on getting every note right and keeping up with the rhythm, the time flew by. Everything blanked out. I wasn't the least bit scared either. I was just so exhilarated by the perfection of the performance, by the music. That's all I wanted to do. It appealed to some meditative part of me."

Jimmy Gaudreau came up to her after the performance, beaming. He kissed Wendy and said, "We might keep you." Her only thought was "Oh, cool." And so the IInd Generation was launched with Wendy on guitar.

The group quickly released two projects, a 45 rpm single and an album, both on the Rome label. The single (ca. 1971) features "Virginia," a composition by Wendy, backed by "Darlin' Corey." The untitled LP (ca. 1972) includes no originals. The all-black album jacket, devoid of band name and album title, was a "mistake," says Wendy. "They didn't have time to get anything printed on there."

With their collective experience singing together, and after all that practice, the band's trios are exceptionally tight. Wendy takes the lead on four songs from the album, including "Legend in My Time." Lynn Hayes Hedgecoth, of California's Homestead Act, had heard Wendy sing this with Codack Special and would add the song to her own repertoire. The disc also included popular rock songs of the day such as "Up Around the Bend," "So Happy Together," and "Old Man" performed bluegrass style. As the *Bluegrass Unlimited* review points out, they weren't the first group to do this, but were "the first to go this far and still maintain their basic bluegrass structure." Wendy's no-frills voice is pure and true. The reviewer called it "warm and sensuous." She wasn't from the "belt it out" school, but there was a certain strength underneath the surface simplicity.

According to writer and lay historian Bill Vernon, "The band soon became one of the top attractions on the bluegrass circuit, playing top festivals and as many as fifty-seven colleges in one year." He quotes Eddie as saying, "We were making so much money, I didn't think we were still playing bluegrass!" Thus, in her short three years with the band Wendy was widely seen. Missy Raines cites her as an influence as does banjo player Sandy Crisco. No doubt others did too.

The band was rocking right along when in the spring of 1973 Martha Hearon moved to Nashville to take a job doing inlay work on instruments for Randy Wood at his Old Time Picking Parlor. Shortly thereafter she met Eddie Adock, and as *Bluegrass Unlimited* reports, "Their romance was immediate." Eddie and Wendy were no longer a couple, but they were still trying to be in the same band together, which, as anyone can imagine, was difficult. Why did she stay?

Why did he stay? "Because it was our band. That's what we did," says Wendy. Nevertheless, the situation was "weird" and Wendy's health was not good. In April, Martha, taught by Eddie, started running the sound system for the band. Soon she was on stage, in the background, playing guitar.

Out of this somewhat awkward configuration—with two women who were both rhythm guitar players, songwriters, lead vocalists, and tenor singers—the IInd Generation brought forth *Head Cleaner* (Rebel, 1974), which included drums and a five-minute "jam" treatment of the two instrumentals, a rarity in bluegrass at the time. The LP featured three original songs by Wendy, including a remake of "Virginia." Martha contributed two songs and a co-write. Wendy and Martha designed the unorthodox album cover, which featured a pen-and-ink drawing of a head with the top part of the skull taken off and various colorful shapes emerging. As *Bluegrass Unlimited* editor Pete Kuykendall wrote, the band's "experimentation within the framework of bluegrass has not made some critics happy." This included his own reviewer, who declared, "Bluegrass it mostly is not."

As Wendy's health failed, Martha's role in the band grew larger. The situation deteriorated and Wendy finally left the band unannounced and flew to Sacramento. Her road days were over. She would spend eight years getting her health back. Wendy has stayed out of music publicly since she left the IInd Generation, but on her own she continues to write and play.

Starting her bluegrass career in 1968, Wendy joins Ginger Boatwright as one of the earliest "modern" women in bluegrass. As someone who was on the scene, how did being there seem to her? Wendy says, "I had no female consorts in the business and missed that more than anything." The other women that she remembers were Sharon and Cheryl White, the "Honey in the Rock ladies," and the Lewis Family women. Of the Lewis Family she says, "Those were chicks, but they weren't chicks I was gonna be able to relate to. There were a lot of supportive women, such as Carol Rumpf, but no women performers." But, of course, there were a few, and one of these, Katie Laur, would later say, "Wendy Thatcher was a real hero to me. I mean a real hero."

Wendy describes the bluegrass world of the early 1970s as "Men, men, hairy-legged men, men, men, men, men, men, and two kinds of women, virgins and whores. So I had to be very careful not to let them all know I was a whore. And that's basically what life was like. No, there weren't any women. I didn't form any friendships at all. I felt really happy around Bill Harrell, and the Duffys were comfortable, but any other performers, no. I didn't bond with anybody. I was a fish out of water."

When asked if Eddie objected to her being friends with other male perform-ers, she replied, "Well, no, but who would I be friends with? Think about it. You don't become friends with other males when you're a chick. And all the guys, especially the traditional guys, like the Stanley crew and the Monroe crew, these are not guys who are gonna be friends to me. Or I'm gonna be friends to. I'm gonna be on my best behavior and try not to besmirch my reputation."

The family atmosphere of most bluegrass festivals forced Wendy into a mold she was not comfortable with. "I wasn't really allowed to do too much, just go out there in my miniskirt, play, pretend like I'm wholesome and then get back out of sight. They weren't ready for me. The only person who appreciated me was Bill Harrell. We'd get together and tell dirty jokes, and laugh, and have fun. And I didn't have to watch my mouth. Eddie said I cussed like a sailor."

Caroline Wright, daughter of the supportive Carol Rumpf, who attended numerous festivals as a child with her cousin Patty, writes: "When Patty and I were young, there weren't many women in bluegrass but we idolized the few that we knew. As little girls, we followed them like puppies at every major festival, as much in awe of their style, whether bumpkin or ballroom, as of their talent . . . But the ultimate goddess of bluegrass was the IInd Generation's Wendy Thatcher, with her single, long, dark braid, smoky gravel voice, and those incredible songs, straight from the heart of the woman we wanted, more than anything to become."

Bluegrass hit me right between the eyes
and led me away by the nose.

—Martha Adcock

MARTHA ADCOCK

O f the many couples who began playing bluegrass together in the early seventies, Martha and Eddie Adock stand out as a team who has hung in there not only as wife and husband but also as a musical unit that still hits the road regularly, often as a duo. In December 2007, after nearly thirty-five years of making music together, the pair toured Japan for the first time, with bass player Tom Gray, playing to sold-out houses everywhere. How have they managed to stay together—and play together—when so many other couples have either split or retired from the road? As Martha told *Bluegrass Now,* "We're lucky that we're of the same temperament that we can manage the situation. We are basically each loners from a rural background—we're loners together."

Martha Hearon Adcock (b. 1949) and older sister, Kay, grew up in Bishopville, "below the bluegrass line in eastern South Carolina." A self-described tomboy,

Martha was "accustomed to male companionship, beginning with Father," and "always preferred it." Her dad, who farmed three thousand acres of cotton, tobacco, and soybeans, also played piano and had studied music at the University of South Carolina. According to Martha, he had "the best voice I ever heard" and "sang in at least a thousand weddings." His "enormous talent," however, kept her from singing around him at home. Her mother, a business major at Winthrop University, also sang and played, and Martha had fiddling grandfathers on both sides. Her own early musical experience included taking classical piano from ages five to sixteen along with forays into ukulele and tenor guitar before finally moving to a full-size guitar. Influenced by groups such as the Kingston Trio and Peter, Paul, and Mary, she became a fingerpicking folksinger. Although she "liked the men's material mostly," she "thought the women's songs and vocals were a fabulous combination." She loved Mary Travers, Joan Baez, and Judy Collins. Positioning herself as "Serious Folk Singer," she performed solo at churches, civic groups, and folk festivals and in bands professional enough to have names like Martha and the Walton Brothers or Erv and Martha.

Graduating from high school at age sixteen in 1966, Martha spent two years at South Carolina's Coker College with art as a focus but found herself playing music rather than studying. After a summer gigging in Myrtle Beach, South Carolina, with the Walton Brothers, she attended the Ringling School of Art in Sarasota, Florida, for a semester. At the end of the term, Martha says, "I had a pretty good idea that it would (1) be hard to make a living at fine art, and that (2) I couldn't see myself ending up behind a desk at Hallmark Cards either." Back home in Bishopville she took some time to think things over. "After some serious deliberation, I chose music."

For the next few years Martha's various jobs included television and newspaper reporter, commercial artist, cook, and waitress. On weekends she would head for the bluegrass festivals and fiddlers conventions she'd discovered. As she puts it, "I'd been bitten and smitten." At a Reidsville, North Carolina, festival in 1971 she got her first dose of "high-level live bluegrass," which she describes as "practically a religious experience for me, complete with the feeling of fireworks going off in my head." She was blown away by the guitar playing of Charlie Waller, Jimmy Martin, Dan Crary, and Bill Harrell.

As Martha notes, Southern festivals in the late sixties and early seventies seemed to be a "man's milieu." This didn't particularly bother her. "I'd always felt as much a part of the 'guy's world' as I did the women's side. I always lived in both worlds, realizing that they were sometimes cruelly divided, but letting it affect me as little as possible, or so I thought." So perhaps it is not surprising that Martha claims that her only role models in bluegrass were men. "I can't really say that any bluegrass women have influenced me at all, certainly not the way the women of folk music inspired me."

The bluegrass records she found in music store bargain bins were mostly by men: Bill Monroe, the Stanley Brothers, Flatt and Scruggs, the Osborne Brothers, Scotty Stoneman. But she did find an album by the Carter Family. Martha waxes eloquent when talking about it:

> I seized the lone copy, and the moment I dropped the needle onto the record back at home, I was theirs. It was like manna from heaven. Those heart songs fit me and instantly made themselves a place in my own heart. The Carter Family became one of my most-beloved groups, and after forty years they still are . . . And the women, Maybelle and Sara: now, *there* are amazing females for you—singers, instrumentalists, creators, recording artists, road warriors, entrepreneurs, gypsy-homebodies, motorcyclists, wives, mothers, and, obviously, human beings.

Eventually she chanced upon an album by the Stoneman Family, featuring Roni and Donna, whom she'd seen on television. As Martha says, "One could hardly think of those girls as 'just' girls. Onstage, that family was like some kind of invading army!" The two sisters, however, were primarily instrumentalists and rarely sang lead, except for the occasional comic song from Roni. Although they were women, they were light-years away from what Martha, the genteelly raised, college-educated, fingerpicking, former folksinger was trying to do.

On stage, aside from the "anonymous [female] pickers" in various band contests at Galax and Union Grove, the only women Martha saw playing were Gloria Belle, the women in the Lewis Family, Betty Fisher, and later the Buffalo Gals. Martha admired Gloria Belle's "strength and dignity" in putting up with Jimmy Martin's "atrocious" onstage demeanor, and she thought Miggie, Polly, and Janis Lewis were "shining models of forbearance" for tolerating their brother Little Roy's "shenanigans" on stage. She also appreciated the fact that these Southern gospel singers were "kind" to the "little hippie girl wearing a headband and weird clothes, living in a bread truck and playing Newgrass." Martha says, "They were some of the sweetest people I ever met."

As Martha realizes from personal experience, "It took a great deal of fortitude to approach bluegrass—a 'man's music' then—as a player even if you were raised, as I was, to believe in yourself and admit to no boundaries." She goes on to say, "Even if a female musician were performing in a positive band environment, touring wasn't easy . . . You sort of have to be cut out for it as well as be willing to learn the skills it takes to survive well out there. Life on the road can be harder on women because they have needs which are not as easily taken care of 'on the fly.' Peeing in the bushes beside the road is a bigger issue for them."

Around 1972 Martha delved even deeper into bluegrass when she landed a job for a short time doing pearl inlay work for C. E. Ward in Charlotte, North Carolina. Although a complete novice, she was "artistic and mechanical minded," and C. E. was willing to take a chance on her and was "generous in showing me what he knew." But in the spring of 1973, having heard that Randy Wood at Nashville's Old Time Picking Parlor could use someone to do inlay work, she lit out for Tennessee. And, some might say, her destiny.

She had only been in town for a couple of weeks, doing instrument repair work as it turned out, when she met Eddie Adcock. There was "an immediate strong connection . . . we felt like we'd known each other before in past lives." When Martha heard him play, she says, "He absolutely blew me away. He was the most incredibly talented musician I'd ever heard. There was nothing he couldn't do on the banjo. It was simply amazing." And when she heard the IInd Generation play, she realized, "This band was exactly what I'd dreamed of creating—bluegrass/folk/pop/jazz/country/blues, everything I wanted, right there in front of me already." The group even had a female lead singer, Wendy Thatcher.

By April, Martha was running sound for the band, which was working the college circuit and could afford a sound technician. Soon she began joining the band on stage, giving the group the unusual configuration of two unrelated female lead singers and guitar players.

Both Wendy and Martha appear on the IInd Generation's second album, *Head Cleaner* (Rebel, 1974). The album is extremely unusual in that it features two women doing all of the lead singing, something virtually unheard of in a mixed-gender band. A male voice, usually Eddie's, joins in only on the harmonies. The *Bluegrass Unlimited* reviewer, too distracted by the band's newgrass approach to give the lead singing much attention, said the album made him think of the Carpenters. In the bluegrass world this was not a compliment.

Before the album's release, however, Wendy departed, leaving Martha as the lone female presence. For the next three decades (and counting) Martha and Eddie would remain together musically and romantically, marrying in 1976. It would be a year or so, however, before she changed her last name to Adcock. As she recalls, "I finally did that because in the mid-seventies it was a boatload of inconvenience to have a different surname than your spouse."

The IInd Generation, with stalwarts Jeff Wisor on fiddle and Johnny Castle on bass, would record two more albums for Rebel, *We Call It Grass* (1975) and *Second Impression* (1976). The name would linger through two CMH albums, *State of Mind* (1976) and *The IInd Generation* (1978), which featured Eddie and Martha as a duo with accompanying rhythm musicians.

The band name would undergo many changes over the years—Eddie Adcock and Martha, Eddie Adcock and Talk of the Town, the Eddie Adcock Band, and finally in 2003 the straightforward Eddie and Martha Adcock. In the mid-eighties the couple would leave bluegrass entirely for a few years to play with David Allan Coe, appearing on three albums with him.

As the names indicate, Eddie was always at the forefront. The *Bluegrass Unlimited* review of *We Call It Grass*, perhaps said it best: "The focus of the group has been and continues to be Eddie Adcock, who seems to exert his influence in every direction. The arrangements, instrumentals, and the vocals all bear his hallmark and he remains without question one of the most talented musicians to ever come down the pike."

Eddie was a creative musical fountainhead with a history in bluegrass that went back to the mid-fifties. He had played with many artists, including Bill Monroe, Mac Wiseman, and Bill Harrell, but was best known through his work with the original Country Gentlemen, now in the IBMA Hall of Fame. Although banjo is his primary instrument, he also plays electric and acoustic guitar with gusto, writes and arranges songs, has a charismatic stage personality, and is one of the best baritone singers in the business.

Although by no means new to music, Martha was relatively new to bluegrass when she met Eddie and joined the IInd Generation. She had a lot of catching up to do. It is to her great and everlasting credit that she managed to carve out a place for herself alongside Eddie and his larger-than-life personality. As she says, "I never begrudged him top billing, because it belonged to him, and it never did anything except help us."

Martha notes that as their career together began to move along, "I began to assume a larger share of the responsibility for the nuts and bolts and the nitty-gritty of sailing our little musical ship." She paid the bills, took care of paperwork, created and sent out promo kits, and later on handled the computer. Eddie kept their vehicles on the road, maintained the sound system, and made most of the phone calls. As Martha says, "Honestly, it takes the both of us to do what we do and keep our ship afloat."

One decision that facilitated their joint musical venture was the choice not to have children. (Eddie has three from a previous marriage). As Martha says, "I felt that a child-oriented lifestyle would require too much self-sacrifice on my part. You might call it selfishness, but I couldn't see giving up my life and my time and creativity to have a kid or kids. Our life was the road. Except for spots here and there, we lived in vehicles for our first fifteen years together. My life—our life—would have had to change radically to accommodate children. Besides, I had Eddie and we had cats."

Coming back to bluegrass in 1987 after their foray with David Allen Coe, Eddie and Martha put together another uniquely configured full bluegrass band called Eddie Adcock and Talk of the Town. With Missy Raines on bass and Susie Gott on fiddle, the group featured three women and Eddie, who sported the same shoulder-length hair as his bandmates. The quartet released one self-titled album (CMH, 1987), on which Eddie did most of the lead singing. When Susie left, the band returned to trio format, performing as the Eddie Adcock Band for the next six years and releasing *The Acoustic Collection* (CMH, 1988).

In 1989 Eddie and Martha began a side venture with the bluegrass super-group the Masters. Although Martha provided rhythm guitar and Missy Raines played bass, the musicians pictured on the covers of the three albums were all men: musical pioneers Kenny Baker, Jesse McReynolds, Josh Graves, and Eddie. When asked about this, Martha replies, "Those guys were the cream of the crop. They're true heroes, and yet they treated us absolutely like we were one of them . . . I used to joke that they were the Masters and we were the Slaves . . . but in truth they never made us feel like the back row was a place to be relegated to. Missy and I had an important job to do and we were proud of it and we tried to do the job as well as we possibly could."

Martha is less sanguine about not being included on the several women-oriented projects that began appearing in the late 1980s and onward. "I have wondered whether it's because I work with a male partner or whether I am seen, even by other women, as simply an adjunct to my husband."

Martha was also making her voice heard along other bluegrass avenues. She served on the IBMA board of directors from 1992 to 1994, one of the few women at the time to do so.

After the couple released two albums as the Eddie Adcock Band, *Dixie Fried* (CMH, 1991) and *Talk to Your Heart* (CMH, 1995), their first Pinecastle CD,

Spirited (1998), was marketed simply as Eddie and Martha Adcock as was their next, *Twograss* (2003).

As Eddie and Martha started to do more duet work, Martha began to get some recognition for the outstanding rhythm guitar work she had always provided. She was featured as a "Master of Rhythm Guitar" in *Flatpicking Guitar Magazine* in 1998, where she commented that rhythm guitar playing is an "overlooked art." She described her role thusly: "You have to be the heart and soul of the beat so that your lead player knows where he is playing." The article notes that "Martha has been the heart and soul of the beat for multi-instrumentalist Eddie Adcock's music for nearly twenty-five years." Still and yet, there was the reference to "Eddie Adcock's music."

Through mid-2008 Martha and Eddie stayed busier than ever. One of the projects that saw fruition that year was *Adcock, Gaudreau, Waller & Gray: The Country Gentlemen Reunion Band,* produced by Eddie and Martha for their own Radio Therapy Records. Then in August the music took a backseat as Eddie underwent elective brain surgery for the tremors in his right hand that had been plaguing him for years. In a process called deep brain stimulation, doctors implanted electrodes in Eddie's brain—while he was awake and playing the banjo—to guide them to the spots where the shaking originated. The whole process was videotaped and clips were later shown on *Good Morning America*. By October, Eddie and Martha were back on stage playing and singing.

Further down the road Martha hopes that one of their next Eddie-and-Martha albums will include a number of her originals, which have been scarce on recent releases. "Earlier Rebel and CMH albums had more of my tunes until we realized they weren't hard-core enough for most." In the meantime, Martha and Eddie are keeping the pedal to the metal, crisscrossing the United States, bringing their own unique brand of duet-style "twograss" to their multitudes of faithful fans.

We started like everyone does—
playing for the PTA or the opening
of a new store in town.

—Raymond W. McLain

THE McLAIN
FAMILY
Alice, Ruth, Nancy Ann

Barely old enough to be called women, Alice and Ruth McLain (b. 1956 and 1958), found themselves smack-dab on the cover of *Bluegrass Unlimited* magazine in October 1972, playing mandolin and bass, respectively, and wearing matching jumpers and headbands that their mother, Betty, had made. They were in the company of their brother Raymond W. (b. 1953), on banjo, and father, Raymond K., on guitar, both wearing jackets of the same boldly striped material. And thus was the bluegrass world at large introduced to the McLain Family Band, from Hindman, Kentucky. Fresh-faced and smiling, the group was the picture of wholesome, a word used often to describe them. More importantly, they were one of the earliest in an increasing number of bands to feature women playing lead instruments, for Ruth used her bass as a third lead instrument and often added a bass break to a song.

The group had been together officially since 1968, when they were known as the Bluegrass State. Playing at home and for local dances had led to a weekly television series in nearby Hazard that lasted for two years. In addition to leading his young charges down the path of bluegrass, their dad, who had a college degree in music theory, was the director of the Hindman Settlement School. When the band was on the road, Betty, who would become their booking agent and manager, often stayed home with the two youngest, Nancy Ann (b. 1965) and Michael (b. 1967). In 1970 father Raymond accepted a job as ethnomusicologist at Kentucky's Berea College, where Alice and her brother Raymond were enrolled as students.

When the bluegrass bug bit, the family began traveling to bluegrass festivals, winning a number of band contests, and making a little money to help with expenses. With their enthusiasm, youth, and a growing professionalism, they were standouts in any crowd. Soon, however, they began to realize that playing in contests was a dead end. They needed to cultivate their own audience, perform their own material, and develop their own sound. And they needed to get themselves booked on some festivals. They started asking promoters if they could play on stage during supper breaks—for free—just for exposure. Bookings soon began rolling in for major events like Bill Monroe's Bean Blossom Festival in Indiana.

During these early years the family made two recordings, one a single around 1969 (Alice was not yet playing mandolin but was singing) and the other an eight-track tape around 1970. They also pragmatically assumed the name that most people were already calling them, the McLain Family Band.

In 1971 the McLains met Italian composer Gian Carlo Menotti, who invited them to play at his Festival of Two Worlds in Italy the next summer. This 1972 trip, which they coordinated with the U.S. State Department, marked the first of fourteen overseas tours that would eventually take them to countries as far away as India, Japan, and the Republic of China. *Bluegrass Unlimited* called them "America's bluegrass ambassadors to the world."

The McLain Family Band released their first LP, self-titled, on their own Country Life Records (1973). It was almost all original material, including seven songs from the pen of their aunt, Rosemary Stovall. In the twenty-two years that the band was together, they would record fourteen albums for the family label. Mixed in with the originals and standards were some unorthodox song choices such as "Stars and Stripes Forever" and "Under the Double Eagle," which starts out with a bass solo. Their arrangements were frequently complex and quirky.

Bluegrass Unlimited reviewers, during the long course of the band's career, didn't quite know what to make of their music. "A mite too cheerful and wholesome" seemed to sum it up best. Overall, reviewers noted that the band was obviously talented and well rehearsed, and the production was polished. They also applauded the band's distinctive style. But they found the music "difficult to categorize." Many reviewers missed that hard edge they had been used to hearing in "standard southeastern bluegrass bands." "They play happy, sunlit bluegrass, even when they do a sad song," said one reviewer. Another spoke of the "complete lack of pain and intensity" in the music. Still the reviewer was quick to say, "Mind you, this isn't a fault, it's a difference." Perhaps Jon Hartley Fox summed it up best: "The dark and haunted side of bluegrass is completely absent from the music of the McLain Family; some people see that as a plus, others as a minus."

Unbelievably, Ruth's amazing bass breaks drew not one comment. At this time most bass players provided rhythm from behind the band and perhaps took a featured solo on one specific show tune. These rarely found their way onto records. Ruth, who at her father's insistence stood up front with the rest of the group, took bass breaks on songs such as "New River Train" and "Take Me Back to Tulsa." In 1974 she was named Most Promising Bass Player by *Muleskinner News* magazine.

The McLains broke new ground in 1973 when they became the first bluegrass band to play with a symphony orchestra. Kentucky composer in residence Phillip Rhodes had written orchestral arrangements for some of their original numbers, and for several summers the band did some mini-festival tours with the Cincinnati Symphony performing these works. Then Rhodes received a grant to write a full-length composition and delivered "Concerto for Bluegrass Band and Orchestra." The group premiered the piece with the Louisville Symphony Orchestra in December 1974 and eventually performed it with a number of other orchestras. Peter Schickele (of P.D.Q. Bach fame) also wrote major orchestral works for them. In 1982 they released an album called *Concerto for Bluegrass Band and Orchestra*.

The band configuration remained stable until early 1977 when Alice's new husband, Al White, joined on lead guitar. He stayed for a couple of years, appearing on one album, and then he and Alice moved to New Mexico, where they played with Bluebird Special. Ruth moved to mandolin, making way for sister Nancy Ann on bass and brother Michael on rhythm mandolin and eventually banjo, although there was always a certain amount of instrument switching in the band. Raymond W. had begun playing more fiddle, and for one year (1979) Tim Owen played banjo. Raymond's wife, Beverly Buchanan, played banjo with the band for a year (1980) while she and Raymond were married. In 1980 Ruth married, and her husband, Michael Riopel, joined the group on guitar. This lineup—two Raymonds, two Michaels, Nancy Ann, and Ruth—would remain intact through 1985, when Ruth and Michael split up. It was this formation that appeared at Carnegie Hall in 1982 and released a live album of the concert, which was sponsored in part by the Ashland (Kentucky) Oil company.

The liner notes from that album provide a small window into the workings of the band:

> During the past eighteen hours, we've flown from a Minnesota concert in one of Ashland's executive planes and were met at the airport by NBC-TV limousines. We've kissed mother Betty, just in from Berea, grandmother Bicky in from Tuscaloosa, and sister Alice with Al White and daughters in from Albuquerque, all six to join us later on the stage. We've slept too briefly, taped for the *Today Show,* ogled our posters on Manhattan street corners, checked out the sound system, the lighting, and made the dry runs necessary for this live album. Best of all, we've greeted the multitude of friends assembled here. We're glad to see that you're a part of this audience now, too, helping to make this monumental time stand still.

In 1978 the McLain Family undertook the gargantuan task of putting on their own festival, which ran every August through 1988. Called the McLain Family Band Family Festival, it was held the first year at Renfro Valley, Kentucky, and afterward at their sixty-acre Big Hill Farm. As its name indicated, the event featured other family bands, including Buck White and the Down Home Folks, the Lewis Family, the Marshall Family, the Foster Family String Band, the Sally Mountain Show (with a young Rhonda Vincent), and Blue Night Express, which included two future Dixie Chicks. With the band constantly on the road, much of the work of organizing and promoting the festival fell to Betty. Some of the festivals were filmed for the Kentucky Educational Television network.

When the festival came to a halt in 1988, the band had been together for twenty years. They had played in more than sixty-two foreign countries and all fifty states, and they had appeared on the Grand Ole Opry, the *Today Show,* at Lincoln Center, and at the Kennedy Center. When patriarch Raymond K.

left the band and moved to Lexington, Kentucky, to start a new career as a librarian, the siblings kept the group together for two more years, including a tour to Brazil in 1989, and then disbanded. Father Raymond died in 2003, and mother Betty in 2011. Today Raymond W. is the director of Morehead State University's Kentucky Center for Traditional Music, while Michael serves as an adjunct instructor of music at Belmont University and plays in a band with his wife, Jennifer. Alice, who teaches first grade, and Al, who is a lecturer in applied music at Berea College, have three children and continue to play for dances and tour overseas with country dance troupes each year. Ruth, married now to Phil Smith, has four children and works for Usborne Educational Books. She has been playing and recording with Ramona Jones and her family since 1988. Nancy Ann, married to Tom Wartman and with five children, also works for Usborne. The McLain Family Band still gets together for concerts every year at places such as the Carter Fold in Hiltons, Virginia, and the Hindman Settlement School, where in 2004 a building was dedicated to Raymond Kane McLain.

THE FLOODGATES OPEN: *The 1970s*

As the seventies rolled around, women seemed, almost magically, to be more visible on the bluegrass scene. Describing this change dramatically in *Finding Her Voice,* Mary Bufwack and Robert Oermann write, "Suddenly, as if from nowhere, there were women fiddlers, singers, banjo pickers, guitarists, and bandleaders at bluegrass festivals, on bluegrass albums, and in bluegrass clubs."

Perhaps women were more visible because many were now stepping forward as instrumentalists, thereby assuming a flashier, more noticeable role in the band. Players like Laurie Lewis on fiddle, Lynn Morris on banjo, Sally Van Meter on Dobro, and a young Rhonda Vincent on mandolin would become well-known faces on the bluegrass scene. Others would make their mark regionally. A surprising number were banjo players: Lauren Seapy, Julie Madru, Pam Gadd, Connie Freeman Morris, Lee Lenker, Susie Monick, Sally Wingate, Louisa Branscomb, Sandy Crisco, Connie Hobbs, Janet Davis, Carolyn Sloan, Pam Hughes, Candi Randolph, Eileen Williams, Mary Cox, Gwen Biddix Flinchum, and Wendy Holcomb. Mandolins were also finding their way into female hands with Beck Gentry, Suzi McKee, Suzanne Thomas, Carol Siegel, Elaine Eliah, Sue Shelasky, Markie Sanders, and Alice McLain leading the way.

Other women were tackling the lead guitar despite being told that "women aren't strong enough to play the guitar." Among those who refused to believe were Suzanne Thomas, Dede Wyland, Lynn Morris, Martha Trachtenberg, Dorothy Baxter, Alice Gerrard, Glenda Faye Knipher (who would record *Flatpickin' Favorites* for Flying Fish in 1987), Wanda Vick, Muriel Anderson, Debbie Bridgewater (Reed), and Marcy Marxer.

Brave souls who did not shy away from the so-called devil's instrument, the fiddle, included Ingrid Fowler, Karen Hirshon, Barbara Lamb, Maureen Riley, Sue Raines, Kristin Wilkinson, Betty Lin, and Carol Nethery. Following in the footsteps of Peggy Brain on Dobro (although she was undoubtedly unknown to them) were Sally Van Meter, Tyra Dean Somers, Bev King, Laurel Bliss, and Cindy Cashdollar, while Cheryl White and Ruth McLain often used their bass fiddles as lead instruments. And these women are merely the tip of the iceberg.

In addition to the family bands that still offered opportunities for women, there were growing numbers of women who did not always play in bands with their partners: Dede Wyland, Lynn Morris, Laurie Lewis, Kathy Kallick, and Lee Lenker. Two women, Katie Laur and Betty Fisher, would break with tradition and lead their own bands. And while the eighties were the heyday of the all-female bands, the Buffalo Gals, the Good Ol' Persons, the Wildwood Girls, and the New Coon Creek Girls all initially formed in the seventies, providing more opportunities for women to shine on lead instruments.

The seventies were also the decade when I began my love affair with bluegrass. Two years into the premed program at the University of Georgia, I clipped an ad from the *Athens Banner-Herald* that read, "Girls-Girls-Girls: Forming an All-Girl Bluegrass Band. If you have musical talent with the following instruments, guitar, mandolin, fiddle, banjo, or bass, call Betty Fisher," and gave a phone number. I met with Betty, but since we both played guitar and no other women answered the ad, that idea died aborning. Later when she put out the call for a bass player I landed the job, although I'd never played bass before. I stayed with her from 1972 to 1974 and recorded two albums. It didn't take long for me to realize that bass players did not get nearly the attention that banjo players did, so I sold my motorcycle to buy a five-string and my college roommates started doing their studying at the library.

At age twenty I was already feeling my feminist oats. I usually went braless, although I did promise Betty that I would wear a foundation garment on stage. When my sisters and I sang together, we routinely changed the gender in traditional bluegrass songs: "*He's* my rose of old Kentucky," "On and on I'll follow my darling, and I wonder where *he* can be," and "How mountain *boys* can love." Betty herself sometimes did this, singing, in "Brush Arbor Meeting," "Years ago when I was just a *girl* in the Carolina hills."

Discovering bluegrass pretty much "wrecked my young life" (as the song goes) and my burgeoning medical career, but during my tenure with Betty, I did manage to attend enough classes to graduate with a BS in food science. I also ran into that mandolin-playing air force pilot Red Henry again at one of Betty's shows and married him ten months later. About that time, as fate would have it, the banjo player in Red's South Carolina bluegrass band bowed out and I was able to step in, even though I'd only been playing banjo for a year. Like many other women in the early seventies, I was more or less welcomed into the group because my husband played in the band.

Looking back, I realize that this was the only possible scenario available to me. I wanted to be a professional banjo player, but as a woman I could not conceive of playing banjo with Lester Flatt or Jim and Jesse. Those doors were so obviously closed to me that thoughts of standing on stage alongside Bill Monroe never entered my mind. Furthermore, being a product of my raising, I could not envision a life plan that didn't include marriage. I could see only this far: graduate from college, get married, have kids. I never considered joining a local male bluegrass band or starting a group on my own. (Twenty-five years later my banjo-playing daughter, Casey, would map out her bluegrass career in some detail: graduate from college, cut an album, buy a truck, move to Nashville, find a job as a banjo player. She accomplished all those things, even though the last proved harder than she had anticipated and required a brief foray into leading her own band.)

When Red got out of the air force in 1975, we formed our own band, Red and Murphy, and moved to Florida, Red's home state, where we would remain, near Gainesville, for the next ten years. We played as a duo or as a trio with my sister Argen Hicks on bass, and eventually as a foursome when we added my sister Nancy on guitar. Later on my sister Laurie, and then Mindy Johnson, took over the bass-playing duties and Tuck Tucker joined us on Dobro. Bill Baker also did time on the bass as did Bob "Hig" Higginbotham on guitar.

In hindsight I can see that I was almost always in the company of other female musicians. Practically in our own backyard were Patty Smith and Debbie Carmichael (now Peck) with Harmony Grits; Linda Crider, playing with her then-husband, Dale, in various aggregations, which often included Red and me; and Polly Johnson with the Sounds of Bluegrass. Slightly further afield were Mary Cox, Liz and Brenda Cross, Melissa and Anne Foster, Pearl Campbell and Belle Terry, and my aunt by marriage, Lynn Hedgecoth—not to mention the numerous women I encountered on stage at festivals. Still I felt, as many women did, that I was the only woman playing bluegrass.

While in Florida we recorded seven vinyl LPs for our own Arrandem label. These albums always featured a number of my original songs, mostly quirky pieces with titles like "My Everyday Silver Is Plastic" and "I Ain't Domesticated Yet." I started writing my own songs because so much of the traditional bluegrass fare simply didn't make sense when sung by a woman: "Will You Be Loving Another Man," "Good Woman's Love," and my favorite example, "Freeborn Man," with the line "I'm a freeborn man, my home is on my back." It's not easy to change the gender in the last one and sing *that* with a straight face!

To pad our income I began teaching banjo lessons at a local folk music store. I liked teaching, and it was here that I began developing my "by ear" teaching style that later would later become the Murphy Method. We started selling our first cassette series in 1982 and have continued on through videos, DVDs, and Internet downloads.

In 1978 my world was turned upside down when our daughter, Casey, was born. Yikes! How could I be "one of the boys" when I was pregnant? When I was, gulp, a mother? I chose not to breast-feed so that I could get back to playing as quickly as possible (and so that Red could help with midnight feedings), but since I was determined not to take Casey on the road, I could not escape the constant frustration of having to find babysitters. The addition of our son, Christopher, in 1981 was not quite so much of a shock. One kid, two kids. I still needed babysitters. Hmmm, this being a woman banjo player was not as easy as I thought it would be.

During our years in Florida, I began writing a monthly column for *Banjo NewsLetter* (1983) and was chosen for inclusion in the masculine-titled book *Masters of the 5-String Banjo* (1988) along with Alison Brown and Lynn Morris, the only other women selected.

By 1986 Red and I felt as if our bluegrass work in Florida had dried up and that a better living would be found farther north. We packed up the U-Haul and moved to Winchester, Virginia, where I found a place to teach at Dalton Brill's Barber and Musician's Shop. I would remain there for two decades.

Putting together another bluegrass band, however, proved harder than we anticipated. We finally landed Karen Spence as bass player and tenor singer, and when we needed a fourth person we scrounged, often coming up with Johnson Mountain Boy David McLaughlin. More often, though, we played as part of Dalton Brill's local band, the Wildcats. Since Dalton played banjo, I moved to guitar. With the kids now in middle and high school, we were finding it harder and harder to hit the road.

Finally Casey and Chris got old enough to pick and we became Red and Murphy and Their Excellent Children, an ostentatious name based on the title of the movie *Bill and Ted's Excellent Adventure*. Casey started playing bass with us at fourteen, and Chris took over the guitar chores when he was twelve. We would record two cassettes with them in the mid-nineties. We did a small amount of traveling, but again their school commitments made it difficult to venture far. Living in northern Virginia offered me the opportunity to take over the "General Store" column for *Bluegrass Unlimited* magazine in December 1987, a wonderful job I continue to hold.

Through the years the balance of our work shifted from primarily playing music to developing and expanding the Murphy Method and teaching banjo lessons. Casey and Chris would eventually leave the nest to further their own bluegrass careers. Casey would play with a number of groups, including the all-female Tennessee HeartStrings and The Dixie Bee-Liners, while Chris plays and records with various artists, including Shawn Camp, Billy Smith, Bawn in the Mash, and his own group, Hardcore Bluegrass.

Today I am content to teach banjo at home, travel to a few summer music camps, play a few local gigs, write about women in bluegrass, and indulge my latest passion—square dancing! Life is good.

In the following section you will find stories of other women who flowered musically in the seventies. Although each story has its own flavor and differences, we all are bound together by our passion for bluegrass and our feeling that we were the only women playing it.

It never occurred to me that
women couldn't play.

—Beck Gentry

BECK
GENTRY

Beck Gentry wanted to be a nurse. She started early by practicing on her dolls, amputating arms and legs and cutting off hair to perform brain surgery. But there was also the music. Beck's instrument of choice, after youthful accomplishments on piano and guitar, was the mandolin. In 1970, when she joined the all-male Ohio River Valley Boys, there were precious few women playing mandolin in working bluegrass bands. There weren't many more when Beck and her then-husband, Roy Gentry, formed the Falls City Ramblers in 1972. It was a wild ride until 1981, when Beck decided that her nursing degree offered more stability and that music would have to take a backseat.

Rebecca Susan Bye (b. 1949), sometimes known as Memphis Beck, grew up near Louisville, Kentucky, the oldest of four children. Her mother was a secretary/bookkeeper and church organist; her father's problems with alcohol meant he didn't always have a job. Beck started picking out piano melodies at age five, and when she was twelve her mom showed her some guitar chords. In high school she played guitar in a folk duo with another girl. After graduating Beck headed into Louisville to attend a Catholic nursing school. When the nuns found out that she played guitar, they tapped her regularly to play for folk masses.

Beck soon started working as a folksinger, alone or with others, appearing at various coffeehouses around town. One of these, the Round Table, featured the Ohio River Valley Boys every Saturday night, with Roy Gentry on banjo. It was the mandolin, however, that caught Beck's ear. She had long loved its sound—not from hearing Bill Monroe, but from hearing Jethro Burns of Homer and Jethro fame. Soon she and Roy were an item and she was borrowing from his extensive record collection and learning to play the little instrument she adored, picking out tunes by ear.

In the spring of 1970 Beck graduated from nursing school and found a job working the night shift in a Louisville hospital. In December of that year she married Roy. Around this same time, through an unfortunate set of circumstances, Roy found himself barred from the Round Table. The Ohio River Valley Boys, however, still had the gig, and in pragmatic bluegrass fashion, they found someone else to play banjo and put Beck on mandolin. "I was not the first-choice replacement or even the fourth, but it was mostly because I kept showing up." Beck realized that she was there by "default." She knew that if she hadn't been married to Roy, she would have never been allowed on stage. Still, it was a job in a bluegrass band and she was excited. She began to do much of the emceeing, since no one else seemed to care about this aspect of the show.

Roy spent days repairing instruments at the Doo-Wop Shop, a music store he owned with bassist Bob Wood. Nights and weekends music flowed at Beck and Roy's farmhouse, where guitarist Jim Webb (not the famous songwriter) was also living. Beck was the only woman who played. "That was when I started figuring out that I was an outcast. I'd be outcast from the women because they didn't like it that I was a musician. They wouldn't talk to me. There was always this underlying opinion that there had to be something other than the music . . . Then I got some of it from the men, because their opinion was [that] you can't possibly be able to play and keep up."

By 1972 the Falls City Ramblers, named in honor of Louisville, the "Falls City," had emerged from these loose musical gatherings. To a core bluegrass sound, the founders—Beck, Roy, Jim Webb, and Bob Wood—added the early blues, swing, and ragtime that they also loved. Their avant-garde musical attitude, hippie appearance, and eclectic material found ready acceptance in the clubs and bars in Louisville and in Dayton, Ohio, particularly among the college crowd. In 1973 they won a band contest at the Louisville Speedway and drove to Nashville to cut a 45 rpm single.

In keeping with the times, the Ramblers were a democratic band, except, as Beck says, "I had to fight for my part of the democracy." This was particularly true when it came to money. In June 1974 the band members chipped in to buy a small farm in China, Indiana, just north of Louisville. As the liner notes to their first album effuse, here they could "grow together with the added benefit of being able to grow their own food." As Beck tells it, "Okay, we'd gone together to buy the farm and actually there were five of us. And the other guys wanted to make me and Roy take one share of our earnings so they could divide it into fourths. So he and I would have a fourth and each of the other guys would have a fourth. And I fought that and fought that. That was one place I really dug my heels in and said no, I'm doing the same amount of work, I get a fifth just like everybody else."

This utopian idea—and the joint mortgage—would prove troublesome to Beck when members started leaving the band. But for a while everyone lived here, including newest members Dave Harvey (fiddle) and Robin Rose (Dobro and washboard). The band was playing fifty-two weeks a year, three to five nights a week, and putting everything they made into the farm. And though they were "living on a shoestring," Beck was able to quit her job as a nurse.

As an oldest female child, Beck perhaps naturally fell into the role of "band mom." "You had to round everybody up and make sure they were going to be there on time." Traveling was no picnic either. In the early days it was "six people in a car with an upright bass." Later Beck would add a baby to the mix.

She also undertook the thankless task of booking and, according to Dave Harvey, did "a phenomenal job." Her cold call to Lou Ukelson of Cincinnati's Vetco Records resulted in the band's first album, *Ain't Nothin' in Ramblin'* (1975). The grab-bag array of songs includes bluegrass, blues, a jug band tune, and a number by Homer and Jethro. Touches of clarinet, saxophone, harmonica, and washboard loudly proclaim that the Falls City Ramblers were not walking the straight-and-narrow bluegrass path. Although the liner notes say that Beck "strums sweet mandolin," she actually *picks* the mandolin, taking solos on five tunes. Jim Webb's pleasant voice is heard most often, with Beck doing the tenor, but she takes the lead on the bluegrassy "Waiting for the Boys to Come Home." Her strongest contribution, however, is her blues delivery on "Red Hot Mama" and Memphis Minnie's "There Ain't Nothin' in Ramblin'." They didn't call her Memphis Beck for nothing.

Bluegrass Unlimited didn't quite know what to make of this young entry into the "string-band revival." The reviewer accused the group of treating their black-derived pieces as "camp" and took them to task for making fun of traditional music, but Beck and Roy loved these old tunes in the same way they loved bluegrass.

The beginning of 1975 found Beck in the family way. She stayed on the road for eight months, playing the mandolin while holding it to her side. During that last month she often had to sit out some songs simply because she could not bear to be on her feet for the five hours a bar gig required. Beck did not find the men sympathetic to the problems of pregnancy. "They thought I was being a wimp."

In August, Beck's only child, Orville Gibson Gentry, was born. Two weeks later the nursing mother was back on the road, Orville in tow. Beck's best friend in bluegrass, Mary Jo Dickman (now Leet), stepped in to help out. Mary Jo says, "I had a bassinet for that baby and for about six weeks I was just following their jobs hoping I wouldn't get fired from mine . . . Orville would scream during the set and I would walk far enough away with him so he didn't disturb the show, and then when she got back between sets then he would calm down and she held him." Trying to be environmentally conscious, Beck stayed away from disposable diapers at first, but soon realized it was foolish to create extra work for herself.

The following year the band released their second album, *Early Indiana Days* (PalmTree, 1976). Except for Beck's strong rendition of Bessie Smith's "Jazzbo Brown," all the pieces are well-crafted originals by various band members. The flavors are neatly divided: one side is blues, ragtime, and Hawaiian; the other is bluegrass. Beck's own hard-core bluegrass "Daddy Don't Drink No More" references her familiarity with this problem. She also gets in plenty of mandolin time, including a unison ride with the clarinet on "Jazzbo" and a mandolin duet with Dave Harvey on "Unreal Reel." Beck's mandolin playing is in many ways more old-timey than bluegrass. Although Jethro Burns was a favorite, she says, "Instinctively I knew there was no point in copying somebody else's style. Your style is who you are. My style is not to play fifty gazillion notes to show how many notes I can play. I stay with a melody line."

The band was on the road continuously. In 1977 they did a weekend at the Childe Harold club in Washington, D.C., and scored a review in the *Washington*

Post. The reviewer wrote, "Best of all was an old-fashioned blues, 'In My Girlish Days,' with vocalist Memphis Beck Gentry singing her heart out." The Ramblers also made their first appearance at O'Lunney's Irish pub in New York, earning a mention in the *New York Times*. After praising the band as "authentic," the reviewer zeroed in on Beck: "The focal point of the Falls City Ramblers is Memphis Beck Gentry . . . She has the plain, almost vibratoless voice and straightforward style of a Kentucky mountain singer, and while these qualities are to be expected from a singer of traditional material, they make her performance of pop and blues material unusual and affecting."

Beck understood that playing music meant "you went out and entertained the audience," and to her, attire was a big part of that. "When I first started playing it was jeans and boots . . . But I actually started dressing up and wearing dresses and skirts. I would look for stuff that maybe was a little on the outrageous side. I would wear hats, I'd put on makeup. It was fun to get ready for a show, kind of a ritual. It helped me get in the mood." On the other hand, the men were inclined to think "the music would carry it. Maybe they would change their shirt, maybe they wouldn't."

By the late seventies "the band was really going downhill fast." In addition to personal frictions, a large overdue-tax notice on the farm added to Beck's anxiety and meant that the band had to keep working to pay it off. In 1978 Roy, who "actually liked to stay home," did so for much of the year while Beck continued on the road with Jim Webb, filling in with musicians as needed. A young Bill Evans, subbing for Roy on banjo, found it exciting to "play all over the eastern part of the country . . . and be a part of what could best be described as a somewhat crazy scene. Beck was a calming force in the middle of a pretty good storm."

For Beck, however, music had ceased to be fun. When Orville started school in 1981, Beck returned to her job as a nurse. The band accused her of being a "traitor," but Beck said, "I'm not living like this anymore. We were living on a farm with no running water, had no phone, sometimes we had a vehicle and sometimes we didn't. I said, 'I'm done with this kind of life.' I didn't want Orville to be living like that either . . . from then on music became a secondary thing again." Beck and Roy still played some locally, but music was no longer the be-all and end-all of Beck's life.

But Beck could never leave music completely behind. Somewhere along the way the Falls City Ramblers morphed into Memphis Beck and the Red Hots, a group that did blues, swing, and old-time. The Red Hots did not record, but

Beck and Roy released a couple of blues-oriented recordings, *Old Photographs* (Vetco, 1984) and *Blues on My Trail* (Papa Lou, 1993). In 1995 they separated.

Music remains in Beck's life. She has helped her friend Mary Jo on several projects, including Mary Jo's solo album, *I Love Bluegrass* (1990), and Mary Jo's duet album with her husband, Charlie (2003). Today Beck and Mary Jo along with Charlie Leet and Mike "Fog" O'Bryan (who played accordion on two albums with the Falls City Ramblers) perform as Nuance and Uncles. Their latest CD is *It's Called Nuance* (2006). Beck now works as a psychiatric nurse in Jeffersonville, Indiana, and counsels people with drug and alcohol problems. But, as ever, she is never far away from her beloved mandolin.

Years ago we played a private party for
Phil Donahue. Some gentlemen were
watching us play and one said to the
other, "D'ya think that's hard to do?"
His friend replied, "I dunno—how
hard can it be? She can do it."

—Suzanne Thomas

SUZANNE THOMAS

It really is all about her voice. The voice of Suzanne Thomas, the voice that Jon Hartley Fox calls "the missing link between Molly O'Day and Alison Krauss." Sure, she was one of the earliest women to play lead mandolin on record, one of the earliest female lead guitar players, and one of the few women to have lengthy careers in two nationally known bands, the Hotmud Family (1970–1984) and the Dry Branch Fire Squad (1990–1999). But it is her voice that, like Windsong perfume, stays on your mind. Reviewer John Roemer, who is not a fan of old-time music, says, "Her voice alone, something like a barroom Emmylou Harris, lifts Hotmud well beyond the rest of the trade and actually makes the traditional approach interesting." Ron Thomason, leader of the Dry Branch Fire Squad, has another take: "She plumbs emotions that are sometimes best left undiscovered."

Even her ex-husband and former bandmate, Dave Edmundson, says, "I still think she is one of the best musicians to ever step on a bluegrass festival stage."

Yet in spite of her enormous talent, Suzanne never became well known to the bluegrass masses and considers herself a "journeyman bluegrass musician, a good utility infielder." She says, "I really don't have any desire to be a star. I like being part of a group. I have a desire to be involved in moments of really good music. I don't care about the other stuff."

Suzanne Thomas (b. 1945), an "assertive first child" with one younger brother, was raised in Dayton, Ohio, in a "little hillbilly heaven" where she grew up hearing old-time and bluegrass music. She also got a large dose of big band music from her father, who for the first ten years of his marriage made a living playing saxophone and clarinet. He came off the road to work as a toolmaker when Suzanne was born but continued to play every weekend until his death. Her mother worked as a salesclerk in a dress shop. Suzanne refers to her parents, both Kentucky natives, as "transplanted hillbillies who got sophisticated." She considers herself a "throwback."

Suzanne took to music early on, plunking out melodies on the piano when she was just five. Years of formal training had her considering a career as a classical pianist, but her small physique posed a problem. "I don't have concert pianist hands. I had the brains for it, but I didn't have the hands." The guitar, however, was a different story. Her mother, paying on time, got one into Suzanne's hands when she was thirteen, but it was five years before she became "obsessed" with the instrument. Her obsession would turn into a lifelong passion for roots music.

Like many young people in the early sixties, Suzanne was listening to folk music. In Dayton, however, when you went "looking for folk music, you would run into hillbillies." The town pulsed with bluegrass. In the bars along Fifth Street you could regularly see the Stanley Brothers, Larry Sparks, Frank Wakefield, Red Allen, Wendy Miller, Mike Lilly, Noah Crase, and Paul Mullins. All men. As Suzanne says, "The community that would play that kind of music were pretty hard core traditional hillbillies and women didn't do that." But women could watch and Suzanne had a fake ID. When she saw the Osborne Brothers, she thought they were "amazing and wonderful." She said to herself, "That's what I want to do. And I did."

But being part of an all-male band was not an option for a teenage girl, although like many women of the time, Suzanne says she never thought about it. "It never crossed my mind that somebody would give me any resistance to doing it or wouldn't accept me doing or wouldn't let me do it. That wasn't a factor for me." Still at some level she had to realize that, talented though she might be, she was never going to play guitar and sing with Ralph Stanley. So she followed a path that was already open to women: she became a folksinger.

After graduating from high school in 1963, the first in her family to do so, Suzanne spent a year at the University of Dayton. While playing in a campus coffeehouse, she met another folksinger, who booked her at a club he ran in Ontario. In the summer of 1964 she grabbed her guitar and headed for Canada. What gives a young woman the spark, the desire, the *ovarios* to strike out on her own and follow such an unconventional path? Suzanne, who has described herself as "real aggressive," says, "At a very early age I saw that boys got better treatment. And I've always been really competitive with guys. I've always wanted to beat them at their own game."

For two years she plied her trade, fingerpicking the guitar in Canada, Ohio, and Indiana. In the fall of 1965 she went back to school at the Dayton Art Institute. In 1966 she married an artist she met there and moved to New York, where her daughter, Miriam, was born in 1969. Here she played occasionally in a rock-and-roll band. "I decided I would be the person who worked and my husband would be the person who stayed home. I was being supportive."

In the summer of 1969 the young family moved to the thriving music community of Yellow Springs, Ohio, where Suzanne was soon getting together with fiddler Dave Edmundson and guitarist Michael Hitchcock. As Dave says, "After a while we started looking around for gigs and thought we should have a banjo player." Thus Rick Good joined the fold. Michael soon bailed, but not before the band had been named. According to Dave, "One night after some enthusiastic partying we started talking about astrology and figured out we had one water, one earth, and two fire signs." They realized that if you put those elements together, you would get hot mud. The "family" came from their "great reverence for the Carter Family." Thus came the Hotmud Family. In 1972 Suzanne and her husband amicably divorced and she and Dave married.

In their early quest for gigs, the trio secured a grant to play Appalachian music for the students in the Dayton public school system. Says Suzanne, "We played all day long five days a week for four months. We got really tight. So that gave us the impetus to keep going." They got hooked up with the Living Arts Center in Dayton in 1974 and ran several programs there for two or three years, including a live, weekly radio broadcast on WYSO at Antioch College that lasted almost twenty years.

From the beginning the Hotmud Family successfully straddled the line between old-time and bluegrass music by using old-time instrumentation—clawhammer banjo and old-time fiddle and mandolin—coupled with bluegrass-style trio singing. As Suzanne said, "Nature abhors a vacuum and the Hotmud Family abhors a duet. Because nobody could stand to lay out . . . We always had to get that other part in there."

Like many young bands of the seventies, the Hotmud Family was a "consortium" that shared the lead singing equally and arranged their vocals through "collaborative effort." It was only later that Suzanne, who had the strongest, most distinctive voice, took on more lead vocals. In other mixed-gender bands of this era, the female lead singer often became the star of the show and then went on to lead her own band, as did Claire Lynch, Laurie Lewis, Kathy Kallick, and Lynn Morris. This was not Suzanne's desire nor her destiny.

The band chose their material carefully. Suzanne says, "We never picked any songs we didn't want to sing for twenty years. We didn't want to end up hating the songs. So we didn't learn any songs we didn't really love." Since each band member could sing all vocal parts, they tested out new material using a variety of harmony stacks to see which one sounded the best. According to Suzanne, "The important thing was the song. The arrangement that worked best for the song was the arrangement that got used. We all wanted to do what was best for the song." Somehow what was best for the songs resulted in vocal equity for the band members.

The Hotmud Family began their recording career in 1974, eventually releasing six Vetco albums, including two on which they backed fiddler Van Kidwell, before moving to Flying Fish in 1979 for two more. The first of these, *Till We Meet Here Again, or Above,* spotlights the versatility of the trio, including Suzanne, who showcases her skills on lead mandolin, lead guitar, clawhammer banjo, and autoharp. Her mandolin playing, the center of "Carbolic Rag" and "Hawkins Rag," was based on a pre-bluegrass style that owed more to ragtime than anything else. The ten vocals, split equally, included "Hello Stranger," "My Wandering Boy," and "Walkin' in Jerusalem." More than thirty years later this album is still eminently listenable. Its magnificence is multiplied when you consider that the band cut these sixteen songs in just six hours and almost every number is a first take.

With their next album, *Stone Mountain Wobble* (1974), the Hotmud Family made a radical one-time foray into country ragtime. This mostly instrumental recording shows off Suzanne's banjo-mandolin playing on decidedly non-bluegrass numbers such as "Black Bottom Strut," "Lindy, Lindy," and "Kansas City Kitty." She also plays solo ragtime piano on "Dallas Rag." By now the trio had expanded to a quartet with the addition of Tom Harley Campbell on bass.

By their third album Suzanne's mandolin-playing days were behind her. On *Buckeyes in the Briarpatch* (1975), their most bluegrassy recording, she takes only one guitar break, on "No School Bus in Heaven." She did, however, sing lead on three songs, including "Ashes of Love" and "Teardrops Falling in the Snow." Dave had taken over on mandolin, making way for a fifth Hotmud, Tom McCreesh, on fiddle. As Suzanne says, "I used to play fiddle till Dave and Rick could play it better, then I went to mandolin. And I played it till Dave could play better than me, then I switched to guitar." With Rick playing exclusively Scruggs-style banjo, the old-time exuberance of their first two albums is somewhat muted. Singer-songwriter material, such as "Rock Salt and Nails" by Utah Phillips, was creeping in, and Suzanne's lead vocal on Neal Allen's "The Singer" gives a taste of the raw emotional power she was capable of bringing to a song.

The band was beginning to tour more, even playing some of the big Southern bluegrass festivals. Suzanne speculates that one of the reasons they were accepted by Southern audiences was that they "dressed up." Early on the guys wore Western shirts with string ties and vests while Suzanne wore green or gold lamé pants or shiny spandex jeans. "We didn't look like a hippie band." When the group first started traveling, Suzanne's daughter, Miriam, went with them. When Mimi started school, however, she would stay with the family who lived across the street, who had five daughters around Mimi's age.

The Hotmuds returned more to their classic, comfortable old-time/bluegrass sound on their last Vetco album, *Years in the Making* (1978). The group apologized on the jacket for not releasing an album in three years: "Sorry you haven't heard from us in such a long time. We've been on the road." The touring had made them an exceptionally well meshed four-piece band (with Jerry Ray Weinert on bass), which translated into their tightest album yet. The quartet "If You Don't Love Your Neighbor," with just guitar and mandolin accompaniment, stacks up with some of the best bluegrass gospel. Part of the strength of this album lies in the fact that Suzanne takes half of the lead vocals. "I Thought I Heard You Calling My Name" allows her to stretch emotionally and wail away. She also takes four well-crafted—and fast—lead guitar breaks.

Live, As We Know It (Flying Fish, 1979), recorded at two different clubs, proves that the Hotmud Family was as competent and tight on stage as they were in the studio. "The Man in the Middle," now a bluegrass standard, surfaces here for the first time, with Suzanne singing lead.

The last album from the band, *Meat and Potatoes & Stuff Like That* (1981), would be their best. They still maintain their eclectic old-time sound, but their arrangements—vocally and instrumentally—are more complex. With the addition of T. J. Lundy on fiddle and Gary Hopkins on bass, they were again five pieces. "Dust Eatin' Cowboys," "Faded Coat of Blue," and "Silver Tongues and Gold-Plated Lies," all singer-songwriter numbers featuring Suzanne's lead vocals, are the high points of the album. *Bluegrass Unlimited* gave the disc a highlight review.

The Hotmud Family was still rolling in 1983 when they appeared on the cover of *Bluegrass Unlimited,* but it was the proverbial kiss of death. In 1984 the group stopped touring. In their last years Greg Dearth had joined on fiddle, and the group had evolved into a "definitive bluegrass band." But fourteen years is a long time for a group to stay together. Constantly being on the road brings out the worst in everyone. Suzanne says, "We just finally self-destructed. We were pretty much doing the same thing we'd been doing for years. It wasn't like we had this big blowup. It was not with a bang but with a whimper." They continued to take occasional jobs as the Hotmud Family, but their heyday was over.

Perhaps their democratic format undermined them. Dave says, in retrospect, that their "egalitarian, share-and-share alike ethos was typical of the hippie sensibility we started from." He calls it "our great strength and eventually our great weakness . . . In the long run it meant every decision rose to the level of encounter-group intensity . . . I always thought it was a bit of a miracle that the Muds lasted for as long as we did."

Suzanne took a job at a senior citizens center in Dayton and discovered she enjoyed working with older adults. In the meantime, Ron Thomason, leader of the Dayton-based Dry Branch Fire Squad, had heard that the Hotmuds had come off the road and called to offer Suzanne a job. Suzanne declined. She was tired of traveling. But Dave needed a job. "Can he sing tenor?" Ron asked. Yes, he could. He was hired.

Suzanne found musical work close to home, singing and playing electric guitar in Sagebrush, a country bar band. She satisfied her need for old-time music by singing in the Kentucky Warblers, a duo with Carol Elizabeth Jones. So for seven years Suzanne rocked along, working a day job, playing music on weekends, and sleeping in her own bed. She might have been temporarily done with bluegrass, but bluegrass was by no means done with her.

The second stage of Suzanne's musical career began in 1990 when she and Dave divorced and he left the Dry Branch Fire Squad. Following the rules of the cosmic circle game, Ron Thomason again asked Suzanne to join the band, and this time she said yes. Suzanne would sing tenor to Ron and play lead guitar and clawhammer banjo.

With Suzanne on board Dry Branch had its strongest lineup ever. As Ron said, "Suzanne is a great, great singer, and once she came into the band it gave us everything I'd ever wanted vocally." Bill Evans, who would do a stint on banjo with the group, said, "Ron met his match artistically when he invited Suzanne to join the band and it raised his game, as well as the entire band's. Their approaches were very similar—be direct, be simple, go for the jugular as quickly as possible."

According to Suzanne, Dry Branch was different from the Hotmud Family "in every way." It had one leader, Ron Thomason. Suzanne would be a side musician, not a member of a feel-good caucus. Unlike the Hotmuds' everlasting trios, the musical backbone of the Dry Branch Fire Squad was duets. There was no part switching, little instrument switching, and usually no fiddle. Unless Suzanne was doing a solo clawhammer number, the banjo was played bluegrass style. And on the nonmusical side there were Ron's sly, humorous monologues, an integral part of the show.

But there was one fundamental similarity: Dry Branch was all about the songs. Ron said, "I actually started Dry Branch just so I could do the songs I really liked. People see us live and say, 'You guys are so ho-ho funny.' And yeah, we're yukkin' it up, but we never make a joke at the expense of the songs. I would absolutely wash my mouth out first."

For the first time, Suzanne was joining a band that included another woman, Mary Jo Leet. (Lisa Ornstein had been a fill-in with the Hotmud Family for a few months in 1977.) Mary Jo had been in the band part-time since 1977 and full-time since 1984, singing high baritone, playing guitar, and doing the occasional solo number. She was married to the bass player, Charlie Leet, who had joined the band in 1989. Longtime friends with Ron Thomason, Mary Jo also booked the group from 1976 until 1984. She and Charlie would stay until 2003.

Playing with Dry Branch gave Suzanne some well-deserved national recognition. The group had been around since 1976 and had a devoted following as well as a long-running contract with Rounder Records. Suzanne would play on five albums with the band and would release her own solo project with the label in 1998.

Although she was hired for her singing, Suzanne's role as lead guitar player was also important. In a band where the vocals reigned supreme and the banjo was sometimes de-emphasized, the guitar became a primary lead instrument, second only to Ron's mandolin playing. The first three albums she recorded with Dry Branch are replete with her understated lead guitar playing. The title song on *Long Journey* (1991) is a prime example. Suzanne plays solo guitar (taking all the lead breaks) on the number as she and Ron wrench all the pathos possible out of a deathbed scenario: "My heart breaks as you take your long journey."

The same year this album came out, Suzanne married Gary Hopkins, the last bass player for the Hotmud Family. "Always marry your bass player, that's my motto," says Suzanne. They live on a small farm in Hillsboro, Ohio.

Suzanne's second album with Dry Branch, *Just for the Record* (1993), follows the same tried-and-true format as the first. One of the highlights is Suzanne's solo rendition of John Prine's "Unwed Fathers" performed with only her claw-hammer banjo. On *Live! At Last* (1996) the audience gets a taste of Suzanne's droll, offbeat humor. Following Ron's introduction, where he brags on her singing and banjo playing, Suzanne steps to the mike and says, with a deadpan, Stepford-wife delivery, "Back home I am famous for my skills at ironing. I love to iron. Housework is my life." Then she wails away at "Red Rocking Chair," a number she popularized with the Hotmud Family.

In 1998 Suzanne recorded what many thought was a long-overdue solo CD, *Dear Friends and Gentle Hearts* (Rounder, 1998). In true Hotmud fashion, each song was a classic—there was no filler. It included two originals by Suzanne, "From the Point of View of Rubye Jane" and "You're Doing Me Wrong, Jim Beam," and reprised two Hotmud favorites, "Faded Coat of Blue" and "Silver Tongue and Gold Plated Lies." Instead of using all-star studio musicians, Suzanne and co-producer Bill Evans paired her up with some of the hottest bands in the business: the Seldom Scene, the Lonesome River Band, IIIrd Tyme Out, Missy Raines and Jim Hurst, and of course Dry Branch Fire Squad. The unusual concept brought out the best in Suzanne, and the album was nominated for IBMA Recorded Event of the Year in 1999.

The last two albums Suzanne did with Dry Branch, *Memories That Bless and Burn* (1999) and *Hand Hewn* (2001), feature a little less of her, although she sings her own "Memories That Bless and Burn" as a lead-off solo. Perhaps it's simply hindsight, but one gets the feeling that the magic is wearing off. The all-gospel *Memories* is primarily quartets, including some pulled from earlier Dry Branch albums. *Hand Hewn*, released after Suzanne had left the band in 1999, features

Ron taking more solo vocals but still spotlights Suzanne singing "The Cuckoo Is a Pretty Bird" with clawhammer banjo. One of the strongest songs here is "Atlanta Is Burning," a duet with Ron, which morphs into a spine-tingling trio when Mary Jo steps in with the high baritone.

On the strength of her solo album, Suzanne was featured on the cover of *Bluegrass Unlimited* in 1998 along with two other women. But once again it proved to be an ill omen, and in 1999 Suzanne parted company with Dry Branch. "It was just time for me to leave," she says. There were other things going on in Suzanne's life outside of music. "This is about the time I started trying to put my life in God's hands."

Today Suzanne says, "I think I'm doing what I'm supposed to be doing. I'm the director of a senior citizens center that is a hangout for active people. I get to do everything I know how to do." She and Gary are heavily involved in their local church, where Suzanne plays guitar in a contemporary Christian band. Suzanne says, "I've turned into this community person. I like being part of the town."

Even though Suzanne found work as a side musician with Dry Branch Fire Squad, which, as she points out, was already woman-friendly, she still feels the sting of having few choices as a woman. "If you're in a band where you're a founding member, you can't get somebody else to hire you. Part of it is that you're not known as a side musician and part of it is that the kind of bands that are up to the level you'd like to be at aren't gonna change the makeup of their band to include someone who happens to be a woman."

Suzanne points out that when all-male bands change vocalists, they just

plug 'em in. And I don't think there's anything wrong with that. Bill Monroe did the same thing. Your band has a sound and when you change personnel you do whatever it takes to preserve that sound. And that's a perfectly legitimate way of running a band. And that's why I was pretty much unemployable. Because I didn't fit a mold, because I wouldn't be easy to plug in some place. I think it has as much to do with my skill set as anything else. I'm a decent rhythm guitar player, and it's not exactly hard to find a decent rhythm guitar player and it's not hard to find a singer in my range.

When it is pointed out that even if this were true, if she had been an adequate male, she could have found work lots of places, Suzanne says, "Probably," then adds, "On the other hand, I wasn't exactly out there begging people to hire me. When I left Dry Branch Fire Squad I didn't want to be on the road. I hadn't been married a real long time, and basically my priorities had changed. What I really wanted was a shot at having a normal life before I was too old to enjoy it. I wanted to be home."

When asked if there is anything particular that she would like people to know about her, Suzanne says, "If you could just put in that I'm very tall. Tall and statuesque." In this all-too-solid world of flesh and bone, this would be a patent untruth. But talent-wise Suzanne Thomas stands tall indeed.

> Anyone who actually believes
> that women can't sing bluegrass
> probably never heard Delia Bell.
>
> —Kathy Kaplan, producer

DELIA
BELL

In the world of bluegrass, where first names such as Gloria Belle, Maybelle, Lulu Belle, and Ola Belle abound, it is surprising to learn that Texas-born Delia Nowell (b. ca. 1935) acquired her last name when she married Bobby Bell. And in the small musical community that is bluegrass, it is perhaps not surprising that Bill Grant, Delia's singing partner for forty-seven years, was a childhood friend of Bobby's.

Delia began harmonizing with Bill Grant when they met at a jam session at his mother-in-law's house in 1959. Since 1972 they have recorded more than twenty-five albums. Their partnership—in business, singing, and songwriting—endured longer than most marriages, from 1959 until 2006. It survived Delia's solo album for County Records (which included Bill); her solo album for Warner Brothers (which did not); her duet with John Anderson, which hit the *Billboard* chart; and the name shift from Bill Grant and Delia Bell to Delia Bell and Bill Grant.

In the beginning, however, Delia was simply a part of the group Bill Grant, Delia Bell, and the Kiamichi Mountain Boys, from Hugo, Oklahoma. When Delia first paired her voice with Bill's, the rancher was already part of the *Little Dixie Hayride* on Hugo's KIHN. Soon they were regulars on the small radio show. Bill started playing mandolin in 1965 and, according to Delia, "For several years we just entertained friends."

The pair didn't hit their stride until, inspired by attending Bill Monroe's Bean Blossom Bluegrass Festival in 1968 and 1969, the Grant family—Bill; his wife, Juarez; and his mother and father—decided to start their own Salt Creek Bluegrass Festival at their ranch in Hugo. The festival opened in August 1969 with Monroe himself as the headliner.

Delia and Bill soon entered the world of recording with a 45 rpm single they made in 1970. The reviewer in *Bluegrass Unlimited,* smitten with Delia's singing, says, "The five stars are for Delia Bell, who sounds much like the Molly O'Day of twenty-five years ago as she belts out this tearjerker. Good female lead singers are all too rare in bluegrass and this gal is really good. When can we hear more of her?"

He would hear more of her on the nine albums that Bill Grant, Delia Bell, and the Kiamichi Mountain Boys would record between 1972 and 1979. Released on their own Kiamichi label, these vinyl records were somewhat typical of the self-produced LPs of the era, recorded in one day (often a Sunday) and issued with stock covers. It is worth noting that Delia is in no way the "star" of any of these recordings. Although members of the band occasionally sing a song or two, the strength of the albums lies in the duets between Delia and Bill. On these Bill always sings lead and Delia sings tenor. Any lead vocals by Delia are done as solos, even though many songs, such as "What About You," "The Memory of Your Smile," and her first recording of "Roses in the Snow," beg for a harmony vocal. Apparently baritone or low tenor singers were in short supply.

Much of the group's material was written by Bill ("Stairway to Heaven" is now a bluegrass classic), with Delia or Juarez contributing the occasional number. Other songs, such as "Blue and Lonesome," "When You Are Lonely," and "I'll Be All Smiles Tonight," were drawn from the standard, but not overdone, bluegrass repertoire. There were even a few new offerings from young songwriters like Tom Harley Campbell ("Man in the Middle") and Tracy Schwarz ("My Pathway Leads to Oklahoma"). Future albums would differ little from this format. The fact that Delia and Bill's music did not change over the years was both the strength and weakness of the act.

Early on Delia's *Bluegrass Unlimited* champion voiced a complaint that today's listeners might find valid. In writing about *There Is a Fountain*, the band's third album, he opined that if it were not for Delia, "there would be little to distinguish them from a number of similar down-home styled bands." He noted that "Ms. Bell does not get enough opportunity to show what she can do. She does sing some excellent tenor on most of the duets, but I wish she had been featured on more than three solo numbers (in fact a Delia Bell solo album would certainly seem in order)."

The reviewer's wish came true when Delia Bell released her first solo recording, *Bluer Than Midnight* (County, 1978). Titled after a Bill Grant original, this solo album by a woman was still somewhat unusual for the time. Even more unusual was the fact that the LP was produced by a woman. Kathy Kaplan, from New York, was a radio deejay, festival emcee, writer of liner notes, occasional contributor to *Bluegrass Unlimited*, early recipient of IBMA's Distinguished Achievement Award (1989), and a big fan of the "Kiamichi Mountain Songbird." The album featured nine solos by Delia, including "God Gave You to Me," "I Want to Be Loved," and the famous "Roses in the Snow," along with three duets with Bill. Her accompanists included the legendary Josh Graves on Dobro and Joe Drumright on banjo.

And though Kathy Kaplan no doubt meant only to praise Delia when she wrote in the liner notes, "Anyone who actually believes that women can't sing bluegrass probably never heard Delia Bell," it is disconcerting that in 1978 this tired old saw—that there were hordes of people who thought women couldn't sing bluegrass—was still making the rounds. For by the late seventies numerous women, including Wilma Lee Cooper, Gloria Belle, Rubye and Shelby Jean Davis, Ginger Boatwright, Laurie Lewis, Kathy Kallick, the Whites, Grace French, Rose Maddox, Dian James, and Jeanie West, were, in fact, successfully singing bluegrass.

True to the times, the *Bluegrass Unlimited* review started out, "Many people have a built-in bias against women performers in bluegrass, particularly the singers . . . One of the main differences between [Delia Bell] and the majority of other women in bluegrass is that she can sing bluegrass lead . . . the way it's supposed to be sung, like Carter Stanley sang it, or perhaps like George Jones might have sung it." Unfortunately, in praising Delia the reviewer is essentially discounting the singing of other women, including the Whites and Wendy Thatcher, who were not from the belt-'em-out school. It would be years before bluegrass would begin to accept the enormous variety of talents that its practitioners—both women and men—would serve up. But it was traditional-sounding women like Delia Bell who helped pave the way for even that.

Delia and Bill made their first of several overseas tours in 1978, which resulted in *Bill Grant and Delia Bell in England* (1979). They were backed by British musicians on steel guitar, piano, twin fiddles, harmonica, and drums. Here the duo's country side surfaces with numbers such as Loretta Lynn's "Blue Kentucky Girl" and "We Must Have Been Out of Our Minds" from Melba Montgomery and George Jones.

By the early eighties the Kiamichi Mountain Boys had disbanded and Delia and Bill were now touring as a duet, often arranging for local musicians to accompany them at their gigs. In 1980 the two moved to the major bluegrass label Rebel Records, where they recorded a pair of albums, the first self-titled (1980) and the second, *Rollin'* (1981). Both were produced by Josh Graves and included Benny Martin on fiddle and Joe Stuart on guitar. These albums are typical Bill Grant–Delia Bell productions, with strong duets, solos from each, original material, and a scattering of the more obscure bluegrass and country numbers.

While Delia and Bill had been busy with their careers, Emmylou Harris had discovered the Kiamichi Mountain Songbird and "Roses in the Snow" and had fallen in love with the singer and the song. Moved by the experience, she recorded an entire bluegrass-flavored album, *Roses in the Snow* (Warner Brothers, 1980). Now she took the Oklahoma vocalist into the studio to produce *Delia Bell* (Warner Brothers, 1983), with Carl Jackson on banjo and Byron Berline on fiddle. Although Bill did not appear on the album, Delia told journalist Juanita Stockton that he "took me to Dallas and saw me off on my way to Los Angeles for the recording session. I never felt so alone in my life when that plane took off." Stockton reports that Bill later flew out "to lend his much-needed moral support." The label released "Flame in My Heart," the duet with John Anderson, as a single and it stayed on the *Billboard* country chart for several weeks. But the next single, "Coyote Song," with its prominent Dobro, banjo, and fiddle (which Delia thought was a bad choice), tanked at number eighty-two, lasting only three weeks.

Here, for the first time, Delia's lead vocals are supported by the superb harmony singing of Emmylou, Carl Jackson, and Holly Tashian. Songs such as "Don't Cheat in Our Hometown" and "This Weary Heart You Stole Away" come alive with the addition of these voices. Although Delia had signed with Warner Brothers for several albums, mergers and cost cutting led to her being dropped. Unfortunately, this would be Delia's last solo effort on any label.

Even though Delia was still under contract to Warner Brothers, she and Bill were able to record for Rounder Records with the stipulation that she not sing more than three or four leads per album. The duo, presented for the first time with Delia's name coming first, released three albums with the label. *The Cheer of the Home Fires* (1984), *A Few Dollars More* (1985), and *Following a Feeling* (1988) paired the two with the red-hot Johnson Mountain Boys, freeing them to do what they did best, which was sing. Guitarist Dudley Connell and mandolin player David McLaughlin provided the occasional low vocal harmony for Delia's leads. Produced by Rounder founder Ken Irwin and Bill Grant, these albums maintained the classic Delia Bell–Bill Grant sound, even though they included fewer of Bill's songs and fewer hard-core traditional numbers. Some of the strongest cuts, "Silver Tongue and Gold Plated Lies," "Foggy Mountain Home," and "Won't You Come and Sing for Me?" came from the pens of newer writers such as John D. Hutchison, Dave Evans, and Hazel Dickens. But it is their stunning version of Hugh Moffit's "Jack and Lucy" that is the high point of all three albums. It is a recording for the ages. Rounder would later compile a selection of these songs on the disc *Dreaming* (1997).

In addition to continuing on with his Salt Creek Park Festival, in 1987 Bill and Delia began co-promoting an annual March Early Bird Bluegrass Show at the Agriplex Auditorium in Hugo. Their partnership in the show would last for almost twenty years.

Delia and Bill's next recordings would be for Old Homestead, which would also reissue some of their older material. There were at least nine recordings for the label, starting with *Dreaming of the Times* (1992) and ending with *We're Not the Jet Set* (2004). *Bluegrass Unlimited* reviewed only three of these, handing out basically solid reviews while grousing about production quality on *Classic Bluegrass Today and Yesterday* (1996) and *Kiamichi Moon* (1997) and lamenting the fact that Delia sang only three leads on the latter.

We're Not the Jet Set would be Delia and Bill's last album together. Health problems were slowing them down, and their closing duet performance came in May 2006. It is fitting that their final *Bluegrass Unlimited* review began by saying, "This is old-time bluegrass. No youngsters with perfect cosmetics here." The magazine, which had consistently applauded the duo's traditional approach for so many years, did so one more time: "Real country music like this that is not watered down or slicked up is a rarity today . . . Delia Bell and Bill Grant are the real deal." Oh, yes, they are.

We didn't depend on men for anything.

—Martha Trachtenberg

BUFFALO GALS

By the 1970s one of the ways that women had found to make a space for themselves in the world of bluegrass was by forming all-female groups or, as they were known back then, all-girl bands. The best known, and possibly the earliest, was New York's Buffalo Gals, then called Buffalo Chips, who were playing as a five-piece band by December 1972. The prime mover behind the group was banjo player Susie Monick, who was with them from their start at Syracuse University through their 1979 finish in Nashville. After playing locally for a couple of years, these aggressive Yankee women booked themselves at Carlton Haney's North Carolina Newgrass Music Festival in April 1974 and then hit the road full-time. Susie says, "We used to say we were like a bunch of guys on the road. We drove the van, fixed our tires, picked up guys, stayed out, partied. We kinda had a real role reversal all around . . . We weren't in the band because we were the girlfriend of the guy." Guitarist Martha Trachtenberg says, "Coming out of a liberal college town in the Northeast, our behavior to us was not outrageous. It was only bold and brash compared to what we saw in the South. We didn't depend on men for anything."

Susie Monick (b. 1952) was raised in Teaneck, New Jersey, the daughter of a scientist father (who invented the Wet Nap) and a homemaker mother. She had one sister, six years older. Music was a part of Susie's childhood, but only as a hobby. "I took a little bit of classical guitar, and then as soon as I started liking it my mom said, 'Now, don't take it too seriously, you're not going to be a musician!'" When Susie entered Syracuse University in 1970, she found a thriving bluegrass and folk music scene. Unbeknownst to anyone else, she brought with her a hidden passion for the banjo, which she had cherished since her summer camp days. "There was this girl, she was really blonde and her name was Patty Black and she played the banjo. I was ten years old and she was like an angel. It was my first crush on a woman, and I was like, 'Wow, she's playing and singing around the campfire. I'd been to camp all my life but [whispers] this girl had a banjo." After that, she says, "I even collected little banjo pins and I always dreamed about it." Thirty years later, she speaks with breathless excitement about going off to college: "Then I heard the banjo again!"

During her first year Susie began playing folk guitar, but in her sophomore year she started taking banjo lessons from Tony Trischka, a leading practitioner of the new melodic style, who lived in Syracuse. Her roommate, Debbie Gabriel, was also learning bluegrass guitar, so they began playing together, performing only instrumentals since neither sang. One day when they were practicing in the lobby of the dorm, Carol Siegel, from West Orange, New Jersey, showed up with a dulcimer, an autoharp, and a voice. Their first gig of record was in February 1972 when Country Kasha played in the main lounge of the dorm. "Country Kasha" was a take-off on Country Granola (itself a play on Crunchy Granola), the name used by the "boy band" from Syracuse that included Tony Trischka. By May 1972 Country Kasha was advertised in the school paper as the "all-girl band" at Hungry Charley's, a restaurant near the university. The mention of the band's gender would become a prominent feature in articles and advertising. Yet, their own hand-lettered flyer for the gig mentioned nothing about being an all-girl band. Instead it proclaimed loudly, "Country Cow Shit," then in smaller letters, "Or, if you prefer, Country Kasha, will be playing their own brand of bluegrass, country, old-timey, raucous shit-kicking music at the late-night place-to-be, Hungry Charlie's [sic]."

By the fall of 1972 Susie and Debbie had moved out of the dorm and were sharing an apartment in a big old house where Tony Trischka and some other male musicians lived. Susie said, "This broadened our musical circle and got us in more with the locals." The band had now settled on the name Buffalo Chips. A December 1972 ad for Hungry Charley's again focused on their gender: "5 chicks putting on some fine sounds." It is unclear exactly who had joined the threesome to make five. At one time, Susie says, they had two fiddlers and a singer named Marty Rix. By 1973 Debbie had dropped out, and the band lineup for that fall included Susie on banjo, Martha Trachtenberg on guitar, Nancy Josephson on bass, Maureen "Mo" Riley on fiddle, with Carol now on mandolin. All were students at Syracuse. Mo was a classically trained violinist who had given her first concert when she was eight. Martha, Carol, and Nancy handled the vocals, with Nancy doing the emceeing.

Martha Trachtenberg (b. 1953) grew up in Long Island, New York, in a house filled with classical and pop music. Her mother was a piano teacher who had majored in music at Smith College. "I don't remember not singing," Martha says. She started pounding the ivories as soon as she could climb up on the bench, and by the time she was seven her mother began giving her lessons. Growing up in the middle of the folk boom, Martha got her first guitar when she was eleven and learned to play "Go Tell Aunt Rhody," "Tom Dooley," and "This Land Is Your Land." She wanted to be Judy Collins, then Joni Mitchell. She started writing songs, "true adolescent drivel," she says, at thirteen. Martha attended summer camps where Carly Simon was a counselor and performers such as Judy Collins and Don McLean dropped in to play. Her mother even bought her a banjo, and she took a few lessons from Roger Sprung but found his emphasis on theory uninspiring, so she quit.

Martha entered Syracuse University in 1971 and soon went to a meeting of the folk music society, which was run by fiddler Tom Hosmer and his girlfriend (now wife), Maria Brace. After the meeting she asked Tom if he could suggest a banjo teacher. Certainly he could. He played in a band with Tony Trischka. Two years later it was Tom who told Martha that Susie was looking for a guitar player for a bluegrass band. Martha says, "I had never held a flat pick in my life at that point. I was strictly a fingerpicking folkie. So I used to play with an absolute death grip on the flat pick. I lived in fear that it would go into the sound hole on stage. I always carried three of them with me on stage. I was petrified, absolutely petrified."

Being in a band was a new experience for Martha. "I'd never played with other people. And when you're in a band, it's like having several mirrors held up to you all the time. I found out that I was short-tempered and intolerant and impatient, which had to be dealt with. I also found out that my timing was really abysmal. I had to work on that." But as she points out, "That was the great thing about the early Gals—none of us were *great* players, we were *all* learning, so we didn't feel self-conscious about making mistakes or having to stop and figure out chords. It was very comfortable for all of us."

A newspaper article from March 1974 gives a glimpse of the band in action. The photo of a gig they played at a Syracuse coffeehouse shows the five women in the scruffy dress of the era: bell-bottom jeans, flannel shirts, work boots, with Susie sporting a cowboy hat. The (male) reviewer had been drawn to the show because it was "billed as a *woman's* bluegrass group [his emphasis]." He wasn't sure what this meant, so he decided to investigate. He liked the show in spite of its "lack of musical tightness." He attributed this to the fact that the group hadn't been together long and that Carol was new to the mandolin. He also said, "The bad jokes and anecdotes are as much a part of the act as the music itself." Apparently the Yankee women already had a good grasp of the genre. We also get a glimpse of the band's college humor with their reworking of "Amazing Grace": "Amazing grass, how sweet the smell . . ."

The Buffalo Chips were not learning their bluegrass music in a musical vacuum. As Martha points out, "There was a remarkable community of male players up there—Tony Trischka, Danny Weiss, Greg Root, Harry Gilmore, Tom Hosmer—and it was a little intimidating to play with them. It's important to note, however, that that was not their intent. They were all supportive and encouraging; good fellas." Others in the area included Walt Michael, Barry Mitterhoff, and Harry Orlove of the group Bottle Hill in Binghamton; while down in Ithaca there was Country Cooking, with Pete Wernick, Joan "Nondi" Leonard, Andy Statman, Russ Barenberg, John Miller, and Kenny Kosek; and from New York City came Matt Glaser, Stacey Phillips, David Bromberg, and Steve Goodman. If one of the girls couldn't make a gig, one of the guys would step in. Tony actually wore a skirt to play at one festival.

In April 1974 the Buffalo Chips moved into big-time bluegrass when they played at Carlton Haney's Newgrass Music Festival. But before booking them, Carlton insisted that they change their name, saying Buffalo "Chips" would offend Southerners. He suggested Buffalo "Gals." Martha says, "As I recall it, his line was 'They know what that means down here!'" (As Carol Siegel points out, perhaps they didn't realize that "buffalo gals" is what hookers in gold-mining camps were called.) But Carlton was a wily promoter who knew that Buffalo *Gals* loudly announced the band's gender. And that's why he had hired them. Martha says, "I'm positive that Carlton Haney hired us solely for our novelty value; he couldn't have cared less if we were terrible players. It was like having a two-headed boy at a carnival. Fortunately, we were good enough to get return engagements based on our ability as entertainers. We faced quite a bit of skepticism when we started out, but any number of the other players took time to teach us licks and give us encouragement, and we largely ignored the men who were blatantly sexist."

This show paved the way for a summer of prestigious festival bookings for the newly named Buffalo Gals. The gigs stretched from Berryville, Virginia, to Ontario, Canada. They also played the Philadelphia Folk Festival in August. The girls were serious about their music, but they did like to party. At one festival, Martha says, the promoter "made the dire mistake of scheduling us for early Sunday morning. We didn't want this to become a habit, so we all hopped onstage in our sleeping bags. Honest to God. We played the first song with our eyes closed, I think. He never put us on in the morning again."

Around this time, Mo decided she didn't want to travel, so in May she was replaced by Sue Raines, another classically trained fiddler, who would stay with the band until August 1975. In May 1974 Susie graduated with a double major in advertising and fine arts. Carol got her degree in education. Martha would spend her final year trying to study while on the road with the band. She graduated in May 1975 with a degree in television-radio and English.

In 1975 the Buffalo Gals released the landmark recording *First Borne* (Revonah), the first album by an all-female bluegrass group. *Bluegrass Unlimited*, apparently unaware of the historical significance of the release, was less than impressed, giving the album a small review in its "Additional Releases" section and saying, "Their singing needs more thrust and distinctiveness, but instrumentally they come out well." Other ears will find the tight vocal trios and the distinctive low-pitched voice of Martha Trachtenberg enthusiastic and inventive. Susie and Sue Raines play almost all of the instrumental leads, while Carol contributes a solid rhythm chop. Martha flat-picks several guitar breaks on the slower numbers—making her one of the earliest women flat-pickers—and also does some fingerpicking.

Martha remembers the recording: "We did one album, thirteen songs, in a two-track studio. Everything was live. There was no such thing as overdubbing. If one person missed something, everybody had to stop and do the whole thing over. Paul Gerry, the owner of Revonah Records, gave us two days to record the whole thing. Pete Wernick came in and helped produce for us, and prevented us from killing Paul outright on the site."

By leading off with Bill Monroe's "Used to Be," a vocal trio, and including "Little Maggie" and "I'll Fly Away," the Gals demonstrated that they could play traditional bluegrass. But the second song, on which they sing "Come On, Baby, Do the Locomotion" in the middle of the instrumental "Foggy Mountain Breakdown" (hence the title "Foggy Mountain Locomotion"), sends a clear signal that the Buffalo Gals were pushing the boundaries of bluegrass. As Susie said, "We learned some of the traditional, but we weren't afraid to stretch out even back then." Martha contributed one original number, the melancholy "About the Road Songs," which included Nancy's bowed bass. "Bluegrass and the Boys," with the line "We could be like Gloria Belle and buy a bluegrass bus," shows that even these "newgrass" women were well aware of Gloria Belle's presence. The album ends with the gospel quartet "I'll Fly Away," on which Martha sings bass. Female gospel quartets are practically unheard of, even today. Was there nothing these brazen Yankee women wouldn't try?

Articles about the group continued to call attention to their gender. The *New York Times* wrote, "The five women who have invaded what has been primarily a man's musical world followed traditional patterns [of instrumentation and repertory] . . . The three singers . . . got the tight, close vocal harmony that is typical of bluegrass, but on solos the traditional high, lonesome tenor was transposed into a friendly soprano. Aside from Miss Monick and Miss Raines, the Buffalo Gals are not exceptional performers, but they project a light-hearted geniality that is much more effective than the tired old hokum many of their male counterparts rely on."

The *Syracuse New Times* mentioned the string of festivals they had recently played, writing, "Although they're competent musicians, these dates are more attributable to their novelty status." One wonders if the writer thinks that boy bands were booked solely on musical merit and not on the basis of whom they knew or what strings they might have pulled. The article goes on to say, "Somewhat surprisingly, given the times and the success they've had emphasizing their sex (it's prominently mentioned on all their posters), none of their music could be interpreted as movement music. 'We're not on an "I Am Woman" trip. In fact, we still call ourselves "girls,"' said Monick."

In a cover article in *Muleskinner News* the Gals elaborated on this subject with interviewer Tony Trischka. Nancy points out that the band had talked many times about the "feminist movement and how it relates to us as musicians in a basically male field . . . Individually, we're into feminism at very different levels. We are entertainers, and don't want to be a political band." Martha adds, "There are five very distinct and separate people in this band, and our involvement in the women's rights movement and our priorities in general are different. The overall band feeling is that we make our statement for women simply by being competent musicians, and beyond that it comes to individual preferences."

In August 1975 fiddler Kristin Wilkinson (b. 1953), from Philadelphia, joined the group, replacing Sue Raines. Kris attended Philadelphia College of the Performing Arts and Stanford University and had played western swing and country before joining the Gals.

In the fall of 1975 Susie recorded a solo instrumental album, *Melting Pots* (Adelphi, 1976), which included Kris Wilkinson as the main fiddler and only other female player. Although this was not the first solo bluegrass instrumental album by a woman—being proceeded by *Twin Sisters* from Vivian Williams and Barbara Lamb (1975), Lena Hughes's unaccompanied fingerpicking guitar album (1970), and Beverly King's Dobro album (1971)—it was by far the most audacious. The surrealistic cover, which was Susie's concept, with its Salvador Dali–like melted banjos, announced that this was not your typical bluegrass recording. Susie, who composed most of the tunes, wanted to have musicians from different musical backgrounds making music that was centered on the banjo. Although Tony Trischka, Jay Unger, and John Hartford played on one or two cuts, most of the players came from outside the bluegrass world, and many, including Dave Amram, were well known in the jazz field. Susie and Kris had been "hanging out" with Dave, who showed them that the fiddle and banjo would work with jazz. He inspired Susie to start "branching out a little more."

The album includes flute, sax, trumpet, French horn, pennywhistle, piano, and drums. The tune titles and liner notes display Susie's offbeat sense of humor. "Wicked Witch Breakdown" was written "after teaching seventy-six banjo students to play 'Cripple Creek.'" About "Devil's Dream/Bluedream" she opines, "What would Freud say?" And "Marmalaid," in 15/4 time, when spelled backward comes out "Dial Amram," which is what Susie did—the night before the recording when she asked him to play on it.

Although the album was not reviewed in *Bluegrass Unlimited*, a 1976 article that profiled Susie and Tony Trischka spoke approvingly of their "inventive music," which sometimes left bluegrass entirely for "spacey excursions into rock, reggae, be-bop, and other forms of jazz."

By the fall of 1976 the Buffalo Gals, who had had enough of the cold and frozen snowy North, moved en masse to Nashville. Carol did not make the move. She said, "I had no desire to live in poverty in Nashville. Living in poverty in Syracuse was fine."

Carol's place on mandolin was taken by twenty-four-year-old Elaine Eliah. Born and raised in Niagara Falls, New York, Elaine left home as soon as she turned eighteen. Already playing some mandolin, she got "turned on to pure bluegrass" in Santa Cruz, California, and learned to play bass "because there were always too many mandolins but anyone who showed up with a bass found a place." She was living in the San Francisco Bay area in 1976 when she "set out to hit a bunch of bluegrass festivals on the east coast and improve my mandolin chops." At a festival in North Carolina, mandolin player Red Rector told her about an all-girl band that was looking for a mandolin player. In August she hitchhiked to Gettysburg, Pennsylvania, to audition. She left for Syracuse with the band that weekend and moved with them to Nashville the following month. She joined Martha and Nancy doing the core vocals.

Although they called Nashville home, the band was traveling almost all the time. As Martha said, "We weren't in Nashville. Our stuff was in Nashville." Shortly after they moved, Kris Wilkinson left the group to do studio work, carving out a successful career for herself in Nashville. Today she composes, orchestrates, and conducts music for film scores, television shows, and chart-topping record releases. She was hard to replace. The band had been branching out into swing bluegrass, which meant not just any run-of-the-mill player would do. They used many fiddlers, including Tanya Dennis, Alex Tottle, and Nelle Levin. Finally in the fall of 1977 Martha and Nancy had grown tired of the grind. Martha says, "What finally made me leave was the realization that we were playing exactly the same gigs year after year. We were playing the same material. It was on a subsistence level and we never earned a lot. And we were never getting into the better venues. It just wasn't happening." Nancy also wanted to be with her boyfriend, now husband, David Bromberg, in California.

Back in New York, Martha was in and out of music, writing songs and having some of them recorded. She got married and had a son. She worked as a copyeditor and as a researcher; she wrote a biography of science fiction writer Anne McCaffrey. Finally in 1999 she released a CD of her own music appropriately titled *It's About Time*. On the CD she thanked her father, saying he "never complained (to me, anyway) when I hit the road with the Buffalo

Gals right after earning the college degree he'd financed and had presumed I'd use to different effect."

Susie and Elaine kept the Buffalo Gals going with Sally Fingerette on guitar, Nancy Garwood on bass, and Nelle Levin on fiddle. However, Susie says this configuration wasn't playing much bluegrass, and in 1979 Elaine, Sally, and Nancy split off to form Gypsy Moon. Reflecting on her time with the Buffalo Girls twenty-five years later, Elaine says, "I wouldn't have missed it for the world." Sally eventually went on to found the Four Bitchin' Babes with Christine Lavin, with whom she still plays. The first "all-girl" bluegrass band had run its course. All-female bands would continue to offer a haven of opportunity for women in bluegrass until the late 1990s, by which time most of them had disbanded or added male musicians. Susie would continue to play with numerous groups, including Ginger Boatwright's Bushwhackers, Holly Tashian's Mother of Pearl, and Richard Dobson and State of the Heart.

Although Susie married in 1983 and divorced in 1989, and has been in other long-term relationships, she does not have children. When asked about this, she replied:

> I think with the music, I saw people who had kids disappear. When people get kids, they don't have time to play music and travel. I think if you're a good parent you can't be flitting around. Some people say, "Boy, we envy you 'cause you have the freedom, you didn't have your kids holding you back." Then you have the person who has the freedom going, "Yeah, but I never got to see that." I could take off tomorrow and go to Europe with a band, so it's exciting and adventurous but it maybe doesn't have as much warm fuzzies as being married or something. I don't think you can do too much of both unless you get into a high income bracket. And then you could take everybody with you."

Today Susie puts a lot of energy into her art, a creative endeavor she put on the back burner for years. Musically, she is happiest now backing up songwriters. In a 2003 email she reported, "Had my Grand Ole Opry debut (televised) with Nanci Griffith last week!!!!!" As she put it so well, "Music is just a big part of my life all the time."

> You don't want an all-girl group because
> the kind of girls that you would want
> are the kind that would leave home
> and you just don't need that.
>
> —Bill Monroe

BETTY FISHER

Thirty-five-year-old Betty Fisher was happily married and living in South Carolina with three young children and a hardworking husband when in 1971 she decided to resurrect a musical career that had lain dormant for seventeen years. Why? Two words: Bill Monroe.

In July of that year, Betty had attended her first-ever bluegrass festival in Lavonia, Georgia, where she had been astounded to see some of the musicians she had known while performing with her father as Betty and Buck at the Carolina Barn Dance. These bluegrass stars—Bill Monroe, Don Reno, Joe Stuart, Mac Wiseman—made a tremendous fuss over Betty, inquiring about Buck and asking if she were playing now. Betty says, "I was absolutely put up on a pedestal that day." Bill in particular told her, "You and your dad were just too good for you not to be doing anything at all." Thus the seed was planted. But the ground had been tilled and fertilized long ago.

Raised in the small community of Crossnore in western North Carolina, Betty Buchanan (1935–2012) was the oldest of four children. Her father, Buck, a sawmill man, played guitar, and almost every weekend the family's house was filled to bursting with people playing music and listening to the Grand Ole Opry. Betty started learning to play chords on the mandolin when she was four. By five she was learning to pick out melodies on the first three strings of the guitar, and by eight she was playing and singing. She and her dad started performing outside their home or church when she was about twelve. Both played guitar and sang, but Betty was the one who played the leads while Buck "seconded" her by playing rhythm. They did some traveling but never went so far out that they couldn't get back on Sunday to attend the Missionary Baptist Church, where Buck was song leader.

Around 1947 Betty and Buck became original members of the Carolina Barn Dance in nearby Spruce Pine. Local talent anchored the show, and every Friday night a Grand Ole Opry performer would be the special guest. Betty got to know all the Opry stars. Hank Snow invited Betty and Buck to go on the road with him, but Buck declined. The duo made several guest appearances on the *Mid-Day Merry-Go-Round* radio program in Knoxville, and Archie Campbell asked them to go to Nashville with his show, but again Buck said no. That was fine with Betty. "I did not have a desire to do any more than we were doing. We were not stars, but the people kinda held you above just the ordinary person walking down the street because you performed."

Buck's work eventually took the family to Charlotte, North Carolina, where Betty finished high school and took an office job. The two did some work on television and played at the Queen City Barn Dance, but Betty was getting tired of the music business, especially since "nothing had really taken off." So when she married J. T. Fisher in 1955, she left her guitar at her parents' house. "I felt like, I've enjoyed this, but it's time to move on and do something else." She soon had three children and was "perfectly happy being a mother and housewife. I did not miss the music at all." Or so she thought.

When she and J. T. moved to Walhalla, South Carolina, around 1962, Betty channeled her energy into horses. This led to trail rides, which led to sing-alongs, which led to someone finding out that Betty played guitar and coaxing her to play. A friend invited her to visit his nearby Western saloon, where she was asked to get up and sing. She enjoyed it so much that she retrieved her forsaken flattop and started playing almost every weekend at the saloon. The music was creeping back in.

Then in 1971 at Lavonia, Betty discovered that the music she had grown up with, now called bluegrass, was alive and well. She wanted back in. She knew she'd need an act that was different. She'd noticed that there weren't any women on stage at Lavonia, except for the Lewis Family sisters, so her thoughts turned to an all-girl group. A group of women would not only be novel, but it would also answer her all-important concern about respectability. Betty knew that "married men didn't always act like they were married. I knew that with me being married and having a family, it wasn't going to work out to have married men in the group. Because there would just be too many problems. Not everybody was as broad-minded as what J. T. was."

Living in Athens, Georgia, now, Betty advertised for female musicians in the local paper, but got only one response. That was just as well, because when Betty saw Bill Monroe the next summer at Lavonia (1972), he discouraged her from forming an all-girl band. His thinking was "the kind of girls that you would want are the kind that would leave home and you just don't need that." Betty was also familiar with this kind of thinking from the days when she and her dad were playing. "Back then, for a woman to be on the road, there just automatically wasn't much to her." More practically, Bill suggested that it would be difficult to find enough girls who played well and were close by. Finally, he didn't think seasoned musicians were the answer, either. "You'd have to break their habits." He recommended finding young—male—musicians so that she could "train them the way you want them."

Betty took Bill's suggestions to heart and pulled together a band of four teenage boys, none of whom she had known before. In October 1972 they entered a band contest in Charlotte, North Carolina, sponsored by festival promoter Roy Martin. Betty wanted her side musicians to dress alike, so she bought pants and matching shirts for the boys, while she wore a floor-length, handmade skirt and blouse.

Entering the contest, the group was yet unnamed. But when an old music friend pointed out that since it was Betty's band, her name should be out front, she named her group Betty Fisher and the Dixie Bluegrass Boys. After the band won the Charlotte contest and also Roy's November contest at Myrtle Beach, the promoter started booking them at most of his big Southeast festivals, paying them expenses only. It was great exposure for the band, but Betty admitted,

"We went through quite a bit of money there for a couple of years." After two contests, however, three of the boys elected not to continue with the band, so Betty found three other young musicians to replace them. Since the bass player was a girl, twenty-year-old Murphy Hicks, the name was amended to Betty Fisher and the Dixie Bluegrass *Band*.

Betty's mode of operating a band was old-school and based on the Bill Monroe model. Two things in particular stood out: the band was never a democracy, and it was backed by J. T.'s money. J. T. also served as Betty's unofficial manager, critic, and cheerleader, and, as Betty says, "He was the one who called the shots." J. T. knew nothing about the music business, but he was born to sell and completely supportive of Betty's musical ambitions.

While J. T. might not have known much about music, he did realize the group needed an album. So in March 1973, although the new configuration had been together for only a few weeks and the mandolin player and bass player were novices on their instruments, the band headed to Nashville to record. *Born to Be Free* (K-Ark, 1973), included five Betty Fisher originals fleshed out with covers of songs from the Country Gentlemen, Jim and Jesse, and the Osborne Brothers. In true low-budget bluegrass fashion, the album was recorded in one day with no overdubs or fixes and mixed by someone with little knowledge of bluegrass. The band was, however, well rehearsed. Betty believed in practice, after which she would frequently fix supper for everyone.

This album gives a glimpse of the other unique aspect of the group: Betty's lead guitar playing. She played instrumentals like "Wheels" and took lead breaks on most of the vocals. Her unusual style was not fancy, but it was assured. Betty had developed her own way of playing as a child, picking out melodies on the treble strings of the guitar, using the downstrokes of a flat pick and two-finger chord formations. If she could hear a song, she could play it, and she wasn't afraid to try. Few women at the time were doing this. Her young band members, unimpressed, wished she could play more like Tony Rice. Betty said, "I don't think I was that great a guitar player. Mine is just very simple picking." Still, when Doc Watson heard her play, he told Betty, "I just want to touch your fingers. Any woman who can pick a guitar like that, I just want to compliment her."

Betty would record three more albums for small labels: *Leaving Town* (1974), *Carolina Mountain Home* (1975), and *I Got a Song to Sing* (1976). During the seventies she and her band worked some of the bigger festivals, including Bill Monroe's Bean Blossom Festival, and played on the stage of the Grand Ole Opry several times. The friendships she had formed during her Betty and Buck days now stood her in good stead. But changes in band personnel were always a problem, and in 1980 Betty called it quits. With no forewarning to the band or to J. T., she announced on stage at a festival that this would be their last show. She finished out what dates she had with other musicians. Playing music wasn't fun anymore.

Part of Betty's frustration was logistical. In 1979 J. T.'s job had taken them to Houston, but Betty's band was still in Atlanta. Flying the group to jobs and having no time to rehearse was difficult. And Betty never did like it when her younger band members preferred socializing and picking in the parking lot to practice. It wasn't that Betty was tired of the music or the fans; she was tired of the grind of leadership.

Soon Betty and J. T. found themselves back in Walhalla, where Betty kept her hand in the music, playing guitar with a Southern gospel group. When their granddaughter Bridget came to live with them, Betty gave up playing to stay at home, work a part-time day job, and care for Bridget. Then in the early 1990s an old friend coaxed her into joining forces to form Betty Fisher, David Deese, and Dixie Bluegrass. Betty was happy to lend her name to the band, but she most emphatically did not want to be the bandleader. "I didn't want the responsibility of having to make a program out and making sure that everybody had on a clean shirt and their trousers were pressed." They recorded two cassettes, but at the end of 1993, when J. T. was diagnosed with colon cancer, Betty pulled out of the band. J. T. died in 1994. Betty lived in Walhalla for another eighteen years, listening to the bluegrass that she still loved but rarely playing her guitar.

When asked what advice she would give to women who are thinking about leading their own bands, Betty said, "The important thing is to decide if you are willing to sacrifice what it takes to be the leader of the group. Make sure you're willing to give it the time and energy. There is a total difference between being a leader and being a band member. But, if that is your dream, go for it."

Betty was diagnosed with cancer in her late seventies. Knowing this, I sent her a copy of her chapter in this book. When she called to thank me, I also thanked her for giving me my first job in a bluegrass band. As we ended our conversation and said good-bye, we both sensed we would never speak again. Our last words to each other were "I love you." Betty died on July 7, 2012.

"Memphis" Beck Gentry
of the Falls City Ramblers,
ca. mid-1970s. (Courtesy
of *Bluegrass Unlimited*)

Delia Bell, Kerrville,
Texas, Bluegrass Fes-
tival, 1975. (Photo by
Rick Gardner)

The Hotmud Family, 1981. L-R: Dave Edmundson, T. J. Lundy, Suzanne Thomas, Gary Hopkins, Rick Good. (Personal collection of author)

Dry Branch Fire Squad, Winterhawk Bluegrass Festival, Hillsdale, New York, 1993. L-R: Mary Jo Leet, Ron Thomason, Suzanne Thomas, Charlie Leet on bass (hidden). (Photo by Penny Clapp)

Buffalo Gals, mid-1970s. L-R: Nancy Josephson, Sue Raines,
Susie Monick (front), Martha Trachtenberg, Carol Siegel.
(Photo by Stephen A. Woiler, courtesy of Carol Siegel)

The Katie Laur Band, 1977. L-R: Jeff Terflinger, Jeff Roberts, Katie Laur.
(Photo by Marty Godbey, courtesy of Frank Godbey)

Betty Fisher,
1978. (Courtesy of
Bluegrass Unlimited)

Dede Wyland, Telluride, Colorado, Bluegrass Festival, 1986. (Photo by Peter Kumble, courtesy of Dede Wyland)

Good Ol' Persons, ca. 1974. L-R: Sue Shelasky, Kathy Kallick, Barbara Mendelsohn, Laurie Lewis, Dorothy Baxter. (Courtesy of Laurie Lewis)

Lynn Morris, ca. mid-1970s. (Courtesy of Lynn Morris)

Laurie Lewis, Beth Weil, and Rich Wilbur playing as Old Friends, ca. 1978.
(Photo by Lars Bourne, courtesy of Laurie Lewis)

The Homestead Act, ca. 1973. L-R: John Hedgecoth, Patsy Trigg, Lynn Hayes
Hedgecoth, Elmo Shropshire. (Courtesy of John and Lynn Hedgecoth)

The Together Tour, en route to Japan, 1997. L-R: Sally Van Meter, Laurie Lewis, Lynn Morris, Kathy Kallick, Markie Sanders. (Personal collection of author)

The Front Porch String Band, late 1970s. L-R: Billy Sandlin, Larry Lynch, Claire Lynch, Murray Ross. (Courtesy of *Bluegrass Unlimited*)

Lee Ann Lenker (Baber) with the Buffalo Chipkickers, 1980. Front, Lee Ann Lenker; back, L-R: Sam Davis, Matthew Guntharp, Hugh Johnson. (Personal collection of author)

Polly Johnson with the Sounds of Bluegrass, Florida Folk Festival, White Springs, Florida, 1970. L-R: Herb Schottland, Polly Johnson, Red Henry, Mike Johnson. (Personal collection of author)

The Hicks Sisters, Mt. Laurel Festival, Clarkesville, Georgia, 1975. L-R: Nancy, Argen, Laurie, Murphy. (Courtesy of Nancy Hodges Johnson, personal collection of author)

Shinbone Alley All-Stars, Nashville, Tennessee, mid-1970s. L-R: Ingrid Fowler, Ed Dye, John Hedgecoth, Lynn Hayes Hedgecoth. (Personal collection of author)

I never had any idea I was making
a statement just by enduring.

—Katie Laur

KATIE
LAUR

Katie Laur (b. 1944), one of the first women in bluegrass to lead her own all-male band, the Katie Laur Band, was in a slight snit. Writing in the *Women in Bluegrass* newsletter, she said:

> I had no notion of being the first woman front-person for a bluegrass band, just as I had no notion that other women weren't doing it. As the years passed I sometimes grew sentimental with the idea of perhaps being the first woman who fronted a non-gospel bluegrass band—can you think of any more qualifiers—but Jeff Roberts [her banjo player] would always remind me of Betty Fisher, a woman I came to gradually resent, even though we had never met, nor have we ever spoken. If you'll recall, Murphy, the minute someone in *Bluegrass Unlimited* held me up as a "first," you were there in the next issue, defending, who else, Betty Fisher! I was shut down again.

Nevertheless, Katie's connection with bluegrass continues today—as performer, radio host, and writer—while Betty's path eventually veered off in other directions.

Nancy Katherine Haley was born into a farming family in Paris, Tennessee. Nancy—or Nancy Kate, as she was called then—grew up surrounded by music. Fiddles, guitars, mandolins, piano, and singing were a part of life for her extended family. When Katie was about five, much of that family moved to Detroit. Like thousands of other displaced country people, the menfolk found work in the automobile factories. Katie's mom worked in an all-night bakery. They maintained connections with home by trooping back to Tennessee as often as possible.

Like other Southerners, Katie's family had a hard time adjusting to life up north. As Katie told *Bluegrass Unlimited*, "They called us hillbillies. We were frightened and shy and intimidated . . . there were just so many things that we didn't understand . . . We went to a restaurant where they served pizza and every one of us ordered a large pizza. It wasn't funny then, it was embarrassing." To ease the loneliness, they would get together on weekends and sing. Although their repertoire included the country songs of Hank Williams, Webb Pierce, and Lefty Frizzell, it also included popular songs like "Shine on Harvest Moon" and "In the Cool, Cool, Cool of the Evening."

Katie was a bit of an anomaly in her own family—an avid reader and a child with imaginary playmates who led her cousins on fanciful adventures. In Detroit, Katie began her study of classical violin (four years) and piano (twelve years), learning to read music and pick out harmony parts. But to this day, she says, "I hate classical music . . . It always seemed so *sissy*. I remember myself at this piano recital in high school. I was wearing a formal and had a gardenia pinned on my bosom. What a *crock*." She also says, "In the mind of my family I couldn't play a stitch—I couldn't play by ear so that didn't count. I had huge big recital pieces but they didn't matter."

Katie's earliest performances were with the Haley Sisters, a quintet with piano accompaniment who played fairs, theaters, and racetracks. As she writes in her inimitable style, "When I was little I sang with my sister, Jackie, and three cousins, Lennon Sisters style, at first in churches, in starched matching dresses with cummerbunds (they always had to let mine out) and bright shiny faces and patent leather shoes that had been shined with Crisco the night before." Later the family moved to Huntsville, Alabama, where on weekends, "Daddy would drag in some guitar player and ply him with liquor and Jackie and I would get to stay up till three in the morning, singing. I learned most of the Hank Williams oeuvre that way. Of course Jackie and I continued to sing duets in church. After church, we'd each take a door and wait for compliments. If we got tears, we counted it as double. Secular or religious, it was singing to us; it was a way of connecting."

The move to Alabama occurred when Katie was about twelve. Here she grew up, gravitating toward music wherever she could find it. Billie Holliday and Patsy Cline became her favorite female singers. Patsy in particular inspired Katie with her soulful, smooth delivery that "didn't sound nasal." She studied journalism at the University of Missouri, but by age nineteen she had married, had a son, and divorced. She married again almost immediately and moved with her husband, engineer Jack Laur, to Cincinnati in 1966. Katie, who had joint custody of her son, left him in Alabama with his father, whom she perceived to be more stable. This caused a painful estrangement from her family, which eventually was resolved.

Adjusting to life in Cincinnati proved difficult. Not only was Katie separated from her family and her music, but "Nancy Laur" was a "miserable failure at being a business wife." Her executive husband had no use for music, and for a few years she gave it up herself. Finally realizing she needed to sing, she took a few guitar lessons. That helped. In her darkest hours, she says, "Singing always healed me." Eventually Katie and her husband separated and she went back to college planning to be a writer. But fate was lurking just inside the door of a hillbilly bar.

One night around 1972 a dejected Katie wandered into Aunt Maudie's and heard Jim McCall, Vernon McIntrye, and the Appalachian Grass. These hard-driving, testosterone-charged good ol' boys had formerly worshipped at the altar of Bill Monroe and Flatt and Scruggs but were now trying to develop a more progressive sound of their own. Katie had what could only be called an epiphany, akin to Saint Paul being hit with a blinding light on the road to Damascus. And like Paul, her name would be changed. Nancy would become Katie. As Katie said, "Life as I knew it was over . . . That was the last thing I remember of any kind of normal life." The band reminded her of home and family and reawakened in her the ferocious love of music that had lain dormant for too long. She started hanging around the bar, and when the guys in the band found out Katie could sing, they asked her to sit in. She began to create a "furor" and draw a crowd.

One night the owner of King's Row, a rival bar near the University of Cincinnati, walked in. As Katie tells it, "He said, 'I would take you for four to five nights a week, but you gotta bring the girl.'" So Katie officially joined Appalachian Grass, who moved operations to King's Row at the beginning of 1973, playing five nights a week. By this time Katie was dating the mandolin player, David Cox, a transplanted Kentuckian. He was responsible for Katie's name change, telling her, "I don't like Nancy for a name, because some woman named Nancy shot me once." Katie says, "He was the quintessential hillbilly."

Eventually the group started going on the road, playing as far away as Florida. Traveling was a leap of faith for Katie. "I felt like I was going off with people I didn't know. You've been working with them all this time, but you don't really know them until you get in the car with them and go a thousand miles away. That takes trust." However, it was her relationship with David that enabled her to travel with the band. Going with him was like "pay[ing] for protection." Speaking bluntly, she says, "Somebody would have wanted you [sexually]."

All Katie knew was that she had to sing and she didn't know any other way to do it. "I did the best I could." Playing the music "overrode everything," including what was turning out to be a difficult relationship with David. But "when we would be sitting around in the day and practicing things, oh, what fun! It was just marvelous."

Katie recorded one album with the band, *Jim McCall, Vernon McIntyre, and the Appalachian Grass* (Vetco, 1973). Their progressive bent resulted in the inclusion of songs like Gram Parsons's "Hickory Wind," on which Katie sang lead, and Utah Phillips's "Rock Salt and Nails." With Jim pounding away at the guitar, Katie's services were not needed there and she was able to put all her energy into her vocals. She provided high harmony to Jim and Vernon on the other selections, most of which were original. Katie received kudos from *Bluegrass Unlimited*: "The addition of vocalist Katie Laur is what seems to really tie the group together. Her singing . . . provides a warmth and sensuousness that an all-male group doing the same arrangements wouldn't be able to manage."

When Jim McCall moved to Florida toward the end of 1974, Katie's tenure with Appalachian Grass was over. Vernon, now the bandleader, elected to keep David but not Katie. Since her relationship with David was falling apart, her departure was "kind of mutual." Still, "It felt like the end of the world. I went around a whole winter grieving." But Vernon had learned that having a woman in the band was good for business, and he hired Meg Davis to take Katie's place.

Katie, however, could not exist without singing, so in 1975 she began playing around the Cincinnati area in a trio with Wayne Clyburn on banjo and Dan

Parker on mandolin. Katie became the leader by "default," since nobody else wanted the responsibility. They called themselves the Katie Laur Band not only because they couldn't think of anything else but also because Katie's name now carried some weight in the Cincinnati bluegrass community. Around this same time John Hartford invited her to join a group of musicians for a bluegrass riverboat cruise. Playing music all day and night and talking about music when they weren't playing proved to be a "watershed" moment for Katie.

Inspired by John and blessed with meeting banjo player Jeff Roberts and fiddler Buddy Griffin, Katie recorded her first album, *Good Time Girl* (Vetco, 1976). Joined shortly thereafter by Jeff Terflinger on mandolin and Rich Flaig on bass, a reorganized, reinvigorated Katie Laur Band hit the road, traveling in a van with no air conditioning and sharing accommodations. "Forget the separate rooms," she says. "I had to bunk with somebody else, just the same as everybody else. I was one of the boys before I knew it couldn't be done."

The group released two more albums, *Cookin' with Katie* (Vetco, 1977) and the feminist-titled *MsBehavin'* (Vetco, 1979). With Katie doing practically all of the lead singing, the sound of the band tended toward the mellow rather than the hard driving, although songs like "Little Bessie" and their fiery instrumentals showed that they could punch it up when they wanted to. Their material was a mixture of traditional bluegrass, country ballads, the occasional classic jazz number like "Ain't Misbehavin'," reworked pop songs like "White Sport Coat," and popular folk numbers. Katie's voice was sweet—pure and true—with a bit of vibrato and sense of hidden power. *Bluegrass Unlimited* called it "refined." She almost sounded classically trained by a teacher who couldn't quite get rid of her Southern accent. The slower numbers, the "torch songs," were her forte. Here her voice could stretch out and shine. But she also easily handled blues numbers like "T for Texas" and "Lovesick Blues."

Good Time Girl is the only Vetco album to feature any of Katie's original songs. Of those three, "He Made a Woman Out of Me" is, by bluegrass standards, positively scandalous: a teenage girl talking about her first sexual experience. The beginning of the song—"Down by the riverside / Underneath the willow tree"—is pure bluegrass. But the explicitness of the next line—"That's where my girlhood died / He made a woman out of me"—is taboo times ten in bluegrass. The resulting pregnancy is not unusual, but the fact that there is no punishment in the song, no murder of the woman by her lover, is certainly not the traditional bluegrass way. Katie says, "I don't know where that song came from. It's just something I totally made up in my head." She adds, "Jeff and Buddy never like to perform it, so we didn't perform it much, because it was a little too 'loose-woman' sounding."

Touring across the country, Katie became more aware of other women in bluegrass: Suzanne Thomas Edmundson, Julie Gray, Pam Gadd, Kathy Chiavola. Katie hung around Suzanne, "because I was scared to death not to. She was so good it was frightening." Pam, she says, "was the first woman player, besides Suzanne, who allowed herself to have quirks like male musicians."

Katie worked the road until finally in the early eighties it just wore her down. Once after driving all night to make a gig, she woke up from a nap in a storage room near the stage to find she didn't know where she was. She was terrified. "I thought I just can't do this anymore. If I do I'm gonna have to start taking drugs or I'm gonna have to start drinking, and I thought enough of myself not to want to do that."

Unable to live without music, Katie became involved with jazz, where, she says, "the situation is a little better for women." Jazz was big in Cincinnati then, and Katie could sing all over town without having to go on the road. She loved it and she was good at it.

The comfortable life that Katie had carved out for herself was shattered in 1989 when her longtime companion, jazz bassist Tom Cahall, was killed by lightning. "It absolutely rocked my world. It was horrendous. I was not myself for a long, long time." Katie turned to bluegrass for solace. As she explained in *Bluegrass Unlimited*, "Jazz had no songs about death . . . It was bluegrass that had the songs about suffering and death that I needed to sing and hear."

Shortly after Tom's death, Katie was invited to host her own show on WNKU radio, just across the Kentucky line from Cincinnati. She called it *Music from the Hills of Home*. Buddy Griffin, her old fiddle player, knew how to run the mixing board, so he joined her on the air. Their good-natured banter appealed to the radio audience. When Buddy left, Katie sought out the rapier wit of Wayne Clyburn, her first banjo player. Their three-hour show is still on the air.

In 1997 the Katie Laur Band, with Jeff Roberts, Jeff Terflinger, and Buddy, returned to the studios for the first time in over twenty-five years to record *Main Street*. Cincinnati's Main Street was the home of Aunt Maudie's, where Katie had met her bluegrass muse long ago. In her one original song on the album, "When Earl Taylor Played the Mandolin for Me," Katie salutes the bar and the musicians who played there: "No matter where I'd roam / Aunt Maudie's was my heart's true home." She also graciously shares the spotlight with two young Cincinnati women, Karin Bergquist and Niki Buerhrig, who turn in a powerful, gut-wrenching performance of Karin's own "Poughkeepsie." Karin also helps her out on the duet "Married Men," in which Katie again tumbles traditional bluegrass boundaries by tackling the taboo subject of married men and sex—from the woman's point of view. The subject surveys her ongoing trysts with several married men, saying, "Never woulda had a good time again / If it wasn't for the married men." Perhaps the song is made palatable to bluegrass listeners by its punishing last line: "All of that time in hell to spend / For kissing the married men."

For several years Katie fronted the Katie Laur All-Girl Bluegrass Band, with Trina Emig on banjo, Linda Scutt on fiddle, Brenda Wolfersberger on bass, and Ma (Elaine) Crow on guitar. "I have always liked the sounds of women's voices," she writes. "There's something about the sound of women's voices that is so sweet—not cloying but comforting, serene. Brenda has a high-baritone range and perfect sense of pitch, Ma is a good lead, and I am, at my age, a wonderful alto. There's a feeling of validation and a blessing I get from being with women."

The idea for the group came together after the women sang with each other in the parking lot following the funeral of guitarist Terry Boswell, forty-six, in 1999. Terry had played with the Wildwood Girls and Kentucky 31 and had been gigging some with Katie. As Katie wrote, "During this time I noticed that Terry's guitar playing was edging up a notch or two." Unfortunately, Terry's goal, to become the female Tony Rice, was never realized.

At the 2001 Appalachian Festival in Cincinnati, Katie's All-Girl Band appeared on the program with the old-time, all-female Reel World String Band and Hazel Dickens. As Katie tells it: "The Reel World musicians had gotten older and we all pointed and laughed at each other back stage . . . but it was warm laughter, the kind that admits to the aging of the body, the easing of competition, and best of all, the softening of the heart. Isn't it odd that a man's voice is cherished for its high lonesome sound? Women have always sounded like that. Our art is shaped by events we can't control. It feels good for me to play music with other women."

Today, in addition to playing music, Katie applies her considerable talents as a wordsmith to churning out a bi-monthly column for *Cincinnati* magazine as well as writing extensively about bluegrass and jazz musicians for various publications. In 2008 she was awarded an Ohio Heritage Fellowship in the performing arts category. In 2010 she would write the *Bluegrass Unlimited* obituary for her friend Jim McCall, a "man of many contradictions."

Katie understood early on that, in spite of her tenure with the Appalachian Grass, she would never be offered work as a side musician. "I didn't imagine I had anything to contribute that men valued in the particular masculine way they choose to perform music, and it would be years before I imagined that women could have a voice. I picked my battles carefully, and I didn't take that one on. I wanted to be able to play, to lead the life of a merry road warrior, and yes, I always wanted to make a statement. I just never had any idea that I was making it just by enduring."

> It took me three years of going to
> festivals to get the nerve to bring
> my guitar out of the case.
>
> —Dede Wyland

DEDE
WYLAND

Milwaukee, Wisconsin, is not one of the first places that comes to mind when you think of bluegrass. But in the early seventies, Dede Wyland (b. 1950), who was quietly attending the University of Wisconsin, had the foundations of her world shaken by the Monroe Doctrine, a young bluegrass band that was playing at a café there. It was, she says, a "life-changing experience." Only shortly before that she had gone to the 1970 Philadelphia Folk Festival, where she had seen Bill Monroe perform. "I'd never heard anything quite like it."

Dede was not unfamiliar with music. She had taken lessons on a variety of instruments, including bass, piano, xylophone, and accordion, but it was the electric guitar lessons that "stuck." Inspired by the Beatles, she and her friend Ann would play together for fun, switching off between lead and rhythm. After her British rock phase, Dede got an acoustic guitar and sang folk music. So when the bluegrass bug bit, she was not musically unprepared. She began studying bluegrass in earnest. She says, "The feeling I had hearing bluegrass music was similar to the feeling of falling in love. It was an infatuation." She bought albums, she took guitar lessons, she went to festivals. And she listened. Still, she says, "It took me three years of going to festivals to get the nerve to bring my guitar out of the case."

Dede was putting herself through college and dropped out before her junior year to earn enough money to finish, but she found herself going down that "music road" and never returned. She honed her bluegrass chops playing in two part-time local bands, the Kenilworth Mountain Boys and the Lost River Ramblers, until she and bandmate Jim Price decided to start a full-time group in 1975. Grass, Food, and Lodging, whose members were all under thirty, toured regionally for four years and made enough of a mark to land between the covers of *Bluegrass Unlimited* in 1978. Here the writer spoke of their "musical integrity" and their "determination to give audiences a highly polished but still traditional program." Dede was the only women in all three of these bands, and it is worth noting that she was not related to or dating any of the band members.

Grass, Food, and Lodging recorded one album, *High Class Bluegrass & Other Road Side Attractions* (1978), on the Rounder subsidiary Ramblin' Records. Although Dede was the lead guitar player in the group, she did not become the lead singer until they went into the studio. As she tells it, "I was just a harmony singer. I would just sing a token lead here and there." Fortunately on the LP she handles the majority of the lead singing, with the men's harmonies stacked below. Her warm, rich voice, pitched slightly on the low side with a hint of vibrato, shows a quiet strength. Although the instrumentals are primarily bluegrass standards, vocals such as "Don't Cry Blue," "If I Needed You," "Tennessee Blues," and the Chris Hillman/Gram Parsons song "Wheels" show a decided leaning toward the current folk-rock scene.

When Grass, Food, and Lodging broke up at the end of 1979, Dede moved to New York with the expressed intention of starting a band with Tony Trischka (banjo), whom she was dating, along with Danny Weiss (guitar) and Barry Mitterhoff (mandolin). Calling themselves Skyline, with the addition of Larry Cohen on electric bass, they recorded three albums for the Flying Fish label. The first, as Skyline, was *Late to Work* (1981); the next two, as Tony Trischka and Skyline, were *Stranded in the Moonlight* (1984) and *Sky-line Drive* (1986). Dede also appeared on Tony's *Fiddle Tunes for Banjo* (Rounder, 1982), singing one song, and on his *Robot Plane Flies over Arkansas* (Rounder, 1983), playing guitar on one tune and singing on another. In addition, with backing from Skyline and other friends, she released a six-song solo cassette, *Look into Your Heart* (1985).

Skyline was a decidedly nontraditional group whose music, according to one *Bluegrass Unlimited* review, was "not for the faint of heart or closed of mind." Tony was already well known for his wildly inventive, no-holds-barred banjo playing and composing and was instrumentally at the forefront of the newgrass movement. Dede shared the lead singing with Danny Weiss and also played twin guitar with him. In arrangements that were worked out in advance, Dede would play the harmony part to Danny's leads. The vocals were drawn from a variety of sources, including Karla Bonoff, Bob Dylan, Willie Nelson, and a couple each from Danny and Dede. "Ticket Back," from *Late to Work,* and "Till It Looks Like Love," from *Stranded in the Moonlight,* were written by Martha Trachtenberg of the Buffalo Gals. This is an early instance of a woman in bluegrass covering songs written by another female bluegrass performer. And though it's difficult to pin down precise influences, Lynn Morris would also record "Wishful Thinking" and Alison Krauss would sing "Lose Again" ten years after Dede had sung them with Skyline.

Dede tells a revealing story about Alison. Rounder Records founder Ken Irwin, who was attending a Skyline gig at Harvard, took Dede out to his car to listen to a tape. Dede said what she heard "sounded like me singing a song called 'I Can't Believe,'" which Skyline had recorded on *Stranded in the Moonlight*. Then Ken said, "That's not you." In fact it was Alison Krauss. Dede marvels, "She was emulating me to the point where I couldn't hear the difference." In fairness Dede also points out that the younger woman was soaking up sounds from everywhere and that when Alison sang a John Cowan song, she also sounded just like him. But Dede was definitely on Alison's radar.

Dede and Tony would marry in 1984 and separate in 1987. In talking about wives and husbands who perform together, Dede says:

> I think different couples work it out differently in different bands. When I met Tony I was playing full-time in a band and touring and so was he, so we met each other as professional musicians. And then our relationship developed.
>
> Then when I moved to New York City, we approached it in the same way, as professional musicians. What tended to happen for us when we went on the road was that we developed a persona. We got into a different mind-set and we were like bandmates while we were touring. And then when we would get home, it would

be like getting to know each other again. When you're traveling with a group of people it's not just your relationship, it's the relationship of five people and you're together all the time. So really our relationship was neutralized in that setting.

And the breakup of the band and the marriage? "I think it had to do with being on the road as much as we were. I wanted to get off the road. And so we just started going in different directions in terms of what we wanted."

Dede headed for Tucson, Arizona, where she stayed from 1987 to 1990, playing with local musicians and teaching voice. She then moved to the Maryland area, where she's been ever since. Initially she managed a Western wear shop in Frederick, Maryland, but in 1994 she began teaching voice almost full-time, giving private lessons and teaching at numerous music camps all over the country. She also continues to play with a variety of local groups and musicians. In 2009 she reentered the recording world with *Keep the Light On* (Patuxent Music), backed by a stellar cast of male musicians, including Wyatt Rice, Darol Anger, and Ira Gitlin.

Looking back, Dede says with modest pride, "I would say it's perhaps accurate to say that back in the seventies and eighties there weren't as many women out there, and I've gotten enough feedback to believe that what I was doing was of some influence." This is no doubt true. When asked about female influences in a questionnaire for the *Women in Bluegrass* newsletter, Martie Erwin Maguire, of the Dixie Chicks, said, "I guess Dede Wyland when she was with Tony Trischka and Skyline was my favorite."

Help me climb that mountain . . .

—Line from a Lynn Morris song

LYNN
MORRIS

When Lynn Morris (b. 1948) recorded her song "Help Me Climb That Mountain" in 1990, she had no idea how prescient it would turn out to be. To be sure, as a woman in bluegrass Lynn had already had many mountains to climb. One of only three women profiled in *Masters of the 5-String Banjo* (1988), Lynn still found it impossible to land a job as a banjo player in a top-notch, all-male band in 1987. Finding that path blocked led to the formation of the Lynn Morris Band in 1988. Leading her own band entailed a hard but steady climb with accolades all along the way: five Rounder albums, three IBMA Female Vocalist of the Year Awards (1996, 1998, 1999), IBMA Song of the Year in 1996 for "Mama's Hand," election to the IBMA board of directors in 1991, and numerous magazine covers, including the redoubtable *Washington Post Magazine* in 2000. She was at the top of her bluegrass game. In the liner notes to her newly released CD *Shape of a Tear* (2003), she said, "There are two things in life that I just know I can't not do. I can't not take in a homeless animal and I can't not play bluegrass." The Universe was fixing to call her on that second one. She was about to meet the biggest mountain in her life. In March 2003, while in the hospital recovering from double knee surgery, Lynn had a stroke.

It was a miracle that she lived. The good news is that she is now almost completely recovered. Mentally she is as sharp as ever—her wicked wit still intact—and physically there is almost no sign of stroke. She walks and drives wherever she pleases. She also manages to communicate effectively, although—and this is the bad news—speech is still somewhat difficult for her, and she is not yet back to form with her music. Still, her ever faithful fans remain hopeful for a comeback.

Born and raised in Lamesa, Texas, the second of four children, Lynn showed an early aptitude for music and started piano lessons when she was six. Unfortunately the fun faded under the glare of her teacher's you-will-learn-to read-music approach. "It was awful. I hated every second of it and I never played the piano again." When she tried guitar at eleven, however, she was allowed to learn her chords by ear and she loved it. "I couldn't get enough of it." The deal with her dad was that she had to play for his friends whenever he asked. The extremely bashful young girl was not thrilled with that arrangement, but fortunately her love for the instrument outweighed her shyness.

When she was sixteen Lynn left home to attend a private girls school in Colorado Springs, Colorado. She stayed there through her graduation from Colorado College in 1972 as an art major. Here, at the advanced age of twenty-one, she discovered bluegrass when she saw the Twenty String Bluegrass Band with Mary Stribling on washtub bass. Hearing the banjo changed her life. It was as simple as that. "I will die if I don't learn how to do this," she thought. She took a few lessons and then was off and running. Everything else came to a halt as Lynn learned to play the five-string. She even took it to bed with her so that she could play at night. "I was eat up with it," she says.

After graduation she moved to Denver, where she and Mary, joined by their (male) friend Pat Rossiter on guitar, formed the City Limits Bluegrass Band in 1972. Mary did all the emceeing. "I stood on stage with City Limits for six years and never said one word out of totally unproductive shyness," Lynn said. After about a year Lynn and Pat started going together. The three-piece group played around the Colorado area until 1978, releasing two albums on Biscuit Records, *Hello City Limits* (1975) and *Live at the Oxford Hotel* (1976), along with four cuts on *Colorado Folk II* (1974).

These records, aimed at the college and skiing crowd, are heavily laced with current favorites such as "Rocky Top," "Fox on the Run," "Friend of the Devil," and "Paradise." By far the most impressive aspect of the recordings is Lynn's banjo playing. "Remington Ride" and especially "Follow the Leader" are difficult banjo tunes, and Lynn plays them both clean and fast as lightning (in a time of few studio overdubs and no computer fixes). It was no wonder that she would win the Winfield (Kansas) National Banjo Contest in 1974 and again in 1981, the only woman to take first place to date. In addition to her Scruggs-style playing, Lynn also plays clawhammer banjo on all three albums. Not many banjo players do both, and so well.

Although Lynn sang lead and harmony with City Limits, she never considered herself a singer and says she wouldn't have become one if City Limits had not needed her voice for their three-part harmonies. "I remember being scared to death to sing . . . I just didn't think I was any good. I didn't know how to get better and was real embarrassed about it. I never went around singing for the fun of it. That wasn't me at all!"

During her City Limits tenure, Lynn initiated her custom of always wearing a dress on stage. She did this with purpose, not wishing to hide the fact that she was a woman. Her floor-length dresses projected an old-fashioned air of femininity and elegance. They seemed to quietly state, "I'm a woman and proud of it!"

When City Limits ended its run in 1978, Lynn and Pat spent the 1979 ski season playing the lodges in Aspen with the band Fire on the Mountain. Lynn was the only woman. She and Pat then did two USO tours with a country band called Little Smoke, in which Lynn, the "token female member," played guitar and banjo and did a little singing. She was asked to put the second tour together herself and hired her friend Junior Brown to play in the group.

In 1981, after her relationship with Pat ended, Lynn moved to North Carolina to play with the all-female Cherokee Rose. But after she had spent only a few months with the band, her father broke his back in an automobile accident and she returned to Texas to help take care of him. The next year, with her dad on the road to recovery, Pete Wernick recommended her for the banjo position with Whetstone Run in College Station, Pennsylvania. At that time the group was all male, but it had originally included Karen Hirshon on fiddle and guitar (1973–1976) and later Celia Wyckoff on bass (1975–1978). On the way to her new job Lynn stopped by a jam session at a club in Austin, Texas, where she met bass player Marshall Wilborn. Sparks flew, and Marshall promised to visit Lynn in Pennsylvania. Skeptical, she replied, "When pigs fly." But sure enough, four months later there he was on her doorstep. (Marshall later named his publishing company Flying Pig Music.) When Whetstone Run's bass player left shortly thereafter, Marshall took over. Although Marshall had played bass in a part-time band in Texas, the Alfalfa Brothers, this was his first full-time professional gig.

Even in 1982 a woman playing as a side musician in an all-male band in which she had no relationship with any of the members was still unusual. For women this was the era of husband-and-wife teams, family bands, or all-female groups. Lynn says she was able to get into Whetstone Run only because Lee Olsen was "absolutely open-minded about that kind of thing." Still Lynn suspects that her joining the group led to the departure of other members.

Lynn and Marshall stayed with Whetstone Run until 1986, recording one album, *No Use Frettin'* (Red Dog Records, 1984). The overall sound of this four-piece band with mandolin is remarkably similar to what would become the sound of the Lynn Morris Band, due in part to Lynn and Marshall's singing eight of the eleven vocals, five of which they wrote. We also get a taste, for the first time, of Lynn's lead guitar playing, a cross-picking style reminiscent of George Shuffler's, which, while not fancy, is absolutely dead-on.

In 1986, as Whetstone Run was beginning to unravel, Marshall took a job with Jimmy Martin. He had been working with Jimmy for only two months when the Johnson Mountain Boys offered him the bass slot. Answering the call, he and Lynn moved to Winchester, Virginia, where they have been ever since. (They would marry in 1989.) Marshall's tenure with that group lasted until March 1988, and for the first time in years, except for a short tour with Laurie Lewis in 1987, Lynn was out of the music business. She found that "demoralizing." Being relegated to "groupie status" did not sit well with her. Standing on the sidelines while Marshall was in one of the most popular bands in the country was also affecting their relationship.

Lynn was not sidelined by choice. She had asked to try out with at least two all-male bands but found she could not even get an audition. Looking back, Lynn says, "I laid myself open to some pretty serious rejection by asking for things that I knew I would be denied, but I was desperate." Many people suggested she find work in one of the all-female bands. But Lynn wasn't having any of that. First of all, she wasn't interested in that particular sound. But more than that, "The point was, I was being denied because I was a woman. And playing with an all-woman group was not going to fix that."

At the time, Lynn also attributed her not being allowed to audition to the fact that she wasn't good enough. Even in 1995 she was still saying "and maybe

I wasn't." However, after leading a band for seven years, Lynn realized that "how good you are is only part of what gets you a job. The other part is how well you fit this group . . . You can't know till you get together and play and maybe things fit and maybe they don't."

One of the groups that Lynn wanted to try out for was the Johnson Mountain Boys. Dudley Connell, lead singer with the group, has this to say: "When Richard Underwood left to pursue a nine-to-five job [in October 1986], Tom Adams was the first person I thought of. He came up and we played a couple of tunes and I knew the Johnson Mountain Boys had a new banjo player. I was blown away by Tom's drive and aggressive banjo style. Our decision to hire Tom was not based on gender, but rather style and musical compatibility. Tom was simply the better choice for us." A number of other male musicians wanted to try out but were also not given auditions. This incident caused strained relationships for a while, but fences have long since been mended and memories of these hard times have softened.

Realizing that "waiting to join an established all-male group was probably going to cost me my career," Lynn felt as if she had no choice but to form her own band. When the Johnson Mountain Boys stopped touring in March 1988, Lynn and Marshall, along with Tom Adams on banjo, formed the Lynn Morris Band. The name was Lynn's "last choice," but since she was going to be the bandleader, it made sense. She would also handle the bookings, finances, emceeing, lead singing, and guitar playing. Lynn knew she sang better when she played rhythm guitar, and, having always thought of herself as a banjo player, she was pleasantly surprised to be getting so much attention for her singing. Finding the right person to play mandolin proved to be a challenge, and that spot remained in flux until 1997 when Jesse Brock committed to the group.

The new band got a huge boost when they signed with Rounder Records, releasing their first, self-titled album in 1990. This recording contains most of the elements that would come to be recognized as the Lynn Morris Band sound: Lynn's signature vocals; her tight duet singing with Marshall; original numbers from each of them; old country songs; compositions from Hazel Dickens; well-crafted songs from newer songwriters; a cut featuring Lynn's clawhammer banjo playing; a taste of her lead guitar work; and a lighthearted vocal from Marshall, complete with bass break. One mark of how strong this first album was is the fact that many of the songs, such as "Little Black Pony," "Help Me Climb That Mountain," and "Handy Man," remained in the band's repertoire for years.

As this album shows, Lynn deliberates carefully over the numbers she chooses to perform. A lover of traditional bluegrass and country music, she understands that these "wonderful old songs" are a sign of the times when they were written, but she finds many of them—which she would enjoy singing—to be at odds with her personal philosophy. "I don't like to sing victim songs or songs completely from the male perspective, especially when it's a male perspective that offers damaging prejudice against women."

Lynn's second album, *The Bramble and the Rose* (1992), followed in the tried-and-true format of the first, but shortly after recording it, in May 1991, Tom Adams went back to the Johnson Mountain Boys, who decided to try it once more with feeling. Lynn was forced to pick up the banjo again. She had not played in almost five years, and her perfectionist self found it "unbelievably hard to try to get my chops back." To most listeners, however, it appeared as if she'd never lost them. She would stay on the banjo until the fall of 1995, when Tom Adams came back for a year.

Unfortunately for fans of Lynn's banjo playing, she did not record an album during these years. Undoubtedly she was much too preoccupied simply trying to keep a band together. When she did record again, *Mama's Hand* (1995), Tom Adams was wearing the picks. But Lynn's three years on banjo had honed her skills to a fine edge on the two original instrumentals she did play on the disc. She is absolutely on fire as she blasts through "Old Rip" in clawhammer style and "Dancing in the Hog Trough" in Scruggs style. She was as good as anybody in the business.

As a bandleader, Lynn was learning a lot. She was also becoming an articulate speaker about the trials and tribulations of being a female bandleader in the world of bluegrass, even while, paradoxically, preferring "not to be thought of as a 'woman' bandleader, but just as a bandleader." Before her stroke she often said that being a bandleader was the hardest thing she'd ever done—"unless it's playing well in the studio."

As a woman from the South reared in the June Cleaver era, Lynn was "definitely raised to defer to male opinion and not to make waves, and to try to be accommodating and get along." She had to learn to be a leader. And she found that "trying to be a 'good woman' and a good leader at the same time is not easy." One of the first things she found out was "how much [a bunch of guys] dislike women who disagree with them. And especially women who want to boss them around and tell them what to do. So the hardest thing to do is to find the middle ground where you can be an effective leader."

Lynn willingly acknowledges that being a bandleader married to a band member complicates things even more. "As married individuals we have all sorts of challenges to work out." She points out that Marshall carries the double burden of having to set an example of how the other musicians should respond to her direction. "It's the ultimate test of a relationship," Lynn says. She found it "especially difficult" to have their relationship "on review twenty-four hours a day." That was in the early years when the band still roomed together to minimize expenses. Lynn and Marshall finally realized they would have to get a separate room for themselves just to survive.

Still she recognizes that being a bandleader is no "piece of cake for a man, either. You're basically taking on the task of making the impossible possible, and the inconvenient worthwhile. You've got all the non-music-related headaches of running a small business and it's a serious challenge to find time for the music."

In 1996, with Tom Adams gone again, Marshall was in despair. He suggested to Lynn that they quit the music business. Lynn simply said, "We can't quit." Fortunately, Ron Stewart arrived on Lynn's doorstep (literally), when Petticoat Junction, in which he was playing mandolin and fiddle, spent the night at Lynn's house. When Lynn heard him play banjo, she nabbed him for that position full-time, after clearing it with Petticoat Junction. When Jesse Brock rejoined the band on mandolin shortly thereafter (he had done a stint in 1992), Lynn had her dream group. Perhaps it is not surprising that the band she calls "the top lineup we've ever had" included two young musicians who had both grown up playing with family bands that included women.

Lynn was overjoyed that she finally had a road band she could record with. *You'll Never Be the Sun* (1999), the first album with Ron and Jesse—and the second produced by Lynn—scored a highlight review in *Bluegrass Unlimited*. The production was vintage Lynn Morris Band, with two exceptions: there were no Lynn or Marshall originals, and there was more fiddle. Ron's work with the band propelled him to an IBMA Fiddle Player of the Year Award in 2000. Ron showed his great respect for Lynn's musical expertise when he chose her to produce his solo album, *Time Stands Still* (Rounder, 2001), which garnered a nomination for IBMA Instrumental Album of the Year in 2002.

With Ron and Jesse still in the band, Lynn recorded her last album to date, *Shape of a Tear* (2003). Lynn put untold hours into its production, overseeing every detail. She wanted it to be her best ever, and she had already set her own bar exceedingly high. In a highlight review, *Bluegrass Unlimited* called it "probably the most musically and emotionally satisfying bluegrass album released so far this year." Marshall's "Goodbye to the Blues" is a stunner, featuring Lynn's exquisite clawhammer playing, her bluesy lead singing, and their tighter-than-ever duet. Lynn's old friend country music star Junior Brown makes a special appearance playing pedal steel and singing harmony on one number.

Lynn's stroke came at almost the same time the album was released. She had chosen to have her knee surgery in March, when bookings were not so numerous. Now her 2003 playing schedule was in shambles. Marshall, who was at Lynn's side when the stroke occurred and who looked after her afterward with unflagging devotion, kept the band together as best he could and salvaged some gigs. He, who normally said little on stage, was now having to do all the emcee work, and he rose to the challenge like a champ. He was also having to deal with all the aspects of running a band that Lynn usually handled: endless phone calls, dealing with cancellations, lining up band members, making travel plans. Most promoters were understanding, and friends, including Dudley Connell, filled in for Lynn. In the months to come, Lynn herself would make some appearances on stage, singing a song or two with the words on a stand in front of her. Her fans were overjoyed to see her, and she positively glowed being among them again at the record table. Still, however, the future of the band was not secure enough to keep Ron and Jesse. Much as they hated to, they had to take positions with other groups. As more time went by, Marshall, too, needed to find steadier work and he joined Michael Cleveland's band, Flamekeeper, in which Jesse was already playing.

Today Lynn continues with her speech therapy, trying to regain her command of language. Her spirits remain high and her smile is always welcoming. In 2009 she took a job running sound for Bill Emerson and Sweet Dixie, allowing her to keep a hand—and an ear—in the bluegrass world. In 2010, in honor of her many achievements in the world of bluegrass, Lynn was given the IBMA Distinguished Achievement Award. She accepted it in person and delivered a heartfelt and beautifully prepared speech. Then, on May 1, 2011, Lynn thrilled her fans by performing an entire set at the Apple Blossom Bluegrass Festival in Winchester, Virginia. Backed by Marshall, Jesse, Ron Stewart, and Tom Adams, she played guitar and banjo and sang her heart out. She received a standing ovation when she stepped on stage and another when she left. Before leaving the stage, she thanked the audience, she thanked the band, she thanked her speech therapist, Darlene Williamson, who was there, and her last words of thanks were these: "I'm alive!"

We thought we could do it because
nobody was saying we couldn't.

—Beth Weil

THE
WOMEN IN
CALIFORNIA

According to many women who live there, bluegrass in California was different from the beginning. Kathy Barwick, who played Dobro with the All Girl Boys, says, "You betcha it's different! I think because there was little or no established (entrenched?) tradition of bluegrass in California, women didn't need as much to 'break in' to something . . . the bluegrass tradition was built by men and women together . . . The Phantoms of the Opry and the Good Ol' Persons really set a standard for women in bluegrass in the Bay Area: this is something women do—and on an equal footing with men."

Or as Beth Weil, who played with Laurie Lewis and Grant Street and the Good Ol' Persons, says, "Music knows no gender here. Men on the West Coast were open to women musicians, even woman bandleaders, because rock-and-roll was that way out here. Joy of Cooking had two women bandleaders [Toni

Brown and Terry Garthwaite], and Ace of Cups was an all-woman rock band. It never occurred to us not to play bluegrass—there weren't the problems of an exclusively male tradition like there were where bluegrass was born on the East Coast. We thought we could do it because there was nobody saying we couldn't."

Yet the Phantoms and the Persons were not formed until the mid-seventies. And there had been bluegrass bands at both ends of California since the late fifties. More to the point, bluegrass historian Neil Rosenberg, who played bluegrass in the Bay Area in the late 1950s, says when he came back to visit in 1978 he found a "*changed* bluegrass scene in which women now *regularly* shared the spotlight with men [emphasis mine]." This seems to imply that before, at least in the 1950s, women in bluegrass were scarce. Yet, as always, they were there. If you looked hard enough, you would find them.

Who were some of these women, the women who tilled the rich California bluegrass soil into the fertile mixture that nurtured the careers of the Good Ol' Persons, Laurie Lewis, Kathy Kallick, Sidesaddle, the All Girl Boys, Alison Brown, and Sara Watkins, to mention just a few?

Neil's Rosenberg's own band, the Redwood Canyon Ramblers, which formed in the summer of 1959, is considered to be the first bluegrass band in the San Francisco area, a band "who paved the way for bluegrass to exist in the Bay area," and which generally consisted of all men. But when one of their members got sick on their very first gig, Betty Aycrigg (stage name Betty Mann), an experienced country and folk performer, filled in on bass. She also played other dates with them.

At the other end of the state, in the Los Angeles area, JoAnn White was playing bass with the Country Boys—her brothers, Clarence, Roland, and Eric—later known as the Kentucky Colonels. While still living in Maine in the early 1950s, the young boys were too bashful to sing, so JoAnn sang with them. When they moved to California in 1954, JoAnn became their first bass player, although this was before they added a banjo player. In a not unusual scenario, she dropped out after a year when she got married. But she was there for a while.

Also in the Los Angeles area was Dian James (ca. 1940–2006), who appeared on two country music shows, the *Hometown Jamboree* radio show in 1953, where she was reportedly backed by "a bluegrass trio," and the *Town Hall Party* television show. She is remembered best for her one bluegrass album, *Dian & the Greenbriar Boys* (Electra, 1963), on which she sings but does not play an instrument.

According to the producer, the album did not sell well, and Dian and the band did not tour in support of it.

In 1966 Marci Rice joined her new husband, Wayne, and his brothers in the San Diego group the Rice Kryspies. She and Wayne had played together in a folk group, and then, as Wayne puts it, Marci "learned the bass well enough to hold down that spot in the band." The group recorded two albums, *Sugar Coated* (1968) and *Reason to Believe* (1970), on both of which Marci played bass and sang. These are probably the earliest bluegrass albums in California to feature a woman playing and singing. When Marci got pregnant in 1971, she dropped out of the band.

Bluegrass Unlimited noted other females in Southern California bands. Fiddler and singer Peggy Moje, from Long Beach, played in Country Coalition, which formed in early 1968. The magazine called her "one of the few female bluegrass fiddlers around." Kathy Marosz was the guitar player and singer with Scott Hambly and the Bluegrass Ramblers, who formed in late 1968. An article for the publication noted that Kathy was also the "leading banjo student" of Bob Leech, the band's banjo player. In the equitable California fashion, both bands have non-gendered names.

A July 1970 San Francisco newspaper article includes a group picture of three bands, each of which includes a woman: Ingrid Herman Fowler, the fiddler with Styx River Ferry; Suzi McKee, who played mandolin with Blue River; and Sue Ericsson, who sang some with High Country but did not play her guitar with the group. Sue (b. 1954) is one of the few women to acknowledge that the bluegrass situation in the Bay Area was "very difficult for me," although she admits that her young age might have had something to do with it. She points out that "if you didn't have an inroad, you just couldn't be there." And by "inroad" she means a connection with a male bluegrass musician.

Even jam sessions were hard to break into. According to Sue, "Picking parties were exclusively the domain of men. If you were a girl, forget it." The women usually ended up in the kitchen, an observation Vivian Williams and Alice Gerrard also made about their parts of the country.

Furthermore, even though Sue loved watching country music shows on television, as she says, "We were hippies. Who were we going to relate to? Who were we gonna be like?" Not like Dolly Parton, whom she saw with the *Porter Wagoner Show*. As far as Sue could tell, there were no role models for what she wanted to do. That's why, for her, the Good Ol' Persons were "such a big deal."

Sue and her older sister Kris, on guitars, and singer Jenny Bedsole were already moving from folk music into edgier country and bluegrass material in 1967 when they formed the group New York Slew, which performed music by the Carter Family, Hank Williams, Patsy Cline, and Bill Monroe. They eventually landed their own night at the Freight and Salvage, a San Francisco acoustic music club. A year or so later Sue started singing some with High Country, getting up to do several songs a set during their gigs at Mooney's Irish Pub. Sometimes she sang with Kris, sometimes in the trio with Butch Waller and Rich Wilbur (whom she was dating). She later provided tenor for three cuts on the band's first album, *High Country* (Raccoon/Warner Brothers, 1971). Bandleader Butch Waller says Sue and Kris were "really good country singers," and Sue is pictured with High Country in an issue of *Bluegrass Unlimited*. Still, when asked if she was part of the band, Sue laughs. She doesn't really know. She feels as if her presence was "tolerated more than celebrated" and that having a woman singing tenor in a hard-core, Monroe-based bluegrass band was "not the thing to do." When Rich left the band around 1971, she stopped performing with the group. Nevertheless she was an inspiration to other women who came up to her to say, "Seeing you there made me have the courage to play bluegrass." Apparently, even in California, playing bluegrass still required courage for women.

Ingrid Herman Reece

Ingrid Herman Reece (1941–1998), with Styx River Ferry, is often mentioned as an influence by other women in bluegrass from California. Ingrid was the only child of big bandleader Woody Herman. Charmaine Lanham, herself a living-room picker in California and later a co-founder of Nashville's Station Inn, credits Ingrid with "getting more women on stage in bluegrass than any other person" and with "opening the door for all women, not just Southern women." Charmaine said that out in California, although women could see Rose Maddox and Patsy Montana on stage, they were thought to be "flukes," because they were women who were raised in the music—women with rural roots. Then along came city-bred Ingrid, who did not pick up a stringed instrument until she was almost twenty.

Ingrid, who had a privileged, if lonely, upbringing in Hollywood, was raised by a nanny and attended private schools. As a young girl she had little interest in the jazz that her father played or her classical piano lessons. But when she attended a local coffeehouse during her senior year in high school (1957–1958), she became enamored with folk music. "I never got over it," she said. She began playing guitar. After a year at the University of California at Riverside, she dropped out in 1959 to marry Tom Littlefield. They had two children, Tommy in 1960 and Alexandra in 1961. But by 1962 Ingrid had divorced and moved to San Francisco, where she met and married Bob Fowler, a guitar player from Alabama, who introduced her to bluegrass through the recordings of Lester Flatt and Earl Scruggs. "I just sort of fell in love with it pretty fast," said Ingrid. But hooking up with a musician was scary to Ingrid. Having seen men and women split up because the man played and the woman didn't, she determined that such a scenario was not going to happen to her. So she jumped into bluegrass with both feet, "driven by fear of being a music widow . . . as much as by the desire to play."

Outspoken, if not downright blunt in a self-effacing way, Ingrid is one of the few women to admit to conflicts between kids and music. "I practically resented the kids because I didn't have enough time to practice." Later her kids spent their summer months in California with their well-to-do grandmother. "It was great for me," Ingrid said, "since I was not crazy about being a mother, and it gave me three months of vacation." When her father's biographer Gene Lees asked her about this "bizarre honesty," she replied, "It prevents the hurt. If I tell you I was a rotten mother, it stops you from saying it to me."

Ingrid also exposes another fear that women of her era often experienced: insecurity about her talent. "I was just sure that, since I had not grown up playing, I had a congenital lack of talent and would never be able to play, never be able to keep up." One imagines that if Ingrid had been thinking like the proverbial young man, she might have assumed that she had a congenital *abundance* of talent, thanks to Woody Herman's genes, and reasoned that she was surely destined to become a fabulous fiddle player.

But with the fiddle in her hand, Ingrid made a strong bluegrass statement. "I took that sucker and made it my own!" Still she never felt she was good enough. She would ask people to show her things but only if they were elementary and she could grasp them easily. She was always afraid they would think her "too slow." So often she didn't ask. "I was too proud. It's too bad, really. I could have learned so much more. Since I didn't have a whole lot of talent, and since I started late in life, my father probably thought I was insane."

Insane or not, in 1967 Ingrid and her husband, Bob, formed one of the first husband-and-wife bluegrass-leaning aggregations in California, Styx River Ferry, with fellow Alabamian Ed Dye. In the first incarnation all three played guitar.

Later that year they added Bruce Nemerov on banjo, Ed Neff on fiddle, and Chuck Wiley on bass. Unfortunately an album the group recorded in 1969 with Jake Tullock and Josh Graves from the Flatt and Scruggs show was never released. In spite of her protests, Ingrid must have been a fairly competent guitar player. Bruce Nemerov says she flat-picked a guitar number like "Salt Creek" in almost every set.

Styx River Ferry was the first band to play at Paul's Saloon in San Francisco, probably around late 1969 or early 1970, when it was still called the Paragon. According to Kathy Kallick, it was Ingrid who convinced the owner of Paul's Saloon to present live bluegrass at his club.

In August 1972 Bob and Ingrid moved to Nashville and in 1974, with three other couples, including Charmaine and Marty Lanham, established the Station Inn, which was patterned after Paul's Saloon. Ingrid continued to play music, working at Opryland for two years. She also took to the stage with a number of groups, including Hubert Davis and the Season Travelers; the all-female Bushwhackers with Ginger Boatwright; and the Shinbone Alley All-Stars, which included her West Coast buddies Ed Dye and John Hedgecoth on Dobro and banjo, along with Gloria Belle on mandolin.

Unfortunately Ingrid's recorded output is small, but it does include *Sentimental Journey* (1994), on which she appeared with Ginger Boatwright; Vassar Clements; and her father, Woody Herman, on clarinet.

In 1982 Ingrid returned to California to take care of her mother, who had breast cancer. This same disease claimed Ingrid on February 21, 1998, at the young age of fifty-six. As her friend and bandmate Ginger Boatwright wrote, "Never in my life have I met anyone so full of the sheer joy of living . . . She loved her children, her friends, her sweethearts, and her music. Music was like breath to Ingrid . . . She played hard, loved hard, and lived hard . . . All with a huge grin and a big laugh."

Markie Sanders

One of the earliest women to claim Ingrid as a role model and inspiration was Markie Sanders (b. 1952). Markie, who started playing bass in 1967, says, "There were no other women when I started." When Markie added singing to her list of bluegrass skills, it was due to the encouragement of Ingrid, who knew how to tease her and make her relax. Markie says Ingrid "never wavered" in her support.

Markie describes the bluegrass scene around San Francisco as "mostly a man's world." With a background in classical piano, she got turned on to bluegrass by the banjo but "hated the singing." When she went "looking for bluegrass" around 1966, she found the Smokey Grass Boys with Rick Shubb on the banjo at a club called Cedar Alley. The band also included David Grisman, Herb Petersen, and a very pregnant Jill Haber (Grisman's wife) on bass. Toward the end of her pregnancy Jill was replaced by Julie Silber. So from the beginning, Markie saw women playing bass in bluegrass bands. She dragged her mother to see the group, whom she described as "so damn hot." Or perhaps that was just Rick.

Soon Markie "dove into bluegrass headfirst" and began taking banjo lessons from Rick. Naturally, they started dating. On one of their first dates, Rick took her to see Lester Flatt and Earl Scruggs. Not long after, they went to a pawnshop and bought a bass. Markie had played around with the bass in the high school orchestra, so she was not a complete novice. Because bass players were scarce, she instantly started playing with "all the good pickers." It didn't hurt that she was partnered with Rick, who was already well established in the bluegrass picking community; "he knew everybody," she says, and thus Markie got to play with the "cream of the crop." Perhaps because she was with Rick she felt accepted from the start and never felt as if she had to prove herself.

From that point on, Markie and Rick, who would marry in the late sixties (and divorce in the mid-eighties), played together in a number of groups, which sometimes included other women. Two of these groups were the seven-piece Diesel Ducks (1967), with Susy Rosenberg (now Thompson) and Sue Draheim on fiddles, and the Hired Hands, with Rich Wilbur, extant until 1974, who played regularly two nights a week at Paul's Saloon for about two years. Then there was the pizza parlor group Blue River Band, which by 1970 with the arrival of Ed Dye had turned into Roaring Blue River, which in turn morphed into Hold the Anchovies, whose rotating membership included Suzi McKee on mandolin, and the "jazz to bluegrass" group Shubb, Wilson, and Shubb, who released a self-titled LP in 1976. *Bluegrass Unlimited* called their music "sort of folkish-jazzish-semi-bluegrass string music, mostly instrumental but with an occasional vocal included almost as an afterthought."

Markie and Rick were also in the first band configuration of High Country in early 1969, but only for a few months, when Rick quit to play with Vern and Ray. Markie would also play bass with Vern and Ray for a number of years, and she and Rick both appear on Vern and Ray's *Sounds from the Ozarks* (Old Homestead, 1974). All of these gigs, especially the regular gig at Paul's Saloon, gave Markie quite a bit of visibility in the bluegrass community, and there were many aspiring women players who saw her and undoubtedly thought, "If she can do it, I can do it!"

The Homestead Act:
Patsy Trigg and Lynn Hayes Hedgecoth

As the 1970s rolled around, women continued to find their way into the California bluegrass scene, their relationships with men still easing the way and often providing the impetus. One of the new groups to form in this fourth decade of bluegrass was the Homestead Act from Sausalito, which solidified around 1971 with Patsy Trigg singing and playing guitar and bass. Before this the group had been a somewhat loose aggregation that played pub gigs, often with Suzi McKee on mandolin. According to a tongue-in-cheek *Bluegrass Unlimited* article (written by the band), John Hedgecoth, Elmo Shropshire, and John Pierson were playing for beer at bar gig in San Francisco when Patsy appeared and asked if she could sit in. The men didn't want her to, because they knew that "a girl that cute couldn't play." In spite of that, they said yes and "after she played and sang a couple of songs, we didn't want her to play, because she intimidated us with her virtuosity." What could they do but ask her to join the group?

Patsy, from Fayetteville, Tennessee, had honed her playing skills in a family band called the Trigg Kids and had put herself through college playing lead guitar in several rock bands. Lynn Hayes (b. 1945), from Oregon, was the next addition to the group. Already a guitar player and singer, she was working as a receptionist at Elmo's veterinary practice when she met John Hedgecoth, was immediately smitten, took a couple of guitar lessons from him, and joined the band soon after. She and John married in 1974. After a brief sojourn in Hawaii playing bluegrass, John and Lynn joined the great bluegrass exodus to Nashville in 1974 and are still together there. Elmo and Patsy divorced, but not before they recorded "Grandma Got Run Over by a Reindeer" in 1979. The Homestead Act's two LPs, *Gospel Snake* (1972) and *Playing Possum* (1974), are some of the earliest bluegrass albums from the Golden State to include women. Their recorded repertoire was, for the most part, nontraditional and included songs such as "Lady Madonna," "Devil in Disguise," and "Catfish John."

The involvement of these California women in bluegrass would provide a solid foundation for those who would follow. These early female musicians were noticed, and their presence made a difference to those who would follow in their footsteps only a few years later. Laurie Lewis and Kathy Kallick were two of those. As Laurie says, "The first time I went to Paul's Saloon, there were women playing lead instruments as integral parts of a band. There was Markie Sanders playing mandolin and bass in the Hired Hands, and of course Ingrid playing fiddle . . . There was Sue Ericsson, who played guitar and was often a guest with bands . . . Live music was all around me with women playing. So it did not seem like it was an odd thing or a thing that was so far out of my realm of possibility that I couldn't do it myself."

You have to realize that it's just a song.
And I can say it's not about me at any point.

—Laurie Lewis

LAURIE LEWIS

Laurie Lewis (b. 1950) is a woman of many talents: singer, fiddler, guitarist, bass player, bandleader, performer, arranger, producer, and teacher. But perhaps her greatest gift is her extraordinarily expressive songwriting. She has a "love affair with the sounds of words together." Her compositions range from ballads to bluegrass, from old-time to torch, from Tex-Mex to calypso, from acoustic funk to heartbreaking country. Her passion, intensity, and willingness to pour every ounce of herself into her singing is reminiscent of none other than one of her own idols, Hazel Dickens. And Laurie does it with seemingly flawless technique and control. Twice named IBMA Female Vocalist of the Year, Laurie has recorded close to sixty original songs spread out over seventeen albums. So far.

Born in Long Beach, California, Laurie lived in Texas until she was three, Michigan until she was eight, and then it was back to Berkeley, where she's been, more or less, ever since. (Her peripatetic family was accompanying her doctor father, who was completing his training.) Music has always been a part of Laurie's life. Her mother's people played traditional Norwegian music, and her dad played flute and piccolo in the Dallas Symphony while he was in medical school. All four of the Lewis children were expected to take music lessons, so Laurie, the second oldest, studied piano briefly and classical violin from ages twelve to seventeen. Her early relationship with the fiddle was rocky. "I loved the instrument and I hated taking lessons." Having to read music was one of the reasons.

But when a friend took her to the annual Berkeley Folk Festival, a teenage Laurie found what would become her life's work and passion. Here she saw Jean Ritchie, Joan Baez, and Doc Watson, and "the whole world of music opened up for me." Inspired, she started teaching herself guitar and later took banjo lessons. When her banjo teacher went away one summer, he left Laurie with his collection of bluegrass albums. She listened to them religiously, feeling like an archeologist, absorbing the sounds. After attending junior college for two years, she dropped out during her fourth year at the University of California, Berkeley, to work as the business manager in a dance studio. She was not playing music at all. "I was a lost soul," she said. But not for long.

The dance studio became the first link in a chain of events that would lead Laurie back to bluegrass. The director's husband, Geoff Berne, played bass and was into the bluegrass scene at Paul's Saloon in nearby San Francisco. When he found out that Laurie had played classical violin, he urged her to try the fiddle. At this same time, Laurie's sister asked Laurie to play at her 1972 wedding, envisioning a folksinger with guitar. But Laurie had something else in mind. Musing over the wedding as the "lovely waltzes" from her favorite Chubby Wise fiddle album danced in her head, Laurie realized that she could learn these tunes by ear. As she says, "A big door opened for me." When Geoff dragged her over to Paul's Saloon, she was "completely smitten."

With her classical violin technique, her excellent ear, and her enormous talent, Laurie was able to plunge right into bluegrass. She began taking fiddle lessons from Paul Shelasky and entering fiddle contests. She took an impressive fifth place in the ladies division at the prestigious Oldtime Fiddlers' Contest in Weiser, Idaho, in 1973, and won the California State Women's Fiddle Championship twice, in 1974 and 1977.

By 1974 Laurie was playing fiddle with the Arkansas Sheiks, an old-time band in Berkeley, which also included Barbara Mendlesohn on clawhammer banjo and hammered dulcimer. The next year Pat Enright asked her to play bass with the Phantoms of the Opry in San Francisco. After six months with the group she moved to fiddle, Paul Shelasky (whom she was dating) switched to mandolin, and Paul's sister Sue took over on bass.

In the midst of this fertile musical mix, Laurie chanced upon a bootlegged copy of Hazel Dickens and Alice Gerrard's 1965 album, *Who's That Knocking*. Laurie loved it. As she said, "Hazel and Alice didn't shy away from the visceral, gritty aspects of the music that were what attracted me as well." These role models would serve her well in her next musical venture—the Good Ol' Persons.

It was Barbara Mendlesohn who suggested that she, Laurie, Dorothy Baxter (lead guitar), Sue Shelasky (mandolin), and Kathy Kallick (bass) get together for a weekly jam. According to Laurie, "It really started out as a woman's support group. But we thought we should set a goal for ourselves, which would be to put together a set to play at Paul's Saloon at jam night." They performed at Paul's in late 1974 and were immediately hired to play one night a week. The band attracted a lot of attention early on, because they were a novelty. Even the name Good Ol' Persons was a joke—a take-off on Frank Wakefield's Good Ol' Boys. Laurie says, "Everybody liked us. The women liked us because we were all women on stage, and the men liked us because we were all girls."

Although the Good Ol' Persons still has the reputation of being an all-female bluegrass band, they were not of one gender for long. Sue soon dropped out and was replaced by her brother Paul. And the band was never bluegrass in the strictest sense of the word, because they didn't have a Scruggs-style banjo player. In fact, they shied away from calling themselves a bluegrass band, saying instead that they played bluegrass music. It was a fine distinction.

The group might have been a novelty to begin with, but the level of musicianship was high. Their first album, *The Good Ol' Persons: California Old-Time Bluegrass Music* (Bay Records, 1977), holds up extremely well after all these years. If there is a defining element, it is the vocal blend of Laurie and Kathy Kallick. Both were already strong singers, and their duet is reminiscent of the close harmonies of Alice and Hazel, without Hazel's hard mountain edge. The Persons drew from a wide variety of musical sources, including old-time, country, folk, swing, Cajun, and Kathy's songwriting. The use of non-bluegrass instruments—piano, hammered dulcimer, spoons, clarinet—presaged Laurie's future solo albums. By the time the LP came out, Laurie had already moved on down the line. Even though she loved harmonizing with Kathy, it was hard to have two lead singers. Kathy would continue to anchor the Good Ol' Persons for another two decades.

For the next couple of years, Laurie played with many different musical aggregations for varying lengths of time. These included Peter Rowan's Free Mexican Air Force; Old Friends, with Nancy Josephson and then Beth Weil on bass; and the Vern Williams Band.

A 1979 article about Old Friends in *Pickin'* magazine, "Banjoless Bluegrass," provides an early glimpse of Laurie. She was already the "front person" and seemed to be "outwardly the most attuned to the path of success, in her own diffident way." The write-up ends with Laurie saying, "People are nuts to play bluegrass for a living—if you want to play as uncommercial a kind of music as bluegrass, you probably shouldn't even try." Naturally, she would not follow her own advice. More than twenty-five years later, she was still saying much the same thing: "I can afford to keep on playing unpopular music. I'm not the sort of person who wants a lot of material stuff. There's a very strong anti-materialist streak which makes even the choice of what we play possible. It makes it work for us."

Playing bass in the Vern Williams Band (1979–1980) has been described by Laurie as one of the "highlights of my musical career." Vern, a singer and mandolin player originally from Arkansas, was a generation older than Laurie. Her comments about this experience are an open window into her musical soul. She says, "Vern would sometimes call me to play fiddle with him, but I was always so scared to do it. I really didn't feel like I was good enough for that band. So I'd try to get him to get Paul Shelasky to play fiddle or someone like that, and I'd wrangle the bass job. And then pretty soon, I got the bass job for a while." As bass player, she says, "I was in heaven, with the best seat in the house for that scraped-clean, unvarnished sound." When Vern and Ray were given an IBMA Distinguished Achievement Award in 1997, Laurie made the presentation. She said Vern told her that if you want to play bluegrass music right, "you've got to spill your guts on stage and then walk in them." It was a lesson she learned well.

Laurie sank her roots deeper into bluegrass soil with her next undertaking, the Grant Street String Band, a group with bluegrass banjo, which she co-founded with Beth Weil in 1979. Like Laurie's previous bands, Grant Street was a democratic organization with "a precise blend of power designed to try and fill all of our various individual needs." As Laurie points out, "All the bands out here in California were communal bands. That was part of the whole thing about bluegrass that was enticing to us out here, the way everybody worked together, the way it wasn't a star-driven music. It was a community music."

In true communal fashion, their self-titled LP (Bonita, 1983) was produced by the band. Laurie, Beth, and guitarist Greg Townsend shared the lead singing and formed the trio. This album featured two of Laurie's original songs, including "The Bear Song." Laurie's songwriting had been ignited by the prolific pen of bandmate Kathy Kallick. Laurie says that Kathy "had this incredibly great thing happening, and all this material that was unavailable to me. I think it was wanting some of that for myself that finally spurred me to write." Striking a blow for feminism, the lyrics in two songs have been changed from their masculine originals: Laurie sings "I'm sure God has *her* way" in Don Stover's "Things in Life," and Beth sings "Will you be ready then, my *sister*" in Bill Monroe's "The Old Crossroads."

The group stayed together long enough to fly their new LP out to the Kentucky Fried Chicken Festival and band contest in Louisville, Kentucky, in 1983, where they took second place. But shortly after that, things began falling apart. Beth quit in 1984 because she found bluegrass "boring." She also admits that she and Laurie "competed fiercely for control of the band" and that she (Beth) had gotten to the point where she was "totally obnoxious." According to Beth, their parting was not pleasant and she and Laurie were estranged for many years. Beth would come back to the band for a short stay six years later having decided that "being a side person was not a bad thing."

Democracy functioned only as long as the original members of the band were together. With Beth gone and Greg the only other original member left, Laurie became the bandleader by default. "I did more lead singing than Greg, so I would write the set lists and that's a position of power." Meanwhile, on the strength of their album, the Grant Street String Band was getting calls to play, so in the time-honored fashion of bandleaders everywhere, Laurie would take the job and then pull together a group.

Leading a band was a job Laurie took seriously. "I truly have always approached performing and putting myself out there with a lot of trepidation, a lot of fear, and I've also luckily been willing to confront that fear so taking on responsibility as a bandleader was another way of confronting that fear. I didn't know I was cut out to be a bandleader until I was forced into it."

In addition to playing music, Laurie had long been working a day job doing repairs at Scoville Violins in nearby San Rafael (Marin County). In 1981 she bought the place herself, thinking that if she didn't, she'd always wonder what it would have been like to own a violin shop. She renamed it Marin Violin. "Part of the reason I decided I wanted to try owning a shop was that it's a good name."

At this point Laurie considered the violin shop her career and music as "just a thing I did on the side." But she had inherited a little bit of money and "I had all these songs I'd been writing." She was not performing them with her bands—that would have been "too pushy" on her part—but she thought it would be nice to record them the way she heard them in her head. She asked her friend Tim O'Brien, from Hot Rize, to produce. He said he would be "honored," and they ended up co-producing.

So it was that Laurie released her first solo album, *Restless Rambling Heart* (Flying Fish, 1986). This recording set the pattern for the many that would follow: funky, non-bluegrass instrumentation (pedal steel, piano, drums), female duets, male-female duets, trios, solos by Laurie, choice material from other songwriters, and little banjo. And though it's never a good idea to take an original composition too literally, her song "I'm Gonna Be the Wind" perhaps reflects some of her feelings about stepping out: "I never tried to stand alone for fear that I might fall . . . but now I'm feeling bold enough to let go my hold." Laurie was beginning to follow her own muse, which was leading her on beyond bluegrass.

Making this album—"that whole creative process"—was a watershed event for Laurie. Suddenly she knew: "This is what I want to do. I don't want to have a violin shop. I just want to play music and I want to do my own stuff." At thirty-six she had found her life's calling. She sold the violin shop and put together Laurie Lewis and Grant Street with Tom Rozum on mandolin and guitar, Tammy Fassaert on bass, Tony Furtado on banjo, and a year later Scott Nygaard on guitar. Laurie had become one of the first of a growing number of women who were leading bluegrass bands with their names out front.

As if leading a new band weren't enough, Laurie also played on the all-female album *Blue Rose* (Sugar Hill, 1989), the brainchild of Cathy Fink and Marcy Marxer. Cathy and Marcy had noticed a preponderance of "superpicker" albums in the 1980s that paired top male players from different bands and had been disappointed that these albums never included any women. To counter this, they talked the Sugar Hill label into sponsoring an all-female recording using Laurie on fiddle, Sally Van Meter on Dobro, Molly Mason on bass, Marcy on guitar and mandolin, and Cathy on guitar and banjo. When this first all-female bluegrass supergroup appeared on the Nashville Network's *New Country,* the producer wanted to provide male session players so that Blue Rose would sound as good on television as they did on the album. Cathy finally convinced the producer to save her money—these women would do their own picking.

At the same time Laurie was working on *Blue Rose* in Virginia, she was recording her second solo album in Nashville, the country-flavored *Love Chooses*

You (Flying Fish, 1989). "I just wanted to try something new," says Laurie. "It's not a bluegrass album." Half of the songs do not include fiddle. Fortunately, this was not a trend, merely Laurie's belief that not every song needs "fiddle all over it."

Hard on the heels of these projects came *Singin' My Troubles Away* (Flying Fish, 1990), her first band album in seven years. Coming into the picture here is a sound that would become almost synonymous with Laurie's music, the duet with Tom Rozum. *Bluegrass Unlimited* called their harmonies "stunning." Laurie says, "I love to have a partner to sing with, crave it deep down inside. And Tom's the same way." On the strength of these various recordings, Laurie received the first of what would be ten straight nominations for IBMA Female Vocalist of the Year (1990–1999). She would win in 1992 and 1994.

Laurie was now taking on the role of producer for other people. Over the years she would produce albums for Scott Nygaard (1991), Peter McLaughlin (1996), Erika Wheeler (1996), Charles Sawtelle (2001), Leah Larson (2004), and Susie Glaze (2008). Laurie says, "I really enjoy the producing role. It's a lot easier to call the shots from the outside." However, she said that finishing the project for friend Charles Sawtelle after his death in 1999 "was some of the most difficult work I have ever done as a producer."

The early magic of the Good Ol' Persons shone again when Laurie and Kathy Kallick joined forces for the duet project *Together* (Kaleidoscope, 1991). That early fit had been so immediately comfortable that Laurie says when she left the band, "it took me awhile to really find my own voice without Kathy's." Laurie and Kathy dedicated "Gonna Lay Down My Old Guitar" to Hazel and Alice (who had recorded it in 1965), with thanks for "breaking trail."

Laurie's next album, *True Stories* (Rounder, 1993), was her strongest project to date. Her songwriting had reached new heights with numbers like "Val's Cabin," "Swept Away," "You'll Be Leaving Me," and "Slow Learner." The opener, "Singing Bird," is a template for what would become one of her signature sounds: intense duets with sparse instrumentation. The small letters at the end of the liner notes speak volumes: "FOR TAR." Tom Rozum.

Then came 1994, a hellacious roller-coaster ride of a year. In March, Laurie, Tom, and bandmate Jerry Logan were involved in a horrific automobile accident in Arizona. Their van flipped twice and Tom was thrown out. Jerry escaped with trauma and bruises, but Laurie fractured her skull and two vertebrae. Tom fractured his shoulder blade and one wrist, dislocated his hip, and nearly severed ligaments in his legs. Laurie was back to playing in a month (guitar only, sitting down); it took Tom three months and he still had to walk with a cane. Their complete recovery would prove to be a "long hard road."

But in September, as if life were offering some small compensation, "Who Will Watch the Homeplace," from *True Stories*, won IBMA Song of the Year and propelled Laurie to her second Female Vocalist of the Year Award. Laurie was also tapped to co-host the IBMA Awards show with John Hartford.

The accident "definitely changed things," Laurie told the magazine *No Depression*. "We didn't want to put stuff off; we just wanted to do what we wanted to do." One of the things they had been meaning to get around to was an album of duets. Spurred on by their brush with death, they accomplished the almost unbelievable task of releasing the first Laurie Lewis and Tom Rozum project, *The Oak and the Laurel* (Rounder), the next year. They took a stark, minimalist approach to the songs, allowing the voices to become the focal point. The project was nominated for a Grammy in the category of Best Traditional Folk Album.

By 1995 Laurie was beginning to recover and, being a big believer in giving something back to the universe, decided to celebrate by riding her bicycle in the June 1995 California AIDs Ride 4, a trek of 583 miles. She was keeping busy musically too. She participated in the mostly all-boy, Grammy-winning production *True Life Blues* (Sugar Hill, 1996), on which she and Kathy Kallick sang the title cut along with "Used to Be." Rounder issued a compilation from her first four albums titled *Earth and Sky: The Songs of Laurie Lewis* (1997), which included three new songs. She flew to Nashville especially to sing "Old Love Letters" with Ralph Stanley for *Clinch Mountain Country* (1998). She also sang with Peter Rowan on *Bluegrass Boy* (1996) and on Craig Smith's self-titled project for Rounder (1997). Tom Rozum stepped into the spotlight with his own solo project, *Jubilee* (Signature, 1998), on which Laurie helped out but kept a low profile.

After a three-year hiatus from her own recording, Laurie brought forth the magnificent solo album *Seeing Things* (Rounder, 1998). This was the first of her own projects on which she was sole producer. "I guess I felt confident enough to call the shots on my own," she says. In the liner notes she talked about the accident, saying, "I suffered a long drought of creativity. I was incapable of doing anything more than just getting by, working through a long physical and emotional process." Determined to get through her writer's block, she went on a retreat, where she wrote "Kiss Me Before I Die," which can only be described as in-your-face acoustic funk. The quieter, contemplative "Angel on His Shoulder" also references the accident, although it mentions no names. But it is the happy, up-tempo opener, "Blue Days, Sleepless Nights," that perhaps addresses the toll of the accident, although with a light touch: "I used to dance out on the edge / I was possessed I could not fall / But nowadays I just inch along that ledge / Afraid to dance, I barely crawl." Knowing that Laurie admittedly writes from her own "personal perspective" makes it hard for the listener not to think these words are personal. In conversation about this song, when admired for her bravery in writing from such a vulnerable place, Laurie is quick to say, "You have to realize that it's just a song. And I can say it's not about me at any point. Or not. So what's the big risk?" When praise for her being gutsy is tendered again, she says quietly, "Well, thank you." And then in the next breath, "See, I'm not gonna tell you." Says the listener, "I know. I noticed that." Then there is loud laughter from both.

In 1999 Laurie went back to bluegrass with a passion, putting together a hard-core bluegrass group and releasing *Laurie Lewis and Her Bluegrass Pals* on Rounder. The seeds for this album had been planted during her recording with Peter Rowan, which was done mostly live in the studio. "It was really, really fun and incredibly exciting to be in there getting all the music down. I probably wanted to grab a little of that excitement for myself." Still she knew that the group—Mary Gibbons, Craig Smith, and Todd Phillips—would not be touring due to day jobs and family commitments.

Bluegrass Pals would be Laurie's last Rounder album. *Winter's Grace* (1999), a Laurie and Tom project, was released by Signature Sounds, the same company that had released Tom's CD. The disc was centered on the winter solstice, and as on *The Oak and the Laurel*, the production was pared down to essentials. Laurie admits that they got into a "less is more" space for a while, although she says, "We've never succeeded in paring it down as much as we kept intending to." She broke new ground by moving Bill Monroe's classic "Christmas Time's A-Coming," from its classic key of E, to the woman-friendly key of A, thus paving the road for all women to do the same while citing Laurie as the authoritative source.

Although *Winter's Grace* would prove to be Laurie's last new project for five years, she was by no means idle. In 2002 she released the compilation *Birdsong* on her own Spruce and Maple label. The project, a benefit for the Audubon Canyon Ranch, was again a way to give something back, this time to her muses. She also published *Earth & Sky: The Laurie Lewis Songbook,* which included the words and music to forty-four of her songs.

Laurie and Tom's third duet album, *Guesthouse* (2004), was on Hightone Records, a Bay Area label. In "O My Malissa" Laurie writes about the courtship of

Bill Monroe's parents, Malissa and J. B. The distinctly feminist-leaning song notes say, "Maybe Malissa was the outstanding fiddler in her musical family, but the pressures of raising eight children seriously cut into her fiddling time. Maybe her famous brother Uncle Pen just had more free time to devote to his craft. We'll never know."

In 2006 Laurie again felt the urge for a bluegrass band and rounded up Craig Smith, Scott Huffman, Todd Phillips, and, of course, Tom to form Laurie Lewis and the Right Hands. Their CD *Golden West* (2006) was a true joint effort, with Scott, Tom, and Laurie sharing the singing load. Laurie says, "It was put together by us all. We just got in the studio and made the arrangements and recorded them." Unlike the Bluegrass Pals, this band is able to hit the road. Although as Laurie says, "I've been away from the bluegrass market, so it's very hard to get fees to support a five piece band—because we're a bunch of old curmudgeons who like to get paid a lot! We just have to pick and choose our places and take little tours." Often she gigs with the full band, and then she and Tom stay out on the road for some additional work. "There's something very easy about traveling as a duo. And it's a lot less expensive." She goes on to say, "I really, really love the band, I just can't afford to have it all the time. And it's not like they are clamoring for work. Everyone has other stuff that they can do." This group is so talented and tight that they were able to record a project while on tour in 2007. Titled *Live* (Spruce and Maple Music, 2008), it is the first performance recording that Laurie has released.

Still, even the best bluegrass band in the world can't provide the sole outlet for Laurie's prodigious creativity. Her latest album, *Blossoms* (Spruce and Maple Music, 2009), features eight new originals and the talents of friends such as Tom Rozum, Kathy Kallick, Nina Gerber, Brittany Haas, Suzy Thompson, Tim O'Brien, David Grier, and a host of others. Perhaps a few lines from one of the songs, "Here Today," give a glimpse into Laurie's thoughts at this point in her life: "We're here today and then we're gone / This life will end just like a song / . . . I've tried to walk the path that winds / And leave just these few tunes behind."

Baby girl, don't cry, I'm not about to die /
Come and kiss your mama, let me dry your eyes.

—Kathy Kallick, "Don't Leave Your
Little Girl All Alone"

KATHY KALLICK

She was a nice Jewish girl living near Chicago. Her mother was a folksinger; her father, a mathematician by trade, played classical guitar. Both parents were exploring roads less traveled. But Kathy Kallick (b. 1952) took "less traveled" into another dimension when she moved to California to become a bluegrass singer, songwriter, and bandleader, a career she has pursued for over thirty years and that shows no signs of stopping.

Born in the Windy City, Kathy grew up in nearby Evanston, Illinois, wanting to be a folksinger like her mom. Dodi had helped establish the coffeehouse scene in Chicago in the mid-fifties and had taken Kathy and her younger brother to her concerts. At age six Kathy was joining Dodi on stage to sing "I'll Fly Away." When she got a nylon-string guitar for her tenth birthday, the first song her mother taught her to play was "All the Good Times Are Past and Gone." Kathy began writing her own songs when she was fourteen—and she hasn't quit yet. Her fifteen albums—eight band albums, four solo albums, two albums for kids, and a landmark duet album with Laurie Lewis—feature eighty originals, not counting the additional verses she has written to other compositions.

After graduating from high school in 1970, it took Kathy awhile to work her way to the West Coast. There was a year's detour at an art school in Kansas City, Missouri, where she got her Martin guitar, followed by a stint waitressing and a five-month tour of Europe. Then she and her boyfriend spent a year in Iowa, where he was learning old-time fiddle and Kathy was learning how to use a flat pick on her guitar. Finally in 1973 she arrived at the San Francisco Art Institute (from which she would graduate in 1977). There in the Bay Area she discovered a lively bluegrass scene, much of which centered on Paul's Saloon. "Painter by day, bluegrass novice by night," Kathy was soon frequenting Paul's and listening to the Phantoms of the Opry with Pat Enright and High Country with Butch Waller. Kathy has high praise for the Saloon. "Paul's provided the opportunity to hear quality music from visiting as well as area bands, plus a place to jam, learn an instrument, or debut a new group. All the bartenders and waitresses were women, and it was ferociously defended as a place where women could go and not be harassed."

Before long Kathy started teaching guitar at Fifth String Guitar, conveniently located next door to Paul's. Soon she and Butch Waller, her bluegrass mentor, were dating. Butch, a mandolin player and Bill Monroe devotee, was an advocate of traditional, Monroe-based bluegrass. Kathy began listening to albums by Monroe (still her favorite singer and songwriter), Jimmy Martin, Del McCoury, the Stanley Brothers, and Larry Sparks. She says, "I didn't only listen to men, but when I started listening to bluegrass, that's a lot of what there was to listen to."

So here she was in 1974, "happily minding my own business when I got hauled out of art school to be in a bluegrass band." The group was the Good Ol' Persons (Barbara Mendlesohn, Laurie Lewis, Dorothy Baxter, and Sue Shelasky), who debuted at Paul's Saloon on jam night for a lark and became a fixture in the Bay Area. Kathy played bass. While the Good Ol' Persons were a novelty in the bluegrass world, the Bay Area had been home to several rock and folk acts fronted by women. Kathy notes, "Janis Joplin, Grace Slick, Tracy Nelson, Terry Garthwaite, Toni Brown, Joan Baez, Barbara Dane, and many others had raised the consciousness of West Coast male musicians. Nobody could ever say that Janis Joplin couldn't rock as hard as a man!"

According to Kathy, "The band was never easily categorized and tended to piss off narrow-minded people for many reasons." Complaints from purists included women singing lead, women singing in nontraditional keys, no Scruggs-style banjo, no suits, and no hats. "So," Kathy says, "we didn't call ourselves a bluegrass band. We said we played bluegrass and when we did, we did." The band's 1977 album included three of Kathy's original songs.

During Kathy's tenure in the Good Ol' Persons, she also landed a gig around 1978 playing guitar and singing lead in the band of eccentric mandolin wizard Frank Wakefield. Amazed by the experience now, she found it a bit "intimidating" then, especially since she felt she was an "unreliable guitar player." Fortunately she was buoyed up by the impeccable rhythm of Frank, Keith Little, Darol Anger, and Todd Phillips. She recorded two albums with Frank, *End of the Rainbow* (Bay, 1980) and *Blues Stay Away from Me* (Takoma, 1980). Markie Sanders played bass on *Rainbow* and shared the job with Sue Shelasky on *Blues*.

While the lineup of the Good Ol' Persons would undergo numerous changes, Kathy remained the cornerstone, eventually moving to guitar. Sally Van Meter (b. 1956) joined in April 1977, playing Scruggs-style banjo and Dobro. Sally's Dobro fit the sound of the band so well that banjo began to take a backseat and was eventually dropped altogether. When Laurie quit a few months later, Paul Shelasky (by then on mandolin) moved to fiddle, and Markie Sanders came in on mandolin and then took over the bass when John Reischman joined in January 1978. The lineup finally solidified in 1980 with Kathy, Sally, Paul, John, and Bethany Raine on bass.

This basic configuration stayed together until 1991 (Paul was replaced by Kevin Wimmer in 1987) and recorded three albums for Kaleidoscope: *I Can't Stand to Ramble* (1983), *Part of a Story* (1986), and *Anywhere the Wind Blows* (1989). Although Bethany Raine did some of the lead singing, the core sound centered on Kathy's strong, crystal-clear vocals; the front-and-center all-female trio (jokingly called the Personettes); and Kathy's original songs. While the band could hardly be called traditional—with three women doing the singing and no banjo—the sound was definitely not as eclectic as that of the original Good Ol' Persons.

Although Kathy had been writing non-bluegrass songs for years, it was a challenge for her to find "material and content" that fit into bluegrass. "There weren't many songs about a woman's experience when I first started singing [bluegrass], and I started writing songs about my experience." She was encouraged in this endeavor by none other than Bill Monroe himself. When the Good

Ol' Persons played Bill's Bean Blossom Festival in 1983, he heard Kathy sing the first real bluegrass number she had written, the up-tempo "Broken Tie" from the *Ramble* album. He told her, "That's a fine bluegrass song," and insisted that she sing it every set. Kathy was heartened that the Father of Bluegrass himself found the story of her family's experience in Illinois a worthy subject. She was off and running.

"Broken Tie" chronicles the breakup of the marriage of Kathy's parents and ends by saying, "The saddest song is the story of a family, many miles apart with a broken tie." Though Monroe liked this "true song" the best, it is the slower "Ellie," from that same album, that is the timeless classic. Ellie is every young woman who grows up with a mother who says, "Girl, don't be trouble or you'll break my heart." So in the tradition of daughters everywhere, Ellie "learns to tell a lie," because "that's easier to do to keep Mama satisfied." Here Kathy follows the standard bluegrass format, which requires the mother to die at the end of the song. It would take nine more years for her to come up with the brilliant "Don't Leave Your Little Girl All Alone," a song in which the ailing mother does not die.

In October 1982 Kathy married Butch Waller, who was still playing with High Country, the band he had founded. Their marriage would last until 1991. Throughout their time together Kathy and Butch played in "parallel bands," often appearing at the same events. They would fill in with each other's groups if needed, but they never played long-term in the same band, and with minor exceptions, they never recorded together. Musically they were headed in different directions. Butch wanted his bluegrass to sound as traditional as possible. When he played Bill Monroe numbers, he wanted them to sound like the records. "I never had that as an option," Kathy says. "I had to figure out a different way to play bluegrass, because I was never going to sound like Bill Monroe."

In 1987 Kathy and Butch's daughter Jen was born. Kathy took Jen with her on the road for the first four years of her daughter's life but found it exhausting. Although plenty of folks volunteered to come along and be nanny, as Kathy says, "Nobody ever signed on for a second tour of duty." She adds, "I don't know of any other band that accommodated a new mother the way they [the Good Ol' Persons] did. Air fare and other expenses for this extra person had to come off the top—and they accepted this! John R. carried Jenny all over Europe in a baby backpack. Everyone was stuck all day in a van with a crying baby and they did their best to entertain her."

With Jen in her life and small children on her mind, Kathy released *What Do You Dream About?* a bluegrass-flavored cassette for children (Kaleidoscope, 1990), which won a Parents' Choice Award. Butch played mandolin on four cuts. The following year saw the release of *Together,* an outstanding duet album with her old singing partner Laurie Lewis. Tragedy also stuck that year when Beth Weil, who had finally achieved her dream of playing bass with the Good Ol' Persons two months earlier, suffered a stroke while performing on stage. She recovered, but the paralysis on her right side ended her playing days. Beth would continue to handle some of the album design for Kathy and the Good Ol' Persons as she had done in the past. Todd Phillips assumed the bass duties.

In 1993 Kathy launched her solo career with an album of originals, *Matters of the Heart.* The first of a four-record deal with Sugar Hill, the disc was by no means bluegrass, although *Bluegrass Unlimited* called it "one of the year's most impressive debut recordings." As the title suggests, these songs are about relationships—matters of the heart—and while their themes are universal—"If you could have talked to me / And I could have talked to you"—several reference the end of Kathy's marriage: "Now that all the anger's done / There's only one thing to tell / Oh, I wish you well."

To promote the album, Kathy put together Kathy Kallick and the Little Big Band with Keith Little (hence the name), Todd Phillips, and John Reischman. The Good Ol' Persons were still together, but they were playing less and less as members pursued individual projects. This was the first time Kathy's name had been out front, and she was "very uncomfortable" with it. The Little Big Band stayed together only three years and never cut a full record together. "It was a band that worked better on paper," Kathy says. With Keith in Nashville and John in Vancouver, there was no easy way to rehearse or work up new material.

Things were also happening in Kathy's life that made it more difficult to tour. In 1994 she had married Peter Thompson, a college professor in Vancouver, who had been "knocked out" by Kathy's songs and her singing long before they met. He threw himself with abandon into supporting Kathy's career. A longtime bluegrass deejay himself, Peter slid easily into the role of manager, publicist, record seller, sound tech, van driver, and money collector. With Jen now in school and able to stay with Butch, with a new solo album and band, and with Peter around to help out, Kathy knew "it was all gonna be easier." Then along came Kathy's second child, Maddy. "Well," Kathy thought, "I've done this before. It can still work." But Maddy was different from Jen and did not take to the road. Even with Peter's willingness to be "Mr. Mom" and stay home, having two kids really slowed

Kathy down. "I couldn't abandon Peter to do too much of that on his own. We're a partnership in parenting and that's when things work best for everybody."

Looking back now, with Jen in her twenties and Maddy a teenager, Kathy has this to say: "Like any mom, you think that when they are little they really need me, but when they get older I can tour. But it turns out an adolescent girl needs her mom around more than ever. So it's pretty much shot twenty years off of my music career. I just don't tour very much. I'm not gonna sacrifice my parenting for my music. So it's the music that has to be sacrificed."

Kathy's albums and songwriting ventured into political territory with her 1995 bluegrassy kids' album, *Use a Napkin (Not Your Mom)*. In addition to funny songs like "Smelly Feet" and "C-H-I-C-K-E-N," Kathy salutes Jackie Robinson's integration of baseball in the Count Basie classic "Did You See Jackie Robinson Hit That Ball?" But it is her song "My Family" that would have been the shocker to many traditional bluegrassers if they had listened closely to the lyrics. As *Bluegrass Unlimited* noted, the song embraces variations of family, "including divorce, step-parents, and interracial marriage." But the review dared not mention the verse about the family with two mothers, "One is 'Mommy,' one is 'Mom.'" At the time, Kathy herself felt very "bold" in putting the notion of "two mommies" in a song. Subtly and with humor, Kathy was bringing her view of the world into bluegrass.

At Peter's urging the Good Ol' Persons celebrated their twentieth anniversary with the release of *Good 'N' Live* (Sugar Hill, 1995), a compilation of numbers drawn from various concerts over the years. *Bluegrass Unlimited* acknowledged the impact of the band, saying, "Their quiet revolution brought acceptance to the idea that women could do more in the bluegrass world than play bass." That same year Kathy took part in the Grammy-winning tribute to Bill Monroe, *True Life Blues,* on which she sang two duets with Laurie Lewis.

Kathy's second solo album, *Call Me a Taxi* (Sugar Hill, 1996), found her heading back into bluegrass with a bang—and a banjo. She made a point of including Lynn Morris and Suzanne Thomas, female musicians who were not on the West Coast. The disc featured some of Kathy's finest songwriting yet. "Thoughts of Love and Home" includes these poignant lines about the consequences of war: "When the dreadful seeds were sown / The hardest work a man has known / Turning earth to bury those who did not live." And there is the enigmatic "True Happy Home": "It was a sad home to live in; it was true happy home." She balanced these thought-provoking numbers with her lighthearted tribute to the fifties, "Griddle in the Middle," and of course the title number.

With the release of *Taxi,* Kathy again needed a touring band, so she tapped Tom Bekeny, Amy Stenberg, and Avram Siegel, all alumni of the Good Ol' Persons. Kathy envisioned another democratic band and made numerous suggestions for a name that would reflect this ideal. The players, however, did not see it that way, and thus the Kathy Kallick Band was born over the protestations of its leader. "Even a benevolent dictatorship role doesn't feel right to me," she told *Bluegrass Unlimited.*

Unlike the Good Ol' Persons, the Kathy Kallick Band considered itself to be an honest-to-goodness bluegrass band. After all, they had Avram's Scruggs-style banjo and they were striving to replicate a traditional sound. The band released its first album, *Walkin' in My Shoes* (1998), on Kathy and Peter's own Live Oak label. When Sugar Hill had shown no interest in renewing Kathy's contract, a bluegrass friend had advised them that putting out your own record was easy and profitable. But as Peter said, "Of course, it turns out to be neither easy nor profitable. But Maddy was in pre-school full-time and I figured I could take it on." Kathy was tired of carefully orchestrated solos and eager to get back to the "roughed-up sound of bluegrass" that she had loved early on. She wanted that spontaneous "conversation" between instruments and players that she feared was being lost.

Living out in California makes Kathy a bit prickly about her band's bluegrass "credentials." As the liner notes to *Walking in My Shoes* state, "There is a tendency to think of West Coast bluegrass as softer, jazzier, and somehow 'other' than traditional. This can be the case but there is also a school of bluegrass in Northern California which has, from the beginning, been steeped in Monroe-based tradition—as well as welcoming to women and original songs."

On *Walkin' in My Shoes* Kathy takes on some even tougher political issues, including the domestic violence of the title track. She sets the stage innocently, using Bill Monroe's classic "You Won't Be Satisfied That Way" as a jumping-off point lyrically and melodically, by singing, "I could leave you any time I want to." But while Monroe's song quickly goes on to brag of sexual prowess ("When I'm gone no more to see you, you won't be satisfied that way"), Kathy slowly works up to the crux of her song, taking five verses to finally say, "Sometimes you're rough and you're mean / You wrecked my house and made me scream / You always say you're sorry for the things you do / But I'm the one who's walkin' in my shoes." True to real life, at the end of the song the woman does *not* leave. Not yet.

Kathy does not consider herself a political songwriter, preferring to think of herself as writing songs that "tell stories from a woman's point of view in a traditional bluegrass context." She refers to "Walkin' in My Shoes," "Burn Down the House," and "Call Me a Taxi" as songs about "women taking charge of their own destiny." Foremost she considers them story songs, songs that pack an "emotional wallop" rather than make a political statement. Nevertheless, more than a few of her story songs deal with issues some would consider both touchy and political.

Kathy's next two albums, *My Mother's Voice* (Copper Creek, 2001) and *Reason and Rhyme* (Copper Creek, 2003), were solo projects. The first of these featured songs Kathy had learned from the folksinging of her mother, Dodi, and the second showcased another collection of originals. Here Kathy thanks guitarist Nina Gerber, who plays on many cuts, for "dragging me kicking and screaming from the comfort of the bluegrass fold and allowing me to find my solo voice." Again Kathy tackles the subject of abuse, this time the sexual abuse of a little girl by her step-grandfather in "Take Care of Your Little Girls." Kathy tells the story simply, calmly, and explicitly, having the grandfather say, "This won't hurt a bit." In the last verse she takes the song in a healing and unexpected direction when she sings, "Now I've got a lover who's my own size / Got nice little hands that look a lot like mine." She also begs mothers to listen to and believe their little girls, because "There ain't a little girl who would lie that way."

Kathy is careful about where she performs sensitive songs of this nature, saying, "I only sing ["Take Care of Your Little Girls"] when I'm playing with Nina Gerber, as she helped invent the guitar part, and the audience that comes to see me and Nina is unusually responsive to gnarly content. Even at that, I have to be up for the response and interactions that the song generates. Suffice it to say, I never sing it at a bluegrass festival! Intense content has to be more subversive for that audience, like, say, 'Walkin' in My Shoes.'"

By 2005 it was back to bluegrass with the Kathy Kallick Band and *Warmer Kind of Blue* (Cooper Creek). Though the band was happy with the completion of the recording, they had been facing hard times having to do with illness and death among family members. In the aftermath Kathy felt they could not recover their musical groove. She decided to stop playing music. She started writing a novel. But she felt sad about leaving the music behind.

Then in March 2006 a blood vessel burst in Kathy's esophagus. Five days in intensive care gave her plenty of time to think. And she thought, "What's up with this not playing music anymore? Here I've been given this gift from a very early age. It's so ungrateful—now that I'm actually not going to die—to hand the gift back and say, 'No thank you, I don't think I'll have that anymore.'" She realized that she felt "compelled to play music in any way I can." But not with the Kathy Kallick Band. She faced the painful task of telling the musicians that she was not going to pursue booking any more gigs for the group. She did it like a woman, talking with each member individually and face-to-face.

She formed a short-lived group called Rustler's Moon, but it "crashed and burned," so she put together another version of the Kathy Kallick Band, this time an all-male ensemble with her old picking buddy Tom Bekeny. Their new CD is called *Between the Hollow and the High-Rise* (Live Oak, 2010). Kathy says, "I'm totally excited, and inspired. It's got me writing a slew of new songs, and playing just for fun. It's a good mix."

With the realization that music is her gift, Kathy is back on her musical path— her feminist bluegrass musical path.

> I live in a feminist household with a feminist husband, who seems to think my writing songs and playing music is important work and he wants to support it, and that enables me to do the little bit that I do. Now my youngest is a teen, and I'm gonna be a senior citizen by the time I'm totally unfettered. But I've still got plenty of time. Some of Bill Monroe's most powerful music was created when he was in his sixties and seventies. And powerful performances. And even as his voice started to slip, he was writing the most amazing tunes and playing with such feeling and passion. That's one of the beauties of the style of music we play. You're never too old to go out and play bluegrass.

I'm learning how to lose you
now and how to carry on.

—Claire and Larry Lynch,
"Some Morning Soon"

CLAIRE LYNCH

Claire Lynch (b. 1954) is articulate about the role of music in her life. "I live for the music," she says. "I burn for it in my soul." Yet for years this mother of two also felt "I can't let my soul go. I have to control it." Time and time again she has chosen family above music, only to find she can't keep the music out. Slowly it comes creeping back in—the jobs appear, the road beckons. So she ventures out, but inevitably commitment to family pulls her back. The classic bluegrass song that appears on her *New Day* album (2006) might have been written about Claire's career: "Up this hill and down, and up this hill again." Now she's definitely up this hill again and apparently free to go as far as she can. The music will not let her stay away.

Hearing Claire's slow, sweet drawl you might think she was Southern born and bred, but not so. The youngest of the three Lutke sisters, she first saw the light of day in Poughkeepsie, New York, and lived in Kingston until she was twelve, when her father's work with IBM took the family to Huntsville, Alabama.

Music was always a part of Claire's life. Her mother played piano, as did her grandmother, and her grandfather played fiddle and mandolin. As a child she sang trios in church with her sisters. When she was around twelve she began playing folk guitar. Religion was also an integral part of her life. "My parents were not just church-goers, but very serious about the scriptures and a personal relationship with God . . . I wouldn't call it a strict religion but more of a getting-to-know God kind of relationship." Today Claire's Christian faith is extremely important to her. Naturally she rebelled against all this religion when she was nineteen—just about the time she found bluegrass.

After graduating from high school in 1972, Claire opted for office work at an insurance company instead of college, although her parents offered to send her. She was doing well at her job but felt herself to be at a "crossroads." One day when her dad asked her what she wanted to do with her life, she says, "I started crying and blurted out that I wanted to work with music, even though I had no idea of how to go about it."

Enter Larry Lynch, a high school friend who was going to college at the University of Alabama in Tuscaloosa and playing in a band called Hickory Wind. In 1974 Claire went to one of his gigs and was "hooked." She and Larry started dating, and soon she found herself playing guitar and singing in the band. In the middle of her religious "backsliding," as she called it, bluegrass would be her outlet. She thought, "I can play this music and not feel guilty about it, because bluegrassers are so wholesome and they do incorporate gospel into it."

Soon the group decided to go full-time. Renaming themselves the Front Porch String Band, the young musicians abandoned college in service to the muse. They worked for three years as the house band at a club in Birmingham and then for six years as a full-time road band. Claire and Larry married in 1976. During this time they released three LPs: their debut *Smilin' at You* (Front Porch Records, 1977), *Country Rain* (Lanark, 1977), and the stunning *Front Porch String Band* (Leather, 1981), later reissued by Rebel.

From the beginning the band's sound was centered on Claire's strong, pure, sweet vocals. Yet Larry's mandolin playing, especially his woody chop, was an essential part of their "groove." Their orientation was progressive—they used electric bass and drums—and their nontraditional, often original, material was intricately arranged and featured unusual chord progressions. Traditional songs were pitched in Claire's key, with the men singing harmony below her.

Their first *Bluegrass Unlimited* review, for *Smilin' at You,* set the tone for those that would follow. Claire's voice was stealing the show. The magazine said, "The most outstanding feature of the band is the singing of Claire Lynch." The reviewer of *Country Rain* ended by referring to the band as "Lynch and company." Their third review pronounced Claire's voice as "the sound around which the Front Porch String Band has constructed this highly listenable [album]." Larry is not mentioned in any of these reviews.

Claire was six months pregnant with her first child, Kegan, when she and Larry decided to quit the road. It was an easy decision for her. Traveling together in one van while the guys smoked inside was miserable. But just before they "retired," Claire cut her first solo album, a country-flavored recording originally titled *Breakin' It* (Ambush, 1982; since rereleased as *Out in the Country* on Copper Creek, 2000). Larry played on just three cuts. Later Claire would write in the Copper Creek liner notes, "I sang all those vocals with morning sickness . . . this is proof that we somehow carry on, isn't it girls?" Claire would not record again for ten years. Though not in print long, this album proved to be a pivotal point in her career. Developing a "life of its own," the disc found its way into the hands of Nashville producer Tony Brown, who invited Claire to sing backup on projects by Patty Loveless, Skip Ewing, and other artists. Patty Loveless would go on to record some of Claire's songs, as would Kathy Mattea, and Claire herself would land a songwriting contract. These were huge breaks. But they were all in the future.

Meanwhile, in Hazel Green, Alabama, Larry went back to school and got a degree in accounting while Claire took a job as assistant to a department head at the University of Alabama in Huntsville. But when Kegan was six months old, the music started creeping back in. Claire and Larry began playing some dates with the Seldom Scene's John Starling, who was living in Alabama. Soon the Front Porch String Band had regrouped with Birmingham musicians Herb Trotman on banjo and Andy Meginniss on electric bass. When word leaked out that Claire and Larry were playing again, the band began getting invitations to appear out of state. By then, 1988, their second child, Christie, had arrived.

Playing festivals meant they needed product to sell, so they recorded *Lines and Traces* (Rebel, 1991), the first Front Porch String Band album in ten years. Reviewers picked up where they had left off a decade ago. The first sentence of the *Bluegrass Unlimited* review elevated Claire to the head of the band: "Are Claire Lynch and the Front Porch String Band back for good?" The second sentence hammered home the point: "Surely for the fans of this exceptional female vocalist, it has been too long between albums." Larry and his bouzouki did get a mention, but he was also referred to as "Claire's husband." Little did anyone realize that this would be the last Front Porch String Band album.

In 1993 Claire got an opportunity to do another solo project, this time for the gospel label Brentwood. *Friends for a Lifetime* included Larry on mandolin but also featured a host of Nashville bluegrass greats such as Alison Brown, Andrea Zonn, Sam Bush, and David Grier. *Bluegrass Unlimited* called it "absolutely the most exciting gospel collection of 1993." Claire was not entirely comfortable with the idea of a solo project. She realized she was the marketable one, but in 1995 she said, "It's not been easy to do . . . But as time goes on, you get used to it . . . It's not like I said, 'I want to be a star. The heck with you guys.' You still have all this guilt. I do, anyway."

With the Brentwood project to promote, Claire and Larry needed a group who could tour full-time. They said good-bye to Herb and Andy and put together a band that included Kenny Smith on guitar and Ronnie Simpkins on bass. By 1995 the lineup had solidified with Missy Raines on bass, Michael McLain on banjo, and Jim Hurst on guitar.

Friends for a Lifetime had a huge impact on Claire's career. The acclaim for the disc, which garnered Claire the first of fourteen nominations for IBMA Female Vocalist of the Year (through 2011), also landed her a contract with Rounder Records. Her label debut, *Moonlighter* (1995), received a Grammy nomination for Best Bluegrass Album. As with *Friends*, the roster of side musicians was deep and also included Larry.

Around 1995, on the strength of Claire's solo projects, the group began to be billed formally as Claire Lynch and the Front Porch String Band. For Claire and Larry this was not an easy transition. Claire acknowledged that they had had "major adjustments to make." But no matter what went on behind the scenes, in public Claire maintained that Larry was a "real gentleman about it."

Happy with the success of *Moonlighter,* Claire still "really, really" wanted her road band on her next album. She got her wish. *Silver and Gold* (1997), featuring her then current band of Larry, Missy, Jim, and Michael, was nominated for a Grammy and propelled her to her first IBMA Female Vocalist of the Year Award. Claire also received her first producing credit, sharing the job with Rich Adler. But in spite of the momentum her career was developing, she and Larry again decided to pull back. Publicly she called it "downsizing"; privately she said, "The kids need a life of their own."

Although touring infrequently, she recorded another album for Rounder, *Love Light* (2000), featuring Larry, Missy, and Jim and listing Claire as sole producer. But again Claire had to come off the road completely, in part due to a successful surgery on her back for a ruptured disc. But there was more. Claire's marriage was crumbling. As her solo career was skyrocketing, Larry was having to take a backseat, and he didn't like it. And who could blame him? When the Front Porch String Band started out, Larry was the experienced player and Claire was the novice. Now a star had been born, and he was in the background.

Believing that the music—her career—was the source of the trouble, Claire gave it up entirely for four years, thinking that would fix things. "I died musically," she says. "I didn't even write." Alas, the sacrifice was futile. Even though the music was gone, the problems remained. Claire now had a troubled marriage and no musical outlet. To earn a living she started a booking agency. "But I went broke, literally, doing that! It gave me a whole new respect for agents, though." For the next five years she would work in retail at a dancewear store.

Finally around 2004 Claire was offered a local gig—for big bucks. Since things didn't seem to be any better without the music, Claire decided she might as well play. She rounded up some nearby musicians and took the job. For the first time, she would be playing without Larry. This seemingly small step was a huge one for Claire. She began playing more local gigs and soon was getting offers that would mean going back on the road. She put together the Claire Lynch Band, calling again on Missy Raines and Jim Hurst and using David Harvey on mandolin. She says, "The Front Porch String Band was not ever my project. It was Larry's and mine. So when I formed the new band . . . I found myself responsible for all the decisions . . . It takes some getting used to, but I'm learning—and it feels pretty good."

In March 2006 she released, and produced, the appropriately titled *New Day*, using her new band along with stalwarts Alison Brown and Andrea Zonn. Her first album in six years, it was also the first that didn't include Larry. (They would officially separate in May 2006.) New responsibility also brought new freedom. "I was more willing to take chances this time out," she said. *New Day* put Claire back in the saddle again. The album features all the elements of a classic Claire Lynch production: strong songs with introspective lyrics and unusual chord progressions, her own originals and co-writes, thoughtful arrangements, and a splash of swing. All of these are in service to the polestar, Claire's voice, which has never been stronger or purer.

Even when Claire does not author the songs, she chooses material that seems to speak to her life. The first song on the album, "Be Ready to Sail," points to the new direction in her life with the words "when a good wind blows your way be ready to sail." If this song speaks to the future, "Love Will Find You Again" acknowledges the hardships of the past, with phrases such as "bird with a broken wing," "traveling your own trail of tears, "shattered dreams," and the last line, "it's hard to see through these tear-stained eyes how the pain could ever end." She closes the album with a song she wrote and dedicated to her mother, "I Believe in Forever," in which she professes her faith in a life hereafter. Still she is also singing about her new life here on earth: "I'm like a child with all my life before me, and each day I live is suddenly brand new."

Being back on the road required a constant influx of new product to sell, so after only a short interval Claire released *Crowd Favorites* (Rounder, 2007), with ten cuts from previous Rounder projects and four new cuts of old material. Then, only two years later, she brought out *Whatcha Gonna Do* (Rounder, 2009), an album of new material that featured her latest band lineup: Mark Schatz, Jason Thomas, and stalwart Jim Hurst. The new project earned her a second IBMA Female Vocalist of the Year Award in 2010 and landed her on the cover of *Bluegrass Unlimited*. Inside the magazine she talked about starting over: "It's just deciding what you need to do and then putting your nose to the grindstone and doing it. It's just a lot of work." Claire Lynch is willing to do that work. Because singing is her life.

I got certain doors opened because I
had a nice smile and I was cute.
I didn't see it as a bad thing.

—Lee Ann Lenker Baber

LEE ANN
LENKER
BABER

Although the seventies were beginning to break wide open for women in bluegrass, their roles as musicians were still often confined to all-female groups or bands that included family or partners. Banjo player Lee Lenker (1955–2008) was an exception. From 1976 until 1982 she played banjo in the Buffalo Chipkickers, an otherwise all-male band based in State College, Pennsylvania. None of these men were related to her, and before she joined the group she hadn't known any of them. In the annals of bluegrass music the Chipkickers are not well known, primarily because they played the college circuit rather than the bluegrass festivals. But, unlike many bands at the time, they were able to make a living playing music full-time.

Lee Ann Lenker was born in Harrisburg, Pennsylvania, the youngest of three sisters. Although her dad was a piano player with a band of his own and her mother sang jazz, Lee didn't encounter bluegrass until 1973 when she heard some male friends playing guitars and banjo with an occasional fiddle. As Lee told it, "I was totally fascinated with the banjo." To her the cheap five-string was "the most beautiful instrument I had ever seen. I was convinced that I would love to learn to play it and that I would be really good at it." Lee's friend loaned her the banjo and showed her how to play three songs. Soon she bought her own fifty-dollar banjo and began learning from *Earl Scruggs and the 5-String Banjo*. "All I did was play banjo every day from then on." She quickly became good and her parents loved it.

After graduating from high school in 1973, she earned an associate's degree from the local community college in 1975. There she began playing in a group called Wheatstraw (not to be confused with the Wheatstraw band from Dayton, Ohio, with Julie Gray Madru on banjo). Around this time she and her dad went to see the Buffalo Chipkickers, who were performing locally. While Lee was chatting with the band members, they asked her if she might be interested in interviewing for the job of banjo player if that came open. She said absolutely.

In the meantime she and her Wheatstraw buddies ventured down to a blue-grass festival in Union Grove, North Carolina, where she saw Susie Monick playing banjo on stage with the Buffalo Gals. An excited Lee thought, "I want to do this. This is totally normal for me to want to do this. This is what I want to be. I had the bug real, real bad. I was gonna be the best banjo player on earth."

Then while walking around the festival with her banjo, the self-described "very brazen" Lee struck up a conversation backstage with fiddle great Vassar Clements. Scheduled to go on next, Vassar had a band but not a banjo player. Without ever hearing her play, he asked Lee to sit in. Stunned, Lee agreed and then they were on. "I couldn't breathe. I couldn't do anything. I could barely play." Vassar even called on her for a banjo tune. Fortunately, she said, "I had learned one song all the way through." After the show, Vassar said, "Girl, now, I know you think you probably made mistakes and you did, but we worked it out, didn't we? Now, the reason I had you do that is you have good timing. You just keep on practicing." To the budding banjo player, Vassar was "a gigantic inspiration."

Lee was not oblivious to the fact that Vassar probably asked her to play be-cause she was a "cute little girl" with long blonde hair. She said, "I thought it was great to have that advantage. I got certain doors opened that wouldn't have been opened because I had a nice smile and I was cute. I felt like if I could get the door open I would legitimize it [with my playing]. So I thought it was okay. I didn't see it as a bad thing."

In 1976 the Buffalo Chipkickers found themselves in need of a banjo player and asked Lee to interview. The Chipkickers, who were founded by guitar player and agent Bob Doyle, were all recent graduates of Penn State University. They had played together during their college days, and the band had turned out to be so successful that they had kept at it. Unlike many bluegrass bands at the time, the Chipkickers ran the group like a business. They did two seasons of touring, fall and spring, playing predominantly colleges but also at fairs and amusement parks.

Lee, who got the job over two other male candidates, later found out that she had been chosen because she was "trainable." The band members wanted someone who was willing to learn rather than someone who was set in their ways. Part of this had to do with the fact that she was so young and had not played in a professional band before. And she was certainly enthusiastic. One can only wonder if they thought a young woman would be more "trainable" than a young man.

An article about the group at the time notes that the Chipkickers "emphasize showmanship . . . Their polished performances lead one to believe that every step, smile, turn, joke, and note have been carefully calculated and rigorously rehearsed." Lee says that in fact their shows were choreographed and that arrangements were worked out to the note, except for individual instrumental breaks. As Bob Doyle put it, "The Chipkickers' primary function is to put on a good show . . . we try to make it exciting and fun for [the audience]." Their repertoire included "Dixie," the Beatles' "I Saw Her Standing There," "Direwolf" (from the Grateful Dead), and an "Orange Blossom Special" finale.

Lee, who was paid a salary of $125 a week, was joining a tightly run, highly polished organization. In addition to playing and singing (Lee sang only harmony), each person had a designated job in the band. Lee was put in charge of public relations, doing the mailings, making copies, going to the post office—jobs that could easily be seen as "women's work." She moved to State College, got her own apartment, and began teaching banjo lessons as she had been doing in Carlisle. Two weeks later she played her first professional job.

Before Lee was hired, it was spelled out that she was expected to be "one of the guys." She would help carry equipment and would share a motel room with one of the men when they were on the road. The band's policy was to rotate roommates so that no one was paired with the same person every time. By talking about these arrangements up front, Lee and her parents "were assured that it would be fine for a twenty-year-old to be touring around the country with a bunch of men." And carrying equipment was no problem for Lee, a tennis player, track star, and gymnast, whose nickname was "Little Herc."

Lee's feelings about being the only female in the band were complicated. "I was scared to death," she said. She wasn't frightened about the sexual aspect, because she felt protected by the professionalism of the band. But having no brothers, she was simply not used to being around men. She didn't know how to communicate or interact with them. "I got in the van and I would just sit there. I wouldn't say anything. I would look out the window." Or she would read a book. Eventually the guys started to tease her about "zoning out" and helped her learn how to get along with them. She became, as they had stipulated, one of them—except in the area of clothing. Lee almost always wore a dress on stage. "I thought you should dress way up for performing. On stage and on tour, I always dressed like a girl." After playing with the Chipkickers, however, she finally got tired of men staring at her legs all the time. "So I started dressing like a guy. I felt like I was getting letched on too much."

Whether it was because she was a girl or because she was a new player, Lee was driven. "My goal was to play a perfect show. When I wasn't able to play my arrangement without a hitch, I came off stage feeling like an absolute jerk. Because the boys did their part and I messed up a note. And I thought everybody in the audience knew." She suffered from stage fright and felt as if she would lose "thirty-five to forty percent" of her playing ability "just walking in front of a crowd." She noted, "Years later people pointed out that because I was a girl I had to be better and that's why I had to be more critical of myself. Because I was going to be criticized more. And that's when it [being a girl] started to make a difference."

Playing with the band was exciting, but jam sessions were something else. "The men banjo players wouldn't even look at me. Wouldn't talk to me. Breaks, no way. I mean I was not even there. I was invisible. And I thought it was my playing, I thought, oh boy, do I need to practice. Growing up in a family full of women that were taught they could do anything and be anything, I had no clue that it was because I was a woman playing a banjo and that was so threatening."

In 1977 Lee became an official endorser for Stelling banjos. Geoff Stelling built her a special banjo with a smaller neck to accommodate her smaller hands. The ad on the back cover of the June 1979 *Banjo NewsLetter* pictures a seated, smiling Lee, looking down at the fingerboard of her banjo, her long hair loose about her face.

The band made two recordings while Lee was with them: *Cleaning Up Our Act* (Chedda, 1976), an album of mostly original songs, and a four-song EP. Lee had been playing banjo for only three years when the album was recorded, but she is already solid in the Scruggs style, staying mostly in the first position, with an occasional melodic riff thrown in. She has a strong right hand, good timing, but doesn't yet play much subtle up-the-neck backup.

In 1981 two members left the group and Lee took over the band, with Bob Doyle still serving as agent. Lee hired replacements, but this was not a happy time for her, as she fought with some of the new players for not being professional enough. "I got very angry with them and they got very angry with me for being angry. I wanted the band to be at the level that it had been with these other guys and I expected that when I hired them." The band did not survive long with Lee at the helm. "There were just too many things I didn't know. I hadn't had the business experience. I really didn't know how to run it successfully." Looking back on that experience, Lee acknowledged that being a woman could have been a big part of the problem, something that she didn't realize at the time. "I always took it personally, thinking I wasn't good at something."

In 1982 Lee moved to Baltimore to attend the University of Maryland, Baltimore County. She received her BA in interdisciplinary studies in January 1985. She had designed her own degree with a focus on audio engineering and the business of music. "I wanted to know everything I'd messed up on. I took all the stuff I could that would make me a good business woman." While there she worked in the campus recording studio as engineer, editor, and producer, as well as banjo player when needed.

One of Lee's more interesting musical experiences while in Baltimore was working as banjo player for Buzz Busby and the Bayou Boys. Buzz, a mandolin player, was one of the pioneers of bluegrass in the Washington-Baltimore area in the 1950s. As a Bayou Boy, Lee stuffed her long hair under a ball cap and wore "boy clothes." With her slim build and her hard-driving banjo playing—a trait stereotypically associated with males—she no doubt easily passed as a boy.

Lee spoke with candor about her own competitiveness. From jam sessions in which she thought male players were trying to "step on" or intimidate female pickers, she learned to "go in and floor everybody." She couldn't "wait to get into a situation to do this. When somebody's being 'I'm so cool and I'm so good' and I walk in there, I just make a point to outplay, outfast, outloud them, and it doesn't matter what they do, I do more." Lee also admitted that she had as much trouble with women as with men. "Men were mad at me because I would play well, and the women were mad at me because I was playing with the men."

In 1986 Lee moved to the Shenandoah Valley of Virginia, where she started her own recording company, Blue Ridge Recording, and taught music and art at an elementary school. She also played in a number of bluegrass groups, including the short-lived, all-female Valley Dolls (with Karen Spence, Susan Spence, and Murphy Henry). In 1995 she married Calvin Baber, a Dobro player, who joined her in the local group Cross Creek. In 2008 Lee was diagnosed with lung cancer. She died on July 31, 2008, at the age of fifty-two and was laid to rest in her favorite attire: blue jeans and a bluegrass T-shirt.

I posted a mention of her passing on the IBMA Listserv and received several responses offline. Larry Carlin wrote, "I am deeply saddened by this news. While I did not know Lee personally, I used to watch her play back in my college days at Penn State, and seeing that band was a huge inspiration to me. So much so that here I am more than thirty years later still playing and writing about bluegrass. In a way Lee was responsible for all of this."

LEADERS OF THE BAND: *The 1980s*

As the 1980s rolled around, a number of women who had begun playing in the seventies were beginning to change the face of bluegrass by assuming the leadership role in their own bands. Although there had been a few other female bandleaders in the past, the time was apparently right for this new trend to take hold. The big three were Laurie Lewis, who put her name out front with Grant Street in 1986; Lynn Morris, who started her own band in 1988; and Kathy Kallick, who had been the de facto leader of the Good Ol' Persons since the early eighties. But there were others, too, like Kate Mac-Kenzie, who was the lead singer with Minnesota's Stoney Lonesome for fifteen years before striking out on her own in 1995. Her bluesy vocals and two solo albums made quite a splash in the bluegrass world until she retired in 1999.

Thus the way had been partly paved when the young Alison Krauss signed with Rounder Records in 1986 and became the head of Union Station in 1989. Her visibility and breathtaking success encouraged other young women not only to take up the fiddle (and other lead instruments) but also to entertain the notion of heading up their own groups. That concept could now be a part of a young girl's dream as mandolin prodigy Sierra Hull would prove in 2008.

The idea of women as side musicians in non-family bands, however, was slow to take hold. Bass player Missy Raines would be one of the first to make a breakthrough, joining Cloud Valley in 1981 and moving through a number of bands until she formed her own group in 2006. Alison Brown also had a high-profile gig playing banjo for three years (1989–1992) with Alison Krauss and Union Station. Cindy Cashdollar (Dobro) and Caroline Dutton (fiddle) both played in the John Herald Band in the early eighties. In an article about the group, a *Bluegrass Unlimited* writer commented, "With the unusual presence of two competent and attractive women performers . . . festival audiences have been enthusiastic." One wonders exactly what the writer thought "unusual": their very presence, their competence, or their attractiveness. Or was it the shocking idea that two attractive women could also be musically competent?

Positions for female side musicians were so rare during this decade that "all-girl" bands played a significant role in providing jobs and stage time for talented women who did not want to lead their own groups. The eighties were prime years for the New Coon Creek Girls, Sidesaddle, the Wildwood Girls, Petticoat Junction, Dixie Reign, Sassygrass, and the Chalker Sisters.

Playing with family members, as always, continued to provide musical opportunities for many women. One of the family groups with staying power proved to be the Isaacs—Joe, Lily, and children Sonya, Becky, and Ben—who became a full-time touring band in 1986. They would begin to hit their stride nationally in 1998 (the year Joe and Lily would separate), showcasing a more contemporary Southern gospel sound on Bill Gaither's *Homecoming* videos. They joined the Gaither tour in 2003. The next year Sonya, who plays a strong lead mandolin, began a run of seven (so far) nominations for IBMA Female Vocalist of the Year. In 2001 *Bluegrass Unlimited* would say, "The Isaacs have unquestionably been one of the most influential bluegrass family gospel groups over the past decade."

And wife-and-husband teams were still going strong. Some of the more prominent long-lived ones were in New England. Peggy Ann and Paul Harvey (fiddle and guitar) founded Connecticut's Traver Hollow in 1980. The group stayed together for well over twenty years and recorded a number of albums. Massachusetts-based Southern Rail, with Sharon Horowitz on bass and husband Jim Muller on guitar, formed in 1979 and celebrated their thirty-year anniversary in 2009. When Hazel and Mac McGee (guitar) started White Mountain Bluegrass in New Hampshire in 1970, Hazel was singing but filling in on bass only occasionally. She took up the instrument full-time around 1982. When the band embarked on its seventh European tour, in 2009, it had recorded a total of ten albums. Over in Kentucky, Ada (guitar) and Jim McCown (banjo) formed the Outdoor Plumbing Company, which lasted from 1972 until 2002, when it morphed into primarily old-time music, with Ada and Jim still at the helm. In the seventies the group recorded three albums, two on the Rebel label.

Instrumentally, the second wave of female banjo players was rolling in. At age twelve banjo player Gena Britt recorded her first album, *Bluegrass in the Sunrise* (1984). She would go on to play with Petticoat Junction, New Vintage, Lou Reid and Carolina, and finally form the Gena Britt Band in 2001. Gena was part of a new generation of female banjo players that would grow to include Robin Roller, Beth Stevens, Ramona Church Taylor, Julie Elkins, Janet Beazley, Donica Christianson, Marcie Malicote (Newhart), Dana Shankman, Trina Emig, Casey Henry, Kristin Scott Benson, and Cia Cherryholmes. In short, things were looking up for women in bluegrass, but we still had a long way to go.

I felt a certain simpatico with the Buffalo Gals.
Some of them didn't even wear bras!
I thought they were very brave.

—Missy Raines

MISSY RAINES

Even as a child in Short Gap, West Virginia, Melissa Kay "Missy" Raines (b. 1962) wanted to be a bluegrass musician. By following her heart, she has carved out a successful career for herself. Seven times her peers have voted her IBMA Bass Player of the Year.

Her memories of seeing the Buffalo Gals set the tone for her life's story:

Most of my early role models were men, and as a very young girl, I spent hours in front of the living room mirror with my guitar, singing into a dust mop and pretending to be Mac Wiseman. While I had been completely inspired and touched by the women (girls) I saw on stage like Cheryl and Sharon White and Ruth McLain, by the time I first saw the Buffalo Gals I was a young teenager and starting to broaden my musical tastes a bit and knew I liked things that were on the edge. They were bold and fearless with their music, their roots, and their feminism. It was like a shot of adrenaline. For the first time, I could see myself on stage through them. I could relate to them in a way I couldn't with any other performer at the time. Even as a kid, I knew I couldn't ever wear the very common "outfits" many groups were wearing then. I liked the individual look. And as much as I loved the traditional sound, I was starving for the more contemporary stuff. They did music from the Andrews Sisters and the Beatles!

Missy's love affair with bluegrass began early. She remembers going to festivals at age five. She says, "I never thought of it as 'starting' anything. Bluegrass was all I ever knew. My parents took me to festival after festival and I got bit by the bug. Instead of wishing I was somewhere else, I planned my life around them."

Missy began playing guitar at age ten with a local family group, the Bluegrass Neighbors, which included two other females. Two years later when she moved to the bass, she knew she had found her instrument. Her second group, Hooker Holler Symphony, included Diana Haines on banjo and originally Diana's then-husband, Jack, on bass. Diana, who later married Ben Eldridge, banjo player with the Seldom Scene, was a decade older than Missy and a "huge influence." "She was gorgeous," Missy says, "and one of the classiest women I have ever known, in the sense that she is graceful in any setting. She could be in a gown and a tiara, but she was also equally as comfortable in her jeans and combat boots and banjo. She was very kind and supportive."

Hooker Holler was headed by Pat Shields, the artist-in-residence for Missy's school, who was very interested in Missy's development both as a bass player and as a person. Before Missy officially joined the group, he was letting her sit in on bass, and when Jack and Diana split, the thirteen-year-old became the bass player.

> I went out every weekend. And many times Pat drove all night back from a gig so I could go to school or do something with my family the next day. He was amazing. He also did a few things that, at the time, were hard to deal with. Like he was worried about me getting a big head. Because I was like the *whiz kid*. I was going around and playing all these festivals, and every time I would come out and play in these jam sessions I clearly was always the belle of the ball. I was a girl and I was playing. He talked to me a lot and tried to keep my head straight.

Missy would stay with Hooker Holler for three years.

Pat also introduced Missy to jazz, bringing in a jazz pianist to the school and making sure Missy was there to watch the bass player. When she was around fourteen, he brought in the Falls City Ramblers, with Beck Gentry on mandolin.

The teenager was excited that her friends would get to see the kind of music she was doing but said, "My schoolmates could not get past Beck Gentry wearing combat boots with a skirt. She was just a little too gritty. I actually got angry with my schoolmates because they were real rude to them, and kind of booed them, and didn't pay attention. Until they got *me* up to play 'Sweet Georgia Brown' with them. And they *loved* that. I was surprised at how much they loved it. They cheered and thought it was really cool."

Missy's next band was the Washington, D.C.–based Stars and Bars, in which she was the only female. They had a regular Thursday-night restaurant gig and worked almost every weekend in the D.C. area, often performing at congressional parties. They recorded one EP.

When Missy graduated from high school in 1980, she knew she wanted to continue to play music. She played with an all-male band in Cleveland for a month or so, but that didn't work out, so she headed to Winston-Salem, North Carolina, for a short stint with the all-female Cherokee Rose. Cherokee Rose had been started by Frances Mundy (Mooney) and Connie Freeman (Morris), but at the time included Louisa Branscomb on guitar, Sally Wingate on banjo, Mindy Johnson (Rakestraw) on bass, and Tyra Dean Somers on Dobro. Louisa was leaving, so when Missy arrived, Mindy moved to guitar. Again things didn't gel, and after a few gigs Missy left. But before hitting the road she got in touch with Bill Evans in Charlottesville, Virginia. Missy said, "Bill had been trying to get me in Cloud Valley for a couple of years. I had sort of kept him at arm's length because I thought that what they were doing was really cool, but I thought they'd never make any money! I called him, and said, 'Is that job still available?' And he said, 'Yeah.' I said, 'Great, I'd like to come tomorrow,' so I did."

Cloud Valley, with whom Missy played from 1981 to 1985, was a young, progressive band whose members were all firmly rooted in traditional bluegrass. Missy joined Bill on banjo, Steve Smith on mandolin, and Charlie Rancke on guitar. The quartet considered themselves an ensemble rather than three side musicians with a leader. Everyone would be featured. The addition of a young woman to the band posed no gender problems for the guys or for Missy. Bill had already worked in two local Virginia groups of mixed gender. One had a woman on bass and the other a woman on guitar. As he put it, "Neither Charlie or myself came from a bluegrass culture that would have made this a charged issue. And in the Charlottesville area, while there were not many female bluegrass musicians, there were lots of female old-time musicians and singer-songwriters." Missy, who had a steady boyfriend at the time, was never personally involved with any band members. Her presence in Cloud Valley was an indication that gender barriers were dropping in some of the newer bands.

The sleeping arrangements that come with travel are often mentioned as a problem with a mixed-gender band, but to Cloud Valley these were not a concern. When they were on the road, Missy roomed with either Bill or Charlie. They usually had separate beds, although if Missy occasionally had to share a bed it was no big deal to anybody, since all they did was sleep. Bill says, "I really viewed Missy as a younger sister—someone who I was responsible for and never viewed her in any other way. We also had much contact with her parents through these years—we were all like extended family." Missy says:

> Being in Cloud Valley was the best thing that ever happened to me. It felt like I'd finally gotten in with a bunch of people who were professional about what they were doing. They never hit on me. None of them. I think it had to do with the kind of people that they were. They were the kind of people who just didn't do that. Maybe if I had made implications that I wanted something like that, maybe they would have. But I wasn't there for that, they weren't there for that, so it was the most comfortable band I've ever been in. And we shared rooms together. And beds together. I look back now and I can't believe it. But it's true. I never felt weird about it at all. It felt cool because we were traveling musicians.

Missy's problems came from another direction.

> Now, I had a hard time in that band for other reasons because of maturity. I didn't want to practice. Bill and I were at each other's throats a lot of the time because he was pushing me, and he was trying to make a band, and I didn't want to be pushed. I didn't have a lot of discipline, and I didn't know what being in a full-time band really meant until I was with them. We spent an enormous amount of time together. It was hard. We bickered, and people got on each other's nerves. But yet we were still trying to make it happen.

Cloud Valley's first album, *A Bluegrass Ensemble* (Outlet Recordings, 1983), received a long and decidedly mixed review from *Bluegrass Unlimited*. In the liner notes Tony Trischka had called the band's sound "orchestral, new age string band music" with a "dazzling kaleidoscope of textures." The reviewer responded sarcastically by saying, "New age kaleidoscopers who are into experimental acoustic music which has surgically removed all traces of country or hillbilly from bluegrass will be dazzled by this album's textures." He did allow that the band was "smooth, inventive, and highly proficient instrumentally." Interestingly, none of the musicians were singled out for comments. Their second album, *Live in Europe* (Strictly Country, 1985), got a shorter, more positive review, in which Missy was called "the band's female bass player" and her singing was applauded. The gender of the other players was not noted. On the song "Haunted Kind," which starts with a bass solo, listeners were treated to Missy's fat-toned, jazz-inflected, creative bass stylings, which would become her trademark. Banjo player Alison Brown called *Live in Europe* "one of my favorites."

Along with debuting a new album in 1983, Missy also began dating Ben Surrat, whom she would marry in 1987. Ben would go on to establish his own recording studio, the Rec Room, in Nashville. He would co-produce and record Missy's solo CD and the debut album from her own group, the New Hip. As Missy says, "Personally, we've been blessed with the 'soul mate' thing. Artistically, we are just enough different with our sensibilities that we offer great perspective to each other. This band [New Hip] is a joint effort in every respect. Even though it's my name out there, he is part of the core of everything we do."

Cloud Valley broke up in the fall of 1985 when marriage beckoned both Steve and Charlie. As Bill says, "The idea of replacing two key members was a bit much for both Missy and me. Trying to find work for an overtly progressive band based out of Virginia wasn't the easiest thing in the world to do, now or then."

Missy was out of a job. But not for long. Eddie Adcock called her to play bass in his and Martha's new bluegrass group, Talk of the Town. Missy says, "The only reason that he called me was because his mother told him to." Mrs. Adcock had seen Missy at many Cloud Valley shows and really liked her. When Eddie called, "It was a *big deal,* because he was this huge person to me." Missy suggested Susie Gott for the fiddle slot, and the band solidified in 1986 with three women and Eddie. In January 1987 they made the cover of *Bluegrass Unlimited*. According to the article, Talk of the Town was "not a leader and his underlings, but a partnership." Still this is not the impression their first self-titled album (CMH, 1987) gives. By then the group had already become Eddie Adcock and Talk of the Town, and on the album Eddie does most of the lead singing and lead playing. Missy said:

> Eddie tried very, very hard not to be the big leader, but the bottom line is musically he's got so much going on that he cannot not be a part of that. It was never mistaken in my mind that I was working for him and it was his band and his name. He tried very hard to listen to what we said but at the bottom things were gonna be his decision. Martha had a lot of input. If she brought in a song, he would do whatever she wanted on that song. Musically I felt like he gave Martha full run.

The long months on the road with Eddie's band gave bluegrass audiences across the country a chance to hear Missy. This exposure landed her on the cover of the new magazine *Bluegrass Now* in 1992, where she was declared "The 'First Lady' of Acoustic Bass."

Susie left after the band's debut album and from then on the group played as a trio. They recorded one more project as Eddie Adcock and Talk of the Town, *The Acoustic Collection* (CMH, 1988), a two-disc set of standards, and then, as *Bluegrass Unlimited* put it, they "complied with truth-in-advertising" and, following a trend in bluegrass, became the Eddie Adcock Band.

During Missy's time with Eddie, the whole band participated in playing with a group of pioneering (male) musicians called The Masters. The six musicians recorded three CDs, one of which, *The Masters*, was named IBMA Instrumental Album of the Year in 1990. Missy recorded one more album with the Eddie Adcock Band, *Dixie Fried* (CMH, 1991), before leaving the group in 1993, although she would continue to play bass on some of their recordings. Of her experience playing with Eddie and Martha, Missy says, "[Eddie] really believed in me. In terms of trying to improvise, he always made me feel like an equal. It was overwhelming at times, but now when I look back I can see he gave me the platform to grow on."

Never without a job for long, Missy joined the Brother Boys in July 1994 for a short ride that she termed "flat-out one of the best times of my life." She was back to being the only female in the group. The Brother Boys were not a bluegrass band but played acoustic music that was an amalgamation of genres. They called their music "new hillbilly." Of this experience, Missy says:

> Musically it opened my heart and my mind up like never before. There's no doubt in my mind I was meant to play with them and get to know Ed Snodderly and Eugene Wolf. Their approach to music is very different. Just the idea that tonight we're gonna play this song this way but tomorrow night we might start it with this kind of a beat. It was so different from anything I've ever done. When I first started doing it, I didn't like it, because I thought, What am I supposed to do? When do I come in? And Ed would just look at me and go, Just come in when you *feel* it. And I'd be like but I don't know how to do that! But at the same time I was drawn to it. I did want to know how to do it but it was uncomfortable, I was out of my comfort zone. But going through that made me realize this is really cool.
>
> That was right after my brother died [1994], and it was a highly emotional time for me. I needed to be with people who were different. I was feeling very alienated from everyone at that time, because Rick was a gay man who died of AIDS. And

I'm a bluegrass bass player in a world where people don't talk about that. I felt like I couldn't talk about it, and all I wanted to do was talk about it. It was just horrible.

Then I met Ed and Eugene, and it was like I was going into this world where if you're different it's just fine and diversity rules. That spilled over into personalities, and I felt like I could just be me and I didn't have to mince words. So it was really nice.

Missy made one CD with the band, *Presley's Grocery* (Sugar Hill, 1996), but Claire Lynch, who was starting to make her presence felt nationally, wanted her for the Front Porch String Band. Missy had filled in with the group on a few Opry gigs, and Claire liked her playing. "She started putting the heat on me big time. She went after me," Missy said. Claire offered a "very sweet deal."

And she was making really good money. And I was looking at this wonderful hippie band that might make a hundred bucks apiece. It wasn't really a contest, but I'm very loyal. I felt like I should stay because I said I would and I wanted to, but I also knew I wanted to make a living, and I certainly liked Claire's music. She was equally creative. And she had so much work and she was on fire, and I had to call Ed and say I just gotta be in this band. The problem was, we'd just made a record and I had actually called Ed while he was sitting in Barry Poss's office trying to get my face on the cover of their CD. It was not good. But Ed forgave me for that and it worked out. So I did the right thing and he knew that, but it was hard.

Perhaps it was her increased visibility with a hot new group, or perhaps it was an overdue reward for long years of toil in the trenches. Whatever the reason, Missy was named IBMA Bass Player of the Year in 1998. At the time she was only the second woman to win an instrumental award in the eight years the awards had been given. That same month, October, Missy released her first solo project, *My Place in the Sun,* on her own label. The mostly instrumental album included swing, jazz, blues, and bluegrass. The *Chicago Tribune* named it one of the Top Five Bluegrass Albums of the Year, and it was nominated for IBMA Instrumental Album of the Year in 1999.

By the mid-nineties Claire Lynch had one of the hottest bands on the circuit. But with two young children at home, she made the gut-wrenching decision to come off the road, and Missy had to find another job. Jim Hurst, the guitar player for the band, was also in the same boat. "So we started thinking how cool it would be to have a duo because then there would be all this musical openness and space and you could do whatever you wanted to do." They decided to go for it, and thus the team of Missy Raines and Jim Hurst (sometimes Jim Hurst and Missy Raines) was born.

Musically it worked. But would people in bluegrass buy a duo? That was the question. And for Missy there was another aspect to consider. "I'd always been in the back and in a supportive role and now I had to step in the front." She knew she would have to sing more and would have to talk to the audience between songs. "And that terrified me." In fact, the whole thing terrified her. She and Jim did not undertake this challenge lightly. Missy said, "We talked more than we played in the first year about what we were gonna do and about what was to be expected and where we saw ourselves."

Then she took the bit between her teeth and began calling people she knew, looking for bookings. Based on her reputation, many of them gave her a shot. Missy and Jim showcased at the IBMA World of Bluegrass in 1999 and, as she said, "It just snowballed." Jim was named IBMA Guitar Player of the Year in 2001 and 2002. And Missy continued to rack up Bass Player of the Year Awards. The duo signed with Pinecastle Records in 2000 and released two CDs: *Two* (2000) and *Synergy* (2003). Both feature only the guitar, bass, and two voices. Each disc received glowing reviews in *Bluegrass Unlimited*, where two different reviewers essentially say that the listener never feels as if anything is missing. Missy's bass work is described as "astonishingly rich, deep, rhythmically impeccable, and melodically amazing." Traveling together as a male-female duo perhaps didn't raise as many eyebrows as in the past, and Missy says she didn't think about it and didn't care, but still, on stage both musicians made a point of mentioning their long-term spouses often by dedicating songs to them.

In 2003 Missy and Jim revised their original plans to include more time for working with their individual bands in 2005. At that time Missy did not even have her own band. However, she had wanted her own group since her days with Cloud Valley, although she knew for a long time that she was not ready. Her fires were fueled when she saw Laurie Lewis showcase at IBMA World of Bluegrass in 1989. Missy said, "That was the only show I saw that came close to what I knew I wanted to do someday." Laurie's 1989 CD, *Love Chooses You*, and the title number fanned the flames. Missy saw the song as "contemporary and good but not country." And not bluegrass, either. Seeing Laurie "going after something on her own that wasn't straight-ahead bluegrass" inspired Missy. "I thought if they are accepting her doing this, then maybe they would accept me doing something equally different." Missy also was "in awe of Lynn Morris's bravery and courage" in starting her own band from scratch. Now, finally, the time felt right.

Getting her new act together took longer than Missy thought, but she showcased Missy Raines and the New Hip at IBMA's World of Bluegrass in 2006. The name referenced Missy's own hip replacement surgery a few years earlier. The group released its self-titled, five-song EP in 2008 and found itself booked on some of the larger bluegrass festivals such as the Grey Fox in New York, the Strawberry Music Festival in California, and Wintergrass in Tacoma, Washington. The young lineup featured Megan McCormick on lead guitar, Mike Witcher on resonator guitar, Ethan Ballinger on mandolin, and Lee Holland on drums. In November 2008 the group signed with Compass Records, releasing their debut CD, *Inside Out*, in early 2009. By the time the album hit the streets, Megan had left to pursue her own musical interests, but she plays and sings on several cuts and co-wrote the title track with Missy.

The year 2010 found Missy and the band writing material for their next Compass recording and performing it live "to see what works and what doesn't." One thing Missy is excited about is the addition of an improv number to their set every night.

> Which means one of us starts an idea, a riff, or a rhythm, completely unrehearsed, and everyone joins in, building on the ideas, listening and playing off of each other. It's a rush of excitement every time for me. It's a feeling of being very much in the moment, of being very alive and very vulnerable at the same time. You're putting yourself out there and it might work or it might not. It makes you really listen to what's going on around you. It's also a bit like the "trust" exercise I've heard of where a person falls back into the arms of the person behind them, trusting they are there. Only you're not just trusting those around you, you have to trust yourself too. I like to think there's this great metaphorical river of music always floating by and all we want as musicians is to be able to jump in, not drown, and let it take us somewhere. Every now and then, if we're lucky and we get out of our own way, it does.

> When my parents told me, "Alison, when
> you grow up you can be anything you want
> to be," I'm pretty sure that banjo picker
> wasn't what they had in mind.
>
> —Alison Brown

ALISON BROWN

Maybe Alison's parents wouldn't have minded so much if they had known that their daughter would be named Banjo Player of the Year by the International Bluegrass Music Association in 1991, the first woman to win that award. And maybe they would have breathed easier if they had known that their daughter would go on to found Compass Records, finding a way to use that MBA from UCLA. In short, Alison has done all right as a banjo player. She is also a Harvard graduate with a BA in history and literature, a former investment banker, and a mother of two. She played banjo and lead guitar for Alison Krauss and Union Station for three years, was the bandleader for folk rocker Michelle Shocked for a year, and is one of only three women included in the book *Masters of the 5-String Banjo*. She has released four solo albums on Vanguard and six on her own Compass label and has been called the "female Béla Fleck." In 2001 she took home the Grammy for Best Country Instrumental Performance for her original tune "Leaving Cottondale." She currently leads her own band, the Alison Brown Quartet, backed by keyboards, drums, and her husband, Garry West, on electric bass. The group focuses on her original music, which contains flavors of jazz, new age, bebop, samba, calypso, Latin, classical, folk, world music, and, yes, bluegrass. She's known as a jazz-grasser in bluegrass circles and a bluegrass player in jazz circles.

What elements came together in Alison's life to lead her down these unusual paths? The oldest of two daughters, Alison (b. 1962) lived in Connecticut until she was eleven. Her father was a lawyer, and her mother was a stay-at-home mom who went back to get her law degree when Alison was ten. By then, Alison says, "She was bored out of her mind. But that's what women did. You stayed home and raised your kids." Her mother's quest for her own career would prove to be a powerful role model for a young girl.

Alison was already learning to play guitar when her teacher brought in the Flatt and Scruggs *Foggy Mountain Banjo* album, an early bible of banjo instrumentals. As Alison said, "The music reached out and tapped me on the shoulder and I've been hooked ever since." Her parents made her continue with guitar for a year before starting banjo lessons. In what would later prove to be a most serendipitous occurrence, the first banjo player Alison saw perform on stage, on her tenth birthday, was a woman—Louisa Branscomb of Boot Hill. "I guess that could explain a lot," says Alison dryly.

Even though Alison's parents cheerfully provided their daughter with lessons, they discouraged her from pursuing music full-time. Music was something you did on the side, something you could talk about at cocktail parties to make you seem more interesting. "My parents created a picture of how I would end up if I did music for a living: a sagging forty-year-old playing 'Rocky Top' at a pizza palace to a ten-person crowd that wanted to hear the jukebox."

Alison had been taking banjo lessons for only a year when her family moved to San Diego. Fortunately Southern California had an active bluegrass scene, which included the Dillards; Berline, Crary, and Hickman; Pat Cloud; Craig Smith; Larry McNeely; and Lauren Seapy, the female banjo player with Lost Highway. As Alison says, "So there was already some kind of role model for me way back then. I don't think I ever thought about it much, but there was another girl playing banjo, so how weird could it be?" There was also the San Diego Bluegrass Club, where she met ten-year-old Stuart Duncan, now eight-time IBMA Fiddle Player of the Year. As Alison said about Stuart, "The two of us forged a musical partnership born out of our mutual love for *Star Trek*, Chef Boyardee lasagna (in a can, of course), and the whole spectrum of bluegrass music from the Stanley Brothers to Andy Statman."

Alison spent the summer of 1977 playing at an amusement park in Los Angeles with Gold Rush, her first real band, with Stuart and banjo whiz John Hickman. Alison played Dobro, learning on the job. The next summer, with Stuart's dad at the wheel, she and Stuart traveled across the country hitting bluegrass festivals as far east as Kentucky and on up into Canada. During her last year of high school she played with a band called High Windows.

Before Alison headed back east for college, she and Stuart recorded an instrumental album called *Pre-Sequel* (Ridge Runner, 1981). Along with standard bluegrass fare, it included originals with clever teenage titles such as "The Great Lasagna Rebellion" and "Bionic Marshmallow." The *Bluegrass Unlimited* reviewer, "suspicious of albums by highly touted teenagers," acknowledged that this one succeeded because Alison and Stuart had a "keen sense of music" and were so good at what they did. He did mention their tendency to "put in all the licks every time when it isn't necessary." Alison's gender was not mentioned. The back of the album included a picture of Stuart dressed as a girl. During their teen years Alison and Stuart, who had the same androgynous hairstyle, were often mistaken for twin brothers or twin sisters. So at a California festival they swapped clothes—Stewart in a dress, Alison in jeans—then went on stage to see if anyone would notice. As the set went on, the audience gradually figured it out, but a lot of folks left the festival thinking Alison played the fiddle!

In the fall of 1980 Alison entered Harvard. She had chosen Harvard over Yale by pulling out her copy of *Bluegrass Unlimited* and comparing the number of bluegrass concerts around Boston to those around New Haven. Boston won. While she was there she co-hosted a weekly radio show called *Living Traditions in Bluegrass*. As the daughter of lawyers, Alison had always taken it for granted that she would go into a profession. So, knowing her parents wanted her to be a doctor, for her first two years she was premed.

At the start of her second year, she joined Boston-based Northern Lights, an all-male group, which was reorganizing, staying until she graduated in June 1984. She recorded one album with the band, *Before the Fire Comes Down* (Revonah, 1983), to which she contributed two original instrumentals. In the *Bluegrass Unlimited* review it was her banjo playing that received the most attention. The reviewer noted her "flawless technique, a fertile imagination, and the taste to keep her talent under control." Again her gender was not mentioned.

Before joining Northern Lights, however, Alison had decided that "it would be great to play banjo with Bill Monroe for the summer." Being a woman of action, she called Bill to ask if she could audition for him. One can only wonder, as Alison did later, what was she thinking? Bill told her she could meet him at Constitution Hall in Washington, D.C., where the band had a gig. Alison spent the evening hanging out with the seventy-year-old patriarch backstage and being introduced to people, but she didn't get to audition. To the cynical eye, these introductions carry more than a faint hint of braggadocio, but to Alison it was all "very innocent." After the show Monroe invited her back to his motel room to audition. The ingenuous Alison, not yet twenty, reasoned that this was okay. "It's Bill Monroe, after all. The Father of Bluegrass Music." She goes on to say, "You deify somebody like that and you tend to not even think of them as human." Once in the hotel room it was clear that Bill would have liked her to stay "for reasons other than auditioning." She did, however, get to play "Sally Goodwin." He told her she played too loud. "But I think any banjo would be too loud at two o'clock in the morning in a hotel room. But he was probably also right." Alison gave him the Harvard Glee Club tie she had brought him and said good-bye.

Looking back on the situation years later, Alison mused, "Here's a guy who's been on the road all his life. And he saw an opportunity. So I'm probably sort of equally to blame for the situation. It's funny to me that I thought that could even work out. Nowadays, if Bill Monroe were still here, I couldn't imagine wanting to put myself in that situation if they would have me. I mean, you can make yourself fit in, but do you want to have to?"

When asked what she was feeling as she left the motel, she replied, "I'm sure I was crushed. I was probably beginning to realize that I'd thought of Bill Monroe as something other than human and then realized that he was just an old road dog."

In June 1984 Alison graduated from Harvard. Playing music then took a backseat as she entered business school at UCLA. While there, she worked as an intern for A&M Records, learning a lot about the business of music from the inside—most of it discouraging. "I didn't find anybody doing any actual work. It was explained to me that you find one big act and it kind of floats the whole infrastructure—the rest was just this kind of charade, people goofing off. I'm one who believes more in hard work."

After graduation she married a lawyer and moved to San Francisco, where she found a job as an investment banker for Smith Barney. She lasted two years in the position. As she told *Banjo NewsLetter* in 1990, "Working morning, noon, and night on financial stuff really sucked." Twelve years later her more reserved observation for *Attaché* magazine was: "There was too much about that kind of work that did not feed my soul." These remarks illuminate two sides of Alison Brown: the spontaneous California kid at heart and the reserved businesswoman. Somehow Alison manages to keep both in peaceful coexistence.

In an attempt to nourish her soul, Alison quit her day job in 1988, setting aside six months to write music, thinking she would like to make another record and then perhaps get a job in a music-related field. She had almost reached the end of her allotted time when Alison Krauss tapped her to fill in with Union Station for a couple of shows in January 1989. Alison stayed for three years, playing on Alison Krauss's 1990 Grammy-winning album, *I've Got That Old Feeling.*

As a result of touring with Alison Krauss, Alison Brown was becoming better known in the international bluegrass community. One of the earliest articles about her, in a 1990 issue of *Banjo NewsLetter*, was alliteratively titled "A Fireball Feminizes the 5-String." In answer to banjo builder Geoff Stelling's query, "What about being a woman in a male-dominated music, playing the most macho bluegrass instrument?" Alison had quite a lot to say:

> Most women have it tough in bluegrass. Intentionally or not, many good bands won't have women. And playing in a band is the key to success in this music. There is also the unbelievably pervasive prejudice that girls can't pick. But men have no natural advantage in banjo; I know women can pick as solid and fast as the guys. But so far all the best banjo players have been men. Just look at the number of women in Tony's and Pete's fine book [*Masters of the 5-String Banjo*]. Things are changing, though. Several hot new bands have women as bandleaders and instrumentalists, not just singers. These women may be able to reach a broader audience than the all-guy bands could. Their success should open things up for other women and create role models so that more young girls take up bluegrass instruments. But women have to support each other.

In 1990 Alison released the first of four solo albums for Vanguard. *Simple Pleasures*, which included Alison Krauss on fiddle, was nominated for a 1991 Grammy in the category Best Bluegrass Album. Flute, cello, and percussion hinted that Alison was already venturing past traditional bluegrass boundaries. The *Bluegrass Unlimited* reviewer noted that "the majority of the tunes on this CD are fairly far from mainstream bluegrass." Her lead guitar work, however, caught his ear, leading him to gush that her banjo playing "is a mere echo of what she can do on the guitar." That year also saw the amicable split between her and her husband. In 1991, aided by the national exposure she received touring with Alison Krauss and in honor of her prodigious talent, Alison Brown was voted IBMA Banjo Player of the Year by her peers. She also moved to Nashville.

By 1992 Alison had left Union Station and released her second solo album, *Twilight Motel,* which featured both Andea Zonn and her old pal Stuart Duncan on fiddles. It also included drums and electric bass and was decidedly less bluegrass than her first. *Bluegrass Unlimited* reviewed the CD in its "On the Edge" section and said that modern banjo playing is being "carried to new heights" by folks like Béla Fleck and Alison Brown.

Alison Krauss and Union Station had appeared on Michelle Shocked's *Arkansas Traveler* album, so in 1992 when Michelle was putting together a band to tour in support of the project, she asked Alison Brown to be her bandleader. Alison in turn hired Garry West, who had toured with Delbert McClinton and Patty Loveless, to be the bass player. Alison and Garry discovered they had a great deal in common, so they not only started a relationship but also talked about starting a record label. They would marry in 1998.

While on tour with Michelle in Australia, Alison and Garry went in search of some indigenous didgeridoo music, which they found on a label called Natural Symphonies. Wanting to release this music in North America, they formed their own label, Small World Music, in 1993. As Alison said in an interview with *Goldmine* magazine, "Our plan was to use this small catalog to develop a distribution network and then launch our own imprint." That same year they put together the Alison Brown Quartet (often referred to as ABQ) to tour and perform Alison's music. The group would include keyboards (John R. Burr) along with drums and percussion (Rick Reed).

The year 1994 saw the release of Alison's third solo album, *Look Left,* which was produced by Garry West and featured the talents of the Quartet along with selected guests. There was no bluegrass on this album of world music. The *Bluegrass Unlimited* reviewer suggests that Alison "may not be a bluegrass player at heart, but a very 'contemporary' musician who has chosen the banjo as her voice." However, Alison herself says, "Even though it might not always sound like it . . . what I've learned from playing bluegrass music is at the core of what I do."

By 1995 Alison and Garry were ready to start their own label, Compass Records, which began on their dining room table. They wanted to create a home for artists they loved who were being ignored by major labels and who were committed to touring in support of their own careers. They wanted to build a company where selling was important but never at the expense of an artist's vision or creativity. That initial year they released four projects, including their first by singer-songwriter Kate Campbell. By 2001 they had released more than one hundred albums. Their catalog would eventually include a diverse selection of roots music, including contemporary folk, jazz, singer-songwriter, Celtic, alt-pop, and bluegrass.

In the beginning Alison said, "It's kind of a challenge to juggle a growing small business on one hand and music on the other, but I love to play so I really don't want to sacrifice that." When the company proved successful, she was able to add, "I'm delighted to have been able to create a situation where I can be both an artist and a businessperson. It really does seem like the best of both worlds to me."

As many people have found, working with your spouse in a business can be problematic. Playing with your partner in a band presents another level of challenges. Alison and Garry do both. As Alison points out, "We're together all the time, which is one of the unique aspects of our relationship. It could sound like a recipe for disaster, but actually it's worked out really well for us." Perhaps Garry's easygoing nature helps. "The synergy of being together all the time has enabled us to do things that we couldn't have accomplished otherwise," Alison says. "It's like one plus one is more than two. But it's a unique situation. It probably wouldn't work the same with another person." With her business background, Alison handles the financing, accounting, royalty accounting, and bill paying. Garry, who is more of a people person, deals directly with the artists and artist management. Other staff members handle sales, marketing, promotion, and radio publicity.

Bands in which the husband is the leader and the wife plays bass conform to age-old patterns of male-female relationships. How does a marriage work when the wife is the leader of the band and the husband plays bass? Alison, who is well aware of the competitive nature of husband-wife relationships from her first marriage, says this role reversal doesn't seem to be a factor in her and Garry's relationship. "He doesn't seem to have a problem playing bass in a band that I front. And he's just as supportive as he can be. He does all the behind-the-scenes legwork and advance work, and he plays bass and that's fine. It's really pretty amazing," she says with a laugh. "I think he's got that bass player team spirit that a lot of bass players seem to have. Because he can only achieve his musical goal by playing in an ensemble, so he really sees himself as part of a group rather than needing to be out front." Garry also produces Alison's records, something that he enjoys and something that Alison has no interest in doing.

Alison's fourth album for Vanguard, the aptly titled *Quartet* (1996), features only the members of her foursome. The *Bluegrass Unlimited* reviewer recognized Alison's deep bluegrass roots, but said, "Brown's muse sings strongest with a jazz voice."

Alison's first release on her own Compass label came in 1998 with the ABQ recording *Out of the Blue*. This one was a little too jazzy for *Bluegrass Unlimited*, which did not review it, even though the cover featured an oversized photo of a banjo pick. *Cleveland Country* magazine said that Alison was "lean[ing] into a Latin direction employing her unique custom built electric nylon-string banjo that has an engaging sound."

In 1998 fiddler Darol Anger put together a supergroup to record an album called *A Christmas Heritage* and do a holiday tour. Included in the venture were Mike Marshall, Todd Phillips, Tim O'Brien, pianist Phil Aaberg, and Alison. That tour worked out so well that the group decided to call themselves New Grange and record a self-titled CD for Compass (1999). As the only female in the group, Alison's observations are interesting:

> It seems to me that men tend to approach music in a more competitive way. It's like we've got a new tune, we're working it out, everybody's trying to carve out their own sonic real estate. Their own place in the tune. My approach—I don't know if this is a female thing or not, it seems to me that it is—is to think of it as an ensemble and approach it as a group. They try to outplay each other, and women try to play *with* each other. It's very interesting. I think that maybe that's why women don't generally tend to try to hone their skills so much as players the way men do.

Alison is no stranger to competitiveness herself. When she was younger she entered a number of contests. "I liked competing and I liked to win, but I find when I'm in a band situation I don't feel like I need to outplay the guy next to me. Maybe it's because I can't. I don't know. Maybe that becomes a convenient excuse. I mean how do you outplay Mike Marshall and Darol Anger?"

On the other hand, she says, touring with New Grange couldn't have been easier or more comfortable. "I was afraid I would go out on the New Grange bus and those guys would—who knows what they might do? It's a bunch of guys on a bus. Your worst-nightmare scenario takes over and instead it wasn't like that at all. These are all modern New Age guys. They aren't gonna do any kind of weird guy stuff. In fact they just sat around reading wine and pasta magazines." Darol Anger, in a tour blog, waxed eloquent about the bus but said the band had not named it: "Gals name their buses, guys don't, and Alison's too busy running her record company to care."

On the whole, Alison thinks, "I've probably benefited more from being a female banjo player than not benefited from it." When asked to elaborate, she says, "It's a smaller pond. I'd rather be called the female Béla Fleck than just some other guy who plays kind of like Béla Fleck but not nearly as good. And I feel like it's created more opportunities than it's taken away. I don't feel like something's been closed off to me that I've missed out on."

When asked about women who have met with closed doors and who have given up, Alison quickly replies:

> Well, how bad do you want it? If you want it bad enough, I think you make it happen. I just couldn't leave music alone, otherwise I'd still be an investment banker. That's what we tell artists here. If you can quit, you should. Because there are a lot of people out there that want it so bad, and there's only a limited number of slots. So you've got to really have a fire in your belly for it, otherwise just go do something else. It'll be easier. It does sound kind of harsh, but I think it is true. The artists who succeed are the ones who would be doing what they do whether or not they had a label or a record out or radio promotion, because it's who they are.

In 2000 Alison returned to the bluegrass roots that were never far away with *Fair Weather* on Compass. Produced by Garry, the album featured bluegrass instruments and bluegrass players and was a mixture of vocals and instrumentals. Of particular interest was the catchy tune "Girl's Breakdown," whose name was a tongue-in-cheek play on "Earl's Breakdown" by Earl Scruggs. *Bluegrass Unlimited* welcomed her back to the fold with a highlight review and said her playing with Béla Fleck on her tune "Leaving Cottondale" was "thirty seconds of absolutely jaw-dropping twin-banjo counterpoint." The folks at the Grammys agreed, naming the number Best Country Instrumental Performance in 2001.

In 2002 the ABQ released *Replay*, a collection of the group's show tunes recorded in the studio over a two-day period. *Bluegrass Unlimited*, in its "On the Edge" section, said the project "offers crisp and inventive jazz banjo playing."

That same year Alison's life changed forever with the birth of her daughter, Hannah. Alison was determined to keeping playing music, so wherever she went, Hannah went, starting with a European tour when she was only three and a half weeks old. "I just feel like I've worked so hard to have the opportunity to go out and play music that I didn't want to let having a baby stand in the way," Alison said. "I knew ultimately that wouldn't be a good thing for me. But I didn't want to miss the experience of having her. I think it's been good for her and it's certainly better for me than giving up playing."

Alison elected to nurse Hannah, figuring it would be easier with the traveling. What she didn't realize is how time-consuming nursing is. Speaking like a true twenty-first-century mother, she says, "When you're doing it, it's just like you're sitting there. You can't really do anything. You can't multi-task." She admits, however, that "it's a lot easier than having to warm a bottle in a foreign country." The hard part for Alison is being at home. "If Hannah is awake it's really hard to practice. The biggest challenge is how to fit that in. And writing, trying to work on stuff for a new record, it's hard to get the mental and physical space to do that. She usually doesn't go to bed till 10:00—she's on musician hours. So by the time she goes to sleep, I'm usually pretty worn out. So it's that time of the day that's the hardest."

With a young child now in her life Alison's next project was appropriately titled *Stolen Moments* (2005). It features the vocal talents of the Indigo Girls, Beth Nielsen Chapman, Mary Chapin Carpenter, and Andrea Zonn, along with the Boomchicks—Thighdalia, Aureola, Ovaria, Fallopia, and Hysteria. Alison wrote a special tune for Hannah, "Musette for a Palindrome," and the liner notes include special thanks to "ALL the babysitters."

Alison seemed to have gotten the hang of being a working mother, because the CDs just kept coming. The year 2007 saw the release of an EP called *Evergreen*, which expanded into a full-length album of the same name in 2008 with a picture of Hannah on the front. The band was billed as the Alison Brown Quartet with Joe Craven, who played mandolin and fiddle. The group's next album, *Alison Brown Quartet Live at Blair with Joe Craven*, was recorded at Vanderbilt University's Blair Auditorium in front of a live audience in 2008.

Meanwhile Compass Records itself was growing with the acquisition of the Green Linnet catalog in 2006, Tayberry Music in 2007, and Mulligan Music in 2008. These labels made the Compass Record Group "the place to go for Celtic and roots music." In 2009 the company could boast nearly six hundred releases. Compass was also becoming a go-to place for hardworking women in bluegrass who were leading their own bands. Dale Ann Bradley signed with the label in 2006 and Missy Raines in 2008. When all three women, including Alison, released albums in 2009, Alison told the *Wall Street Journal*, "It's kind of a sisterhood, really . . . women are leading the charge with the most interesting bluegrass." Alison's *The Company You Keep* was a disc of thoughtful, jazz-inflected instrumentals featuring nine original tunes from Alison, who publishes with her own Brown Knows Music. The title "The Clean Plate Club" could only have come from a parent. And Alison was now the mother of two, having welcomed son Brendan into the family on April 10, 2007. She saluted her son with "Waltz for Mr. B."

Way back in 1990 Alison noted in an interview that things were changing in bluegrass with the emergence of women as bandleaders. Today, however, there are still few women side musicians. When asked about her thoughts on this, Alison made a comparison to the business world. "In business, I've heard people say that women who are in upper levels of management don't tend to necessarily support and nurture the women underneath them the way men will do. I think it's kind of a minority mentality. It's like I've got to keep fighting for myself; there's not room to help somebody else." Yet, after saying that, she says pointedly:

> Well, the two great opportunities I had as a side person were both as a result of a woman hiring me. Alison Krauss and Michelle Shocked both gave me a tremendous amount. And for example if [fiddler] Andrea Zonn wanted to play in the ABQ, she *knows* she has a standing invitation any time. But it's because she's a great musician, it's not because she's a woman. I guess that's where it needs to start. You need to have the chops, and then if you do, I don't think it should matter what gender you are. But sometimes it does.
>
> Unfortunately I think it's still true that women instrumentalists as a whole aren't as strong as their male counterparts. I don't know why that's true. But it just seems to be. They tend to be great singers, but not as strong players. Maybe it's because they *can* sing. Maybe that's why I worked so hard playing the banjo, because that's what I did. As women we're very lucky to live in the times we do and to have grown up in the times we have. Imagine wanting to play music if you'd been born even seventy years ago.

In the early days, we were just like a rolling
pajama party. We slept together, we ate together,
we picked together, we practiced together.
We sometimes lived together.

—Andrea Roberts,
founder of Petticoat Junction

ALL-FEMALE BANDS

For the roughly twenty-five years that they existed in some number, from 1972 to 1996, all-female bands, or "all-girl" bands as they are usually called, served an extremely important function. For females who were not part of a family group or partnered with a male musician, they became a way to break into the business, providing access to festival stages and an opportunity to play at a professional level. And for young women, as for young men, playing in a road band with your peers offered fun, excitement, and camaraderie. Trying to maintain an all-estrogen lineup, however, often proved to be an insurmountable obstacle. Many all-girl groups folded when they could not find female replacements for departing musicians. Others chose to open their ranks to men rather than quit playing.

Hope springs eternal, however, and the twenty-first century finds a new generation of primarily young women sowing their first musical oats in all-female groups with wonderful band names such as Della Mae (Boston), the Hillbettys (Seattle), Giddyup Kitty (Colorado), Sweet Potato Pie (going strong for a decade down in North Carolina), Red Molly (a trio with banjo in the New York area), and Ma Crowe and the Lady Slippers with the powerful Trina Emig on banjo (Cincinnati).

The Dixie Chicks are undoubtedly the most famous of the all-female groups, but the Buffalo Gals and the Good Ol' Persons were two of the earliest. Other well-known groups include the New Coon Creek Girls, Petticoat Junction, the Wildwood Girls, Sugar in the Gourd, Sidesaddle, the All Girl Boys, Ranch Romance, Tennessee HeartStrings, and Carolina Rose, which Lorraine Jordan turned into Carolina Road when she added men. Additional configurations, some of short duration, were Bluegrass Liberation, the Bushwhackers, Dixie Reign, Sassygrass, the Dixie Belles, the Bar Belles, the Chalker Sisters, the Happy Hollow String Band, Cherokee Rose, Girls Nite Out, the Valley Dolls, Mother of Pearl, High Hills, and the Barefoot Nellies.

The Happy Hollow String Band, from North Carolina, a group of teenage girls who played together from 1974 to 1979 and billed themselves as "bluegrass with a feminine touch," featured Sandy Crisco (now Hatley) on banjo. In a 1983 *Banjo NewsLetter* article, she wrote about "The Plight of a Lady Banjo Picker." Among her wry observations was this: "Restrooms have always posed a problem. Recently, while jamming at a local picking parlor, I inquired as to the location of the ladies room. The fellow picker scratched his head, blushed, and smiled. 'Most of them just step out back. We, uh, don't get too many ladies.'"

Ken Irwin, of Rounder Records, reports recording an all-female group called the Country Girls on August 8, 1971, during a field trip to the Elizabethton, Tennessee, area. He says, "As I remember, they played mostly for fun, but we were surprised to find an all-women's band at that time." Their repertoire, which featured the Scruggs-style banjo, included "Randy Lynn Rag," "Little Maggie," and "Rocky Top." Susan Taylor played banjo, Anita Grindstaff played guitar, Kate Ensor played fiddle, and Jeanie and Bonnie Estep filled out the rest of the quintet.

Bluegrass Liberation, although short-lived and virtually unknown today, may actually have been the first modern, all-female bluegrass band, since they formed (as near as anyone can figure) in the spring of 1972 in Winston-Salem,

North Carolina, with Sally Davis (now Wingate) on banjo, Louisa Branscomb on lead guitar, Erica Hunter on rhythm guitar, and Lynn Grey (now Salls) on bass. Sally (b. 1949), who was raised in Wilmington, Delaware, had been bitten by the banjo bug when she heard her brother's friend playing. "I knew I had to create that sound myself . . . The obsession lasted quite a while."

In 1964 she started taking banjo lessons from the great Ted Lundy, who was originally from the Galax, Virginia, area. "After that," she says, "I lived to jam at Sunset Park on Sundays." The famous country music park in West Grove, Pennsylvania, just a half hour from Sally's house, featured big-name country and bluegrass acts every weekend. It also sponsored contests. Sally entered the Fourth of July banjo contest there in 1965 and 1966 and took second place each time, once losing to banjo whiz Larry McNeely, who would go on to play with Glen Campbell. Sally moved from jamming in the fields to playing on stage with Alex and Ola Belle Campbell and the New River Boys and Girls, but she stopped when the musician's union demanded that she join. "I returned to the fields," she said. One of her fondest memories is of playing backstage with Earl Scruggs.

Sally's parents insisted that she go to college, so in 1967 she arrived at Randolph Macon Women's College in Lynchburg, Virginia. The next year she met Louisa Branscomb (b. 1949), who was born in upstate New York but raised in Alabama. Louisa, who had been writing songs since she was a child, started playing guitar at seventeen and was learning to flat-pick her Martin. Soon Sally and Louisa were playing in an all-female group at the college that included Sally on banjo, Louisa on guitar, Ann Ashburn (now Ciani) on mandolin, and Martha VanLandingham on washtub bass.

Louisa spent her junior year in England, and by the time she came back, Sally, a philosophy major, had decided that she wanted to be a professional musician when she graduated. "Consequently," Sally says, "the school year of 1970–1971 was a very busy musical year." Early in that year, Sally and Louisa played at a bar in Lynchburg called Henry's, sometimes joined by (male) fiddler Bonnie Beverly, who later played for Don Reno. In November 1970 Sally joined Bonnie's all-male band, the Virginia Buddies, playing banjo and singing. She recorded a 45 rpm single with Bonnie featuring "Orange Blossom Special," but unfortunately the banjo is inaudible.

In August 1971 Sally and Louisa moved to Winston-Salem, where they formed Bluegrass Liberation the next year. The only commercial recording of the band is "Old Joe Clark," played by Sally, Louisa, and Lynn in a jam session that was captured in April 1972 for the album *48th Union Grove Fiddler's Convention*. The group did not stay all female for long, as Lynn soon moved away and was replaced by Howard Eury. The band broke up in October 1973 when Sally married Mark Wingate, the fiddle player with Chicken Hot Rod. Sally would play with Cherokee Rose in the early eighties and then twenty years later with the all-female Tennessee HeartStrings, appearing on the group's self-titled 2002 album.

Louisa, who began playing banjo after Bluegrass Liberation broke up, has continued with her songwriting and music even while holding down a day job as a psychologist. She has played in numerous groups, including Boot Hill, formed in February 1976 with three men, and the all-female groups Cherokee Rose and Gypsy Heart and later with Born Gypsy. But she became best known for writing the song "Steel Rails," which was recorded by Alison Krauss.

More widely known were the Wildwood Girls (originally the Wildwood Pickers), from the Chicago area, who did not purposefully intend to be an all-female band when they formed in late 1976 with Kim Koskela, sixteen, on banjo, her older sister Robin helping out with the vocals, Muriel Anderson on guitar, and Kathy Jones on fiddle. Their first bass player was a man, and early on they used a male fiddle player. But by 1980 when Kim's mom, Cory, and younger sister Sue joined on bass and mandolin, the configuration become all female and stayed that way until Kim "retired the band" in 1999. Throughout the twenty-three years the band was together, Kim was the mainstay of the group. In 1982 the group changed its name to the Wildwood Girls and, according to Kim, "got twice as many bookings."

The Wildwood Girls did a number of overseas tours for the USO and Department of Defense, worked as the house bluegrass band at Dollywood for five years, and were regulars at Bill Monroe's Bean Blossom Festival in Indiana for ten years. They also claim to be the "first all-girl band to play traditional bluegrass on the Grand Ole Opry."

While the Koskela women held down the banjo, mandolin, and bass slots, they used a number of different fiddlers, including Kathy Jones, Sandra Shelton, Barbara Good, Lois Pittman, Cathy Kannapel, Peggy White, and Hollis Brown. When Muriel Anderson left after six years (she went on to play with Chet Atkins), the guitar slot was filled by, among others, Michelle Roberts, Mitzi Oden, and Terry Boswell. Laura Walker, Chris Bennett, and Nancy Cardwell all handled the bass duties when Cory left.

The Wildwood Girls released a total of six recordings, with their initial two LPs, *First Harvest* (1980) and *Family Reunion* (1983), on their own Clogging

Chickens label. Their third, *Bluegrass in My Heart* (1987), was on Atteiram, and their last recording, the CD *Goodnight Soldier* (1992), was on the Wildwood Girls label. When asked in 1987 if they ever had any problems "being an all-girl band," Cory replied, "Unfortunately we've run into some promoters that didn't hire us because we are women."

Unlike the Wildwood Girls, the New Coon Creek Girls were all-female by design when they formed in 1979 and remained so until 1997, when they bowed to necessity and added two men. The last all-female configuration of the band, one of their strongest lineups, included Vicki Simmons on electric bass, Ramona Church Taylor on banjo, Dale Ann Bradley on guitar, and Kathy Kuhn on fiddle.

Founded by John Lair for the Renfro Valley Barn Dance in Kentucky, the New Coon Creek Girls were held together by the stubbornness and devotion of bass player Vicki Simmons (b. 1954), who became the leader. "Nobody would do this, and nobody would do that, and I wanted to play so bad, I'd do whatever it took to get them to play . . . 'Cause I was eat up with it. I mean, it was bad." When she joined Jan and Kelli Cummins (banjo and guitar) and fiddler Betty Lin, who had already been appearing on the Barn Dance as a trio, Vicki was performing on stage for the first time. And though she'd been playing guitar since she was twelve, mostly at family gatherings, she'd been a bass player for a mere three weeks. The band worked one night a week for three years, and Mr. Lair paid her twenty-five dollars a week.

For months the group didn't even have a name; they were simply called "The Girls." Then Mr. Lair got the blessing of Lily May Ledford, who had founded the original Coon Creek Girls in 1937, and the New Coon Creek Girls were launched.

By 1983 folks in the Renfro Valley listening area were wanting to hire the New Coon Creek Girls for local events such as fairs. This was a chance for the women to make extra money, and Vicki was all for it. Mr. Lair, however, wanted them to sign an exclusive contract with Renfro Valley. As Vicki says, "And you had to sign it. See, that's what he did to the original Coon Creek Girls. He had them in bondage pretty much for years. And I knew that . . . But I said, 'I'm not gonna sign anything that puts me just staying here at Renfro Valley. And he says, 'Well, I don't need you.' I said, 'It's been nice knowing you. Thank you for my first job.' And I was out the door."

Free now to chart their own course, the women quickly recorded their first album, *How Many Biscuits Can You Eat* (RCM, 1983). Vicki was doing the booking, and their ad in the March 1984 *Bluegrass Unlimited* proclaimed them "Eastern Kentucky's Finest & Prettiest Bluegrass Band." The band's second album, *Home Sweet Highway* (1987), was on the Rutabaga label, the next three were on Turquoise, and then came four for Pinecastle Records. Their ninth album, *Our Point of View* (1996), boldly proclaimed "featuring Dale Ann Bradley" on the cover. This was the last album to use the name New Coon Creek Girls. All subsequent albums would be solo projects by Dale Ann. After two albums on Pinecastle and one each on Doobie Shea and Mountain Home, Dale Ann signed with Compass Records, where Alison Brown produced Dale Ann's albums *Catch Tomorrow* (2006) and *Don't Turn Your Back* (2009).

Over the years, the New Coon Creek Girls had many personnel changes, but Vicki and her bass remained the one constant. Other band members have included Cathy Lavender, Wanda Barnett, Pam Gadd, Pam Perry, Annie (Kaser) Carpenter, Deanie Richardson, Carmella Ramsey, Phylls Jones, Jennifer Wrinkle, Michelle Birkby, and Kim Bibb. Many times, to Vicki's dismay, the band has served as a training ground for female musicians, usually fiddle players, who then leave to play with country music stars. As she says, "It's aggravating that these major country artists come right smack dab to this band and yank somebody. We're talking Patty Lovelace, we're talking Holly Dunn, we're talking Pam Tillis, we're talking Bill Anderson, Reba McEntire." Banjo player Pam Gadd and mandolinist Pam Perry also went on to have successful country music careers with the all-female Wild Rose (1988–1992). Finding replacement band members had long been a headache for Vicki. As late as 1996 she was saying, "It still is a problem. We still have yet to find somebody else to play mandolin. That's the hardest thing to find. It's probably increased some, the pool, but not a lot. It's still hard to find good [players]. I mean you can find rather mediocre [players], but to find people who are really outstanding on their instrument, that's hard."

They thought about using men many times. As Ramona Church Taylor put it, "We've come bad close to doing it." Vicki added, "Because right now the standard of the music, we've set it so high that it's up there. If a girl can't cut it, we'll get somebody who can . . . I wouldn't want to let the music suffer just to have four girls up there." Finally in 1997 the band had to bite the bitter bullet and add men to the group. Pregnant with her second child, Ramona had decided to come off the road for that most common of working mother tribulations: child-care issues. With one-third of their extremely strong female trio gone, Vicki and Dale Ann decided not to try to duplicate their current sound, but to go for a totally different sound.

Obviously, with the addition of men, the band could no longer be called the Coon Creek Girls. But it was Vicki's idea to call the group Dale Ann Bradley and Coon Creek. Vicki says that Dale Ann, who had been with the group since 1992, is "the best singer I ever heard." But even after years with the group, audiences did not know Dale Ann by name. Vicki points out that women who lead their own bands don't have this problem: Claire Lynch, Lynn Morris, Alison Krauss, Laurie Lewis. "Dale Ann kinda got lost in there," says Vicki. The change worked, because not only was the band nominated by the IBMA for Emerging Artist of the Year in 1998 and 2002, but also Dale Ann was nominated for Female Vocalist of the Year in 2002, and every year from then on, winning the award from 2007 through 2009 and again in 2011.

Around 2004 the name of the band was changed again to the Dale Ann Bradley Band, in keeping with the current trend of naming groups after the featured performer. Then in 2006 the unthinkable happened: Dale Ann, wanting a musical change, parted company with Vicki. As Vicki told *Bluegrass Unlimited,* "We were business partners, music partners, the whole bit. I've had trouble figuring it out. This wasn't something I wanted. I hope it all works out." Dale Ann told the magazine, "I've never had to do anything like this before. My musical soul had to have a change. Sometimes, in order to stay in the ball game, this is what has to happen."

A year later Vicki reported that she and Dale Ann had been able to work through this painful time in their relationship and were hoping to get back to writing songs together. Vicki rediscovered her love of the clawhammer banjo and began performing again as a regular on the Renfro Valley Barn Dance, where the director of entertainment was her old bandmate Pam Perry Combs. Then in the summer of 2008 Vicki developed a brain aneurysm and while in the hospital for surgery suffered a stroke. She was on the mend and even playing some when she began to have seizures. Friends were heartbroken to see her progress now recede. Still, Vicki is a determined woman, and if there is any way she can get back to playing, she will.

At the same time that the New Coon Creek Girls were forming in Kentucky (1979), Sidesaddle was just getting off the ground in Northern California. Original members Lee Anne Welch on fiddle, guitarist Diana Deininger, and Karen Quick on bass were soon joined by Sonia Shell on banjo and Kim Elking on mandolin. In this configuration the band released two albums: *Saratoga Gap* (Faultline, 1985) and *The Girl from the Red Rose Saloon* (Turquoise, 1988). Their third album, *Daylight Train* (Turquoise, 1991), featured new members Sheila

Hogan McCormick on bass and Jackie Miller on guitar. Then, like its eastern counterpart, Sidesaddle made the decision to survive by adding male members sometime after 1991, changing the name to Sidesaddle & Co. With this lineup the group released three more albums, the latest being *Queen for a Day* (2005). The band continues to feature the talents of Lee Anne Welch and Kim Elking.

One of the last of the well-known girl groups, Petticoat Junction, was put together by Andrea Roberts and Sonya Yoder in September 1987. The band, which lasted for ten years, served as a training ground for some powerful female musicians, including Robin Roller, Kristin Scott Benson, Gena Britt, Gail Rudisill, Sally Jones, Holly O'Dell, Dawn Watson, Amanda Mathis, and Amy Baker. Although reluctant to claim leadership of the group—"I never have done the leader thing very well"—Andrea was the one consistent member down through the years.

Raised on a diet of country music in Windfall, Indiana, twelve-year-old Andrea was bitten by the bluegrass bug when her mom and dad dragged their budding rock-and-roller to her first bluegrass festival, in Martinsville, Indiana. To her surprise, she "totally fell in love with it." Finding a lot of kids her own age to hang out with helped. The next year she started taking banjo lessons, and soon she sold her flute to buy a bass. Her first band, the Bluegrass Rebels, was made up of two girls and two boys, all fourteen. She played bass and Jennifer Demarcus played guitar. They recorded one 45 rpm single. But even at that young age she and Jennifer decided they wanted to start an all-girl band. So Andrea moved to banjo, they enlisted the services of their friend Michelle Chapin to play bass, and called themselves Southern Comfort. Often they worked shows as a three-piece group, because it was hard to find a girl to play another lead instrument. Occasionally they enlisted the help of a male friend to play mandolin or fiddle. At age sixteen Andrea took a break from bluegrass to play electric bass with some of her neighbors in a country band. At first the idea of playing in bars seemed glamorous, but the novelty soon wore off and it was back to bluegrass.

During her first year at vocational school, Andrea, eighteen, began playing guitar and singing tenor with Gary Adams and the Bluegrass Gentlemen, making the five-hour trip to Detroit every weekend with her mother. This was her first all-male band. When their former guitar player returned, Andrea was without a band for only a few months before becoming the bass player for Wendy Smith, a male mandolin player, and his group Blue Velvet. She stayed with Wendy's band for two years, graduating from vocational school during her tenure. She then took her musical dreams to Nashville, where she found herself alone in a large city knowing not a soul and feeling intimidated by the whole Nashville scene. "I'm never gonna play again," she thought. "Every hamburger flipper is a player and singer."

Andrea attended the Sunday-night jam sessions at the Station Inn but was too afraid to join in. The generally all-male assemblage was not exactly welcoming. Finally she decided, "I just want to play." At one of the sessions she suggested a song she wanted to sing: "Rose of Old Kentucky" in the key of D. She was aware that she was going out on a limb here, because although the song was a familiar one, the key of D was not where Bill Monroe had done it. She was immediately drawing attention to her Otherness by singing in a girl's key. But she'd already had experience with that when she was learning banjo as a kid and going to jam sessions. As she told it: "I'd wander up and you've got the occasional fellow who'd go, 'Isn't she cute? A little girl with a banjo case.' I'd get it out and say, 'I want to sing such and such in E.' 'That's not where it was recorded,' [he'd say]. And I'd say, 'I'm not Lester Flatt.' That used to irritate me and it made jamming not much fun."

But now at the Station Inn, she was dying to sing. Fortunately one of the fiddle players said, "Cool, I love getting to do something different." Andrea was off and running. They asked her to sing song after song. Her confidence in her music was restored.

While attending the IBMA Trade Show and Fan Fest in 1987 with her friend Sonya Yoder, Andrea came up with the idea of forming an all-female band. The only other girl groups she knew of were the Wildwood Girls and the New Coon Creek Girls. She thought there was room for another. But they needed a name. As Andrea said, "We didn't want to be a river, or a mountain, or a steam, or the something-something girls." They were looking for something catchier. While listening to records one day, the Flatt and Scruggs recording of "Petticoat Junction" came on. They had their name. "It sounds like girls, but doesn't say it." The first configuration of Petticoat Junction included Andrea on guitar, Sonya on mandolin, Virginia Brawner on bass, Lori Howie on banjo, and fiddler Kim Bibb. The band started out "great guns," playing their first festival at Bean Blossom, Indiana, in June 1988. Then the usual happened: Kim got married and Sonya didn't want to travel. The band "fizzled out."

This would be the pattern for the life of the band: struggling to find women to play and then struggling to replace them when they left. The difficulty was that the women not only had to play bluegrass, but they also had to be free to travel, often for little or no money. The pool of women who fit these criteria seemed extremely small.

However, Robin Roller settled in on banjo for six years, and fiddler Gail Rudisill, who at first was still in high school but flew down every weekend to play, was on board for three years. With Lori Harmon on bass, Andrea, on guitar, had achieved a solid configuration. Then Lori left. Andrea, however, had learned to keep her eyes open all the time. "If I saw a girl playing any instrument I would ask her name, where was she from, and get phone numbers." Thus she had a contact for Gena Britt, a banjo player from North Carolina, who had just graduated from high school. Andrea called her. "We need a bass player. Are you willing to play bass?" Gena said, "I don't know how." Andrea said, "I'll teach you." And she did. Two weeks later the band played the IBMA showcase. This configuration—Gena, Gail, Andrea, and Robin—lasted for two years, from August 1990 to August 1992. They released two projects for Pinecastle: the gospel cassette *Hand of the Higher Power* (1991), and the CD *Lonely Old Depot* (1993). *Bluegrass Unlimited* said the band "comprises some of the finest vocalists in bluegrass today" and called Gena and Andrea "phenomenal lead singers."

But Gena missed playing the banjo. She went back to North Carolina to join New Vintage, a regional group that went on to achieve some level of national prominence, with Gena's driving banjo and strong singing being a key element in the band.

Andrea now moved to bass to accommodate Amy Baker on guitar, but the upheavals continued. Finally in June 1996 they added their first permanent male member to the band, Ron Stewart. Andrea said, "I hate to say it, but in a way I was starting to feel like we were sacrificing our musicianship to continue just trying to find females. *Any* female as long as she was female, if she could hold an instrument. We had to have that to continue." Sally Jones, in the group from 1995 until it folded, added, "Rather than hiring someone who could really play, we had to hire someone who was just learning to play." Ron would stay with the group for just over a year, leaving (with no hard feelings) to join the Lynn Morris Band. Petticoat Junction's last performance was at the IBMA Fan Fest in 1997.

Although the music was always important to Andrea, in the early days there was also an element of pure fun involved. Then, as Andrea said, "The older we got, we kinda got separate lives. Everybody was doing other things." With constant turnover, Andrea felt like they were "spinning their wheels, relearning the same old songs over and over." They never seemed to get past the stage of teaching new members the old material, often having to teach them the bluegrass style at the same time.

One reason Andrea was excited about not being an all-girl band was because they would no longer be in competition for the "all-girl band" slot at festivals. As Sally Jones said, "It's really odd, because there are hundreds and hundreds of male bands, but if we call a festival that is already having the New Coon Creek Girls, they will say, 'We already have a girl band.' But all the female bands are very different. There's no confusing the sound of one from the other."

Andrea says wistfully, "We were still a novelty. And that frustrated me beyond words. I would tell emcees please don't introduce us as 'pretty little gals' or 'one of the finest all-girl bands.' We just want to be a band. And that's why we were all so thrilled that [being an all-girl band] is over. You can't call us an all-girl band anymore. We're just a band. We're released from that." "When asked if she thought it was a mistake to start out as an all-girl band, Andrea said, "No. It had its time. I think at that moment it went well because that's what it was." And Andrea certainly doesn't think she could have been the leader of a "guy band."

Although the situation has changed somewhat in recent years, in 1996 Petticoat Junction had some strong words to say about the difficulty of women singing lead in jam sessions. Andrea said, "I've been in a jam with great musicians and they say, 'Sing one!' And I'm thinking, 'Yeah, you don't really want me to do that B. As soon as I tell you what key I want, you're gonna give me the evil eye.' So I say, 'Let's do "Little Cabin Home on the Hill" in B.' 'What? In B [said in a real whiny tone]?' 'Yes, in B and kick it off if you can.'" Sally sympathetically added, "I never sing lead in a jam. Never. Chris [Jones, her husband] plays every Tuesday night in Franklin and every Tuesday night goes, 'Come and sing some lead.' Uh-uh." Sally also points out that when she or Andrea gets called up for a grand finale, when all bands are invited on stage for one last number, "They will kick off a song and say, 'Why don't you sing a verse?'" Andrea chimes in, "Every finale you do the grand slam ending in the key of A [a low key for women]." She demonstrated by singing a little bit of "Will the Circle Be Unbroken" in a low-pitched voice. Sally says, "So we always have to go, 'We can't. Sorry.'" Still they both admit that now is a better time than any for girls to come up as bluegrass singers. According to Sally, "The girls now go, 'I wanna be a Lynn or a Laurie or an Alison or a Suzanne.' They have those people. Who did we have?"

The idea of all-female groups had not yet run its course in 1989 when the All Girl Boys, a "traditional band with modern ideas," formed out in the San

Francisco Bay area. Original members Kathy Barwick on Dobro and lead guitar, Mary Gibbons on rhythm guitar, and Chris Lewis on mandolin were alumni of a mixed-gender group, the Fog City Ramblers, who had a weekly gig at Paul's Saloon in San Francisco for four years and did some touring in the West. These women were joined by Debby Cotter on banjo and Bethany Raine on bass. Sonia Shell would later take Debby's place, and Carolyn Cirimele would replace Bethany. The All Girl Boys showcased at IBMA in 1991 and released one CD, *Heart's Desire* (1994). And though the band never officially broke up, they simply stopped booking when Chris Lewis moved to Nashville in 1997. She would join the all-female Tennessee HeartStrings in 2001.

As more women began leading their own bands and as a few more mixed-gender bands began appearing, the desperate need for all-female bands quietly receded. Or perhaps they faded away in part because keeping an all-female band together was simply too hard. As Kathy Barwick so eloquently put it, "Finding replacement band members is hard enough without eliminating the vast majority of pickers out there—men."

I love music. I love music of any form
that moves me. I don't care where it comes from.

—Alison Krauss

ALISON
KRAUSS

Alison Krauss (b. 1971) has been called "the biggest thing to happen to bluegrass since Flatt and Scruggs." She has won more Grammys—twenty-six in all—than any other female artist. She has recorded with Sting, James Taylor, and Robert Plant, with Brad Paisley, Dolly Parton, and Ralph Stanley. She signed with Rounder Records when she was fourteen and has released more than a dozen Rounder albums, which now routinely sell millions. Her combined sales are greater than those of any other bluegrass act. Her voice can be heard on numerous movie soundtracks from *Midnight in the Garden of Good and Evil* to *O Brother, Where Art Thou?* She appears on late-night television with David Letterman and Jay Leno. She has produced a Grammy-nominated album for country superstar Alan Jackson. And she has achieved the Holy Grail of country and bluegrass music: she is a member of the Grand Ole Opry.

Yet her career initially caused great angst for many in the bluegrass community who didn't know whether to love her or leave her alone. A *Bluegrass Unlimited* reviewer, wondering if readers would want to buy *Now That I've Found You,* a CD with "little bluegrass" on it, finally gave up, saying, "Many a bluegrass purist has been seen casting principles aside when Alison Krauss steps up to the microphone."

Alison's story begins with her family—mother Louise, father Fred, and older brother, Viktor—living quietly in Champaign, Illinois. Louise and Fred took parenting seriously and put their two children into every program imaginable, including music. Violin was five-year-old Alison's choice of instrument, and she stuck with classical lessons until age eleven, when she started to chafe at the rigid confines of the music. Fiddle contests, which Alison began entering at age eight, offered the thrill of competition along with freedom from the printed page. Soon Alison was studying the music of the great contest champions like Randy Howard and Mark O'Connor, and bluegrass fiddler Stuart Duncan. She took first place at the prestigious Winfield, Kansas, fiddle championship in 1984 and by 1985 had added state championships from Illinois, Indiana, and Tennessee to her trophy case.

Through these contests Alison would become friendly rivals then fast friends with Andrea Zonn (b. 1969), another young Illinois violinist who was also venturing on beyond classical music. The two would hang out in each other's homes, talking about music (and boys) and working out twin fiddle arrangements. Andrea would go on to carve out a successful career as a fiddler, playing in Vince Gill's band for over thirteen years and touring with Lyle Lovett, James Taylor, and Alison Brown.

In addition to being immersed in fiddle music, Alison was also listening to Foreigner, Lynyrd Skynyrd, Stevie Wonder, Huey Lewis, Bad Company, and the sound tracks from *Grease* and *Saturday Night Fever*. Bluegrass was not yet on her radar. All that changed in 1983 when she joined Silver Rail, a bluegrass band that included songwriters John Pennell and Nelson Mandrell. John introduced her to the music of J. D. Crowe and the New South, Ricky Skaggs and Boone Creek, the Bluegrass Album Band, the New Grass Revival, and Tony Rice. "I went nuts on it," Alison says. "I really didn't listen to anything else for a while." The novice bluegrasser went "cuckoo" when she saw Rhonda Vincent. "I was thirteen and she was about twenty-one . . . She was so beautiful. I was just speechless, and then she sang . . . Her singing was so feminine and I loved that. To see someone be very strong and yet incredibly feminine was so appealing."

In 1985 Alison started working some with the Indianapolis-based Classified Grass. In addition she made her first album, the all-instrumental *Different Strokes,* with her brother, Viktor, and Bruce Weiss from Silver Rail. Hearing Alison's well-developed, contest-style fiddling on the standards "Dusty Miller" and "Grey Eagle" is not surprising. But the funky, jazzy sounds of "Nick's Noodle" (from the fiddling of Richard Greene) stretch far beyond traditional boundaries.

Alison's life certainly could not be called run-of-the-mill, yet there were other young musicians who were traveling along much the same path. But change was in the wind. In the summer of 1985 Classified Grass sent an un-solicited cassette to Ken Irwin at Rounder Records. On the fourth number Ken heard something special: Alison singing lead on a gospel song. In a classic understatement Ken says, "I really, really liked her voice." He phoned her to ask for more music and soon was listening to a demo that included four songs by John Pennell. On the strength of this tape, on May 10, 1986, Ken and his partners signed Alison to Rounder Records, having never heard her in person. According to Ken, this was "extremely unusual." She was two months shy of her fifteenth birthday.

Meanwhile, in the fall of 1985, John Pennell had formed Union Station with Alison's friend Andrea Zonn on fiddle. When Andrea left for Nashville in the spring of 1986, Alison replaced her. Working now with two bands, Alison played with whomever called first. Todd Rakestraw, who was in this early version of Union Station, said, "Alison's mom traveled with us most of the time if it was an overnight thing and occasionally her dad would go. But we were like her older brothers so we all watched out for her, and John, being the oldest, kinda looked out for everybody."

Independently of Ken's operations, Union Station had been booked to play the prestigious Newport Folk Festival in August 1986. This high-profile appear-ance garnered Alison a full page in *People Weekly* magazine, where her irreverent charm went on display nationally for the first time: Not only does she want to play and sing better, she also wants to "burp better." Not wanting to be seen as "hick with no teeth" she asserts, "I don't wear plaid shirts and I don't plow." Alison was off and running.

Alison's first project for Rounder, *Too Late to Cry* (1987), was a solo album—Rounder had signed Alison, not Union Station. Produced by Ken Irwin, the album featured some of the top guns in bluegrass: Sam Bush, Jerry Douglas, and Tony Trischka. Alison chose all of the material, including six songs by John Pennell. Looking back on the record fifteen years later, Alison says, "Of course

I over sang and over played, but what can I say? I was using too much Aqua Net. My hair was way too big and way too stiff." *Bluegrass Unlimited* hailed her as "the dominating female voice of the modern era" and said, presciently, that "the entire music world is in for an adventure of the first magnitude." With plenty of banjo there was no quarrel about this album being bluegrass.

What does this first record reveal about the young and future star? As a fiddler and singer her talent was obvious. Not a songwriter herself, she was already a superb song catcher, a task she is "passionate" about. She credits mentors John Pennell and Nelson Mandrell with giving her a "sense of song." "There's nothing like finding the right song," she says. She looks for the "timeless quality" of a song. "I don't like things that are so specific that that's the only way you can think about them." She also wants songs that "truly move me," songs that have "that sadness, that dark feeling . . . I love being in a studio and singing a song that makes you feel crappy."

On this first album Alison has not found the marvelously controlled whispery delivery for which she is now famous. She would not arrive at this style until her fourth record, *Every Time You Say Goodbye*. On her first three projects she sings with incredible power and precision, pulling out all the stops in a manner reminiscent of the full-bore approach of her friend Rhonda Vincent and of John Cowan, another singer whom she admired. *Bluegrass Unlimited* would later criticize her "forcefulness" as a singer, saying, "She has a tendency toward shrillness when she pushes too hard."

With an album under her belt, Alison skipped her last two years of high school to start at the University of Illinois in the fall of 1987. She would attend for a year and a half. One of the subjects she studied was voice. Within a few months she signed with the Nashville booking agency Keith Case and Associates and began her long "special, working dysfunctional relationship" with Denise Stiff, who would remain her manager for over twenty years.

In the spring of 1988 Alison ducked out of classes for three weeks to play on the Masters of the Folk Violin Tour, produced by the National Council for the Traditional Arts. She and pianist Barbara MacDonald Magone, the only other female performer on the tour, roomed together. Tour organizer Joe Wilson had hired Alison to represent the Texas long-bow fiddle style, but she was soon playing duets with Claude Williams, the legendary jazz violinist. As Joe said of Claude, "He was old [eighty-one] and well-wrinkled, but small, compact, and dapper. She was beautiful and young, and a wee bit shy, and they played beautifully together. They were a vision on stage. He adored her." The *New York Times* liked her fiddling and thought her voice had a "thin but attractive twang." The limited edition, self-titled cassette—made to sell on next year's coast-to-coast tour, on which Alison also played—showcased Alison's powerhouse vocals on "I Can't Get You Off of My Mind" and "Wayfaring Stranger" along with her prowess with the bow on two fiddle tunes. Banjo player Bill Evans, who saw the tour in California, said, "There was no question that she was the smash hit of that show. The audience response at the Berkeley show was incendiary."

Alison Krauss and Union Station: Two Highways (1989) marked the emergence of Alison's name at the head of the band. Since Rounder was banking on the young singer, the label wanted her name out front. Thus Alison joined the vanguard of a tiny but growing number of women-fronted bands that included Laurie Lewis and Grant Street and the Lynn Morris Band. Alison's situation, however, was different: not only was she much younger, but she also did not have a husband, partner, or relative in the band. Her success would do much to fuel the movement toward women-led bands in the future.

Two Highways initiated the pattern of alternating a solo album with a band album. Alison revels in the band experience. She loves playing full-time with "people who challenge me musically." She enjoys working with a group that has been road-tested and is comfortable playing together. And she values what her bandmates have to say: "Their opinions are worth more to me than anybody's opinion . . . more than any record label's opinion . . . If they like what I've done, I know it's okay." As Alison's solo projects began to venture into non-bluegrass waters, her band albums became the expression of her bluegrass soul.

When Mike Harman left in early 1989, Alison called on Alison Brown to fill in on banjo for a couple of gigs. The young Harvard graduate would stay for three years. Having two unrelated women playing lead instruments in the same band was practically unheard of except in all-female bands. Together the two Alisons were breaking new ground.

The IBMA premiered its awards show in 1990, and with the exception of the other women in the vocal category, Alison Krauss was the lone female presence, with five nominations. She won only Female Vocalist of the Year, a feat she would repeat in 1991, 1993, and 1995. To date, no woman has won IBMA Fiddle Player of the Year.

Alison's second solo album, *I've Got That Old Feeling* (1990), became her commercial breakthrough, winning her the first in a long line of Grammys. Even before receiving this prestigious award, her music had found its way into the hearts of the national press. *Newsweek* raved about her fiddling, and *USA Today* said that both her fiddle and voice would "surprise anybody who expects bluegrass to drone." *Rolling Stone* profiled her in its "New Faces" section and declared, "Krauss makes traditional bluegrass seem utterly contemporary."

But in appealing to a wider audience, Alison had alienated some hard-core bluegrass fans. The disc received a scathing review in *Bluegrass Unlimited*. Unsurprisingly, the reviewer's first volley invoked the phrase "isn't exactly bluegrass." He poured fuel on the fire by adding that it "isn't much of any-thing." He groused about "over-production," said the songs were "not up to previous material," and closed by saying the album was "a squandering of her tremendous musical gift."

Two decades later one wonders what the fuss was about. All things consid-ered, this album was not terribly different from Alison's first two. True, it has less banjo on it, but the Dobro takes up the slack admirably—if there is any slack. The drums, on three cuts, are audible but not obtrusive, the touches of piano tasteful, and Alison is still delivering the goods with gusto. As for the material, "Steel Rails" would go on to become a modern bluegrass standard.

This review launched another round of "What is bluegrass?" in the pages of *Bluegrass Unlimited*. A reader wrote in saying he was "glad to see BU pan Alison's recording." He bellyached, "Why can't people be satisfied with bluegrass the way it is? If I were where Alison Krauss is in her career I'd be satisfied." His letter sparked a passionate response from Dry Branch Fire Squad bandleader (and Rounder artist) Ron Thomason. "Whether you like *I've Got That Old Feeling* or not, if you're in the bluegrass business, you should be darned glad Alison Krauss won the Grammy. Ken Irwin and Rounder did good business in promoting her and we all benefited."

One of the most significant spin-offs from the album was the video of the title song, "I've Got That Old Feeling." This was the first video that Rounder had produced and the first bluegrass video considered for regular rotation on CMT and The Nashville Network. It would go on to win the CMT award for Independent Video of the Year in 1991, thus opening the door for other bluegrass artists like Rhonda Vincent and Nickel Creek. Alison's career was kicking into high gear, and according to Ken Irwin, the video was a "key ingredient."

Meanwhile Alison was being tapped to play on recordings by her friends in the bluegrass world. Her appearance on Butch Baldassari's *Old Town*, playing twin fiddles with pal Andrea Zonn, was one of the first. Even her disgruntled *Bluegrass Unlimited* reviewer liked her work here, calling it "sassier, hotter, tastier and bolder than anything she's done previously." As late as 1990 it was still unusual for a woman to appear on an album as a side musician. These bluegrass albums helped establish Alison as a power player, not just a talented female vocalist. Her early work included albums by Alison Brown (1990), Northern Lights (1991), Tony Furtado (1992), Jerry Douglas (1992), and a cut on Michelle Shocked's *Arkansas Traveler* (1992).

By early 1990 Alison had almost completely revamped her band, picking up three members of the group Dusty Miller: Adam Steffey, Tim Stafford, and Barry Bales. Banjo player Ron Block would join shortly after to complete the configuration—now referred to as AKUS—that would appear on her fourth album, *Every Time You Say Goodbye* (1992). With a project that included plenty of banjo, Alison found her way back in the good graces of *Bluegrass Unlimited*, where the happy reviewer called her "the brightest star on the bluegrass horizon." Here, for the first time, Alison sublimates her powerful, full-throated vocals for what became her signature sound: a soft, whispery touch under immaculate control.

In addition to myriad other honors, in July 1993 Alison reached a high-water mark when she became a member of the Grand Ole Opry. Although technically the first bluegrass artist to join in twenty-nine years (since Jim and Jesse and the Osborne Brothers in 1964), Ricky Skaggs, who joined in 1982, and the Whites, inducted in 1984, were both deeply rooted in bluegrass.

Alison, who enjoyed working in the studio, now turned her skills to arranging and producing *Everybody's Reaching Out for Someone* (Rounder, 1993) for her friends and vocal soul mates, the Cox Family, a bluegrass group from Louisiana. Alison had fallen in love with the group's music in the late eighties and Sidney Cox had already supplied her with several songs, including "I've Got That Old Feeling." There is some speculation that her vocal style began to change after hearing the singing of Suzanne and Evelyn Cox. This was Alison's first in an impressive list of outside producing credits that would expand to include Nickel Creek, Reba McEntire, and Alan Jackson. Her next production venture, *Alison Krauss and the Cox Family: I Know Who Holds Tomorrow* (1994), would win a Grammy. She also produced two more albums for the group: *Beyond the City* (1995) and *Just When We're Thinking It's Over* (1996).

Artists from other genres were now asking Alison to guest on their projects. One of the earliest of these was a duet with Alan Jackson on his *Honky Tonk Christmas* (1993). The next two years would include recordings with Phish, Dolly Parton, Linda Ronstadt, and Shenandoah. More important career-wise was "When You Say Nothing at All," a cut on the Keith Whitley tribute album.

In 1994 Alison and the band, which now included Dan Tyminski, opened a number of arena shows for Garth Brooks. This was enormous exposure for Alison but "not something I'd want a steady diet of," she said. She didn't like having to plug in the instruments to be heard. "You've worked on your own tone, trying to make that sound good, and you plug it in and all that goes down the toilet." Also, as she told the *New York Times,* "You can't hear, you don't know if you're singing in tune. All the joy of hearing the person next to you sing is gone." Perhaps this experience was part of the reason Alison never jumped the fence to become the next flavor-of-the-month country music star.

Alison's fifth recording, *Now That I've Found You: A Collection* (1995), became Rounder's first platinum-selling album and would eventually go double platinum. Sales were propelled by "When You Say Nothing at All," which received airplay on major country stations, and the video of the song, which was in heavy rotation on CMT.

Still, the sensitive singer was conscious of the reaction of bluegrass fans to the new compilation. In the pages of *Bluegrass Unlimited,* Alison goes to great lengths to explain that her solo albums and outside projects are a way "to branch out and have fun." She is not pretending that songs like "Baby, Now That I've Found You" are bluegrass. "I think we definitely do bluegrass and then we do stuff that isn't, and I'd never put it under the same label." She understands that her branching out "offends some people." But drawing the conclusion that every pioneer has had to reach, she says, "Why should we not do something 'cause you're afraid of making somebody mad, you know?"

When Alison walked off with four Country Music Association Awards in 1995, including the Horizon Award and the award for Female Vocalist of the Year, talk surfaced about her becoming a country star. In fact, major labels had been courting Alison for years—and she had been listening. "I felt it would be stupid not to meet." When she was making her second album, she even came "close" to going elsewhere but realized she was happy at Rounder. "Switching to a major just never seemed like the right thing to do, because we were *already* doing the right things. We had our needs met, and we were making the records we wanted to make."

In 1995 Alison's growing success propelled her into the arms of a major sponsor, Martha White Foods, and for several years the band crossed the country in the Martha White Bluegrass Express bus. This was the first time the corporation had sponsored a bluegrass band since the days of Lester Flatt and Earl Scruggs. The crowning touch was the inclusion of "Alison Krauss's Winning Cornbread" in the Martha White recipe leaflet. Even a Grammy-winning, platinum-selling, female fiddle champion could not escape the cultural expectation that she should still be able to turn out a pan of prizewinning cornbread.

After all the hoopla surrounding *Now That I've Found You,* Union Station enjoyed circling the wagons to make *So Long, So Wrong* (1997), the first album on which Dan Tyminski makes a substantial appearance. His own brush with fame as the singing voice of George Clooney in *O Brother, Where Art Thou?* was still a few years off. *Bluegrass Unlimited* opined that the album "makes one happy that, if bluegrass needs an ambassador in the mainstream world, Alison is our current representative." The new alt-country magazine *No Depression* called the band the "standard-bearers of contemporary bluegrass." The black-and-white CD cover showed the five musicians in unsmiling mode. Perhaps as "standard-bearers" they felt they needed to project a serious demeanor.

Alison has always insisted on keeping her private affairs closely guarded, consequently there was little fanfare when in November 1997 she married Pat Bergeson, guitarist with Lyle Lovett's band. Her brother, Viktor, also played bass in the group. Pat would appear on Alison's album, *Forget About It*.

Adam Steffey's departure after *So Long, So Wrong* made room for the official addition of Jerry Douglas, "the greatest Dobro player who has ever lived," according to Alison. Jerry, who already had a flourishing solo career, would receive special billing as well as a spot on the show to showcase his own brilliant work.

In August 1999 Alison released the solo album *Forget About It*. The disc was not reviewed by *Bluegrass Unlimited,* who deemed it "alt-country." However, the album was right down the alley for *No Depression*, who applauded Alison for continuing to follow her own muse with a "healthy disregard for both the jealous embrace of bluegrass exclusivists and her own commercial success."

The month before, Alison and Pat had celebrated the birth of their son, Sam. Two years later Alison became a single mother when she and Pat divorced and she received custody of the toddler. From now on Sam would come first, although Alison would continue a hectic schedule of recording and touring, taking Sam and a caregiver on the road with her in a separate bus. Meredith Bub, who was Sam's on-the-road nanny from 2002 to 2005, says, "[Alison's] the best mother I've ever seen. I've learned so much from her, as far as being a good mom, and just being selfless. She is utterly patient, interested in every aspect, and she listens to everything he has to say."

The birth of a baby is expected to bring change. The release of a movie? Not so much. Yet the Coen brothers' film *O Brother, Where Art Thou?* (2000) turned the world of roots music on its ear. The sound track, on which Alison sang three songs, would go on to sell almost seven million copies with virtually no airplay. The resurrected Stanley Brothers' number "Man of Constant Sorrow," featuring the voice of Dan Tyminski, became an instant classic. In the blink of an eye, acoustic music was all the rage. Why now? What underground steam had *O Brother* tapped in to?

While many factors contributed to this "overnight" fascination with acoustic music, the *Journal of Country Music* sees Alison's career "as the foundation, if not the set-up." With airplay on country radio, videos on CMT, national press coverage, and appearances on television, she had done much to keep bluegrass in the public eye during the previous decade.

The movie spawned a wealth of projects in which Alison and the band participated, including the documentary film and sound track *Down from the Mountain* (2001), the Down from the Mountain Tour (2002), and the follow-up Great High Mountain Tour (2004), which added music from the movie *Cold Mountain*.

The TV broadcast of the 44th Annual Grammy Awards (2002) put the icing on an already very rich cake. A host of musicians from the *O Brother* sound track, including Alison and the band, made a magnificent showing, performed three songs, and took home a total of eleven Grammys, including Album of the Year. When the Dixie Chicks awarded a Grammy to "Man of Constant Sorrow," Natalie Maines said, "In case you haven't heard, bluegrass kicks ass!" Although somewhat overshadowed by the *O Brother* tumult, Alison's own new band project, *New Favorite* (2001), picked up three Grammys, including one for Best Bluegrass Album.

Alison was not only paving the way as a female bandleader and popular culture conduit to bluegrass, but she was also tramping through uncharted territory for women in the powerful role of producer. Although her first three albums were produced by others—Ken Irwin, Bil VornDick, and Jerry Douglas—she, with Union Station, took over the reins on her fourth album and her hand has been at the controls ever since. She had already served as producer for the Cox Family and was becoming known for her deliberate crafting of songs, her willingness to experiment, and her attention to detail. Now she began getting calls to produce for others.

Nickel Creek was the first. Alison's musical ventures were having a tremendous impact on the young musicians following in her wake. To this band of teenagers—Sara Watkins and her brother Sean, plus Chris Thile—she was, as Sara says, the "queen of bluegrass . . . the icon." Sean says, "She set a standard for keeping an open mind-set for things . . . and it's very inspiring." Encouraged by her support and interest, the group asked her to produce their self-titled Sugar Hill debut (2000). She introduced the young musicians to her creed of the timeless album, which meant limiting flash and dazzle in favor of turning out a disc that people would listen to again and again. The band enjoyed working with her so much that they asked her to produce their second recording, *This Side* (2002).

Producing Nickel Creek brought Alison to the attention of Reba McEntire. When the country music superstar heard the group's video on CMT, she asked Alison to produce a selection for her *Greatest Hits Volume III: I'm a Survivor* (2001). Reba's well-developed studio ethic is to move fast, sing the song a few times, and get out; Alison, on the other hand, likes to explore endless possibilities. Acknowledging their differences, the two women agreed to work together on "Sweet Music Man," a song Alison chose. Reba gave her producer a good solid hour of singing, trying Alison's many suggestions without complaint and nailing each one. When the session was over, Reba left immediately for her Broadway performance of *Annie Get Your Gun*. As she headed for the door, Alison told her, "That's one of the best musical experiences I ever had. I can't even really believe how amazing you are." Reba replied, "Well, I'm a good doer, and you're a good thinker-upper."

Alison would venture into country music territory again a few years later when Alan Jackson asked her to produce a bluegrass album for him. The honky-tonk heartthrob was only the second male country star, behind Toby Keith, to have an album produced by a woman. The decidedly non-bluegrass *Like Red on a Rose* (2006), which was nothing like Alan's previous records, turned out to be a collection of slow, reflective songs about love, family, and growing older. The disc received three Grammy nominations but lost Best Country Album to the Dixie Chicks.

Somehow in the middle of all these projects, Alison and the band found time to deliver an onstage recording, *Live* (2002), filmed in concert at Louisville, Kentucky. The DVD, released the following year, gives the viewer the pleasure of seeing Union Station in action. The show is tight, the music stunning, the band a relaxed but well-oiled machine whose members obviously love what they are doing. But beyond the music there is the unexpected delight of Alison's quirky commentary, which provides a break from the barrage of what she calls "the sad, pitiful numbers that we do all the time."

The band does four songs before Alison steps to the mike and thanks the audience for coming. She says, "This is one of the most beautiful theaters, if not the prettiest, that I think that we've ever got the chance to play in. It's unbelievable . . . [pause] . . . I especially like the naked people." Bada-bing! Laughter! She immediately has the audience in the palm of her hand. (She is referring to the statues that grace the sides of the Louisville Palace, which the camera thoughtfully zooms in on for viewers to see.)

Well aware that her albums have been criticized for their abundance of introspective, navel-gazing material, Alison uses this common knowledge to tease the crowd. She starts by mentioning the first time she heard "The Lucky One." "I was going, 'Oh, what a great song. I love this song. There's only one thing wrong with it though. It's happy.'" Pause. Laughter. "And I thought, 'Well, maybe we can talk to him [the writer] about it. Maybe we can get him to change it. Instead of a positive experience we want a negative experience. 'Cause we don't want anybody leaving our shows feeling good." Large laughter and clapping.

And what did the unassuming diva choose to wear for her first live DVD? Unlike the flashy, short, low-cut dress that Rhonda Vincent would wear in her own Rounder DVD a few years later, Alison is dressed simply in a light blue denim skirt that falls just below the knee; a short-sleeved, high-necked, black-ribbed sweater top; and sensible wedge sandals. The "undisputed star" of bluegrass music keeps it casual.

Casual definitely was not the order of the day when in February 2004 Alison became one of the few country acts to ever appear at the Academy Awards. She sang two songs from the film *Cold Mountain,* including "You Will Be My Ain True Love" with Sting. Ironically her performances were overshadowed by her shoes, a pair of four-inch stiletto sandals covered in two million dollars' worth of diamonds. (The daughters of the designer, Stuart Weitzman, were big fans.) As is her wont, Alison joked about her appearance. "I just want the folks back home to be proud. To say, 'She sang in tune and didn't forget the words. And she didn't fall off them shoes.'"

Alison's third consecutive band album, *Lonely Runs Both Ways,* was unusual not for its music but for its cover. For the first time Alison appears in glamorous attire—a slinky, turquoise evening gown cut low enough to show cleavage. Was this in response to Rhonda Vincent's raising the glamour bar for women in bluegrass? Alison's bandmates have not changed their attire in any way.

In 2007 Alison released her first solo project in eight years, *A Hundred Miles or More: A Collection.* In addition to five new songs, the album gathers gems from Alison's many side projects, such as "Whiskey Lullaby" with Brad Paisley and "How's the World Treating You?" with James Taylor. Although Alison clearly enjoys exploring the dark side of relationships, two songs from this collection reveal her romantic side. In talking about "Simple Kind of Love," with the lyrics "I want a simple love like that, always giving, never asking back," she says, "That's the hope of every little girl, the selfless love of a man." And of the song "Lay Down Beside Me" (with English rocker John Waite), she comments, "It's a dream for a woman to hear those things." Things like "Lay down beside me, love me, and hide me and kiss all the hurting of this world away."

The cover photo of the album is a complete reversal from the sexy Alison of *Lonely Runs Both Ways*. Here she walks along the beach, eyes demurely cast down, her short dress topped by a long white coat, the sleeves of which cover her hands. With lengthy, tousled blonde hair, she looks like an innocent little girl. Since Alison is widely known for calling her own shots, one wonders about this radical change. Is Alison now intentionally positioning herself against the brash, in-your-face sexiness of Rhonda Vincent and the other country stars she is competing with?

Before Alison hit the road that summer to promote *A Hundred Miles*, she and Union Station did a shorter spring tour with guitar maestro Tony Rice. With Alison and the band handling the singing, their performances packed arts centers in selected Southern cities. Alison was on cloud nine. As she said, "Tony Rice is my biggest influence. He was my hero. The first time I was ever star-struck was watching Tony . . . And the standard of making records, when I think about what I'd want one of my records to be like, Tony is what comes to mind."

Tony also appeared on Alison's hour-long television special that aired in August 2007 on GAC, the Great American Country channel. Recorded live in a Nashville studio (the musicians are wearing headphones), the show also featured duet appearances with James Taylor, Brad Paisley, and John Waite. There is no audience, no chitchat, and little movement save that of fingers on strings. With nothing to distract the viewer, all that is left is, of course, the song. As James Taylor said, "The material is so over-the-top emotional and her delivery of it is so cool, so detached, and so technical that it's like hot chocolate sauce on vanilla ice cream."

In October of the same year Alison made possibly the biggest leap of her career when she released *Raising Sand*, a duet album with Led Zeppelin's Robert Plant. A project that spanned musical genres, it garnered five Grammys, including Album of the Year, Best Contemporary Folk/Americana Album, Best Pop Collaboration with Vocals, and Best Country Collaboration with Vocals.

Way back in 1995 when Alison was asked to comment on her place in country music history, she said simply, "I want to make good records. That's my goal. I want this record to be better than the last one. I want to sing more in tune, play more in tune. I don't have any solo ambitions. I'm part of something with them [Union Station]."

More than a decade later her friend and longtime bandmate Ron Block gave Alison the highest praise imaginable when he said, "She's come to a new place in her singing and expression of that inner person that just blows me away . . . She gets better with each record."

Alison Brown, 1976. (Courtesy of Alison Brown)

Cloud Valley, early 1980s. L-R: Charlie Rancke, Steve Smith, Bill Evans, Missy Raines. (Courtesy of *Bluegrass Unlimited*)

Cherokee Rose, early 1980s. L-R: Louisa Branscomb (seated on floor), Tyra Dean Somers (seated on chair with banjo), Mindy Johnson, Sally Wingate (standing). (Courtesy of *Bluegrass Unlimited*)

Sally Davis (Wingate) at the banjo contest at Sunset Park in West Grove, Pennsylvania, July 4, 1965. Sally, the only woman (in shorts), took second place to Larry McNeely, second from left. (Courtesy of Sally Wingate)

Bluegrass Liberation, 1972. L-R: Sally Davis (Wingate), Louisa Branscomb, Lynn Grey (Salls), Erica Hunter. (Courtesy of Sally Wingate)

New Coon Creek Girls, early 1980s. L-R: Cathy Lavender, Jan Cummins, Wanda Barnett, Vicki Simmons. (Courtesy of Wanda Barnett)

Last all-female configuration of the New Coon Creek Girls, 1996. L-R: Dale Ann Bradley, Kathy Kuhn, Vicki Simmons, Gena Britt. (Personal collection of author)

Pam Gadd, IBMA World of Bluegrass, 1998.
(Photo by Garland Gobble, personal collection of author)

Sidesaddle, ca. 1992. L-R: Sonia Shell, Lee Anne Welch, Sheila McCormick, Jackie Miller, Kim Elking. (Personal collection of author)

Petticoat Junction, 1991. L-R: Andrea Roberts, Gail Rudisill, Robin Roller, Lori Harman. (Personal collection of author)

All Girl Boys, ca. 1994. L-R: Kathy Barwick, Sonia Shell, Mary Gibbons,
Chris Lewis, Carolyn Cirimele. (Personal collection of author)

The Tennessee HeartStrings, 2002. L-R: Karen Pendley, Marilyn Barclay, Bo Jamison,
Chris Lewis, Sally Wingate. (Personal collection of author)

Alison Krauss and Union Station with Roy Clark on the set of *Hee Haw*, early 1990s. L-R: Adam Steffey, Tim Stafford, Alison Krauss, Barry Bales, Roy Clark, Alison Brown. (Courtesy of Alison Brown)

The Vincent Family, mid-1970s. L-R: Johnny, Carolyn, Rhonda. (Courtesy of Rhonda Vincent)

Kristin Scott Benson and Laurie Lewis, Sachsenheim, Germany, 2001.
(Courtesy of Laurie Lewis)

Blue Night Express (pre–Dixie Chicks), McLain Family Band Festival, Berea, Kentucky, 1986. Marti Erwin, Sharon Gilchrist, Troy Gilchrist, Emily Erwin. (Courtesy of Jean-Marc Delon)

Blue Night Express on stage (pre–Dixie Chicks), McLain Family Band Festival, Berea, Kentucky, 1986. L-R: Sharon Gilchrist, Troy Gilchrist, Marti Erwin, Emily Erwin. (Courtesy of Jean-Marc Delon)

Cherryholmes, 2003. Front, Molly; middle, Sandy, Cia; back,
L-R: B. J., Jere, Skip. (Personal collection of author)

Sara Watkins, IBMA World of Bluegrass, 1998, when she was playing with
Nickel Creek. (Photo by Garland Gobble, personal collection of author)

Amanda Kowalski, bass; Sierra Hull, mandolin; Michelle Porter, mandolin. IBMA World of Bluegrass, 1998. (Personal collection of author)

The Dixie Bee-Liners, 2010. L-R: Buddy Woodward, Rachel Renee Johnson (Boyd), Brandi Hart, Casey Henry, Sav Sankaram (Photo by James Joseph Bray, courtesy of the Dixie Bee-Liners)

Trina Emig, ca. late 1990s. (Personal collection of author)

Sweet Potato Pie, 2011. L-R: Sandy Whitley, Chrystal Richardson, Sonya Stead, Katie Springer. (Photo by Julia Wade, courtesy of Sweet Potato Pie)

The Daughters of Bluegrass receiving their Recorded Event of the Year Award at the 2009 IBMA Awards show. (Photo by David Roye, courtesy of Dixie Hall)

TOO MANY TO COUNT: *The 1990s and Beyond*

Now that the doors had been opened (or pried apart some might say), the 1990s and beyond saw more and more women— both the young and the seasoned—leading their own bands. The most prominent, of course, was Alison Krauss, who began her long string of Grammy wins in 1990. Alison's rampant success acted as a bulldozer, widening the opportunities for the women who followed in her wake.

A decade later Rhonda Vincent moved into national prominence with her first Rounder album while newcomer Sierra Hull's own Rounder debut in 2008 propelled her to four IBMA Mandolin Player of the Year nominations. It is no surprise that the young player found a role model in Rhonda, whose mandolin playing and singing were also dropping jaws when she was a kid.

And if it was still unlikely that first- or second-generation bandleaders such as Ralph Stanley and Ricky Skaggs would be hiring any women, the testosterone-charged Grascals, a new collaboration of established male players, stepped up to the plate and tapped banjo whiz Kristin Scott Benson to join their highly visible, tightly organized group.

As always, family bands such as the extraordinarily successful Cherryholmes, along with myriad local groups such as North Carolina's Wells Family (sisters Jade, Sara, Eden, and mother Debi), continued to provide a safe environment for young women to test their mettle and their wings.

And of course reigning over all, for a time, were the Dixie Chicks, who, while not totally embraced by the bluegrass community, insisted on playing banjo and fiddle on their live shows, DVDs, and records, thereby putting these two hillbilly-tinged instruments on the radar for their millions of fans who might not have encountered them otherwise.

In addition the surprising success of the movie *O Brother, Where Art Thou?* in 2000 sent veteran female country music artists scurrying to hop on the bluegrass bandwagon. Dolly Parton released three bluegrass-inflected CDs on Sugar Hill, *The Grass Is Blue* (1999), *Little Sparrow* (2001), and *Halos and Horns* (2002), with the first winning IBMA Album of the Year in 2000. The acoustic-flavored *Mountain Soul* (2001) from Patty Loveless, which featured the fiddle playing of Deanie Richardson, was nominated for IBMA Album of the Year.

Rounder Records also used the *O Brother* phenomenon as a springboard to release three "Women's Bluegrass Collections" that showcased their deep roster of female artists: *O Sister* (2001), *O Sister 2* (2002), and the all-gospel *The Angels Are Singing* (2002). While not the first all-female compilations, with the clout of the Rounder label and the drawing power of Alison Krauss, who had a cut on all three projects, these CDs enjoyed wide circulation.

The achievements of women on the national scene broke ground for women at the local and regional level. Women who were new to the business could now more easily step into the role of bandleader, and they often used other women as side musicians, which was an important new development in bluegrass.

Valerie Smith, "a heretofore unknown but undeniably major league talent," earned those enthusiastic remarks and a highlight review from *Bluegrass Unlimited* for her debut CD, *Patchwork Heart* (1997). From the first configuration of her band Liberty Pike, with Sheila Wingate on bass, Valerie has almost always used women in her group, including bass players and vocalists Casey Grimes and Jessica Lee and guitarist Megan McCormick. A recent lineup featured nine-year band veteran Becky Buller on fiddle (and clawhammer banjo and guitar) and Rebekah Long on bass (and mandolin, fiddle, and guitar). Valerie's newest CD, *Blame It on the Bluegrass* (2010), was produced by Becky and engineered by Rebekah.

In the early days of her career Valerie caused some consternation in the bluegrass world because she did not play an instrument. The *Women in Bluegrass* newsletter addressed this topic, asking, "Is this a gender-related issue?" and "Why are no men doing this?" To which Valerie responded by saying, "Who makes the rules?" and "Where is the rule that says a musician *has* to play an instrument on stage?" She opined that her voice is her strongest instrument and that she puts most of her energy into singing and songwriting. Still, lately she has been playing fiddle, mandolin, and guitar on stage while continuing to let others handle the picking chores in the studio.

Jeanette Williams is another bandleader of long standing who did not at first play an instrument. She joined the Virginia group Clearwater in 1989 as a tenor singer and married founder Johnnie Williams in 1991. Shortly thereafter she became the lead singer, and around 1996 the band changed its name to Jeanette Williams and Clearwater. Her solo release, *Cherry Blossoms in the Springtime* (1999), brought this "relatively unknown talent" to national prominence, and soon the group was being billed as the Jeanette Williams Band. By 2009 *Bluegrass Unlimited* was calling her "one of the premier singers in bluegrass." Jeanette has not shied away from using other female musicians in the group. Marsha Bowman, Sandra Baucom, Ramona Church, and Donica Christiansen have all done stints on the banjo with her during the past ten years. And she herself took up the bass in 2002.

Honi Deaton, who fronts the band Dream, first flexed her bluegrass chops in Idaho as bass player for the Grasshoppers in the mid-nineties with her banjo-playing husband, Randy Glenn. Like many other women, Honi landed her position when the original player quit. After she and Randy parted ways, she remained with the Grasshoppers until 2001, when she met bluegrass musician Jeff Deaton. Six months later they were married and living in Georgia, Jeff's home state. Not wanting to be traveling in separate groups, she and Jeff decided to start their own band. As Honi says, "It was actually Jeff's idea to put my name out front." Over the years Honi has featured several women as side musicians, including Kristin Scott Benson on banjo and Shirley Seim on fiddle.

Mandolin player Lorraine Jordan's original concept for a band was the all-female Carolina Rose, which she organized in 1997. This soon morphed into the mixed-gender band Ramona Church and Carolina Road, which by 2006 had become Lorraine Jordan and Carolina Road. But perhaps her greatest pioneering venture was coming up with the concept for the Daughters of Bluegrass albums, aided originally by Gena Britt. This trio of recordings originated with *Daughters of American Bluegrass,* which was a nominee for IBMA Recorded Event of the Year in 2005. The second, *Back to the Well,* won that award in 2006, as did *Bluegrass Bouquet* in 2009. These CDs feature women doing all the picking and the singing, and the third included women handling the production, engineering, and mixing as well. These albums have brought national attention to many under-recognized artists such as Linda Lay, Heather Berry, Lisa Ray, Julie Elkins, and Rebecca Frazier.

Other women-led bands of this era include Michelle Nixon and Drive, Carrie Hassler and Hard Rain, Beth Stephens and Edge, Amy Gallatin and Stillwaters, Frances Mooney and Fontanna Sunset, Robin Roller and the High Rollers, the Patty Mitchell Band, the Judith Edelman Band, the Lizzie Long Band, the Bertye Maddux Band, the Tina Adair Band, and the Katie Penn Band. There are also a number of solo female artists such as Donna Hughes, Melonie Cannon, Sharon Cort, and Alicia Nugent, whose recordings and shows feature full bands.

The twenty-first century also brought a host of young women to the forefront, and none has been more prominent than Sierra Hull (b. 1991), who now leads her own band, Highway 111. The Tennessee native picked up the mandolin when she was eight years old and hasn't put it down yet. Nominated five times for IBMA Mandolin Player of the Year (2008–2012), she is the only woman (so far) to have attained this lofty recognition from her peers. Sierra, however, was a fast learner right out of the gate. By age eleven she had guested on the Grand Ole Opry twice, once with her idol Alison Krauss. When she was ten she released her first CD, *Angel Mountain* (2002), on an independent label, and in 2008 she made her Rounder Records debut with *Secrets,* which she co-produced with Ron Block, banjo player for Alison Krauss. In addition to a heavy touring schedule, she found time to attend the prestigious Berklee College of Music in Boston, graduating in 2012.

Sierra's musical journey demonstrates that while some things have changed significantly for women, others have, unfortunately, remained the same. Even though she found a marvelous role model in Alison Krauss ("She's my main hero"), Sierra still had the experience (or the feeling) of being "the only female around" in jam sessions. On the other hand, she was able to say, "I remember seeing a Rhonda Vincent CD in Walmart one time, and then it kind of dawned on me, I was like 'Wow, a woman holding a mandolin.' I thought, 'Man, that'll be me someday . . . I'll be grown and be a woman and be a mandolin player.'" A watershed moment indeed!

Other up-and-coming young women of this era include fiddler Brittany Haas with Crooked Still; Analise, Jocelyn, and Shelby Gold, the three sisters from Gold Heart, on mandolin, lead guitar, and fiddle, respectively; mandolin player Amber Burks; Frankie Nagle on banjo and lead guitar; the Martin sisters, with Janice on banjo, Larita on resonator guitar, and Jeana on fiddle; Carmen Gibes on banjo with Cats and the Fiddler; fiddler Katie Nakamura; and multi-instrumentalist Sarah Jorosz, whose music has lately moved into the Americana realm. California lead guitarist Molly Tuttle was awarded the first Hazel Dickens Memorial Scholarship in 2011 and began her studies at Berklee College of Music in 2012.

One encouraging development over the last two decades has been the growth in the number of mixed-gender bands. One of the most prominent of these is the SteelDrivers, with Tammy Rogers on fiddle. Their self-titled debut album (Rounder, 2008) was nominated for IBMA Album of the Year in 2008, and the group was named IBMA Emerging Artist of the Year in 2009. Like her Nashville bandmates, Tammy has a long track record in the music business, including stints with Dusty Miller (bluegrass) and country stars Reba McEntire, Trisha Yearwood, and Patty Loveless. She is also a respected studio session player in Music City.

Other mixed-gender bands have included the Peter Rowan and Tony Rice Quartet, with Bryn Davies on bass and Sharon Gilchrist on mandolin; Sugarbeat, with Sally Truitt on bass; The Dixie Bee-Liners; Cross-Eyed Rosie; Some Assembly Required; Monroe Crossing; Common Ground; Silver Dagger; the WBT Briarhoppers, who in 2009 added banjo player Alana Flowers, their first female in seventy years; the short-lived Due West, with Megan Lynch and Cindy Browne; Bull Harman and Bull's Eye, with Robin Roller on banjo and Tammy Harman on bass; Mountain Laurel, with Kathy Barwick on Dobro; and Wild Blue Yonder, with sisters Laura Wallace Knight and Cindy Wallace and Melissa Wade.

One of the doors that has remained the most tightly closed for women (in spite of Kristin Scott Benson's presence in the Grascals) is the opportunity to play as a side musician in a high-profile band. Reflecting this situation is a recent article in Banjo NewsLetter titled "Young Guns of Bluegrass," which profiled six young men—and no women—who are all playing banjo with up-and-coming nationally prominent bands. Banjo player and feminist Casey Henry responded to this article with a blog post titled "Where Are the Girls?" in which she asked several pointed questions: "Are the girls really not there?" Or "Are the girls, as is so often the case, playing in family bands and thus discounted or ignored?" And "Do our cultural constraints make it harder for girls to become 'young guns' with all the aggression, assertiveness, mastery, self-confidence, and even violence that that implies?" She proposed writing her own article about young women who are "out there, on stage, playing for money." To his everlasting credit, editor Donald Nitchie agreed, saying, "Good idea. I should have thought of this. Duh."

Casey's blog entry generated a bevy of responses from readers who mentioned quite a few young women they knew about—Sarah Ward, Maggie Mackay, Katie Norton, Gina Furtado, Alana Flowers, Molly Tuttle, Haley Stiltner, Grace Van't Hof, and Katy Clark. Male banjo student Marty Bacon also chimed in with a comment that warmed my heart and gave me a chuckle: "All I ever wanted to do was 'pick like a girl!' Kristin Scott Benson, Gena Britt, Julie Elkins, Casey Henry, Murphy Henry." We've come a long way, ladies.

> I don't think people should applaud me for playing
> in a male band, they should applaud Larry and the
> band for hiring me; that's where the barrier is.
>
> —Kristin Scott Benson

KRISTIN
SCOTT
BENSON

September 1, 1995, was a memorable day in the life of banjo player Kristin Scott. A sophomore at Nashville's Belmont University, she was missing the start of classes to play her first gig with the Larry Stephenson Band at a bluegrass festival in Maine. It was also a milestone, albeit unnoticed, for women in bluegrass. This was the first time a female banjo player who was unconnected in any way with the players in an otherwise all-male band had joined a well-established, nationally known bluegrass band as a side musician. Kristin was neither mother, wife, daughter, sister, aunt, cousin, in-law, girlfriend, nor leader of the band. She was not a singer. And she was playing the banjo, the instrument that many think defines the sound of bluegrass music.

The Larry Stephenson Band might not have had the drawing power of Alison Krauss or Ralph Stanley, but Larry was definitely in the major leagues and he had his own bus. A well-known tenor singer and mandolin player, he had worked with Bill Harrell for four years and the Bluegrass Cardinals for five before forming his own band in 1989. The new group was featured on the cover of *Bluegrass Unlimited* in 1990. Six years later, when Larry's band again graced the front of the magazine, Kristin Scott was holding the banjo. A glass ceiling had been shattered. The question was, would other bands follow Larry's lead?

Even Kristin herself was not aware of the significance of her achievement. "I never felt like the first," she says. For her the trail had been blazed by bass player Missy Raines. "She pioneered the sideman job for a woman who's not involved with any of the guys or related to them. She was already accepted in all-male configurations, was already respected, and it wasn't unusual for her to play in a band with all guys even if it wasn't her routine job." Kristin also mentions fiddler Gail Rudisill, who had joined Continental Divide shortly before Kristin went with Larry. But Continental Divide was a new band and Gail's stay was short-lived. In addition, Kristin brings up Gloria Belle, who played with Jimmy Martin off and on for years. Yet none of them was doing what Kristin was doing: playing banjo in a widely recognized all-male band. "I didn't think of it as being that important. I was just happy to have the job."

Kristin (b. 1976), from Union, South Carolina, had been playing the banjo for only six years when she joined Larry, but she had bluegrass in her blood. Her grandfather Arval Hogan had been the mandolin player and tenor singer for Whitey and Hogan, a popular North Carolina group in the 1940s. She started playing mandolin when she was five and the next year won first place on the instrument in the junior division at the South Carolina Fiddler's Convention. But the mandolin never inspired her like the banjo would, and her parents always had to hound her to practice.

Bluegrass lovers themselves, Kristin's parents took their daughter to festivals regularly. She didn't pay a whole lot of attention, however, until she heard Doyle Lawson with Scott Vestal on banjo when she was nine. Her initial interest was visual: these were young men and their music excited her. Christmas 1989 brought Kristin her first banjo. Now her parents were annoyed because she never put it down. Kristin had found her instrument.

Two years later Kristin joined her first band, Furman Boyce and the Harmony Express, a gospel group based in nearby Woodruff, South Carolina. The band traveled throughout the South playing churches and bluegrass festivals, and for the first three months Kristin's parents were right there alongside their fifteen-year-old until they deemed the situation trustworthy. The earliest formation of the group, which also included three other women, Sherrill Boyce, Peggy Cooke, and Johnnie Sue Allen, recorded one album, *Through Heaven's Door* (Atteiram, 1993).

Kristin stayed with Harmony Express long enough to record a second album and then joined Nashville's all-female Petticoat Junction in 1994 during the last half of her senior year. Her ever supportive parents white-knuckled it as their daughter drove the four hundred miles to Nashville several times a month. No matter how late the band got back in on Sunday night, Kristin always left immediately to drive home to catch a few winks before school on Monday. The road she traveled, Interstate 40, includes a long stretch through the Blue Ridge Mountains. One night Kristin's mother woke up to find her husband walking the floor. "What are you doing?" she asked. "I'm helping Kristin drive across the mountains," he said. "I think my parents worried a lot more than I realized," Kristin says wryly.

Although Kristin's work with Petticoat Junction gave her national exposure, she still says, "Sometimes since we were an all-female band I think we were looked at as a novelty and not taken as seriously by other musicians, but I never felt singled out, obviously."

In the fall of 1994 she moved to Nashville to attend Belmont University. During her first semester she had a class with bass player Jill Snider, who played in the band Wild and Blue with her sister Jan, on guitar, and Jan's husband, Dave Harvey, on mandolin and fiddle. Kristin said, "I think the biggest reason I joined Wild and Blue was to get to play with Dave. I know at the time he was by far the best instrumentalist I'd ever played with, and I knew I could learn from him. And I knew I would be challenged in that situation." She was with Wild and Blue for only six months when she got the opportunity to audition for the Larry Stephenson Band. One of the recommendations came from Larry's bass player Matthew Allred. Kristin wanted a steady paying gig and Larry could provide one. "I never subscribed to the theory that because I was a female I was destined to play in bands with other females or mixed bands. I just thought if there was an open gig that I wanted, I would audition for it." She said, "I'll always be indebted to Larry for hiring me. I was only nineteen years old and nobody knew who I was, but he hired me anyway."

According to Larry, however, some prominent male bluegrassers strongly advised him not to hire Kristin. "It's gonna be a mistake. You can't do this. You can't have a girl running up and down the road on a bus with you." Larry simply said, "I'm gonna do it. She's a great banjo player." "It will never work," they warned. But it did work—for five years. Yet even in 1995 people who saw Kristin with the band often assumed she was married to one of the musicians or that she was Larry's daughter. Some no doubt thought she was his girlfriend. Kristin, recognizing that she was an anomaly, said wistfully, "I wish there were more females in bands that weren't linked to one of the members. It seems the only way to become prominent as a female is to be a lead singer or front your own band." She did not want to be either. She thought it was "cool to be a total sideman."

Larry described Kristin as "a good person with her head on straight and who played great . . . She outplayed everybody that auditioned . . . She was the best person for the job at the time." To Larry, Kristin's sterling reputation made a big difference. He did not want even a hint of sexual scandal or innuendo. "I didn't want anybody in the band that everybody was gonna be whispering behind our backs, 'What bunk's she sleeping in this weekend?' I was still trying to get going myself. We were doing well, but I didn't want anything to stop it dead in its tracks." So Larry was taking quite a risk.

Since much of the unease about having a woman in a band seems to revolve around sex, perhaps it helped that Kristin was already dating another banjo player when she was hired. When she broke up with him, it was only a short time before she started dating mandolin player Wayne Benson, whom she eventually married. So when Kristin says, "The guys that I travel with never think of me romantically. I can't imagine dating any of them and I don't think any one of them could imagine dating me," perhaps it is because in their view she was simply off-limits. If she had been unattached, perhaps it would have been a different story. Or perhaps it is simply Kristin's own personality. Whatever the reason, Kristin's above-reproach performance and long tenure with the Larry Stephenson Band provided proof that a woman could indeed perform as a side musician in an all-male band.

Shortly after joining Larry's band, Kristin released a self-produced cassette, *Kristin Scott,* helped out by Wayne Benson, her new bandmates, and fiddler Gail Rudisill, who had played with her in Petticoat Junction. The tunes included some of the most difficult in the extended banjo repertoire: "Follow the Leader," "Bye Bye Blues," and "Charmaine." Her new visibility landed her on the cover of *Banjo NewsLetter,* an honor few women attain, where her recording garnered a glowing review. Ian Perry wrote that Kristin played with "exceptional taste and timing, not to mention a youthful exuberance that many players lose as the years go by."

Kristin also played on three of Larry's albums: *I See God* (Pinecastle/Webco 1996), *On Fire* (Pinecastle, 1998), and *Two Hearts on the Borderline* (Pinecastle, 2000). Her appearance on the third received high praise in the *Bluegrass Unlimited* review: "Her banjo playing . . . is a fine example of how to get a lot done without going over the top. Her phrasing and timing are impeccable." The magazine's 1996 cover article about the band said that although Kristin was "personally quiet and unassuming, she can 'drive' the banjo with the very best and is extremely skillful and tasteful in playing to complement the vocalists." There was no mention of her gender, the fact that she was the lone female in this four-piece group, or her groundbreaking role as a side musician.

In 1998 Kristin graduated summa cum laude from Belmont with a bachelor's degree in business administration with a major in marketing and minor in music business. Although Larry's band worked quite a bit by bluegrass standards, as a single person Kristin always found it necessary to hold a day job to make ends meet. As she said, "I either was in school and with Larry, working and with Larry, or in school and working and with Larry."

The following year Kristin played banjo on Mark Newton's *Follow Me Back to the Fold: A Tribute to Women in Bluegrass* (Rebel, 2000), on which several women were featured as side musicians. Kristin did all of the banjo work except for the three songs that featured Lynn Morris. The project went on to win the IBMA Recorded Event of the Year 2001.

Mark arranged an album release party at the famous Birchmere in Washington, D.C., in the spring of 2000. Here Laurie Lewis had a chance to work with Kristin for the first time. In the liner notes to Kristin's second solo CD, *Straight Paths* (Pinecastle, 2002), Laurie said, "I felt immediately comfortable with her sense of time and her sensitive ear for ensemble work. Both being a bit on the shy side, we barely said more than a couple of short sentences to each other, but I filed her name away in my mental Rolodex of banjo prospects." For Kristin, this meeting turned into a European tour with Laurie and her band in 2001. As Laurie wrote, "It's a big leap of faith to go on the road with someone you barely know, but Kristin struck me as a real band player. By this I mean someone who is more concerned with the communal effort of making good music than with using the stage as a platform to say, 'Hey! Over here! Look at me!'"

The year 2000 was a banner year for Kristin. In April she married Wayne Benson, mandolin player for the award-winning IIIrd Tyme Out, whom she had been dating for three years, and they purchased a house in Murfreesboro, Tennessee. Kristin also bought her 1933 Gibson banjo, a major financial commitment, since banjos of that era now run to five figures. She was aided in that decision by her dad, a construction worker, who told her, "I own the best backhoe that I can get . . .You need to own the best banjo that you can get." Kristin, thrifty by nature, had been saving for the banjo for years. She said, "I had ordered water at restaurants instead of Coke and little things like that to save for a banjo."

Although Kristin was well aware that if she left Larry's band there would be no banjo-picking jobs of equal caliber available to her, she still opted out in 2000. She and Larry's bass player, Mickey Harris, were partnering with their mutual friend Sally Jones in the risky venture of starting a new band, the Sidewinders. Both players were interested in having more input in a group. As Kristin said, "That's kind of the ultimate artistic statement, to form something and have it be completely new."

Kristin has nothing but the highest praise for her five years with Larry's band. "Larry was always great to me. Never did 'girl stuff' ever get to be a problem. I'm so indebted to him. Nobody's ever treated me better than he has. I'm convinced that that was without a doubt the best thing that ever happened to me just because I was there a long time and I got to play a lot."

When word got out in bluegrass circles that Kristin was leaving, it was only natural that several women called Larry hoping to audition for the banjo or bass slot. To them, Larry's band seemed like a ray of sunshine in an otherwise bleak landscape, an open door that could provide an opportunity to play with a high-caliber band. After all, he'd hired Kristin. Perhaps, to borrow from Christine Lavin, he really was a "sensitive New Age guy." At least one of them was stunned when Larry said he wasn't going to hire any more women. The blow was crushing. When questioned about this four years later, Larry said, "You know, we go through life and say things sometimes we wished we didn't say? If I had it to do over again, I would have never quite put it that way. And yet I did mean that. I meant it in the sense that if I would have hired another female would she have been as good as Kristin? No, I don't think so. I don't think they could have stood up to what Kristin was doing at the time." Larry also mentioned the singing. He wanted to keep the sound of his male trio, which featured him singing a high lead with two men singing harmony beneath him, and he also wanted to do some male gospel quartets. And there was another reason. He didn't want people saying, "Well, he just hired another girl." He didn't want to become known as the band with the girl banjo player.

In the five years Kristin was with Larry, no other woman had been hired to play banjo in a high-profile band. Although Kristin had worked out extremely well, having a woman in the band still made Larry's band an anomaly. Although the time was apparently not yet right for mixed-gender bands to become the norm, there were other breakthroughs. Fiddler and singer Jenee Keener, nineteen, another Belmont student, joined Larry Cordle and Lonesome Standard Time in 2002, staying long enough to record two albums with him. She then left to play country music with Terri Clark.

Kristin's new Sidewinder bandmate Sally Jones was married to Chris Jones, who already had his own band, the Night Drivers. Yet the couple had chosen not to become a husband-and-wife bluegrass team. As Sally tells it:

> I would have had no problem being considered just Chris's wife in the band. My own parents farmed together in Canada and were literally partners in every activity. Chris was the one who maintained that I was a singer, songwriter, piano and guitar player all on my own when he met me, and to toss all my musical identity to play together would be the wrong kind of sacrifice. His model was of a successful Broadway actress mother who was determined to go her own way. He felt I would never discover my own potential in the husband-wife playing scenario, particularly in bluegrass, where many people would always defer to the man. Chris also understood that we had different styles and approaches, and the nuances of each would be lost in an amalgam. That we are both lead singers and guitar players and songwriters is a strong part of that argument. In the end, I think he was right to push me into my own path. I have grown tremendously, faced things that I would have always relied on him to face for us, and developed my own vision for my music. Our marriage is if anything stronger because of it.

With whiz kid Cody Kilby on mandolin, the Sidewinders were a true mixed-gender band, in which no members were related or paired up romantically. Kristin worked with Sally from August 2000 until September 2002, when this version of the band fizzled out as everyone's lives began to move in different directions. Kristin was heartbroken. However, even as the band was unraveling she received an offer to join Honi Deaton and Dream, a talented start-up group based in north Georgia. Honi, one of the new wave of talented young female bandleaders, would be featured on the cover of *Bluegrass Now* in February 2004. Kristin said, "It's like God was so cool to me, because I haven't been without a job really since I was fifteen years old." Kristin stayed with Honi from September 2002 until March 2004, recording one CD, *What Should Have Been*.

In April 2004 Kristin got the opportunity to join Larry Cordle and Lonesome Standard Time, a well-known band who twice had won IBMA Song of the Year for songs penned by Larry. His "Murder on Music Row" was named

Country Music Association Song of the Year in 2001. Kristin was back with a well-established band. She stayed with Larry Cordle until 2006 and played on his 2007 album, *Took Down and Put Up*.

Kristin landed this job the way many male players get jobs: she was recommended by players she had worked with before. Booie Beach, Cordle's guitar player, had been in the Larry Stephenson Band, and Chris Davis, the new mandolin player, had been in Dream. When Cordle needed a banjo player, they both gave her strong recommendations. When she was younger, Kristin had wanted to "not even know any of the guys before the audition. Just get a job because of how you play—that's the way it's supposed to be." But now that she has a few bands under her belt, Kristin knows that usually "it's all just who you know and who you play with."

In 2004 the decision to have children also loomed large. "We just can't decide. Our hearts are definitely softening towards children. Wayne always says, 'If I had to give up playing music to have children, we would never have them. So there's no way I'm gonna force you to do that.' But I really believe if I ever do have a kid, I picture it being normal with me at home. So it's hard to figure out what you want." Kristin figured it out, however, and Hogan Wayne Benson arrived on October 2, 2006. In December of the same year, Kristin rejoined Larry Stephenson, who was working more than Larry Cordle. Soon after Hogan was born, Kristin and Wayne realized that if they both intended to travel they would have to move closer to family. So they relocated to South Carolina, about an hour from Kristin's parents, who care for Hogan when his own mom and dad are on the road.

And if Kristin's life weren't exciting enough, in October 2008 she was named IBMA Banjo Player of the Year, only the second woman to win this prestigious award. She became a four-time winner in 2011. Asked if this had been a goal of hers, she replied, "No, I never thought it was possible." The month following her win, she joined the Grascals, an award-winning group of seasoned musicians who in four short years had served as Dolly Parton's 2004 opening act, released three Rounder albums, and been named IBMA Entertainer of the Year twice in a row. Kristin came highly recommended for the job, this time by her friend and mentor, the legendary banjo player Sonny Osborne. Of course, she had also been playing steadily in top-tier bands for over a decade, and she knew these musicians and they knew her; plus she had a stellar reputation, not only for her playing, but for her work ethic. Still the fact that an all-male band would hire a woman with a two-year-old baby is notable.

Kristin quickly got to work on her third solo CD, *Second Season* (Pinecastle, 2009), an all-instrumental project that she produced. In addition to husband Wayne, she enlisted old band buddies Larry Cordle, Sally Jones, Mickey Harris, Cody Kilby, and Larry Stephenson to help her out.

As far being a "normal" stay-at-home-mom, Kristin now says:

Life isn't always what we envision it, is it? I've finally come to realize that I'm always going to want to play music. During every phase of my life I thought the desire would subside, but it never does. In college I thought, "After I graduate, I'll want to pursue a normal career," but I didn't. Then I thought I wouldn't want to be gone all the time after I was married. Wrong again! The biggie was, "After I have kids, I won't want to play." And while having a child has been the most rewarding experience of my life, it didn't diminish my love for playing music. I've found peace in realizing that I'm always going to want to do this. It's part of who I am. Wayne and my family are incredibly supportive and I couldn't do it without them.

She's one I like a lot these days because she just went
totally bluegrass, and she's trying to get as much
edge as she can—which is unusual for women.

—Hazel Dickens

RHONDA
VINCENT

When Rhonda Vincent's two-page *Bluegrass Unlimited* ad for her Ragin' Live
Tour appeared in March 2005, showing her in a sleeveless black dress with a
plunging neckline, several enraged subscribers canceled their subscriptions. To
them, there was no place in bluegrass music for cleavage. But Rhonda is charting
her own course in bluegrass couture and remains undeterred and unrepentant.
For every grandparent who cancels a subscription, another brings a granddaughter to one of her shows and says to Rhonda, "My granddaughter's got a
favorite song and can't wait to see what you're gonna wear." Rhonda is trying
to walk that thin chalk line and appeal to both audiences. So far, the woman the
Wall Street Journal called "the new queen of bluegrass" is keeping her balance.

Rhonda (b. 1962), the seven-time IBMA Female Vocalist of the Year from
Greentop, Missouri, has been playing music professionally since she was three

years old. Five generations of Vincents have put rosin to bows and picks to strings, so for Rhonda playing music wasn't a choice. Nor was it for her mother, Carolyn (b. 1943), when she married guitar-playing Johnny Vincent in 1961. As Carolyn says humorously, "My husband told me I had to play or get out." Luckily she already played a little piano and enjoyed singing harmony. The extended Vincent family, which included Johnny's father, Bill, played dances almost every week, and Carolyn carved out a spot pounding out rhythm on the ivories.

Johnny (b. 1940) had been playing guitar since he was eleven. But music might not have become his life's work if he hadn't broken his neck in an automobile accident in 1964. He was paralyzed for three months and not expected to walk again. From tough Missouri stock, he eventually learned to get around with a cane. While recuperating he began playing the banjo, and the Vincent family added that to their not-yet-bluegrass sound. Before the accident both he and Carolyn had worked at the Florsheim shoe factory, but afterward Johnny was unable to return. Rhonda says, "Music became the absolute, constant focal point and something that drove him to get as good as he is and to drive us to play with such intensity every night."

Rhonda made her recording debut at five, singing "How Far Is Heaven" with her mother on an album titled *Boyd Halford and the Sally Mountain Singers*. That same year the family group began playing a live television program in Ottumwa, Iowa, sixty miles from Greentop. Needing a name for the band, they called themselves the Sally Mountain Show after a nearby mountain. Their show aired Friday mornings at 6:00 A.M. While it was no doubt hard on young Rhonda, it was doubly hard on Carolyn (and Aunt Kathryn), who had to be back for their jobs at the shoe factory.

When Bill began to suffer seriously from emphysema, Johnny looked for jobs that would be easier on his father than dances. In 1970 he found steady work for the family, playing at the Frontier Jamboree in nearby Marceline every Saturday night. They would stay there for five years. The show frequently featured national country music stars, and Rhonda met them all. Johnny was the guitar player in the house band and also played banjo with the now pared-down Sally Mountain Trio. Bill, who found it hard to stand up and play bass, moved to guitar, so Carolyn learned to play bass. The group soon included one-year-old Darrin (b. 1969), who at a very young age would sing "Me and Jesus." Eight-year-old Rhonda, not yet playing an instrument, was advertised as a main attraction—the little girl singer with the powerful set of lungs. Since she was getting tremendous response from the audience, Johnny naturally thought she should be paid.

The manager had other ideas: "When she starts picking an instrument, she gets paid." Johnny had a mandolin in her hands the next week. Rhonda was proud to be able to add another ten dollars to the family coffer. In 1972 Bill Vincent died, but the Sally Mountain Trio kept going. Until Darrin took over on guitar when he was about nine, Johnny would hire other musicians to fill that spot.

For years the Vincent family also went out on the road with the owner of the Jamboree, singer Buck Cody, traveling as far as Oklahoma. Often it was only overnight, but occasionally they were out for as much as a week. Carolyn had her hands full with two and eventually three children, including the baby, Brian (b. 1974). Sometimes Johnny's mother would go with them; other times they would leave the boys with her. But Rhonda always went along. It is no wonder that today Rhonda calls her life on the road "living my dream." As her mother says, "That's all she knows."

In 1971, realizing the family needed some merchandise to sell at their appearances, Johnny arranged for nine-year-old Rhonda to record her first solo single. She says, "I spent hours rehearsing my songs so I would do a good job." And she did. She belted out a Dolly Parton–inspired version of "Muleskinner Blues" and with the brashness of youth also tackled Martha Carson's "Satisfied." Her mandolin chop demonstrates her already impeccable sense of timing.

Bluegrass festivals, still fairly new at the time, offered a golden performance opportunity for a family band. One of the earliest festival appearances by the Sally Mountain Show was a band contest in Knob Noster, Missouri, on Friday, July 13, 1973, which just happened to be Rhonda's thirteenth birthday. With those auspicious numbers lining up, the Vincents won the contest and were booked for the following year.

That year also saw the release of the Sally Mountain Show's first album, *Joshua* (1974), which featured ten of their most requested gospel numbers. The cover, typical for bluegrass bands at the time, shows the four Vincents, including pint-sized Darrin, wearing matching dresses and shirts, which Carolyn had made. The title song includes a punchy mandolin break from Rhonda, whose well-developed lead playing shows up here for the first time.

In January 1975 the Vincents moved to southeast Texas for about three months to play a second Frontier Jamboree in Harlingen. They lived in their fifteen-foot camper, and Rhonda attended seventh grade. Carolyn, at first on maternity leave from the factory and then flying back and forth, finally quit her day job. When they returned from Texas, she decided to go to beauty school, graduating in

1976. As a hairdresser she could work when the family was not on the road and supplement their musical income.

One job they held steadily for seven years was at the weeklong Missouri State Fair. They performed from 1:00 P.M. until 1:00 A.M. every day on the Show-Me Riverboat. *Pretty Fair Bluegrass* (1975), a collection of crowd-pleasers, is a nod to their work at the fair. The album was paid for by the owners of the riverboat, who generously turned the album over to the Vincents when they got their money back. Rhonda says, "So many people like that helped us out." "Rocky Top" and "Midnight Flyer" reflect the influence of the Osborne Brothers, whose close harmonies the Vincents studied with care. Rhonda made her recording debut on fiddle, playing on a new cut of "Muleskinner Blues."

At some point the young Rhonda, tired of singing "Muleskinner Blues" on every show, complained to her father. Johnny was clear about what would be done: "I don't care if you've done it a million times. If those people want to hear it, you've got to do it for them." And she's still doing it.

From 1975 to 1978 the Vincents found summer work at Silver Dollar City in Branson, Missouri. They played eight hours a day, five days a week and lived in a camper in a nearby campground. On the weekends they were off to a festival. Is it any wonder that around this time a teenage Rhonda become disenchanted with performing? Johnny had a cure for that. He took her to see the Stoneman Family, with Donna Stoneman on the mandolin. Rhonda was captivated. "I knew I wanted to play just like her. I was reinvigorated. She was so aggressive. It was like watching a madwoman up there on stage." The Vincents left Silver Dollar City when the venue balked at paying Darrin, nine, who was playing several instruments and singing. Johnny was adamant: "If you don't pay my son, then we can't be here." So they left. Carolyn was worried, but Johnny was confident they would make it.

Their third album, *Blue Ribbon Bluegrass* (1976), featured more complex Osborne Brothers numbers ("Pathway of Teardrops" and "Bluegrass Melodies") and four lead vocals by Rhonda, who again plays both mandolin and fiddle. Although Carolyn says they were "pushing Rhonda because of the singer she was," she by no means dominated these early albums. Johnny, Carolyn, and Darrin all took turns singing lead.

Four years would pass before the Sally Mountain Show would release another album. Rhonda suspects they spent that time paying off the motor home they bought. The Vincent family had gone from traveling in a station wagon, to a pickup camper, to a fifteen-foot camper, to a twenty-five-foot camper, and then to a motor home. Carolyn did all the driving. When they picked up their first bus from owners Jim and Jesse McReynolds in Nashville, Carolyn says, "Jesse got in with me and taught me how to shift gears. He let me drive it back. Then I had to drive it clear home, five hundred-some miles. I had to learn how to double clutch. I ground gears for quite a while."

Amid all this traveling, Rhonda continued her education. In 1980 she graduated from high school, and in the fall, still living at home, she entered Northeast Missouri State University (now Truman State) in Kirksville. She would complete two years on an accounting track before surrendering to her first love, music.

The Sun's Coming Up (1980) was the first Sally Mountain album to be reviewed by *Bluegrass Unlimited*. The reviewer had not heard of the band before but was impressed. Eighteen-year-old Rhonda was singled out for her "powerful, country-style lead" vocals on songs like "Roses in the Snow" and for her "tasty mandolin and fiddle backup."

Around this time Rhonda met Herb Sandker, her future husband. Herb, manager and deejay at a club in Kirksville, was putting together a band for a dance and looking for a fiddle player. Hearing about Rhonda, he talked to Johnny, who told him she could play, with one caveat: he and his electric guitar came with the deal. Was he keeping an eye on his daughter? "We'd always done everything together, so I guess so," Rhonda says. "And I was eighteen and wasn't old enough to go into a club without my parents." She also says, "We couldn't get into much trouble, because we were playing all the time. We were always with the family. I guess that's a good thing."

The fifth Sally Mountain LP, *I Came on Business for the King* (1981), an all-gospel project, was the first album to be produced by Rhonda. From then on she would produce or co-produce all of her bluegrass recordings. The entire album was recorded live in only three hours. Rhonda sang lead on nine numbers while Carolyn and Johnny supplied the almost sensual, tight, stacked-down harmony. Rhonda also played triple fiddles on "Just Any Day Now," demonstrating not only her mastery of that instrument but also her arranging ability. The *Bluegrass Unlimited* review pronounced her "clearly a rising star" and compared her to Molly O'Day. The reviewer also said, "As Rhonda Vincent goes, so goes the Sally Mountain Show."

The teenage Rhonda was feeling her musical oats. "I was experiencing New Grass Revival and learning every Sam Bush break on the *Fly Through the Country* album. I was learning every break Buck White had on every album. I was studying all this music, having new ideas, and wanting to do more contemporary things. I'd write a song and Darrin and I would sit back in the back for hours, putting together arrangements."

When they would have people over to their house to pick, Rhonda would struggle to find places to put in all the new licks she was learning. She says, "But he [her dad] never deterred me from doing that. In fact he even started singing 'Good Woman's Love' [recorded by the New Grass Revival] just so I could play that break. That is pretty amazing. He always let us spread our wings and check stuff out, but he was smart enough to know when it came down to entertaining the audience, yes, we're gonna do the 'Muleskinner Blues.'"

The next album, *Lavender Lullaby* (1983), was the first to reflect Rhonda's expanding range of musical and production talents. There were four original numbers, lush twin fiddles, and contemporary arrangements. Rhonda had also begun to overdub harmony vocals to some of her own leads. Darrin had taken over most of the bass playing, and Carolyn's diminishing role in the music suited her fine. "I always liked to sit back and watch the kids," she says. Rhonda remembers, "They would let us do whatever we needed to do. There was never any question of you should let your mom do this. Whatever it takes for this song, that's what you did." Nevertheless, the album disappointed the *Bluegrass Unlimited* reviewer, who took Rhonda to task for sharing the spotlight with the family when she was clearly star material. He suggested that the group "come up with a way to create a 'band sound' without minimizing the contributions of Rhonda Vincent."

On Christmas Eve 1983 Rhonda entered a new phase of her life when she married Herb Sandker, whom she had been dating for three years. Newly wed, she continued to play with the Sally Mountain Show and make albums. Their seventh, *Sheltered in the Arms of God* (1985), received a scathing review in *Bluegrass Unlimited*. Although the reviewer liked her "spare, but imaginative arrangements," he said, "she'll have to stop making 'family' albums in which everybody else gets a chance to experiment with lead singing." Reaching out beyond traditional bluegrass instrumentation, Rhonda brought in pedal steel on two numbers to good effect.

Before this review came out, however, Rhonda had taken the plunge—albeit a short one—into country music. In the spring of 1985 she had appeared on The Nashville Network's program *You Can Be a Star* and was seen by country music great Jim Ed Brown, who hired her on the spot to play fiddle, mandolin, and guitar and sing on his show. She stayed only six months. She describes this, the first time she had been away from the security of her family, as being "my first experience in the real world." Many things worked against her: Rhonda didn't like the big-city atmosphere of Nashville, she quickly tired of doing the same three or four songs over and over, flying home to play with the Sally Mountain Show was stressful, and the job put a huge strain on her recent marriage. She was also no longer the star of the show. She had gone from being the center of attention in her family band to being a backup vocalist. With her talent, energy, and drive, that had to feel confining. Rhonda bailed. She went back to Missouri.

While she was away, however, her spot in the band had been filled by twelve-year-old Alison Krauss. Rhonda says, "Dad made her wear my dresses. I don't think she'd ever had a dress on. She thought they were so dorky. But now she understands why we matched and why we did what we did."

Carolyn had also taken her own smaller plunge. She went to school to become an emergency medical technician. Beautician, EMT, performer. Carolyn likes to keep busy. As she says, "I don't read, I don't crochet, or sew. I'm not a TV person either."

In October a year later another big change occurred in Rhonda's life when her daughter Sally Lea was born. And like her mother before her, she played right through the pregnancy. The Sally Mountain Show also released their eighth album, *Holdin' Things Together* (1987), whose title song, with the line "Holding things together, ain't no easy thing to do," perhaps spoke to Rhonda's life: a husband, a baby, a family band, and an enormous talent hungering for wider acclaim.

Carolyn and Johnny also started a new venture. Johnny had bought some land in nearby Queen City at auction, and in 1987 they held their first bluegrass festival there, calling the place Sally Mountain Park. Eventually they were doing two festivals a year, although by 2009 they had cut back to one long weekend in July. The Sally Mountain Show is the host band, and Rhonda is one of the featured acts. In 2004 Carolyn herself made fifty blackberry pies to sell—all from scratch, including the crust!

Back in the arms of her family, Rhonda began writing to major bluegrass labels, looking for a solo record deal. She signed with Rebel, entering the bluegrass big leagues but still thinking of this phase in her career as a stepping-stone to a major country contract.

The title of her first Rebel album, *New Dreams and Sunshine* (1988), announced a new beginning. Recorded not long after she had returned from Nashville, the project reflected Rhonda's divided musical self. Half bluegrass and half country, the disc included drums, steel, and Buck White's piano. Rhonda also brought in the vocal talents of Kathy Chiavola, Charley Louvin, and David Parmley, and for the first time called on high-profile bluegrass musicians such as Béla Fleck,

Jerry Douglas, and Bobby Hicks to help out. She herself took a less active role as an instrumentalist. Her steady mandolin chop is heard throughout, but she takes only one mandolin break, a jazzy solo on "Country Rain." *Bluegrass Unlimited*'s half-page review called the music "terrific" and waxed eloquent about her voice, speaking of power, intensity, and "a growing ability to touch the softer sounds without losing emotional strength." It likened her to "Rose Maddox under control." At the end of this year of new beginnings, Rhonda's daughter Tensel Lea was born.

Rhonda's second Rebel album, *A Dream Come True* (1990), garnered a highlight review in *Bluegrass Unlimited*. The reviewer gave some well-deserved attention to Rhonda's mandolin playing, saying, "She plays with a tasteful, understated style, and an unusually clean, 'woody' tone." The recording, minus pedal steel and drums, seemed to be consciously striving for a more solid bluegrass sound. Studio musicians were again called in, and for the first time ever Johnny and Carolyn did not appear. The recording was named Best Bluegrass Album of 1990 by *Billboard* magazine.

Amid the excitement of releasing her second solo album, Rhonda experienced a heartbreaking tragedy. She lost her third daughter, three-day old Brooke Lea, to a heart defect on July 11, 1990. *Bound for Gloryland* (Rebel, 1991), a gospel project done with the Sally Mountain Show, was dedicated to Brooke. Knowing that the whole family had recently suffered such a devastating loss makes songs like "A Heart That Will Never Break Again" and "Precious Jewel" seem particularly poignant. Moving away from the slicker production of Rhonda's solo albums, this recording showcases what the Vincent Family did best: pour out their hearts in song.

Timeless and True Love (1991), Rhonda's third solo album for Rebel, again utilized the talents of studio musicians, including Alison Brown on banjo. The recording featured both country and bluegrass material and arrangements, perhaps mirroring the split that Rhonda was still feeling. People continued to tell her that she had a great voice for country music, and *Bluegrass Unlimited* agreed, saying, "She's presently a country singer of the best neo-traditional kind." What was she to do?

Then fate tiptoed in. While Rhonda was in the studio recording *Timeless and True Love*, James Stroud of Giant Records heard her and soon signed her to the label. Rhonda was back in country music.

Rhonda now describes her five years in country music as being "the school of hard knocks." One thing she balked at was giving up production control. She didn't like being told what songs she was going to record, who was going to play on the sessions, or having to ask if she could overdub her own harmony. Giant released two albums, *Written in the Stars* (1993) and *Trouble Free* (1996), which, according to writer Jon Weisberger, featured "top-notch" material, "outstanding singing," and a band that "cooked." With the second disc, Rhonda said, "I really thought we were on the way." But when the promotion team was fired, the whole shooting match fell to pieces. If things had gone well with these recordings, perhaps Rhonda would have stayed in country music. Good sales, radio airplay, a little recognition, a few awards, and bluegrass might not have seen the return of the prodigal daughter. But the same Fate (or was it Grace?) that had brought her into country music would now lead her home.

Rhonda looked for another label, but the same issues of control came up again. Rhonda said, "The question really came down to whether I was willing to make the concessions you need to make in order to work in that environment, and I wasn't." She wanted to be in charge of her life and her music. Still, Rhonda was not quite ready to look at music as a business in the same way that Nashville did. For now, as she told a newspaper, "I was not going to unbutton my shirt or my pants or whatever seems to be the marketing strategy . . . In Nashville [music] is looked at as a business, and I just had a love for the music." Rhonda's own marketing strategy would change, but that would take awhile. And when it did change, she would be the one calling the shots.

Like Scarlett O'Hara returning to the red earth of Tara, Rhonda returned home to Missouri to regroup. She started playing bluegrass again with some friends, and by the fall of 1996 she had assembled a group called the Raje. Herb came up with the band name, using the first letters from the names of the band members: Rhonda, Allen, Joey, and Earl (Irl). It was supposed to be pronounced "rage," but naturally everyone in bluegrass called it "rahj." When these musicians moved on, Rhonda officially changed the spelling to Rage, a name appropriate for the high-energy music she delivers on stage.

While her band was in this embryonic period, Rhonda put together *Yesterday and Today* (1998), a compilation of songs from previous recordings, including some of her country songs. Released on the Lighthouse label, it was a retrospective of a career that began with "How Far Is Heaven," recorded with her mother, and ended with her own daughters singing the same song with her. After a six-year absence from the pages of *Bluegrass Unlimited,* Rhonda received a highlight review. The reviewer said she had "one of the most amazing voices in all of gospel, bluegrass, and country music."

That same year Rhonda finally landed on a label that would let her have "complete control" over making her own albums, Rounder Records. The company was already home to many women in bluegrass, including Alison Krauss, Hazel Dickens, Lynn Morris, and Laurie Lewis. She was also chosen to co-host the IMBA Awards show with Ricky Skaggs.

Rhonda's debut album with Rounder was aptly titled *Back Home Again* (2000). In the liner notes she says, "this is the first recording . . . that truly captures my music, voice, and style, as well as creating a defining 'sound.'" Instead of using members of the Rage (which caused some hard feelings), Rhonda brought in high-caliber bluegrass players like Ron Stewart, Jerry Douglas, and Bryan Sutton. *Bluegrass Unlimited* put Rhonda on its cover in April and reviewed the CD in May, saying, "it is great to have her back home where she belongs." The album was nominated for IBMA Album of the Year but lost to Dolly Parton's *The Grass Is Blue,* on which Rhonda had sung harmony. However, she was more than compensated for that loss by winning her first award as Female Vocalist of the Year.

Rhonda was also taking care of business and after much hard work landed a sponsorship from Martha White Foods, a brand name long associated with Lester Flatt and Earl Scruggs and, more recently, Alison Krauss. She began traveling in a bus emblazoned with the Martha White logo, and the company put her face on their nationally distributed packages of blueberry muffins. Her next album would include a Rage recording of "The Martha White Theme."

Rhonda's second Rounder project, *The Storm Still Rages* (2001), is her first bluegrass album to graphically indicate that she was beginning to cultivate a more sensual image. The cover of the CD is a head-and-shoulders glamour shot of Rhonda, beautiful as a model with glistening lips and big, almond-shaped, blue eyes. The inside cover is another head-and-shoulders photo of Rhonda this time with her eyes closed, wearing a shoulderless red dress with a plunging neckline. Cleavage is not yet shown but is tastefully suggested.

For the first time on any of her bluegrass albums, Rhonda does not play an instrument on most cuts and takes only two short mandolin breaks. When questioned about this, Rhonda explains that in May 2000 she had been knocked unconscious by a falling light pole at a show and had ruptured a disc, which would go undiagnosed for a year. She had gradually lost the use of her right arm and was in horrific pain. Refusing to come off the road, she sometimes had to hire a fill-in mandolin player. Fearing she would never sing again, she finally had surgery in December. "They sliced right there at my vocal cords. Now I've got a plate and four screws directly behind my Adam's apple." *The*

Storm Still Rages was recorded during this time period, and the fact that Rhonda played at all is remarkable.

Meanwhile, in 2001 Rhonda and the Rage won IBMA's coveted Entertainer of the Year Award, the only female-fronted band to win since Alison Krauss and Union Station (1991 and 1995). Rhonda also took home her second Female Vocalist of the Year Award. Her awards show outfit had set tongues wagging. The white floor-length gown—backless to her waist and partially cut out in front—showed some serious skin. "In poor taste" was one of the kinder remarks.

The cover of Rhonda's next CD, *One Step Ahead* (2003), was a radical departure from traditional bluegrass album art. The photo of Rhonda reveals her movement toward a funky, in-your-face, upscale image. Dressed in leather, she stands superimposed against the gray background of a busy city street, mandolin by her side. Her red crop-top displays cleavage and midriff. There was no doubt about it—she looked sexy. Things were definitely changing.

Since Rhonda was just regaining the use of her right arm when *One Step Ahead* was being recorded, she again did little playing. "It was so much easier to have Aubrey [Haynie] go in and lay down the tracks." One highlight of the CD was the inclusion of up-and-coming young fiddler Molly Cherryholmes, who played her own instrumental "Frankie Belle." Rhonda took a full-length mandolin break, on which her ability to play traditional, in-your-gut bluegrass was still evident.

In the spring of 2005 Rhonda released her most adventurous project yet: *Ragin' Live* on CD and DVD. She was also back in the saddle instrumentally, propelling the band with her insistent mandolin chop. Rhonda finally felt she had the right group—Kenny Ingram, Josh Williams, Hunter Berry, and Mickey Harris—to do a live recording. And after the success of the DVD from Alison Krauss, Rounder also supported the idea.

Recorded during two performances in St. Louis, Missouri, the smooth, high-quality production is a magnificent tour de force both musically and visually. With this DVD Rhonda ratcheted things up a notch for bluegrass performers. She shines in her myriad roles as singer, picker, emcee, down-to-earth star—and mother—to show that apparently she can do it all. She takes several breaks, including a full-length solo on the rapid-fire banjo instrumental "Road Rage." All of this is done in a short, sleeveless black dress with a plunging neckline and high heels. Rhonda may sing with the power of Rose Maddox, but visually she's Tina Turner—without the shimmy.

Of course the project didn't come off without a hitch, as Rhonda is quick to admit. For her it was "one of the most traumatic experiences of my life." Never having done a DVD before—and not being the executive producer herself—Rhonda had expected to find the taping organized and running smoothly. Alas! Of the twenty-five songs they shot on a Monday night, only one was usable. The event, she says, was a "fiasco." It had run three and a half hours long, and Rhonda was so flummoxed she even forgot the words to "Muleskinner Blues." She says, "I left there thinking I was gonna have to borrow about two hundred thousand dollars, pay [for the project], and throw it in the trash. It was horrendous."

Instead, Rhonda stayed up all night and completely reorganized everything. She called on her husband, Herb, to take over the production reins. He gathered everyone together and said, "Folks, it's crunch time." According to Rhonda, "Tuesday night everybody buckled down." The results are spectacular. And Monday night's unusable footage provided the outtakes.

With the DVD behind her, Rhonda was free to tackle other projects. In 2004 Herb had formed Upper Management to handle Rhonda's tour schedule. Now the two of them bought a home in Nashville, and in 2005 she opened her own recording studio, Adventure Studios, right in the house. Her next three albums would all be recorded there. The couple also launched their own travel agency, Bogie's Travel, through which Rhonda began to book her own bluegrass cruises. In addition to the Rage, the 2010 lineup included country music star Gene Watson and Next Best Thing, the band her daughters Sally and Tensel had formed. Rhonda is quick to credit Herb for supporting all her projects. "My husband is the strength of everything I do. My dad gave me free rein and Herb is the same way."

Rhonda would not stay out of the studio for long. In 2006 she released two projects, *All-American Bluegrass Girl* and *Beautiful Star: A Christmas Collection*. A line in the title song of the first reveals that Rhonda, too, has been on the receiving end of the insult disguised as a compliment that so many women have heard: "All my life they told me / You're pretty good for a girl." The cover, belying the stereotypical image of "all-American girl," features Rhonda posed suggestively on a green chair, knees conspicuously together, wearing a short, green cocktail dress with a plunging neckline.

This photo sparked a conversation with writer Edward Morris of CMT.com. Rhonda said that all her recent covers are strictly for "marketing purposes" and that she was encouraged in that direction by a woman who told her that she had not wanted to come hear her play, because Rhonda's promotional photo looked "boring." From then on she began to be more daring during her cover shoots. Even the front (and back) of the Christmas CD showed cleavage.

In 2008 Rhonda released her seventh Rounder album, *Good Thing Going*, which included five songs she wrote or co-wrote. Here Rhonda used members of her own group sparingly and again brought in big-name bluegrass players. In 2009, however, she brought the Rage back into the studio for *Destination Life*, which she co-produced with longtime fiddler Hunter Berry, now engaged to her daughter Sally. (They would marry in 2010.) As *Bluegrass Unlimited* said, "When you've got a road band this good, why look elsewhere?"

Missing from the Rage lineup, however, were the familiar faces of Kenny Ingram on banjo and Josh Williams on guitar. Changes in band personnel are a normal part of the music business, but Rhonda has a reputation for being hard to work with and is well aware of it. Bob Black, an early Rage banjo player (1997–1998), described her approach as "authoritarian." Having worked with Bill Monroe, however, he was used to that. He said in some ways Rhonda reminded him of Monroe: "There was never any doubt as to who was in charge." A good teacher, she taught Bob to sing the low tenor part and was demanding when it came to getting the vocals right. "She knew exactly what she wanted." That early version of the Rage was apparently not what she had in mind, because she fired the whole band in 1998.

Of her bandleading, Rhonda says, "I learn every day. I continually soak in a new idea or how can I do this better. I've definitely made a lot of mistakes in doing this. I think the band members I've had in my group have taught me. One of the first things Darrin told me was, 'You need to tell people exactly what you expect of them.'" A departing band member told her the same thing.

Rhonda now hands new musicians a written job description with a list of duties, guidelines, and expectations. "They're very well paid, but it's because we *do* everything. We schlep the merch, they drive the bus." (In 2005 they hired a bus driver.) But her expectations are large. "What I instill in them now is that when you join this group, I expect you to do anything that needs to be done." This had been Carolyn Vincent's own mantra in the Sally Mountain Show: she sewed the outfits, she did the cooking and cleaning, she handled the merchandise, she drove the bus. Rhonda knows that people complain about her switching band members often, "But they don't know why, and a lot of times you can't tell them."

When asked if her reputation for being hard-nosed comes from being a woman, Rhonda replies, "I think some of it comes from that. I've had band members that don't really consider what I'm saying is serious. But they eagerly accept the check when I write it." Rhonda is aware of many of the unflattering stories that circulate about her but says, "I'm secure in who I am and what I do, so I don't worry about it. People are always gonna talk. The more success that you attain, the more people you have trying to shoot you down. I've got that really strong family, and I have a very supportive husband, and my husband is gonna be the first to tell me when I've done something wrong."

When asked if she takes a lot of flak for her outfits, she replies, "I don't think they tell me to my face." She hears only the positive remarks. When it comes to clothes, Rhonda listens to her daughters. "I don't have that knowledge myself. But now I'm getting it. Tensel has a sense of style, and that's what she wants to do and I listen to her."

Another woman Rhonda has paid close attention to is Dolly Parton. "I'm a huge fan of hers. I've also watched her business savvy and her sense of style, and what she does." Dolly has returned the admiration, using the younger singer on five of her own albums starting in 1992, and writing a testimonial for Rhonda's first Rounder album. Dolly enthused, "What a talent. What a beauty. What a special human being. I love this album and I love this girl."

Rhonda agrees that her packaging has helped broaden her appeal to include people who would not normally listen to bluegrass. "Yes, it has! Thank God for Rounder, who, without compromising the music, is able to take some of our songs and put them on CMT. It's just grown our audience. I don't feel like I have done anything different from what I would ever do. But they're exposing us not only to the traditional bluegrass fan but also to a whole nother audience and to a younger one. We're seeing every age at our show. And I just think it's wonderful."

Still and yet, after eight albums for Rounder, Rhonda parted company with the label, releasing her next project, *Taken* (2010), on her own Upper Management Music imprint. Again she used the Rage in the studio to good effect, garnering a highlight review from *Bluegrass Unlimited,* which effused, "It's hard to imagine how she will top these performances." Instead of trying to top them, Rhonda returned to the country side of music and released *Your Money and My Good Looks* (Upper Management, 2011), which paired her with country crooner Gene Watson. The disc, with its "classic sixties honky-tonk style" of music, was not reviewed by *Bluegrass Unlimited.*

With her obvious staying power and her myriad accomplishments, Rhonda still has one goal left, one wish that has not yet been granted. "It's always been a dream to be a member of the Grand Ole Opry . . . Just to get to perform there is an honor. To be a member would be the ultimate." To paraphrase an old country song, "If hard work brought fame / In life's crazy game / She'd be a legend in her time." And she would be a member of the Grand Ole Opry. Time alone will tell if Rhonda gets to live this part of her dream.

> Name one other banjo player who wears Prada.
> And I don't mean Prada overalls.
>
> —Natalie Maines

THE
DIXIE
CHICKS

Dixie Chicks. Superstars. Winners of twelve Grammy Awards. Ninth on the list of top-selling women artists in any genre, with over thirty million albums sold. In the country field only Reba McEntire and Shania Twain have done better. These three talented women—Emily Robison, Martie Maguire, and Natalie Maines—are glamorous, outspoken, controversial, fiercely independent, and business-minded. After the wild success of their first two Sony albums, they boldly sued the record company for a bigger slice of the pie and won their own label imprint, Open Wide Records. Furthermore, as *No Depression* magazine says, "Their daring and success have made it possible for any number of acts to have a fiddle or banjo back on the radio." No little feat. But before any of this happened, they played bluegrass.

Martie (b. 1969) and Emily Erwin (b. 1972) began life parented by a mother, Barbara, who played classical violin and a father, Paul, who loved country music. The family, including older sister Julie, moved to Dallas, Texas, around 1974, where Barbara soon had all three girls enrolled in Suzuki violin lessons. Martie ventured into fiddling when she was twelve. She says, "My father is the main reason [I started bluegrass]. He loved bluegrass and country and with my involvement [on fiddle] we made it a family affair every weekend. I was really looking for a kind of music I could make my own."

Hearing the banjo at festivals inspired Emily to start taking lessons when she was ten. Not only did she love the sound and think it was "cool," but also, the former tomboy says, "I always wanted to beat the boys at whatever was going on; I was always very competitive when I was little. I think playing the banjo was not a thing for a girl to do, and that gave me a thrill, to do something the boys were doing."

Like many precocious bluegrass youngsters with supportive parents, Martie and Emily became part of a kids' band. In the summer of 1982 Martie joined Blue Night Express, a group that already included Sharon Gilchrist (b. 1972) on mandolin; her brother Troy, eleven, on guitar; and two other young boys. When the banjo player left, who better to fill the slot than Emily? When the bass player departed, all three girls shared bass-playing duties.

Booked by father Sid Gilchrist, "Texas's youngest bluegrass band" appeared at festivals in the Midwest and Southeast every weekend of the summer. For several years during the winter months they played three nights a week at Judge Roy Bean's, a restaurant in Dallas. Toward the end of the band's career, they even entertained on a street corner in Dallas's new, ritzy West End Market, an open guitar case in front of them to collect the substantial tips. But when Martie headed to college in 1987, after placing second at the Walnut Valley Fiddle Championship in Winfield, Kansas, the band essentially broke up.

Meanwhile, two women who would become the other half of the original Dixie Chicks were also busy playing music and holding down day jobs. Folksinger Robin Lynn Macy (b. ca. 1958) had moved from Missouri to Dallas in 1981 to teach math at a private boys school. Her spare time was devoted to acting in local theater productions. She joined the bluegrass group Danger in the Air as it was forming around 1986. The lone female, she played guitar, sang lead, and was soon dating the banjo player, James McKinney.

Danger in the Air was a progressive bluegrass band who paid as much attention to their stage show as to their music. According to Andy Owens, mandolin player with the group, Robin "had very good stage presence, [paid] much attention to dress, and could really sell a song." James, fresh from a stint at Opryland, taught the group to "always smile, always look at the crowd, always look at the person in the band who is singing or soloing, never say a negative thing on stage, never show weakness, never admit a mistake, always talk positively about all the band members." The future Dixie Chicks, who were fans, were taking notes.

With Robin and Andy pushing the band aggressively, Danger in the Air became quite a regional success. Andy says, "Robin was a tireless marketer and promoter." The group was a big influence on Blue Night Express, and Robin was one of the few female performers the young musicians saw with regularity. As Sharon Gilchrist said, "She's so dynamic. We all really looked up to her."

Danger in the Air would release two cassettes, the self-titled first in 1988; the second, *Airtight,* in 1990. Both feature well-executed, complex trios of modern material like the gender-altered Beatles tune "I Saw Him Standing There" and the Monkees' "I'm a Believer." Although there were three vocalists in the group, Robin did the majority of the lead singing. The combination of the voices in harmony, which mesh amazingly well, is considerably stronger than those of the individual singers. The early Dixie Chicks would add this to their bag of tricks.

The fourth original Dixie Chick, Laura Lynch (b. ca. 1958), was also leading a busy life. Raised in West Texas, Laura had a degree in speech communications from the University of Texas at Austin and had held several jobs, including that of television newscaster in El Paso. Married in 1980 and divorced a few years later, she was a single mom to daughter Asia. She was dating mandolin player Dave Peters, her former guitar teacher, and playing off and on in a Houston band called Fat Chance. According to a bandmate, she was already a "cowgirl fashion freak" with numerous cowgirl outfits and matching boots. Robin and Laura had become friends after meeting at a festival around 1987, and sometimes Laura would join Danger in the Air on stage for a song or two.

It was out of this fertile musical mélange that the Dixie Chicks would emerge. How and when the four women got together initially is not clear. *Chick Chat,* an irreverent newsletter the Chicks sent to their fans (1991–1997), dates their "anniversary" as March 1989. Perhaps that is when they began living-room rehearsals for what became their debut gig: playing on a street corner in Dallas' historic West End that summer, turf well known to Martie and Emily. When this first gig netted them several hundred dollars in tips right off the bat, the women knew they had put together a winning combination. Before long they had decided on a name. Driving to an audition, the women heard the Little Feat song "Dixie Chicken" on the radio and decided on the spot that they would be the Dixie Chickens, soon shortened to Dixie Chicks. Laura points out, "As far as marketing goes, it was brilliant."

Danger in the Air, however, was doing well and for a while Robin played in both bands. This created conflicts, and the 1990 release of *Airtight* coincided with the disintegration of the Texas version of the band. For Martie and Emily the formation of the Dixie Chicks came at a troubled time in their lives: their parents were separating. The sisters would eventually turn this trauma into a song, "You Were Mine," which would appear on their first Sony album, along with a personal note from Emily thanking their parents for "letting me borrow your baggage for the song."

The Dixie Chicks formed in a bluegrass world that was beginning to burgeon with women, even if no one was noticing. Martie recalls seeing the Cox Family, the Lewis Family, Rhonda Vincent, the Shoemaker Family, Lynn Morris, and Claire Lynch. Sharon Gilchrist mentions fiddler Tammy Rogers, the Whites, Emmylou Harris, Rhonda Vincent, and Ruth and Alice McLain. Sharon's and Martie's favorite was Dede Wyland, with Tony Trischka and Skyline, a "stellar singer and rhythm guitarist" who was "very gracious" toward her younger admirers. Texas native Lynn Morris even provided a homegrown role model for Emily's banjo playing, having twice won the Winfield banjo contest, in 1974 and again in 1981. So when the Chicks came along, although the trail was still new, there were at least blaze marks.

From the beginning the Chicks concentrated not only on the music but also on the economics. As Emily told the *Journal of Country Music,* "Oh, we had our little business running, definitely. I think that was a lot of the Robin and Laura influence. From the beginning it was very much a business—that was not a concession. You can have your art, but you can be smart about how you promote yourself. We were the ultimate self-promoters . . . We got an office, and we printed our own T-shirts." Emily, who would put aside college to play music, felt as if she were getting a hands-on business degree.

Robin and Laura handled booking and promotion. Laura told writer James Dickerson, "Marketing that band was the only thing I thought of. When I woke up in the morning, I thought about how I would market the band. I knew that was all I brought to the band. I didn't bring great musical prowess. I didn't bring a great, LeAnn Rimes–type voice. I didn't bring a dewy, youthful presence. I brought marketing."

Robin now brought her well-entrenched connections to bear on behalf of the Dixie Chicks. Danger in the Air also lent a helping hand, using the band as an opening act at clubs and even sharing their set at the Kerrville Folk Festival that year. ("Guess who was booked back the next year," says Andy Owens.)

In November, however, just as the Chicks were getting off the ground, Laura left for a six-month gig at a tourist attraction in Japan with the Texas Rangers, a five-piece band that Dave Peters put together. Marvin Gruenbaum, the fiddler for the job, says, "Laura was highly committed to a future with the Dixie Chicks and was always listening to tapes of our sets and trying to improve her singing." Laura played guitar, and when the bass player left, she took over for him. Already she was singing "I Want to Be a Cowboy's Sweetheart," which would appear on the Chicks' first album. Her dozen or so cowgirl outfits with matching boots sometimes made going through customs difficult.

Laura's absence didn't stop the Chicks. Patty Mitchell Lege (b. 1966), newly married, filled in for Laura till she got back in June. As Patty says, "The Dixie Chicks were really starting to take off around Texas, had quite a few bookings, and needed someone fast. I bought a bass and learned how to play pretty quick." Patty was no stranger to performing, having grown up playing bluegrass with the Mitchell family band, Bluegrass Southland. Her parents also ran a bluegrass festival at Mitchell Park in Perrin, Texas, where Blue Night Express had played many times.

With Laura back from Japan and Patty on mandolin, the Chicks won first place in the band contest at the Telluride Bluegrass Festival in June 1990. Patty then made a graceful exit, and Sharon Gilchrist filled in on mandolin until she left for Nashville's Belmont College, where she would major in mandolin performance. Then in September and October 1990, the Dixie Chicks went into the studio, with Dave Peters on mandolin, and emerged with their first album, *Thank Heavens for Dale Evans* (1991).

The band went all out on this self-produced recording, hoping from the start to attract a major label. *Bluegrass Unlimited* appreciatively noted that "everything about this project reflects a sense of quality and attention to detail." On the cover the women espouse a retro-cowgirl look with pants, tailored cowgirl shirts, and 1940s hair. Inside, the fiddle and banjo tear through modern bluegrass arrangements as well as western swing numbers such as "The Cowboy Lives Forever" (whose last line is sung as "the cow*girl* lives forever"), "I Want to Be a Cowboy's Sweetheart," and "Thank Heavens for Dale Evans," complete with three-part yodeling. Martie characterized their style as "an acoustic, nostalgic Western cowgirl sound." The *Journal of Country Music* called it "impeccably played, NPR-worthy cowgirl kitsch and spirited bluegrass."

Instrumentally Martie's fiddle playing is the standout. Perhaps that is no surprise, since she had studied violin performance in college. Robin does most of the lead singing while all four women contribute harmonies. The Chicks had a hand in writing only three of the songs. By 1992 the Chicks had sold more than twelve thousand copies of the disc, big numbers for a regional bluegrass band.

With an album to hustle, the women kept the pedal to the metal all summer, traveling now with a road manager and sound engineer, Jim Humphrey. They showcased that fall at the IBMA World of Bluegrass and soon signed with Nashville booking agency Buddy Lee Attractions, which also booked Bill Monroe. Not long after, they hired a manager, Nashville's David Skepner, who had also managed Loretta Lynn.

Later that fall the band recorded a Christmas single called "Home on the Radar Range," with two songs, "Christmas Swing" and "The Flip Side." For the first time they used a drummer, Tom Van Schaik, and brought in producer Larry Seyer, who had produced Danger in the Air. The Chicks must have liked the results, because both men surfaced again on their second album.

In spite of everyone's best efforts, *Thank Heavens for Dale Evans* was not their ticket to the big time. So in the winter of 1992 the Chicks headed back to the studio to try again. According to a Dallas newspaper, all four women were feeling "the make-or-break pressure" the year would bring. Tears in the studio were mentioned.

Perhaps that pressure determined the shift in direction that their second album took. *Little Ol' Cowgirl* (1992) includes a variety of styles: western swing, Irish, folk, rhythm-and-blues, gospel, and, the best song on the disc, an original tongue-in-cheek torch song, "Pink Toenails." The recording featured banjo and fiddle, yet it wasn't bluegrass. For the first time hints of Lloyd Maines's pedal steel drift in, yet it wasn't hard-core country. The album just couldn't seem to light. But the biggest change, right there on the first number, was the use of drums. The women knew that these might alienate some of their fans, but as Martie said, "[We] have to make a living and you can't do that playing bluegrass." A subtler difference was that Laura was now singing more leads than Robin.

The summer of 1992 found the Chicks once again hitting the road hard in support of the album. Touring in a van pulling a trailer, the six-piece entourage now included drummer Tom Van Schaik. *Chick Chat* reported, "We need vintage western clothing, a mute driver, an unlimited Mary Kay credit line, a record deal, and a pedicurist. Not in that order."

Then that fall *Chick Chat* casually dropped a bombshell: the departure of Robin Macy. "We're going to miss our singin' and songwritin,' guitar pickin' pal Robin and we hope all her dreams come true." According to the newsletter, Robin had this to say: "On July 28, 1992, my official Dixie Chicks wristwatch suddenly quit ticking. 'This must be a sign,' I gasped. It was then I knew it was time to move on and take a road less traveled. So to all my friends, thanks for the many memories. And for now I bid a fond farewell." From then on, the Chicks would be a trio. With side musicians.

The party line was that Robin was a "purist" and objected to the direction the music was taking. However, her playing with the progressive Danger in the Air seems to belie this notion. With two lead singers in the band, conflict was bound to erupt. No doubt things got heated and personalities got involved, a fact the Chicks wisely have kept under wraps. Eventually lawsuits would be filed.

Matt Benjamin was the new guitarist, and the Chicks were now landing the occasional prestigious gig. They performed at a Dallas Cowboys halftime show, sang the "Star-Spangled Banner" at a Texas Rangers game, and in January 1993 they played at the Tennessee Inaugural Ball in Washington, D.C.

Still pursuing that elusive brass ring, the band released a third album, *Shouldn't a Told You That,* at the end of 1993. The sound was more unified than that of *Little Ol' Cowgirl,* and with the exception of the torch song "Planet of Love," the direction was consistently country. Lloyd Maines's pedal steel and plenty of fiddle helped, while the banjo had been toned down in favor of Emily's Dobro. The women were willing to experiment with many things—except giving up their instruments. As Emily told an interviewer, "Men dominate the musical virtuosity field at the moment and I, along with Laura, and Martie, love that fact that we are the band, as well as the vocalists."

The December 1993 *Chick Chat* announced the new album and thanked the band's legal department for "herding them through" all the paperwork. Perhaps it was this association with lawyers that precipitated a section in the newsletter titled "Big Bidness Babes": "Held our first Bored of Directors meetin' . . . there has been a rise in 'net earnings and nerve endings' according to the little 'number thing' you push the buttons on and it spits out a little roll of paper tape . . . 'Til that meeting the only thing we'd ever done on our (kinda) oak conference table was lay out barbecue buns, Chinese food containers, and cowboy shirts!"

The women were making a point of trivializing the business side of their organization, a stance that is almost impossible to imagine a male band taking. Were they catching flak for "getting above their raising"? Was there growing jealousy over their success? Bluegrass music has long had an uneasy relationship to its business side, preferring to pretend that most musicians play for love, not money. But the Chicks were no-nonsense when it came to money. Perhaps that in itself was disturbing to some people. Were their fans—or peers—becoming uncomfortable with their big-business approach?

Interest from a major label was just over the horizon, but until then it was back to the same old grind: hit the road and hope for a break. The Chicks were beginning to get some national exposure. They appeared on TNN's *Nashville Now* and later irreverently opined in *Chick Chat,* "We were pleasantly surprised to find out that Emily wears the same shade of pancake makeup as Ralph Emery."

The year 1994 kicked off with the Chicks' first European tour, summer brought a spot on *CBS This Morning* with Paula Zahn, and fall found them on their longest tour to date, hitting eighteen cities in their pink RV. In her downtime Martie answered the *Women in Bluegrass* questionnaire, writing a note on the back of the envelope that said, "What a great idea! Us girls have to stick together!"

But perhaps the most significant event of the year was the appearance of manager Simon Renshaw. Simon was the penultimate piece of the puzzle, and with his practiced hand on the wheel, the Chicks were headed for stardom. He was impressed with their talent, if not with their repertoire—"they performed these songs which were pretty bad"—and thought that if they were willing to move into a "contemporary country music space," he could make things happen. He did. On June 16, 1995, the Chicks signed a contract with Sony. The "developmental deal" meant the label would give them money to make a demo, and if Sony liked it they might sign the band to a record contract. The next day Martie married Ted Siedel. *Chick Chat* reported, "The most commonly asked question when we tell people that Martie is getting married is, 'Will she stay in the band?' Hello! It's the '90s!!!"

What happened next comes in all colors and sizes. The short version is that the label did not like Laura's voice, and perhaps her age, thirty-seven. She was replaced by twenty-one-year-old Natalie Maines. The machinations are a bit murky and perhaps in the long run unimportant. In print Martie said, "Laura views the change as a 'passing of the baton.'" Laura responded, "It can't really be characterized as a resignation. There are three Dixie Chicks and I'm only one." She did say age was a factor and that she understood. Perhaps she did. In print Laura continues to be a good sport about the split. (And why not? After leaving the Chicks she married her high school sweetheart, who had hit the Texas Lottery!) The former Chick had one request: "Never say I quit, even if it's the easy thing to do."

Natalie (b. 1974), the daughter of Lloyd Maines and the final piece of the puzzle, turned out to be a perfect fit. "It was destiny," Emily told *People* magazine. The leather-lunged firecracker from Lubbock, Texas, had grown up singing and said, "I always knew I was definitely going to do music." After graduating from high school in 1992, Natalie attended West Texas A&M for a year, then enrolled at South Plains College in Levelland, Texas, for another year. Although not a part of the school's well-known bluegrass music program, she took piano and guitar, studied music theory and voice, and sang in student-produced television shows. According to director Cary Banks, her guitar teacher, Tim McCasland, not only "fueled her interest in the 'open G chord,' but in arguing politics as well." Cary, who has known Natalie all her life, says, "From a very early age, Natalie had a big powerful voice, a fabulous ear, and keen musical instincts and I watched her really hone and perfect her stage presence and performance skills while she was here." After South Plains she studied voice at Boston's Berklee College of Music in the spring of 1995, spent the pivotal summer of that year in Lubbock at Texas Tech, and then in November joined the Dixie Chicks.

In signing with Sony the Dixie Chicks left the world of bluegrass far behind, although Emily would be featured on the cover of *Banjo NewsLetter* in July 2000. The venerable magazine declared that she was "doing as much as anybody today to raise the banjo's visibility and enhance its hip factor."

For the last time, in December 1997 the Chicks would make a bawdy announcement of an album in *Chick Chat*: "The days of penny pinching and scraping together sofa change to make independent albums are over—sort of. We learned from it all, developing as a band (growing our musical boobies you could say) and we wouldn't trade those experiences for the world, so now we are proud to announce that our first album on Monument Records is here!"

Wide Open Spaces (1998) would go on to sell twelve million copies; their second, *Fly* (Monument, 1999), ten million. Both albums featured Emily's banjo and Dobro and Martie's fiddle, which was one of the reasons they had signed with Sony. Says Emily, "There was no question as to whether we were going to be playing our own instruments on our album."

Even a sensitive bluegrass ear has to listen closely, though, to detect the banjo on *Wide Open Spaces*. The first number to hit the *Billboard* chart, "I Can Love You

Better," is both banjo- and fiddle-free. It was only with their second chart hit, the number-one song "There's Your Trouble," that bluegrass sounds emerge, the fiddle prominently and the banjo—that red-headed stepchild—faintly at the end. The four other songs that made the charts feature fiddle, but little or no banjo.

As Emily explains, "Because it was our first major label album, we had to temper everything a bit." Or as producer Blake Chancy put it, "Getting the banjo on country radio literally scared me to death. It hadn't been on for ten years. Now all these people are introducing the banjo on their records because it's accepted, and that's one hundred percent directly related to Emily."

Fly featured even more banjo. Emily explains, "We had a lot more rein to use." Ten songs charted and four of these included easily audible banjo. "Sin Wagon" featured not one but two in-your-face banjo solos, played in the modern chromatic style.

As Emily told *Banjo NewsLetter*, it is important to her that she be seen playing an actual banjo on stage. On the Chicks' first major tour (1999) Emily played a Crossfire banjo, which is shaped like an electric guitar. As she said, "A lot of people didn't know what it was . . . and I want it to be very clear that I'm playing the banjo." So she switched to a banjo that looks like a banjo.

The Dixie Chicks were racking up the awards. Both *Wide Open Spaces* and *Fly* won Grammys for Best Country Album. After winning the Country Music Association Horizon Award in 1998, the Chicks were named CMA Entertainer of the Year in 2000, the same year *Fly* won the association's Album of the Year and then in 2002 Vocal Group of the Year.

But the Chicks, sitting on top of the world, were not happy. They felt that they were being denied millions of dollars in royalties by Sony. Suits and countersuits ensued, and while lawyers sorted things out, the Chicks returned to Texas, where, just for fun, they started working on a few acoustic-flavored songs with Lloyd Maines at the console. Soon they had a full-fledged album on their hands. Appropriately titled *Home,* the project was eventually released in the fall of 2002 on the Chicks' own imprint, Open Wide Records, formed as part of their settlement with Sony.

Although this return to their musical roots coincided with the success of the sound track to the movie *O Brother, Where Art Thou?* and the intense revival of all things acoustic, this radical departure from a clearly successful format was seen by some as being "outside the boundaries of common sense." Eventual sales of over six million albums and a Grammy for Best Country Album proved that the Chicks knew what they were doing. However, even with the full-throttle bluegrass arrangements of "White Trash Wedding" and "Li'l Jack Slade," *Home* was more modern country than anything else. It had enough banjo, though, to receive an on-the-edge review in the pages of *Bluegrass Unlimited*.

Following on the heels of the *Home* CD came the Chicks' first full-length DVD, *An Evening with the Dixie Chicks* (February 2003), taped at a concert in the Kodak Theater in Hollywood. Described as a "ramped-up record release party" and filmed for an NBC television special, the DVD features a track-by-track rendition of *Home* plus, as Natalie put it, "some songs you recognize." The six-piece acoustic backup band includes Lloyd Maines along with bluegrass stalwarts Bryan Sutton and Adam Steffey, conservatively dressed in suits and ties.

Unlike later DVD offerings, *An Evening with the Dixie Chicks* includes some earthy Chick emcee work. Here's Martie explaining why they won't be touring until April of next year: "We kinda took a hiatus when Natalie got knocked up. And now Emily's knocked up so now we gotta take another hiatus." An obviously expectant Emily, who would give birth to son Gus in November, effortlessly picks her instrument sideways, in the fashion of pregnant banjo pickers everywhere.

The Chicks, riding high, were featured on the cover of *People* magazine in February 2003. Then in March, at the beginning of their Top of the World Tour in London, as war with Iraq loomed on the horizon, Natalie made an off-the-cuff, onstage remark: "Just so you know, we're ashamed the president of the United States is from Texas." And the fur started flying. As CMT music journalist Chet Flippo noted, "The reaction was unprecedented in country music history." Radio stations banned records, fans smashed CDs, and the country music community split along the lines of "free speech advocates" versus "patriots." That summer Natalie received a death threat so specific—"You will be shot dead at your show in Dallas"—that the FBI and Texas Rangers were called in. Natalie's remarks and the surrounding hoopla were henceforth known as "The Incident."

As time would tell, the Chicks not only survived; they prospered. In the midst of the controversy—and after their tastefully nude appearance on the cover of *Entertainment Weekly* in May—the Chicks suited up for the North American leg of their tour, which resulted in the dual release *Live* on CD and *Top of the World Tour: Live* on DVD (November 2003). This DVD captures the power of angry Chicks in action. Although completely professional at every turn, with high-wattage smiles set on stun, their performances seem to crackle with extra energy, as if the women were channeling their frustrations and rage at the media frenzy into their music. Or perhaps they were simply going all out for the thousands of loyal fans who chose not to boycott the show. It was not until the release of the documentary film *Shut Up and Sing* (2006), which chronicled this tour from behind the scenes, that fans would learn what courage it took for the Chicks to keep on keeping on.

In 2003 Chet Flippo had ended his CMT.com commentary about The Incident with a "Memo to Natalie Maines": "You're an artist? You have a message? Hey, put it in a song. We'll listen to that. But otherwise—shut up and sing." Three years later the Chicks did just that, bouncing back with *Taking the Long Way* (May 2006), which included the in-your-face single and video "Not Ready to Make Nice." This time the Chicks, who had written only sparingly for their other projects, co-wrote all fourteen numbers, pouring out their ire in song. Not only was this album light-years away from bluegrass (significant banjo only on "Lubbock or Leave It"), but it was also less country than anything they had done before. In everything from song selection, to rock producer Rick Rubin, to the wall-of-sound mix in which the voices compete with the instruments, the album sounded like rock music. *No Depression* called it "adult alternative."

Taking the Long Way went double platinum by January 2007 and earned five Grammys, including Best Country Album and Album of the Year. Many people saw this as a vindication of the Dixie Chicks and free speech. On the other hand, if the country music community was listening (as Chet Flippo had said they would), they apparently didn't like what they were hearing. The Chicks were blackballed by the Country Music Association, receiving no award nominations. And despite the now-familiar predictions of boycotts, their Accidents and Accusations Tour went well.

Only a few months after *Taking the Long Way* was released, *Shut Up and Sing*, the award-winning documentary covering the Dixie Chicks and the controversy surrounding Natalie's remarks, was also released. Using film shot at the start of the Top of the World Tour in March 2003 (including footage of The Incident in London), the documentary reveals the impact the controversy had on the Chicks individually and as a group. Here Martie, Emily, and Natalie come to life as real people—sometimes in rollers and often without makeup. Their fears in the face of death threats are revealed, as is their bravery in continuing to perform: "I'll call you tonight. If I don't get shot," jokes Emily. Viewers also witness the hurt, confusion, and eventually anger they felt at being rejected by the country music community that they had been a part of all their lives. Yet they did not falter, they did not fail, and they did not fold. As Emily said, "We're a sisterhood. We go through the good, the bad, and the ugly together."

With small children weaving in and out of the documentary, it is obvious that in the downtime between albums all three Chicks had been busy with non-musical endeavors. Martie, now married to Gareth McGuire, welcomed twin girls in April 2004 and a third daughter in 2008. Emily, who married Charlie Robison in 1999, followed suit with twins in April 2005. She and Charlie would divorce amicably in 2008. And Natalie's second marriage, to Adrian Pasdar in 2000, had yielded two sons, Slade in 2001 and Becket in July 2004.

The Chicks took a well-earned rest in 2007, staying close to hearth and home, venturing out only to perform a few shows at a newly opened theater in Los Angeles. One section of the country music community made a peace offering in the form of a CMA nomination for Vocal Group of the Year. But as Emily admits, with kids entering school, things will be different. As of now the Chicks seem to be keeping a low profile. And, sad to say, a reputable fan website is now referring to them as "former Dixie Chicks." But in 2010 Emily and Marty resurfaced with *Courtyard Hounds* (Columbia), which is also the new name for the duo. Emily does most of the lead singing, and the twelve songs were all written or cowritten by her and Martie. Although Lloyd Maines played on the CD, Natalie was conspicuously absent. *Rolling Stone* called it "one of the year's better country records."

If the bluegrass elements in the Dixie Chicks' music were less audible on their CDs during their hard-core country years, they continued to make the banjo and fiddle visible to millions of people every time they hit the stage or released a DVD. As Emily told NPR's Melissa Block: "I always take personal offense any time I'm watching any show or cartoon or anything where something backasswards is about to happen and they start the banjo music . . . There are stereotypes to be torn down and if I can help in that I will."

We had three strikes against us. We were a family
band, we had kids, and we had women.

—Sandy Cherryholmes

CHERRYHOLMES
Sandy, Cia, Molly

The family made the cover of *Bluegrass Unlimited* in May 2005, a mere six years after they started performing. At the center of the photo, three closely aligned youthful women with instruments look straight into the camera: sisters Cia and Molly, and mother, Sandy. To the left are two handsome young men with guitar and fiddle: brothers B. J. and Skip. On the far right, an anomaly: an older man with a long white beard wearing a baseball cap and overalls paired with a sleeveless muscle shirt that reveals a large tattoo on his hefty bicep. Father, Jere, bandleader and emcee. They are Cherryholmes, a band embodying that most appealing of American dreams: the idea that hard work leads to success, especially when it is coupled with talent, energy, and the guiding hands of two firm but loving parents. Their path to fame, however, began with heartache, the loss of oldest daughter and sister, Shelly, twenty, in 1999. Each of their albums has been dedicated to her memory.

The Cherryholmes Family Band, as they were first called (after a brief flirtation with Spirit High Ridge), seemed to come out of nowhere and take the bluegrass world by storm. In reality they lived in a primarily Latino neighborhood seven miles from downtown Los Angeles. The first incarnation of the group included Cia, fifteen, on guitar; Molly, seven, and B. J., eleven, on fiddles; mother, Sandy, and Skip, nine, on mandolins; and father, Jere, on bass. (An older son is not in the band.) The children were homeschooled by Sandy, so it was easy to add bluegrass to a curriculum that already included Irish step dancing.

But the family had been musical all along. Sandy, who was classically trained in piano and operatic singing, played the piano in church while Jere played bass or guitar. Cia started playing folk guitar around age eleven and accompanied her friends when they all sang in church. She and Shelly often sang together for fun, especially when doing the dishes, and loved classic 1960s rock music. Yet early on there was a glimmer of bluegrass—family bluegrass and female bluegrass. As Cia says, "For years we grew up listening to the Lewis Family. Without even knowing what bluegrass music was. They were a big influence on us without [our] even realizing they were an influence."

Within a few months of its formation, the family band was playing gigs in public. The siblings were all crackerjack musicians, and Sandy added step dancing to the act so that the band was able to put on a lively, entertaining show that was quickly musically solid. Soon Jere decided that a bluegrass band needed a banjo player. Cia was the chosen one. Skip took over on guitar.

At first the seventeen-year-old rebelled. As she told *Bluegrass Now,* "I really didn't want to play, I guess because everybody made fun of banjos." However, she goes on to say, "The motivation came from knowing I was going to be on stage regardless of what I wanted to do. Because we had shows booked it wasn't 'Can you do this?' it was 'You are going to do this.' I was playing eight to ten hours a day for several months, then dropped down to about four hours a day after a while." She took some lessons early on from banjo jazzmeister Pat Cloud. Pat recalls, "She was already very talented and was an excellent student with a great ear. She absorbed everything I offered to her and her natural talent was very obvious. I wish I could say that I had a greater influence on her, but she is and has been very much her own person when it came to banjo."

By summer of 2001 the family was playing some of the biggest festivals on the West Coast, including the Huck Finn Jubilee. In 2002 the band was doing well enough for Jere to quit his day job as a carpenter. They sold their house in California and for a while lived in two trailers parked on some land they owned in Arizona. However, they were on the road so much, they actually spent little time there. Three years later they relocated to Nashville. However, as late as October 2007, Jere told CMT.com, "We don't actually have a home . . . We live on the bus on the road. That's about three hundred days a year." Those few other days they often parked the bus at a friend's home near Nashville. "He has a little two-bedroom bachelor flat on top of his garage and we let the kids go up there . . . Sandy and I have always slept on the bus."

The Cherryholmes Family Band began recording early on, producing their first three projects from home. Although their first two cassettes, with Cia still on guitar, are no longer available, their debut CD, *Still a Little Rough around the Edges* (2001), shows that they were studying pioneers Bill Monroe, Flatt and Scruggs, and Ralph Stanley. The cover portrays the band as Depression-era itinerants complete with campfire and tent. Their next CD, *Dressed for Success* (2002), is still heavy on traditional bluegrass but also includes five original numbers from various family members. Its cover, too, continues the Dust Bowl imagery, this time with the family piled on a Jed Clampett–like truck. This recording, however, took place in a professional studio in California. By their fifth recording, *Bluegrass Vagabonds* (2003), released under their new name, Cherryholmes, their flirtation with hillbilly imagery is over. They are pictured on the stage of the Grand Ole Opry, the women in long, cranberry-colored skirts and white blouses, the men in white hats and ties. The self-released project was produced by Rhonda Vincent's brother Darrin, who was then playing with Ricky Skaggs. More than half of the selections were originals. The group received its first full-length review in *Bluegrass Unlimited,* who declared their outlook "very promising." On the strength of this album they were nominated for the IBMA's Emerging Artist of the Year Award in 2004.

In the liner notes to each of these CDs, as well as those that would follow, careful readers will note an important aspect of the Cherryholmes family creed: their Christian beliefs. Each CD offers a thank-you to God and his son, Jesus Christ. Jere is quoted most often on the subject. As he told *Bluegrass Unlimited,* "In the entertainment industry, I think it's important to be grounded in faith and in God because your values are so challenged. Our standards are that we don't want to change ourselves to become part of the pop culture." Cia's faith, too, is an integral part of her life. She interprets the group's success as a sign that they are on the right path. She says, "As long as God has it in his plan for us to be doing this, we'll know if we need to quit."

In 2005 the road warriors signed with Skaggs Family Records, eventually releasing four more albums chock-full of original material: *Cherryholmes* (2005), *Cherryholmes II: Black and White* (2007), *Cherryholmes III: Don't Believe* (2008), and *Cherryholmes IV: Common Threads* (2010). The first three received Grammy nominations for Best Bluegrass Album. Cia also garnered a nomination for IBMA Female Vocalist of the Year in 2005, and her song "Brand New Heartache" was nominated for Song of the Year in 2006. In 2005 Cherryholmes was the surprise winner of the IBMA's prestigious Entertainer of the Year Award, an unprecedented achievement for a fledgling group. Then in 2007 Cia cracked the all-male lineup as a nominee for Banjo Player of the Year, losing to Tony Trischka.

Although new to the scene, the band was becoming savvy about shaping its image for maximum market appeal as the startling and primarily black cover of *Black and White* indicates. The musicians, clad in all black, including the men's hats, are boxed in on three sides by chain-link fencing with lightning bolts shooting out from all sides. The instruments, hands, and faces provide the only spots of color. When the *Bluegrass Unlimited* review pointed out that the band was demonstrating "exactly what popularity in today's bluegrass world demands," it was referring to the music, with its "variety of strong lead singers" and "distinctive original material." However, having a CD with graphics that appeal primarily to the younger audience is also a part of the package.

Cia takes her songwriting seriously, and in their 2008 cover appearance in *Bluegrass Unlimited* she mentioned that one of the reviewers of *Black and White* had said "he'd like to see me try to write a little deeper." Thus on *Don't Believe* she consciously tried to "branch out a little bit more, so not everything is in the same vein."

In addition to the family's projects, Cia has appeared as a backup singer on albums by other artists such as Jim Lauderdale, Alicia Nugent, J. D. Crowe, and Bradley Walker. But it was her banjo playing that landed her an endorsement with Huber Banjos and a spot on the company's all-banjo-instrumental CD *Have a Cuppa 'Jo* (2005), where she appears with six other Huber endorsers, all male. The backup musicians were also all male. Cia was entering testosterone-charged territory. Few women have had starring roles on albums that feature male super-pickers.

Sandy and Cia shared some of their thoughts about gender and music with *Bluegrass Unlimited*. Sandy says, "To me the best mandolin players to learn from are usually men. That's not to say there aren't some good women mandolin players, but I've not sat down and listened to them, to learn from, other than Donna Stoneman . . . A circle of women playing bluegrass don't seem to have that thing I see in my boys." And Cia says, "I think a man is naturally more aggressive . . . We've definitely been more influenced by the men than the women, because we've chosen to pattern ourselves after them." Perhaps these thoughts stem from the fact that Jere encourages his wife and daughters to play "like men." Nevertheless, there was a lot of groundbreaking work done by women to enable folks like Sandy, Cia, and Molly to get on stage and "play like men." And the article about Cia in *Banjo NewsLetter* was still, unfortunately, titled "Bluegrass Darling."

In 2007 Cia herself graced the cover of *Bluegrass Now,* where she was interviewed by another young female banjo player, Casey Henry. In part of the interview that didn't make it to print, Cia elaborates on gender issues. When asked if she feels overlooked because she is a woman playing in an extremely entertaining family band, she replies, "I believe that being a woman player you should always be judged on your ability, not because you're a woman. I don't want people to make exceptions for me just because I'm a woman." She also denies that any bluegrass women were role models and proclaims the Stanley Brothers to be her biggest influence. When asked if she wishes there were more women playing bluegrass "just so they would be there or so you would have them to look up to," she responds, "Not really, because at this point I feel like we're creating our own thing. When we first started we were trying to imitate people but the people we were imitating were Del McCoury and Jimmy Martin."

Gender issues aside, Cia candidly shares that she is "making a really good living" playing with her family. In fact, she had just bought a new Ford Expedition. "We're all on salary and we have the creative freedom to do what we want." She continues, "I can speak for all my siblings, and none of us have any desire to go and play with anybody else . . . This is a better gig than most people are gonna get."

But as the Bible and the Byrds say, "To everything there is a season," and in January 2011 Cherryholmes announced through their Web page that they were "officially disbanding." As their farewell letter said, "With spouses to consider and differing career aspirations, [our young folk] deserve the freedom to choose their own paths without the extreme interdependence that exists in a family business."

Will these extremely talented young women, Cia and Molly, be able to carve out a musical path without the support of the family unit? Will they want to? Can they find jobs as side musicians? Will they start their own band? Will their brothers find the road easier? The next chapter lies ahead.

Not Just Pretty Good for a Girl!

From the stories of these remarkable female musicians, we can clearly see that women have been a part of bluegrass music right from the beginning. We can also observe that their roles have broadened and changed considerably over the years. From being primarily partnered with husbands or family members and playing rhythm guitar or bass, women have stepped up to the plate on every instrument in the bluegrass field. Even a quick survey of top players reveals Sierra Hull and Rhonda Vincent on mandolin, Alison Krauss and Laurie Lewis on fiddle, Kristin Scott Benson and Cia Cherryholmes on banjo, Sally Van Meter and Jennifer Kennedy Meredith on Dobro, Missy Raines and Amanda Kowalski on bass, and Alison Brown and Marcy Marxer on lead guitar. Numerous women are now leading their own bands, a few women are finding work as side musicians in male bands, mixed-gender bands are becoming more common, and, inspired by the visible success of Alison Krauss and Rhonda Vincent, more young women than ever are taking up bluegrass instruments.

Yet in spite of these advances, women are still underrepresented at festivals both as side musicians and bandleaders ("We've already booked our woman-led band") and even at jam sessions. At the 2010 IBMA World of Bluegrass, Saburo Inoue, the editor of the Japanese bluegrass magazine *Moonshiner,* snapped a shot of a late-night private picking session in a hotel room. Here Sierra Hull is pictured playing her mandolin in the midst of six male musicians who are surrounded by a larger circle of male listeners. The good news is that in the past there might not have even been the one woman—and she almost certainly would not have been a bandleader whose musical prowess commands the respect of a high-powered pickers like Ron Block and Clay Hess.

Perhaps because women are still scarce at high-profile venues such as festivals, awards shows, television shows and documentaries, and radio programs—all of which provide enormous visibility and often spark monstrous mounds of publicity and buzz ("Did you see Sammy Shelor and the Lonesome River Band, with

Steve Martin, on the David Letterman Show?")—women themselves sometimes *still* can't see the other women who are out there. A 2011 publicity sheet from an all-female band boldly proclaims, "With the obvious lack of female musicians in the bluegrass world, [the band] fills a unique niche." Granted, there is undoubtedly a bit of sophism present here ("Hire us! We're different!"), but the "hook" wouldn't work if many people didn't already believe it.

The IBMA Awards themselves, which originated in 1990, provide a condensed look at how far women have come—and how far we still have to go. These prestigious honors, voted on by the professional musicians that comprise this bluegrass trade organization, are the highest form of national recognition that artists can receive from their peers in the industry. Viewed as a whole over a period of twenty-one years, these awards indicate that bluegrass music is still apparently considered—in some categories—to be a "man's music."

For instance, no group with a woman in it has ever received the IBMA's Vocal Group of the Year Award. (Can women sing bluegrass?) Only one group, Nickel Creek, has been named Instrumental Group of the Year (2001), and only two albums—featuring a total of three women, two of them side musicians—have won the award for Instrumental Performance of the Year. (Can women really pick?) Lack of recognition for women in these categories indicates that the battle for a woman's worthiness in bluegrass is far from over.

Voters seem slightly more comfortable with women as entertainers, since the IBMA's Entertainer of the Year Award has gone to groups that include women four times: Alison Krauss and Union Station in 1991 and 1995, Rhonda Vincent and the Rage in 2001, and Cherryholmes in 2005. And as the twenty-first century dawned, things finally began loosening up slightly for bands with women with the IBMA's nod for Emerging Artist of the Year, a category that originated in 1994, going to Nickel Creek in 2000, Kenny and Amanda Smith in 2003, and the SteelDrivers in 2009. And thanks to Alison Krauss and once to Dolly Parton, the Album of the Year Award has gone to women four times. (To be scrupulously fair, the four collaborative albums that have won, including the sound track to *O Brother, Where Art Thou?* all include a smattering of women.)

However, the situation remains bleak in the association's Instrumental Performer category. While Alison Brown and Kristin Scott Benson have been named Banjo Player of the Year, and Missy Raines has captured the bass player honors numerous times, never has a woman received the award for guitar, fiddle, mandolin, or Dobro. Few, other than mandolin player Sierra Hull, have even been nominated.

The highest honor that the organization can bestow on a bluegrass musician is induction into the IBMA Hall of Fame. Since its inception in 1991 thirty-five acts, comprising sixty-five individuals, have been voted in. Six of these are women, and it took eleven years for the first two, Sara and Maybelle Carter, to be inducted (2001). Miggie, Janis, and Polly Lewis joined them in 2006, and Louise Scruggs was added in the "Non-Performer" category in 2010. At the very least, where is Alison Krauss? Where are Hazel and Alice? Where are the Stonemans?

It has been noted that carving out a career in bluegrass is tough for men, too. Life on the road is hard and financial rewards are meager, especially in the beginning. Men often continue to play because there is a wife or partner back home who is willing to work a day job and take care of the family. But from the life stories of these female musicians, we can see that most women in bluegrass have to contend with obstacles that many men don't confront. From the cultural conditioning of Roni Stoneman, who took up the bass and gave her banjo-picking job to her husband because he was a man; to Laurie Lewis, who chose to play bass with the Vern Williams Band because she didn't think she was good enough on the fiddle; to the child-care issues that keep Kathy Kallick off the road because her girls need their mother close by; to the choice of Missy Raines not to have children; to the fact that the earliest women in bluegrass had few children—these are all issues that men, for the most part, don't have to deal with. And we must never lose sight of the fact that women who wanted to play bluegrass were often told that they were not capable of playing as well as their male friends, that bluegrass is for boys, that the banjo is a man's instrument. Surmounting that initial hurdle is huge. Readers may snicker at the title of this book, but it takes a hardheaded, bound-and-determined, thick-skinned woman to continually shrug off the comment "You're pretty good for a girl." As Ola Belle Reed sang, "I've endured, I've endured. How long must I endure?"

Perhaps the best response to this question is the colloquial "We're getting there" or the even more down-to-earth "We're getting 'er done!" My hope is that this book will begin to shed some light on the women who were out there first, paving the way, and those who are out there now singing (and picking) their hearts out. As Alison Brown said, "The female voice in bluegrass is loud and clear at the moment." For, indeed, with fresh new faces and power pickers like Sierra Hull, Brittany Haas, Rachel Renee Johnson (now Boyd), Frankie Nagle, and Molly Tuttle joining road warriors such as Rhonda Vincent, Alison Krauss, and Claire Lynch, the future for women in bluegrass has never looked brighter.

Abbreviations used: *BNL: Banjo NewsLetter*; *BN: Bluegrass Now*; *BU: Bluegrass Un-limited*; *MN: Muleskinner News*; *WIB: Women in Bluegrass* newsletter.

Introduction

The "future of bluegrass music" quote is found in Murphy H. Henry's *BNL* column and Peter Wernick's letter to *WIB*. The "barren of bluegrass" quote is from Henry's liner notes to *M and M Blues*. Information on Betty Aycrigg comes from Sandy Rothman's article in *BU*. Charles Wolfe's quote is from the *Old-Time Herald*, while the quote from Wayne Daniels is from *BU*. Hazel Dickens's quote is from an interview with the author.

In the Beginning: The 1940s

Historians who consider 1945 as the starting date for bluegrass include Mayne Smith, who, in his seminal 1965 article, "Introduction to Bluegrass," wrote, "Bill Monroe and his Blue Grass Boys played the first bluegrass in 1945." In *Blue-grass: A History* Neil Rosenberg frames the question thusly: "Did bluegrass date from 1939 when Bill Monroe organized and brought his Blue Grass Boys to the Grand Ole Opry, or from 1945–48 when his most famous band . . . was active?" Bill Malone, in *Country Music, U.S.A.*, says, "[Bluegrass] did not assume its present fully developed form until the post–World War II period, particularly from 1945 to 1948." Mark Humphrey writes, in the liner notes to the 1992 Columbia boxed set *The Essential Bill Monroe and His Blue Grass Boys*, "Scholars . . . are given to squabble over minor differences, but most heartily echo the statement [Alan] Lomax made to *Esquire*'s readers in 1959: 'Bluegrass began in 1945.'"

Information on Betty Amos comes from a phone interview with her. Betty Harper first came to the author's attention via Urban Hagland's letter to *BU*,

September 1984, and Walt Saunders turned that lead into an interview with Betty for his column in that same magazine in May 2010. Patricia Glaze Stone provided a short synopsis of the musical career of her mother, Ginny Payne Glaze.

SALLY ANN FORRESTER

All biographical information about Sally Ann Forrester comes from the master's thesis "Come Prepared to Stay. Bring Fiddle": The Story of Sally Ann Forrester, the Original Blue Grass Girl," by Murphy H. Henry. Originally this information came from interviews with Sally Ann's son, Bob Forrester, who also graciously offered the use of his mother's scrapbooks, letters, yearbooks, autograph books, photo albums, and other memorabilia.

Data on Monroe's 1945 Columbia recordings can be found in Mark Humphrey's liner notes to the Columbia boxed set *The Essential Bill Monroe and His Blue Grass Boys, 1945–1949*. The idea that Sally Ann was hired as a "favor" to her fiddling husband, Howdy, also found its way into print courtesy of these same notes. The comment that Sally Ann was "holding Howdy's place" in the band was one the author heard mentioned frequently when Sally Ann's name came up in casual bluegrass conversation.

Information on tent shows comes from Jack Hurst's comments in *Nashville's Grand Ole Opry* and from Grant Alden's interview with David Wilds in *No Depression*. The idea that Monroe was following in the footsteps of Roy Acuff when he added accordion to the band comes from John Rumble's liner notes to the MCA boxed set *The Music of Bill Monroe from 1936 to 1994*. Roy Acuff's comments are from *Roy Acuff: The Smoky Mountain Boy*, by Elizabeth Schlappi. The video footage of Sally Ann is found on *"Doc" Ramblin' Tommy Scott Presents Hillbilly Music and Western Swing*, Volumes 1 and 2.

WILMA LEE COOPER

Many of Wilma Lee's direct quotes as well as much historical data come from a live, on-air interview with WSM's Eddie Stubbs on February 5, 2001. Eddie also provided some information by email. Other bits of history and quotes are drawn from an oral interview with Wilma Lee and Stoney by Doug Green on December 3, 1973, which is on file at the Country Music Hall of Fame library, as well as Robert Cogswell's article and discography in the *JEMF [John Edwards Memorial Foundation] Quarterly*. Other sources consulted include Carl May's 1976 *MN* article; Bruce McGuire's liner notes to the 2006 Wilma Lee and Stoney

Cooper Bear Family boxed set; articles in *BU* by Wayne Daniel, Doug Green, and Ray Thigpen; and liner notes from Robert Oermann and Colin Escot.

Information on Wilma Lee's high school days comes from the Elkins High School yearbook, *The Tiger*. Confirmation of her business diploma came from the office of Davis and Elkins College. Her stroke was reported on www.cmt.com, February 27, 2001. Record reviews from *BU* include those by Frank Godbey, Les McIntyre, John Roemer, and Walter V. Saunders.

ROSE MADDOX

Almost all of the biographical information on Rose Maddox comes from *Ramblin' Rose: The Life and Career of Rose Maddox,* by Jonny Whiteside, and from his "Maddox Brothers and Rose" entry in the *Encyclopedia of Country Music.* Her last public appearance was described at www.electricearl.com. Other information is found in Charlie Seeman's liner notes to *Rose Maddox, The One Rose: The Capitol Years,* and the accompanying discography by Patrick Milligan and Richard Weize. Record reviews from *BU* are by John Roemer and Walter V. Saunders.

OLA BELLE CAMPBELL REED

Much of Ola Belle's history can be found in Judy Marti's article in the *Old-Time Herald*; *A Hot-Bed of Musicians* by Paula Hathaway Anderson-Green; and *BU* articles by Victor Evdokimoff and Rhonda Strickland. The discography in *Hot-Bed* was also useful. Ola Belle's quote about being a hillbilly is found in both *Hot-Bed* and the *Herald.* Other direct quotes come from her unpublished autobiography, *High on a Mountain,* which was furnished to the author by Elena Skye. The chapter also relies on Lawrence A. Waltman's book *Sunset Park 50th Anniversary Album, 1940–1990* and his *Sunset Park: A Video Documentary*, which includes the quote from Gene Lowinger. Dick Spottswood's email list of 45 rpm records was also most helpful.

The Second Decade: The 1950s

Information on Lou Osborne can be found at www.ham.muohio.edu/bluegrass/index.htm and in Neil Rosenberg's *BU* column. Information on Mary and Bill Reid also comes from Rosenberg's column and from Jerry Steinberg's liner notes to the CD *Bill and Mary Reid: Early Radio Favorites* and his own *BU* article. *BU* was also the source for facts about LaVaughn Lambert Tomlin (Bob Carlin article), Dottie Lou Martin (Al Green article), and Jackie Dickson (Arlie

Metheny article). Onie Baxter was profiled by Nancy Pate in *WIB* and by S. R. Daugherty in *BU*.

Frank Johnson, who played bass with Juanita and Lucky Saylor, put the author in touch with their banjo player at the time, Hubert Graham King, who provided a photo and personal historical data by email. Ira Gitlin's *BU* article backs this up with a slightly different date.

A detailed history of Lillimae Whitaker's career was provided by Ivan and Deanna Tribe in *BU*. Lillimae's quote about the mandolin player is from Derek Halsey's *BU* article, and the quote about her singing style is from Frank Godbey's review in the magazine. Bonnie Lou and Buster were subjects of a *BU* article by Ivan Tribe, and further facts come from Gary Reid's liner notes to *Carl Story: Angel Band—Early Starday Recordings*. Tribe also wrote about Rex and Eleanor Parker for *BU,* and Howard Dorgan included them in his book *The Airwaves of Zion*. The women of the Upper Cumberland are found in *Grassroots Music in the Upper Cumberland*, edited by William Montell.

BESSIE LEE MAULDIN

Bill Monroe's introduction is from a live recording at New York University, 1963, courtesy of David Dees. Information on Bessie Lee's personal life comes from the Richard D. Smith biography *Can't You Hear Me Callin'?* Ralph Rinzler's reference is found in Tom Ewing's *The Bill Monroe Reader. Bill Monroe and His Blue Grass Boys: An Illustrated Discography* by Neil Rosenberg provided listings of the songs on which Bessie Lee played.

The quote "aroused considerable consternation" is found in *True Life News,* 2nd ed., 2001, edited by Sandy Rothman. Del McCoury's quote is found in Smith, note 110. Monroe's quote about Bessie Lee's singing is from a live show in California, 1955, courtesy of David Dees. Bessie Lee's earliest singing is found on a live recording in Alabama, ca. 1952, courtesy of James Bryan and Neil Rosenberg. Other live recordings from the 1950s include one from Rising Sun, Maryland, in 1957, courtesy of David Dees. The live recording from South Georgia is courtesy of C. P. Heaton. Quotes from the Newport Folk Festival are found on the CD *Bill Monroe with Del McCoury and Bill Keith: Two Days at Newport, July 1963.*

VALLIE CAIN

Vallie's introductory quote is from Mike Pittard's article in *Blueprint*. Johnnie Whisnant's quote is from a Walt Saunders *BU* article. Much of the Cain history comes from another Saunders article in *BU*. Other personal and musical information comes from a collection of Vallie's and Benny's memorabilia in the possession, at the time, of Andrew Acosta. Their home recordings were courtesy of Ford Cave. Vallie's quote about their singing is from *Blueprint*. Richard K. Spottswood wrote the review of their second album for *BU*.

GRACE FRENCH

The Frenches were profiled by Rick Lang in *BU*. Much of Grace's history comes from the publication *My Country*, edited by Ruth Dennett. Other facts come from the questionnaire Grace filled out for the *WIB* newsletter. Richard K. Spottswood wrote the band's first *BU* review.

THE LEWIS FAMILY: MIGGIE, POLLY, JANIS

The quote from Janis Lewis is from her *WIB* questionnaire, as is her quote about her mother's playing. Much of the family's history comes from Lance LeRoy's *The Lewis Family: 45 Years on the Stages of America, a Retrospective*, 1996. Other bits and pieces come from articles in *BU* by Brett F. Devan, Gary Henderson, Lance LeRoy, Don Rhodes, and Barbara Taylor. Their first *BU* record review was written by Richard K. Spottswood; their second by George B. McCeney; their third by Richard K. Spottswood; and the 1975 review by Frank J. Godbey. Shindig in the Barn listings were found in the "Personal Appearance Calendar" of *BU*. Information on Lizzy Long's band is found at www.littleroyandlizzy.com (accessed September 25, 2012).

THE STONEMANS: PATSY, DONNA, RONI

Roni's introductory quote is from the *WIB* newsletter. Most of the family's historical data comes from Ivan Tribe's *The Stonemans: An Appalachian Family and the Music That Shaped Their Lives*. Additional information is found in Norm Cohen's chapter in *Stars of Country Music*, as well as Tribe's *BU* articles. Don Rhodes and Wayne Daniels also wrote about the family for *BU*. Roni's autobiography, *Pressing On*, co-written with Ellen Wright, was quite useful. Buzz Busby's life is detailed in a *BU* article by Rhonda Strickland. Interviews with Patsy, Roni, and Peggy Brain, parts of which were published in *WIB*, were most helpful.

The video clip of the Bluegrass Champs playing on *Arthur Godfrey's Talent Scouts* is from the personal collection of Archie Warnock. Don Owens's career was chronicled by Conway Gandy in *BU*. Mike Seeger's liner notes to *American Banjo: Three-Finger and Scruggs Style* provided information on Roni's participation in the project; emails added clarification. The reporter's review of the Stoneman appearance at the University of Illinois is related in Tribe's biography.

BU reviews are by Murphy H. Henry, George B. McCeney, and Richard K. Spottswood. The two movies the Stonemans are in, *Hell on Wheels* and *Road to Nashville,* are on DVDs from Rhino Home Video. Rhonda Vincent's quote is from Chicago's *City Talk Newspaper*, a clipping in a Rounder publicity package.

MARGIE SULLIVAN

Much of the Sullivan Family history comes from their autobiography, *The Sullivan Family: Fifty Years in Bluegrass Gospel Music,* edited by Patricia Martinez. Direct quotes come from this and the author's interview. Other biographical information comes from Doug Green in *BU* and from Margie's *WIB* questionnaire. The 1967 *BU* review is by Richard K. Spottswood. Later *BU* reviews are by George B. McCeney and Walter V. Saunders. The *BNL* profile is by Murphy H. Henry.

The Numbers Are Growing: The 1960s

Information on Janet Davis comes from her *WIB* questionnaire, her online profile at www.janetdavismusic.com, and from Wayne Shrubsall's *BNL* article. The quote about Carolyn Smith is from Richard K. Spottswood's *BU* review. Details about the Marshall Family are found in a Glenn Roberts *BU* article and a John Roemer *BU* review. Valeda Greer was mentioned in two *BU* articles. A phone call to Jim Greer confirmed the information about his sisters Bonnie and Valeda.

JEANIE WEST

Dates and biographical tidbits come from Jeanie's *WIB* questionnaire. Information on recordings was gleaned from many sources, including Thomas Stern's Association for Recorded Sound Discussion List at http://cool.conservation-us .org/byform/mailing-lists/arsclist/2006/07/msg00215.html. The liner notes to many of Harry and Jeanie's albums, including *Songs of the Southland,* can be found at www.folkways.si.edu. Fred Bartenstein provided a copy of *Southern Mountain Folksongs and Ballads* from his personal collection as well as much information on recordings. Neil Rosenberg's quote is from *Bluegrass: A History*. Les McIntyre's review of *Roots of Bluegrass* is in *BU*.

BETTY AMOS WITH JUDY AND JEAN

The early photograph of Betty with the banjo is found in *Not Too Old to Cut The Mustard:"Jumping"Bill Carlisle and Friends Talk about His Life and the Country Music Business,* by Anita Capps. Information about Betty's tenure with Carlisle is also found here along with a discography. The story about the plane crash, written by Judy Lee Schreiber, can be found online at www.pinetreeline.org. Other historical information is from "Judy's Life in Country Music," by Judy Lee Schreiber, online at http://community-4.webtve.net.

The male recorder collector is Tom Armstrong, who made this comment in an email to the author. He also graciously provided a compilation of the band's recordings from his personal collection. A list is available at www.tomarmstrongmusic.com. Judy Lee also sent a compilation CD of the band's recordings from her personal collection. Judy's quote about softball can be found at www.elder.com.

GLORIA BELLE

Gloria Belle was profiled by Murphy H. Henry in *WIB*; her *WIB* questionnaire was also helpful in providing dates. Mike Seeger's report on the banjo contest is from the publication *gardyloo,* July 1959, courtesy of Pete Kuykendall. Information on Lois Johnson and Penny Jay comes from Chris Skinker's liner notes to the Bear Family boxed set *Jimmy Martin and the Sunny Mountain Boys.* Clarence Greene penned the 1969 description of Jimmy Martin on stage for *BU.* Mark Newton's quote is found on his website, www.marknewtonband.com. Gloria Belle's participation in the 2001 IBMA Awards show along with her part in other IBMA events were reported by Murphy H. Henry in various issues of *WIB,* including 21 (Fall 1999), 13 (Fall 1997), and 9 (Fall 1996). *BU* reviews are by Les McIntryre, Walter V. Saunders, and Richard K. Spottswood.

HAZEL AND ALICE

Biographical details about the lives of Hazel and Alice come from a variety of sources, including Mary Battiata in the *Washington Post Magazine,* Jack Bernhardt in the *Old-Time Herald,* Debbie Brightwell at www.ibluegrass.com, Bill Friskic-Warren in *No Depression,* Alice Gerrard in *Sing Out!,* Alice and Hazel's liner notes to the CD *Hazel Dickens and Alice Gerrard: Pioneering Women of Bluegrass,* Geoffery Himes in the *Baltimore City Paper,* Katie Laur in *Country Living* magazine, Madelyn Rosenberg in *BU,* Ron Thomason in *BU,* Caroline Wright in *BN,* and Mimi Pickering's documentary film *Hazel Dickens: It's Hard to Tell the Singer from the Song.* Direct quotes from Alice and Hazel come from these same sources or from author interviews.

The author of the introductory quote is given as "jon da peripatetic poet." Neil Rosenberg's quote is from *Bluegrass: A History.* The first quote from Laurie Lewis is found in *WIB.* Laurie's second quote is from her liner notes to the CD *Guest House.* Hazel's honorary doctorate speech was printed in *WIB.* The quote from the *Old-Time Herald* is in a review by Jon and Marcia Pankake. Alison Krauss's quote is from the DVD *It's Hard to Tell the Singer from the Song.*

Reviews mentioned include Dave Wilson in *Broadside,* J. B. Goddard in the *Village Voice,* an unknown author in *Time,* and Frank J. Godbey in *BU.* Also quoted are Bruce Winkworth liner's notes to the CD *Newport Folk Festival: Best of Bluegrass, 1959–1966* and Charles Wolfe's liner notes to the CD *Hazel & Alice.* Alice graciously sent scans of early reviews and articles.

DOTTIE EYLER

Biographical information comes from Walter V. Saunders in *BU,* an unknown author in *BU* (February 1968), Charles Brumley in *BU,* Lilli Butler in *Blueprint,* and Dottie Eyler's *WIB* questionnaire. The *BU* reviews quoted are by Frank J. Godbey and Art Menius. Bonnie Eyler emailed a complete discography.

VIVIAN WILLIAMS

Vivian Williams related Bill Monroe's quote and the story of playing with him in *WIB.* Biographical information comes from Claire Levine in *WIB. BU* reviews are by Richard K. Spottswood, Joseph C. Hickerson, and Dick Kimmel.

BETTIE BUCKLAND

Biographical information on Bettie comes from an author interview with her son, Andrew, who also provided a cassette copy of the Moonlighters' demo tape.

RUBYE DAVIS

Much biographical information on Rubye Davis comes from Murphy H. Henry's article in *WIB.* Other historical details are found in *BU* articles by Bruce Nemerov and Brett F. Devan. The "soul of the Season Travelers" quote is from Dan Loftin's obituary for Rubye in *WIB,* as is his ending quote. *BU* reviews are by George B. McCeney and John Roemer.

GINGER BOATWRIGHT

Background information can be found in *BU* articles by Frank Overstreet, Alana White, Lee Grant, and Janice McDonald and by Julie Koehler in *BN*. Ginger's direct quotes come from these sources, from Murphy H. Henry in *WIB,* and from Ginger's own article in *WIB*. Other historical data come from the liner notes to the CD *Red, White, and Blue(grass): Guaranteed,* by Jerry W. Hammond and Mariel R. Dickson. Some dates come from Ginger's *WIB* questionnaire. Information on Randy Wood and the Old Time Picking Parlor is from the Janice Brown McDonald article in *BU*. Ginger's influence was reported by five women in their *WIB* questionnaires. *BU* reviews were written by Frank J. Godbey, George B. McCeney, and Jon Hartley Fox.

THE WHITES: PAT, SHARON, CHERYL, ROSIE

The history of the Whites was gathered from articles by Bob Allen, Douglas Green, Boris Weintraub, and Steven M. Robinson in *BU* and from Marilyn Kochman in *Frets*. Biographical and recording information was also found online at www.cmt.com and at www.classactentertainment.com. *BU* reviews include those by Frank J. Godbey, Jim S. Griffith, and John Roemer. Direct quotes are found in Allen, Robinson, Green, and Weintraub.

WENDY THATCHER

Caroline Wright's quotes are from *WIB*. Quotes from Wendy are from the author's interview. The quote from Katie Laur was in an email to the author. Biographical details were gleaned from articles in *BU* by Pete Kuykendall and Bill Vernon. The history of the Country Gentlemen by Glenn Roberts in *BU* was also useful. Reviews in *BU* are by Frank J. Godbey.

MARTHA ADCOCK

Many of the personal details of Martha's history were provided by her in written form to the author. This includes her *WIB* questionnaire. Most of her direct quotes come from this. She also provided a discography. Other background information comes from Bob Peelstrom, Pete Kuykendall, Don Rhodes, and Bill Vernon in *BU* and Eddie Collins in *BN*. Dan Miller wrote the *Flatpicking Guitar Magazine* article. Martha and Eddie's division of labor was spelled out by Missy Raines in an email to the author. Reviews in *BU* are by Frank J. Godbey and George B. McCeney.

THE MCLAIN FAMILY: ALICE, RUTH, NANCY ANN

The McLain Family history was chronicled in *BU* articles by Chandler Davis, Marty Godbey, and Christopher M. Strong; *BU* reviews were written by Richard K. Spottswood, Walter V. Saunders, Jon Hartley Fox, and Jim S. Griffith. Other background information is from Stephanie P. Ledgin's article in *Pickin'* magazine and Wayne Shrubsall's in *BNL*. Raymond W. McLain's introductory quote is from *BNL*. Raymond K. McLain's obituary by Loyal Jones, online at www.mclains.com, was useful, as was the guide to the McLain Family Band records at www.berea.edu. Festival ads in *BU* provided a historical timeline for the family festival.

The Floodgates Open: The 1970s

Marcy Marxer related the quote about women and the guitar in *Flatpicking Guitar Magazine*.

BECK GENTRY

Details of Beck's life and quotes from her are from the author's interview and follow-up emails, parts of which appeared in *WIB*. Mary Jo Leet's quotes are from that same interview. Dave Harvey's quotes are from a phone interview with the author. Jim Webb cleared up some points in a phone interview. Bill Evans made his comments in an email to the author. Reviews are by Joseph McLellan in the *Washington Post*, Robert Palmer in the *New York Post*, and Richard K. Spottswood in *BU*.

SUZANNE THOMAS

Background information and most of Suzanne's quotes come from interviews with the author and from her *WIB* questionnaire. Information about Mary Jo Leet also comes from author interviews and emails. Parts of these interviews appeared in an article by Murphy H. Henry in *WIB*. Jon Hartley Fox provided personal observations of Suzanne's role in the band in an email to the author. Other historical facts come from articles by Bob Cantwell, Murphy H. Henry, and Ron Thomason in *BU*.

DELIA BELL

Information on Delia Bell's career is found in *BU* articles by Ralph Dice, Don Rhodes, Juanita Stockton, and Barry Brower. *BU* reviews are by Walter V.

Saunders, Nancy Pate, Jon Weisberger, and Robert C. Buckingham. Information on Kathy Kaplan comes from her *BU* obituary by Bill Vernon. Walt Saunders allowed the author to borrow all of Delia Bell's albums.

BUFFALO GALS

Background information comes from an interview with Susie Monick and follow-up emails with the author. Carol Siegel and Martha Trachtenberg also provided corroborating detail by email. Henry Koretzky's unedited interview with Martha was also useful; an edited version appeared in *BU*. Most of the direct quotes come from these. Elaine Eliah, Kristin Wilkinson, Sally Finger-ett, Nancy Josephson, Bill Knowlton, Peter Wernick, and Tony Trischka also answered numerous questions by email. Other bits of trivia and some quotes come from a Tony Trischka interview with the Buffalo Gals ghostwritten by Martha Trachtenberg in *MN*. Mike Greenstein's article in *BU* also helped tie some information together. The *BU* review is by Richard K. Spottswood.

Country Kasha's first gig was advertised in a dated mimeographed dormi-tory flyer. The school paper at Syracuse University was the *Daily Orange*. Bruce Hornstein wrote the March 1974 newspaper article. The *New York Times* article was written by John S. Wilson, the *Syracuse New Times* article by J. K. of the newspaper's music staff. All of these clippings are from Susie's personal collec-tion.

BETTY FISHER

Betty's quotes and most of her life story come from an interview with the author, parts of which were published in *WIB*. A few details come from the author's personal observations.

KATIE LAUR

Much of Katie's historical narrative comes from an interview with the author followed by emails and phone calls bolstered by her *WIB* questionnaire and her own articles in *WIB*. Katie also wrote about Terry Boswell in *WIB*. Other details come from articles by Dan Geringer in *Ohio* magazine, John Eliot in *MN,* and Carin Joy Condon and Marty Godbey in *BU*. Derek Halsey's own interview with Katie was useful. Parts of it were published in his "Oh Sister Thou Hast Been Here All Along" article for *Gritz* magazine. *BU* reviews are by Frank J. Godbey and Richard K. Spottswood. Russell McDivitt provided a CD copy and liner notes of the Appalachian Grass recording. Fred Bartenstein emailed his personal recollections of the genesis of the *Good Time Girl* CD. Wayne Clyburn shared his memories of Katie's early days with the Appalachian Grass by email.

DEDE WYLAND

Dede's background information and quotes come from an interview she did with Ira Gitlin and follow-up emails with the author. Richard D. Smith's article in *BU* was also useful. The *BU* review quoted is by Alan J. Steiner.

LYNN MORRIS

Background information and quotes from Lynn come from interviews with the author, parts of which were published in *WIB,* as well as articles by Frank Overstreet in *Bluegrass Music News*, Joan McCarthy in the *Bluegrass Chronicle*, Mary Battiata in the *Washington Post Magazine*, Joe Romano in *BN,* and Art Menius and Geoffrey Himes in *BU*. Her *WIB* questionnaire was also useful. Marshall Wilborn helped clear up some points about the lineup of the Lynn Morris Band. Dudley Connell shed some light on the choice of banjo player for the Johnson Mountain Boys. David McLaughlin also talked about the situation in personal conversation with the author. The personnel of Whetstone Run was described by Mia Boynton in *BU*. The *BU* review is by Rick Anderson. The author was on hand personally for Lynn's appearance at the Apple Blossom Festival.

THE WOMEN IN CALIFORNIA

In addition to author interviews and emails, information on these women comes from *BU* articles by Sandy Rothman, Peter V. Kuykendall, Tom Riney, Lou Curtis, Wayne Rice, and John Donnelly in the *San Francisco Sunday Examiner and Chronicle*. Information on JoAnn White comes from an author's conversation with Roland White. Information on Dian James comes from Richie Unterberger at www.mudcat.org and the uncredited liner notes to her album *Dian and the Greenbriar Boys*. A view of the early life of Ingrid Herman Reece comes from Gene Lees's biography of Woody Herman. Most of her quotes are from here. Other quotes about her come from Murphy H. Henry's article in *WIB*. Information on the Homestead Act comes from Lynn Hedgecoth's *WIB* questionnaire and an uncredited *BU* article, December 1971. The *BU* review is by Frank J. Godbey. The final quote from Laurie Lewis is from Claire Levine's article in *WIB*.

LAURIE LEWIS

Information on and quotes from Laurie come from interviews and emails with the author, her *WIB* questionnaire, and her own liner notes to various projects. Her story was fleshed out using articles by Claire Levine in *WIB* and *No Depression*, Alan Senauke in *Sing Out!* Mary Larsen in *Fiddler* magazine, Richard Saltus in *Pickin','* Laurie Lewis and Murphy H. Henry in *WIB*, Joe Carr and Ira Gitlin in *BU*, and Peter Wernick's liner notes to the Grant Street String Band CD. The *BU* review is by Jon Hartley Fox. Laurie's quote about a singing partner is from an uncredited Hightone Records press release. Pat Enright confirmed information about the Phantoms of the Opry by email.

KATHY KALLICK

Biographical information and quotes from Kathy come from interviews and emails with the author. Peter Thompson also provided additional details via emails and a self-published on-air interview with Kathy, parts of which ran in *WIB*. Much information on the Good Ol' Persons comes from a Laurie Lewis interview and Kathy's own article in *WIB*. Murphy H. Henry also wrote about Kathy for *WIB*. Other information comes from *BU* articles by Kerry Dexter, Claire Levine, Chris Lewis, J. D. Kleinke, and Stephanie Davis. *BU* reviews are by Jon Hartley Fox and David Royko.

CLAIRE LYNCH

Claire's story was collected by the author in several interviews and emails. Part of one interview was published in *WIB*. Additional information was gleaned from her *WIB* questionnaire and articles by Susan Atteberry Smith in *BN* and Larry Nager, Chris Stuart, and Jerry Wilson in *BU*. *BU* reviews are by James S. Griffith, John Roemer, Frank J. Godbey, Alan J. Steiner, and Les McIntryre. Claire's quotes about the Front Porch String Band not ever being her project and her willingness to take chances are from an uncredited Rounder publicity sheet for her CD *New Day*.

LEE ANN LENKER BABER

Most of Lee Ann's biographical information and quotes come from an interview she did with the author. She also shared numerous clippings, contracts, and press kit items. The article quoted is by Roger Williams, which is also where Bob Doyle's quip originated.

Leaders of the Band: The 1980s

Kate MacKenzie was profiled in *BU* articles by Steven Earl Howard and Jamie Peterson. Her *WIB* questionnaire was also helpful. Information on the Isaacs comes from a *BU* article by Glenn Roberts Jr. and from www.cmt .com. The review on the Isaacs in *BU* is by Les McIntyre. Facts about Traver Hollow come from Glenn R. Huffer's liner notes to their 1984 album, *Genuine Acoustic Bluegrass,* Peggy Harvey's *WIB* questionnaire, and dates of *BU* reviews. Information on Southern Rail comes from Rich Stillman's notes to their thirtieth-anniversary CD, *On the Road from Appomattox.* Hazel McGee's story is outlined by Fran Larkin in *WIB,* Dave Haney in *BU,* and the band website, www .whitemountainbluegrass.com. Ada McCown filled out a *WIB* questionnaire, the three Outdoor Plumbing Company albums were reviewed by *BU* (September 1973, August 1977, December 1984), and www.goldtone.com provided the dates for the band's bluegrass focus and Jim's switch to old-time music. The website www.appalshop.org advertised Ada and Jim's old-time performance in 2010 and referred to them as "mainstays of the bluegrass and old-time scene for decades." The John Herald Band was profiled in *BU* by R. J. Kelly.

MISSY RAINES

Missy shared her story with the author by phone, in follow-up emails, and via her *WIB* questionnaire. Bill Evans added details and answered questions by email. Helpful articles include those by Bob Peelstrom and Bill Vernon in *BU* and Nancy Cardwell in *BN*. *BU* reviews are by John Roemer, Alan J. Steiner, David J. McCarty, and Henry Koretzky. Alison Brown's quote is from the liner notes to Missy's first CD, *My Place in the Sun.*

ALISON BROWN

Alison's history comes from an interview with the author as well as follow-up emails and her *WIB* questionnaire. Her beginning quote comes from her IBMA keynote address as does her quote about Stuart Duncan; the speech was published in *WIB*. Additional information and quotes come from articles by Geoff Stelling (*BNL*), Parke Puterbaugh (*Attaché*), Louisa Branscomb (*BN*), Lee Zimmerman (*Goldmine*), Ira Gitlin (unpublished interview), Dave Rakich (*Cleveland Country Magazine*), Russell Hall (*Performing Songwriter*), Irena Pribylova (*BNL*), Shelton Clark (*Acoustic Musician*), and Barry Mazor (*Wall Street Journal*). *BU* reviews are by Rick Anderson, Jon Hartley Fox, Frank J. Godbey,

Dick Kimmel, J. D. Kleinke, and David Royko. Information on Compass Records comes from company press releases and www.compassrecords.com.

ALL-FEMALE BANDS

Band information comes primarily from interviews and emails with band members, including Andrea Roberts (Petticoat Junction), Sally Wingate (Bluegrass Liberation, HeartStrings), Louisa Branscomb (Bluegrass Liberation, Boot Hill), Erica Hunter (Bluegrass Liberation), Lynn Grey Salls (Bluegrass Liberation), the Coon Creek Girls (Vicki Simmons, Ramona Church Taylor, Dale Ann Bradley, Kathy Kuhn), Lee Ann Welch (Sidesaddle), and Kathy Barwick (All Girl Boys). Portions of the Coon Creek Girls interview appeared in an article by Murphy H. Henry for *WIB*. Henry also discussed the addition of men to the New Coon Creek Girls in *WIB*. The quote about the All Girl Boys is from Jon Hartley Fox in his *BU* review. Information on the Wildwood Girls comes from *BU* articles by Jim Scribbins, Arlie Metheny, and Nancy Cardwell, and from *BU* record reviews. Additional information on Sidesaddle is from www.sidesaddleandco.com and Lee Ann Welch's *WIB* questionnaire. Jerry Keys provided the names of the Country Girls. Various band press releases were also useful, particularly those of new groups Della Mae and Giddyup Kitty. Internet sources include www.sweet-potato-pie.com; www.myspace .com/redmollyband; www.facebook.com/pages/Red-Molly; www.facebook .com/hillbettys; and www.macrowemusic.com.

ALISON KRAUSS

Information on Alison's life and quotes from her come from articles by Nancy Grant (*Frets*); Roy Kasten (*No Depression*); Chris Jones (*BN*); Jim Bessman (*Journal of Country Music*); Jon Weisberger (*BN*); Charlene A. Blevins (*Acoustic Musician*); and Jack Tottle, Thomas Goldsmith, Geoffrey Himes, and Jay Orr in *BU*. Her quote about her diamond-studded shoes is from Lisa Lee's article at www .cmt.com. Roger Catlin originally said Alison is the "biggest thing to happen to bluegrass since Flatt and Scruggs." He was quoted in *BU* by Joe Ross.

BU reviews are by Allan Walton, Les McIntyre, Jon Hartley Fox, J. D. Kleinke, Paul A. Sacks, and David Royko. Other reviews are by Bob Townsend and Jon Weisberger in *No Depression*. The *New York Times* article is by Stephen Holden; the *Rolling Stone* article is by David Wild. Information about Alison's first video is from Ken Irwin in *BU*.

The *USA Today* quote is from David Zimmerman and was noted in *BU* by Jack Tottle, who also mentioned Bill Christophersen's remark in *Newsweek*. Richard Dale was the author of the letter to the editor in *BU*. Alison's quote about burping is from an uncredited writer in *People Weekly* magazine, August 11, 1986. Alison's *New York Times* quote about singing in tune is from Jim Macnie's liner notes to *Now That I've Found You*.

Information on Alison's sponsorship by Martha White is found in Murphy H. Henry's "General Store" column in *BU*, June 1996. Statistics on the *O Brother* sound track come from *Billboard*. Information and quotes from Meredith Bub come from Caroline Wright in *BN*. Information on Andrea Zonn comes from a *BN* article by Dave Higgs. The Sara Watkins quote is from an article by Eddie Collins in *BN*, the Sean Watkins quote is from the Bessman article, and Ron Block's quote is from Goldsmith. David Dees provided a copy of the *Masters of the Folk Violin* cassette, and Bruce Weiss sent a copy of the *Different Strokes* cassette.

Too Many to Count: The 1990s and Beyond

Sierra Hull was profiled in articles by Leon Alligood (*The Tennessean*), Geoff Edgers (*Boston Globe*), a publicity sheet from GoodStuff PR, Jewly Hight (*Nashville Scene*), Randy Rudder (*BU*), and an Alison Krauss publicity email (from www.AlisonKrauss.com). Sierra Hull's graduation from Berklee is reported on her website, www.sierrahull.com (accessed September 25, 2012). The final quote from Alison Brown also comes from the Hight article. Information on Molly Tuttle was found at www.mollytuttle.net and www.scbs.org (accessed September 25, 2012).

Information on Valerie Smith comes from articles by Timothy Jones (*BN*), a Bell Buckle publicity flyer, www.valeriesmithonline.com, and her own letter to *WIB*. David Royko wrote the quoted review in *BU*. Information on Jeanette Williams comes from stories by Nancy Cardwell in *BN* and *BU*. Quotes come from *BU* reviews by Alan J. Steiner and Archie Warnock III. Information on Honi Deaton comes from articles by Casey Henry (*BN*), Amy Reinholds (*BN*), and Derek Halsey (*BU*). Information on Lorraine Jordan comes from her *WIB* questionnaire and articles by Jack Bernhardt (*BU*) and Joe Ross (*BN*). Information on Tammy Rogers and the SteelDrivers comes from a Rounder Records publicity flyer.

The "Young Guns in Bluegrass Article" in *BNL* was written by Michael Brantley. The names of mixed-gender bands and up-and-coming players come from various band publicity flyers, CDs, and emails that were sent to *BU* for the "General Store" column.

KRISTIN SCOTT BENSON

Kristin shared her history in interviews and emails with the author. Additional information came from articles by Chris Cioffi and Casey Henry in *BNL*, Jon Weisberger and Nancy Cardwell in *BN,* and Brett F. Devan in *BU*. Information on Honi Deaton is from an article by Casey Henry in *BN*. Sally Jones corresponded with the author via email; Larry Stephenson by phone. Information on Jenee Keener is from the *BU* "General Store" column of February 2002 and Dave's Diary at www.nucountry.com.au. Reviews are by Ian Perry (*BNL*) and Robert C. Buckingham (*BU*). Larry Stephenson was profiled in *BU* by Don Rhodes.

RHONDA VINCENT

Much of Rhonda's background information and many quotes come from the author's interview with her. Her mother, Carolyn Vincent, was also interviewed. Both filled out *WIB* questionnaires. Other information comes from articles by Jon Weisberger (*BU*), Brett F. Devan (*BU*), Arlie Metheny (*BU*), Derek Halsey (*Gritz*), Steve Romanosky (*Sing Out!*), and Loretta Sawyer (*BN*). Additional quotes are from Mary Houlihan (*City Talk*), David Potorti (*Independent Weekly*), and Rhonda's *Ragin' Live* DVD. *BU* reviews are by Robert C. Buckingham, Les McIntyre, Jon Hartley Fox, Frank Godbey, John Roemer, J. D. Kleinke, Bob Allen, and Murphy H. Henry. Craig Havighurst dubbed Rhonda "the new queen of bluegrass" in the *Wall Street Journal*. Rhonda's quote about being on the Opry is from Jessica Phillips (www.countrystandardtime.com). The phrase "classic sixties honky-tonk style" belongs to John Lupton (www.countrystandardtime .com). Information on Rhonda's leaving Rounder was found at www.cmt.com (February 19, 2010), and the marriage of Hunter Berry was reported by John Lawless at www.bluegrasstoday.com.

Julia Yokum and Ed Rosenkrans provided scans of early Sally Mountain Show album covers; Tom Henderson made copies of early Sally Mountain Show albums.

THE DIXIE CHICKS

Background information on and quotes from the Dixie Chicks come from articles by Ira Gitlin (*BNL*), Richard Skanse (*Journal of Country Music*), James L. Dickerson's book *Dixie Chicks: Down-Home and Backstage*, Jim Jerome (*People*), Jeremy Helligar and Chris Rose (*People*), Josh Tyrangiel (www.time.com), and

Renee Clark (*Dallas Life*). Information on Blue Night Express is from Sharon Gilchrist via email. Andy Owens sent his personal recollections via fax, sent copies of the Danger in the Air cassettes, and answered many questions by email. Henry Moore provided the author with a copy of the Chicks' first album.

Additional information and quotes come from a Blue Night Express publicity brochure (ca. 1985, courtesy of Jean-Mark Delon), Martie Maguire's *WIB* questionnaire, www.cmt.com, http://dixiechicks.msn.com, www.riaa.com, www.npr.org, www.grammy.com, and www.cmaawards.com. Judy Cain's website, www.chickoholic.tripod.com (also named www.dixiechickshenhouse.com), and www.dixie-chicks.com, with their online versions of "Chick Chat," were extremely helpful.

These Dixie Chicks DVDs provided information and quotes: *Shut Up and Sing, Top of the World Tour: Live,* and *An Evening with the Dixie Chicks.* Reviews include those by Barry Mazor (*No Depression*), Murphy H. Henry (*BU*), David J. McCarty (*BU*), and Jody Rosen (www.rollingstone.com). Randy Rudder quoted Natalie Maines's statement about the president in an article for *Country Music Goes to War.* Natalie's introductory quote is from the Chicks' interview with Melissa Block on NPR's *All Things Considered.*

CHERRYHOLMES

Information and quotes about Cherryholmes come from articles by Nancy Cardwell (*BU*), Casey Henry (*BN* and *BU*), Larry Wine (*BNL*), Frank Goodman (www.puremusic.com), http://cherryholmes.musiccitynetworks.com, and Edward Morris (www.cmt.com). Additional information comes from Casey Henry's unedited interview with Cia Cherryholmes. *BU* reviews are by Allan Walton and Art Menius.

Conclusion

A complete list of IBMA Award recipients and Hall of Fame members can be found at www.ibma.org. The publicity flyer is from Coaltown Dixie. The photo by Saburo Inoue was published in *Moonshiner* magazine. Alison Brown's quote is from Jewly Hight's article in the *Nashville Scene.*

ABBREVIATIONS USE

AM	*Acoustic Musician*
BNL	*Banjo NewsLetter*
BC	*Bluegrass Chronicle*
BMN	*Bluegrass Music News*
BN	*Bluegrass Now*
BU	*Bluegrass Unlimited*
FGM	*Flatpicking Guitar Magazine*
JAF	*Journal of American Folklore*
JEMFQ	*John Edwards Memorial Foundation Quarterly*
JCM	*Journal of Country Music*
MN	*Muleskinner News*
ND	*No Depression*
OTH	*Old-Time Herald*
WIB	*Women in Bluegrass newsletter*

SOURCES

"AKUS—Great High Mountain Tour." www.AlisonKraus.com. April 29, 2004. Accessed April 30, 2004.

"Alison Krauss Is No Cornball When It Comes to Fancy Fiddlin'." *People* 26, no. 6 (1986).

Allen, Bob. Review of *Rhonda Vincent: Yesterday and Today*. *BU* 33, no. 6 (1998): 61.

————. "The Whites." *BU* 35, no. 11 (2001): 60–64.

Alligood, Leon. "Where the Bluegrass Grows." *Nashville Tennessean*. October 12, 2003. Life section.

Anderson, Rick. Review of *Alison Brown: Fair Weather*. *BU* 35, no. 3 (2000): 66.

————. Review of *Lynn Morris Band: Shape of a Tear*. *BU* 38, no. 2 (2003): 75.

Anderson-Green, Paula Hathaway. *A Hot-Bed of Musicians: Traditional Music in the Upper New River Valley–Whitetop Region*. Knoxville: University of Tennessee Press, 2002.

Battiata, Mary. "A High and Lonesome Sound." *Washington Post Magazine.* June 24, 2001. 8–15, 21–24.

———. "On the Road with the Ghost of Bill Monroe." *Washington Post Magazine.* June 25, 2000. 10–15, 23–28.

Bernhardt, Jack. "Hard Working, Hard Driving Carolina Road." *BU* 38, no. 4 (2003): 72–75.

———. "With a Song in Her Heart: The Musical Journey of Alice Gerrard." *OTH* 9, no. 8 (2005): 24–30.

Bessman, Jim. "Alison Krauss: Mountain Mama." *JCM* 23, no. 1 (2002): 10–16.

Blevins, Charlene A. "Alison Krauss and Union Station: It's a Band Thing." *AM* 2, no. 6 (1995): 8–13, 21.

Block, Melissa. "Dixie Chicks Return: *Taking the Long Way*." *All Things Considered.* National Public Radio. May 23, 2006. www.npr.org/player/v2/mediaPlayer .html?action=1&t=1&islist=false&id=5424238&m=5425715. Accessed August 29, 2011.

Boatwright, Ginger. "Friends Remember Ingrid." *WIB* 15 (Spring 1998): 2–3.

Boynton, Mia. "Whetstone Run: Past and Present." *BU* 15, no. 1 (1978): 51–53.

Branscomb, Louisa. "Alison Brown: A Graceful Balancing of Bluegrass and Business." *BN* 10, no. 7 (2000): 26–29.

Brantley, Michael. "Young Guns of Bluegrass." *BNL* 37, no. 6 (2010): 40–43.

Brooks, Robert. "The All-Inclusive Dixie Chicks Page." www.dixie-chicks.com/ dlife392.shtml. Accessed August 30, 2011.

Brower, Barry. "Bill Grant and Delia Bell: Living Life the First Time Around." *BU* 23, no. 3 (1988): 16–18.

Brown, Alison. "Alison Brown: Embrace It All." *WIB* 31 (December 2002): 2–5.

———. Liner notes to *Alison Brown: Stolen Moments*. Compass Records 7 4400 2, 2005.

———. Liner notes to *Missy Raines: My Place in the Sun*. No label. MR CD 1001, 1998.

Brumley, Charles. "The Carroll County Ramblers." *BU* 12, no. 8 (1978): 43–45.

Buckingham, Robert C. Review of *Delia Bell and Bill Grant: We're Not the Jet Set*. *BU* 39, no. 4 (2004): 77.

———. Review of *The Larry Stephenson Band: Two Hearts on the Borderline*. *BU* 34, no. 12 (2000): 72–73.

———. Review of *Rhonda Vincent: Back Home Again*. *BU* 34, no. 11 (2000): 84.

Bufwack, Mary A., and Robert K. Oermann. *Finding Her Voice: The Saga of Women in Country Music*. New York: Crown, 1993.

Butler, Lilli. "Carroll County's Dottie Eyler." *Blueprint* (December 1982).

Cantwell, Bob. "The Hotmud Family: It's Current to Us." *BU* 11, no. 10 (1977): 52–58.

Capps, Anita. *Not Too Old to Cut the Mustard: "Jumping" Bill Carlisle and Friends Talk about His Life and the Country Music Business.* Johnson City, TN: Overmountain Press, 2000.

Cardwell, Nancy. "Cherryholmes and the Bluegrass Dream." *BU* 39, no. 11 (2005): 42–47.

———. "Jeanette Williams: Making Music, Touching Lives." *BN* 10, no. 8 (2000): 20–21, 34–36.

———. "Jeanette Williams: She's Got Her Walkin' Shoes On." *BU* 39, no. 4 (2004): 56–60.

———. "Kristin Scott Benson Talks Banjo." *BN* 12, no. 2 (2002): 22–25, 36–37.

———. "Missy Raines." *BN* 2, no. 5 (1992): 4–7.

———. "The Wildwood Girls." *BU* 27, no. 11 (1993): 32–36.

Carlin, Bob. "L. W. Lambert: True Banjo Picker." *BU* 33, no. 9 (1999): 38–43.

Carr, Joe. "Laurie Lewis: Shining Star of Bluegrass Music's New Golden Era." *BU* 31, no. 9 (1997): 34–39.

Cherryholmes. "Cherryholmes Bid Farewell and Best Wishes." January 12, 2011. http://cherryholmes.musiccitynetworks.com/index.htm?inc=5&news_id=19247. Accessed January 24, 2012.

Cioffi, Chris. "Kristin Scott." *BNL* 24, no. 12 (1997): 8–14.

Clark, Renee. "Local Heroes: Can the Dixie Chicks Make It in the Big Time?" *Dallas Life Magazine.* March 1, 1992. www.dixie-chicks.com/dlife392.shtml. Accessed August 30, 2011.

Clark, Shelton. "Alison Brown: Her Aim Is True." *AM* 2, no. 11 (1996): 8–13.

Cogswell, Robert. "'We Made Our Name in the Days of Radio': A Look at the Career of Wilma Lee and Stoney Cooper." *JEMFQ* 11, no. 38 (1975): 67–79.

———. "Wilma Lee and Stoney Cooper Discography." *JEMFQ* 11, no. 38 (1975): 89–94.

Cohen, Norm. "Early Pioneers." In *Stars of Country Music,* ed. Bill C. Malone and Judith McCulloh, 3–39. New York: De Capo Press, 1975.

Collins, Eddie. "Eddie and Martha: Big Creativity in a Small Package." *BN* 11, no. 11 (2001): 18–20, 31, 33, 40.

———. "Sara Watkins." *BN* 12, no. 4 (2002): 22–25.

Condon, Carin Joy. "Katie Laur." *BU* 28, no. 12 (1994): 56–63.

Cooper, Wilma Lee, and Stoney Cooper. Transcript of interview by Douglas B. Green. December 3, 1973. Frist Library and Archive, Country Music Foundation, Nashville, Tennessee.

Curtis, Lou. "Scott Hambly and the Bluegrass Ramblers." *BU* 4, no. 2 (1969): 10.

Dale, Richard. "Letters: The Presence." *BU* 25, no. 8 (1991): 9–10.

Daniel, Wayne W. "The Serious Side of Roni Stoneman." *BU* 24, no. 12 (1990): 46–50.

————. "Wilma Lee Cooper: America's Most Authentic Mountain Singer." *BU* 16, no. 8 (1982): 12–17.

Daugherty, S. R. "Passing the Torch and Keeping It Lit: The Story of J. N. and Onie Baxter." *BU* 37, no. 5 (2002): 42–45.

Davis, Chandler. "Bluegrass Family—Family Bluegrass." *BU* 7, no. 4 (1972): 5–8.

Davis, Stephanie. "Good Ol' Persons." *BU* 19, no. 4 (1984): 25–27.

Dawson, Dave. "Dave's Diary: Terri Clark—Pain to Thrill." December 15, 2003. www.nucountry.com.au/articles/diary/december2003/151203_terrieclark.htm. Accessed August, 29, 2011.

Dennett, Ruth. "Bob and Grace French: Sweethearts of New England Bluegrass." *My Country* no. 38 (June 1984): 1, 4, 8–16.

Devan, Brett F. "The Early Career of an American Original: The Musical Lewis Family." *BU* 27, no. 5 (1992): 18–26.

————. "The Larry Stephenson Band: Making a Strong Case for Mainstream Bluegrass Music." *BU* 30, no. 12 (1996): 42–45.

————. "The New Coon Creek Girls: A Legend Lives On with Overdrive." *BU* 23, no. 5 (1988): 8–14.

————. "The Sally Mountain Show." *BU* 18, no. 3 (1983): 33–35.

————. "Still Making Bluegrass History: The Sensational Lewis Family." *BU* 30, no. 3 (1995): 34–38.

Dexter, Kerry. "Kathy Kallick." *BU* 30, no. 2 (1995): 38–42.

Dian and the Greenbriar Boys. Uncredited liner notes. Elektra, EKL-233, 1963.

Dice, Ralph. "Bill Grant: Oklahoma Bluegrass Man." *BU* 16, no. 7 (1982): 8, 10–11.

Dickens, Hazel. "Hazel Dickens Speaks." *WIB* no. 16 (Fall 1998): 8.

Dickens, Hazel, and Alice Gerrard. Liner notes to *Pioneering Women of Bluegrass*. Smithsonian/Folkways, SF CD 40065, 1996.

Dickerson, James L. *Dixie Chicks: Down-Home and Backstage*. Dallas: Taylor Trade, 2000.

Dixie Chicks. *Chick Chat*, 1992–1997. www.dixiechickshenhouse.com. Accessed January 2, 2012.

————. *Chick Chat*, 1992–1997. http://chickoholic.tripod.com/DixieChicks/id24.html. Accessed August 30, 2011.

————. *An Evening with the Dixie Chicks: Live from the Kodak Theatre*. Directed by Joel Gallen. Woolly Puddin' Films/Open Wide/Monument/Columbia, CVD 55322, 2003.

————. *Shut Up and Sing*. Directed by Barbara Kopple and Cecilia Peck. Woolly Puddin' Films/Weinstein Company, 79970, 2006.

————. *Top of the World Tour: Live*. Produced by the Dixie Chicks and Lloyd Maines. Open Wide/Monument/Columbia, CVD 56366, 2003.

Donaghey, Bob. "Valerie Smith." *BU* 33, no. 6 (1998): 50–52.

Donnelly, John. "The Country Vibes." *San Francisco Sunday Examiner and Chronicle.* July 12, 1970.

Dorgan, Howard. *The Airwaves of Zion.* Knoxville: University of Tennessee Press, 1993.

Edgers, Geoff. "The Road to Nashville: Sierra Hull, 12, Rises in Bluegrass with Help from Alison Krauss." *Boston Globe.* May 30, 2004. http://pqasb.pqarchiver .com/boston/access/645053981.html?FMT=ABS&date=May+30%2C+ 2004. Accessed May 11, 2010.

Eliot, John. "Cincinnati, Ohio: Bluegrass Hot Spot." *MN* 5, no. 5 (1974): 8–14.

Escott, Colin. Liner notes to *The Very Best of Wilma Lee and Stoney Cooper and the Clinch Mountain Clan.* Varese Sarabande Records, 302 066 323 2, 2002.

Evdokimoff, Victor. "Ola Belle Reed." *BU* 35, no. 12 (2001): 50–53.

Ewing, Tom, ed. *The Bluegrass Reader.* Chicago: University of Illinois Press, 2000.

Flippo, Chet. "Shut Up and Sing?" Nashville Skyline. CMT.com. March 24, 2003, www.cmt.com/news/nashville-skyline/1470672/nashville-skyline-shut -up-and-sing.jhtml. Accessed August 29, 2011.

Foster, Alice. See Gerrard, Alice.

Fox, Jon Hartley. Liner notes to *Suzanne Thomas: Dear Friends and Gentle Hearts.* Rounder CD 0423, 1998.

————. Review of *Alison Krauss and Union Station: Two Highways. BU* 24, no. 8 (1990): 28.

————. Review of *The All Girl Boys: Heart's Desire. BU* 29, no. 3 (1994): 72–73.

————. Review of *Ginger Boatwright: Fertile Ground. BU* 26, no. 4 (1991): 54–55.

————. Review of *Kathy Kallick: Matters of the Heart. BU* 28, no. 11 (1994): 74–75.

————. Review of *Laurie Lewis and Grant Street: Singin' My Troubles Away. BU* 25, no 8 (1991): 48.

————. Review of *The McLain Family: Sunday Singing. BU* 19, no. 8 (1985): 38.

————. Review of *Northern Lights: Before the Fire Comes Down. BU* 20, no. 3 (1985): 43.

————. Review of *The Sally Mountain Show: I Came on Business for the King. BU* 18, no. 5 (1983): 31.

————. Review of *The Sally Mountain Show: Lavender Lullaby. BU* 19, no. 3 (1984): 33.

Friskics-Warren, Bill. "Coal Miner's Sister." *ND* 20 (March-April 1999): 73–85.

Gandy, Conway H. "Don Owens: The Washington, D.C., Connection." *BU* 22, no. 5 (1987): 68–72.

Geringer, Dan. "Katie Laur: Queen of Cincinnati Bluegrass, A-Pickin' and A-Grin-nin'." *Ohio* (November 1980): 58–61.

Gerrard, Alice. "Hazel Dickens: As Country as I Could Sing." *Sing Out!* 21, no. 1 (1971): 2–7.

————. Song notes to *Pieces of My Heart*. Copper Creek C-0134, 1994.

————. (Written as Alice Foster.) "The Southern Folk Festival." *BU* 3, no. 10 (1969): 10.

Gitlin, Ira. "Emily Robison: Banjo Chick." *BNL* 27, no. 9 (2000): 14–19.

————. "Forgotten Blue Grass Boy: Lucky Saylor." *BU* 27, no. 11 (1993): 38–43.

————. "Laurie Lewis and Grant Street: I'm Gonna Be the Wind." *BU* 24, no. 10 (1990): 24–31.

————. "Union Station's Other Alison." Unpublished article. January 1991.

Godbey, Frank J. Review of *Alison Brown and Stuart Duncan: Pre-Sequel. BU* 17, no. 1 (1982): 58.

————. Review of *Buck White and the Down Homers* [Down Home Folks]. *BU* 7, no. 3 (1972): 12.

————. Review of *The Front Porch String Band. BU* 15, no. 10 (1981): 32.

————. Review of *Hazel Dickens and Alice Gerrard: Who's That Knocking? BU* 13, no. 8 (1979): 20.

————. Review of *Jim McCall, Vernon McIntryre, and the Appalachian Grass. BU* 8, no. 9 (1974): 21.

————. Review of *The Lewis Family: Absolutely Lewis. BU* 10, no. 4 (1975): 22.

————. Review of *Lillimae and the Dixie Gospelaires: There's a Big Wheel. BU* 10, no. 10 (1976): 28.

————. Review of *Lou Christie: Three Brothers. BU* 8, no. 6 (1973): 17.

————. Review of *More of the Carroll County Ramblers. BU* 9, no. 8 (1975): 19.

————. Review of *Red, White, and Blue(grass): Very Popular. BU* 8, no. 7 (1974): 14.

————. Review of *The Sally Mountain Gang: The Sun's Coming Up. BU* 17, no. 5 (1982): 35.

————. Review of *The II Generation: Head Cleaner. BU* 9, no. 8 (1975): 18.

————. Review of *Shubb, Wilson and Shubb. BU* 11, no. 9 (1977): 27.

Godbey, Marty. "The Katie Laur Band." *BU* 12, no. 7 (1978): 14–17.

————. "The McLain Family Band." *BU* 15, no. 8 (1981): 12–16.

Goddard, J. B. Review of *Who's That Knocking? Village Voice*. October 28, 1965.

Goldsmith, Thomas. "Alison Krauss: Then and Now." *BU* 42, no. 2 (2007): 34–38.

————. "Alison Krauss and Union Station, 1995." *BU* 29, no. 12 (1995): 42–46.

————. "Alison Krauss: What Inspires Me." *BU* 42, no. 1 (2007): 24–27.

Goodman, Frank. "A Conversation with Sandy Cherryholmes." www.puremusic .com. February 2006. Accessed January 31, 2010.

Grant, Lee. "In Tune with Ginger Boatwright." *BU* 31, no. 6 (1996): 40–42.

Grant, Nancy. "Champaign Fiddler Alison Krauss." *Frets* 10, no. 12 (1988): 40–43, 48.

Green, Al. "Tiny Martin's Countrysiders." *BU* 5, no. 3 (1970): 22–23.

Green, Douglas B. "Buck White and the Downhomers." *BU* 7, no. 11 (1973): 7–10.

———. "The Sullivan Family: Goodwill Ambassadors of Bluegrass Gospel." *BU* 15, no. 4 (1980): 11–15.

———. "Wilma Lee and Stoney Cooper." *BU* 8, no. 9 (1974): 25–27.

Greene, Clarence H. "Carolina Opry Features Jimmy Martin." *BU* 4, no. 5 (1969): 2–3.

Greenstein, Mike. "Expanding the Horizons: Susie Monick and Tony Trischka." *BU* 11, no. 6 (1976): 18–21.

[Greer, Jim.] "Jim Greer and the Mac-O-Chee Valley Folks." *BU* 2, no. 12 (1968): 10.

Griffith, James S. Review of *Buck White and the Down Home Folks: Poor Folk's Pleasure*. *BU* 13, no. 9 (1979): 26.

———. Review of *The Front Porch String Band: Smilin' at You*. *BU* 12, no. 2 (1977): 35.

———. Review of *The McLain Family Band: On the Road*. *BU* 11, no. 11 (1977): 38.

Haglund, Urban. "Another Female Bluegrass 'First.'" *BU* 19, no. 3 (1984): 6.

Hall, Russell. "Alison Brown: Compass Records." *Performing Songwriter* (June 1999): 37–39.

Halsey, Derek. "Down from the Mountain with Rhonda Vincent." *Gritz*. March 2002. www.gritz.net/new_gritz/inner_views/rhonda_vincent.html. Accessed March 18, 2002.

———. "Honi Deaton and Dream: You Never Know Where Bluegrass Will Find You." *BU* 42, no. 3 (2007): 44–48.

———. "Lillimae and the Dixie Gospel-Aires." *BU* 38, no. 10 (2004): 36–38.

———. "O Sister Thou Hath Been There All Along." *Gritz*. June 2002. Now posted at http://swampland.com/articles/view/title:o_sister_thou_hath_been_there_all_along__women_in_bluegrass. Accessed August 30, 2012.

———. Unpublished interview with Katie Laur. Cincinnati, Ohio, ca. 2002. Originally posted at http://communities.msn.com/VintageBluegrassers. Accessed March 11, 2002.

Hammond, Jerry W., and Mariel R. Dickson. Liner notes to *Red, White, and Blue(grass): Guaranteed*. Ginn Music Group CD GMG 5002, 1997.

Haney, Dave. "White Mountain Bluegrass." *BU* 19, no. 8 (1985): 49–53.

Hatley, Sandy Crisco. "Bluegrass with a Feminine Touch: The Plight of a Lady Banjo Picker." *WIB* 3 (April-June 1995): 7.

Havighurst, Craig. "The New Queen of Bluegrass." *Wall Street Journal*. April 14, 2000.

Helligar, Jeremy, and Chris Rose. "Feather Friends." *People* (September 28, 1998): 167–68.

Henderson, Gary. "Lewis Family: The First Family of Gospel Song." *BU* 4, no. 12 (1970): 2–4.

Henry, Casey. "Cherryholmes." *BU* 43, no. 5 (2008): 20–23.

———. "Cia Cherryholmes: Singing, Playing, Rising Star." *BN* 17, no. 4 (2007): 22–27.

———. Cia Cherryholmes. Unedited interview, December 3, 2006.

———. "Honi Deaton: Dreaming Her Way to Bluegrass Stardom." *BN* 14, no. 2 (2004): 24–27.

———. "Kristin Scott Benson: Banjo Player of the Year." *BNL* 36, no. 6 (2009): 8–15.

———. "Where Are the Girls?" Murphy Method Blog. April 7, 2010. http://blog .murphymethod.com/2010/04/07/where-are-the-girls. Accessed January 24, 2012.

Henry, Murphy H. "All-Female Bands: A Thing of the Past?" *WIB* 13 (Fall 1997): 7.

———. "The Banjo Teacher: For Girls Only." *BNL* 10, no. 9 (1983): 16–17.

———. "Bay Area Wibbers." *WIB* 22 (Winter 2000): 1.

———. "Betty Fisher: From Bandleader to Side Musician." *WIB* 19 (Spring 1999): 7–11.

———. "Betty Fisher: The Leader of the Band." *WIB* 18 (Winter 1999): 2–6.

———. "Change of Life." *WIB* 1 (September 1994): 7.

———. "'Come Prepared to Stay. Bring Fiddle': The Story of Sally Ann Forrester, the Original Blue Grass Girl." Master's thesis, George Mason University, 1999.

———. "Early Woman Dobro Player Located." [Peggy Brain.] *WIB* 5 (October-December 1995): 1.

———. "General Store." *BU* 30, no. 12 (1996): 22.

———. "General Store." *BU* 37, no. 8 (2002): 12.

———. "How Mountain Girls Can Pick: The World's Greatest All-Female Jam, 73 Strong!" *International Bluegrass* 19, no. 6 (1995): 5.

———. "I'm Not About to Die: The Voices of Women in Bluegrass." *WIB* 8 (Summer 1996): 5–8.

———. "Ingrid." *WIB* 15 (Spring 1998): 4–6.

———. Liner notes to *M and M Blues*. Arrandem Records AR-80, 1992.

———. "Memphis Beck: There Was No One to Tell Me I Couldn't." *WIB* 32 and 33 (April and September 2003): 2–9, 2–8.

———. "Old Friends: Margie and Enoch Sullivan." *BNL* 32, no. 11 (2005): 7–10.

———. "On the Road: Owensboro '93." *BNL* 21, no. 1 (1993): 14–15.

———. "Queen of the Scratch Vocals: Suzanne Thomas." *BU* 33, no. 6 (1998): 34–38.

———. Review of *The Dixie Chicks: Home*. *BU* 37, no. 11 (May 2003): 84.

———. Review of *Rhonda Vincent: Destination Life*. *BU* 44, no. 4 (2009): 83.

———. Review of *The Stonemans: Patsy, Donna, and Roni*. *BU* 44, no. 3 (2009): 59–60.

———. "Roni Stoneman: Comedy and Tragedy Go Hand in Hand." *WIB* 29 (May 2002): 2–8.

———. "Rubye Davis: I Do Have a Name and I Was Part of That Band, Too." *WIB* 30 (August 2002): 2–9.

———. "Spotlight on Claire Lynch." *WIB* 5 (October-December 1995): 3–7.

———. "Spotlight on Gloria Belle." *WIB* 6 (Winter 1996): 3–7.

———. "Spotlight on Lynn Morris." *WIB* 3 (April-June 1995): 4–6, 8.

———. "Spotlight on the New Coon Creek Girls: Eat Up with Playing." *WIB* 7 (Spring 1996): 3–7.

———. "Spotlight on Patsy Stoneman: The Young'un with the Strongest Backbone." *WIB* 9 (Fall 1996): 4–8.

———. "Take Your Pillow from Home and Don't Ever Let Them Have Your Guitar." *WIB* 4 (July-September 1995): 3–6.

Hickerson, Joseph C. Review of *Fiddle Jam Session: Recorded at Fiddle Contests in Weiser, Idaho, and Missoula, Montana. BU* 2, no. 9 (1968): 15.

Higgs, Dave. "Andrea Zonn: Love Goes On." *BN* 14, no. 5 (2004): 32–37, 53.

Hight, Jewly. "Generation by Generation, Women's Profiles in Bluegrass Have Risen." October 1, 2009. www.nashvillescene.com/nashville/generation-by -generation-womens-profiles-in-bluegrass-have-risen/ Content?oid=1202875. Accessed November 17, 2009.

Himes, Geoffrey. "From the Hills: How Mid-Century Migrants from the Mountains Brought Bluegrass—and More—to Baltimore." *Baltimore City Paper.* January 12, 2000.

———. "Lynn Morris: She Will Be the Light." *BU* 34, no. 2 (1999): 26–31.

———. "On the Lookout for Jerry Douglas." *BU* 36, no. 12 (2002): 36–40.

Holden, Stephen. "Review/Music: Six Fiddle Virtuosos Demonstrate a Wealth of Folk Styles." *New York Times.* March 7, 1988.

Hornstein, Bruce. "Bluegrass in Coffeehouse; Buffalo Chips Performs." *Syracuse Spectator.* March 8, 1974.

Houlihan, Mary. "She Found Her Home—and Heart—in Bluegrass." *Chicago City Talk.* March 9, 2001.

Howard, Steven Earl. "Stoney Lonesome Keeps Honing the Sound on Red House." *BU* 27, no. 8 (1993): 28–33.

Huey, Steve. "The Whites Biography." www.cmt.com/artists/az/whites_the/bio .jhtml. Accessed January 7, 2008.

Huffer, Glenn R. Liner notes to *Traver Hollow: Genuine Acoustic Bluegrass.* Fishtraks FTLP-453, 1984.

Humphrey, Mark A. Liner notes to *The Essential Bill Monroe and His Blue Grass Boys, 1945–1949.* Columbia Records Boxed Set, C2K 52478, 1992.

Hurst, Jack. *Nashville's Grand Ole Opry.* New York: Harry N. Abrams, 1975.

"The Isaacs Biography." www.cmt.com/artists/az/isaacs/bio.jhtml. Accessed January 21, 2012.

Inoue, Saburo. "October 30, 2010: Last Day of the Convention of WOB (World of Bluegrass) sponsored by the IBMA." *Moonshiner* 28, no. 4 (2011): 2.

Irwin, Ken. "Ken's Korner." *BU* 25, no. 6 (1990): 22.

Jerome, Jim. "Trio Grande." *People* 59, no. 4 (2003): 95–100.

Jon da peripatetic poet. Review of *Won't You Come and Sing for Me: Hazel Dickens and Alice Foster. Berkeley Barb* (November 30-December 6, 1973): 23.

Jones, Chris. "More Than Words: Nelson Mandrell." *BN* 8, no. 10 (1998): 44, 46.
———. "Songwriters: John Pennell." *BN* 8, no. 6 (1998): 16–17.

Jones, Loyal. Obituary for Raymond Kane McLain. www.mclains.com/Daddy. Accessed November 11, 2005.

Jones, Timothy. "Gospel Profile: Valerie Smith." *BN* 15, no. 8 (2005): 61.

Judd, Naomi, with Bud Schaetzle. *Love Can Build a Bridge.* New York: Villard Books, 1993.

Judy. "Dixie Chicks Henhouse." http://chickoholic.tripod.com/DixieChicks/index.html. Accessed August 30, 2011.

Kallick, Kathy. "Don't Leave Your Little Girl All Alone." On *Laurie Lewis and Kathy Kallick: Together.* Rounder CD 0318, 1995.
———. "Kathy Kallick Speaks." *WIB* 22 (Winter 2000): 9.

Kallick, Kathy, with Peter Thompson. "More from Kathy Kallick." *WIB* 22 (Winter 2000): 10–11.

Kaplan, Kathy. Liner notes to *Delia Bell: Bluer Than Midnight.* County 768, 1978.

Kasten, Roy. "The Bluegrass Rose Blooms: Alison Krauss Follows the Sounds within Her Heart with Union Station by Her Side." *ND* 43 (January/February 2003): 58–71.

Kelly, R. J. "The John Herald Band." *BU* 17, no. 8 (1983): 10–15.

Kimmel, Dick. Review of *Alison Brown: Twilight Motel. BU* 28, no. 1 (1993): 77.
———. Review of *Vivian Williams: Fiddler. BU* 14, no. 7 (1980): 32.

Kleinke, J. D. "Omigrass Anyone? The Good Ol' Persons and the Can't-Label-Us-Blues." *BU* 25, no. 9 (1991): 18–24.
———. Review of *Alison Brown: Simple Pleasures. BU* 25, no. 11 (1991): 67.
———. Review of *Alison Krauss: I've Got That Old Feeling. BU* 25, no. 6 (1990): 51.
———. Review of *Rhonda Vincent: A Dream Come True. BU* 25, no. 8 (1991): 47.

Kochman, Marilyn. "Buck White: You Can Take the Boy Out of the Country . . ." *Frets* 3, no. 3 (1981): 28–30.

Koehler, Julie. "Ginger Boatwright: Laughter and Music Are Really the Best Medicines." *BN* 10, no. 10 (2000): 24–27, 40, 44.

Koretzky, Henry. "Martha Trachtenberg: 'A Ticket Back' to Bluegrass." *BU* 38, no. 3 (2003): 46–48.

————. Review of "Jim Hurst and Missy Raines: Synergy." *BU* 38, no. 6 (2003): 65–66.

Kreps, Daniel. "The Hold Steady's 'Heaven Is Whenever' and More New Reviews." Rolling Stone.com. May 4, 2010. www.rollingstone.com/music/news/the-hold-steadys-heaven-is-whenever-and-more-new-reviews-20100504. Accessed August 9, 2011.

Kuykendall, Pete. "II Generation." *BU* 9, no. 9 (1975): 10–15.

————. "The Kentucky Colonels." *BU* 3, no. 10 (1969): 3–4.

[Kuykendall, Pete]. "Carroll County Ramblers." *BU* 2, no. 8 (1968): 13.

Lacy, Shari. "Fret Wizard Sierra Hull Releases First Teaching DVD with AcuTab March 16th." Goodstuffpr.com. March 15, 2010. Accessed March 16, 2010.

Lang, Rick. "Bob and Grace French: Pioneers of Bluegrass Music in New England." *BU* 37, no. 4 (2002): 60–65.

Larkin, Fran. "Spotlight on Hazel McGee." *WIB* 14 (Winter 1998): 2–5.

Larsen, Mary. "Laurie Lewis on Fiddling." *Fiddler* 1, no. 1 (1994): 26–30.

Laur, Katie. "Hazel Dickens." *Country Living*. N.p., n.d.

————. "Katie Laur Speaks." *WIB* 16 (Fall 1998): 9–10.

————. "The Sound of Women's Voices." *WIB* 27 (September 2001): 10–11.

————. "Tribute to Terry Boswell." *WIB* 21 (Fall 1999): 13.

Lawless, John. "Mr. and Mrs. Hunter Berry." Bluegrasstoday.com. June 11, 2010. http://bluegrasstoday.com/13767/mr-and-mrs-hunter-berry. Accessed January 13, 2012.

Ledgin, Stephanie P. "On the Road and Off: Talking with the McLain Family Band." *Pickin'* 4, no. 6 (1977): 6–19.

Lee, Lisa. "Cinderella Krauss Tries on Her Slippers." February 27, 2004. www.cmt.com/news/country-music/1485404/cinderella-krauss-tries-on-her-slippers.jhtml. Accessed January 21, 2012.

Lees, Gene. *Leader of the Band: The Life of Woody Herman.* New York: Oxford University Press, 1995.

LeRoy, Lance. *The Lewis Family History/Picture Book: 45 Years on the Stages of America—A Retrospective.* Hendersonville, TN: Dulany Printing. 1996.

Levine, Claire. "Coming into Her Own: Kathy Kallick's Bluegrass Evolution." *BU* 35, no. 5 (2000): 42–45.

————. "Laurie Lewis: Committed to Being Me." *WIB* 22 (Winter 2000): 2–5.

————. "Laurie Lewis and Tom Rozum: Ten Years After." *ND* 51 (May-June 2004): 26–27.

————. "Why Ruin a Good Hobby? Fiddler Vivian Williams." *WIB* 10 (Winter 1997): 4–6.

Levine, Claire, and Beth Weil. "Beth Weil: There Was Nobody Saying We Couldn't." *WIB* 22 (Winter 2000): 6–8.

Lewis, Chris. "The Good Ol' Persons Celebrate Twenty Years." *BU* 31, no. 4 (1996): 20–22.

Lewis, Laurie. "Laurie Lewis Presents Alice Gerrard with Distinguished Achievement Award." *WIB* 28 (January 2002): 2.

———. Liner notes to *Charles Sawtelle: Music from Rancho deVille*. Acoustic Disc ACD 44, 2001.

———. Liner notes to *Guest House*. High Tone Records, HCD 8167, 2004.

———. Liner notes to *Kristin Scott Benson: Straight Paths*. Pinecastle PRC 6502, 2002.

———. Liner notes to *Seeing Things*. Rounder CD 0428, 1998.

———. Liner notes to *Winter's Grace*. Dog Boy Records, SIG 1251, 1999.

Lewis, Laurie, and Tom Rozum. Liner notes to *The Oak and the Laurel*. Rounder CD 0340, 1995.

Little, Keith. "Rose Maddox Reflections." Personal correspondence with author, 2007. Parts later published as "Rose Maddox: Reflections" in *BU* 42, no. 11 (2008): 39–40.

Loftin, Dan. "To That Mansion in the Sky: Rubye Davis 1937–2002." *WIB* 31 (December 2002): 11.

Lupton, John. Review of *Gene Watson and Rhonda Vincent: Your Money and My Good Looks*. www.countrystandardtime.com/d/cdreview.asp?xid=4686. Accessed January 12, 2012.

Lynch, Claire. Liner notes to *Out in the Country*. Copper Creek CCCD-0184, 2000.

Lynch, Claire, and Larry Lynch. "Some Morning Soon." From *Front Porch String Band: Lines and Traces*. Rebel REB-CD-1689, 1991.

Macnie, Jim. Liner notes to *Alison Krauss: Now That I've Found You*. Rounder CD 0325, 1995.

Malone, Bill C. *Country Music, U.S.A.* Austin: University of Texas Press, 1968.

Marti, Judy. "A Banjo Pickin' Girl: The Life and Music of Ola Belle Campbell Reed." *OTH* 3, no. 6 (1992/1993): 17–22.

Marxer, Marcy. "Marcy Marxer: Fair Morning Hornpipe." *FGM* 10, no. 6 (2006): 50–51.

May, Carl. "Wilma Lee and Stoney Cooper: Twenty Years on the Grand Ole Opry." *MN* 7, no. 6 (1976): 12–13.

Mazor, Barry. "For Their Next Act . . . Dixie Chicks: Taking the Long Way." *ND* 63 (May-June 2006): 122–23.

———. "The Sisterhood of Bluegrass." *Wall Street Journal*. Arts and Entertainment. July 8, 2009.

McCarthy, Joan. "Lynn Morris: The Woman behind the Band." *BC* (May 1996): 10.

McCarty, David J. Review of *Dixie Chicks: Thank Heavens for Dale Evans*. *BU* 25, no. 12 (1991): 69.

————. Review of *Missy Raines and Jim Hurst: Two. BU* 35, no. 8 (2001): 58.

McCeney, George B. Review of *II Generation: We Call It Grass. BU* 10, no. 12 (1976): 42, 44.

————. Review of *The Lewis Family: Time is Moving On. BU* 2, no. 7 (1968): 12.

————. Review of *Red, White and Blue(grass): Pickin' Up. BU* 9, no. 7 (1975): 17.

————. Review of *The Stonemans: Country Hospitality. BU* 13, no. 2 (1984): 34.

————. Review of *The Sullivan Family: Brush Arbors. BU* 4, no. 1 (1969): 37–38.

McDonald, Janice Brown. "The Doug Dillard Band." *BU* 20, no. 4 (1985): 14–15.

————. "Randy Wood: Woodworking Wizard." *BU* 23, no. 11 (1989): 35–38.

McIntyre, Les. Review of *Alison Krauss: Too Late to Cry. BU* 22, no. 9 (1988): 65.

————. Review of *Claire Lynch: Friends for a Lifetime. BU* 28, no. 7 (1994): 68.

————. Review of *Down Home Bluegrass: Hubert Davis and His Season Travelers. BU* 6, no. 9 (1972): 11.

————. Review of *Gloria Belle: The Love of the Mountains. BU* 21, no. 8 (1987): 40.

————. Review of *Gloria Belle and Tennessee Sunshine: He Leadeth Me. BU* 35, no. 10 (2001): 58.

————. Review of *Harry and Jeanie West: Roots of Bluegrass. BU* 17, no. 10 (1983): 44.

————. Review of *The Isaacs: Stand Still. BU* 35, no. 12 (2001): 74.

————. Review of *Wilma Lee Cooper. BU* 17, no. 4 (1982): 22–23.

McGuire, Bruce A. Liner notes to *Wilma Lee and Stoney Cooper: Big Midnight Special.* Bear Family Records Boxed Set, BCD 16751 DK, 2007.

McLain Family. Liner notes to *The McLain Family Band: In Concert at Carnegie Hall.* Country Life Records CLR-12, 1982.

McLellan, Joseph. "The Falls City Ramblers." *Washington Post.* November 4, 1977.

Menius, Art. "Finding the Roses among the Brambles: The Lynn Morris Band." *BU* 28, no. 4 (1993): 18–26.

————. Review of *Cherryholmes: Cherryholmes II—Black and White. BU* 42, no. 9 (2008): 72–73.

————. Review of *Leroy Eyler and the Carroll County Ramblers: The Best of All Things. BU* 29, no. 2 (1994): 60.

Metheny, Arlie. "Bill and Juarez Grant's Salt Creek Park: Nineteen Going on Twenty." *BU* 23, no. 3 (1988): 19–23.

————. "Larry and Jackie Dickson: They Love the Little Ones." *BU* 18, no. 12 (1984): 57–59.

————. "Missouri's Vincent Family and Their Sally Mountain Show." *BU* 23, no. 1 (1988): 24–26.

————. "The Wildwood Pickers." *BU* 22, no. 5 (1987): 59–60.

Miller, Dan. "Masters of Rhythm Guitar: Martha Adcock." *FGM* 2, no. 2 (1998): 40–42.

Montell, William Lynwood, ed. *Grassroots Music in the Upper Cumberland*. Knoxville: University of Tennessee Press, 2006.

Morris, Edward. "Rhonda Vincent Goes *All American* on New Album." June 2, 2006. www.cmt.com/news/country-music/1533497/rhonda-vincent-goes-all -american-on-new-album.jhtml. Accessed August 29, 2011.

———. "Ricky Skaggs: Cherryholmes' Incessant Touring Supports New Album." October 10, 2007. www.cmt.com/artists/news/1571618/20071010/ skaggs_ricky.jhtml. Accessed February 19, 2008.

Morris, Lynn. "Help Me Climb That Mountain." *The Lynn Morris Band*. Rounder 0276, 1990.

———. Liner notes to *Shape of a Tear*. Rounder 116 610 509-2, 2003.

Nager, Larry. "Claire Lynch Knows What She's Gonna Do." *BU* 44, no. 3 (2009): 26–29.

Nemerov, Bruce. "Hubert Davis: Down Home Banjo Picker." *BU* 11, no. 7 (1977): 18–21.

New Times Music Staff. "Wild Nights: Local Women's Bluegrass Band." *Syracuse New Times*. December 1974.

Newton, Mark. Liner notes to *Follow Me Back to the Fold*. Rebel REB-CD-1764, 2000.

Oermann, Robert K. Liner notes to *Wilma Lee Cooper: Classic Country Favorites*. Rebel Records, REB-CD-1122, 1996.

Orr, Jay. "Lucky Ones All: Member of Alison Krauss + Union Station Pursue Solo Work, Remain Dedicated to the Band." *BU* 36, no. 12 (2002): 28–32.

Overstreet, Frank. "Lynn Morris and Marshall Wilborn: America's Bluegrass Team." *BMN* (Summer 1992): 9, 11.

———. "Red, White, and Blue(grass)." *BU* 8, no. 1 (1973): 27.

Palmer, Robert. "Ramblers Present Old-Fashioned Country Music." *New York Times*. October 1, 1977.

Pankake, Jon, and Marcia Pankake. Review of *Hazel Dickens and Alice Gerrard: Pioneer-ing Women of Bluegrass*. *OTH* 5, no. 8 (1997).

Pate, Nancy. "Maternity Guitar." *WIB* 7 (Spring 1996): 8.

———. Review of *Delia Bell and Bill Grant: Kiamichi Moon*. *BU* 32, no. 10 (1998): 69.

Peelstrom, Bob. "Down Home with Eddie and Martha Adcock." *BU* 37, no. 3 (2002): 32–37.

Perry, Ian. Review of *Kristin Scott*. *BNL* 24, no. 12 (1997): 8.

Peterson, Jamie. "Let Them Talk about Kate MacKenzie." *BU* 30, no. 9 (1996): 38–42.

Phillips, Jessica. "Bluegrass 'Queen' Rhonda Vincent Has Her Sights Set on Opry." The Front Porch. October 15, 2009. www.countrystandardtime.com/ blog/TheFront Porch/entry.asp?xid=505. Accessed January 12, 2012.

Pickering, Mimi. *Hazel Dickens: It's Hard to Tell the Singer from the Song*. Appalshop Video, 2001.

Pittard, Mike. "Benny and Vallie Cain: Still the 'Right Combination.'" *Blueprint* 4, no. 7 (1983): 5–6, 14.

Potorti, David. "Bringing It All Back Home: Turned Off by Nashville's Faith Hill Factor, Rhonda Vincent Returns to Bluegrass." *Durham (NC) Independent Weekly Online.* March 14, 2001. www.indyweek.com/durham/current/music .html. Accessed March 19, 2001.

———. "A Few Old Memories." *Durham (NC) Independent Weekly.* March 22–28, 2000.

Pribylova, Irena. "Alison Brown." *BNL* 22, no. 3 (1995): 12–16.

Price, Deborah Evans. "Blue Skies for Bluegrass." *Billboard.* October 9, 2004.

Puterbaugh, Parke. "The Brain and the Banjo." *US Airways Attaché.* (February 2002): 40–43.

Rakich, Dave. "Compass Records: Nashville's Coolest Independent Label." *Cleveland Country Magazine* 7, no. 3 (1998): 6.

Reed, Ola Belle, with Josh Dunson. "High on a Mountain: The Story and Songs of Ola Belle Reed." Unpublished manuscript. Reed Papers 20010. Southern Life Folk Collection. Wilson Library. University of North Carolina, Chapel Hill. 1977.

Reid, Gary. Liner notes to *Carl Story: Angel Band—Early Starday Recordings.* Gusto Records GT7-0548-2, 2008.

Reinholds, Amy. "By Leaps and Bounds: The Grasshoppers Jump into Professional Bluegrass." *BN* 9, no. 11 (1999): 26–27, 33.

Review of *Who's That Knocking? Time.* October 1, 1965.

Rhodes, Don. "1029: The Lewis Family." *BU* 8, no. 10 (1974): 13–16.

———. "Delia Bell: The Way It's Supposed to Be." *BU* 16, no. 7 (1982): 9, 12–13.

———. "Larry Stephenson: Taking Control of the Spotlight." *BU* 25, no. 3 (1990): 28–33.

———. "Pop Lewis." *BU* 9, no. 6 (1974): 11–12.

———. "Roni Stoneman." *BU* 11, no. 11 (1977): 13–17.

Rice, Wayne. "The Rice Kryspies." *BU* 3, no. 12 (1969): 23.

Riney, Tom. "The Country Coalition." *BU* 3, no. 4 (1968): 12.

Rinzler, Ralph. Liner notes to *American Banjo: Three-Finger and Scruggs Style.* Smithsonian Folkways CD SF 40037, 1990. Originally issued as Folkways 2314, 1957.

Roberts, Glenn, Jr. "Country Gentlemen: Forty-Five Years." *BU* 37, no. 2 (2002): 28–34.

———. "Makin' a Joyful Noise: The Isaacs." *BU* 32, no. 6 (1997): 24–29.

———. "The Marshall Family." *BU* 11, no. 12 (1977): 16–24.

Robinson, Steven M. "The Whites: Living in the Name of Love." *BU* 20, no. 12 (1986): 14–19.

Roemer, John. Review of *Cloud Valley: A Bluegrass Ensemble*. BU 18, no. 3 (1983): 42.

———. Review of *The Front Porch String Band: Country Rain*. BU 13, no. 2 (1978): 32.

———. Review of *The Hotmud Family: Meat and Potatoes and Stuff Like That*. BU 16, no. 7 (1982): 25.

———. Review of *Hubert Davis and the Season Travelers: It's Bluegrass Time Again*. BU 11, no. 7 (1977): 24.

———. Review of *The Marshall Family: Requests*. BU 11, no. 8 (1977): 27.

———. Review of *Rhonda Vincent: Timeless and True Love*. BU 26, no. 12 (1992): 66–67.

———. Review of *Rose Maddox: Reckless Love and Bold Adventure*. BU 11, no. 11 (1977): 39.

———. Review of *The Sally Mountain Show: New Dreams and Sunshine*. BU 23, no. 9 (1989): 51.

———. Review of *The Sally Mountain Show: Sheltered in the Arms of God*. BU 20, no. 9 (1986): 58.

———. Review of *The Whites: A Lifetime in the Making*. BU 35, no. 6 (2000): 64.

———. Review of *Wilma Lee and Stoney Cooper*. BU 11, no. 7 (1977): 22.

Romano, Joe. "The Lynn Morris Band: More Fun Than It's Ever Been!" *BN* 9, no. 6 (1999): 4–6.

Romanoski, Steve. "Rhonda Vincent: All the Rage in Bluegrass." *Sing Out!* 47, no. 2 (2003): 36–45.

Rosenberg, Neil V. *Bill Monroe and His Blue Grass Boys: An Illustrated Discography*. Nashville: Country Music Foundation Press, 1974.

———. *Bluegrass: A History*. Chicago: University of Illinois Press, 1985.

———. Liner notes to *Laurie Lewis and Her Bluegrass Pals*. Rounder 1161-0461-2, 1999.

———. Liner notes to *Won't You Come and Sing For Me?* Folkways Records FTS 31034, 1973.

———. "Thirty Years Ago This Month: December 1955." *BU* 20, no 6 (1985): 6.

———. "Thirty Years Ago This Month: July 1951." *BU* 16, no. 1 (1981): 6.

Rosenburg, Madelyn. "Hazel Dickens." *BU* 36, no. 3 (2001): 30–34.

Ross, Joe. "Guest Editorial: Bluegrass R.I.P.?" *BU* 25, no. 8 (1991): 26.

———. "Lorraine Jordan: Hard Work and Drive Pay Off." *BN* 17, no. 2 (2007): 26–29.

Rothman, Sandy. "Editor's Notes." *True Life News*. 2nd ed. (Spring 2001).

———. "Rambling in Redwood Canyon: The Routes of Bay Area Bluegrass, Part One." *BU* 25, no. 11 (1991): 50–60.

———. "Rambling in Redwood Canyon: The Routes of Bay Area Bluegrass, Part Two." *BU* 25, no. 12 (1991): 58–66.

————. "Rambling in Redwood Canyon: The Routes of Bay Area Bluegrass, Part Four." *BU* 26, no. 2 (1991): 60–68.

Royko, David. Review of *Alison Brown: Look Left. BU* 29, no. 3 (1994): 75.

————. Review of *Alison Brown: Quartet. BU* 31, no. 3 (1996): 69.

————. Review of *Alison Brown Quartet: Replay. BU* 37, no. 5 (2002): 61.

————. Review of *Good Ol' Persons: Good 'n' Live—Twentieth Anniversary Collection. BU* 31, no. 2 (1996): 74.

————. Review of *Valerie Smith: Patchwork Heart. BU* 32, no. 8 (1998): 57.

Rudder, Randy. "In Whose Name? Country Artists Speak Out on Gulf War II." In *Country Music Goes to War,* ed. Charles Wolfe and James E. Akenson, 208–26. Lexington: University Press of Kentucky, 2005.

————. "Sierra Hull: Ready for the Big Time." *BU* 42, no. 12 (2008): 48–51.

Rumble, John. Liner notes to *The Music of Bill Monroe from 1936 to 1994.* MCA Records Boxed Set, MCAC/D4-11048, 1994.

Sacks, Paul A. Review of *Alison Krauss and Union Station: Every Time You Say Goodbye. BU* 27, no. 6 (1992): 49.

Saltus, Richard. "Old Friends: Banjoless Bluegrass." *Pickin'* 6, no. 9 (1979): 36–38.

Saunders, Walter V. "Benny and Vallie Cain." *BU* 6, no. 11 (1972): 7–12.

————. "Johnny Whisnant Musical History: Part III." *BU* 5, no. 2 (1970): 17–22.

————. "Leroy Robert Eyler, 1930–1995." *BU* 30, no. 2 (1995): 25.

————. "Notes and Queries." *BU* 44, no. 11 (2010): 20–21.

————. Review of *Alison Krauss and Union Station: So Long So Wrong. BU* 32, no. 2 (1997): 59–60.

————. Review of *Bill Grant, Delia Bell and the Kiamichi Mountain Boys: There Is a Fountain. BU* 11, no. 5 (1976): 26.

————. Review of *Bill Grant/Delia Bell: When the Angels Come for Me/Beneath the Old Pine Tree. BU* 5, no. 5 (1970): 19.

————. Review of *Delia Bell: Bluer Than Midnight. BU* 13, no. 7 (1979): 25.

————. Review of *Gloria Belle: A Good Hearted Woman. BU* 13, no. 8 (1979): 19.

————. Review of *Maddox Brothers and Rose, 1946–1951, Vol. 1 and Vol. 2. BU* 12, no. 6 (1977): 22.

————. Review of *The McLain Family Band: Country Ham. BU* 9, no. 7 (1975): 18.

————. Review of *The McLain Family Band: Country Life. BU* 10, no. 4 (1975): 23.

————. Review of *The McLain Family Band: Kentucky Wind. BU* 12, no. 7 (1978): 23.

————. Review of *The Sullivan Family: Working on a Building. BU* 7, no. 3 (1972): 14.

————. Review of *Wilma Lee Cooper and the Clinch Mountain Clan: A Daisy a Day. BU* 15, no. 5 (1980): 33.

Sawyer, Loretta. "Rhonda Vincent: She's Come Full Circle and Her Future Looks Bright." *BN* 9, no. 10 (1999): 22–25, 42.

Schlappi, Elizabeth. *Roy Acuff: The Smoky Mountain Boy*. 2nd ed. Gretna, LA: Pelican
         Publishing, 1993.

Scott, Tommy. *"Doc" Ramblin' Tommy Scott Presents Hillbilly Music and Western Swing, Vol. 1
         and Vol. 2*. Video. No label, no number, no date.

Scribbins, Jim. "The Wildwood Pickers: A Sincere, Attractive Family Thrives on
         Traditional Bluegrass." *BU* 16, no. 8 (1982): 18–22.

Seeger, Mike. "Five-String Banjo Picking Contest." *Gardyloo* 4 (July 1959): 23–24.

———. Liner notes to *American Banjo: Three-Finger and Scruggs Style*. Smithsonian/
         Folkways CD SF 40037, 1990.

———. Liner notes to *Mountain Music Bluegrass Style*. Folkways FA2318, 1959. Reis-
         sued as Smithsonian/Folkways CD SF 40038, 1991.

Seeman, Charlie. Liner notes to *Rose Maddox: The One Rose—The Capitol Years*. Bear
         Family Records Boxed Set, BCD 15743-1 DI, 1993.

Senauke, Alan. "Laurie Lewis: Far from the Hills of Home." *Sing Out!* 37, no. 4
         (1993): 11–19.

Shirk, Miriam. "Jim Greer and the Mac-O-Chee Valley Folks." *BU* 5, no. 10 (1971): 27.

[Shropshire, Elmo?] "The Homestead Act." *BU* 6, no. 6 (1971): 18.

Shrubsall, Wayne. "Janet Davis." *BNL* 21, no. 3 (1994): 6–11.

———. "Raymond W. McLain." *BNL* 10, no. 12 (1983): 5–10.

Skanse, Richard. "Dixie Chicks: Bringing It All Back Home." *JCM* 22, no. 2 (2002):
         12–19.

Skinker, Chris. Liner notes to *Jimmy Martin and the Sunny Mountain Boys*. Bear Family
         Records, BCD 15705 EI, 1994.

Smith, Lee. Liner notes to *Pieces of My Heart*. Copper Creek C-0134, 1994.

Smith, Mayne. "An Introduction to Bluegrass." Reprinted in *BU* 1, no. 3 (1966): 1–4.
         Originally published in *JAF* 78, no. 309 (1965): 245–56.

Smith, Richard D. *Can't You Hear Me Callin': The Life of Bill Monroe, Father of Bluegrass*.
         New York: Little, Brown, 2000.

———. "The Skyline's the Limit." *BU* 18, no. 4 (1983): 11–14.

Smith, Susan Atteberry. "Claire Lynch and the Front Porch String Band." *BN* 7, no. 11
         (1997): 4–7, 9.

Smith, Valerie. "No Boundaries in the Creative Process." *WIB* 20 (Summer 1999): 7.

Spottswood, Richard K. Review of *Benny and Vallie Cain: More of Benny and Vallie Cain*.
         BU 9, no. 6 (1974): 21.

———. Review of *Buffalo Gals: First Borne*. *BU* 10, no. 7 (1976): 21.

———. Review of *Clyde and Marie Denney and the Kentuckians*. *BU* 4, no. 3 (1969):
         23–24.

———. Review of *The Falls City Ramblers: Ain't Nothin' in Ramblin'*." *BU* 9, no. 11
         (1975): 21.

————. Review of *Gloria Belle: Today I Can Smile / Baby, You Gotta Be Mine. BU* 1, no.
    12 (1967): 12.
————. Review of *Katie Laur Band: Good Time Girl. BU* 11, no. 4 (1976): 23.
————. Review of *The Lewis Family: Shall We Gather at the River. BU* 1, no. 11 (1967): 10.
————. Review of *The Lewis Family Sing in Gospel Country. BU* 5, no. 2 (1970): 38.
————. Review of *The McLain Family Band: Troublesome Creek. BU* 20, no. 8 (1986): 34.
————. Review of *Presenting the Sullivan Family in Blue Grass Gospel. BU* 1, no. 9
    (1967): 10–11.
————. Review of *Rainbow Valley Boys and Sweetheart: Green Grass of Home. BU* 1, no. 7
    (1967): 8.
————. Review of *Singing All Day and Dinner on the Ground with Jimmy Martin and the
    Sunny Mountain Boys. BU* 5, no. 7 (1971): 18.
————. Review of *Vivian Williams and Barbara Lamb: Twin Sisters. BU* 10, no. 8
    (1976): 20.
————. Review of *Vivian Williams: Lee Highway Ramble / Back Up and Push. BU* 2, no. 4
    (1967): 13.
————. Review of *White Lightning: The Singing Swinging Stoneman Family. BU* 1, no.
    12 (1967): 10.
Stecher, Jody. Liner notes to *Heart of a Singer*. Rounder Records, CD 0433, 1998.
Steinberg, Jerry. "Bill Reid." *BU* 28, no. 10 (1984): 61–62.
————. Liner notes to *Bill and Mary Reid: Early Radio Favorites*. Old Homestead,
    OHCD-4011, 1998.
Steiner, Alan J. Review of *Cloud Valley: Live in Europe. BU* 20, no. 8 (1986): 32.
————. Review of *Front Porch String Band: Lines and Traces. BU* 28, no. 10 (1992):
    63–64.
————. Review of *Jeanette Williams: Dreams Come True. BU* 29, no. 11 (1995): 75.
————. Review of *Tony Trischka and Skyline: Stranded in the Moonlight. BU* 19, no. 7
    (1985): 32.
Stelling, Geoff. "Alison Brown: A Fireball Feminizes the 5-String." *BNL* 17, no. 3
    (1990): 5–7.
Stillman, Rich. Liner notes to *Southern Rail: On the Road from Appomattox*. Railway
    Records SRCD0609, 2009.
Stockton, Juanita. "Bill Grant and Grant's Bluegrass and Old-Time Music Festival in
    Hugo, Oklahoma." *BU* 38, no. 7 (2004): 38–42.
Stoneman, Roni, as told to Ellen Wright. *Pressing On: The Roni Stoneman Story*. Urbana:
    University of Illinois Press, 2007.
Strickland, Rhonda. "Buzz Busby: A Lonesome Road." *BU* 21, no. 5 (1986): 16–29.
————. "Ola Belle Reed: Preserving Traditional Music without Killing It." *BU* 17,
    no. 12 (1983): 40–46.

Strong, Christopher M. "Several Thousand McLains." *BU* 16, no. 10 (1982): 72–73.

Stuart, Chris. "Claire Lynch: A Sense of Balance." *BU* 40, no. 2 (2005): 40–44.

Sullivan, Enoch, and Margie Sullivan, with Robert Gentry. *The Sullivan Family: Fifty Years in Bluegrass Gospel Music.* Many, LA: Sweet Dreams Publishing, 1999.

Taylor, Barbara. "Mom Lewis." *BU* 9, no. 6 (1974): 10.

Thigpen, Ray. "Wilma Lee Cooper." *BU* 23, no. 5 (1988): 59–61.

Thomason, Ron. "Guest Editorial." *BU* 25, no. 10 (1991): 10–12.

———. "Hazel Dickens: Only a Woman." *BU* 16, no. 8 (1982): 23–26.

———. "The Hotmud Family: Fertile Ground With Deep Roots." *BU* 18, no. 6 (1983): 10–15.

———. Liner notes to *Just for the Record.* Rounder C 0306, 1993.

———. Liner notes to *Suzanne Thomas: Dear Friends and Gentle Hearts.* Rounder CD 0423, 1998.

Tottle, Jack. "Alison Krauss and Union Station." *BU* 25, no. 12 (1991): 20–27.

Townsend, Bob. Review of *Alison Krauss and Union Station: So Long, So Wrong. ND* 8 (March/April 1997).

Tribe, Ivan M. "Charlie Monroe." *BU* 10, no. 4 (1975): 12–19.

———. "Patsy Stoneman: Portrait of a Survivor." *BU* 23, no. 9 (1989): 45–49.

———. "The Return of Donna Stoneman: First Lady of the Mandolin." *BU* 17, no. 12 (1983): 16–26.

———. "Rex and Eleanor Parker: The West Virginia Sweethearts." *BU* 10, no. 10 (1976): 18–25.

———. *The Stonemans: An Appalachian Family and the Music That Shaped Their Lives.* Urbana: University of Illinois Press, 1993.

———. "Through the Years with Bonnie Lou and Buster Moore." *BU* 16, no. 11 (1982): 52–56.

Tribe, Ivan, and Deanna Tribe. "Lillimae: In the Men's World of Bluegrass." *BU* 11, no. 2 (1976): 26–30.

Trischka, Tony, with Martha Trachtenberg. "Buffalo Gals: Female Grass." *MN* 6, no. 11 (1976): 8–11.

Tucker, Sherri. *Swing Shift: "All-Girl" Bands of the 1940s.* Durham, NC: Duke University Press, 2000.

Tyrangiel, Josh. "Music: Dixie Divas." August 26, 2002. www.time.com/time/magazine/article/0,9171,1003093,00.html. Accessed August 9, 2007.

Unterberger, Richie. Liner notes to *Dian and the Greenbriar Boys.* CD reissue. www.mudcat.org. Accessed December 12, 2007.

"Valerie Smith to Release Fifth Album and First All-Gospel Album." Bellbucklerecords.com. September 12, 2006.

Vernon, Bill. "Eddie Adcock and Talk of the Town: Band on the Cutting Edge." *BU* 21, no. 7 (1987): 12–19.

————. Obituary for Kathy Kaplan. *BU* 18, no. 8 (1984): 10.

————. "Southern Rail." *BU* 27, no. 4 (1992): 20–26.

Vincent, Rhonda. Liner notes *Rhonda Vincent: Back Home Again.* Rounder 11661-0460-2, 2000.

————. "Rhonda Vincent and the Rage: Ragin' Live." Rounder DVD 11661-0553-9, 2005.

Waltman, Lawrence A. *Sunset Park: Fiftieth Anniversary Album, 1940–1990.* West Grove, PA: Sunset Park. 1991.

————. *Sunset Park: A Video Documentary.* P. J. March Productions, 1993.

Walton, Allan. Review of *Alison Krauss: Now That I've Found You—A Collection. BU* 30, no. 1 (1995): 83–84.

Warnock, Archie III. Review of *Jeanette Williams: Thank You for Caring. BU* 43, no. 8 (2009): 47.

Weintraub, Boris. "Buck White and the Down Home Folks." *BU* 16, no. 5 (1981): 9–13.

Weisburger, Jon. "Alison." *BN* 13, no. 5 (2003): 26–29, 42.

————. Review of *Alison Krauss: Forget About It. ND* 23 (September/October 1999): 106–107.

————. Review of *Delia Bell and Bill Grant: Classic Bluegrass Today and Yesterday. BU* 31, no. 12 (1997): 70.

————. "Rhonda Vincent." *BU* 34, no. 10 (2000): 38–42.

————. "Sally Jones and the Sidewinders: On Stretching the Boundaries and Being Yourself." *BN* 11, no. 3 (2001): 24–29.

Weize, Richard, and Patrick Milligan. Discography for *Rose Maddox: The One Rose—The Capitol Years.* Bear Family Records Boxed Set, BCD 15743-1 DI, 1993.

Wernick, Pete. "Keynote: Bones to Pick." *WIB* 17 (Fall 1998): 8–9.

————. Liner notes to *Grant Street String Band.* Flat Rock Records FR 103, 1995.

White, Alana. "Ginger Boatwright." *BU* 23, no. 3 (1988): 29–33.

White, Roland, and Diane Bouska. *The Essential Clarence White.* Diane and Roland Music, 2009.

Whiteside, Jonny. "Maddox Brothers and Rose." In *Encyclopedia of Country Music,* ed. Paul Kingsbury. Oxford: Oxford University Press, 1998.

————. *Ramblin' Rose: The Life and Career of Rose Maddox.* Nashville: Country Music Foundation Press and Vanderbilt University Press, 1997.

Wild, David. "New Faces: Alison Krauss." *Rolling Stone.* November 15, 1990.

Wilds, David, and Grant Alden. "Honey Wilds: The Wilds, The Innocent, The Grand Ole Opry." *ND* 4 (Summer 1996): 48–55.

Wilgus, D. K. Liner notes to *Harry and Jeanie West: Country Music in the Blue Grass Style.* Originally Prestige/International 13049, 1960. Reissued by Prestige, PRCD-24238-2, 2000.

————. Liner notes to *Roaming the Blue Ridge with Jeanie West*. Prestige/International 13038, 1960.

Williams, Roger. "Bach to Bluegrass." *Penn Stater* (January/February 1980): 5, 14.

Williams, Vivian. "Gigging with Big Mon." *WIB* 8 (Summer 1996): 3–4.

Wilson, Dave. Review of *Who's That Knocking? Broadside*. n.d.

Wilson, Jerry. "Claire Lynch: In Her Own Words." *BU* 28, no. 11 (1994): 22–26.

Wilson, John S. "Lively Bluegrass Played at Seaport by the Buffalo Gals." *New York Times*. June 7, 1975.

Wine, Larry. "Cia Cherryholmes: Bluegrass Darling." *BNL* 32, no. 4 (2005): 44–45, 47.

Winkworth, Bruce. Liner notes to *Newport Folk Festival: Best of Bluegrass 1959–1966*. Vanguard 187/89-2, 2001.

Winston, Nat. Foreword to *Earl Scruggs and the 5-String Banjo*, by Earl Scruggs, 6–8. New York: Peer International, 1968.

Wolfe, Charles. Liner notes to *Hazel and Alice*. Rounder CD 0027, 1995.

————. "Samantha Bumgarner: The Original Banjo Pickin' Girl." *OTH* 1, no. 2 (1987/1988): 6–9.

Wright, Carolyn. "Bluegrass Girl." *WIB* 11 (Spring 1997): 1.

————. "Hazel Dickens: A Bridge between Two Worlds." *BN* 11, no. 12 (2001): 16–19, 33.

————. "State of the Union: Meredith Bub Talks about Her Job." *BN* 13, no. 10 (2003): 36.

————. "The Voice: Dale Ann Bradley." *BU* 41, no. 8 (2007): 26–31.

Zimmerman, Lee. "Compass Records: Alison Brown's Label Finds Its Own Diverse Musical Direction." *Goldmine* (May 3, 2002).

AUTHOR INTERVIEWS AND EMAILS

Adcock, Martha. Emails January 10, 2008; February 7, 2008; March 17, 2008; April 25 and 30, 2008; May 28, 2008; June 29, 2008; August 3, 2008.

Amos, Betty. Telephone interview, November 13, 2009.

Baber, Lee Ann Lenker. Personal interview, January 19, 2003.

Baldassari, Butch. Telephone interview, May 15, 2007.

Banks, Cary. Email August 11, 2007.

Bartenstein, Fred. Email February 13, 2007; December 6, 2007.

Barwick, Kathy. Email January 5, 2008.

Belle, Gloria. Personal interview, September 24, 1995. Telephone interview, January 5, 2005.

Black, Bob. Telephone interview, March 10, 2005.

Boatwright, Ginger. Email February 17, 2008.

Brain, Peggy. Telephone interview, 1995.

Branscomb, Louisa. Emails September 10 and 22, 2003; April 7, 2004; March 17, 2009.

Bray, Shera. Emails September 6 and 11, 2003.

Brooks, James. Telephone interview, October 12, 2006.

Brown, Alison. Personal interview, May 29, 2003.

Bub, Meredith. Email September 17, 2007.

Buckland, Andrew. Telephone interview, February 22, 2004. Emails August 26, 30, and 31, 2000; September 26, 2000; October 18, 2000.

Bussard, Joe. Telephone interview, March 9, 2004.

Cardwell, Nancy. Telephone conversation, February 13, 2004. Email January 23, 2006.

Carlin, Larry. Email August 19, 2008.

Cloud, Pat. Email March 1, 2008.

Clyburn, Wayne. Emails February 10 and 14, 2007.

Connell, Dudley. Emails January 30, 2007; October 24, 2007.

Cooper, Wilma Lee. Live on-air interview by Eddie Stubbs, February 5, 2001.

Davis, Janet. Emails February 25, 2010.

Davis, Rubye. Personal interview, April 10, 2002.

Delon, Jean-Mark. Emails July 31, 2007; August 1, 2007.

Dickens, Hazel. Personal interview, January 18, 2004. Telephone interview, November 6, 2004;

Dye, Ed. Telephone interview, January 14, 2000.

Edmundson, Dave. Emails March 22, 2007; April 17, 2007.

Eilts, Leo. Emails July 29, 2007; August 9, 2007.

Eliah, Elaine. Emails February 17 and 19, 2003; March 28, 2003.

Ellis, Tony. Telephone interview, November 11, 2004.

Emerson, Bill. Email July 14, 2008.

Enright, Pat. Emails February 24 and 25, 2004.

Ericsson, Sue. Telephone interview, December 8, 2007.

Evans, Bill. Emails June 9, 2004; July 11, 2004; January 8, 2007; March 17, 2007; April 17, 18, and 19, 2007; May 15, 2007.

Eyler, Bonnie. Emails December 10 and 12, 2007; January 19, 2012.

Eyler, Dottie. Telephone interview, January 17, 2005.

Fingerette, Sally. Emails February 18 and 27, 2003.

Fink, Cathy. Email November 11, 2006.

Fisher, Betty. Personal interview, March 9, 1998.

Fox, Jon Hartley. Emails March 21, 2007.

French, Grace. Emails September 11, 2003; February 25, 26, 27, and 29, 2004; January 15 and 17, 2005; December 13, 2007.

Gentry, Beck. Personal interview, January 30, 2003. Emails March 12 and 18, 2003; February 20, 2007; March 11, 2007.

Gerrard, Alice. Personal interview, November 17, 2003. Telephone interview, November 6, 2004. Emails December 18, 2003; October 17, 2007; November 8 and 14, 2007; April 22, 2011, May 4, 2011.

Gilchrist, Sharon. Emails August 31, 2007; September 5, 2007.

Gilchrist, Troy. Email August 15, 2007.

Gray, Tom. Emails January 17 and 18, 2004.

Greer, Jim. Telephone interview, January 13, 2012.

Gruenbaum, Marvin. Emails July 30 and 31, 2007.

Haney, Carlton. Telephone interviews, January 9, 2004; May 15, 2004.

Harvey, Dave. Telephone interview, February 15, 2007. Email February 23, 2007.

Hedgecoth, John. Emails February 17, 19, and 21, 2004.

Hunter, Erica. Email October 22, 2003.

Irwin, Ken. Telephone interview, May 2, 2007. Emails May 6, 2005 (with input from Brad Paul and Art Menius); December 5, 2006; May 3 and 14, 2007; July 3, 2007

Jones, Sally. Email June 5, 2004.

Josephson, Nancy. Email February 19, 2003.

Kallick, Kathy. Telephone interview, January 16, 2007. Emails January 23, 2007; October 22 and 31, 2007; July 10, 2008; December 9 and 10, 2007; December 2, 2009.

Keith, Bill. Telephone interview, November 2, 2004.

Keys, Jerry. Email January 23, 2012 (forwarded by Frank Godbey).

King, Bev. Emails March 3, 2010.

King, Hubert Graham. Emails July 22 and 26, 2008.

Knowlton, Bill. Email March 23, 2004.

Koretzky, Henry. Email March 31, 2003.

Laur, Katie. Telephone interview, February 3, 2007. Emails February 4, 5, and 6, 2007; July 7, 2008.

Lee, Judy. Emails September 24, 2009; November 16, 2009.

Leet, Mary Jo. Personal interview, January 30, 2003. Emails April 20, 2007; November 30, 2009.

Lewis, Laurie. Telephone interview, November 17, 2006. Emails October 25, 2003; August 8, 2005; June 9, 2006; December 5, 2006; July 10, 2008.

Long, Elizabeth. Emails January 9, 2010; April 6, 2010.

Lynch, Claire. Personal interview, July 1, 1995. Telephone interview, October 24, 2006. Emails August 12, 1997; October 25 and 26, 2006; February 9, 2008; August 16, 2010. Posting to BGListserv (via Ken Irwin) December 7, 1997.

Magone, Barbara MacDonald. Telephone interview, July 14, 2007. Email July 19, 2007.

McGraw, Sharon. Telephone interview, April 21, 2005.

McKee, Suzi. Telephone interviews, January 3 and 5, 2008.

McLain, Raymond W. Email November 14, 2005.

McLain, Ruth (Smith). Emails November 12 and 13, 2005; January 20, 2010; December 7, 2011.

Milovsoroff, Ann. Email January 25, 2004.

Mitchell, Patty. Emails July 30, 2007; August 2 and 17, 2007.

Monick, Susie. Personal interview, November 23, 2002. Emails February 18, 2003; March 4, 2003; September 26, 2003; March 15 and 24, 2004; April 1, 2004.

Morris, Lynn. Personal interview, March 29, 1994. Telephone interview, January 23, 2007.

Munde, Alan. Email July 31, 2007.

New Coon Creek Girls (Vicki Simmons, Ramona Church Taylor, Dale Ann Bradley, Kathy Kuhn). Personal interview, March 2, 1996.

Nitchie, Donald. Email April 8, 2010.

Owens, Andy. Personal correspondence via fax August 13, 2007. Emails August 10 and 14, 2007.

Perry, Pam. Emails October 24, 2010.

Pitts, Randy. Emails December 5 and 7, 2006.

Raines, Missy. Telephone interview, June 19, 2004. Emails June 12, 13, and 15, 2004; October 26, 2006; January 24, 2008; December 10, 2009; January 23, 2010.

Rakestraw, Todd. Emails May 3 and 8, 2007.

Reed, Doria. Email July 7, 2007.

Rice, Wayne. Emails January 19, 2004; December 9 and 13, 2007.

Roberts, Andrea, and Sally Jones. Personal interview, December 14, 1996.

Roberts, Andrea. Emails June 9, 2004; July 7, 2008; March 12 and 22, 2010.

Rosenberg, Neil. Email January 10, 2004.

Salls, Lynn Grey. Emails May 3, 2004; January 22, 2008.

Sanders, Markie. Telephone interviews, January 12 and 20, 2000. Emails January 5, 7, and 8, 2008; February 7, 2010.

Saunders, Walt. Emails January 4, 2005; January 6, 2005.

Scott-Benson, Kristin. Telephone interview, May 26, 2004. Emails May 24, 2004; June 6, 8, and 9, 2004; January 6 and 7, 2008.

Seeger, Mike. Telephone interview, December 9, 2003. Emails January 9 and 16, 2006.

Shropshire, Elmo. Email March 1, 2004.

Shubb, Rick. Emails February 16, 17, and 26, 2004.

Siegel, Carol. Emails September 25, 2003; April 7, 2004.

Simmons, Vicki. Telephone interview, January 8, 2008.

Spottswood, Dick. Email June 10, 2006.

Stafford, Tim. Email May 15, 2007.

Stephenson, Larry. Telephone interview, June 8, 2004.

Stockton, Judith. Email April 26, 2003.

Stoneman, Donna. Telephone conversations, January 15, 2000; February 10, 2000; January 21, 2006.

Stoneman, Patsy. Personal interview, September 24, 1996. Telephone interview, October 12, 2007.

Stoneman, Roni. Talk recorded at Maryland Banjo Academy, April 19, 1997. Telephone conversations July 19, 1998; May 21, 2002; January 13, 2003.

Stubbs, Eddie. Email December 8, 2003.

Sullivan, Margie. Telephone interviews, November 8, 2005; January 4, 2012.

Thatcher, Wendy. Telephone interview, July 4, 2004. Emails April 1, 2001; March 25, 2003; December 9 and 11, 2007.

Thomas, Suzanne. Personal interview, May 11, 1998. Telephone interviews, March 18, 2007; April 19, 2007. Email January 20, 2010.

Thomason, Ron. Email to IBMA Listserv, April 23, 2011.

Thompson, Peter. Emails December 18 and 20, 2006; January 3, 4, and 17, 2007.

Trachtenberg, Martha. Telephone interview, March 27, 2004. Emails March 19, 2000; November 19 and 20, 2002; February 17, 2003; March 16, 22, and 25, 2004.

Trischka, Tony. Emails February 22, 2003.

Vincent, Carolyn. Telephone interview, April, 14, 2005. Email April 21, 2005.

Vincent, Rhonda. Telephone interview, April 7, 2005. Emails April 20, 2005; April 1, 2008.

Waller, Butch. Emails December 9 and 12, 2007.

Weiss, Bruce. Telephone interview, September 14, 2007.

Welch, Lee Ann. Emails January 13, 2008; July 9, 2008.

Wernick, Peter. Email September 10, 2003.

West, Jeannie. Telephone interview, November 15, 2004.

White, Roland. Telephone interview, January 7, 2011.

Wilborn, Marshall. Telephone interviews, January 23 and 30, 2007.

Wilkinson, Kristin. Email March 27, 2004.

Williams, Vivian. Emails September 2, 3, and 4, 2003; February 23 and 29, 2004; January 14 and 15, 2005.

Wilson, Joe. Telephone interview, May 16, 2007. Email May 16, 2007.

Wingate, Sally. Emails February 21, 2003; March 17, 2003; September 10, 2003; November 11 and 22, 2003; April 1, 2004.

Wyland, Dede. Interview by Ira Gitlin, November 29, 2007. Emails July 8, 2008; March 12, 2009.

Yokum, Julia. Emails March 25, 2005; April 25, 2005.

Aaberg, Phil, 300

A & M Records, 296

"About the Road Songs," 212

Accidents and Accusations Tour, 372

Ace of Cups, 242

Acoustic Collection, The, 173, 289

Acuff, Roy, 16, 17, 19

Adams, Tom, 130, 237, 238, 240

Adcock, Eddie, 161–66, 171–74, 288–89

Adcock, Gaudreau, Waller, & Gray: The Country Gentlemen Reunion Band, 174

Adcock, Martha Hearon, 2, 93, 165–66, 168–74

Adelphi Records, 57, 213

Adler, Rich, 272

Adventure Studios, 357

"Agate Hill," 133

"Ain't Misbehavin'," 225

Ain't Nothin' in Ramblin', 188

"Ain't Nothin' in Ramblin'," 189

Airtight, 363, 364

AKUS, 322

Alabama Folk Heritage Award, 90

Alex and Ola Belle and the New River Boys and Girls, 35, 37, 39, 306

Alfalfa Brothers, 236

Alice and Hazel. *See* Hazel and Alice

Alice Gerrard and Mike Seeger, 132

Alice, Gail, & Sharon: The Road to Agate Hill: Music From Southwest Virginia and Beyond, 132

Alison Brown Quartet, 294, 298, 302

Alison Brown Quartet Live at Blair with Joe Craven, 302

Alison Krauss and the Cox Family: I Know Who Holds Tomorrow, 322

Alison Krauss and Union Station, 282, 293, 298, 356, 382

Alison Krauss and Union Station: Live (CD), 326

Alison Krauss and Union Station: Live (DVD), 326

Alison Krauss and Union Station: Two Highways, 320

All-American Bluegrass Girl, 357

All Girl Boys, 241, 242, 305, 314, 315

Allen, Johnnie Sue, 339

Allen, Neal, 196

Allen, Red, 57, 77, 193

Allen, Steve, 70, 77

All in One Evening, 39

"All the Good Times Are Past and Gone," 260

"All the Guys Who Turn Me On Turn Me Down," 78

"Amazing Grace," 210

Ambush Records, 271

American Banjo Three-Finger and Scruggs Style, 3, 74, 117

Amos, Betty, 11, 94, 100–103, 122, 159

Amos, Ed, 100

Amram, Dave, 213

Amy Gallatin and Stillwaters, 334

Anderson, John, 202, 205

Anderson, Muriel, 182, 307

Andrea, Roberts, 304, 311–14

Angel Mountain, 334

"Angel on His Shoulder," 257

Angels Are Singing, The, 332

Anger, Darol, 232, 262, 300, 301

"Angry Brown Eyes," 57

"Another Lonesome Morning," 163

Anthology of American Folk Music, 119

Antioch College, 119, 121, 194

Anywhere the Wind Blows, 262

Apple Blossom Bluegrass Festival (Winchester, Va.), 240

Arco Label, 43

Arhoolie Records, 11, 32, 33, 125

Arkansas Sheiks, 251

Arkansas Traveler, 298, 322

Arkie and His Hillbillies, 29

Arrandem Records, 4, 184

Arsenault, Louis, 144

Art Davis and the Rhythm Riders, 18

Arthur Godfrey's Talent Scouts, 73

Asch, Moe, 122

"Ashes of Love," 193

Ash Grove, The, 70, 77

Ashley, Clarence, 119

Atlanta Country Music Hall of Honor, 44

"Atlanta Is Burning," 200

Atlanta Symphony, 152

Atteiram Records, 308, 339

Auldridge, Mike, 109

Aunt Maudie's, 223, 226

Authentic Bluegrass, 61

Aycrigg, Betty (Betty Mann), 3, 242

Baber, Calvin, 280

"Baby, Now That I've Found You," 323

Back Home Again, 355

Back Porch Bluegrass, 145

Back to the Well, 334

"Back Up and Push," 140

Bacon, Marty, 336

"Bad Moon Rising," 80

Baez, Joan, 97, 117, 162, 169, 251, 261

Bailes, Walter, 87

Bailey Brothers, 100, 105, 110

Bailey, Danny, 105, 106, 110

Baker, Amy, 311, 313

Baker, Billy, 50, 123

Baker, Bobby, 117

Baker, Kenny, 46, 52, 142, 158, 173

Baldassari, Butch, 321

Bales, Barry, 322

Balfa Brothers, 124

Ballinger, Ethan, 292

Banjo Newsletter, 335; women on cover, 278, 340, 369; women profiled in, 90, 297, 305, 370, 378; women writing for, 1, 94, 184

"Banjo Picking Girl," 106

"Banjo Signal," 80

Banjo Songs of the Southern Mountains, 97

Banks, Cary, 369

"Banks of the Ohio," 106

Bar Belles, 305

Barefoot Nellies, 305

Barenburg, Russ, 210

Barnett, Connie, 103

Barnett, Wanda, 309

Barney Schreiber and the Hayshakers, 101

Barrows, April, 154

Barwick, Kathy, 241, 315, 335

Baucom, Sandra, 333

Baum, Clyde, 44

Baxter, Dorothy, 182, 252, 261

Baxter, Iona "Onie," 44

Baxter, J. N., 44

Bay Records, 252

Be Good Tanyas, 10

"Be Ready to Sail," 274

Beach, Booie, 344

Bean, Bob, 72, 80

Bean Blossom, Indiana, Festival, 203; bands with women who played there, 89, 124, 176, 203, 219, 263, 307, 312

Bear Family Records, 21

"Bear Song, The," 254

Beatles, The: inspiration, 229, 285; songs recorded bluegrass style, 153, 277, 363

"Beaufort County Jail," 127

Beautiful, 95

Beautiful Bouquet, A, 33

"Beautiful Hills of Galilee," 129, 130

Beautiful Star: A Christmas Collection, 357

Beazley, Janet, 283

Bedsole, Jenny, 244

Been There Still, 133

Before the Fire Comes Down, 295

Bekeny, Tom, 266, 268

Bell, Bobby, 202

Bell, Delia, 44, 136, 202–6

Belle, Gloria, 5, 67, 104–12, 202; in bands with other women, 103, 246; mentioned by other women, 2, 4, 119, 170, 212, 338; mention of pioneering "firsts," 93, 94, 143, 156, 204

Belle, Lulu (Wiseman), 10, 37, 202

Belmont University, 179, 343, 365; Kristin Scott Benson at, 337, 339, 341

Benjamin, Matt, 367

Bennett, Chris, 307

Benny and Vallie and the Country Clan, 54

Benny and Vallie Cain and the Country Clan, 57

Benny Cain and his Country Cousins, 55, 56

Benson, Hogan Wayne, 344

Benson, Kristin Scott, 283, 336, 337–45; in bands with other women, 311, 333; ground-breaking banjo player, 112, 381, 382; hired by Grascals 332, 335

Benson, Wayne, 340, 341, 344, 345

Berea College, 176, 178, 179

Bergeson, Pat, 324

Bergquist, Karin, 227

Berkeley Folk Festival, 251

Berklee College of Music, 334, 335, 369

Berline, Byron, 33, 152, 205

Berline, Crary, and Hickman, 294

Berne, Geoff, 251

Berry, Heather, 334

Berry, Hunter, 356, 358

Bertye Maddux Band, 334

Best of All Things, The, 137

Beth Stephens and Edge, 334

Betty Amos and Her All-Girl Band, 106

Betty Amos with Judy and Jean, 101

Betty and Buck, 216, 217, 219

Betty Buckland and the Moonlighters, 144

Betty Fisher and the Dixie Bluegrass Band, 2, 219

Betty Fisher and the Dixie Bluegrass Boys, 218

Betty Fisher, David Deese and Dixie Bluegrass, 220

Betty Harper and the Black Mountain Boys, 11

Between the Hollow and the High-Rise, 268

Beverly, Bonnie, 306

Beyond The City, 322

Bibb, Kim, 309, 312

Big Ball in Monterey, 77

"Big Midnight Special," 24

Bill and Mary Reid and the Melody Mountaineers, 42

Bill and Ted's Excellent Adventure, 185

Bill Emerson and Sweet Dixie, 240

Bill Grant and Delia Bell, 202

Bill Grant and Delia Bell in England, 205

Bill Grant, Delia Bell, and the Kiamichi Mountain Boys, 203, 205

Bill Monroe and the Blue Grass Boys, 2, 9, 47, 145; Howdy Forrester with, 14, 16, 18; Sally Ann Forrester with, 13, 16, 17, 19; Bessie Lee Mauldin with, 46, 48, 52, 53; *See also* Monroe, Bill

Bill Monroe's Bean Blossom Festival. *See* Bean Blossom, Indiana, Festival

Bill Monroe's Hall of Honor (Bean Blossom, Ind.), 90

Billboard (Billboard's Country Music Chart): Delia Bell, 202, 205; chart action of bands over the years, 24, 78, 101; Dixie Chicks, 369, 370; individual songs that charted, 28, 36, 102, 152; The Whites, 157, 159, 160

Billboard (magazine), 353

"Bionic Marshmallow," 295

Birchmere, The, 341

Birdsong, 258

Birkby, Michelle, 309

Biscuit Records, 234

Bitter End, The, 70

Black, Bob, 358

Black, Patty, 208

"Black Bottom Strut," 196

"Black Lung," 125, 129

Black Poodle, The (nightclub), 78

Blake, Nancy, 156

Blake, Norman, 152

Blame It On the Bluegrass, 333

Bledsoe, Deb, 6

Bliss, Laurel, 182

Block, Melissa, 373

Block, Ron, 322, 329, 334, 381

Blood Oranges, 36

Blossoms, 259

"Blue and Lonesome," 203

Bluebird Special, 178

"Blue Days, Sleepless Nights," 258

Blue-Eyed Janie (Stroud), 60

Bluegrass: A History, 3

Bluegrass Album Band, 317

Bluegrass Bouquet, 334

Bluegrass Boy, 257

Blue Grass Boys. *See* Bill Monroe and the Blue Grass Boys

"Bluegrass Breakdown," 74

Bluegrass Breakdown (newsletter), 6

Bluegrass Cardinals, 338

Bluegrass Champs, 69, 72, 73, 74

Bluegrass Ensemble, A, 287

Bluegrass Five, 44

Bluegrass Hoedown, 142

Bluegrass in My Heart, 308

Bluegrass Inn, The, 147, 148, 149

Bluegrass Instrumentals, 47

Bluegrass in the Sunrise, 283

Bluegrass Liberation, 305–7

"Bluegrass Melodies," 349

Bluegrass Neighbors, 285

Bluegrass Now, 6; women on cover, 289, 343, 378; women quoted in, 155, 168, 375

Bluegrass Rebels, 311

Bluegrass Southland, 365

"Blue Grass Special," 17

Bluegrass Spectacular, 70 Songs, 57

Bluegrass State (band), 176

Bluegrass Tarheels, 2

Bluegrass Travelers, 107

Bluegrass Unlimited, 3, 6, 83, 135, 185; early days, 65, 102, 121, 124, 133; women on cover, 55, 66, 89, 158, 159, 164, 175, 197, 200, 274, 288, 338, 355, 374

Bluegrass Vagabonds, 376

Bluegrass Youth All-Stars, 1

Blue Kentucky Girl, 159

"Blue Kentucky Girl," 205

"Blue Moon of Kentucky," 32, 98

Blue Night Express, 178, 362, 363, 365

Blueprint, 57

Blue Ribbon Bluegrass, 349

Blue Ridge Connection, 94

Blue Ridge Mountain Boys, 44

Blue Ridge Recording, 280

Blue Ridge Records, 11

Blue River, 243, 247

Blue Rose, 255

Blue Rose (group), 255

Bluer Than Midnight, 204

Blue Sky Boys, 58, 97

Blues on My Trail, 191

Blues Stay Away From Me, 262

Boatwright, Ginger, 93, 150–56, 166, 204; with Bushwhackers, 153, 215, 246

Boatwright, Grant, 151, 152, 153, 155

Bob's Barn, 18

Bob Wills and the Texas Playboys, 14

Boggs, Dock, 119, 124

Bogie's Travel, 357

Bomstein, Sam, 73
Bonita Records, 253
Bonnie Lou and Buster (Moore), 43, 110
Bonoff, Karla, 231
Boone Creek, 317
Boot Hill, 294, 307
Born Gypsy, 307
Born To Be Free, 219
Boston Folk Festival, 144
Boswell, Terry, 227, 307
Bottle Hill, 210
"Bottle of Wine," 78
Bound For Gloryland, 353
Bowman, Marsha, 333
Boyce, Sherrill, 339
Boyd Halford and the Sally Mountain Singers, 347
Brace, Maria, 209
Bradley, Dale Ann, 302, 308, 309, 310
Brain, Peggy, 3, 69, 73, 182
Bramble And the Rose, 238
Brand, Oscar, 97
"Brand New Heartache," 377
Brand New Old-Time Fiddle Tunes, 141
Branscomb, Louisa, 2, 4, 182; in bands, 286, 294; with Bluegrass Liberation, 306–7
Brawner, Virginia, 312
Bray, Harley, 142
Bray, Shera, 142
Bray Brothers, 142
Breakin' It, 271
Brentwood Records, 272
Bridgewater, Debbie (Reed), 182
Brill, Dalton, 185
Brislin, Kate, 131
Britt, Gena, 283, 311, 313, 334, 336
Broadside, 123
Brock, Jesse, 237, 239
"Broken Tie," 263
Bromberg, David, 210, 214
Brooks, Garth, 323
Brooks, Harold, 38

Brooks, James "Jim," 38
Brother Boys, 289
Brown, Alison, 242, 293–303, 317, 383; album work with others, 272, 273, 309, 353; high profile, 184, 381, 382; with Alison Krauss, 282, 320, 322
Brown, Earl, 77
Brown, Ferrell, 77
Brown, Hollis, 307
Brown, Jim Ed, 351
Brown, Junior, 235, 240
Brown, Reverend Pearly, The, 124
Brown, Toni, 261
Brown, Tony, 271
"Brown County Breakdown," 48
Browne, Cindy, 335
Brown Knows Music, 303
Brumfield, Deacon, 38
"Brush Arbor Meeting," 183
Bryan, Evelyn (Miss Evelyn), 105
Bryan, James, 147
Bryant, Donnie, 55
Bub, Meredith, 324
Buchanan, Beverly, 178
Buck and Family Live, 159
Buckeyes in the Briarpatch, 196
Buckland, Andrew, 143
Buckland, Bettie, 4, 93, 94, 143–45
Buck Mountain Ramblers, 100
Buck White and the Down Home Folks, 178, 148
Buck White and the Down Home Folks [Buck White and the Down Homers], 158
Buck White and the Down Home Folks: In Person at Randy Wood's Old-Time Picking Parlor, 158
Buck White and the Down Homers, 158, 159. *See also* Down Homers
Buddy Lee Attractions, 366
Buerhrig, Niki, 227
Buffalo Chipkickers, 275, 276, 277, 278
Buffalo Chips, 207, 209, 210
Buffalo Gals, 159, 207–15, 231; early

all-female band, 182, 305; mentioned as influence, 170, 276, 284
Bufwack, Mary, 3, 10, 181
Bull Harman and Bull's Eye, 335
Buller, Becky, 333
Bumgarner, Samantha, 10, 98
Burkett, Elizabeth, 156
Burks, Amber, 335
"Burn Down the House," 267
Burns, Jethro, 187, 189
Burr, John R., 298
Bury Me Beneath The Willow," 17, 97
Busby, Buzz, 57, 58, 279; and Stonemans, 72, 77, 83
Bush, Gene, 147
Bush, Sam, 272, 318, 350
Bushwhackers, 153, 154, 156, 215, 246, 305
Buzz Busby and the Bayou Boys, 279
"Bye Bye Blues," 340
By the Sweat of My Brow, 129

Cahall, Tom, 226
Cain, Andre Paul, 57, 58
Cain, Benny and Vallie, 54, 75
Cain, Benny, 55, 56, 57, 58
Cain, Vallie, 3, 41, 54–58, 136
Cain's Academy, 14
California AIDs Ride 4, 257
Callaway, Sudie, 103
Calling Me Home: Songs of Love and Life, 133
Call Me a Taxi, 256
"Call Me a Taxi," 267
Camp, Shawn, 185
Camp Springs, N.C., Festival, 66
Campbell, Alex, 36, 37, 38, 39
Campbell, Archie, 217
Campbell, Arthur, 36
Campbell, Dockery, 36
Campbell, Ellen, 36
Campbell, Glen, 306
Campbell, Kate, 299
Campbell, Pearl, 184

Campbell, Ola Belle. See Reed, Ola Belle Campbell
Campbell, Tom Harley, 196, 203
Canaan Records, 65
Cannon, Melonie, 334
Can't You Hear Me Callin', 47
"Can't You Hear Me Callin'," 51
Capitol Records, 28, 31, 159
"Carbolic Rag," 195
Cardwell, Nancy, 6, 307
Carlin, Larry, 280
Carlisle, Betty. See Amos, Betty
Carlisle, Bill, 101
Carlisles, The, 100
Carlton Haney's North Carolina New Grass Festival, 207, 210
Carmichael, Debbie. See Peck, Debbie
Carnegie Hall, 178
Carolee Singers, 24, 25
Carolina Barn Dance, 216, 217
Carolina Mountain Home, 219
Carolina Neighbors, 43
Carolina Road, 305, 334
Carolina Rose, 305, 333
Carolina Songbird, 46, 50
Carpenter, Annie Kaser, 309
Carpenter, Beth Nielsen, 302
Carpenter, Karen, 152
Carpenter, Mary Chapin
Carpenters, The, 171
Carrie Hassler and Hard Rain, 334
Carroll County Ramblers, 135, 136, 137
Carson, Martha, 67, 101, 348
Carter, Anna (Mrs. Jimmie Davis), 67
Carter, Jason, 138
Carter, Maybelle, 10, 383; guitar style, 64, 125; influence of, 37, 98, 123, 170
Carter, Sara, 10, 98, 123, 170, 383
Carter Family, The: influence of, 98, 114, 119, 170, 194; listened to, 29, 93; performed music of, 122, 244
Carter Fold, The, 179
Carve That Possum, 133

Carver, Bill, 23
Case, Jimmy, 72
Cash, Johnny, 65
Cash, Johnny and June, 52
Cashdollar, Cindy, 182, 282
Castle, Johnny, 172
Cas Walker Show, 106, 108, 110, 112
Catch Tomorrow, 309
"Catfish John," 248
Cats and the Fiddler, 335
CBS This Morning, 368
Ceili Music, 160
Cellar Door, The, 162
Chain, Hazel, 85
Chalker Sisters, 282, 305
Chancy, Blake, 370
Chapin, Michelle, 311
"Charmaine," 340
Chedda Records, 279
Cheer of the Home Fires, The, 206
Cherokee Rose, 235, 286, 305, 307
Cherry Blossoms in the Springtime, 333
Cherryholmes, 332, 374–79, 382
Cherryholmes, 377
Cherryholmes II: Black and White, 377
Cherryholmes III: Don't Believe, 377
Cherryholmes IV: Common Threads, 377
Cherryholmes, B. J., 374, 375
Cherryholmes, Cia, 374, 375, 376, 377, 378, 379
Cherryholmes, Jere, 374, 375, 376, 378
Cherryholmes, Molly, 374, 375, 378, 379
Cherryholmes, Sandy, 374, 375, 376, 378
Cherryholmes, Shelly, 375
Cherryholmes, Skip, 374, 375
Cherryhomes Family Band, 375
Chesapeake Records, 37
Chiavola, Kathy, 154, 156, 226, 352
Chicago Tribune, The, 290
Chick Chat, 363, 366, 367, 368, 369
"C-H-I-C-K-E-N," 265
Chicken Hot Rod, 307
"Chicken Under the Washtub," 138

Childe Harold club, 189
Chism, Terry, 156
Chris, Davis, 344
Chris Jones and the Night Drivers, 343
Christiansen, Donica, 283, 333
"Christmas Swing," 366
"Christmas Time's A-Coming," 258
Chuck Wagon Gang, 65, 67
Church, Porter, 72, 75, 77, 83
Church, Ramona. *See* Taylor, Ramona Church
Ciani, Ann Ashburn, 306
Cincinnati Symphony, 177
"Cindy," 117
Cirimele, Carolyn, 315
City Limits Bluegrass Band, 234, 235
City Limits: Live at the Oxford Hotel, 234
Claire Lynch and the Front Porch String Band, 271, 272
Claire Lynch Band, 272
Clark, Johnny, 24
Clark, Katy, 336
Clark, Roy, 81
Clark, Terri, 343
Classic Bluegrass Today and Yesterday, 206
Classified Grass, 318
"Clay County Miner," 125
Cleaning Up Our Act, 279
"Clean Plate Club, The," 303
Clearwater, 333
Clements, Vassar, 152, 154, 246, 276
Cleveland Country, 300
Clinch Mountain Country, 257
Cline, Patsy, 61, 223, 244
Clinton Codack and Wendy Special, 163
Clogging Chickens Label, 307
Clooney, George, 324
Cloud, Pat, 294, 375
Cloud Valley, 282, 286, 287, 288, 291
Cloud Valley: Live in Europe, 287
Clyburn, Wayne, 224, 226
Clyde and Marie Denny and the Kentuckians, 45, 95

Clyde Joy and the Country Folk, 60
CMA Awards (Country Music Association): Album, 370; Entertainer, 370; Female Vocalist, 323; Horizon, 323, 370; Song, 344; Vocal Group, 70, 79, 370, 373
CMH Records: Eddie Adcock bands, 172, 173, 174, 288, 289; Stonemans, 81, 82
Coal Mining Women (CD), 129
Coal Mining Women (DVD), 129
Coats, Bill, 94
Coats, Sue, 94
Codack Special, 163, 164, 165
Cody, Buck, 348
Coe, David Allan, 173
Coen Brothers, 160, 324
Cogswell, Robert, 23
Cohen, Joe, 123
Cohen, Larry, 230
Cold Mountain, 325, 327
Cole, Nat King, 119
Collins, Judy, 169, 209
Colorado Folk II, 234
Coltman, Robert, 19
Columbia Records, 13, 17, 24, 42, 373
Come All You Coal Miners, 125
"Come Back to Me in My Dreams," 17, 18
"Come On-a My House," 119
"Come On, Baby, Do the Locomotion," 212
"Come Walk With Me," 24
Common Ground, 335
Company You Keep, The, 303
Compass Records, 298; Alison Brown recordings on, 293, 300, 301; other women on 292, 302, 309
Compton, Mike, 147
Concerto for Bluegrass Band and Orchestra, 177
"Concerto for Bluegrass Band and Orchestra," 177
Connell, Dudley, 130, 206, 237, 240
Continental Divide, 338

"Coo Coo Bird," 119
Cook, Joe, 89
Cook, Vicki, 89
Cooke, Jack, 49, 117
Cooke, Peggy, 339
Cookin' With Katie, 225
Cooper, Carolee, 22, 24
Cooper, Stoney, 20, 21, 22, 24, 25; death, 21, 26; on Dobro, 23
Cooper, Wilma Lee, 58, 61, 20–27, 156; early woman in bluegrass, 3, 10, 12, 12, 204; influence, 2, 67, 94, 105, 119, 136
Copper Creek Records, 133, 267, 271
Cordle, Larry, 344, 345
Cornelius, Mary Ann, 94
Cort, Sharon, 334
Cotter, Debby, 315
Cotton, Elizabeth "Libba," 5, 124, 132, 162
Country Boys, 242
Country Clan, 56
Country Coalition, 243
Country Cooking, 210
Country Cow Shit, 201
Country Favorites, 74
Country Gentlemen, 49, 57, 58, 219; Eddie Adcock and, 162, 163, 172
Country Girls, 305
Country Granola, 208
Country Heritage, 6, 95
Country Heritage Music Store, 95
Country Kasha, 208
Country Rain, 270, 271
"Country Rain." *See* "Good Morning Country Rain"
County Records, 158, 202, 204
Courtyard Hounds, 373
Cousin Emmy, 10, 23, 24
Covered Wagon Gang, 135, 136
Cowan, John, 231, 319
"Cowboy Jim," 123
"Cowboy Lives Forever, The," 365
Cox, David, 224
Cox, Evelyn, 322

Cox, Gene, 73, 74, 78, 80
Cox, Mary, 4, 182, 184
Cox, Sidney, 322
Cox, Suzanne, 322
Cox Family, 322, 325, 364
"Coyote Song," 205
Crary, Dan, 169
Crase, Noah, 193
Craven, Joe, 302
Crider, Dale, 184
Crider, Linda, 184
"Cripple Creek," 78, 79, 82, 213
Crisco, Sandy. *See* Hatley, Sandy Crisco
Crist, Carol, 140
Crooked Still, 335
Cross, Brenda, 184
Cross, Liz, 184
Cross Creek, 280
Cross-Eyed Rosie, 335
Crossroads Records, 140
Crosstown, 94
Crowd Favorites, 274
Crowe, Ma (Elaine), 305
"Cry of the Wild Goose, The," 119
"Cuckoo Is a Pretty Bird, The," 200
Cummins, Jan, 308
Cummins, Kelli, 308
Curtis, Danny, 117
"Custom Made Woman Blues," 127
Cuttin' the Grass, 82

"Daddy Don't Drink No More," 189
"Daddy Stay Home," 74
Daisy a Day, 26
Dale Ann Bradley and Coon Creek, 310
Dale Ann Bradley Band, 310
"Dallas Rag," 196
Dallas Symphony, 251
Dalton Brill and the Wildcats, 185
Dalton Brill's Barber and Musician's Shop, 185
"Dancing in the Hog Trough," 238
Dane, Barbara, 261

Danger in the Air, 362, 365, 366; Robin Macy and, 363, 364, 367
Danger in the Air, 363
Daniel, Wayne, 5
Darlene, Donna, 101
"Darlin' Corey," 165
Daughters of American Bluegrass, 334
Daughters of Bluegrass, 334
Davies, Bryn, 335
Davis, Hubert, 146, 147, 148, 149
Davis, Janet, 4, 94, 182
Davis, Jim, 94
Davis, Luther, 132
Davis, Meg, 224
Davis, Rubye, 146–49, 156, 204
Davis, Sally. *See* Wingate, Sally
Davis, Shelby Jean, 147, 148, 204
Davis and Elkins College, 21
Daylight Train, 310
Dean, Jimmy, 11, 74
Deanie, Richardson, 309, 332
Dear Friends and Gentle Hearts, 199
Dearth, Greg, 197
Deaton, Honi, 333, 343
Deaton, Jeff, 333
Decca Records, 25, 108
"Deep River Blues," 161
Deininger, Diana, 310
Delia Bell, 205
Delia Bell and Bill Grant, 202, 206
Deliverance, 61
Dell, Georgia, 98
Della Mae, 305
Demarcus, Jennifer, 311
Demolition String Band, 36
Denison, Suzanne, 6
Dennis, Tanya, 214
Destination Life, 358
"Devil in Disguise," 248
Deville, Joy, 90
"Devil's Dream," 140, 213
Dian and the Greenbriar Boys, 29, 242
Dickens, Arnold, 116, 117

Dickens, Bertie Mae, 132
Dickens, Hazel, 2, 111, 113–34, 156, 227; albums, 4, 94, 252, 335; influence of, 5, 250; songwriter, 206, 237; thoughts on other female artists 51, 107, 346
Dickens, H. N., 114
Dickens, Robert, 116
Dickens, Sarah, 114
Dickens, Thurman, 125
Dickens, Velvie, 115
Dickerson, James, 364
Dickerson, Ronnie, 89
Dickman, Mary Jo. *See* Leet, Mary Jo
Dickson, Jackie, 44
Dickson, Larry, 44
"Did You See Jackie Robinson Hit That Ball?" 265
Diesel Ducks, 247
Different Strokes, 318
Dillard, Doug, 154
Dillards, The, 61, 145, 294
"Direwolf," 277
"Dirty Old Egg-Suckin' Dog," 78
"Dixie," 277
Dixie Bee-Liners, The, 185, 335
Dixie Belle and Goober (Buchanan), 16
Dixie Belles, 305
Dixie Bluegrass Festival, 89
"Dixie Breakdown," 105, 111
"Dixie Chicken," 364
Dixie Chicks, 178, 232, 361–73; fame in bluegrass 305, 332; at the Grammys, 325, 326
Dixie Chicks: Live, 371
Dixie Fried, 173, 289
"Dixieland For Me," 158
Dixie Reign, 282, 305
Dixon, Don, 77
Dobro Dozen, A, 94
Dobro Nut, 6
Doing It By the Book, 160
Dollywood, 307
"Do Lord," 105

"Dominique," 77
"Donna Mite," 79
Don Owens' Jamboree, 73
"Don't Cheat in Our Hometown," 205
"Don't Cry Blue," 230
"Don't Leave Your Little Girl All Alone," 260, 263
"Don't Put Her Down, You Helped Put Her There," 127, 128
"Don't That Moon Look Lonesome," 11
Don't Turn Your Back, 309
Doobie Shea Records, 309
Doub, Mary Tyler, 6
Doug Dillard Band, 154
"Doug's Tune," 145
Douglas, Jerry, 324, 325, 353, 355
Down From the Mountain (CD), 325
Down From the Mountain (film), 325
Down From the Mountain (tour), 160, 325
Down Home Bluegrass, 148
Down Home Kids, 158
Down Homers, 44, 157. *See also* Buck White and the Down Homers
Doyle, Bob, 277, 279
Draheim, Sue, 247
Dream (band), 333
Dream Come True, A, 353
Dreaming, 206
Dreaming of the Times, 206
Dressed For Success, 376
Drumright, Joe, 204
Dry Branch Fire Squad, 114, 321; Suzanne Thomas and, 192, 197–200
Dry Branch Fire Squad: Live! At Last, 199
Due West, 335
Duffy, John, 162, 166
Duffy, Nancy, 162, 166
Duncan, Stuart, 294, 298, 317
Dunn, Holly, 309
"Dust Eatin' Cowboys," 197
"Dusty Miller," 318
Dusty Miller (band), 322, 335

Dutton, Caroline, 282
Dye, Ed, 245, 246, 247
Dylan, Bob, 95, 231

"Each Season Changes You," 158
"Earl's Breakdown," 301
Earl Scruggs and the 5-String Banjo, 4, 276
Early Indiana Days, 189
Earth & Sky: The Laurie Lewis Songbook, 258
Earth and Sky: The Songs of Laurie Lewis, 257
East Tennessee State University, 121
Eddie Adcock and Martha, 172
Eddie Adcock and Talk of the Town (band),
    172, 173, 288, 289
Eddie Adcock and Talk of the Town, 173
Eddie Adcock Band, 172, 173, 289
Eddie and Martha Adcock, 172, 174
Edmundson, Dave, 193, 194, 196, 197, 198
Edwards, Billy, 107
"Eighteen Wheels A-Rolling," 101, 102
Eldridge, Ben, 285
"Eleanor Rigby," 153
Eliah, Elaine, 214, 215
Elking, Kim, 310, 311
Elkins, Julie, 283, 334, 336
"Ellie," 263
Ellis, Tony, 49, 50
Emerson, Bill, 55, 72, 77, 97, 162, 240
Emery, Ralph, 368
Emig, Trina, 227, 283, 305
End of the Rainbow, 262
Enright, Pat, 252, 261
Ensor, Kate, 305
Entertainment Weekly, 371
Ericcson, Kris, 244
Ericcson, Sue, 243, 244
Erv and Martha, 169
Erwin, Barbara, 362
Erwin, Julie, 362
Erwin, Martie Maguire, 361–73
Erwin, Paul, 362
Esoteric Records, 97
Estep, Bonnie, 305

Estep, Jeanie, 305
Eury, Howard, 307
Evans, Bill, 190, 198, 199, 286, 320
Evans, Dave, 206
Evening with the Dixie Chicks, An, 371
Evergreen, 302
Everybody's Reaching Out For Someone, 322
Every Time You Say Goodbye, 319, 322
Ewing, Skip, 271
Eyler, Bonnie, 135, 136, 137
Eyler, Dale, 135, 136
Eyler, Dottie, 135–37
Eyler, Leroy, 135, 136, 137

"Faded Coat of Blue," 197, 199
Fairchild, Raymond, 106
Fair Weather, 301
Falls City Ramblers, 186, 187, 188, 190,
    191, 285
Family Reunion, 307
Famous, The, 72, 73, 75, 76
Fantasy Label, 99
Farmington Bluegrass, 11
Fassaert, Tammy, 255
Fat Chance, 363
Faultline Records, 310
Favorite Gospel Songs, 97
Ferris, Ed, 77, 162
Fertile Ground, 154
Festival of Two Worlds, 176
"Feudin' Banjos," 61
Few Dollars More, A, 206
Few Old Memories, A, 130
"Few Old Memories, A," 130
Fiddle Jam Sessions, 140
Fiddle Tunes for Banjo, 230
Fiddling Down the Oregon Trail, 142
*Finding Her Voice: The Saga Of Women in
    Country Music*, 3, 10, 181
Fingerette, Sally, 215
Fink, Cathy, 10, 36, 255
Fire on the Mountain (band), 235
First Borne, 211

First Family of Country Music, The, 182

First Generation (plaque), 62

First Harvest, 307

Fisher, Betty, 2, 170, 182, 216–20, 221

Fisher, J.T., 217, 218, 219, 220

Flaig, Rich, 225

"Flame in My Heart," 205

Flatpickin' Favorites, 182

Flatpicking Guitar Magazine, 174

Flatt, Lester, 2, 183, 312; with Bill Monroe, 9, 18; with Earl Scruggs, 24, 37, 245, 247, 323, 355

Fleck, Bela, 293, 298, 301, 352

Flinchum, Gwen Biddix, 2, 182

"Flint Hill Special," 145

Flippo, Chet, 371, 372

"Flip Side, The," 366

Flowers, Alana, 335, 336

Fly, 369, 370

"Fly Away Pretty Little Bird," 129

Flying Fish Records, 132, 154, 182, 230; Hotmud Family on, 195, 196; Laurie Lewis on, 255, 256

Fly Through the Country, 350

Fog City Ramblers, 315

Foggy Mountain Banjo, 294

"Foggy Mountain Breakdown," 73, 212

"Foggy Mountain Home," 206

"Foggy Mountain Locomotion," 212

Folk Variety Label, 99

Folkways Records, 5, 39, 119, 122; American Banjo: Three-Finger and Scruggs Style, 3, 74, 117; Hazel and Alice, 4, 123, 124, 126, 127, 129, 131; Jeanie West, 97, 99

Following a Feeling, 206

Follow Me Back to the Fold: A Tribute to Women in Bluegrass, 111, 160, 341

"Follow the Leader," 235, 340

"Footprints in the Snow," 13, 31, 32, 55

Foreigner, 317

Forget About It, 324

Forrester, Bob, 15, 18, 19

Forrester, Emmie, 16

Forrester, Howdy, 13, 15, 17, 19; with Bill Monroe, 14, 16, 18

Forrester, Joe, 15, 17, 18, 19

Forrester, Sally Ann, 1, 3, 10, 12, 13–19; with Bill Monroe, 9, 11

48th Union Grove Fiddler's Convention (album), 307

Foster, Anne, 184

Foster, Jeremy, 119, 121, 122

Foster, Melissa, 184

Foster Family String Band, 178

Four Bitchin' Babes, 215

Fowler, Bob, 245

Fowler, Wally, 64

Fox, Jon Hartley, 177, 192

Foxfire, 110

"Fox on the Run," 148, 235

Frances Mooney and Fontanna Sunset, 334

"Frankie Belle," 356

"Franklin County Moonshine," 101, 102

Frank Wakefield's Good Ol' Boys, 252

Frazier, Rebecca, 334

Fred Pike, Randy Hawkins, and the Country Nighthawks, 61

"Freeborn Man," 184

Freight and Salvage, The, 244

"Freight Train," 161, 162

French, Bob, 59, 60, 61, 62

French, Grace, 41, 59–62, 204

Friendly Variety Show, The, 87

"Friend of the Devil," 235

Friends For a Lifetime, 272

Friends of Sally Johnson, 142

Frizzell, Lefty, 117, 222

"From the Point of View of Rubye Jane," 199

Front Porch Records, 270

Front Porch String Band, 270, 271, 272, 273, 290

Front Porch String Band (album), 270

Frost, Robert, 112

Furman Boyce and the Harmony Express, 338, 339

Furtado, Gina, 336
Furtado, Tony, 255, 322

Gabriel, Debbie, 208, 209
"Gabriel's Call," 123
Gadd, Pam, 182, 226, 309
Gailey, Wayne, 31
Gaither, Bill, 282
Galax, Virginia, Fiddlers' Convention, 121
Gann, Nelson, 48
Garthwaite, Terry, 242, 261
Garwood, Nancy, 215
Gary Adams and the Bluegrass Gentlemen, 311
Gary Epley and the Cheerful Valley Gang, 105
"Gathering Storm," 129
Gaudreau, Jimmy, 161, 163, 164, 165
Gay, Connie B., 71
Gay Time, 71
Gena Britt Band, 283
Gentry, Beck, 83, 182, 186–91, 285, 286
Gentry, Orville Gibson, 189, 190
Gentry, Robert, 90
Gentry, Roy, 186, 187, 188, 198, 190, 191
Gerber, Nina, 259, 267
Gerrard, Alice, 4, 93, 94, 113–35, 182, 252; about other women, 48, 51, 107, 243
Gerry, Paul, 107, 212
Gerteis, Margaret, 62
GFA Label, 154
Ghost Town, 106
Giant Records, 353, 354
Gibbons, Mary, 258, 315
Gibes, Carmen, 335
Giddyup Kitty, 305
Gilchrist, Sharon, 335, 362, 363, 364, 365
Gilchrist, Sid, 362
Gilchrist, Troy, 362
Gill, Vince, 317
Gillespie, Gail, 132, 133
Gilmore, Harry, 210

"Girl From Galax," 76
Girl From the Red Rose Saloon, The, 310
"Girl I Left In Sunny Tennessee, The," 98
"Girl in the Blue Velvet Band, The," 98
"Girl's Breakdown," 301
Girls Nite Out, 305
Gitlin, Ira, 232
Gladden, Texas, 119
Glaser, Matt, 210
Glassie, Henry, 39
Glaze, Ginny Payne, 11
Glaze, Susie, 256
Glenn, Randy, 333
Gloria Belle and Tennessee Sunshine, 111
Gloria Belle and the Green Mountain Travelers, 107
Gloria Belle Sings and Plays Bluegrass in the Country, 94, 107
Gloryland Records, 95
"God Gave You To Me," 204
Gold, Analise, 335
Gold, Jocelyn, 335
Gold, Shelby, 335
Golden West, 259
Golden West Girls, 101
Gold Heart, 335
Goldmine, 298
Gold Rush, 295
"Gonna Lay Down My Old Guitar," 256
Good, Barbara, 307
Good, Rick, 194, 196
"Goodbye Old Pal," 17
"Goodbye to the Blues," 240
Good N' Live, 265
Good Hearted Woman, 109
Goodman, Herald, 14, 15
Goodman, Steve, 210
Good Morning America, 174
"Good Morning Country Rain," 158, 353
Goodnight Soldier, 308
"Goodnight Soldier," 17
Good Ol' Persons, 32, 182, 242, 305; influence of 241, 243; Kathy Kallick

and 261, 262, 263, 264, 265, 266, 267;
Laurie Lewis and 252, 256
Good Ol' Persons: California Old-Time Blue-grass Music, The, 252, 262
Good Thing Going, 358
Good Time Girl, 225
"Good Woman's Love," 184, 351
Gospel Snake, 248
Gott, Susie, 173
"Gotta Travel On," 38
Graham, Randy, 110
Grammy Awards, 160, 257, 265, 272, 325, 377; Alison Brown, 294, 301; Dixie Chicks, 316, 370; Alison Krauss, 297, 316, 320, 321, 322, 324; Rose Maddox, 11, 33
"Grandma Got Run Over By a Reindeer," 248
Grand National Fiddle Championship, 141
Grand Ole Opry, 23, 79, 360; Alison Krauss, 316, 322; appearances on, 67, 75, 89, 178, 215, 219, 307, 334, 376; influence of listening to, 114, 217; members of, 14, 16, 21, 24, 25, 30; Bill Monroe, 47, 53; Whites, 157, 159
Grant, Bill, 44, 202, 203, 204, 205, 206
Grant, Dale, and Ginger, 151
Grant, Juarez, 203
Grant and Ginger, 151
Grant Street String Band, 241, 253, 254
Grascals, 332, 335, 344
Grass, Food, and Lodging, 230
Grasshoppers, 333
Grass is Blue, The, 332
Grassroots Music in the Upper Cumberland, 3, 44
Grateful Dead, 277
Graves, Buck, 24. *See also* Graves, Josh
Graves, Josh, 173, 204, 205, 246
Gray, Julie, 276, 226, 182. *See also* Madru, Julie
Gray, Sally, 6
Gray, Tom, 49, 55, 109, 168

GRC Records, 152, 153
Grease, 317
Great American Country (GAC), 328
Great High Mountain Tour, 160, 325
"Great Lasagna Rebellion, The," 295
Green, Doug (Ranger Doug), 141, 158
Green, Joe, 142
"Greenback Dollar," 98
Green County Stump Jumpers, 121
Greene, Richard, 318
Green, Green Grass of Home, 61
Greenhays Records, 132
Green Linnet Records, 302
Greenwich Village, 97
Greer, Bonnie, 95
Greer, Jim, 95
Greer, Valeda, 95
Greer Sisters and Little Brother Jimmy, 95
Grey, Lynn (Salls), 306
"Grey Eagle," 141, 318
Grey Fox Festival, 6, 292
"Griddle in the Middle," 265
Grier, David, 259, 272
Grier, Lamar, 83, 121, 122, 125
Griffin, Buddy, 225, 226
Griffith, Nanci, 215
Grimes, Casey, 333
Grindstaff, Anita, 305
Grisman, David, 121, 122, 124, 247
"Groundhog," 77
Gruenbaum, Marvin, 365
Gruhn, George, 155
G-Stringers, 144
Guesthouse, 258
Gypsy Heart, 307
Gypsy Moon, 215

Haas, Brittany, 259, 335, 383
Haber, Jill, 247
Haggard, Merle, 33
Haines, Diana, 285
Haines, Jack, 285
Hale, Donnie, 30, 33

Haley, Jackie, 222, 223
Haley Sisters, 222
Hall, John, 55
Hall, Tom T., 65, 82
Halos and Horns, 332
Hamilton County Bluegrass Band, 6
Hand of the Higher Power, 313
"Handy Man," 237
Haney, Carlton, 30–31, 48; festivals, 66, 207, 210, 211
Haney, Wilma Jean, 42
Haney Family, 42
Happy Goodman Family, 64
Happy Hollow String Band, 305
"Happy On My Way," 87
Hardhitting Songs For Hard Hit People, 129
Harding, Earla, 6
Hardly Strictly Bluegrass Festival, 131
Harlan County, USA, 129
Harman, Mike, 320
Harman, Tammy, 335
Harmon, Buddy, 65
Harmon, Lori, 313
Harmony Grits, 184
Harmony Pie, 132
Harmony Sisters, 132, 133
Harmony Sisters: The Early Years, The, 132
Harper, Betty, 11
Harrell, Bill, 166, 167, 169, 172, 338
Harris, Emmylou, 157, 159, 163, 192, 205, 364
Harris, Ludie, 18
Harris, Mickey, 342, 345, 356
Harry and Jeanie West: Country Music in the Bluegrass Style, 97
Harry and Jeanie West Fine Musical Instruments, 99
Hartford, John, 213. 225, 257
Hartz, Danita, 141
Harvard Square, 144
Harvard University, 231, 293, 295, 296, 320
Harvey, Dave, 188, 189, 273, 339

Harvey, Jan Snider, 339
Harvey, Paul, 283
Harvey, Peggy Ann, 283
Hatley, Sandy Crisco, 305, 165, 182
"Haunted House," 73
"Haunted Kind," 288
Have A Cuppa 'Jo, 377
Hazel Dickens Memorial Scholarship, 335
Hawker, Ginny, 130, 131
"Hawkins Rag," 195
Haynie, Aubrey, 356
Hazel and Alice, 113–34, 252, 256, 383. *See also* Hazel Dickens and Alice Gerrard
Hazel and Alice, 126
Hazel Dickens and Alice Gerrard, 4, 51, 94, 252. *See also* Hazel and Alice
Hazel Dickens and Alice Gerrard, 126
Head Cleaner, 166, 171
"Head Over Heels," 147
"Heartaches Keep on Coming," 73
Heartbreak Hotel, 154
Heart of a Singer, 28, 130
Heart of Gold, 155
Heart's Desire, 315
"Heart That Will Never Break Again, A," 353
Hedgecoth, John, 246, 248
Hedgecoth, Lynn Hayes, 165, 184, 248
Hee Haw, 69, 81
Hee Haw Honeys, 81
Heilbrun, Carolyn, 1
He Leadeth Me, 111
Hello City Limits, 234
Hell on Wheels, 79
"Hello Stranger," 195
"Hello To the Blues," 101
"Help Me Climb That Mountain," 233, 237
"He Made a Woman Out of Me," 225
Henry, Casey, 1, 183, 184, 185, 283, 335, 336, 378
Henry, Christopher, 184, 185
Henry, Murphy Hicks, 221, 280, 336. *See also* Hicks, Murphy
Henry, Red, 2, 183, 184, 185

Herald Angels, 132
"Here Today," 259
Herman, Woody, 154, 244, 245, 246
Herrmann, Irene, 132
Hess, Clay, 381
Hickman, John, 33, 294, 295
Hickory Records, 24
Hickory Wind, 270
"Hickory Wind," 224
Hicks, Argen, 2, 183
Hicks, Bobby, 353
Hicks, Claire, 2
Hicks, Jack, 158, 159
Hicks, Laurie, 2, 183
Hicks, Murphy, 219. See also Henry, Murphy Hicks
Hicks, Nancy, 2, 183
High Class Bluegrass & Other Road Side Attractions, 230
High Country (band), 243, 244, 247, 261, 263
High Country (High Country), 244
High Country (Kenny Baker and Joe Greene), 142
"High Ground," 152
High Hills, 305
"High On A Mountain Top," 36
Hightone Records, 258
Highway 111, 334
High Windows, 295
Hill, Joe, 129
Hill, Katy, 119
Hillbettys, 305
Hillbilly Ranch (Boston), 61, 144
Hillbilly Ranch (Maine), 44
"Hills of Glory," 50
Hi-Lo Country, The, 33
Hindman Settlement School, 176, 179
Hinson, Marlene, 2
Hired Hands, 247, 249
Hirshon, Karen, 235, 182
Hitchcock, Michael, 194
Hobbs, Connie, 2, 4, 182

Hobbs, Pam, 2
Hobbs, Smiley, 124
Hoffman, Richard, 147
Hogan, Arval, 338
Holcomb, Roscoe, 132
Holcomb, Wendy, 182
Hold the Anchovies, 247
Holdin' Things Together, 352
"Holdin' Things Together," 352
Holland, Lee, 292
Holliday, Billie, 223
Hollon, Noah, 42
Hollyding, 133
Hollywood Hillbilly Jamboree, 18
Hollywood Records, 65
Hollywood Troubadour, 77
Home, 370, 371
Homemade American Music, 114, 132
"Home on the Radar Range," 366
Homer and Jethro, 187, 188
Homestead Act, 165, 248
Home Sweet Highway, 309
Hometown Jamboree, 242
Honey in the Rock, 166
Honi Deaton and Dream, 343
Honky Tonk Christmas, 322
Hooker Holler Symphony, 285
"Hopelessly in Love," 36
Hopkins, Gary, 197, 199, 200
Horowitz, Sharon, 283
Hosmer, Tom, 209, 210
Hotmud Family, 192, 194, 195, 196, 197, 198, 199
Hot Rize, 114, 255
Howard, Randy, 317
"How Far Is Heaven," 347, 354
Howie, Lori, 312
How Many Biscuits Can You Eat, 308
"How's the World Treating You?" 327
"How Will I Explain About You?" 47
Huber Banjos, 377
Hubert Davis and the Season Travelers, 146, 246

Huck Finn Jubilee, 376

Huffman, Scott, 259

Hug, Barbara, 140

Hughes, Donna, 334

Hughes, Lena, 213

Hughes, Pam, 182

Hugo, Oklahoma, Festival, 44, 66, 95, 203

Hull, Sierra, 282, 331, 334, 381, 382, 383

Humphrey, Jim, 366

Humphrey, Mark, 4

Hundred Miles Or More: A Collection, A, 327

Hungry Charley's, 208, 209

Hunter, Erica, 306

Hurst, Jim, 199, 272, 273, 274, 290, 291

Hurt, Mississippi John, 119, 162

Husky, Junior, Sr., 49

Hutchison, John D., 206

Hylton, Randall, 65

"I Ain't Domesticated Yet," 184

"I Ain't Gonna Work Tomorrow," 23

"I Believe I'm Entitled to You," 55

"I Believe in Forever," 274

IBMA Annual Awards: Album, 239, 289, 290, 332, 335, 355, 382; Banjo Player, 293, 298, 344, 377, 382; Bass Player, 284. 290, 291; Distinguished Achievement Award, 21, 33, 39, 67, 70, 90, 112, 114, 118, 204, 240, 253; Emerging Artist, 310, 335, 376, 382; Female Vocalist, 233, 250, 256, 257, 272, 274, 282, 310, 320, 346, 355, 356, 377; Fiddle Player, 138, 239, 294, 320; Guitar Player, 155, 291; Instrumental Album, 239, 289, 290; Mandolin Player, 331, 334; Recorded Event, 111, 199, 334, 341; Song, 130, 233, 257, 343, 377

IBMA: Awards Show, 1, 111, 257, 320, 355; Board of Directors, 173, 233; Hall of Fame, 5, 49, 67, 172, 383; Trade Show and Fan Fest, 111, 131, 312, 313; World of Bluegrass, 111, 291, 292, 366, 381

"I Came On Business For the King," 350

"I Can Love You Better," 369

"I Can See God's Changing Hand," 87

"I Can't Believe," 231

"I Can't Find Your Love Anymore," 130

"I Can't Get You Off Of My Mind," 320

"I Can't Stand to Ramble," 262

Ida Lee Nagger, 81

"If I Needed You," 230

"If It Ain't Love (Let's Leave It Alone)," 160

"If Mommy Didn't Sing," 103

"If You Don't Love Your Neighbor," 196

"I Got A Song to Sing," 219

IIIrd Tyme Out, 199, 341

IInd Generation: Martha Adcock and, 171, 172; Wendy Thatcher and, 161, 164, 165, 166, 167

"I Know What It Means To Be Lonesome," 99

"I'll Be All Smiles Tonight," 203

"I'll Fly Away," 212, 260

"I Love Bluegrass," 191

"I'm a Believer," 363

"I'm Gonna Be the Wind," 255

"I'm Just Here to Get My Baby Out of Jail," 17

"I'm Lonely Tonight," 11

In A Little Village Churchyard, 99

"In Despair," 51

Indigo Girls, 302

I Need The Prayers of Those I Love: Old Time Sacred Picking & Singing, 99

In God's Eyes, 158

Ingram, Kenny, 356, 358

"In My Girlish Days," 190

Inoue, Saburo, 381

Inside Out, 292

Inside the Gate, 154

Instrumental Tribute to Brother Oswald, 94

International Bluegrass, 6

International Bluegrass Music Museum (IBMM), 62, 111

"In the Cool, Cool, Cool of the Evening," 222

Ironing Board Lady, 81
Irwin, Ken, 128, 206, 231, 305, 318, 321, 325
Isaacs, Becky, 282
Isaacs, Ben, 282
Isaacs, Joe, 282
Isaacs, Lily, 282
Isaacs, Sonya, 282
Isaacs, The, 282
"I Saw Her Standing There," 277
"I Saw Him Standing There," 363
I Saw the Light, 47
I See God, 341
"Is Zat You Myrtle?" 101
"I Thought I Heard You Calling My Name," 196
It's Called Nuance, 191
"It's Hard to Tell the Singer From the Song," 130
It's Hard to Tell the Singer From the Song (album), 130
It's Hard to Tell The Singer From the Song (film), 114
"It's Might Dark to Travel," 152
"It Wasn't God Who Made Honky-Tonk Angels," 50
"I've Endured," 36
"I've Got My Future On Ice," 108
I've Got That Old Feeling, 297, 320, 321
"I've Got That Old Feeling," 322
"I Want to be a Cowboy's Sweetheart," 365
"I Want To Be Loved," 204
"I Wonder How the Old Folks are at Home," 77

"Jack and Lucy," 206
Jackson, Alan, 316, 322, 326
Jackson, Carl, 89, 205
Jackson, Mahalia, 67
Jackson, Wanda, 117
"Jambalaya," 61
James, Dian, 29, 204, 242
Jamup and Honey, 16

Janet Davis Music Company, 94
Jarrell, Tommy, 114, 132, 133
Jay, Penny (Helen Morgan), 108
"Jazzbo Brown," 189
J. D. Crowe and the Kentucky Mountain Boys, 164
J. D. Crowe and the New South, 317, 377
Jeanette Williams and Clearwater, 333
Jeanette Williams Band, 333
Jeanie West: Country Bluegrass featuring Harry West, 99
Jeff, Roberts, 221, 225, 226
Jesus Has Called Me, 43
Jim and Jesse and the Virginia Boys, 2, 89, 183, 219, 322, 350
Jim McCall, Vernon McIntyre and the Appalachian Grass, 224
Jim McCall, Vernon McIntyre and the Appalachian Grass (band), 223
Jimmy Martin and His Sunny Mountain Boys, 104, 108
Joan Baez, 97
Joe Val and the New England Bluegrass Boys, 61, 62
John Herald Band, 282
Johnson, Arnold, 157
Johnson, Lois, 103, 106, 108
Johnson, Mindy (Rakestraw), 183, 286
Johnson, Peggy, 44, 157
Johnson, Polly, 184
Johnson, Rachel Renee (Boyd), 383
Johnson Mountain Boys, 185, 206, 236, 237, 238; Gloria Belle and, 110, 111; Hazel Dickens and, 114, 128, 130
"Jole John," 101
jon da peripatetic poet, 113
Jones, Carol Elizabeth, 130, 197
Jones, Chris, 314, 343
Jones, George, 117, 204, 205
Jones, Grandpa, 81
Jones, Kathy, 307
Jones, Patsy, 87
Jones, Phylls, 309

Jones, Ramona, 179
Jones, Rebecca, 36
Jones, Sally, 311, 313, 314, 342, 343, 345
Jones and Leva, 130
Joplin, Janis, 152, 261
Jordan, Gilda, 103
Jordan, Lorraine, 305, 333
Jorosz, Sarah, 335
Josephson, Nancy, 209, 212, 214
Joshua, 348
Journal of American Folklore, 3
Journal of Country Music, 325, 364, 366
Journey of August King, 129
Joy of Cooking, 241
Jubilee, 257
Judd, Naomi, 113
Judd, Wynonna, 113
Judith Edelman Band, 334
"July, You're a Woman," 152
"Just a Closer Walk With Thee," 55
"Just Any Day Now," 350
Just For the Record, 199
Justice, Kay, 130, 131
Just When We're Thinking It's Over, 322

Kaleidoscope Records, 256, 262, 264
Kallick, Dodi, 260, 267
Kallick, Kathy, 204, 242, 246, 249,
    260–68, 283; bandleader, 182, 195,
    281; Laurie Lewis and, 252, 254, 256,
    257, 259; on Rose Maddox, 32, 34
Kannapel, Cathy, 307
"Kansas City Kitty," 196
Kaplan, Kathy, 202, 204
K-Ark Records, 219
Kate and Bill, 150
Kathy Kallick and the Little Big Band, 264
Kathy Kallick Band, 266, 267, 268
Katie Laur All-Girl Bluegrass Band, 227
Katie Laur Band, 221, 225, 226
Katie Penn Band, 334
Katz, Nancy, 142
Kave, Ford, 55

Kave, Virginia, 55
Keener, Jenee, 343
"Keep on the Sunny Side," 160
Keep the Light On, 232
Keith, Bill, 49, 51, 52, 106
Keith, Toby, 326
Keith Case and Associates, 319
Kenilworth Mountain Boys, 230
Kennedy Center, 178
Kenny and Amanda Smith, 382
Kentucky Colonels, 242
Kentucky Educational Television, 178
Kentucky Fried Chicken Festival, 254
Kentucky Sweethearts, 16
Kentucky 31, 227
"Kentucky Waltz," 13, 17
Kentucky Warblers, 197
Kerrville Folk Festival, 365
Kiamichi Moon, 206
Kiamichi Mountain Boys, 205
Kiamichi Mountain Songbird, 204, 205
Kiamichi Records, 203
Kidwell, Erma, 57
Kidwell, Van, 195
KIHN (Hugo, Okla.), 203
Kilby, Cody, 343, 345
King, Beverly, 6, 94, 182, 213
King, Joy, 110
King Records, 75
King's Row, 223, 224
Kingston Trio, 94, 169
Kirby, Oswald, 94
"Kiss Me Before I Die," 257
Kitty Label, 42
KMMJ (Grand Island, Neb.), 22
Knee Deep in Bluegrass, 46
Knight, Laura Wallace, 335
Knipher, Glenda Faye, 182
"Knoxville Girl," 97
Koppel, Barbara, 129
Kosek, Kenny, 210
Koskela, Cory, 307, 308
Koskela, Kim, 307

Koskela, Robin, 307
Koskela, Sue, 307
Kowalski, Amanda, 381
Krauss, Alison, 131, 192, 231, 307,
    316–29, 337, 352; awards, 382, 383;
    bandleader, 310, 331, 356; Alison
    Brown and, 293, 297, 298, 303; influ-
    ence, 334, 381; Rounder Records and,
    128, 282, 322, 355
Krauss, Fred, 317
Krauss, Louise, 317, 318
Krauss, Viktor, 317, 318, 324
Kristin Scott, 340
KTRB (Modesto, Cal.), 29
Kuhn, Buck, 154
Kuhn, Kathy, 308
Kuykendall, Marion, 6
Kuykendall, Pete, 55, 57, 121, 122, 166
KVOO (Tulsa, Okla.), 14, 15
KWFT (Wichita Falls, Tex.), 15

Lambert, LaVaughn (Tomlin), 43
Lambert, L. W., 43
Lambert, Pee Wee, 83
Lanark Records, 270
Lanham, Charmaine, 244, 246
Lanham, Marty, 246
Lantana Ramblers, 45
Larry Cordle and Lonesome Standard
    Time, 343
Larry Stephenson Band, 337, 339, 340, 344
Larson, Leah, 256
Late to Work, 230, 231
Lauderdale, Jim, 377
Laur, Jack, 223
Laur, Katie, 166, 182, 221–28
Laurie Lewis and Grant Street, 241, 255,
    320
Laurie Lewis and Her Bluegrass Pals, 258
Laurie Lewis and Her Bluegrass Pals, 258
Laurie Lewis and the Right Hands, 259
Laurie Lewis and the Right Hands: Live, 259
Lavender, Cathy, 309

Lavender Lullaby, 351
Lavin, Christine, 215, 342
Lavonia, Ga., Bluegrass Festival, 2, 216,
    218
Lawson, Doyle, 338
Lay, Linda, 334
"Lay Down Beside Me," 328
Leading Role, The, 36
Leary, Gerry, 26
Leary, Jake, 21, 22, 26
Leary, Wilma Lee. See Cooper, Wilma Lee
Leary Family, 21
Leather Records, 26, 270
"Leaving Cottondale," 294, 301
Ledford, Lily May, 132, 308. See also Lily
    May Ledford and the Coon Creek Girls
Led Zeppelin, 328
Lee, Jessica, 333
Lee, Judy (Alice Schreiber), 101, 102, 103
Leech, Bob, 243
"Lee Highway Blues," 76
"Lee Highway Ramble," 140
Lees, Gene, 245
Leet, Charlie, 191, 198
Leet, Mary Jo (Dickman), 131, 189, 191,
    198, 200
Leftwich, Brad, 133
Lege, Patty Mitchell, 365
"Legend in My Time," 165
"Legend of the Dogwood Tree," 24
Lenker, Lee Ann (Baber), 182, 275–80
Leno, Jay, 316
Leonard, Joan "Nondi," 210
Lester Flatt and Earl Scruggs, 24, 37, 245,
    247, 312, 323, 355
Lester Flatt and the Nashville Grass, 2
"Letter From My Darling," 51
Letterman, David, 316, 382
Leva, James, 130
Levin, Nelle, 214, 215
Lewis, "Mom" (Pauline Holloway), 63, 64,
    65, 66, 67
Lewis, Chris, 315

Lewis, Esley, 63

Lewis, Huey, 317

Lewis, Janis, 2, 3, 63, 64, 67, 68, 170, 383

Lewis, Laurie, 34, 182, 204, 242, 249,
  250–59, 291, 355, 381; bandleader,
  195, 281, 310, 320; as fiddle, 181, 381;
  and Hazel and Alice, 114, 123, 131; and
  Kathy Kallick, 261, 264, 265; working
  with other women, 236, 341

Lewis, Little Roy, 63, 66, 68, 170

Lewis, Miggie, 2, 3, 63, 64, 66, 67, 170,
  383

Lewis, Mosley, 63

Lewis, Polly, 2, 3, 63, 64, 66, 67, 170, 383

Lewis, Roy "Pop," 63, 64, 66, 67

Lewis, Talmadge, 63

Lewis, Travis, 67, 68

Lewis, Wallace, 63, 64, 67

Lewis Brothers, 64

Lewis Family, 41, 63–68, 159, 178; influence, 2, 166, 170, 218, 364, 375

Lewis Family Tradition, 68

Liberty Pike, 332

Lifetime in the Making, A, 159

Lighthouse Label, 354

Like Red on a Rose, 326

"Li'l Jack Slade," 371

Lillimae and the Dixie Gospel-Aires, 43

Lilly Brothers, 61

Lilly, Mike, 193

Lily May Ledford and the Coon Creek
  Girls, 10, 119. *See also* Ledford, Lily May

Lin, Betty, 182, 308

Lincoln Center, 178

"Lindy, Lindy," 196

Lines and Traces, 271

Little, Keith, 33, 262, 264

"Little Bessie," 121, 225

"Little Birdie," 106

"Little Black Pony," 237

Little Feat, 364

Littlefield, Alexandra, 245

Littlefield, Tom (father), 245

Littlefield, Tommy (son), 245

"Little Georgia Rose," 51

"Little Girl In Tennessee," 74

"Little Maggie," 212, 305

"Little Margaret," 98

Little Nell Walker Band, 44

Little Ol' Cowgirl, 366, 367

Little Orphan Girl, 14, 15

"Little Rosewood Casket," 23

Little Smoke, 235

Little Sparrow, 332

Live, As We Know It, 196

Live Oak Label, 266, 268

Liza Jane and Sally Anne, 158

Lloyd, Darrell, 91

Loftin, Dan, 149

Logan, Jerry, 256

Logan, Tex, 124

Lo, I Am With You, 43

Lonely Old Depot, 313

Lonely Runs Both Ways, 327, 328

Lonesome River Band, 199, 381

"Lonesome Road Blues," 74

Long, Mike, 111

Long, Rebekah, 333

Long Journey, 199

"Long Journey," 199

Look Into Your Heart, 231

Look Left, 298

"Loose Talk," 31

"Lord I'm Coming Home," 108

"Lorena," 57

Lorraine Jordan and Carolina Road, 305,
  334

"Lost Ball in the High Weeds," 77

Lost River Ramblers, 230

Lou and Sonny Osborne and the Stoney
  Mountain Boys, 42

Lou Osborne and the Osborne Family, 42

Lou Reid and Carolina, 283

Louisiana Hayride, 101, 103

Louisville Symphony Orchestra, 177

Louvin, Charley, 352

Love Chooses You, 291
Loveless, Patty, 335, 271, 298, 332
Love Light, 273
Love of the Mountains, The, 110
"Lovesick Blues," 225
"Love the One You're With," 153
Lovett, Lyle, 317, 324
"Love Will Find You Again," 274
Loyal Records, 87, 88
"Lubbock Or Leave It," 372
"Lucky One, The," 327
Lundy, T. J., 197, 306
Lundy, Ted, 38
Lyle, Rudy, 83
Lynch, Christie, 271
Lynch, Claire, 150, 151, 195, 269–74,
    290, 310, 364, 383
Lynch, Kegan, 271
Lynch, Larry, 269–73
Lynch, Laura, 363, 364–69
Lynch, Megan, 335
Lynn, Loretta, 205, 366
Lynn Morris Band, 233, 236, 237, 239,
    313, 320
Lynyrd Skynyrd, 317

Mackay, Maggie, 336
MacKenzie, Kate, 281, 282
Mac-O-Chee Valley Folks, 95
Macon, Uncle Dave, 119
Ma Crowe and the Lady Slippers, 305
Macy, Robin Lynn, 362–67
Maddox, Cal, 29, 30
Maddox, Charlie, 29
Maddox, Cliff, 29, 30
Maddox, Don, 30
Maddox, Fred, 29, 30
Maddox, Foncy, 29
Maddox, Lula, 29, 30
Maddox, Rose, 28–34, 58, 98, 201; early
    woman in bluegrass, 3, 10, 11; influ-
    ence of, 105, 107, 117, 244, 353, 356
Maddox Brothers and Rose, 28, 29, 30

*Maddox Brothers and Rose 1947–1951, Vol. 1
    and 2,* 32
Madru, Julie Gray, 276, 226, 182. *See also*
    Gray, Julie
Magnificent Music Machine, 82
Magone, Barbara McDonald, 319
Mainer, Wade and J. E., 97
Maines, Lloyd, 366, 367, 369, 370, 371,
    373
Maines, Natalie, 325, 361, 368, 369, 371,
    372, 373
Main Street, 226
"Making Believe," 158
Malicote, Marcie (Newhart), 283
"Mama's Hand," 130, 233
Mama's Hand, 238
Mandrell, Nelson, 317, 319
M & M Blues, 4
"Man in the Middle, The," 197, 203
"Man of Constant Sorrow," 325
"Mannington Mine Disaster, The," 125, 129
Manzer, Cathy, 80
"Maple Sugar," 111
Marin Violin, 254
"Marmalaid," 213
Marosz, Kathy, 243
"Married Men," 227
Marshall, Donna, 95
Marshall, Judy, 95
Marshall, Mike, 300
Marshall Family, 95, 178
Martha and the Walton Brothers, 169
Martha White Bluegrass Express, 323
Martha White Foods, 323, 355
"Martha White Theme," 355
Martin, Benny, 205
Martin, Dottie Lou, 43, 44
Martin, Janice, 335
Martin, Jeana, 335
Martin, Jimmy, 42, 236; Gloria Belle and
    104, 106, 108–10, 170, 338; influence
    of 169, 261, 378
Martin, Larita, 335

Martin, Roy, 218
Martin, Slim, 43
Martin, Steve, 382
Martin, Wilma, 43
Martinez, Patricia, 90
Marty Raybon and the American Bluegrass
    Express, 2
Marxer, Marcy, 10, 36, 182, 255, 381
"Mary Dear," 57
"Mary Johnson," 127
Mason, Molly, 255
Masters, The, 289
Masters, The (group), 173, 289
Masters of the 5-String Banjo, 184, 233,
    293, 297
Masters of the Folk Violin Tour, 319
Matewan, 129
Mathis, Amanda, 311
Mattea, Kathy, 271
Matters of the Heart, 264
Mauldin, Bessie Lee, 3, 41, 46–53
McBride, Kenny, 55
McCaffrey, Anne, 214
McCall, Jim, 223, 224, 227
McCasland, Tim, 369
McClinton, Delbert, 298
McCormick, Megan, 155, 292, 333
McCormick, Sheila Hogan, 310
McCormick Brothers, 106
McCoury, Del, 36, 49, 52, 138, 261, 378
McCown, Ada, 283
McCown, Jim, 283
McCreesh, Tom, 196
McEntire, Reba, 309, 322, 326, 335, 361
McGee, Hazel, 283
McGee, Mac, 283
McGraw, Sharon, 6
McGuire, Gareth, 373
McKee, Suzi, 182, 243, 247, 248
McKinney, James, 362, 363
McLain, Alice, 2, 175–79; early mandolin
    player, 94, 182; influence, 364
McLain, Betty, 175, 176, 178, 179

McLain, Jennifer, 179
McLain, Michael, 176, 178, 179, 272
McLain, Nancy Ann, 176, 178, 179
McLain, Raymond K., 175–79
McLain, Raymond W., 175–79
McLain, Ruth, 2, 175, 177, 178, 179, 182;
    influence, 284, 364
McLain Family, 175–79
McLain Family Band, 175, 176
McLain Family Band, 176
McLain Family Band Family Festival, 178
McLaughlin, David, 130, 185, 206
McLaughlin, Peter, 256
McLean, Don, 209
McLerie, Jeanie, 132
McNeely, Larry, 294, 306
McReynolds, Jesse, 173, 350
"Me and Jesus," 247
Meat and Potatoes & Stuff Like That, 197
Meginniss, Andy, 271
Melting Pots, 213
Memories That Bless and Burn, 199
"Memories That Bless and Burn," 199
"Memory of Your Smile, The," 203
Memphis Beck, 186, 189, 190. *See also*
    Gentry, Beck
Memphis Beck and the Red Hots, 190
Mendlesohn, Barbara, 251, 252, 261
Menotti, Gian Carol, 176
"Mental Cruelty," 31
Mercury Records, 117, 153
Meredith, Jennifer Kennedy, 381
MGM Records, 70, 78, 83, 163
Michael, Walt, 210
Michael Cleveland and Flamekeeper, 240
Michelle Nixon and Drive, 334
Michelson, Albert, 119
Mid-Day Merry-Go-Round, 217
Midnight Flyer," 349
Midnight in the Garden of Good and Evil, 316
Mike Seeger: Second Annual Farewell Reunion,
    117
Miller, Jackie, 311

Miller, John, 210

Miller, Sonny, 37, 38

Miller, Wendy, 193

Milovsoroff, Ann, 52

"Milwaukee, Here I Come," 104, 108

Missy Raines and Jim Hurst (band), 199, 273, 291. *See also* Raines, Missy

Missy Raines and the New Hip, 155, 292. *See also* Raines, Missy

Misty River, 10, 19

Mitchell, Bill, 142

Mitchell, Joni, 209

Mitchell Family, 365

Mitterhoff, Barry, 130, 210, 230

Moffit, Hugh, 206

Moje, Peggy, 243

"Molly and Tenbrooks," 31

Monday, Jerry, 79, 80

Monick, Susie, 4, 154, 182, 276; and Buffalo Gals, 207–15

Monroe, Bill, 4, 65, 83, 96, 183, 187, 200, 296, 366; Sally Ann Forrester and 11, 14; influence, 23, 152, 164, 170, 212, 223, 261, 312, 358, 376; influence on Betty Fisher, 216, 218, 219; influence on Hazel and Alice, 114, 119, 123, 124; influence on Kathy Kallick, 262, 263, 265, 266, 268; influence on Laurie Lewis, 254, 258, 259; influence on Donna Stoneman 42, 72, 74, 75, 76, 78, 79; influence on Dede Wyland, 229, 244; Bessie Lee and 3, 46, 47, 48, 50, 51, 52, 53; Rose Maddox and, 28, 30, 31, 98; side musicians, 106, 145, 147, 158, 172; Sullivan Family and 87, 88, 89, 90; Vivian Williams and 138, 141. *See also* Bill Monroe and the Blue Grass Boys

Monroe, Carolyn, 46, 47, 48, 52

Monroe, Charlie, 43, 97, 109, 119

Monroe, J. B., 259

Monroe, James, 52

Monroe, Malissa, 259

Monroe, Melissa, 47, 50, 67

Monroe Brothers, 47, 58

Monroe Crossing, 335

Monroe Doctrine, 229

Montana, Patsy, 29, 244

Monterey Folk Festival, 77

Montgomery, Melba, 205

Monument Records, 369

Mooney's Irish Pub, 244

Moonlighter, 272

Moonlighters, The, 143, 144, 145

Moonshine Kate, 10

Moonshiner, 381

Morehead State University's Kentucky Center for Traditional Music, 179

More of Benny and Vallie Cain, 57

Morgan, Tom, 55, 97

Morris, Connie Freeman, 2, 182, 286

Morris, Edward, 357

Morris, Lynn, 182, 231, 233–40, 265, 355, 364; bandleader, 195, 281, 291, 310; banjo player, 4, 181, 184, 341; and Hazel Dickens, 114, 130, 131

Mother of Pearl, 215, 305

Mountain Folk Dance and Music Festival, 97

Mountain Home Records, 309

Mountain Laurel (band), 335

Mountain Music Bluegrass Style, 5

Mountain Soul, 332

MsBehavin', 225

Muhlenbrink's Saloon, 152

"Muleskinner Blues," 348, 349, 351, 357

Muleskinner News, 177, 212

Muller, Jim, 283

Mulligan Music, 302

Mullins, Paul, 193

Mundy, Frances (Mooney), 2, 286

"Murder On Music Row," 343

Murphy, John, 80

Murphy Method, The, 184, 185

"Musette For a Palindrome," 302

"My Better Years," 123

"My Dirty, Lowdown, Rotten, Cotton
  Pickin' Little Darlin'," 78
*My Epitaph: A Documentary in Song and
  Lyric*, 39
"My Everyday Silver Is Plastic," 184
"My Family," 265
"My Little Girl," 57
My Mother's Voice, 267
"My Pathway Leads to Oklahoma," 203
My Place in the Sun, 290
"My Wandering Boy," 195

Nagle, Frankie, 335, 383
Nakamura, Katie, 335
Nashville Kitty Kats, 109
Nashville Network, The, 255, 321, 351
Nashville Now, 368
National Council for the Traditional Arts,
  319
National Folk Festival, 21
National Heritage Award, 35, 39, 113, 132
National Oldtime Fiddlers' Contest, 138
Natural Symphonies Label, 298
"Nature Boy," 119
Neff, Ed, 246
Nelson, James, 6
Nelson, Tracy, 261
Nelson, Willie, 231
Nemerov, Bruce, 246
Nethery, Carol, 182
New Coon Creek Girls, 182, 282, 305,
  308–10, 312, 314
New Country, 255
New Day, 269, 273
New Dreams and Sunshine, 352
New Favorite, 325
"New Freedom Bell," 42
New Grange, 300
New Grange, 300
New Grass Revival, 317, 350, 351
New Hip, The, 155, 288, 292
New Lost City Ramblers, 125
Newport Folk Festival, 50, 124, 318

Newport Folk Festival, 124
New Riders of the Purple Sage, 114
New River Boys and Girls, 35, 36, 37, 39,
  306
New River Ranch, 5, 37, 38
New River Records, 38
"New River Train," 57, 177
Newsweek, 320
Newton, Mark, 111, 160, 341
New Vintage, 283, 313
New York Slew, 244
New York Times, 319, 323
Next Best Thing, 357
Nickel Creek, 10, 321, 322, 325, 326, 382
Nickel Creek, 326
"Nick's Noodle," 318
Nickson, Dave, 144
"Nine Pound Hammer," 97
Nitchie, Donald, 336
"Nobody Loves Me," 17, 18, 19
No Depression, 257, 324, 361, 372
"No Help Wanted," 101
"No Never No," 125
North Carolina Folk Heritage Award, 132
North Carolina Ridge Runners, 37
Northern Lights, 295, 296
Norton, Katie, 336
"No School Bus in Heaven," 196
"Not Ready to Make Nice," 372
No Use Frettin', 236
Now That I've Found You: A Collection, 317,
  323, 324
NPR (National Public Radio), 366, 373
Nuance and Uncles, 191
Nugent, Alicia, 377, 334
Nygaard, Scott, 255, 256

Oak and the Laurel, The, 257, 258
O'Brien, Tim, 255, 259, 300
O Brother, Where Art Thou? 157, 160, 316,
  324, 325, 332, 370, 382
O'Bryan, Mike "Fog," 191
O'Connor, Mark, 317

O'Day, Molly, 10, 192; influence, 98, 105, 107, 111, 114, 119; women compared to, 88, 203, 350

O'Dell, Holly, 311

Oden, Mitzi, 307

Oermann, Robert, 3, 10, 27, 181

O'Hara, Scarlett, 254

Ohio Heritage Fellowship, 227

Ohio River Valley Boys, 186, 187

Okeh Records, 70

Olabelle (group), 36

Ola Belle Reed, 39

Ola Belle Reed and Family, 39

Ola Belle Reed Homecoming Festival, 36

Old Crossroads, The," 31, 32, 254

Old Crossroad, The, 43

Old Dominion Barn Dance, 30

Old Friends, 253

"Old Home Place," 145

Old Homestead Records, 78, 82, 99, 206, 247

"Old Joe Clark," 106, 306

"Old Love Letters," 257

"Old Man," 165

"Old Man at the Mill," 145

Old Photographs, 191

"Old Rip," 238

"Old River," 130

Old Town, 321

"Old Train," 33

Old-Time Herald, 5, 114, 118, 133, 134

Old Time Picking Parlor, 153, 154, 165, 171

Old-Time Way, The, 132

Olsen, Lee, 236

"O My Malissa," 258

"On and On," 51

O'Neill, Trish, 6

"One I Love Is Gone, The," 124

One Morning in May," 119

One Step Ahead, 356

On Fire, 341

"Only the Leading Role Will Do," 36

On The Move, 138

On The Road, 81

Open Wide Records, 361, 370

Opryland, 246, 363

"Orange Blossom Special," 76, 82, 141, 277, 306

Original Country Gentlemen, 49, 172

Orlove, Harry, 210

Ornstein, Lisa, 198

Osborne, Bobby, 42

Osborne, Lou (Willliams), 42

Osborne, Sonny, 42, 145, 344

Osborne Brothers, 2, 33, 42, 79, 121, 322; influence, 170, 193, 219, 349

O Sister, 332

O Sister 2, 332

Our Point of View, 309

Outdoor Plumbing Company, 283

Out in the Country, 271

Out of the Blue, 300

Outlet Recordings, 287

Owen, Tim, 178

Owens, Andy, 362, 363, 365

Owens, Buck, 31, 33

Paisley, Brad, 316, 327, 328

Paley, Tom, 97

Palmer, John, 107

Palm Tree Records, 189

Papa Lou Records, 191

"Paradise," 235

Paragon, The, 246

Parents' Choice Award, 264

Parish, Leone, 132

Parish, Roscoe, 132

Parker, Conizene, 43

Parker, Dan, 224

Parker, Rex and Eleanor, 43

Parker, Rexana, 43

Parker Family, 43

Parmley, David, 352

Parsons, Gram, 224, 230

Part of a Story, 262

Parton, Dolly, 114, 243, 332, 344, 382;
    and Alison Krauss, 316, 322; and
    Rhonda Vincent, 348, 355, 359
Pasdar, Adrian, 373
Pasdar, Becket, 373
Pasdar, Slade, 373
Patchwork Heart, 332
"Pathway of Teardrops," 349
Patsy Stoneman Show, 77
Patterson, Charlie, 144, 145
Patty Mitchell Band, 334
Patuxent Music, 82, 232
Paul's Saloon, 246, 247, 249, 251, 252,
    261, 315
Payne, Myrtie, 11
P.D.Q. Bach, 177
Peck, Debbie, 156, 184
Pennell, John, 317, 318, 319
People, 369, 371
People Weekly, 318
Perry, Ian, 340
Perry, Pam, 309, 310
Personettes, 262
Peter, Paul, and Mary, 169
Peter Rowan and Tony Rice Quartet, 335
Peter Rowan's Free Mexican Air Force, 253
Peters, Dave, 363, 365
Petersen, Herb, 247
Petticoat Junction, 239, 282, 283, 304,
    305, 311–14; Kristin Scott Benson
    with, 339, 340
"Petticoat Junction," 312
Phantoms of the Opry, 241, 242, 252, 261
Philadelphia Folk Festival, 211, 229
Phil and Vivian Williams Live! 142
Phillips, Lewis, 67, 68
Phillips, Stacey, 210
Phillips, Todd, 258, 259, 262, 264, 300
Phillips, Utah, 196, 224
Phish, 322
Pickin', 253
Pickin' Up, 152
Pieces of My Heart, 133

Pierce, Don, 75
Pierce, Webb, 222
Pierson, John, 248
Pike County Boys, 117
Pinecastle Records, 173, 291, 309, 313,
    341, 345
"Pink Toenails," 366
Pioneer Dance Tunes of the Far West, 142
Pioneering Women of Bluegrass, 129, 131
Pittard, Mike, 57, 58
Pittman, Lois, 307
"Planet of Love," 367
Plant, Robert, 316, 328
Playing Possum, 248
"Poor Ellen Smith," 98
Poor Folk's Pleasure, 159
Pop Stoneman and His Little Pebbles, 72
Poss, Barry, 290
"Poughkeepsie," 227
Prairie Home Companion, 131
"Precious Jewel," 353
"Precious Memories," 32
*Presenting the Sullivan Family in Blue Grass
    Gospel*, 88
Pre-Sequel, 295
Presley, Elvis, 64, 101
Presley's Grocery, 290
Pressing On, 81
Prestige Records, 29, 96, 97, 98, 99
Pretty Fair Bluegrass, 349
"Pretty Little Miss," 51
Price, Jim, 230
Prine, John, 199
Purkey, Elaine, 131
"Put Me in Your Pocket," 17

Quartet, 300
Queen City Barn Dance, 217
Queen For a Day, 311
Quick, Karen, 310

Raccoon Records, 244
Radio Therapy Records, 174

Rage, The, 356–59, 382
Ragin' Live (CD), 356
Ragin' Live (DVD), 356
"Rag Time Annie," 57
Rainbow Park, 37
Rainbow Valley Boys, 60, 61
Rainbow Valley Boys and Sweetheart, 61
Rainbow Valley Folks, 62
Raine, Bethany, 262, 315
Raines, Missy, 155, 284–92, 302, 338, 381, 382, 383; influences on, 112, 165; as a side musician, 173, 199, 272, 273, 282
Raines, Rick, 289
Raines, Sue, 182, 211, 213
Rainwater, Cedric (Howard Watts), 18
Raising Sand, 328
Raje, The, 354
Rakestraw, Todd, 318
Ralph Rinzler Memorial Concert, 131
Ralph Stanley and the Clinch Mountain Boys, 2
Ramblin' Records, 230
"Ramblin' Woman," 127
Ramona Church and Carolina Road, 334
Ramsey, Carmella, 309
Ranch Romance, 141, 305
Rancke, Charlie, 286
Randolph Macon Women's College, 306
Randolph, Candi, 182
"Randy Lynn Rag," 305
"Rawhide," 51, 78
Raymond, Beverly, 61
RCA Records, 70, 78, 80, 83
RCM Records, 308
Reason and Rhyme, 267
Reason to Believe, 243
Reba McEntire: Greatest Hits Volume III: I'm A Survivor, 326
"Rebel Girl," 129
Rebel Records, 26, 57, 95, 107, 110, 111, 160, 166, 171, 172, 174, 205, 270, 271, 283, 341, 352, 353

Reckless Love & Bold Adventure, 33
Rec Room, The, 288
Rector, Red, 106, 214
Red and Murphy, 183, 184, 185
Red and Murphy and their Excellent Children, 185
Red Dog Records, 236
"Red Hot Mama," 188
Red Molly, 305
"Red Rocking Chair," 199
Red, White and Blue(grass), 151–55
Red, White and Blue(grass) and Company, 153
Redwood Canyon Ramblers, 3, 242
Reece, Ingrid Herman, 147, 154, 182, 243, 244–46
Reed, David, 37, 39
Reed, Ola Belle Campbell, 3, 10, 11, 12, 35–39, 58, 202, 383; influence 2, 5, 23, 119; other women playing with, 95, 124, 306
Reed, Ralph "Bud," 37
Reed, Ralph, Jr., 37
Reed, Rick, 298
Reel World String Band, 227
Reischman, John, 262, 263, 264
"Remington Ride," 235
Renfro Valley Barn Dance, 308, 310
Reno, Don, 30, 31, 105, 216, 306
Reno and Smiley, 31
Renshaw, Simon, 368
Replay, 301
Requests, 95
Resophonic Echoes, 6
"Restless Rambling Heart," 255
Revival Records, 86
Revonah Records, 107, 211, 212, 295
RHD Records, 148
Rhodes, Philip, 177
Rice Kryspies, 243
Rice, Marci, 243
Rice, Tony, 151, 219, 335; and IInd Generation, 161, 163, 164; influence 227, 317, 328

Rice, Wayne, 243
Rice, Wyatt, 232
Richard Dobson and State of the Heart,
   215
Rich-R-Tone Records, 23
Riders in the Sky, 141
Ridge Runner Records, 159, 295
Riley, Maureen "Mo," 182, 289
Rinzler, Ralph, 3, 46, 51, 83, 121, 126,
   131
Riopel, Michael, 178
Ritchie, Jean, 97, 251
Rittler, Dickie, 116
Riverside Records, 97
Riversong/Benson Records, 65
Rix, Marty, 209
"Road Not Taken, The," 112
Road To Agate Hill, 132, 133
Road to Nashville, 79
Roamin' the Blue Ridge With Jeanie West, 29,
   94, 96, 97
Roaring Blue River, 247
Robbins, Ed, 145
Robbins, George, 14
Robbins, Pig, 65
Robbins, Sudie, 14, 18, 19
Roberts, Michelle, 307
Robin and Linda Williams, 10
Robin Roller and the High Rollers, 334
Robinson, Jackie, 265
Robison, Charlie, 373
Robison, Emily, 361–73
Robot Plane Flies Over Arkansas, 231
"Rock Salt and Nails," 196, 224
"Rocky Road Blues," 13, 17
"Rocky Top," 109, 148, 235, 294, 305, 349
Roemer, John, 192
Rogers, Tammy, 335, 364
Roller, Robin, 283, 311, 313, 334, 335
Rollin', 205
Rolling Stone, 321, 373
"Roll in My Sweet Baby's Arms," 32
Romaine, Anne, 124, 125

Ronstadt, Linda, 322
Root, Greg, 210
Roots of Bluegrass, 99
Rose, Artie, 97, 99
Rose, Robin, 188
Rose, Wesley, 24
Rose Maddox Sings Bluegrass, 28, 75, 94, 96
Rosenberg, Neil, 3, 4, 52, 98, 119, 242,
   247
Rosenberg, Suzy. See Thompson, Suzy
"Rose of Old Kentucky," 183, 312
Rose of the West Coast Country, 33
Roses in the Snow, 159, 205
"Roses in the Snow," 203, 204, 205, 350
Rossiter, Pat, 234
Rough Hewn, 199
Rounder Records: and Hazel and Alice,
   113, 125, 126, 127, 128, 129, 130; and
   Alison Krauss, 282, 316, 318, 320, 321,
   322, 323, 327, 332; and Wilma Lee,
   25, 26; and Laurie Lewis, 256, 257,
   258; and Claire Lynch, 272, 273, 274;
   and Lynn Morris, 233, 237, 239; and
   Suzanne Thomas, 198, 199; and various
   artists, 36, 39, 206, 230, 231, 334, 335,
   344; and Rhonda Vincent, 331, 355,
   356, 358, 359
"Roving Gambler," 57
Rowan, Peter, 144, 145, 253, 257, 258,
   335
Rozum, Tom, 255, 256, 257, 259
Rubin, Rick, 372
"Ruby, Are You Mad at Your Man," 24
Rudisill, Gail, 311, 313, 338, 340
Rumpf, Carol, 166, 167
Rustler's Moon, 268
Rutabaga Records, 82, 309
Rutland, Georgia Slim, 15, 18
R-V-B Label, 61

Saddle Mountain Roundup, 14, 15
"Sally Goodwin," 296
Sally Mountain Park, 352

Sally Mountain Show, 178, 347, 351, 358; albums, 348, 349, 350, 352, 353
Sally Mountain Trio, 347, 348
"Salt Creek," 246
Salt Creek Bluegrass Festival (Hugo, Okla.), 203, 206
Salt of the Earth, 160
"Salty Dog Blues," 73
Sammy Shelor and the Lonesome River Band, 381
Sanchez, Felipe, 18
Sanders, Markie, 182, 246–49, 252
Sandker, Brooke Lea, 353
Sandker, Herb, 350, 351
Sandker, Sally Lea, 352
Sandomirsky, Sharon, 132
Sandy Records, 87
Saratoga Gap, 310
Sassygrass, 282, 305
"Satisfied," 348
Saturday Night Fever, 317
Saunders, Walt, 56, 58
Sawtelle, Charles, 256
Sayles, John, 129
Saylor, Juanita, 44
Saylor, Lucky, 44, 388
"Scars From an Old Love," 123
Schatz, Mark, 274
Schickele, Peter, 177
Schreiber, Alice. See Lee, Judy
Schreiber, Barney, 101
Schreiber, Betty, 101
Schwarz, Tracy, 125, 126, 128, 130, 203
Scott, Sandra, 19
Scott, Tommy, 18
Scott Hambly and the Bluegrass Ramblers, 243
Scoville Violins, 254
"Scraps From Your Table," 130
Scutt, Linda, 337
Seapy, Lauren, 182, 294
Sebolt, Dave, 150, 152
"Second Fiddle To An Old Guitar," 102

Second Helping, 132
Second Impression, 172
Second Season, 345
Secrets, 334
Security Records, 37
Seeger, Charles, 116
Seeger, Mike, 5, 74, 105; and Hazel and Alice; 116, 117, 119, 120, 125, 126, 128, 131, 132
Seeger, Pete, 139
Seeger, Ruth, 116
Seeing Things, 257
Seim, Shirley, 333
Seldom Scene, 49, 130, 163, 199, 271, 285
Sentimental Journey, 154, 246
Seyer, Larry, 366
"Shackles and Chains," 61
"Shady Grove," 78
Shall We Gather at the River, 65
Shanklin, Bob, 116
Shankman, Dana, 283
Shape of a Tear, 239
Shaver, Billy Joe, 65
Shaw, Linda, 6
"She Has Wings (and She Knows How To Fly)," 152
Shelasky, Paul, 251, 252, 253, 262
Shelasky, Sue, 182, 252, 261, 262
Shell, Sonia, 310, 315
"She'll Be Coming Round the Mountain," 18
"Shelly's Winter Love," 33
Sheltered in the Arms of God, 351
Shelton, Sandra, 307
Shenandoah, 322
Shendandoah Cut-ups, 2, 30
Shendandoah Valley Trio, 50
Shepherd, Jean, 61, 102
Shepherd College, 131
Shields, Pat, 285
Shinbone Alley All-Stars, 246
Shindig in the Barn, 66
"Shine on Harvest Moon," 222

Shivaree! 97

Shocked, Michelle, 293, 298, 322

Shoemaker Family, 364

Shouldn't a Told You That, 367

Shropshire, Elmo, 248

Shubb, Rick, 247

Shubb, Wilson, and Shubb, 247

Shubb, Wilson, and Shubb (group), 247

Shuffler, George, 236

Shut Up and Sing, 372

Sidesaddle, 242, 282, 305, 310, 311

Sidesaddle & Co., 311

Sidewinders, 342, 343

Siedel, Ted, 368

Siegel, Avram, 266

Siegel, Carol, 182, 208, 210

Siegel, Peter, 121, 123

Signature Sounds, 258

Silber, Julie, 247

Sills, Bobby, 103

Silver and Gold, 272

"Silver Dagger," 335

Silver Dollar City, 349

Silver Rail, 317, 318

Silverstein, Harry, 25

"Silver Tongues and Gold-Plated Lies," 197

Simmons, Vicki, 308, 309, 310

Simon, Carly, 209

Simon and Garfunkel, 113, 128

Simpkins, Ronnie, 272

"Simple Kind of Love," 328

Simple Pleasures, 297

Sims, Diane, 6

Sinatra, Frank, 119, 162

"Sin City," 33

"Singer, The," 196

Singing All Day And Dinner on the Ground, 108

"Singing All Day And Dinner on the Ground," 108

"Singing Bird," 256

Singing Nun, The, 77

Singing Time Down South, 65

Singin' My Troubles Away, 256

"Single Girl, Married Girl," 98

Sing Out! 46

"Sin Wagon," 370

Sipsey, 154

Sipsey River Band, 156

Sixteen Radio Favorites: Alex Campbell, Ola Belle, and Deacon and the New River Boys, 38

Skaggs, Molly, 160

Skaggs, Ricky, 159, 160, 317, 322, 332, 355, 376

Skaggs Family Records, 377

Skepner, David, 366

Skyline. *See* Tony Trischka and Skyline

Sky-line Drive, 230

"Slewfoot," 78, 106

Slick, Grace, 261

Sloan, Carolyn, 182

"Slow Learner," 256

Small World Music, 298

"Smelly Feet," 265

Smiley, Red, 30, 31, 107

Smilin' At You, 270, 271

Smith, Arthur, 15

Smith, Bessie, 189

Smith, Billy, 185

Smith, Carolyn, 95

Smith, Craig, 257, 258, 259, 294

Smith, Emma, 6

Smith, Harry, 119

Smith, Kenny, 272, 382

Smith, Lee, 133

Smith, Mayne, 3, 4

Smith, Phil, 179

Smith, Richard D., 46, 47

Smith, Steve, 286, 288

Smith, Valerie, 332, 333

Smithsonian Folklife Festival, 126

Smithsonian Folkways Records, 131

Smokey Grass Boys, 247

Smoky Mountain Ballads, 97

Smothers Brothers, 70

Snider, Jill, 339
Snodderly, Ed, 289
Snow, Hank, 55, 217
"Snow Deer," 55
"So Happy Together," 165
"Soldier's Joy," 106
So Long, So Wrong, 324
Some Assembly Required, 335
"Somebody Touched Me," 50
"Somebody's Waiting for Me," 80
Somers, Tyra Dean, 182, 286
Songcatcher, 129
Songs of the Southland, 99
Sons of the Pioneers, 29
Sony Records, 361, 364, 368, 369, 370
Sounds From the Ozarks, 247
Sounds of Bluegrass, 184
Southern Belle Label, 110
Southern Comfort, 311
Southern Folk Festival, 124
Southern Gospel Singers, 43
Southern Mountain Folksongs and Ballads, 97
Southern Rail, 283
South Plains College, 369
Southwest Baptist College, 14
Sparks, Larry, 193, 261
Spence, Karen, 280
Spence, Susan, 280
Spicher, Bobby, 101
Spicher, Buddy, 65
Spirited, 174
Spirit High Ridge, 375
Splitting the Licks, 94
Spottswood, Dick, 121
Sprout Wings and Fly, 114
Spruce and Maple Label, 258, 259
Sprung, Roger, 209
Stafford, Tim, 130, 322
"Stairway to Heaven," 203
Stanley, Ralph, 49, 107, 194, 332, 337; his
    festival, 89, 95; influence, 2, 164, 376;
    recordings with women, 207, 316
Stanley Brothers, 66, 121, 193, 325; influ-
ence, 114, 119, 123, 170, 261, 295,
    378
Stanton, Jim, 23
Star, Trigger, 106
Starday Records, 38, 43, 65, 75, 76, 101,
    388
Starks, Juanita, 29
Starling, John, 271
Stars and Bars, 286
"Stars and Stripes Forever," 176
"Star-Spangled Banner, The" 367
Station Inn, 244, 246, 312
Statman, Andy, 210, 295
Stauber, Tom, 133
Stecher, Jody, 28, 130
SteelDrivers, 335, 382
"Steel Rails," 307, 321
Steffey, Adam, 322, 324, 371
Stelling, Geoff, 278, 297
Stelling Banjos, 278
Stenberg, Amy, 266
Stephenson, Larry, 337, 339, 340, 344, 345
Steve Allen Show, 70, 77
Stevens, Beth, 283, 334
Stewart, Ron, 239, 240, 313, 355
Stiff, Denise, 319
Still a Little Rough Around the Edges, 376
Stiltner, Haley, 336
Sting, 316
Stockton, Juanita, 205
Stolen Moments, 302
Stonehouse Label, 82
Stoneman, Billy, 74
Stoneman, Donna, 2, 3, 31, 32, 42, 69–83,
    106, 122, 170, 349, 378
Stoneman, Eddie, 71
Stoneman, Ernest "Pop," 70, 71; and Blue-
    grass Champs, 74, 75; death, 79, 80, 82;
    and his Little Pebbles, 72, 73; and The
    Stonemans (group), 76, 77, 78
Stoneman, Hattie Frost, 70, 71, 82
Stoneman, Jimmy, 69, 70, 72, 73, 74, 79,
    80, 81

Stoneman, Nita, 71
Stoneman, Patsy (Murphy), 69–83
Stoneman, Scott (Scotty), 55, 78, 81, 170;
    and Bluegrass Champs, 69, 72, 73; as
    fiddler, 70, 80, 82; recordings 74, 76,
    77
Stoneman, Van, 70, 72, 74, 79, 80, 81
Stoneman, Veronica "Roni," 69–83, 105,
    143, 122, 170, 383
Stoneman Family: 28 Big Ones, The, 75
Stonemans, The, (TV show), 78
*Stonemans: An Appalachian Family and the
    Music That Shaped Their Lives,* 82
Stonemans: Live! 78
Stonemans: Patsy, Donna, Roni, 69–83
Stonemans: Patsy, Donna & Roni, 82
Stone Mountain Wobble, 195
Stoneway Records, 148
"Stoney, Are You Mad At Your Gal," 24
Stoney Cooper and His Clinch Mountain
    Boys, 23
"Stoney Creek," 145
Stoney Lonesome (band), 281
Storm Still Rages, The, 355, 356
Story, Carl, 43, 388
Stovall, Rosemary, 176
Stover, Don, 55, 254
Straight Paths, 341
Stranded in the Moonlight, 230, 231
Strange Creek Singers, 125, 126
Strange Creek Singers, 125
Strawberry Festival, 292
Stribling, Mary, 234
Strictly Country Records, 288
String Bean (David Akeman), 17
Stuart, Joe, 205, 216
Stuart, Marty, 36, 89
Stubbs, Eddie, 23, 27
Styx River Ferry, 243, 244, 245, 246
Sugarbeat, 335
Sugar Coated, 243
Sugar Hill Records, 159, 255, 257, 264,
    265, 266, 290

Sugar in the Gourd, 305
Sugar Shack, 34
Sullivan, Arthur, 85, 86
Sullivan, Aubrey, 85
Sullivan, Emmett, 85, 86, 87, 90
Sullivan, Enoch, 85–90
Sullivan, J. B., 85
Sullivan, Jerry, 87
Sullivan, Lesa, 87, 89, 90
Sullivan, Margie, 2, 3, 42, 84–91
Sullivan, Susie, 85
Sullivan, Wayne, 90
*Sullivan Family: Fifty Years in Bluegrass Gospel
    Music, The,* 90
Sullivan Family: Live in Holland, 90
Sullivan Records, 65
Sunday Show, The, 151
Sunny Mountain Boys, 104, 109
Sun's Coming Up, The, 350
Sunset Park, 5, 37, 38, 39, 95, 105, 107
Sunshine Bluegrass Boys, 2
Surrat, Ben, 288
Sutton, Bryan, 355, 371
Swan, Jimmy, 88
"Sweet Georgia Brown," 286
"Sweet Music Man," 326
Sweet Potato Pie, 305
"Swept Away," 256
Swing Shift, 6
Synergy, 291
Syracuse New Times, 212
Syracuse University, 207, 208, 209

"Take Care of Your Little Girls," 267
"Take Me Back to Tulsa," 177
Taken, 359
Taking the Long Way, 372
Takoma Records, 33, 262
"Talking Fiddle Blues," 76
Talk to Your Heart, 173
Tall Timber, 141, 142
"Tall Timber," 48
Tall Timber Boys, 53, 140

Tall Timber Gang, 140, 141
Tashian, Holly, 205, 215
Tate, Tater, 106, 107
Taubman, Alyse, 117
Tayberry Music, 302
Taylor, Earl, 57, 226
Taylor, Hilton, 85
Taylor, James, 316, 317, 327, 328
Taylor, Ramona Church, 283, 308, 309,
    333, 334
Taylor, Red, 142
Taylor, Susan, 305
Taylor, Tut, 153
"Teardrops Falling in the Snow," 196
"Teen Angel," 162
Telluride Bluegrass Festival, 365
"Tennessee Blues," 230
Tennessee Cut-ups, 30
Tennessee Heartstrings, 19, 185, 305, 307,
    315
Tennessee Valley Boys, 15
Terflinger, Jeff, 225, 226
Terry, Belle, 184
Tew, Richard, 91
Texas Rangers, 365, 367, 371
Texas Roundup, 18
Texas Troubadour Theater, 90
"T for Texas," 225
Thank Heavens For Dale Evans, 365
"Thank Heavens for Dale Evans," 366
Thatcher, Wendy, 93, 161–67, 171, 204
"Them Toad Suckers," 153
"There Ain't Nothin' in Ramblin'," 189
"There Goes My Everything," 78
There Is a Fountain, 204
"There Is a Time," 61
"There's a Big Wheel," 24
"There's Your Trouble," 370
Thevis, Michael, 152, 153
"They'll Never Keep Us Down," 129
They'll Never Keep Us Down: Women's Coal
    Mining Songs, 129
Thile, Chris, 325

"Things in Life," 254
$35 and a Dream, 11, 33
"Thirty Pieces of Silver," 24
This Is Rose Maddox, 33
"This Land Is Your Land," 209
This Side, 326
"This Weary Heart You Stole Away," 205
"This World Can't Stand Long," 23
Thomas, Danny, 70, 77
Thomas, Jason, 274
Thomas, Ralph, 157
Thomas, Suzanne, 131, 182, 192–201,
    226, 265
Thomason, Ron, 131, 192, 197, 198, 321
Thompson, Bobby, 81
Thompson, Maddy, 264, 265, 266
Thompson, Peter, 264, 265, 266
Thompson, Sue, 142
Thompson, Suzy Rosenberg, 247, 259
Thompson, Tommy, 16
Thoroughbred/Daywind Records, 54
Thorpe, Sister Rosetta, 67
"Thoughts of Love and Home," 265
Through Heaven's Door, 339
"Ticket Back," 231
Tillis, Pam, 309
"Till It Looks Like Love," 231
Till We Meet Here Again or Above, 195
Time, 123
Time Is Moving On, 65
Timeless and True Love, 353
Time Stands Still, 239
Tina Adair Band, 334
Tiny Martin and the Countrysiders, 43
Toby Stroud and the Blue Mountain Boys, 60
Today Show, 178
Together, 256, 264
Tom, Brad, and Alice, 133
Tom Dooley, 209
Tomlin, LaVaughn Lambert, 43
Tony Trischka and Skyline, 230, 231, 232,
    364. See also Trischka, Tony
Took Down and Put Up, 344

Too Late to Cry, 318
Top of the World Tour, 371, 372
Top of the World Tour: Live, 371
Tottle, Alex, 214
Tottle, Jack, 121
Town Hall Party, 242
Townsend, Greg, 253
Trachtenberg, Martha, 182, 207, 231; and
    Buffalo Gals, 208, 209, 210, 211, 212,
    213, 214
"Train 45," 108
"Train on the Island," 124
"Tramp on the Street," 23
Travel On: Alex Campbell and Ola Belle, and the
    New River Boys, 38
Traver Hollow, 283
Travers, Mary, 169
Trenwith, Colleen, 6
Tribe, Ivan, 71, 80, 82, 83
Tribute to Molly O'Day, A, 111
Tribute to Roy Acuff, A, 25
Trigg, Patsy, 248
Trigg Kids, 248
Trischka, Tony, 287, 318, 377; and Buffalo
    Gals, 208, 209, 210, 212, 213; and
    Skyline, 230, 232, 364
Trotman, Herb, 271
Trouble Free, 354
"True Happy Home," 265
"True Life Blues," 13, 257
True Life Blues, 257, 265
True Stories, 256, 257
Truitt, Sally, 335
Tubb, Ernest, 55, 114
Tucker, Sherrie, 5, 6
Tucker, Tuck, 184
Tullock, Jake, 246
"Tumbling Tumbleweeds," 158
"Turkey Knob," 145
Turkey Pluckers, 139, 140
Turner, Tina, 356
Turquoise Records, 309, 310
Tuttle, Molly, 335, 336, 383

Twain, Shania, 361
Twenty String Bluegrass Band, 234
Twilight Motel, 298
Twin Sisters, 142, 213
Two, 291
Twograss, 174
Two Hearts on the Borderline, 341
Tyminski, Dan, 323, 324, 325

UCLA, 293, 296
UCLA Folk Festival, 77
Ukelson, Lou, 188
Uncle Earl, 10
Uncle Pen, 259
"Uncle Pen," 31, 51, 110
"Under The Double Eagle," 82, 145, 176
Underwood, Richard, 130, 237
Union Station, 282, 297, 298, 318, 324,
    325, 326, 328, 329. *See also* Alison
    Krauss and Union Station; AKUS
"Unwed Fathers," 199
"Up Around the Bend," 165
"Up This Hill and Down," 269
USA Today, 320, 400
"Use a Napkin (Not Your Mom)," 265
"Used To Be," 48, 212, 257

Vale, Jerry, 162
Valley, The, 95
Valley Dolls, 280, 305
"Val's Cabin," 256
Vance, Jenny, 19
Vanderbilt University, 147, 302
Vanguard Records, 97, 293, 297, 300
VanLandingham, Martha, 306
Van Meter, Sally, 181, 182, 255, 262, 381
Van Schaik, Tom, 366
Van't Hof, Grace, 336
Vassar University, 144
Veach, Rachel, 16
Vern and Ray, 247, 253
Vernon, Bill, 165
Vern Williams Band, 33, 253, 383

Verve/Folkways Records, 122
Very Popular, 152
Vestal, Scott, 338
Vetco Records, 188, 191, 195, 196, 224, 225
Vick, Wanda, 182
Village Voice, 123
Vincent, Bill, 347, 348
Vincent, Brian, 348
Vincent, Carolyn, 347–53, 358
Vincent, Darrin, 347–49, 351, 358, 376
Vincent, Johnny, 347–50, 352, 353
Vincent, Rhonda, 178, 331, 346–60, 364, 376, 382, 382; clothes, 327, 328; and Sierra Hull, 332, 334; and Alison Krauss, 317, 319, 321; mandolin player, 83, 181, 381
"Virginia," 165, 166
Virginia Buddies, 306
VornDick, Bil, 325
Voyager Recordings, 140, 142

Wade, Melissa, 335
Wagoner, Porter, 243
"Wait a Little Longer Please, Jesus," 50
Waite, John, 328
"Waiting For the Boys to Come Home," 188
Wakefield, Frank, 57, 79, 83, 193, 252, 262
Walker, Bradley, 377
Walker, Cas, 105, 106, 108, 110, 112
Walker, Laura, 307
Walker, Nell, 44
"Walking in Jerusalem," 50
"Walking My Lord Up Calvary's Hill," 24
Walking My Lord Up Calvary's Hill, 25
"Walkin' In My Shoes," 267
Walkin' In My Shoes, 266
Wallace, Cindy, 335
Wallace, George, 88
Wallace, Lureen, 88

Waller, Butch, 34, 244, 261, 263
Waller, Charlie, 72, 169, 174
Waller, Jen, 263
Wall Street Journal, 302, 346
"Waltz For Mr. B.," 303
Wamboldt, Lil, 61
Ward, C. E., 171
Ward, Sarah, 336
Warmer Kind of Blue, 267
Warner, Chris, 136
Warner, Creola, 45
Warner, Greer, 45
Warner, Willie Gene, 45
Warner Brothers Records, 202, 205, 244
Wartman, Tom, 179
Washington Post, 190, 191
Washington Post Magazine, 114, 233
Washington Square, 97
Watkins, Sara, 242, 325
Watkins, Sean, 325
Watson, Dawn, 311
Watson, Doc, 219, 251
Watson, Gene, 357, 359
"Wayfaring Stranger," 320
WBT Briarhoppers, 335
Weavers, The, 119
Webb, Jim, 187, 188, 190
Webco Records, 110, 341
We Call It Grass, 172
Weil, Beth, 241, 253, 264
Weinert, Jerry Ray, 196
Weisberger, Jon, 354
Weiss, Bruce, 318
Weiss, Danny, 210, 230, 231
Weitzman, Stuart, 327
Welch, Gillian, 6
Welch, Lee Anne, 310, 311
We'll Die in the Pig Pen Fighting, 133
Wells Family, 332
Wells, Debi, 332
Wells, Eden, 3332
Wells, Jade, 332

Wells, Kitty, 5, 50, 61, 114, 117

Wells, Sara, 332

"We Must Have Been Out of Our Minds,"
  205

Wendy Smith and Blue Velvet, 311

We're Not the Jet Set, 206

Wernick, Pete, 210, 212, 235

West, Brendan, 303

West, Everett, 99

West, Garry, 294, 298, 299, 300, 301

West, Hannah, 301, 302

West, Harry, 96, 97, 98, 99, 119

West, Jeanie, 29, 32, 94, 96–99, 204

West Texas A&M, 369

West Virginia Music Hall of Fame, 131

"West Virginia Polka," 24

"What About You," 203

"Whatcha Gonna Do," 274

"What Do You Dream About?" 264

What Should Have Been, 343

What's That? 154

Wheatstraw (Pennsylvania band), 276

Wheatstraw (Ohio band), 276

Wheeler, Erika, 256

Wheeling Jamboree, 101, 105, 164

Wheels (instrumental), 219

Wheels (vocal), 230

"When Earl Taylor Played the Mandolin
  For Me," 226

"When He Reached Down His Hand For
  Me," 55

"When I Lay My Burdens Down," 38

When You Are Lonely," 203

"When You Say Nothing At All," 322, 323

Where the Wild, Wild Flowers Grow, 36

"Where the Wild, Wild Flowers Grow," 36

Whetstone Run, 235, 236

"Whiskey Lullaby," 327

Whisnant, Johnny, 54, 55

Whitaker, Charlie, 42

Whitaker, Lillimae, 42, 43

Whitcomb, Dale, 151

White, Al, 177, 178, 179

White, Barbara, 2

White, Buck, 44, 148, 157–60, 178, 350,
  352

White, Cheryl, 2, 44, 148, 157–60, 166,
  182, 284

White, Clarence, 242

White, Eric, 242

White, Gwen, 2

White, JoAnn, 242

White, Melissa, 159

White, Pat, 44, 157–60

White, Peggy, 307

White, Roland, 242

White, Rosie, 157, 159

White, Sharon, 2, 44, 148, 157–60, 284

"White Dove," 110

White Mountain Bluegrass, 283

White Pine Girls, 140

White Rose, 26

Whites, The, 157–60, 204, 322, 364

Whiteside, Jonny, 28, 29, 32, 34

"White Sport Coat," 225

"White Trash Wedding," 371

Whitey and Hogan, 338

Whitfield, J. G., 88

Whitley, Keith, 322

"Who'll Stop the Rain," 80

Who's That Knocking, 94, 122, 123, 252

"Who Will Watch the Homeplace," 257

"Why Did You Wander," 147

"Wicked Path of Sin," 23

"Wicked Witch Breakdown," 213

Wide Open Spaces, 369, 370

"Widow Maker," 108, 110

Wilborn, Marshall, 130, 235, 236, 237,
  239, 240

Wilbur, Rich, 244, 247

Wild and Blue, 339

"Wild Bill Jones," 97

Wild Blue Yonder, 335

Wild Rose, 309

Wilds, David, 16
Wilds, Honey, 16
"Wildwood Flower," 74, 80
Wildwood Girls, 182, 227, 282, 305, 307,
   308, 312
Wildwood Girls Label, 308
Wildwood Pickers, 307
Wiley, Chuck, 246
Wiley, Paul, 141
Wilgus, D. K., 97, 98
Wilkinson, Kristin (Kris), 182, 213, 214
Williams and Bray, 142
Williams, Claude, 319
Williams, Eileen, 182
Williams, Hank, 55, 117, 222, 223, 244
Williams, Hob, 85
Williams, Jeanette, 333
Williams, Johnnie, 333
Williams, Josh, 356, 358
Williams, Mason, 153, 155
Williams, Phil, 139–42
Williams, Vern, 33, 253, 383
Williams, Vivian, 53, 93, 94, 138–42, 213,
   243
Williamson, Darlene, 240
"Willie's Winter Love," 33
"Will Jesus Wash the Bloodstains From
   Your Hands," 130
"Will the Circle Be Unbroken," 125, 314
"Will You Be Loving Another Man," 184
*Wilma Lee and Stoney Cooper: Big Midnight
   Special*, 21
Wilma Lee Cooper, 26
Wilson, Joe, 319
Wimmer, Kevin, 262
WINC (Winchester, Va.), 55, 56
"Winchester Cathedral," 78
Wind in the Willows, 147
Winfield (Kansas) Banjo Contest, 235, 364
Winfield (Kansas) Fiddle Contest, 317,
   362
Wingate, Mark, 307
Wingate, Sally, 4, 182, 286, 306

Wingate, Sheila, 332
Winston, Nat, 4
Wintergrass, 6, 292
Winter's Grace, 258
Wise, Chubby, 18, 122, 251
Wiseman, Mac, 100, 172, 216, 284
Wisor, Jeff, 172
Witcher, Mike, 292
With Babies and Banners, 129
WJBF-TV (Augusta, Ga.), 64
WLS Barn Dance, 37
WNKU (Highland Heights, Ky.), 226
Wolf, Eugene, 289
Wolf, Kate, 34
Wolfe, Charles, 5, 15, 127
Wolfersberger, Brenda, 227
Woman Alive! 128
Women in Bluegrass, 1, 146, 148, 153, 221,
   232, 333, 368
Wonder, Stevie, 317
Won't You Come and Sing For Me, 4, 123
"Won't You Come and Sing for Me," 206
Wood, A. L., 164
Wood, Bob, 187
Wood, Randy, 153, 165, 171
Wood, Shirley, 103
Woods, Arthur "Shorty," 37
Wooten, Art, 16
Wooten, Gene, 26
"Working Girl Blues," 127
Working on a Road, 43
"World is Waiting For the Sunrise, The," 78
World Pacific Label, 77
World's Fair (Knoxville, Tenn.), 110
"Wreck on the Highway," 23, 24
Wright, Caroline, 161, 167, 391
Wrinkle, Jennifer, 309
Written in the Stars, 354
WSVA (Harrisonburg, Va.), 21
WWNC (Asheville, N.C.), 23
WWVA (Wheeling, W. Va.), 22, 23, 101,
   164
Wyckoff, Celia, 235

Wyland, Dede, 182, 229–32, 364
Wyncote Records, 74
WYSO (Yellow Springs, Ohio), 194

"Yablonski Murder (Cold Blooded Murder), The" 125, 129
Yale University, 295
Yates, Wayne, 77
Years in the Making, 196
Yearwood, Trisha, 335
Yesterday and Today, 354
Yoder, Sonya, 311, 312
"You Are My Sunshine," 55
You Can Be a Star, 351
"You Gave Me a Song," 131
"You'll Be Leaving Me," 256
"You'll Find Her Name Written There," 117

"You'll Get No More of Me," 130
You'll Never Be the Sun, 239
Young, Neil, 155
"You're a Flower Blooming in the Wildwood," 98
"You're Doing Me Wrong Jim Beam," 199
Your Money and My Good Looks, 359
You've Been a Friend to Me, 132
"You Were Mine," 364
"You Will Be My Ain True Love," 327
"You Won't Be Satisfied That Way," 266

Zahn, Paula, 368
Zanzinger, Gei, 39
Zonn, Andrea: with Alison Brown, 298, 302, 303; and Alison Krauss, 317, 318, 321; with Claire Lynch, 272, 273

MURPHY HICKS HENRY is a professional banjo player, teacher, and writer living in Virginia. She founded the *Women in Bluegrass* newsletter and has written regularly for *Bluegrass Unlimited* and *Banjo Newsletter*. She is also the co-creator of The Murphy Method, a series of instructional videos on playing the banjo and other bluegrass instruments.

Music in American Life

Only a Miner: Studies in Recorded Coal-Mining Songs   *Archie Green*

Great Day Coming: Folk Music and the American Left   *R. Serge Denisoff*

John Philip Sousa: A Descriptive Catalog of His Works   *Paul E. Bierley*

The Hell-Bound Train: A Cowboy Songbook   *Glenn Ohrlin*

Oh, Didn't He Ramble: The Life Story of Lee Collins, as Told to Mary Collins
       Edited by Frank J. Gillis and John W. Miner

American Labor Songs of the Nineteenth Century   *Philip S. Foner*

Stars of Country Music: Uncle Dave Macon to Johnny Rodriguez   *Edited by*
       Bill C. Malone and Judith McCulloh

Git Along, Little Dogies: Songs and Songmakers of the American West   *John I. White*

A Texas-Mexican *Cancionero*: Folksongs of the Lower Border   *Américo Paredes*

San Antonio Rose: The Life and Music of Bob Wills   *Charles R. Townsend*

Early Downhome Blues: A Musical and Cultural Analysis   *Jeff Todd Titon*

An Ives Celebration: Papers and Panels of the Charles Ives Centennial Festival-
       Conference   *Edited by H. Wiley Hitchcock and Vivian Perlis*

Sinful Tunes and Spirituals: Black Folk Music to the Civil War   *Dena J. Epstein*

Joe Scott, the Woodsman-Songmaker   *Edward D. Ives*

Jimmie Rodgers: The Life and Times of America's Blue Yodeler   *Nolan Porterfield*

Early American Music Engraving and Printing: A History of Music Publishing in America
       from 1787 to 1825, with Commentary on Earlier and Later Practices
       Richard J. Wolfe

Sing a Sad Song: The Life of Hank Williams   *Roger M. Williams*

Long Steel Rail: The Railroad in American Folksong   *Norm Cohen*

Resources of American Music History: A Directory of Source Materials from Colonial
       Times to World War II   *D. W. Krummel, Jean Geil, Doris J. Dyen, and Deane L. Root*

Tenement Songs: The Popular Music of the Jewish Immigrants   *Mark Slobin*

Ozark Folksongs   *Vance Randolph; edited and abridged by Norm Cohen*

Oscar Sonneck and American Music   *Edited by William Lichtenwanger*

Bluegrass Breakdown: The Making of the Old Southern Sound   *Robert Cantwell*

Bluegrass: A History   *Neil V. Rosenberg*

Music at the White House: A History of the American Spirit   *Elise K. Kirk*

Red River Blues: The Blues Tradition in the Southeast   *Bruce Bastin*

Good Friends and Bad Enemies: Robert Winslow Gordon and the Study of American
       Folksong   *Debora Kodish*

Fiddlin' Georgia Crazy: Fiddlin' John Carson, His Real World, and the World
       of His Songs   *Gene Wiggins*

America's Music: From the Pilgrims to the Present (rev. 3d ed.)   *Gilbert Chase*

Secular Music in Colonial Annapolis: The Tuesday Club, 1745–56   *John Barry Talley*

Bibliographical Handbook of American Music   *D. W. Krummel*

Goin' to Kansas City   *Nathan W. Pearson, Jr.*

"Susanna," "Jeanie," and "The Old Folks at Home": The Songs of Stephen C. Foster
       from His Time to Ours (2d ed.)   *William W. Austin*

Songprints: The Musical Experience of Five Shoshone Women   *Judith Vander*

"Happy in the Service of the Lord": Afro-American Gospel Quartets in Memphis
    Kip Lornell

Paul Hindemith in the United States   *Luther Noss*

"My Song Is My Weapon": People's Songs, American Communism, and the Politics
    of Culture, 1930–50   *Robbie Lieberman*

Chosen Voices: The Story of the American Cantorate   *Mark Slobin*

Theodore Thomas: America's Conductor and Builder of Orchestras, 1835–1905
    Ezra Schabas

"The Whorehouse Bells Were Ringing" and Other Songs Cowboys Sing   *Collected
    and Edited by Guy Logsdon*

Crazeology: The Autobiography of a Chicago Jazzman   *Bud Freeman, as Told to Robert Wolf*

Discoursing Sweet Music: Brass Bands and Community Life in Turn-of-the-Century
    Pennsylvania   *Kenneth Kreitner*

Mormonism and Music: A History   *Michael Hicks*

Voices of the Jazz Age: Profiles of Eight Vintage Jazzmen   *Chip Deffaa*

Pickin' on Peachtree: A History of Country Music in Atlanta, Georgia   *Wayne W. Daniel*

Bitter Music: Collected Journals, Essays, Introductions, and Librettos   *Harry Partch;
    edited by Thomas McGeary*

Ethnic Music on Records: A Discography of Ethnic Recordings Produced
    in the United States, 1893 to 1942   *Richard K. Spottswood*

Downhome Blues Lyrics: An Anthology from the Post–World War II Era   *Jeff Todd Titon*

Ellington: The Early Years   *Mark Tucker*

Chicago Soul   *Robert Pruter*

That Half-Barbaric Twang: The Banjo in American Popular Culture   *Karen Linn*

Hot Man: The Life of Art Hodes   *Art Hodes and Chadwick Hansen*

The Erotic Muse: American Bawdy Songs (2d ed.)   *Ed Cray*

Barrio Rhythm: Mexican American Music in Los Angeles   *Steven Loza*

The Creation of Jazz: Music, Race, and Culture in Urban America   *Burton W. Peretti*

Charles Martin Loeffler: A Life Apart in Music   *Ellen Knight*

Club Date Musicians: Playing the New York Party Circuit   *Bruce A. MacLeod*

Opera on the Road: Traveling Opera Troupes in the United States, 1825–60
    Katherine K. Preston

The Stonemans: An Appalachian Family and the Music That Shaped Their Lives
    Ivan M. Tribe

Transforming Tradition: Folk Music Revivals Examined   *Edited by Neil V. Rosenberg*

The Crooked Stovepipe: Athapaskan Fiddle Music and Square Dancing in Northeast
    Alaska and Northwest Canada   *Craig Mishler*

Traveling the High Way Home: Ralph Stanley and the World of Traditional Bluegrass
    Music   *John Wright*

Carl Ruggles: Composer, Painter, and Storyteller   *Marilyn Ziffrin*

Never without a Song: The Years and Songs of Jennie Devlin, 1865–1952
    Katharine D. Newman

The Hank Snow Story   *Hank Snow, with Jack Ownbey and Bob Burris*

Milton Brown and the Founding of Western Swing   *Cary Ginell, with special assistance
      from Roy Lee Brown*

Santiago de Murcia's "Códice Saldívar No. 4": A Treasury of Secular Guitar Music
      from Baroque Mexico   *Craig H. Russell*

The Sound of the Dove: Singing in Appalachian Primitive Baptist Churches
      Beverly Bush Patterson

Heartland Excursions: Ethnomusicological Reflections on Schools of Music   *Bruno Nettl*

Doowop: The Chicago Scene   *Robert Pruter*

Blue Rhythms: Six Lives in Rhythm and Blues   *Chip Deffaa*

Shoshone Ghost Dance Religion: Poetry Songs and Great Basin Context   *Judith Vander*

Go Cat Go! Rockabilly Music and Its Makers   *Craig Morrison*

'Twas Only an Irishman's Dream: The Image of Ireland and the Irish in American Popular
      Song Lyrics, 1800–1920   *William H. A. Williams*

Democracy at the Opera: Music, Theater, and Culture in New York City,
      1815–60   *Karen Ahlquist*

Fred Waring and the Pennsylvanians   *Virginia Waring*

Woody, Cisco, and Me: Seamen Three in the Merchant Marine   *Jim Longhi*

Behind the Burnt Cork Mask: Early Blackface Minstrelsy and Antebellum American
      Popular Culture   *William J. Mahar*

Going to Cincinnati: A History of the Blues in the Queen City   *Steven C. Tracy*

Pistol Packin' Mama: Aunt Molly Jackson and the Politics of Folksong   *Shelly Romalis*

Sixties Rock: Garage, Psychedelic, and Other Satisfactions   *Michael Hicks*

The Late Great Johnny Ace and the Transition from R&B to Rock 'n' Roll
      James M. Salem

Tito Puente and the Making of Latin Music   *Steven Loza*

Juilliard: A History   *Andrea Olmstead*

Understanding Charles Seeger, Pioneer in American Musicology   *Edited by Bell Yung
      and Helen Rees*

Mountains of Music: West Virginia Traditional Music from *Goldenseal*   *Edited by John Lilly*

Alice Tully: An Intimate Portrait   *Albert Fuller*

A Blues Life   *Henry Townsend, as told to Bill Greensmith*

Long Steel Rail: The Railroad in American Folksong (2d ed.)   *Norm Cohen*

The Golden Age of Gospel   *Text by Horace Clarence Boyer; photography by Lloyd Yearwood*

Aaron Copland: The Life and Work of an Uncommon Man   *Howard Pollack*

Louis Moreau Gottschalk   *S. Frederick Starr*

Race, Rock, and Elvis   *Michael T. Bertrand*

Theremin: Ether Music and Espionage   *Albert Glinsky*

Poetry and Violence: The Ballad Tradition of Mexico's Costa Chica   *John H. McDowell*

The Bill Monroe Reader   *Edited by Tom Ewing*

Music in Lubavitcher Life   *Ellen Koskoff*

Zarzuela: Spanish Operetta, American Stage   *Janet L. Sturman*

Bluegrass Odyssey: A Documentary in Pictures and Words, 1966–86   *Carl Fleischhauer and Neil V. Rosenberg*

That Old-Time Rock & Roll: A Chronicle of an Era, 1954–63   *Richard Aquila*

Labor's Troubadour   *Joe Glazer*

American Opera   *Elise K. Kirk*

Don't Get above Your Raisin': Country Music and the Southern Working Class   *Bill C. Malone*

John Alden Carpenter: A Chicago Composer   *Howard Pollack*

Heartbeat of the People: Music and Dance of the Northern Pow-wow   *Tara Browner*

My Lord, What a Morning: An Autobiography   *Marian Anderson*

Marian Anderson: A Singer's Journey   *Allan Keiler*

Charles Ives Remembered: An Oral History   *Vivian Perlis*

Henry Cowell, Bohemian   *Michael Hicks*

Rap Music and Street Consciousness   *Cheryl L. Keyes*

Louis Prima   *Garry Boulard*

Marian McPartland's Jazz World: All in Good Time   *Marian McPartland*

Robert Johnson: Lost and Found   *Barry Lee Pearson and Bill McCulloch*

Bound for America: Three British Composers   *Nicholas Temperley*

Lost Sounds: Blacks and the Birth of the Recording Industry, 1890–1919   *Tim Brooks*

Burn, Baby! BURN! The Autobiography of Magnificent Montague   *Magnificent Montague with Bob Baker*

Way Up North in Dixie: A Black Family's Claim to the Confederate Anthem   *Howard L. Sacks and Judith Rose Sacks*

The Bluegrass Reader   *Edited by Thomas Goldsmith*

Colin McPhee: Composer in Two Worlds   *Carol J. Oja*

Robert Johnson, Mythmaking, and Contemporary American Culture   *Patricia R. Schroeder*

Composing a World: Lou Harrison, Musical Wayfarer   *Leta E. Miller and Fredric Lieberman*

Fritz Reiner, Maestro and Martinet   *Kenneth Morgan*

That Toddlin' Town: Chicago's White Dance Bands and Orchestras, 1900–1950   *Charles A. Sengstock Jr.*

Dewey and Elvis: The Life and Times of a Rock 'n' Roll Deejay   *Louis Cantor*

Come Hither to Go Yonder: Playing Bluegrass with Bill Monroe   *Bob Black*

Chicago Blues: Portraits and Stories   *David Whiteis*

The Incredible Band of John Philip Sousa   *Paul E. Bierley*

"Maximum Clarity" and Other Writings on Music   *Ben Johnston, edited by Bob Gilmore*

Staging Tradition: John Lair and Sarah Gertrude Knott   *Michael Ann Williams*

Homegrown Music: Discovering Bluegrass   *Stephanie P. Ledgin*

Tales of a Theatrical Guru   *Danny Newman*

The Music of Bill Monroe   *Neil V. Rosenberg and Charles K. Wolfe*

Pressing On: The Roni Stoneman Story   *Roni Stoneman, as told to Ellen Wright*

Together Let Us Sweetly Live   *Jonathan C. David, with photographs by Richard Holloway*

Live Fast, Love Hard: The Faron Young Story   *Diane Diekman*
Air Castle of the South: WSM Radio and the Making of Music City   *Craig P. Havighurst*
Traveling Home: Sacred Harp Singing and American Pluralism   *Kiri Miller*
Where Did Our Love Go? The Rise and Fall of the Motown Sound   *Nelson George*
Lonesome Cowgirls and Honky-Tonk Angels: The Women of Barn Dance Radio
    Kristine M. McCusker
California Polyphony: Ethnic Voices, Musical Crossroads   *Mina Yang*
The Never-Ending Revival: Rounder Records and the Folk Alliance   *Michael F. Scully*
Sing It Pretty: A Memoir   *Bess Lomax Hawes*
Working Girl Blues: The Life and Music of Hazel Dickens   *Hazel Dickens*
    and Bill C. Malone
Charles Ives Reconsidered   *Gayle Sherwood Magee*
The Hayloft Gang: The Story of the National Barn Dance   *Edited by Chad Berry*
Country Music Humorists and Comedians   *Loyal Jones*
Record Makers and Breakers: Voices of the Independent Rock 'n' Roll Pioneers
    John Broven
Music of the First Nations: Tradition and Innovation in Native North America
    Edited by Tara Browner
Cafe Society: The Wrong Place for the Right People   *Barney Josephson,*
    with Terry Trilling-Josephson
George Gershwin: An Intimate Portrait   *Walter Rimler*
Life Flows On in Endless Song: Folk Songs and American History   *Robert V. Wells*
I Feel a Song Coming On: The Life of Jimmy McHugh   *Alyn Shipton*
King of the Queen City: The Story of King Records   *Jon Hartley Fox*
Long Lost Blues: Popular Blues in America, 1850–1920   *Peter C. Muir*
Hard Luck Blues: Roots Music Photographs from the Great Depression   *Rich Remsberg*
Restless Giant: The Life and Times of Jean Aberbach and Hill and Range Songs
    Bar Biszick-Lockwood
Champagne Charlie and Pretty Jemima: Variety Theater in the Nineteenth Century
    Gillian M. Rodger
Sacred Steel: Inside an African American Steel Guitar Tradition   *Robert L. Stone*
Gone to the Country: The New Lost City Ramblers and the Folk Music Revival
    Ray Allen
The Makers of the Sacred Harp   *David Warren Steel with Richard H. Hulan*
Woody Guthrie, American Radical   *Will Kaufman*
George Szell: A Life of Music   *Michael Charry*
Bean Blossom: The Brown County Jamboree and Bill Monroe's Bluegrass
    Festivals   *Thomas A. Adler*
Crowe on the Banjo: The Music Life of J. D. Crowe   *Marty Godbey*
Twentieth-Century Drifter: The Life of Marty Robbins   *Diane Diekman*
Henry Mancini: Reinventing Film Music   *John Caps*
The Beautiful Music All Around Us: Field Recordings and the American
    Experience   *Stephen Wade*

Then Sings My Soul: The Culture of Southern Gospel Music   *Douglas Harrison*

The Accordion in the Americas: Klezmer, Polka, Tango, Zydeco, and More!
Edited by Helena Simonett

Bluegrass Bluesman: A Memoir   *Josh Graves, edited by Fred Bartenstein*

One Woman in a Hundred: Edna Phillips and the Philadelphia Orchestra   *Mary Sue Welsh*

The Great Orchestrator: Arthur Judson and American Arts Management
James M. Doering

Charles Ives in the Mirror: American Histories of an Iconic Composer   *David C. Paul*

Southern Soul-Blues   *David Whiteis*

Sweet Air: Modernism, Regionalism, and American Popular Song   *Edward P. Comentale*

Pretty Good for a Girl: Women in Bluegrass   *Murphy Hicks Henry*

The University of Illinois Press
is a founding member of the
Association of American University Presses.

————————————————

Designed by Kelly Gray
Composed in 11 / 14 Perpetua Std
by Celia Shapland
at the University of Illinois Press
Manufactured by Thomson-Shore, Inc.

University of Illinois Press
1325 South Oak Street
Champaign, IL 61820-6903
www.press.uillinois.edu